THE UNESCO CONVENTION ON THE DIVERSITY OF CULTURAL EXPRESSIONS

THE UNESCO CONVENTION ON THE DIVERSITY OF CULTURAL EXPRESSIONS

A Tale of Fragmentation in International Law

Toshiyuki Kono
Steven Van Uytsel
(eds.)

intersentia
Cambridge – Antwerp – Portland

Intersentia Publishing Ltd.
Trinity House | Cambridge Business Park | Cowley Road
Cambridge | CB4 0WZ | United Kingdom
Tel.: +44 1223 393 753 | Email: mail@intersentia.co.uk

Distribution for the UK:
Hart Publishing Ltd.
16C Worcester Place
Oxford OX1 2JW
UK
Tel.: +44 1865 517 530
Email: mail@hartpub.co.uk

Distribution for the USA and Canada:
International Specialized Book Services
920 NE 58th Ave. Suite 300
Portland, OR 97213
USA
Tel.: +1 800 944 6190 (toll free)
Email: info@isbs.com

Distribution for Austria:
Neuer Wissenschaftlicher Verlag
Argentinierstraße 42/6
1040 Wien
Austria
Tel.: +43 1 535 61 03 24
Email: office@nwv.at

Distribution for other countries:
Intersentia Publishing nv
Groenstraat 31
2640 Mortsel
Belgium
Tel.: +32 3 680 15 50
Email: mail@intersentia.be

The UNESCO Convention on the Diversity of Cultural Expressions. A Tale of Fragmentation in International Law
Toshiyuki Kono and Steven Van Uytsel (eds.)

ISBN 978-94-000-0003-2
D/2012/7849/94
NUR 820

British Library Cataloguing in Publication Data. A catalogue record for this book is available from the British Library.

FOREWORD

The editors are very pleased to present *The UNESCO Convention on the Diversity of Cultural Expressions: A Tale of Fragmentation in International Law*. This book aims at discussing the UNESCO *Convention for the Promotion and Protection of the Diversity of Cultural Expressions* ("Convention on the Diversity of Cultural Expressions") from the viewpoint of its potential relationships with other fields of international law.

It is generally known that one of the main driving forces behind this Convention was the inability of the international trade regime to properly deal with cultural expressions and more specifically to deal with the audiovisual sector. This deadlock in the trade regime inspired civil society to take action and look for a new forum to discuss, and eventually adopt, an international instrument defending the cultural content of the audiovisual sector, thus putting in place the special trade measures required for its protection.

These initiatives of civil society resulted in a shift towards UNESCO. Within a relatively short span of time, UNESCO did not only initiate negotiations, it also adopted a new binding international instrument. The shift of venue had more implications than only the adoption of a new instrument. Trade was no longer the only issue at stake. The negotiators raised issues of tangible and intangible cultural heritage, human rights law issues and development law issues. All of these issues, some more explicitly than others, were addressed within the Convention on the Diversity of Cultural Expressions.

Cultural heritage, human rights and development issues, just like trade, are dealt with in other international legal instruments. Yet, the new UNESCO Convention on the Diversity of Cultural Expressions also purports to have something to say on these issues. To what extent this Convention effectively has any influence on the other international legal instruments is the subject of this book. To draw this study of the fragmentation of international law to an end, we have opted to add a section that examines the extent to which the Convention on the Diversity of Cultural Expressions has an influence on the legislation of two jurisdictions, Europe and South Africa.

This book has been a long journey. The contributors deserve our warm gratitude for their patience. We thank them for staying with us until the end of the project.

We would like to acknowledge the help of Carol Lawson and Yuji Matson for their linguistic editorial work. Finally, we would like to thank Tom Scheirs from

Intersentia for his continued belief in the project. Together with the professionalism and dedication of his staff, he has contributed greatly to the successful completion of it.

Toshiyuki Kono & Steven Van Uytsel
Fukuoka, 1 May 2012

CONTENTS

PART I. THE CONVENTION ON THE DIVERSITY OF CULTURAL EXPRESSIONS REVISITED

PART II. HERITAGE LAW & THE CONVENTION ON THE DIVERSITY OF CULTURAL EXPRESSIONS

PART III.
HUMAN RIGHTS & THE CONVENTION ON THE DIVERSITY OF CULTURAL EXPRESSIONS

PART VI.
IMPLEMENTATION OF AND VIEWS ON THE CONVENTION ON THE DIVERSITY OF CULTURAL EXPRESSIONS

LIST OF ABBREVIATIONS

AD Agreement	Anti-dumping Agreement or Agreement on Implementation of Article VI of the General Agreement on Tariffs and Trade 1994
ASEAN	Association of Southeast Asian Nations
AsgiSA	Accelerated and Shared Growth Initiative for South Africa
AVMS	Audiovisual Media Services Directive
AU	African Union
Cariforum	Caribbean Forum of ACP States
CEDAW	International Convention on the Elimination of All Forms of Discrimination Against Women
CESCR	Covenant on Economic, Social, and Cultural Rights
CIA	Central Intelligence Agency
CLAC	Centres de lecture et d'animation culturelle
CNUCED	Conférence des Nations Unies sur le commerce et le développement
COP	Conference of Parties
CRC	Convention on the Rights of the Child
CSCE	Commission on Security and Cooperation in Europe
CT	Custom Territories
CUSFTA	Canada-United States Free Trade Agreement
Cultural Diversity Declaration	Universal Declaration on Cultural Diversity
DAC	Department of Arts and Culture
DACST	Department of Arts, Culture, Science and Technology
DSB	Dispute Settlement Body
DSU	Understanding on Rules and Procedures Governing The Settlement of Disputes
DTI	Department of Trade and Investment
EC	European Community
ECJ	European Court of Justice
EC Treaty	Treaty establishing the European Community
ECHR	European Convention for the Protection of Human Rights and Fundamental Freedoms

EIA	Economic Integration Agreement
ELIAMEP	Hellenic Foundation for European and Foreign Policy
EU	European Union
FCC	Federal Communications Commission
FCNM	Framework Covenant for the Protection of National Minorities
FESTAC	Festival of the Arts and Culture
FICDC	International Federation of Coalitions for Cultural Diversity
FTA	Free Trade Agreement
GATT	General Agreement on Tariffs and Trade
GATS	General Agreement on Trade in Service
GNI	Gross National Income
GSP	Generalized System of Preferences
HDI	Human Development Index
IACHR	Inter-American Commission on Human Rights
ICCPR	International Covenant on Civil and Political Rights
ICERD	International Covenant on the Elimination of All Forms of Racial Discrimination
(I)CESCR	(International) Covenant on Economic, Social and Cultural Rights
ICH Convention	Convention for the Safeguarding of Intangible Cultural Heritage
ICIC	International Committee for Intellectual Cooperation
ICRMW	International Covenant on the Protection of the Rights of All Migrant Workers and Members of Their Families
IFCD	International Fund for Cultural Diversity
IGC	Intergovernmental Committee
IICI	International Institute of Intellectual Cooperation
ILM	International Legal Materials
ILO	International Labour Organization
ILO Convention No.169	ILO Convention concerning Indigenous and Tribal Peoples in Independent Countries
INCP	International Network on Cultural Policy
IMF	International Monetary Fund
IPRs	Intellectual Property Rights
ITO	International Trade Organization
JIPSA	Joint Initiative for Priority Skills Acquisition
KORUS FTA	Korea-US Free Trade Agreement

Languages Charter	European Charter for Regional or Minority Languages
lit.	litera
LNTS	League of Nations Treaty Series
MAI	Multilateral Agreement on Investment
Marrakesh Agreements	Marrakesh Agreements Establishing the World Trade Organization
MFN	Most-Favoured Nation
MINMEC	(South African) Ministers and Members of the Executive Council
MPAA	Motion Picture Association of America
NAFTA	North American Free Trade Agreement
NEPAD	New Partnership for Africa's Development
NGO	Non-Governmental Organization
OECD	Organization for Economic Cooperation and Development
OIF	Organisation Internationale de la Francophonie
PCC	Protocol on Cultural Cooperation
Recommendation 1043	Recommendation 1043 on Europe's Linguistic and Literary Heritage
REIO	Regional Economic Integration Organizations
RTA	Regional Trade Agreement
SACAN	South African Chapter of Arterial Network
SACCD	South African Coalition for Cultural Diversity
SADC	South African Development Community
SAMRO	South African Music Rights Organization
SCM Agreement	Agreement on Subsidies and Countervailing Measures
SPS Agreement	Agreement on the Application of Sanitary and Phytosanitary Measures
TEC	Treaty on the European Community
TFEU	Treaty on the Functioning of the European Union
TIC	(South African) Technical Intergovernmental Committee
TRIPS	Agreement on Trade-Related Aspects of Intellectual Property Rights
TWF	Television without Frontiers Directive
UDHR	Universal Declaration of Human Rights
UK	United Kingdom
UN	United Nations
UNCTAD	United Nations Conference on Trade and Development

UNDM	Declaration on the Rights of Persons Belonging to National or Ethnic, Religious and Linguistic Minorities
UNDRIP	United Nations Declaration on the Rights of Indigenous Peoples
UNESCO	United Nations Educational, Scientific and Cultural Organization
UNISA	University of South Africa
UNTS	United Nations Treaty Series
US	United States
USA	United States of America
USTR	United States Trade Representative
UTECA	Unión de Televisiones Comerciales Asociadas
v.	versus
Vienna Convention	Vienna Convention on the Law of Treaties
WIPO	World Intellectual Property Organization
World Heritage Convention	Convention Concerning the Protection of the World Cultural and Natural Heritage
WTO	World Trade Organization

INTRODUCTORY PART

POSITIONING THE CONVENTION ON THE DIVERSITY OF CULTURAL EXPRESSIONS

THE CONVENTION ON THE DIVERSITY OF CULTURAL EXPRESSIONS

Beyond a Trade and Culture Convention

Toshiyuki KONO* and Steven VAN UYTSEL**

1. INTRODUCTION

What had to become the Convention for the Protection and Promotion of the Diversity of Cultural Expressions ("Convention on the Diversity of Cultural Expressions")[1] was to put an end to a century long controversy in international trade.[2] This controversy centred on how to deal with audiovisuals, which were considered to carry a cultural content. Because of this cultural content, it was argued that they could not just be governed by the same trade principles as other goods and services. The ultimate failure of the trade regime to find a response to this controversy was the *leitmotiv* for regulatory action outside the trade regime. Many countries had therefore, as Nina Obuljen indicates, "the expectation to negotiate a trade treaty, a culture friendly trade treaty"[3] within the framework of UNESCO.

Opposed to the creation of a trade treaty were the countries who saw the rationale of the newly to establish international instrument "to promote cultural development and intercultural dialogue."[4] Obuljen sides with this view and expresses that it would be a "mistake to look at the Convention as an instrument

---

* Professor of Law, Kyushu University Faculty of Law.

** LL.B (1994) & LL.M. (1997) (University of Antwerp); LL.M (1998) & LL.D. (2005) Kyushu University. Associate Professor, Kyushu University Faculty of Law.

1 *See* Convention on the Protection and Promotion of the Diversity of Cultural Expressions, 20 October 2005, *U.N. Doc. CLT-2005/CONVENTION DIVERSITE-CULT REV.* [hereinafter "Convention on the Diversity of Cultural Expressions"].

2 *See* T. VOON, *Cultural Products and the World Trade Organization*, 2007, 173–202; I. BERNIER, "Trade and Culture", in P.F.J. MACRORY, A.E. APPLETON, and M.G. PLUMMER (eds.) *The World Trade Organization: Legal, Economic and Political Analysis* Vol. II, 2005,787–8.

3 N. OBULJEN, "From Our Creative Diversity to the Convention on Cultural Diversity", in N. OBULJEN and J. SMIERS (eds.), *UNESCO'S Convention on the Protection and the Promotion of the Diversity of Cultural Expressions: Making it Work*, 2006, 19.

4 Id.

whose only goal is to ensure special treatment of culture in trade negotiations or to confirm the sovereign rights of states to adopt cultural policies. While these aspects are important, in assessing the possible impact of the Convention it is important to look at the broader debates that have been taking place over the past decade or more, which go well beyond trade concerns."[5]

Based upon the volume of intellectual spinoffs dealing with the Convention on the Diversity of Cultural Expressions, the impression may grow that this Convention eventually is a trade related one.[6] Why else would most, if not all, discussion link to the relationship between the Convention on the Diversity of Cultural Expressions and the WTO? If a broader context was at play during the negotiations, would it not be possible that Convention on the Diversity of Cultural Expressions has something to contribute to the already existing UNESCO conventions on culture, the human rights instruments, or some other areas that may not be so obvious? Yet, the non-trade issues of the Convention on the Diversity of Cultural Expressions have barely received any attention.[7]

---

5 Id., at 20.

6 *See, e.g.*, A. Herold, *European Film Policies in EU and International Law: Culture and Trade – Marriage or Misalliance?*, 2010, 341–8; Ch. Germann, *Diversité Culturelle et Libre-Echange a la Lumière du Cinéma: Réflexions Critiques sur le Droit Naissant de la Diversité Culturelle sous les Angles du Droit de l'UNESCO et de l'OMC, de la Concurrence et de la Propriété Intellectuelle*, 2008, 357–70; R. J. Neuwirth, *The Cultural Industries in International Trade Law: Insights from the NAFTA, the WTO and the EU*, 2006, 345–1; A. Dahrendorf, "Free Trade Meets Cultural Diversity: The Legal Relationship between WTO Rules and the UNESCO Convention on the Protection of the Diversity of Cultural Expressions", in H. Schneider and P. Van den Bossche (eds.), *Protection of Cultural Diversity from a European and International Perspective*, 2008, 31; J. Wouters and B. De Meester, "Cultural Diversity and the WTO: David Versus Goliath", in H. Schneider and P. Van den Bossche (eds.), *Protection of Cultural Diversity from a European and International Perspective*, 2008, 85; J. Wouters and B. De Meester, "The New UNESCO Convention on Cultural Diversity and the WTO Law: A Case-Study in Fragmentation of International Law", 42 *J. World Trade* 205 (2008); Ch. B. Graber, "The New UNESCO Convention on Cultural Diversity: A Counterbalance to the WTO", 9 *JIEL* 553–74 (2006); M. Hahn, "A Clash of Cultures? The UNESCO *Diversity Convention* and International Trade Law", 9 *JIEL* 515–52 (2006); T. Voon, "UNESCO and the WTO: A Clash of Cultures?", 55 *ICLQ* 635–52 (2006); J. Wouters and B. De Meester, "UNESCO's Convention on Cultural Diversity and WTO Law: Complimentary or Contradictory?" (K.U. Leuven Institute for International Law, Working Paper no. 73, 2005), *available at* http://law.kuleuven.be/iir/nl/wp/WP/WP73e.pdf (last visited 2 February 2012); T. Broude, "Cultural Diversity and the WTO: A Diverse Relationship" (2005), *available at* www.asil.org/insights/2005/11/insightcomment051121_000.html (last visited 2 February 2012); J. Pauwelijn, "The UNESCO Convention on Cultural Diversity, and the WTO: Diversity in International Law-Making?" (2005), *available at* www.asil.org/insights/2005/11/insights051115.html (last visited 2 February 2012).

7 *See, e.g.*, F. Macmillan, "The UNESCO Convention as a New Incentive to Protect Cultural Diversity", in H. Schneider and P. Van den Bossche (eds.), *Protection of Cultural Diversity from a European and International Perspective*, 2008, 163 (highlighting copyright issues); J. Wouters and B. De Meester, "The Implementation by the European Community of the UNESCO Convention on Cultural Diversity" (Leuven Centre for Global Governance Studies, Policy Brief No. 8, 2008), *available at* http://ghum.kuleuven.be/ggs/publications/policy_briefs/pb06.pdf (last visited 2 February 2012) (covering the legal issues regarding the

The current book is inspired by the dichotomy identified as underlying the Convention on the Diversity of Cultural Expressions. If at all there has been an impact on the trade regime by the Convention on the Diversity of Cultural Expressions, it is also worthwhile to investigate on whether there is a broader spectrum affected by this Convention. In order to facilitate the understanding of this dichotomy and thus the possible scope of the Convention on the Diversity of Cultural Expressions, this chapter will introduce on the one hand the tension between trade and culture and on the other hand the efforts of UNESCO to broaden the scope of culture beyond the heritage sphere. The latter proved to be essential for allocating UNESCO as the appropriate venue to deal with the failure of the trade regime to take appropriate action regarding the trade and culture tension. At the same time, it has had an impact on the contents of the negotiations.

This introductory Chapter to the book is structured as follows. This Chapter will start out in Section 2 by depicting the long history of tension between trade and culture. The journey will start from the early concerns that several European countries had towards the trade imbalance that existed in the audiovisual sector around the end of World War I. After World War II, GATT offered a response to the cultural concerns in the audiovisual sector, which was at that time still limited to the cinematographic industry. The limited scope in coverage of GATT, brought the audiovisual sector again to the forefront of the trade negotiations in the Uruguay Round of Trade Negotiations. The result of these negotiations was a standstill in the framework of GATS. As WTO and its agreements did not further provide any hope for cultural considerations, Section 3 will introduce the initiatives to raise the awareness of the cultural arguments and the need to address them in a new legal instrument. UNESCO was pointed out as the appropriate international organization for this purpose. Section 4 will look at the negotiation of the new instrument to indicate that culture and trade quandary has only been one of the concerns of the negotiators. The broad spectrum of the Convention on the Diversity of Cultural Expressions warrants an investigation into whether this Convention has been able to have an impact on all the areas envisaged at the time of the negotiation. This will be answered in the different contributions to this book. A summary of these arguments will be provided in Section 5.

---

implementation by the EU); R. Craufurd Smith, "The UNESCO Convention on the Protection and Promotion of the Diversity of Cultural Expressions: Building a New World Information and Communication Order?", 1 *International Journal of Communication* 24 (2007) (covering besides the trade issues also the development issue and minority group issues); R. Albro, "Managing Culture at Diversity's Expense? Thoughts on the UNESCO's Newest Cultural Policy Instrument", 35 *J. Arts Management, Law and Society* 247 (2005) (engaging with the concept of diversity, such as how and why it matters, to whom it may apply, and how it may vary for different cultural subjects).

2. TRADE VERSUS CULTURE, A TENSION WITH A HISTORY

2.1. THE AFTERMATH OF WORLD WAR I: A DESTROYED EUROPEAN FILM INDUSTRY

At the end of the 19th and the beginning of the 20th century, Europe, France and Italy in particular, had a very thriving cinematographic film industry. In fact, they were dominating the cinematographic film industry internationally. This was partly made possible by an attempt of the American producers, distributors and exhibitors of films to stabilize their business, which was characterized by a devastating struggle for power. They chose for a rapid expansion of cheap film theatres all over the country, which would be able to run several films in one program. As a result, many more films were needed because of this new system. The American cinematographic film industry, even by concentrating on their domestic market alone, could not fulfil the sharp rise in demand. European films filled the gap.[8]

This picture drastically changed due to World War I. Capital necessary for making films was drained away to support the war fronts. Film industry personnel were being forced to join the army. The industry's raw-stock factories switched to manufacturing munitions. With this shift to a war economy, European film makers were not able to maintain a steady production of cinematographic films. Some film makers, especially in France, were even near a complete cessation of their production. This had an enormous impact on the United States film market. By loosing their main film suppliers, the United States film industry faced even more than before the need to step up their film production. They had to become self-sufficient to sustain an exhibition system they had just created.[9]

The armistice had also profound effects outside the United States, as European films were also prominently present elsewhere. The curtailment of the European industry now meant that these markets had to look for another source of supply. They found it in the United States, where the film industry, after overcoming its occupancy with struggles for domestic power, showed more and more interest in the international market. They eagerly stepped in to fill the by the war created vacuum.[10] This brought the United States film industry to be the

---

8 *See* K. Thompson and D. Bordwell, *Film History: An Introduction*, 2nd ed. 2003, 33–56.

9 *See* id., at 56.

10 *See* id., at 56–7 and 85; *See also* W. M. Shao, "Is there no Business Like Show Business? Free Trade and Cultural Protectionism", 20 *Yale J. Int'l L.* 105, 127–128 (1995) (stating that the export of United States' cinematographic films increased from 32 million feet of films to 235 million feet of films over a period of twelve years. Further, the author points out that by the 1920's, several states had already noticed that the United States' cinematographic films accounted for about four fifths of all cinematographic film screenings in the world).

world leader from the post-World War I era, a position that up until today has not been successfully challenged.

Whereas the European filmmakers reverted to competition to regain their position, they realized in the early 1920s that the United States business advantage of their film industry had grown too big to compete. Even if competition was possible, it too often meant a negative effect on the distinctive character that the various European filmmakers used to have. To shelter their cinematographic film industry, protective barriers were erected in Europe. Some countries installed import quotas, while others implemented screen quotas. Prompted by these barriers, the United States State Department lodged complaints with several of the European countries.[11] However, this remained without success, setting the tone for future disagreements about the cinematographic film industry – later extended to the audiovisual sector as a whole – in the process of trade negotiations.

2.2. THE HAVANA CHARTER: CONDITIONED SCREEN QUOTAS

World War II weakened Europe again, due to which they were in no position to make strong demands. The United States film industry saw its chance for returning to a free-for-all competition. Backed by the United States Department of State,[12] the film industry could obtain the elimination of most of the pre-war quotas on American films.[13] The by far most known bilateral agreement from that time is the Blum-Byrnes Agreement (1946), in which the Prime Minister Léon Blum and US Secretary of State James Byrnes reduced the guaranteed exhibition time for French movies to sixteen weeks per year.[14] These agreements had dramatic consequences. A huge drop in the domestic film production paralleled the tremendous increase of United States film imports. To rectify the situation, several European countries reverted back to import quotas or screen quotas, supplemented by extensive subsidy schemes for domestic films.[15]

11 *See* Shao, *supra* note 10, at 129.

12 It was the opinion of the United States officials that all communicative means should be used to prevent the Left to make headway in Western Europe. American films were seen, by the Bureau of Psychological Warfare, as one of the means to achieve this purpose. Moreover, President Truman, for example, secretly supported propaganda schemes that included the promotion of American film export, in order to fight the spread of communism in Europe. That this had to be done was also backed by the United States officials' conviction that all means of communication would be appropriate to spread American ideals to the destabilized areas.

13 *See* Bernier, *supra* note 2, at 748.

14 *See* Thompson and Bordwell, *supra* note 8, at 374.

15 *See* id., at 374–5; Th. H. Guback, *The International Film Industry, Western Europe and America Since 1945*, 1969, 22–3.

This renewed protectionist drive, characterizing the pre-war 'beggar-they-neighbour'[16] economic policies, was one of the stimuli to elevate the negotiations about trade restrictions to the multilateral level. It was perceived that these self-interested economic trade policies contributed to instability in international relations.[17] Only a liberalized world market would be able to make an end to the ever-returning trade conflicts between countries. In order to achieve this ideal of a free and liberalized world trade order, the war victors proceeded with the drafting of a new charter for world trade, the Havana Charter (1948). This stillborn Charter had to provide, among others, a solution for the trade conflict between the United States and Europe about the protection of the latter's film industry.

The draft of the Havana Charter included, what Clair Wilcox calls, a recognition that the cinematographic film is entitled to protection against foreign competition.[18] Article 19 of the Havana Charter stipulated that countries were allowed to adopt screen quotas under certain conditions.[19] The United States Department of State explicitly made clear that this protection should not be linked with cultural considerations. In doing so, they denied the cinematographic film industry an intrinsic value worth protecting. The Department of State rather focused on the monetary aspect of films, by arguing that the earning power of films gave them a special status.[20]

2.3. GATT'S CONFIRMATION OF PROTECTIONIST MEASURES IN THE FORM OF SCREEN QUOTAS

Without waiting for the completion and entering into force of the Havana Charter, less then half of the participating states began in 1946 negotiations to eradicate discriminatory tariffs and other trade barriers employed in the trade of goods. This led to the General Agreement on Tariffs and Trade[21] in 1947 (GATT 1947). During the negotiations of the GATT 1947, the cultural industries got particular attention. France wanted to shield this industry from the forces of liberalization by including a cultural exclusion clause in the GATT 1947.[22] Opposition from the United States, which saw this industry as part of the

16 *See* Shao, *supra* note 10, at 109.

17 *See* J. H. Jackson, *The Jurisprudence of GATT and the WTO: Insights on Treaty Law and Economic Relations*, 2000, 21.

18 *See* C. A. Wilcox, *Charter for World Trade*, 1949, 77.

19 *See* Bernier, *supra* note 2, at 754.

20 *See* id.; *See also* J. H. Jackson, *World Trade and the Law of GATT*, 1969, 293 n.1.

21 *See* General Agreement on Tariffs and Trade 1947, 1 January 1948, *available at* www.wto.org/english/docs_e/legal_e/gatt47.pdf *LT/UR/A-1A/1/GATT/1* (last visited 2 February 2012).

22 *See* P. S. Grant and Ch. Wood, *Blockbusters and Trade Wards: Popular Culture in a Globalized World*, 2004, 356.

entertainment industry and thus not worthwhile a different protection than other goods, prevented the inclusion of such a clause.[23]

Nevertheless, to accommodate the existing protective national laws, there was sensitivity for granting a special treatment to the cinematographic film industry.[24] This industry, especially in Europe, had once more to recover from the disruptive effects of a war. The negotiators could therefore agree on a special treatment for the film industry and incorporated Article IV.[25] This Article sets out special rules for screen quotas for cinematographic films. Pursuant to Article IV, states were allowed to reserve screen time for their domestic films. However, this Article called upon its member States to enter in negotiations on the limitation, liberalization and, eventually, elimination of these screen quotas.[26]

The exemption of screen quotas from the national treatment and most favourite nations treatment, has led to discussion as to what the motive could have been to incorporate it. The United Kingdom, Norway and, at that time, Czechoslovakia have pointed to cultural considerations to insert screen quotas within GATT,[27] an explanation with which John Jackson seems to agree in his work entitled *World Trade and the Law of GATT*.[28] Domestic cultural policies, he argues, more than reasons of economics and trade, urged the different states to accept the cinematographic film exception.[29] The historical review of Article IV, prepared by the GATT Secretariat in 1990, joined this interpretation.[30] The United States, however, have always emphasized that the economic value of cinematographic films lies beyond the special treatment. Recently, however, a change in communication is visible. Rather than emphasizing the economic value, they seem to hold that purely historical facts explain the insertion of the screen quotas. A devastated European film industry could only recover with special treatment. Leaving the films to the competitive forces of the market

23 *See* Herold, *supra* note 6, at 269.

24 *See* R.J. Neuwirth, "The Cultural Industries and the Legacy of Article IV GATT: Rethinking the Relation of Culture and Trade in the Light of the New WTO Round", 3 (Europe-Russia Conference Series, Carleton University, November 22–23, 2002), *available at* http://papers.ssrn.com/sol3/papers.cfm?abstract_id=1352171 (last visited2 February 2012).

25 *See* Bernier, *supra* note 2, at 754; *See also* R. L. Van Harpen, "Mamas, Don't Let Your Babies Grow Up to Be Cowboys: Reconciling Trade and Cultural Independence", 4 *Minn. J. Global Trade* 169, n.18 (1995).

26 This provision constitutes an exception to the national treatment obligation of Article III of the GATT 1994, to the MFN treatment obligation of Article I:1 of the GATT 1994 and to the obligation to eliminate quantitative restrictions of Article XI of the GATT 1994.

27 Second Session of the Preparatory Committee of the United Nations Conference on Trade and Development, *Doc. EPCT/TACF/SR/10* (Geneva 1947).

28 *See* J. H. Jackson, supra note 20.

29 *See* id., at 293; *See also* R.L. Van Harpen, "Mamas, Don't Let Your Babies Grow Up to Be Cowboys: Reconciling Trade and Cultural Independence", 4 *Minn. J. Global Trade* 167 (1995).

30 *See* GATT Doc. MTN.GSN/AUD/W/1 (4 October 1990).

would have meant that the European film industry would not be able to secure adequate screen time.[31]

By allowing screen quotas, the controversy surrounding the film industry did not end. It was rather the start for further discussions. As technology advanced, other forms of media became widespread around the 1960s. Several countries applied trade restrictions to this other forms of media, in particular to television programming. The United States, during the Nineteenth Session of the Contracting Parties to GATT in 1961, urged to set up a working party within the framework of GATT to examine whether GATT 1949 could be applied to these trade restrictions.[32]

Three points of view emerged within this Working Party, of which two accept that television programs are products within the scope of GATT 1949. The division between these two views was determined on whether televisions programs are distinct from cinematographic films or not. Hence, the distinction was important regarding the application of the Article IV GATT 1949. The United States, by denying the similarity of the products, rejected the application of Article IV GATT 1949,[33] while Canada, among others, advocated for a similar treatment.[34] France, on the other hand, favoured a completely different stance, in that it was not convinced that television programs would be that easily categorize as products. Therefore, a suggestion was made to postpone any decision on this issue.[35]

France's suggestion seemed to have coincidently gained prevalence. In a search for a recommendation, the Working Party made several drafts. However, the divergent views made the adoption of any recommendation impossible. This outcome did not mean that no progress was made. Due to the divergence, a prudent stance towards Article IV GATT 1949 became prevalent. Further, France's viewpoint opened the discussion of considering a different categorization for the audiovisual sector.[36] As will be seen in next section, the plea was ultimately won by those who favoured the audiovisual sector as a service rather than a product.

---

31 *See* WTO, Council for Trade in Services, "Communication from the United States, Audiovisual and Related Services", *Doc. S/CSS/W/21*, §19 (18 December 2000).

32 *See* J. Filipek, "Culture Quotas: The Trade Controversy over European Community's Broadcasting Directive", 28 *Stan. J. Int'l L.* 340 (1992).

33 *See* id., at 341 (The United States held the position that: 1) there does not exist a widespread network of television stations that can guarantee that a certain element of competition is at work. The lack of television stations meant that there existed only a limited competitive bidding for the television programs; 2) the government usually operates the television stations, due to which there is insufficient pressure on broadcasters to seek the most popular programming and greater freedom for governments to restrict imports).

34 *See* Filipek, *supra* note 32, at 342.

35 *See* id.

36 *See* id.

2.4. THE URUGUAY ROUND: FROM CULTURAL SPECIFICITY TO CULTURAL EXCEPTION

The question on how to categorize the audiovisual sector arose again after about twenty-five years and this in the framework of the eighth round of multilateral trade negotiations, which started in 1986 in Punta del Sol, Uruguay. The Uruguay Round, the name under which these negotiations are generally known, did not start out by focusing on this question as one of the main issues. To the contrary, the audiovisual sector did not pose much of a problem at the beginning of the Uruguay Round. No state objected at the Ministerial Conference in Montreal in 1988 to the confirmation that the principles of GATT would be applicable to the audiovisual sector as well. It was only when the European Community adopted its Broadcasting Directive in 1989 that the audiovisual sector became one of the major issues,[37] with the creation of an Audio-Visual Working Group within the Group of Negotiations on Services as a result.[38]

The European Union did not have any specific strategy towards the talks in the Audio-Visual Working Group. Only after the French filmmakers contested to the liberalization of the audiovisual media, fearing that the Uruguay Round might lead to the dismantling of protective barriers, French politicians became sensible to what is really at stake for the audiovisual media in the Uruguay Round. Subsequently, the French government insisted Europe should negotiate a specific status for the audiovisual media.[39]

The main strategy followed by the European Union was to seek a special or specific treatment of the audiovisual sector under GATS.[40] The idea grew in the

---

37 *See* id., at 343; *See also* L.L. Garret, Comment, "Commerce versus Culture: The Battle Between the United States and the European Union over Audiovisual Trade Policies", 19 *N.C.J. Int'l & Com. Reg.* 553, 561 (the US and the EU started to disagree about the proper classification of audiovisuals).

38 *See* Filipek, *supra* note 32, at 343.

39 *See* Thompson and Bordwell, *supra* note 8, at 707 (stipulating that the counter attack of the French to keep the audiovisuals out of the liberalizations talks occurred around 1992). *See also* J. B. Prowda, U.S. "Dominance in the 'Marketplace of Culture' and the French 'Cultural Exception'", 29 *NYU Int'l L. & P.* 193, 199–8 (1996–7); T. W. Chao, Comment, "GATT's Cultural Exemption of Audiovisual Trade: The United States May have lost the Battle but not the War", 17 *U. Pa. J. Int'l Econ. L.* 1127, 1141, n. 82–4 (all including statement of French politicians made around 1993, a time when the Uruguay Round was about to reach its end goals). It is even been said that Even when the president of the European Commission, Jacques Delors, proclaimed in October 1989 that the audiovisual sector was not a merchandise like any other, no specific strategies emerged within the EU or among its member States.

40 *See* S. Cahn and D. Schimmel, "The Cultural Exception: Does it Exists in GATT and GATS Framework? How Does it Affect or is it Affected by the Agreement on TRIPS", 15 *Card. Arts and Ent. L. J.* 294–5 (1997); *See also* M. E. Footer and Ch. B. Graber, "Trade Liberalization and Cultural Policy", 3 *J. Econ. L.* 116, 118 (2000) (we can deduct this from Leon Brittan's intervention – Leon Brittan was the European Commissioner responsible for the GATT negotiations – in the European Parliament on July 14, 1993. During this intervention he admitted that the European Commission did not succeed in their main objective of making the other parties to accept the cultural specificity of the audiovisual sector).

European Council that certain sectors should be treated separately because of their specificity. The audiovisual sector reveals this specificity by the fact that it includes – at least partially – a cultural component.[41] This cultural component justifies that the audiovisual sector would not be treated identical to other sectors. In practice, the specificity clause would mean that the WTO members adopt sectorial annexes to GATS, which contain express exceptions to the most favoured nation treatment and to the national treatment principle and permissions to deny access to imports of audiovisual services.

The cultural specificity clause in the Uruguay Round would have included the audiovisual sector in the liberalization process of GATS. At the same time, the clause would have enabled the European Union to maintain its Television without Frontiers Directive and to continue subsidizing national film production. In doing so, national and local cultural identities would also be preserved.[42]

France, supported by a majority of the European film industry, lobbied for a more radical strategy. Several reasons were advanced.[43] First, the cultural specificity would only end in the sole protection of the actual applicable audiovisual policies. Countries would have to abide by the specific commitments they made. Second, the United States might press for the further liberalization of the audiovisual sector once it is included in GATS.[44] Third, experts pointed to the vagueness of the cultural specificity clause. The vagueness would make it not only difficult for the United States and the European Union to agree on what the concept covers, but also for a dispute resolution panel. In such a case the dispute resolution panel might interpret the concept narrowly, so that it becomes most likely an unfavourable concept for the European Union. Having learned about what is really at stake, the European Parliament revoked its support for the cultural specificity clause in September 1993. Instead, the Parliament declared itself in favour of a cultural exception clause.

The cultural exception sought to give the audiovisual sector the status of exception to GATS' liberalization obligations, similar to GATS exceptions for public health and national security. Three options remained. First, a derogation

---

41 *See* F. Dehousse and Fr. Havelange, "Aspect Audiovisuels des Accords du GATT Exception ou Spécificité Culturelle?", in C. Doutrelepont (ed.), *L'Europe et les Enjeux du GATT dans le Domaine de L'Audiovisuel*, 1994, 123.

42 *See* Cahn and Schimmel, *supra* note 40, at 294–5 (Cahn and Schimmel point to the fact that the cultural specificity clause would enable states to maintain their quota system and to further subsidize their national film industries. The European Commission saw two more reasons in order to defend this cultural specificity clause. First, the inclusion of the audiovisual media in GATS would legally protect the sector against unilateral action taken by another Member of GATS. Second, by including the audiovisual media, the European Commission prevented the creation of a dangerous precedent of excluding sectors.

43 *See* J.-J. Plantin, "Exception Culturelle Contre Spécificité Culturelle: Les Enjeux", 5 *Revue de la SACD* 10–1 (1993).

44 *See* Cahn and Schimmel, *supra* note 40, at 294–5.

of the most favoured nation clause could be sought. European negotiators did not even propose this option, because such derogation would only be temporarily and limited by the national treatment clause. Second, a cultural exception clause similar to NAFTA's cultural exception clause could be negotiated, leaving space for retaliatory action. The option was not further considered. Third, a cultural exception clause could be negotiated in Article XIV of GATS final draft. Article XIV of GATS provides a means of taking measures as long as they are not arbitrary and unjustifiable discrimination. The European negotiators defended that culture could be a basis for taking measures restricting trade and that it could be added as a subdivision in this article. The threat behind this proposal would be that the cultural exception would be narrowly construed.[45]

Being confronted with two opposing views on the position that should taken towards the audiovisual media, the then twelve ministers of culture of the European Union met in Belgium in October 1993.[46] They discussed the status culture, alias the audiovisual media, should get in the Uruguay Round. Their position was adopted in a six part resolution, known as the 'Six Informal Requirements of Mons'.[47] That resolution sought to:

(1) To request an *ad hoc* exemption from the MFN clause in order to enable EU member states to maintain privileged relations with states outside the European Union and with whom no economic integration agreements exist;
(2) To obtain the continuity and extension of public aid and subsidies;
(3) To maintain the opportunity for regulating the present modes of broadcast transmission as well as future technologies in this regard;
(4) To maintain the opportunity to develop every political aid to the audiovisual sector in all its aspects (creation, production, diffusion, radio diffusion, distribution and exploitation);
(5) To exclude the audiovisual sector from the principle of progressive liberalization;
(6) To maintain the *acquis communautaire*, notably the results achieved by the TVSF Directive[48]

In order to achieve the aim set forward in the Six Informal Requirements to a full extent, the ministers advocated that adding a cultural exception to Article XIV GATS' final draft would be the most appropriate. This Article XIV GATS'

45 *See* id., at 298.
46 *See* Cahn and Schimmel, *supra* note 40, at 294; *See also* Dehousse and Havelange, *supra* note 41, at 123.
47 *See* Dehousse and Havelange, *supra* note 41, at 123.
48 Id., at 124 (translation by the authors); an informal description is also given by Cahn and Schimmel. *See* Cahn and Schimmel, *supra* note 40, at 294.

final draft would have allowed a state to take measures restricting trade as long as they are not arbitrary and unjustifiable discrimination.[49]

The Six Informal Requirements could not just be neglected. The European Commission, in charge for the negotiations, therefore amended its position in order to safeguard the existing quota and subsidy systems. The European Commission worked out a proposal in which the Member States to the WTO would only be bound by the principles of free trade to the extent that they have committed themselves. Most favoured nation treatment, national treatment and market access would only be applicable if a Member State would choose for it.[50] Further, the Commission aimed at creating the possibility to object to progressive liberalization of the audiovisual sector and to incorporate a cultural specificity clause in Article XV GATS (subsidies) and the Annex on Article II (MFN Exemptions).[51] However, the European Council disfavoured this approach. In December 1993, the Council vowed its support for a cultural exception and ordered not to negotiate for anything less than the objectives defined in the Six Informal Requirements of Mons.[52]

2.5. THE CREATION OF A LEGAL STANDSTILL WITHIN GATS

The United States strongly objected to the idea of keeping the audiovisual sector out GATS, creating basically an impasse. The negotiators could not else than admit that they could only agree to disagree.[53] The major key point of the agreement to disagree was to create a legal standstill in the liberalization of the audiovisual sector. In other words, the impact of the inclusion of the audiovisual sector in GATS, brought about by the principles of market access, national treatment and most-favoured-nation, had to be neutralized. The means to achieve this end were commitments and exemptions.[54]

---

49 *See* D. Atkinson, "Cultural Diversity: The Right of States and Governments to Support Culture in the light of the Changing Regulatory Framework of International Trade, Towards an International Instrument" §2.1 (2001), *available at* www.incp-ripc.org/w-group/wg-cdg/reader/rightofstates_e.shtml (last visited 2 February 2012) (The threat behind this proposal would be that exception to the general prohibition against discrimination would be narrowly construed).

50 *See* Dehousse and Havelange, *supra* note 41, at 123.

51 *See* id., at 124.

52 *See* id., at 124.

53 *See* Cahn and Schimmel, *supra* note 40, at 298–9; *See also* B. de Witte, "Trade in Culture: International Legal regimes and EU Constitutional Values, in J. Scott and G. De Burca (eds.), *The EU and the WTO: Legal and Constitutional Issues*, 2001, 243; Footer and Graber, *supra* note 40, at 118.

54 *See* T. Kono, "The UNESCO Convention for the Protection and the Promotion of the Diversity of Cultural Expressions", in K. Alexander and M. Andenas (eds.), *The World*

Commitments overcome the burden of market access and national treatment. Member States will only be obliged to abide by the principles of market access and national treatment if they wish so. To make that wish obvious, the Member States have to expressly confirm their commitment to these two principles. These commitments appear in schedules. The schedules are complex documents in which each Member State identifies the service sectors or sub sector to which and to what extent it will apply the market access and national treatment obligations.[55] The commitments regarding market access and national treatment, supplemented with the possible limitations on these principles, apply to the four modes of supply that constitute the definition of trade in services in Article I of the GATS: (1) cross-border supply, (2) consumption abroad, (3) commercial presence, and (4) presence of natural persons.[56] Only negotiations can unwind the commitments once undertaken.

Unlike the case for market access and national treatment, the principle of most-favourite nation treatment (MFN treatment) applies automatically to all services within the scope of GATS. Article II:1 states that with respect to any measure covered by GATS, each WTO member shall accord immediately and unconditionally to services and service suppliers of any other member treatment no less favourable that it accords to like services and service supplier of any other country. There is, however, a possibility to keep the measures inconsistent with the most favourite nation principle on the condition that these inconsistent measures have been listed either at the end of the Uruguay Round or, if later, the date of accession. There is no possibility for WTO members to seek new exemptions under this Article, not even for existing measures that had escaped their attention during the Uruguay Round or, in case of recent WTO members, the accession process. In short, the MFN treatment applies in general to all internationally traded services, except for the exemptions made during the

Trade Organization and Trade in Services, 2008, 873–89 (giving a detailed overview of these commitments and exemptions).

55 *See* World Trade Organization, *Guide to Reading the GATS Schedules of Specific Commitments and the List of Article II (MFN) Exemptions, available at* www.wto.org/english/tratop_e/serv_e/guide1_e.htm (last visited 2 February 2012).

56 The modes of supply should be understood in the following way: cross-border supply – the possibility for non-resident service suppliers to supply services cross-border into the Member's territory; consumption abroad – the freedom for the Member's residents to purchase services in the territory of another Member; commercial presence – the opportunities for foreign service suppliers to establish, operate or expand a commercial presence in the Member's territory, such as a branch, agency, or wholly-owned subsidiary; presence of natural persons – the possibilities offered for the entry and temporary stay in the Member's territory of foreign individuals in order to supply a service. *See* P. A. Messerlin, S. Siwek, and E. Cocq, *The Audiovisual Services Sector in the GATS Negotiations*, 2003, 15; *See also* Ch. B. Graber, *Handel und Kultur im Audiovisionsrecht der WTO Völkerrechtliche, ökonomische und kulturpolitische Grundlagen einer globalen Medienordnung*, 2003, 183; World Trade Organization, *GATS Explained, available at* www.wto.org/english/thewto_e/whatis_e/tif_e/agrm6_e.htm#commitments (last visited 2 February 2012).

Uruguay Round or the accession process. It is thus conceptualized as a once-only opportunity.[57]

2.6. NEGOTIATING FURTHER LIBERALIZATION OF THE AUDIOVISUAL SECTOR

By creating this unique structure for GATS, WTO members could continue to protect their audiovisual sector as they had been doing so far. The least that can be said, is that the WTO members do not show any reticence in using this unique structure in order to protect their audiovisual sector. Hence, one could even state that a *de facto* cultural exception has been created. The original plan was to give only a temporary character to the *de facto* cultural exception. Negotiations would resume after a period of 5 years. Results of these negotiations should be reached after another period of 5 years, since the MFN exemptions have, in principle, only a legal basis for a period of 10 years. 2000 and 2005 should have been crucial years for GATS, but nothing changed.[58]

Following the build in agenda of Article XIX GATS, WTO members started negotiations in January 2000 in order to achieve a higher standard of liberalization of services.[59] The negotiations got their real start with the Doha Ministerial Conference in November 2001, where it was agreed to follow a request-offer approach based on the existing list of commitments.[60] While initial requests were due for 30 June 2002, initial offers had to be presented before

---

57 *See* R. Adlung, "The GATS Turns Ten: A Preliminary Stocktaking", 4 (WTO Staff Working Paper ERSD 2004-05), *available at* www.wto.org/english/res_e/reser_e/ersd200405_e.doc (last visited 2 February 2012); Until October 2000, 420 exemptions have been made, involving more than two-thirds of the WTO members. These exemptions are mainly situated in the sector of services that have attracted relatively few commitments, in particular the various transport sectors (35 per cent) and the audiovisual sector (20 per cent) *See* id., 3-4.

58 *See* Wouters and De Meester, "Cultural Diversity and the WTO: David Versus Goliath", in H. Schneider and P. Van den Bossche (eds.), *supra* note 2, at 118-9 and 118 n. 149.

59 Only four WTO members (Japan, the United States, Brazil, and Switzerland) formulated GATS 2000 negotiation proposals directly mentioning the audiovisual sector. *See* Communication from Japan, The Negotiations on Trade in Services, *S/CSS/W/42* (22 December 2000), paragraphs 36-37; *See* Communication from the United States, Audiovisual and Related Services, *S/CSS/W/21* (18 December 2000), ANNEX A; *See* Communication from Brazil, Audiovisual Services, *S/CSS/W/99* (9 July 2001); *See* Communication from Switzerland, GATS 2000: Audio-visual Services, *S/CSS/W/74* (4 May 2001); *See* Communication from Canada, Initial Canadian Negotiating Proposals, *S/CSS/W/46* (14 March 2001) paragraph 9; France used even stronger terms to reiterate the doctrine of cultural specificity. *See* de Witte, *supra* note 53, at 244; *See* B. Marre, "Rapport d'Information sur la Préparation de la Conférence Ministérielle de l'OMC à Seattle", 139 (30 septembre 1999), *available at* www.assemblee-nationale.fr/europe/rap-info/i1824.pdf (last visited 2 February 2012).

60 *See* World Trade Organization, "Technical Aspects of Requests and Offers" (2002), *available at* www.wto.org/english/tratop_e/serv_e/requests_offers_approach_e.doc (last visited 2 February 2012).

31 March 2003. Request relating to the audiovisual sector have not been made.[61] Offers, to the contrary, have been formulated.

If we compare the offers made and the post-Uruguay situation of GATS, there is not much of a change. The EU has not formulated any offer regarding the audiovisual sector. The EU market access restrictions in the audiovisual sector would be able to remain in effect. Even if the MFN exemptions' period of legal existence is not prolonged, the omission of specific commitments in the audiovisual sector means that foreign films and television programs still face the broadcast quotas within all EU markets. The EU neglected to go along with the United States, Japan, and Brazil that urged in the negotiations proposals to increase the number of positive commitments.

Not only has the EU refrained from making any offer in the audiovisual sector, so has Canada. Canada, which requires all over the air television broadcasters to program at least 60 per cent of their annual broadcast time with programming certified as Canadian content, still keeps all cultural services out of GATS by not making any commitment. In Australia, where 50% of programming broadcast between 6 a.m. and midnight must be of Australian origin, GATS would not alter this situation. The Australian offer does not stipulate any specific commitment in this regard. The offer of India and China do not substantially differ from the specific commitments they have made so far, due to which market access and national treatment is only applicable to a limited number of sub-sectors. Based on the absence of any offer of the Republic of Korea, Korea seems to express its satisfaction with the present commitments it made. These, or better the absence of any further commitments, allow Korea to require the cinemas to show Korean films 146 days out of a year.[62]

Substantial commitments in the audiovisual sector and its sub-sectors have not been made. Notwithstanding the switch in position of the United States towards openness of a cultural consciousness in trade, due to which we might nurse hopes that the Doha Round would solve an old problem in the trade liberalization, an analysis of the offers regarding specific commitments prudently compels the conclusion that a solution within WTO might not be for tomorrow.

---

61 There exist four types of requests, which are not mutually exclusive. First, a WTO member may request of another the addition of sectors that are not included in its schedule. Second, a request may ask the removal of existing limitations or reducing its level of restrictiveness. Third, a WTO member may request of another for additional commitments under Article XVII. Fourth, a request may relate to the removal of MFN exemptions. The exchange of requests as a process has traditionally been purely bilateral. It is simply a process of letters being addressed from the requesting participants to their negotiating partners. The WTO secretariat does not have any role in this process.

62 *See* MESSERLIN, SIWEK, and COCQ, *supra* note 56, 26.

3. CULTURAL TENSIONS IN THE TRADE REGIME

3.1. CIVIL SOCIETY GROUPS TAKE INITIATIVE

The audiovisual industry has been a stumbling block in the trade liberalization negotiations for several decades. The trade negotiators have tried to reconcile the opposing views of how to deal with this industry. Up until now, they have not succeeded in this task. The relationship between trade and the audiovisual sector proved to be so sensitive, that has been opted for politically safe solution. WTO Members have been given the option to choose how fast and to what extent they will open their audiovisual markets. To this end, a special structure was created for the trade in services.

Not necessarily satisfied with this outcome, several civil society groups, advocating a degree of protection for the audiovisual industry, and culture at large, started to take action.[63] The Canadian Cultural Industries Sectoral Advisory Group on International Trade ("SAGIT") called upon the Canadian

[63] By making reference to Ivan Bernier, Toshiyuki Kono has indicated that several events explain the increased interest of civil society groups in dealing with the audiovisual sector. Kono describes roughly that "[f]irst, the OECD negotiations on a Multilateral Agreement on Investment failed in 1998. During these negotiations, France argued in favor of an exception for cultural industries in the following clause: "Nothing in this agreement shall be construed to prevent any Contracting Party to take any measure to regulate investment of foreign companies and the conditions of activity of those companies, in the framework of policies designed to preserve and promote cultural and linguistic diversity." A consensus was lacking during the Uruguay Round, so was it during the OECD negotiations on MAI as well. France withdrew from the negotiations, bringing them to an immediate halt. Second, the failure of the third Ministerial Conference in Seattle in 1999 has revealed that greater awareness should be shown regarding the impact globalization and trade liberalization may have on cultures understood in a sociological and anthropological sense. Following these events, influential people pointed out that "backlash against globalization is much more than economics" [...] and "...The fact is we are witnessing the first stirrings of a cultural backlash against globalization whose effects are likely to be significant and far-reaching" [...]. Faouzia Zouari states that the precedence that economic imperatives take over social and political values, backed by the prodigious expansion of the information highway, is challenging national identities, sometimes driving them into retreat and even into aggressively asserting counter-models. [...] In this context, Canada puts the *Cultural Industries Sectoral Advisory Group on International Trade* (SAGIT) in place by the Canadian Department of Foreign Affairs and International Trade in order to respond to the friction between cultural diversity and globalization. Canada is, around the same time, also the driving force behind the *International Network on Cultural Diversity,* a forum to civil society to debate on cultural diversity, and the Working Group on cultural Diversity and Globalization within INCP. Since the INCP is at this moment the only intergovernmental organization actively involved in the project on cultural diversity, I limit the major discussion on this Network." Kono draws on the following sources: I. Bernier, "A UNESCO International Convention on Cultural Diversity", *in* Ch. B. Graber, M. Girsberger and M. Nenova (eds.), *Free Trade versus Cultural Diversity* 68–71 (2004); F. Bergsten, "Backlash against Globalization" (speech held at Trilateral Commission in Tokyo, May 9, 2000), *available at* www.iie.com/publications/papers/paper.cfm?ResearchID=377 (last visited 2 February 2012); J. Rifkin, "World Culture Resists Bowing to Commerce", Los Angeles Times, July 2, 2001; F. Zouari, "Synthese des

government in its report, entitled *New Strategies for Culture and Trade: Canadian Culture in a Global World*, to take further initiative.[64] More in specific, the report recommended that Canada should take the lead in calling on other countries to develop a new international instrument on cultural diversity. This new instrument should emphasize the difference of cultural goods and services from other products and services and prescribe rules appropriately adjusted to this distinct character.

The idea of developing a new international instrument on trade and cultural goods and services was further pursued by the International Network for Cultural Diversity ("INCD"), an international non-governmental organization, composed of artists, cultural producers, professional organizations and academics. Within the framework of countering the adverse effects of globalization on culture, the INCD endorsed the need for a new legally binding international instrument protecting cultural goods and services from the negative consequences of gradually progressing liberalized trade regime at its annual meeting in Santorini in 2000.[65]

Under the impulse of the Minister of Canadian Heritage, Sheila Copps, several ministers of culture met informally in 1998.[66] This informal meeting resulted in the establishment of the International Network on Cultural Policy ("INCP") one year later. This network at the ministerial level of 72 States[67] aims at exchanging views on the emerging cultural policy issues.[68] One of these issues

---

Raport et des Contributions" 7, available at http://confculture.francophonie.org/TrvxPrep/pdf/Synthese.pdf (last visited 2 February 2012).

64 *See* The Cultural Industries Sectoral Advisory Group on International Trade The Cultural Industries Sectoral Advisory Group on International Trade, "New Strategies for Culture and Trade: Canadian Culture in a Global World" (February 1999), *available at* www.international.gc.ca/trade-agreements-accords-commerciaux/fo/canculture.aspx?lang=en (last visited 2 February 2012).

65 *See* INCD Secretariat, Canadian Conference of the Arts, "Summary Report on The Artist, Culture and Globalization and The Founding Meeting of the International Network for Cultural Diversity" (December 2000), *available at* www.incd.net/santorini.html (last visited 2 February 2012).

66 *See* id., at 25.

67 *See* International Network on Cultural Policy, "Member Countries", *available at* http://incp-ripc.org/members/index_e.shtml (last visited 2 February 2012).

68 *See* Kono, *supra* note 54, at 894–6 (where the author indicates that "to achieve the aim of a new instrument, several working groups have been formed within the INCP. One of these working groups is the Working Group on Cultural Diversity and Globalization, established during the annual ministerial meeting of 1999 taking place in Oaxaca. A real breakthrough for this working group came a year later. The Working Group's discussion paper at the Santorini annual ministerial meeting, *International Responses to the Challenges Facing Cultural Diversity*, was so favorably welcomed that the mandate of the Working Group was extended. Besides working on the development of a vision, principles and common objectives related to cultural diversity, the ministers agreed that the Working Group should elaborate the framework and scope of a new international instrument to protect cultural diversity. A report was submitted to the ministers at the 2001 annual meeting. At the same meeting, the ministers of the INCP agreed to give a two-year mandate to the Working Group to continue developing the international instrument").

discussed was the idea of drafting a new convention on cultural diversity, which the culture ministers publicly supported during their meeting in Lucerne in 2001.[69]

In this context, it is not surprising that, in 2003, a Canadian network of artist organizations and trade organizations of producers, known as the Coalition for Cultural Diversity, formulated request for a binding instrument via Jacques Chirac, at that time the President of France. The request was made during the second meeting of this civil society organization, which was hosted by the French Comité de Vigilance pour la Diversité Culturelle in Paris.[70]

3.2. SHIFTING THE VENUE

The public support resulted in the preparation of a draft document of such a new international instrument. Extremely active in this respect was the INCP. At their annual meeting in 1999, which took place in Oaxaca, they established the Working Group on Cultural Diversity and Globalization ("Working Group").[71] Their discussion paper, *International Responses to the Challenges Facing Cultural Diversity*, was so favourably welcomed that their mandate was extended at the Santorini annual meeting.[72] It was also decided, Kono informs us, that "[b]esides working on the development of a vision, principles and common objectives related to cultural diversity, [...] the Working Group should elaborate the framework and scope of a new international instrument to protect cultural diversity."[73] The latter mandate was extended by two years in 2001.[74]

The agenda of the mandate in 2001 was twofold. In the report of the Working Group of the Oslo meeting, it was stated that "[t]he first part of the mandate is to write a draft text of an instrument that would focus on the promotion and preservation of cultural diversity in the face of globalization, including the

---

69 *See* International Network on Cultural Policy, Ministerial Meetings, "International Network on Cultural Policy 4th Annual Ministerial Meeting Lucerne September 24–26 2001 – Final Report" (Lucerne, September 2001), *available at* http://incp-ripc.org/meetings/2001/index_e.shtml (last visited 2 February 2012).

70 *See* Obuljen, *supra* note 3, at 26.

71 *See* International Network on Cultural Policy, Ministerial Meetings, "Second INCP Annual Ministerial Meeting – Oaxaca, Mexico, September 20 and 21, 1999 – Final Report" (Oaxaca, September 1999), *available at* http://incp-ripc.org/meetings/1999/index_e.shtml (last visited 2 February 2012).

72 *See* International Network on Cultural Policy, Ministerial Meetings, "Third INCP Annual Ministerial Meeting – Santorini, Greece, September 27–28, 2000 – Final Report" (Santorini, Spetember 2000), *available at* http://incp-ripc.org/meetings/2000/santorini2/index_e.shtml (last visited 2 February 2012).

73 *See* Kono, *supra* note 54, at 897.

74 *See* International Network on Cultural Policy, Ministerial Meetings, "Lucerne Statement" (Lucerne, September 2001), *available at* http://incp-ripc.org/meetings/2001/statement_e.shtml (last visited 2 February 2012).

impact of trade liberalization, prejudicial trade practices and rapid technological advancement on cultural products and policies. The second part of the mandate on this instrument is a study on key governance issues for the instrument will be led by Switzerland, including where it could be housed, notions of enforceability, etc. will complement the draft text."[75] The latter task was given to a special team within the Working Group, named the Special Policy Research Team on Governance Issues.[76]

After having been notified of the results of the drafting process during INCP's annual meeting in 2002, the ministers of culture agreed that the draft would constitute an appropriate basis for the further development of an enforceable agreement to preserve and promote cultural diversity. The Working Group was asked to provide a refined text of their proposal taking the following points into consideration in order to develop, what has been termed within the INCP, the International Instrument on Cultural Diversity ("IICD")[77]:

- Deepening the elaboration of the Instrument's rights and obligations regarding cultural policies in the context of globalization and technological change.
- Elaborating the needs of developing countries, both in terms of obligations and international co-operation, within the Instrument text.
- Addressing the linkages to other agreements and institutions, which should be studied further to enable the Instrument to achieve its objectives.
- Ongoing advocacy and awareness raising on the importance of cultural diversity and the international instrument and the crossovers with other international agendas.[78]

The Ministerial Meeting in Cape Town also considered the venue of IICD. Three options, all being elaborated on by the Special Policy Research Team on Governance Issues, were being discussed: the WTO, UNESCO or a stand alone

---

75 *See* INCP's Working Group on Cultural Diversity and Globalization, "Meeting Report" (Oslo, November 2001), available at http://incp-ripc.org/w-group/wg-cdg/oslo/1101report_e.shtml (last visited 2 February 2012); *See also* International Network on Cultural Policy, Ministerial Meetings, "Theme 2 – Cultural Diversity and Globalization: Consideration of an International Instrument on Cultural Diversity" (Lucerne, September 2011), *available at* http://incp-ripc.org/meetings/2001/rt2-synthesis_e.shtml (last visited 2 February 2012).

76 *See* International Network on Cultural Policy, Ministerial Meetings, *supra* note 74; *See also* International Network on Cultural Policy, Ministerial Meetings, "Report for Ministerial Consideration: An International Instrument on Cultural Diversity from the Working Group on Cultural Diversity and Globalization 2001–2002" (Cape Town, October 2002), *available at* http://incp-ripc.org/meetings/2002/consideration_e.shtml (last visited 2 February 2012).

77 *See* International Network on Cultural Policy, Ministerial Meetings, *supra* note 69.

78 *See* International Network on Cultural Policy, Ministerial Meetings, "Report for Ministerial Consideration", *supra* note 76.

agreement.[79] WTO was disfavoured because of the draft, even though it had commercial aspects in it, was culturally inspired.[80] The option of a stand alone agreement was criticized because of the lack of an institutional sponsorship may have a negative impact on the acceptance of the instrument and the funding of it, but also because it complicates the integration of the new instrument in the existing international legal fabric.[81] UNESCO was described as "the (natural) benchmark agency to serve as depositary for such an instrument in the medium to longer term."[82] Nevertheless, several questions regarding the thrust of the INCP in UNESCO and the interest of UNESCO Members in a new instrument had to be answered.[83]

A meeting between INCP representatives and the Director General of UNESCO had to be organized to address the feasibility of achieving this objective.[84] Ministers of the INCP met with the Director General, Koichiro Matsuura, in February 2003.[85] Matsuura indicated his willingness to launch the process of elaborating a convention on cultural diversity in UNESCO. A promise was made to seek for a mandate in this regard at the UNESCO General Conference in October 2003.[86] The choice for UNESCO was logical, given the several attempts since the 1980 to reconcile culture and economics in order to achieve development.

3.3. DEVELOPMENT AND CULTURE

Development has long been conceptualized as a process of economic growth, a rapid and sustained expansion of production, productivity and income per head.[87] This conceptualization has been prominently present in the early development thinking of the United Nations.[88] Culture had relatively few meaning for this concept of development. The main policies on culture therefore

79 *See* International Network on Cultural Policy, Ministerial Meetings, "Strategic Options for a New International Instrument on Cultural Diversity" (Cape Town, October 2002), *available at* http://incp-ripc.org/meetings/2002/strategic_e.shtml (last visited 2 February 2012).

80 *See* id., §1 The IICD and the WTO.

81 *See* id., §3 The IICD as a Stand Alone Agreement.

82 *See* id., §2 The IICD and the UNESCO.

83 *See* id.

84 *See* Bernier, *supra* note 63, at 65.

85 *See* International Network on Cultural Policy, Ministerial Meetings, "Sixth INCP Annual Ministerial Meeting – Opatija, Croatia, October 16 to 18 2003 – Final Report" (Opatija, October 2003), *available at* http://incp-ripc.org/meetings/2003/finalreport_e.pdf (last visited 2 February 2012).

86 *See* Bernier, *supra* note 63, at 65.

87 *See* World Commission on Culture and Development, *Our Creative Diversity: Report of the World Commission on Culture and Development*, 1995, 22.

88 *See, generally,* R. Jolly, L. Emmerij, Dh. Ghali and Fr. Lapeyre, *UN Contributions to Development Thinking in Practice*, 2004; L. Emmerij, R. Jolly and Th. G. Weiss, *Ahead of the Curve, UN Ideas and Global Challenges*, 2001.

developed in a different direction. The UN organization that got culture under its mandate, UNESCO, focused on tangible cultural objects. A number of conventions, recommendations and charters were adopted to back up the principle of a common cultural heritage towards buildings and monuments. The measures were all agreed upon between 1954 and the 1970s.[89]

The clinical separation of culture and development started to break down in the 1960s, when it became obvious that development project were jeopardized by only focusing on the introduction of technical improvements within a community. Such improvements were often not accepted as they were running counter to the principles to which these communities adhered. The awareness that such principles might exist, led to the introduction of cultural readjustments in economic development planning. Jean Meynaud, writing in a 1963 UNESCO publication, suggests that "the study of cultural models helps us to situate the individual again in his social context."[90]

Toshiyuki Kono has elsewhere[91] referred to Lourdes Arizpe, who indicates that "the challenge of relating culture to development was taken up for the first time by governments at the World Conference on Cultural Policies held in Mexico City in 1982." MONDIACULT, as this conference became known, highlighted the cultural dimension of development by stating that "balanced development can only be insured by making cultural factors an integral part of the strategies designed to achieve it; consequently, these strategies should always be devised in the light of historical, social, and cultural context of each society."[92]

The breakthrough of the idea to link culture and development came with the resolution declaring 1988–97 the *Decade for Cultural Development (1988–1997)*.[93] Within this framework, the General Assembly of UNESCO adopted in 1991 a resolution requesting the Director-General, Federico Mayor, in co-operation with the Secretary-General of the United Nations, Boutros Boutros-Ghali, to "establish an independent World Commission on Culture and Development comprising women and men drawn from all regions and eminent in diverse disciplines, to prepare a *World Report on Culture and Development* and proposals for both urgent and long-term action to meet cultural needs in the context of development."[94]

89 *See* T. Kono, "UNESCO and Intangible Cultural Heritage from the Viewpoint of Sustainable Development", in A. A. Yusuf (ed.), *Standard Setting in UNESCO: Normative Action in Education, Science and Culture*, 2007, 237–41.

90 Quoted in L. Arizpe, "The Intellectual History of Culture and Development", in V. Rao and M. Walton (eds.), *Culture and Public Action*, 2004, 171.

91 *See* Kono, *supra* note 89, at 242–3.

92 Arizpe, *supra* note 90, at 174.

93 *See* C. B. Graber, *Handel und Kultur im Audiovisionsrecht der WTO Völkerrechtliche, ökonomische und kulturpolitische Grundlagen einer globalen Medienordnung*, 2003, 86.

94 UNESCO, General Assembly, "World Report on Culture and Development", *26C/Resolution 3.4.* (7 November 1991), *available at* http://unesdoc.unesco.org/images/0009/000904/090448e.pdf (last visited 2 February 2012).

Once the UNESCO resolution was endorsed by the General Assembly of the United Nations, the World Commission started its activities under the leadership of Javier Pérez de Cuéllar. The Commission finished its work with its 1995 report *Our Creative Diversity.*[95] The main message of this report was to indicate that development goes beyond the mere production of goods and services. Development embraces also concerns for the human well-being. This implies that the various things a person may value doing or being should be reflected in development policies.[96] Based on this report, UNESCO published its First World Culture Report, called *Culture, Creativity and Markets.* The report dealt with the question of what effect the globalizing economy could have on cultural diversity.[97]

This general trend of discussing the position of culture in gradually liberalizing trade system continued. UNESCO released a document called *Culture, Trade and Globalization: Questions and Answers,* in which it investigated the pressures cultural diversity was facing due to trade liberalization and globalization.[98] In 1999, an expert symposium followed to discuss whether culture should be regarded as a form of merchandise like no other.[99] In the same year, the *First Round Table of Ministers of Culture* was held discussing culture and creativity in a globalized world.[100] One year later, the experts and ministers met again. The former discussed how the role of UNESCO could be strengthened in order to promote cultural diversity in a context of globalization,[101] while the latter debated the challenge cultural diversity could play within the marketplace.[102]

A decade of research, reports, meeting and colloquia resulted in drafting and adopting a *Universal Declaration on Cultural Diversity* (Cultural Diversity

95 *See* WORLD COMMISSION ON CULTURE AND DEVELOPMENT, *Our Creative Diversity: Report of the World Commission on Culture and Development,* 1995.

96 *See* A. SEN, *Commodities and Capabilities*, 1985; V. RAO and M. WALTON, "Culture and Public Action; Relationality, Equality of Agency, and Development", RAO and WALTON, *supra* note 90, at 12.

97 *See* UNESCO, *World Culture Report 1998: Culture, Creativity and Markets*, 1998.

98 *See* UNESCO, *Culture, Trade and Globalization: Questions and Answers*, 2000.

99 *See* UNESCO, "Culture, the Market and Globalization, Culture: A Form of Merchandise like Another? (Symposium of Experts, 14–15 June 1999), *available at* http://unesdoc.unesco.org/images/0012/001228/122892eo.pdf (last visited 2 February 2012).

100 *See* UNESCO, "Reflections on Cultural Diversity – Conferences and Round Tables", *available at* http://portal.unesco.org/culture/en/ev.php-URL_ID=35258&URL_DO=DO_TOPIC&URL_SECTION=201.html (last visited 2 August 2010) (examining the liberalization issue and culture under the theme of *Culture and Creativity in a Globalized World*).

101 *See* UNESCO, ROUND TABLE OF MINISTERS OF CULTURE, "2000–2010 Cultural Diversity: Challenges of the Marketplace", *CLT/2000/ME/H/2* (11–12 December 2000), *available at* http://unesdoc.unesco.org/images/0015/001591/159175F.pdf (last visited 2 February 2012).

102 *See* UNESCO, "Cultural Diversity in the Light of Globalization: The Future of the Cultural Industries in East and Central Europe" (Symposium of Experts, 30 June – 1 July 2000), *available at* http://unesdoc.unesco.org/images/0012/001228/122893eo.pdf (last visited 2 February 2001).

Declaration),[103] adopted by the General Assembly of UNESCO in 2001.[104] Culture should be awarded a special place within the globalizing world, so that multiple cultures can exist next to each other. Recognizing that cultural is something special is necessary, according to the Declaration, because cultural diversity is, as source of innovation and creativity, important for humanity, just like biodiversity is for nature.

Stating that cultural diversity is important is one thing. The Declaration continues with locating the current danger. Imbalances in flows and exchanges of cultural goods and services at the global level threaten this cultural diversity. Such imbalances should inspire States to define their policies in a way that it can stimulate the recovery and the distribution of diversified goods and services. The policies should start from the premise of the specificity of cultural goods and services, as vectors of identity, values and meaning. In doing so, the policies should reject the view that they are mere commodities or consumer products. State intervention is, moreover, important due to the incapability of the market to adjust the imbalanced flow of cultural goods and services.

3.4. A DUAL CONCEPT OF CULTURE

The discussion on development and culture reveals a double stance towards how these concepts can be linked. Whereas the early developmental practitioners were dealing with the modification of developmental policies to fit the cultural background of the communities for which these policies were created, the debate gradually expanded towards the use of culture and its products and services for development.

Bernier has identified the cause of such an evolution by referring to the definition of culture as it was formulated during MONDIACULT conference.[105] This conference coined that culture should be understood as "the whole complex of distinctive spiritual, material, intellectual, and emotional features that characterize a society or social group. It includes not only the arts and literature, but also the modes of life, the fundamental rights of the human being, value systems, traditions and beliefs."[106] This definition of culture comprehends besides creational concept of culture, in the form of arts and literature, also sociological or anthropological concept of culture, in the form of lifestyles, basic

103 Universal Declaration on Cultural Diversity, 2 November 2001, *available at* http://portal.unesco.org/en/ev.php-URL_ID=13179&URL_DO=DO_TOPIC&URL_SECTION=201.html (last visited 2 February 2012) [hereinafter "Cultural Diversity Declaration"].

104 *See* BERNIER, *supra* note 63, at 72–3.

105 *See* id., at 66–7.

106 UNESCO, "Mexico City Declaration on Cultural Policies", Sixth Recital (World Conference on Cultural Policies, Mexico City, 26 July – 6 August 1982), *available at* http://portal.unesco.org/culture/en/files/35197/11919410061mexico_en.pdf/mexico_en.pdf (last visited 2 February 2012).

human rights, traditions and beliefs. Jan Wouters and Maarten Vidal proclaim that the former understanding of the concept of culture presupposes the individual as creator of culture, while the latter conceptualization of culture sees the individual as a product of culture.[107]

The lack of a univocal concept of culture has its implication of cultural policies. A cultural concept in which the individual is regarded as the creator of culture focuses on the individual. He should be given the opportunity to innovate,[108] requiring the setting up of an environment to do so. This requires policies that are oriented towards the individual and the protection of what he produces. A shift occurs when culture is conceptualized as something that shapes the individual. It is important for the individual to have access to his culture.[109] This entails policies that ensure the access to one's own culture and respect for someone else's culture.

UNESCO has more than once indicated that it is at the same time "mediator and catalyzer for cultural exchange and a counsel and guard for the respect of fundamental cultural liberties."[110] Indeed, UNESCO has been largely involved in both the "exchange of cultural creations and the protection of cultural creators."[111] UNESCO's involvement in the *International Covenant on Economics, Social and Cultural Rights*,[112] its adoption of the *Declaration of Principles of International Cooperation*,[113] its adoption of the *Universal Copyright Convention*,[114] its cooperation in the *International Convention for the Protection of Performers, Producers of Phonograms and Broadcasting Organizations*,[115] its adoption of the *Convention concerning the Protection of the World Cultural and Natural Heritage*,[116] its *Recommendation on the Status of the Artist*, its adoption of the Cultural Diversity Declaration[117] and its adoption of the *Convention for the Safeguarding of Intangible Cultural Heritage*[118] have been referred to as

---

107 *See* J. Wouters and M. Vidal, UNESCO and the Promotion of Cultural Exchange and Cultural Diversity, in Yusuf (ed.), *supra* note 89, at 148–9.

108 *See* id., at 149.

109 *See* id.

110 Id.

111 Id.

112 *See* Covenant on Economic, Social and Cultural Rights, 16 December 1966, 993 U.N.T.S. 3.

113 *See* Declaration of Principles of International Cultural Co-operation, 4 November 1966, *available at* http://unesdoc.unesco.org/images/0011/001140/114048e.pdf#page=82 (last visited 2 February 2012).

114 *See* Universal Copyright Convention, 6 September 1952, 216 *UNTS* 133.

115 *See* International Convention for the Protection of Performers, Producers of Phonograms and Broadcasting Organisations, Article 3, 26 October 1961, 496 *U.N.T.S.* 44 (1961).

116 *See* Convention Concerning the Protection of the World Cultural and Natural Heritage, 16 November 1972, *available at* http://portal.unesco.org/en/ev.php-URL_ID=13055&URL_DO=DO_TOPIC&URL_SECTION=201.html (last visited 2 February 2012).

117 *See* Cultural Diversity Declaration, *supra* note 95.

118 *See* Convention for the Safeguarding of the Intangible Cultural Heritage, 17 October 2003, *U.N. Doc. MISC/2003/CLT/CH/14.*

exemplifying either one or both of the cultural dimensions within UNESCO's framework.[119]

Out of the instruments just mentioned, the Cultural Diversity Declaration closely linked to the new instrument for which UNESCO was solicited as the host. This soft law instrument embraces both concepts of culture. Above we have stated that one major theme within the Cultural Diversity Declaration was globalization and its impact on the diversity of cultural goods and services. However, the Cultural Diversity Declaration frames the concept of cultural diversity also in terms of common heritage of humanity, linking it with the language of two of the most important standard setting instruments of UNESCO. By incorporating the heritage aspect, the Cultural Diversity Declaration, just like the World Heritage Convention and the Intangible Cultural Heritage Convention, had to stress the idea of the importance of cultural diversity across generations. This ethical call requires generations to respect anyone's culture, because only this can ensure access to later generations.

Cultural diversity is within the Convention on the Diversity of Cultural Expressions also seen as offering a possible offspring for cultural pluralism. Cultural pluralism is perceived as the "policies for the inclusion and participation of all citizens,"[120] so guaranteeing "social cohesion, the vitality of civil society and peace."[121] Wouters and Vidal further point out that the Declaration contributes to strengthening the importance of democracy in modern international law, because it links cultural pluralism with a democratic society.[122]

Human rights are called upon to defend cultural diversity, because defending cultural diversity is inseparable from respect for human dignity. The Cultural Diversity Declaration is firm on the understanding that the defence for cultural diversity cannot extend to the point that cultural diversity is used for infringing upon or limiting any human right guaranteed by international law. The cultural human rights are further identified as enabling the environment for cultural diversity.

With the dual dimension of culture explicitly present in the instrument that, as we will see in the next section, has been declared to be the basis of what had to become the Convention on the Diversity of Cultural Expressions, negotiations within UNESCO were bound to incorporate another level of complexity into what the trade and culture quandary already was.

---

119 *See, e.g.*, Wouters and Vidal, *supra* note 99, at 149–58. *See also* Bernier, *supra* note 63, at 72 (where he gives a theoretized summary of these conventions).

120 Cultural Diversity Declaration, *supra* note 95, Article 2.

121 Id.

122 *See* Wouters and Vidal, *supra* note 99, at 162.

4. NEGOTIATING IN THE WAKE OF A CENTURY'S LONG TENSION

4.1. THE TRADE AND CULTURE DEBATE GOVERNS

The broader perception of the role UNESCO could fulfil towards culture, made it possible for negotiations to start in order to create a new standard setting instrument to protect local cultures from the effects of globalization. The initial mandate for working out this new instrument was given to a group of 15 experts who had to deliberate in their personal capacity of how that instrument should look like.[123] The Report on the First Meeting of Experts on the Draft of an International Convention on the Protection of the Diversity of Cultural Contents and Artistic Expressions reads as a continuation of the trade and culture debate.[124]

The general agreement among the experts was that the achievements of the Cultural Diversity Declaration should serve as a basis for the new instrument. Already at the beginning it was pointed out by some experts that the Cultural Diversity Declaration could not as a whole be part of the new instrument.[125] At the end, the new instrument was only to cover the "diversity of cultural content and artistic expressions,"[126] and not cultural diversity as a whole.

From the beginning of the expert meetings, the diversity of cultural content and artistic expressions was situated in the framework of the trade and culture controversy that had grown in the trade regime. A more clear indication of this understanding could not be found than in the statement that the new instrument had to underscore the need for a balance between culture and trade.[127] To achieve this balance, the new instrument had to clarify the dual nature of goods and services bearing a cultural content or showing an artistic expression. The dual nature implies that the cultural goods and services have symbolic value besides an economic value.[128]

---

123 *See* UNESCO, General Conference (32nd session), "Desirability of Drawing up an International Standard-Setting Instrument on Cultural Diversity", *32C/Resolution 34* (October 2003), *available at* http://unesdoc.unesco.org/images/0013/001331/133171e.pdf (last visited 2 February 2012).

124 *See* UNESCO, "First Meeting of Experts (category VI) on the First Draft of an International Convention on the Protection of the Diversity of Cultural Contents and Artistic Expressions", CLT/CPD/2003-608/01 (Paris, 17–20 December 2003).

125 *See* id., at 3.

126 Id. (it should be noted that many of the experts have nevertheless referred to the new instrument as the Convention on the Diversity of Cultural Expressions. Also, when developing the draft proposals, many experts just used cultural diversity as a concept that could be guiding the rights and obligation setting. See, e.g., *See* UNESCO, Second Expert Meeting, "Consolidated Draft Proposals by the Experts", *CLT/CPD/2004/602/2*, at 3, 5, 6, and 11 (19 March 2004).

127 *See* UNESCO, *supra* note 109, at 3.

128 *See* id., at 5.

Unlike the attempts in the trade regime, where the dual nature had to find its expression in a cultural exemption, a cultural exception, or a cultural specificity clause, the experts envisaged the conceptualization of the dual nature as a 'cultural recognition'.[129] This basically meant that the new instrument had to validate rights and obligations in relation to cultural goods and services. The experts thereby embraced the idea that the new convention should have a purely cultural objective.[130] It is stated in the Report on the First Meeting of Experts on the Draft of an International Convention on the Protection of the Diversity of Cultural Contents and Artistic Expressions that this was to seek not to modify rights and obligations of States had under other international agreements.

Nevertheless the position that the new instrument should not interfere with existing rights and obligations, much attention was paid by the experts on how the new instrument should relate to GATT, GATS and TRIPS.[131] Of all other international conventions that could have any importance for the new instrument, only the Convention for the Safeguarding of Intangible Cultural Heritage was explicitly mentioned.[132] Again, this further confirms the trade oriented focus of the early negotiations of what had to become the Convention on the Diversity of Cultural Expressions.

The trade orientated content of the early discussions is also reflected in the language. 'Consumers',[133] 'products and services',[134] 'industries'[135], 'WTO and GATS',[136] 'imperfections of the market',[137] or 'market pressures'[138] are often used concepts.

4.2. PROMOTION OF CULTURAL DEVELOPMENT

The trade orientated thinking extended also to the development issue. Once international assistance and cooperation were identified as an important means to develop and strengthen cultural industries in developing countries, the expert report indicated that this would enable the developing countries to position themselves in the domestic and international market for cultural goods.[139]

---

129 *See* id., at 3.
130 *See* id., at 7.
131 *See* id., at 6–7.
132 *See* id., at 7.
133 *See* id., at 3.
134 *See* id., at 3–6.
135 *See* id., at 5.
136 *See* id., at 2 and 7.
137 *See* id., at 2.
138 *See* First Expert Meeting, "List of Key Points of the First Expert Meeting" 1 (9 February 2004) (unpublished document on file with the authors) [hereinafter "List of Key Points"].
139 *See* UNESCO, *supra* note 109, at 8.

There was no unanimous acceptance as to how this end should be achieved. Some experts preferred to concentrate the assistance and cooperation on the production and distribution capacity of developing countries that face vigorous competition from imports from industrialized countries.[140] Other experts have put partnerships forward as a solution.[141] These partnerships could encompass preferential treatment of cultural products from developing countries, support for cultural institutions, or co-production agreements with the audiovisual sector.

Only a single expert suggested adopting an approach that may have gone beyond the mere trade aspect. By relying on Chapter 5 of the Intangible Cultural Heritage Convention, the expert advocated for broadening the international assistance and cooperation to the specific problem of preserving and promoting.[142] However, this line of thinking did not find its way to the proposals following the first Expert Meeting.[143]

4.3. NON-TRADE RELATED ISSUES BRIEFLY DISCUSSED

Even though the trade related aspects may have been dominant, the influence of the anthropological concept of culture can also be seen in the discussion. The most obvious statement that the new instrument is not limited in content to a cultural perspective on trade, is the strong preference of the experts to treat this new instrument as having a purely cultural objective and being of an essentially cultural nature.[144]

Immediately before making this statement, the experts stressed the fact that the new instrument should be consistent with the various UNESCO standard-setting instruments. One of the more important instruments was the Intangible Cultural Heritage Convention.[145] The Intangible Cultural Heritage Convention does go beyond a cultural concept that can be linked with trade.[146]

Another incorporation of a broader cultural concept has been achieved via a reference to the Cultural Diversity Declaration. The Cultural Diversity Declaration was perceived as an essential source for drafting the new instrument.[147] Concerns appearing in that Declaration have therefore also been

---

140 *See* id.

141 *See* id.

142 *See* id.

143 *See* UNESCO, Third Expert Meeting, "Consolidated Draft – Convention on the Protection and Promotion of the Diversity of Cultural Expressions", *CLT/CPD/2004/603/01* (27 May 2004).

144 *See* id., at 7.

145 *See* id.

146 *See* T. Kono (ed.), *Intangible Cultural Heritage and Intellectual Property: Communities, Cultural Diversity and Sustainable Development*, 2009.

147 *See* UNESCO, *supra* note 109, at 3.

taken up in the discussions on the new instrument. Cultural diversity, as has been pointed out in the Universal Declaration, essentially links with human rights. The warning not to use the new instrument to defend undesirable practices and cultural expressions has been reaffirmed by the experts. Human rights principles proclaimed in international instruments should have primacy over the diversity claim.

When summarizing the key issues of the discussions of the first Expert Meeting, the language becomes general.[148] The rights and obligation section could be read as opening the possibility of adopting appropriate measures for achieving diversity without having any trade related content. In a diversity of formulations have the experts expressed their desire that the new instrument should confirm the right of states to take appropriate measures in favour of protecting and promoting cultural diversity.[149] It is only at a few points that a direct link is made to the trade debate, especially when these appropriate measures are linked to market access, dual nature of cultural products and the limitations of GATS.[150] However, this kind of references is certainly not the bulk of the text.

5. REDIRECTING THE FOCUS

5.1. THE EXPERTS EMBRACE CULTURE IN ALL ITS ASPECTS

Little attention was being paid to non-trade related issues in the first Expert Meeting. The discussions of the first meeting were gathered into a first draft proposal,[151] followed by several reworked versions.[152] Even in these proposals the trade issues remained. Several of the articles in these draft proposals bore

148 *See* List of Key Points, *supra* note 123, at 3.

149 *See* id.

150 *See* id., at 3 n.5 and bullet point 5(4) and (5).

151 *See* UNESCO, Second Expert Meeting, "Consolidated Draft Proposals by the Experts", *CLT/CPD/2004/602/2* (19 March 2004).

152 *See* Second Expert Meeting, "Draft Proposal" (31 March 2004) (unpublished manuscript on file with the authors); UNESCO, Third Expert Meeting, "Consolidated Draft – Convention on the Protection and Promotion of the Diversity of Cultural Expressions", *CLT/CPD/2004/603/01* (27 May 2004); Third Expert Meeting, "Draft Version" (30 May 2004) (unpublished manuscript on file with the authors); Third Expert Meeting, "Convention on the Protection and Promotion of the Diversity of Cultural Contents and Artistic Expressions – Draft Version (31 May 2004) (unpublished manuscript on file with the authors); Third Expert Meeting, "Provisional Draft Version – 3rd Meeting of Experts" (8 June 2004) (unpublished manuscript on file with the authors); Third Expert Meeting, "Provisional Draft Version – 3rd Meeting of Experts" (11 June 2004) (unpublished manuscript on file with the authors); UNESCO, "Preliminary Draft of a Convention on the Protection of the Diversity of Cultural Contents and Artistic Expressions", *CLT/CPD/2004/CONF-201/2* (July 2004).

resemblance to issues discussed in the trade and culture quandary or in the first Expert Meeting. The language has not always been as direct as in the early discussions within the trade framework.

The idea that states should have the right to adopt regulation reserving a portion of their space to national goods and services indirectly refers to the quota systems that have been developed in the trade regime.[153] Comments of the experts seem to confirm this. In one of the footnotes to the article in which the above-mentioned idea was introduced, David Throsby reminds the experts of a discussion they had earlier on protective measures.[154] One of these protective measures, as is apparent from the text, is quotas. Even though Tyler Cowen had argued against such kind of protective measures,[155] Throsby makes the point that no conclusive statement in favour or disfavour can be made.[156] Therefore, the new instrument should not a priori exclude the possibility of taking this kind of measures.[157]

Another reference to the trade and culture debate is to be found in the reference to the specificity of cultural goods and services. Some experts have situated that in the objective section for the new instrument,[158] others thought it better fits in the principles section,[159] and still other prefer to incorporate it in the rights section. The specificity has also been included in the preamble section in some of the other drafts developed by the experts.[160]

Globalization and trade liberalization is another example of how the trade and culture debate has, if not direct than indirect, entered the discussion on the new instrument.[161] Free trade and trade liberalization has been identified as the cause of globalization, which in turn is been perceived as posing a threat to many of the domestic cultural goods and services. In the various proposals of the experts, a justification for the new instrument or for taking measures based upon this instrument is globalization.

153 *See* UNESCO, Third Expert Meeting, *supra* note 137, at 17–9 (27 May 2004); This idea has been kept in the subsequent draft proposals. *See* Third Expert Meeting, *supra* note 137, Article 6(3)(a) (30 May 2004); Third Expert Meeting, *supra* note 137, Article 6(2)(a) (31 May 2004); Third Expert Meeting, *supra* note 137, 6(2)(a) (8 June 2004); Third Expert Meeting, *supra* note 137, Article 6(2)(a) (11 June 2004); UNESCO, *supra* note 137, Article 6(2)(a) (July 2004).

154 *See* UNESCO, Third Expert Meeting, *supra* note 137, at 19 n.52 (27 May 2004).

155 *See* id.

156 *See* id.

157 *See* id. (also Mr. Parekh makes an argument that quotas are sometimes necessary, *See* id., at 8).

158 *See* UNESCO, Second Expert Meeting, *supra* note 136, at 2.

159 *See* id., at 5.

160 *See* UNESCO, Third Expert Meeting, *supra* note 137, at 3 (27 May 2004).

161 *See* UNESCO, Second Expert Meeting, *supra* note 136, at 1; Second Expert Meeting, *supra* note 137, 1 Preamble (31 March 2004); UNESCO, Third Expert Meeting, *supra* note 137, at 3 (27 May 2004); Third Expert Meeting, *supra* note 137, at 2 (31 May 2004); Third Expert Meeting, *supra* note 137, at 1 (11 June 2004); UNESCO, *supra* note 137, at 2 (July 2004).

The trade and culture debate entered in a little less disguised way the section of development. The experts expanded the development section towards economic development in audiovisual sector. The proposals made by the experts include creating production capacities,[162] supporting the emergence of local markets,[163] and facilitating access to international markets.[164] A direct reference to the trade and culture debate could be found in the suggestion to encourage the signing of cinematographic and other audiovisual co-production and co-distribution.[165] From the third meeting of independent experts, preferential treatment and partnership formation was added.[166]

Even though the above-mentioned remains of the trade and culture debate, the experts have increasingly emphasized the non-economic nature of the new instrument. 'Consumption' as a part of the definition of cultural policy has, for example, been changed to 'access to'.[167] The underlying reasoning for this change would probably be similar to the one developed by one of the experts when debating the concept of 'goods and services.' The expert emphasized that not everything is a matter of commercial exchange and therefore suggested replacing 'goods and services' it by 'objects, activities and services.'[168] However, his

162 *See* UNESCO, Second Expert Meeting, *supra* note 136, Chapter III.3.2.a; Second Expert Meeting, *supra* note 137, Article V.3.2.a (31 March 2004); Third Expert Meeting, *supra* note 137, Article 12(2)(a) (31 May 2004); Third Expert Meeting, *supra* note 137, Article 12 (8 June 2004); UNESCO, *supra* note 137, Article 12(2)(a) (July 2004).

163 *See* UNESCO, Second Expert Meeting, *supra* note 136, Chapter III.3.2.b; Second Expert Meeting, *supra* note 137, Article V.3.2.b (31 March 2004); Third Expert Meeting, *supra* note 137, Article 12(2)(b) (31 May 2004); Third Expert Meeting, *supra* note 137, Article 12(2)(b) (8 June 2004); UNESCO, *supra* note 137, Article 12(2)(b) (July 2004).

164 *See* UNESCO, Second Expert Meeting, *supra* note 136, Chapter III.3.2.c; Second Expert Meeting, *supra* note 137, Article V.3.2.c (31 March 2004); UNESCO, Third Expert Meeting, *supra* note 137, Article 8(2) (27 May 2004); Third Expert Meeting, *supra* note 137, Article 8(3) (30 May 2004); Third Expert Meeting, *supra* note 137, Article 12(2)(c) (31 May 2004); Third Expert Meeting, *supra* note 137, Article 12(2)(c) (8 June 2004); UNESCO, *supra* note 137, Article 12(2)(c) (July 2004).

165 *See* UNESCO, Second Expert Meeting, *supra* note 136, Chapter III.3.5; Second Expert Meeting, *supra* note 137, Article V.3.4 (31 March 2004); UNESCO, Third Expert Meeting, *supra* note 137, Article 11 (27 May 2004); Third Expert Meeting, *supra* note 137, Article 12 (30 May 2004); Third Expert Meeting, *supra* note 137, Article 14 (31 May 2004); Third Expert Meeting, *supra* note 137, Article 14 (8 June 2004); UNESCO, *supra* note 137, Article 14 (July 2004).

166 *See* UNESCO, Third Expert Meeting, *supra* note 137, at 28 (27 May 2004); Third Expert Meeting, *supra* note 137, Article 13 (30 May 2004); Third Expert Meeting, *supra* note 137, Article 17 and 18 (31 May 2004);Third Expert Meeting, *supra* note 137, Article 14 (8 June 2004); UNESCO, *supra* note 137, Article 17 (July 2004).

167 *See* Second Expert Meeting, "Draft Proposal" 6 (3 April 2004) (unpublished manuscript on file with the authors) (in Chapter III.6, the experts discussed the definition of cultural policy, which originally included consumption. 'Consumption' was replaced by 'access.' This change did not change anymore in the independent expert meetings. *See, e.g.*, UNESCO, Third Expert Meeting, *supra* note 137, Article 5.6 (27 May 2004); UNESCO, *supra* note 137, Article 4.7 (July 2004)).

168 *See* UNESCO, Third Expert Meeting, *supra* note 137, I Article 1(b) (27 May 2004).

suggestion was not accepted in the stage of the, partly because the provision he was commenting on disappeared out of the draft proposal.

More important than the few changes in terminology is the overall possibility to read beyond the trade and culture debate in the provisions that the experts have been suggesting. The experts emphasize the sovereign right of states to ensure the protection and promotion of the diversity of cultural expressions.[169] That this general restatement of the sovereignty may entail a broad understanding of culture can be deducted from the experts' suggestions to link this right with cultural heritage, cultural life, pluralism and cultural and linguistic diversity.[170]

As the expert meetings progressed, express language was barely retained. A choice was made for vague and indirect language when they developed the rights of states in relation to the diversity of cultural expressions. The emphasis was put on 'appropriate cultural policies' that 'protect and promote the diversity of cultural expressions.' A further denominator of the cultural policies was the 'particular circumstances and the needs' of the State Party.[171] A similar approach was taken for identifying the obligations of states. The draft texts referred to the creation of opportunities to create, produce, disseminate, distribute or have access to cultural expressions.[172] The experts also agreed that appropriate cultural policies should especially be sought when the expressions are threatened or in a situation of vulnerability.[173]

The experts elaborated only in a few cases the vague and general language by providing a non-exhaustive list of possible measures.[174] Even though the list of exemplary list of measures, it has to be understood that the generally formulated rights and obligations still have to be interpreted according to the objectives and the principles guiding the new instrument. At the end of the independent expert meetings, only few of these objectives and principles entail an offspring of the trade or culture debate. The specificity or distinctive nature of cultural goods and services is hereof an example. Other objectives and principles are more closely linked to an anthropological and sociological understanding of culture. Human rights and fundamental freedoms are called upon to set the framework in which the diversity of cultural expressions should operate. Equal dignity of all cultures, especially in of importance for minorities and indigenous people, is being proclaimed as a principle without which diversity is not attainable. In

169 *See* id., III Article 5(1); This Article still remained in the draft. *See* UNESCO, *supra* note 137, III Article 5.1 (July 2004).

170 *See, e.g.*, UNESCO, *supra* note 137, Preamble (July 2004).

171 *See, e.g.*, Third Expert Meeting, *supra* note 137, Article 6 (31 May 2004).

172 *See* id., Article 7.

173 *See* id., Article 8.

174 *See* id., Article 6 (the list of possible measures are mainly related to trade issues, as they involve reserving a portion of space in their territory for production and distribution of cultural goods and services, providing subsidies to cultural industries, guaranteeing the viability of independent cultural industries, etc.).

other objectives and principles trade and culture issues can be read as much as anthropological and sociological issues. Solidarity and cooperation may apply to cultural policies involving trade issues, but also anthropological issues. A line of thought is applicable to the principle of balance, openness and proportionality.[175]

5.2. THE INTERGOVERNMENTAL MEETINGS AFFIRM THE BROAD CULTURAL APPROACH

The Intergovernmental Meeting of Experts on the Preliminary Draft Convention on the Protection of the Diversity of Cultural Contents and Artistic (Intergovernmental Meeting of Experts) expressions followed up the work of the independent experts.[176] At its first session, which was held from 20 to 25 September 2004, the Intergovernmental Meeting of Experts decided to establish a Drafting Committee.[177] This Committee took as a basis for its deliberations the text of 15 July 2004, which was the product of the independent experts. The structure of that draft text was not questioned. The Drafting Committee rather suggested alternative formulations, refinements or cautions, based upon the comments that were given by the UNESCO Member States, fifteen non-governmental organizations, three intergovernmental organizations, UNCTAD, WTO and WIPO.[178]

The alternative formulations provided the Intergovernmental Meeting with a whole range of options. Every aspect of the independent expert's draft convention was closely looked at to decide on whether the provision was an appropriate reflection of what the future standard setting instrument had to be. The result was a voluminous document with on average four to seven alternatives, with the alternatives for the title with increasing to sixteen.[179] The alternative

175 *See* UNESCO, Third Expert Meeting, *supra* note 137, III Article 5(2) (27 May 2004) (where it was explained that the objectives, principles and the scope have to be taken into consideration when elaborating this sovereign right). This Article still remained in the draft. *See* UNESCO, *supra* note 137, III Article 5.2 (July 2004). It should be stated that some of the objectives or principles included trade related issues. At the early stage of negotiations, the trade related issues were mentioned explicitly. The principles of free trade in cultural products were incorporated in the draft. *See* UNESCO, Third Expert Meeting, *supra* note 137, I Article 4(b) (27 May 2004). This principle was not retained. *See* UNESCO, *supra* note 137, I Article 2 (July 2004).

176 *See* UNESCO, "Preliminary Draft Convention on the Protection of the Diversity of Cultural Contents and Artistic Expressions: Preliminary Report of the Director General", *CLT/CPD/2004/CONF.201/1*, at 6 (July 2004).

177 *See* UNESCO, "Preliminary Draft Convention on the Protection of the Diversity of Cultural Contents and Artistic Expressions: Text Revised by the Drafting Committee 14–17 December 2004", *CLT/CPD/2004/CONF/607/6*, at 5 (23 December 2004).

178 *See* id.

179 *See* id.

formulations were often followed by comments of the Drafting Committee.[180] For the title sections,[181] the Drafting Committee considered the inclusion of promotion and the replacement of the cultural content and artistic expressions by cultural expressions.[182] In many of the comments, Drafting Committee expressed their preference to keep the original text or to give prevalence to one of the options.[183]

With the refinements, the Drafting Committee and the Intergovernmental Meeting of Experts envisaged to bring the new instrument in line with the other UNESCO instruments or to provide more detail. The former can be exemplified by the discussion that arose regarding the concept of 'vulnerability'. This concept was considered to be opposed because it is foreign to other UNESCO instruments. Both the World Heritage Convention and the Intangible Cultural Heritage Convention refer to danger, which is then defined as a threat. Therefore, it was suggested to replace vulnerability by 'serious threat.'[184] Regarding the

180 *See* id., at 9, 22, 23, 24, 25, 26, 28, 29; 30, 31, 32, 33, 34, 35, 37, 38, 40, 41, 42, 43, 46, 47, 50, 51, 53, 54, 55, 58, 59, 61, 62, 68, 70, and 72.

181 *See* id., at 8 (providing the following alternatives for the title: OPTION 1 Convention on the protection and promotion of the diversity of cultural contents and artistic expressions; OPTION 2 Convention on the promotion and protection of the diversity of artistic and cultural contents and expressions; OPTION 3 Convention on the preservation, promotion and protection of the diversity of cultural contents and artistic expressions; OPTION 4 Convention on the protection, preservation, development and promotion of the diversity of cultural contents and artistic expressions; OPTION 5 Convention on the promotion of the diversity of cultural contents and artistic expressions; OPTION 6 Convention on the preservation and promotion of the diversity of cultural contents and artistic expressions; OPTION 7 Convention on the promotion and development of the diversity of cultural contents and Expressions; OPTION 8 Convention on the protection and promotion of the diversity of cultural contents and Expressions; OPTION 9 Convention on the protection and promotion of cultural diversity and cultural expressions; OPTION 10 Convention on the development and preservation of the diversity of cultural contents and expressions; OPTION 11 Convention on the protection and promotion of the diversity of cultural expressions; OPTION 12 Convention for the preservation and promotion of the diversity of cultural expressions; OPTION 13 Convention on the preservation and promotion of cultural expressions; OPTION 14 Convention on the protection and promotion of cultural diversity; OPTION 15 Convention on the protection of cultural diversity; OPTION 16 Convention on cultural diversity).

182 *See* id., at 9; *See also* UNESCO, Secretariat, "Summary of the Comments and Amendments Submitted by the States and the NGOs with regard to [Preliminary Draft Convention on the Protection of the Diversity of Cultural Contents and Artistic Expressions]", *CLT/CPD/2004/CONF.607/2*, at 3 (December 2004) (indicating that the inclusion of 'promotion' was advocated for by several UNESCO Member States).

183 *See* UNESCO, *supra* note 177, at 21, 28, 29; 30, 31, 32, 33, 34, 35, 37, 38, 40, 41, 42, 43, 46, 47, 50, 51, 53, 54, 55, 59, 61, 66, 68, 70, and 72.

184 *See* UNESCO, General Conference, "Preliminary Report by the Director-General on the Progress Achieved During the Third Session of the Intergovernmental Meetings of Experts on the Preliminary Draft Convention on the Protection of the Diversity of Cultural Contents and Artistic Expressions", *33C/23*, at 6 (11 August 2005) (discussion in this section the First session of the Intergovernmental Meeting of 20–24 September 2004); *See also* UNESCO, Secretariat, *supra* note 182, at 9–10 (indicating that the formulation of the article dealing with vulnerable cultural expressions was under much scrutiny by the UNESCO Member States and NGOs).

latter, the Drafting Committee made a suggestion to list up the instruments that contributed to cultural diversity rather than only referring to the Convention on the Diversity of Cultural Expressions.[185]

Cautions were formulated to language that possibly came to close to the one used in the commercial realm. 'Protect' was being questioned because it may recall the concept of protectionism. However, as the concept of protection is also well used within the UNESCO standard setting instruments on culture, the word 'protect' has been kept.[186] The phrase 'more balanced' was criticized because it could reflect that trade does not pay enough attention to cultural products.[187] Another caution that was formulated was to avoid any kind of overlap with the World Heritage Convention and the ICH Convention when international cooperation and assistance was being set up.[188]

Neither the alternative formulations nor the refinements had the capability to affect the reading of the provisions of the new instrument. Even with the suggested alternatives or refinements, it would still be possible to interpret the new instrument to contribute both to the trade and culture debate as well as to the more anthropological view on culture. With formulating the cautions, the Drafting Committee further prevented that the new instrument would be pushed in a one sided direction.

The second session of the Intergovernmental Meeting of Experts, which was organized between 31 January and 11 February 2005, brought in some more non-trade related issues.[189] It was suggested to expand the objective section to include objective of linking culture with development and promote interculturality.[190] The former was objective received further attention of the

185 *See* UNESCO, *supra* note 177, at 16 Paragraph 13 ("*Referring* to the provisions of the international instruments promulgated by UNESCO relating to cultural diversity, the exercise of cultural rights, and the protection of the cultural heritage, and in particular the Universal Declaration on Cultural Diversity, Convention for the Protection of the World Cultural and Natural Heritage, Convention for the Safeguarding of the Intangible Cultural Heritage and agreements of the World Trade Organization on cultural goods and services, such as the General Agreement on Trade in Services, General Agreement on Tariffs and Trade, Agreement on Trade-Related Aspects of Intellectual Property Rights and the Agreement on Subsidies and Countervailing Measures," was suggested as a refinement of "*Referring* to the provisions of the international instruments promulgated by UNESCO relating to cultural diversity and the exercise of cultural rights, and in particular the Universal Declaration on Cultural Diversity,").

186 *See* id., at 22.

187 *See* id., at 25; *See also* UNESCO, Secretariat, *supra* note 182, at 6 (giving warnings that the content of the new convention should not be excessively economic connoted. Further,).

188 *See* UNESCO, *supra* note 177, at 65.

189 *See* UNESCO, "Preliminary Report by the Director-General Containing two Preliminary Drafts of a Convention on the Protection of the Diversity of Cultural Contents and Artistic Expressions", *CLT/CPD/2005/CONF.203/6*, at 8 (3 March 2005) (discussing the second session of the intergovernmental meeting).

190 *See* id., at 9.

experts in the elaboration of the section on international cooperation,[191] while the latter was only defined in the objective section as "cultural interaction with the spirit of building bridges among people."[192] By emphasizing these two elements, the new instrument would be less trade orientated compared to very early drafts.

The third session of the Intergovernmental Meeting of Experts, held between 25 May and 3 June 2005, revealed the tension behind the new instrument. The experts took the time for a thorough review of the whole draft to see whether the provisions captured the spirit of what the new instrument should be. At this stage, we see UNESCO Member States raising objections. Several of the objections came from the United States. The US opposed to references to the dual nature of cultural goods and services or the inclusion of cultural industries the principle of international cooperation. Also, the provision in the draft giving the right to protect domestic cultural industries or the provision regulating the relationship with other conventions was subject of the US objections. It is obvious that the US feared an overly protective convention in the sphere of trade. However, as indicated above, many of the provisions allow for a much broader reading. None of the discussions in the third session on the draft proposal changed this perspective.[193] This remained so in the final and adopted version of the Convention on the Diversity of Cultural Expressions.[194]

If the Convention on the Diversity of Cultural Expressions is indeed the product of a congruence of several ideological streams, the Convention should have a broader impact than only on trade. To what extent this presumption is

---

191 *See* id. (dealing with Article 12 to 15: promotion of international cooperation; the promotion of the central role of culture in sustainable development; the preferential treatment due to developing countries; and vulnerable forms of cultural expressions); *See also* UNESCO, SECRETARIAT, *supra* note 182, at 11–2 (stipulating that the UNESCO Member States were a driving force behind the reformulation of the cooperation provisions, with one provision explicitly dealing with economics).

192 Id., 19 (annex to the report containing the preliminary draft of a convention on the protection of the diversity of cultural contents and artistic expressions); *See also* UNESCO, SECRETARIAT, *supra* note 182, at 4 (it should be stipulated that the UNESCO Member States have put a great emphasis on human rights and social cohesion).

193 *See, e.g.*, CHAIRPERSON OF THE INTERGOVERNMENTAL MEETING, "Preliminary Draft of the Convention on the Protection of the Diversity of Cultural Contents and Artistic Expressions", *171 EX/INF.18* (April 2005); UNESCO, THIRD INTERGOVERNMENTAL MEETING OF EXPERTS, Discussion Documents (25–31 May 2005) (unpublished manuscript on file with the authors); UNESCO, THIRD INTERGOVERNMENTAL MEETING OF EXPERTS "Preliminary Draft of the Convention on the Protection of the Diversity of Cultural Expressions – Revised Text" (2 June 2005) (unpublished manuscript on file with the authors); UNESCO, THIRD INTERGOVERNMENTAL MEETING OF EXPERTS "Preliminary Draft of the Convention on the Protection of the Diversity of Cultural Expressions – Revised Text" (3 June 2005).

194 *See* Convention on the Diversity of Cultural Expressions, *supra* note 1; *See also* Y. Donders, "The History of the UNESCO Convention on the Protection and Promotion of the Diversity of Cultural Expressions", in SCHNEIDER and VAN DEN BOSSCHE (eds.), *supra* note 2, at 22 (indicating that the multipurpose objectives of the convention find their origin in the fact the negotiators where divided as what the purpose of the convention should be).

correct will be the subject of this book. Next section will summarize the main positions towards this presumption. Each of these summaries is further elaborated in the respective chapters to follow.

6. TRADE AND BEYOND, MAPPING OUT THE BOOK

The Convention on the Diversity of Cultural Diversity started out with a strong emphasis on trade and development. The Convention had to stimulate the non-mainstream audiovisual industry, which was for a large part situated in developing countries. The experts in both the independent and the intergovernmental committees gradually expanded the scope of the Convention to also include other issues. The Convention was being positioned within the already heritage law of UNESCO. Human rights language entered the Convention, with references to minorities and indigenous people. Together with the original negotiating themes of trade and development, the Convention on the Diversity of Cultural Expressions encroached upon various fields of law in which international legal instruments already existed. The aim of this book is to investigate to what extent the Convention on the Diversity of Cultural Expressions regulates within these fields of law and hence is contributing to the fragmentation of international law.

Before entering in detail into the debate of fragmentation, Part One will remind the reader of the content of the Convention on the Diversity of Cultural Expressions and the fierce debate on whether it is a cultural or trade convention. *Rostam Neuwirth* systematically introduces all the provisions of the Convention, covering also the major frictions that existed during the negotiation process. Each of the provisions is then subject to a critical review. The contribution of *Carol Balassa* will familiarize us with the position taken by the United States towards the negotiations of the Convention on the Diversity of Cultural Expressions and their end-result. The fear of an overly strong convention in the field of 'trade and culture' pushed the United States to be rather reluctant to give support. *Ivan Bernier* disagrees with the view that the Convention is limited to trade. To the contrary, he advocates for a broad cultural content underlying the entire Convention. Does the Convention on the Diversity of Cultural Expressions have an influence on the trade regime only? Or, to the contrary, could an argument be made that the Convention on the Diversity of Cultural Expressions intersects with other cultural related fields of law?

Culture has been the focus of earlier UNESCO legislative acts. Part Two investigates the relationship between the earlier heritage law, embodied in the World Heritage Convention and the ICH Convention, and the Convention on the Diversity of Cultural Expressions. *Frederico Lenzerini* argues that the

Convention on the Diversity of Cultural Expressions has had a great bearing on the concept of culture. Against this background, he indicates that the Convention on the Diversity of Cultural Expressions could give a broader dimension to the World Heritage Convention's essential concepts and provide complementary protection to heritage sites based upon their belonging to a community. Conflicts between the two conventions seem to settle in favour of the World Heritage Convention. *Steven Van Uytsel* and *Toshiyuki Kono* focus on the ICH Convention. Their argument is based upon the premise that the ICH Convention and the Convention on the Diversity of Cultural Expressions share a common object and objective, due to which both conventions supplement each other in terms of achieving greater visibility and accessibility for cultural expressions. It is further argued that the soft wording of the obligations in the Convention on the Diversity of Cultural Expressions will prevent potential conflicts and that, if conflicts do arise, the conflict-regulating provisions seem to give priority to the ICH Convention.

The extensive use of human rights language in the Convention on the Diversity of Cultural Expressions warrants a human rights analysis of the Convention. Part Three deals with various aspects of human rights. *Yvonne Donders* approaches the Convention on the Diversity of Cultural Expressions from a cultural rights perspective to conclude that cultural rights are neither promoted or protected, nor seen as the guardian of cultural diversity. The only positive off-spring of the Convention on the Diversity of Cultural Expressions for cultural rights is its increased visibility as a human right. The relationship between civil and political rights and the Convention on the Diversity of Cultural Expressions is dealt with by *Eva Brems*. She argues that the Convention on the Diversity of Cultural Expressions includes provisions that can further the right of cultural expression and the right of access to cultural information as long as non-restrictive measures are chosen to implement the Convention. Her analysis further shows that any fear of the Convention being the basis of human rights infringements is unjustified. *Anna Meijknecht* takes up the references to minorities and indigenous people to discuss how their position has been changed by the adoption of the Convention on the Diversity of Cultural Expressions. To do so, she examines whether the conventions dealing with minorities and indigenous people aim at establishing cultural diversity. Even though her conclusion is not so positive on this point, her view of the Convention on the Diversity of Cultural Expressions is not all negative. The Convention on the Diversity of Cultural Expressions may empower minorities and indigenous people.

Part Four places the Convention on the Diversity of Cultural Expressions within the framework of the trade and intellectual property regime. *Rostam Neuwirth* will familiarize us with the milestones in the trade and culture debate, in order then to see how the Convention on the Diversity of Cultural Expressions has changed the landscape of the trade regime. To do so, Neuwirth reflects upon recent WTO and European Court of Justice jurisprudence, as well as insights gained from regional trade agreements. *Tania Voon* analyses the relationship between the Convention on the Diversity of Cultural Expressions and the substantive law of the WTO. Her arguments centre on an analysis of the WTO disciplines affecting trade in goods and services that could conflict with cultural policies to argue that uncertainty on the side of the WTO regarding the interpretation of its provisions hampers an extensive implementation of the Convention on the Diversity of Cultural Expressions. However, she contends that both international instruments leave enough leeway to successfully prevent serious conflicts between their respective rights and obligations. *Branislav Hazucha* details the debate on intellectual property and cultural diversity, which he perceives as running parallel with the divide between emphasizing the role of the market and promoting state intervention in order to achieve a diversity of cultural expressions. Hazucha argues that intellectual property is not a governmental intervention hampering a form of cultural diversity, *i.e.* diversity of cultural expressions. He points out that intellectual property has evolved to stimulate diversity and that reliance solely on the market may not work to achieve diversity. At the same time, he points out that intellectual property must be understood as part of all the policy instruments to achieve diversity, otherwise inefficient outcomes will be the result.

Development has received major attention both during the negotiations of the Convention on the Diversity of Cultural Expressions and in the Convention itself. Part Five will deal with two different aspects of development. *Liliane Richieri Hanania* and *Hélène Ruiz-Fabri* focus on international cooperation for development to analyse whether the obligations under the Convention on the Diversity of Cultural Expressions negatively impact international trade obligations. The answer put forward by both of them is negative, due to the weak formulation of the provision in the Convention on the Diversity of Cultural Expressions. *David Throsby* engages with the concept of sustainable development by discussing how this concept links to cultural diversity. This discussion is then taken as a starting point to investigate whether the Convention on the Diversity of Cultural Expressions is promoting sustainable development. In developing this analysis, Throsby points out that the Convention more than once seems to take the direction of a cultural policy convention rather than a convention on the diversity of cultural expressions.

Part Six introduces two views on implementing the Convention on the Diversity of Cultural Expressions. *Evangelia Psychogiopoulou* deals with the Convention on the Diversity of Cultural Expressions in a European context. Europe, as being a proponent of the Convention, has quickly embraced the end-result of the negotiations. Notwithstanding this fact, the argument made in this chapter is that the European Union is only selective in implementing the prescriptions of the Convention on the Diversity of Cultural Expressions. Warnings about this kind of patchwork approach, but also causes of it, are discussed in this chapter. *Christina Rautenbach* explains the meaning of the Convention on the Diversity of Cultural Expressions for a developing country, South Africa. Even though South Africa has not yet implemented the Convention on the Diversity of Cultural Expressions in its legislation, political leaders have fully embraced the ideas of the Convention. A mandate rests therefore on the responsible ministries governmental to work out a strategy to fully implement the Convention on the Diversity of Cultural Expressions in South Africa's cultural legislation and policy. However, a cautious note is given to the fragmented approach within the government, which may impede an effective implementation of the Convention.

PART I

THE CONVENTION ON THE DIVERSITY OF CULTURAL EXPRESSIONS REVISITED

THE CONVENTION ON THE DIVERSITY OF CULTURAL EXPRESSIONS

A Critical Analysis of the Provisions

Rostam J. NEUWIRTH*

Ultimately, we find that the relationship between international hard- and soft-law instruments cannot be characterized in a universal or invariant fashion. Rather, we contend that the interaction of hard and soft law depends on the respective power of the key players, the degree of distributive conflict among them, the constellation and character of regimes within a given regime complex, and the distinct politics of implementation.[1]

1. THE TEXT OF THE CONVENTION ON THE DIVERSITY OF CULTURAL EXPRESSIONS REVISITED

After two years of negotiations the *Convention on the Protection and Promotion of the Diversity of Cultural Expressions* ("Convention on the Diversity of Cultural Expressions") was finally adopted by the General Conference of UNESCO on October 20, 2005 in Paris.[2] Following the deposit of the 30th instrument of ratification, the Convention on the Diversity of Cultural Expressions finally entered into force on March 18, 2007.[3] The adoption and subsequent entry into

* *Mag. iur.* (University of Graz), *LL.M.* (McGill), *Ph.D.* (EUI), Associate Professor at the Faculty of Law of the University of Macau; Email: rjn@umac.mo.

1 G.C. SHAFFER and M.A. POLLACK, "Hard vs. Soft Law: Alternatives, Complements, and Antagonists in International Governance", 94 *Minnesota Law Review* 706, 799 (2010).

2 The various stages in the negotiation history of the Convention are well documented. *See, e.g.*, UNESCO, EXECUTIVE BOARD, "Report of the Director-General on the Progress Achieved During the Third Session of the Intergovernmental Meeting of Experts on the Preliminary Draft Convention on the Protection of the Diversity of Cultural Contents and Artistic Expressions", *172 EX/20* (11 August 2005).

3 *See* Convention on the Protection and Promotion of the Diversity of Cultural Expressions, 20 October 2005, *U.N. Doc. CLT-2005/CONVENTION DIVERSITE-CULT REV.* [hereinafter "Convention on the Diversity of Cultural Expressions"].

force of the convention thus meant a clear decision by the international community in favour of UNESCO over the WTO as the international host organization entrusted with the reconciliation of cultural and trade policies. Before its adoption, several policy options were on the table. In institutional terms, the options consisted mainly of seeking a solution to the culture and trade quandary to be negotiated either inside the WTO, or else outside the WTO in a different forum. The first option was criticized for a possible bias in favour of trade issues over cultural issues, whereas the adoption in a non-WTO forum was disapproved because of a possible lack of legal strength in terms of the absence of an effective and legalistic dispute settlement mechanism.[4] In substantive regulatory terms, the options first included a possible amendment to the WTO agreements,[5] notably by virtue of the inclusion of a cultural exception, a so-called '*exception culturelle*', or the drafting of an enabling clause for culture or adoption of a cultural waiver.[6] Another option, as advocated by the International Network on Cultural Policy ("INCP"), propagated the idea of negotiating a separate international legal instrument in the context of a new international organization.

Finally, a decision was made in favour of UNESCO, marking an important turning point in terms of both institutional linkages and regulatory means. Both aspects are important for a legal consideration of the Convention's eventual impact on the realm of international trade. In order to substantiate the differences between the present Convention and a mere cultural exception clause(s) enshrined in one or more WTO administered agreements, the present chapter thus yields a brief review of the content, purpose and objectives enshrined in the main legal provisions of the Convention on the Diversity of Cultural Expressions.

2. THE TITLE

The title of a convention, written at length or abbreviated, not only helps to identify its regulatory content or purpose but also serves as a first reference in different contexts such as public debate or the simple search for documents in catalogues or electronic databases. From this viewpoint, I deemed the present Convention's title to be too long and, despite the plethora of words listed, "not

4 *See* T. Voon, "UNESCO and the WTO: A Clash of Cultures?", 55 *International and Comparative Law Quarterly* 635, 636–8 (2006) (providing a brief discussion on this issue).

5 R.J. Neuwirth, *The Cultural Industries in International Trade Law: Insights from the NAFTA, the WTO, and the EU*, 2006, 303–18.

6 C. Carmody, "When 'Cultural Identity was not at Issue': Thinking About Canada – Certain Measures Concerning Periodicals", 30 *Law & Pol'y Int'l Bus.* 231 (1999).

very revealing in terms of its content and regulatory scope".[7] Equally, I found the direct juxtaposition in the title of "protection" and "promotion" in the context of the diversity of cultural expressions – even if it is capable of provoking interesting tension for further thought –[8] to appear contradictory rather than informative.[9] In this respect it was interesting to ask why the use of the predominant concept of "cultural diversity" was not retained for the Convention on the Diversity of Cultural Expressions as it was used in the debate preceding its adoption.[10] My fear was clearly that the introduction of new terms or concepts may prove problematic because it usually takes some time to anchor their meaning in general usage and might simply hamper a fruitful debate from taking place because colloquists in a debate might not be speaking about the same issue. Moreover, I expressed the following concerns:

> The sudden change of terminology may be harmful to the continuity of the debate because it is capable of dissociating the present convention from the achievements of the past. Finally, it may also be confusing when considering, for instance, the basic objectives of the convention as reflected in the Preamble which, at the beginning, frequently refers – in stark contrast to the title – to the concept of cultural diversity. This could create the impression that the objective and scope of the convention is considerably beyond the impression derived from the title.[11]

These fears appeared realistic despite the useful consideration of the drafters' intention to narrow down its scope in order to give it more precision and more legal weight. However, subsequent developments instantly showed that several commentators indeed used "cultural diversity" rather than the "diversity of cultural expressions" when talking about the Convention on the Diversity of Cultural Expressions.[12] As a vindication of these fears, one commentator

---

7 R.J. Neuwirth, ""United in Divergency": A Commentary on the UNESCO Convention on the Protection and Promotion of the Diversity of Cultural Expressions", 66 *Heidelberg Journal of International Law* 819, 831 (2006), *available at* www.zaoerv.de/66_2006/.cfm#Heft4 (last visited 2 February 2012).

8 On this tension, see the remarks to Articles 7 and 8 Convention on the Diversity of Cultural Expressions, *infra* Section 7.

9 Id.

10 *See* Universal Declaration on Cultural Diversity, 2 November 2001, *available at* http://portal.unesco.org/en/ev.php-URL_ID=13179&URL_DO=DO_TOPIC&URL_SECTION=201.html (last visited on 2 February 2012); UNESCO, Executive Board, "Preliminary Study on the Technical and Legal Aspects Relating to the Desirability of a Standard-Setting Instrument on Cultural Diversity", *32 C/52* (12 March 2003).

11 Neuwirth, *supra* note 3, at 831.

12 Note the various references to the Convention by way of cultural diversity; *see, e.g.* A. Riding, "Next lone U.S. dissent: Cultural diversity pact", *The New York Times*, at E3 (12 October 2005); M. Hahn, "A Clash of Cultures? The UNESCO Diversity Convention and International Trade Law", 9 *J.I.E.L.* 515 (2006); C.B. Graber, "The New UNESCO Convention on Cultural Diversity: A Counterbalance to the WTO?", 9 *J.I.E.L.* 553 (2006); A. Khachaturian, "The New Cultural Diversity Convention and its Implications on the WTO International Trade Regime: A Critical Comparative Analysis", 42 *Tex. Int'l L. J.* 191 (2006); J.H.B. Pauwelyn,

confused the UNESCO *Universal Declaration on Cultural Diversity* ("Cultural Diversity Declaration") with the Convention on the Diversity of Cultural Expressions.[13]

3. THE PREAMBLE

The preamble preceding the text of a treaty, as well as the annexes attached to it, form an integral part of the whole.[14] As such, a preamble first provides a useful source for the interpretation of the text of a treaty in the process of its application. Secondly, it is possible under certain circumstances that single passages contained in the preamble itself may formulate legal obligations for the Parties to it, making them fit for direct application.[15] Finally, and of greatest relevance in the present context, a preamble may contain useful information about the principal aim, underlying reasoning, envisaged field of application and scope of the treaty. A preamble is particularly useful for the evaluation of the data and the kind of reasoning admitted to and used in the drafting process. In short, its text provides a general impression of the rationale underlying the debate that preceded, or perhaps even triggered, the negotiations for the respective treaty.

With regard to new or recently adopted treaties, such as the present Convention, a preamble is thus a useful device for drawing some general preliminary conclusions about the potential implications the new treaty may have for existing treaties or agreements. Ideally, a critical reader may also look at the preamble from the viewpoint of the international legal order as a whole and try to determine the implications the new treaty may have on its unity, stability and efficiency in the present state. With regard to old treaties adopted some time in the past, a preamble still contains important information about the context and scope of the past debate leading to its adoption, which can and should be critically weighed and balanced against the present state (principle of

---

"The UNESCO Convention on Cultural Diversity, and the WTO: Diversity in International Law-Making?", *ASIL Insights* (2005), *available at* www.asil.org/insights/2005/11/insights051115.html (last visited 2 February 2012); J. Wouters & B. de Meester, "The UNESCO Convention on Cultural Diversity and WTO Law: A Case Study in Fragmentation of International Law", 42 *J. World T.* 205 (2008); C. Balassa, "America's Image Abroad: The UNESCO Cultural Diversity Convention and U.S. Motion Picture Exports", at 16–8 (Paper Presented at a conference held in Washington, D.C. by the Curb Center for Art, Enterprise and Public Policy at Vanderbilt, on 24 April 2008).

13 *See* E.K. Slattery, "Preserving the United States' Intangible Cultural Heritage: An Evaluation of the 2003 UNESCO Convention for the Safeguarding of the Intangible Cultural Heritage as a Means to Overcome the Problems Posed by Intellectual Property Law", 16 *DePaul-LCA Journal of Art and Entertainment Law* 201, 209 (2006).

14 *See* Vienna Convention on the Law of Treaties, 23 May 1969, 1155 *UNTS* 331, Article 31 (2) [hereinafter "Vienna Convention"].

15 *See, e.g.*, St. Schepers, "The Legal Force of the Preamble to the EEC Treaty", 6 *European Law Review* 356, 357–8 (1981).

evolutionary treaty interpretation).[16] Such critical comparison, carried out in the process of a historic-teleological interpretation, is gaining special significance in fast-evolving regulatory fields such as those of technology, trade and culture, which all form important elements of the so-called "culture and trade linkage debate" in pursuit of greater global cultural diversity.

3.1. SUBSTANTIAL REMARKS

Condensed in 21 Recitals altogether, the Preamble isolates a number of topics related to the Convention's scope, and summarizes the basic considerations which resume not only past experiences but also the dominant reasoning at the time of the drafting, in addition to the expression of major aspirations for the future.[17] First and foremost, the Preamble sets out some basic considerations linked to cultural diversity, namely that it is both a defining characteristic and common heritage of humanity, responsible for the rich and varied world that forms the basis for the sustainable development of communities, peoples and nations by increasing the range of choices and nurturing human capacities. Furthermore, Recitals 4 and 5 of the Preamble recall the links between cultural diversity on the one hand, and democracy, tolerance, social justice, and human rights and fundamental freedoms on the other, as well as mutual respect between peoples and cultures as preconditions for national and international peace and security.[18] These considerations clearly draw from painful experiences of world wars and civil wars in the past, partly transformed into the mandate given in the *Constitution of the United Nations Educational, Scientific and Cultural Organization* itself.[19]

---

16 *See* Appelate Body Report, "United States – Import Prohibition of Certain Shrimp and Shrimp Products", *WT/DS58/AB/R*, §130, n. 109 (12 October 12, 1998) (In this case, the Appellate Body of the WTO DSB stated that "where concepts embodied in a treaty are "by definition, evolutionary", their "interpretation cannot remain unaffected by the subsequent development of law ... Moreover, an international instrument has to be interpreted and applied within the framework of the entire legal system prevailing at the time of the interpretation.").

17 See K. Stenou, *UNESCO and the Issue of Cultural Diversity: Review and strategy, 1946–2004 – A study based on official documents*, 2004, *available at* http://unesdoc.unesco.org////154341mo.pdf (providing us with a broad overview on cultural diversity).

18 *See, e.g.*, P. Leuprecht, "International Law: The Difficult Acceptance of Diversity", 30 *Vt. L. Rev.* 551 (2006); A. Yupsanis, "The Concept and Categories of Cultural Rights in International Law – Their Broad Sense and the Relevant Clauses of the International Human Rights Treaties", 37 *Syracuse J. Int'l L. & Com.* 207, 262 (2010).

19 *See* Constitution of the United Nations Educational, Scientific and Cultural Organization, 16 November 1945, 52 *UNTS* 275, Article I (1) ("Purposes and Functions") (defining the purpose of UNESCO as to "contribute to peace and security by promoting collaboration among the nations through education, science and culture in order to further universal respect for justice, for the rule of law and for the human rights and fundamental freedoms

As another issue for consideration, Recital 6 emphasizes the strategic role of culture in the development of cooperation and the eradication of poverty.[20] Consequently, the Preamble recognizes the highly elastic nature of the concept of culture which frequently changes across time and space making it adverse to definition and regulation.[21] This volatile quality of the concept of culture is essentially the precondition for the diversity that is embodied "in the uniqueness and plurality of the identities and cultural expressions of the peoples and societies making up humanity". Recital 8 then moves on to another important aspect of cultural diversity, that found in the importance of traditional knowledge and its positive contribution to sustainable development, already legally recognized by virtue of the 2003 *Convention for the Safeguarding of Intangible Cultural Heritage*.[22] For the sake of greater coherence, the reference to traditional knowledge as a source of intangible and material wealth would ideally have been combined with the reference to intellectual property rights in Recital 17.

Continuing the narration and specification, the next paragraph stresses the need to take measures aimed at protecting the diversity of cultural expressions, especially where they are threatened with extinction. Recital 10 moves back to the more general level of culture and emphasizes its importance for social cohesion and particularly the enhancement of the role of women in society. The subsequent three recitals are dedicated to the freedom of thought, expression and information in connection with the role of the media and cultural products as the transmitters for the free flow ideas and exchanges between cultures. These

---

which are affirmed for the peoples of the world, without distinction of race, sex, language or religion, by the Charter of the United Nations.") [hereinafter "UNESCO Constitution"].

20 *See, e.g.*, UNCTAD, "Report of the Expert Meeting on Audiovisual Services: Improving Participation of Developing Countries", *TD/B/COM.1/56*, at 2 (4 December 2002); G. Pagniet, "Industries de la culture et développement", 194 *Le Courrier ACP* 42 (2002) (characterizing the role of the culture and cultural products in the field of development as follows: "*Phénomène social aux caractéristiques très diverses et aux multiples ramifications, les industries culturelles doivent être étudiées à travers les divers sous-secteurs qui les composent. Au fil du temps, une prise de conscience de plus en plus forte des enjeux liés aux "industries culturelles" a abouti à l'idée que culture et développement sont intimement liés*"). *See also* Partnership Agreement 2000/483/EC between the Members of the African, Caribbean and Pacific Group of States of the one part, and the European Community and its Member States, of the other part (the "Cotonou Agreement", *O.J. L 317/3* (15 December 2000), Article 27 ("Cultural Development").

21 Theodor W. Adorno asserted the difficulties linked with the formulation of cultural policies by pinpointing that the essence of culture itself is negated when subjected to administration and planning because culture is particularly nurtured by concepts such as autonomy, spontaneity and criticism; *See* Th. W. Adorno, "Culture and Administration", in Th. W. Adorno (ed.), *The Culture Industry: Selected Essays on Mass Culture*, 1991, 107, 123.

22 *See* Convention for the Safeguarding of the Intangible Cultural Heritage, 17 October 2003, *U.N. Doc. MISC/2003/CLT/CH/14* [hereinafter "ICH Convention"]. *See also* Recommendation on the Safeguarding of Traditional Culture and Folklore, 15 November 1989, *available at* http://portal.unesco.org/en/ev.php-URL_ID=13141&URL_DO=DO_TOPIC&URL_SECTION=201.html (last visited 2 February 2012).

three paragraphs can practically be read as a brief summary of a previously important aspect of UNESCO's efforts, namely the establishment of a new information order.[23]

Most relevant for cultural diversity, Recital 14 expresses the underlying link between language and culture, or in other words, between linguistic and cultural diversity, provided by the intellect as the prime perceptive agent in the inspiration, creation and development of content and meaning.[24] It also pays tribute to the insoluble links between language and education on the one hand, and education and culture on the other.

In partial reference to Recitals 6, 8 and 9, Recitals 15 and 16 stress the importance of the vitality of cultures, manifested in the "freedom to create, disseminate and distribute their cultural expressions" and of cultural interaction and creativity for the benefit of progress of society at large.

The next set of Recitals contain various trade aspects on the issue of cultural diversity. First, Recital 17 emphasizes the importance of intellectual property rights in sustaining those involved in cultural activity, by ensuring that they (especially artists) will receive revenues for their artistic and creative efforts. Second, Recital 18 enters the heart of the culture and trade debate by restating the dual, *i.e.* cultural and economic, nature of cultural activities, goods and services, based as they are on the reasoning that they not only form the basis for significant commercial transactions but also "convey identities, values and meaning". This statement merely restates the Cultural Diversity Declarations, which calls cultural goods and services "commodities of a unique kind" and defines them as follows:

> In the face of present-day economic and technological change, opening up vast prospects for creation and innovation, particular attention must be paid to the diversity of the supply of creative work, to due recognition of the rights of authors and artists and to the specificity of cultural goods and services which, as vectors of identity, values and meaning, must not be treated as mere commodities or consumer goods.[25]

Third, Recital 19 then notes the challenges posed by the processes of globalization and notably the rapid development of information and communication technologies. These challenges, on the one hand, afford unprecedented conditions for enhanced interaction between cultures, yet also threaten the world's cultural diversity, especially in view of the widening gap

---

23 *See, generally,* C. Breunig, *Kommunikationspolitik der UNESCO: Dokumentation und Analyse der Jahre 1946 bis 1987*, 1987.

24 *See, generally,* Y.M. Lotman, *Universe of the Mind – A Semiotic Theory of Culture*, 1990, 237 (elaborating on the entwinement of the mind and culture).

25 Universal Declaration on Cultural Diversity, 2 November 2001, *CLT-2002/WS/9*, Article 8 (2002) [hereinafter "Cultural Diversity Declaration"].

between rich and poor countries. In this regard, the unprecedented pace of change surfaces, as the Convention fails to mention the concept of the creative economy, which only gained wider acceptance after the signing of the Convention. However, Recital 19 already hints at some important challenges related to and summarized by the concept of the creative economy.[26] The last two recitals refer to the mandate of UNESCO and the provisions of international instruments related to cultural diversity and the exercise of cultural rights adopted by it, such as, notably, the 2001 Cultural Diversity Declaration.[27]

3.2. THE PREAMBLE REVISITED

The various provisions of the Convention on the Diversity of Cultural Expressions will have to be interpreted in light of the considerations listed in the Preamble. As usual, the Preamble also provides useful background information about the purpose (telos) for the adoption of the Convention on the Diversity of Cultural Expressions as well as about the debate on the diversity of cultural expressions in particular and on the 'culture and trade debate' in general. When read and interpreted systematically, it also reflects relatively well the need for a holistic approach not only to the issue of cultural diversity but to global governance, which, in other words means that the overall goal of protecting and promoting the world's cultural diversity cannot be achieved without considering other valuable objectives of the international community, such as democracy, sustainable development, human rights, and international trade to mention but a few. More concretely, it also reflects the fragmented character of the institutional framework as well as the various international legal instruments governing the issue of cultural diversity only. This is reflected in the various references to the concepts of cultural heritage, intangible cultural heritage and traditional knowledge as well as intellectual property rights, which are of great significance for the objectives formulated in the Convention on the Diversity of Cultural Expressions. This has been underlined for the relationship between intellectual property rights and cultural diversity as follows:

> To smooth tensions and frictions in the field of cultural production, it is essential that the institutions responsible for cultural affairs and intellectual property policies understand that the only way to achieve efficient protection and promotion of

---

26 *See* UNCTAD, *World Creative Economy Report 2010: Creative Economy: A Feasible Development Option*, *available at* www.unctad.org//docs/_en.pdf (last visited 2 February 2012); UNCTAD, *World Creative Economy Report 2008: The challenge of assessing the creative economy towards informed policy-making*, *available at* www.unctad.org//docs/c20082cer_en.pdf (last visited 2 February 2012). *See also* J. Howkins, *The Creative Economy: How People Make Money From Ideas*, 2002; R.J. Neuwirth, "(De)Regulating the Creative Economy", 1 *Journal of Creative and Knowledge Society* 44–62 (2011) (providing a more legal perspective).

27 Cultural Diversity Declaration, *supra* note 21.

> cultural diversity on the local, regional and global level is to strike an appropriate and adequate balance between individual cultural policies, *i.e.* intellectual property and other cultural policies. The CD Convention can assist the contracting parties to achieve a balance between individual policies and to calibrate an adequate role for intellectual property regimes as means of protecting and promoting a diversity of cultural expressions.[28]

Similar findings have been made for the relation between cultural property, cultural relics, intangible cultural heritage, cultural and biological diversity as well as investment law.[29] In this regard, the Preamble fails to provide explanatory references to the institutional context of the Convention on the Diversity of Cultural Expressions, its relation to other agreements and the rule of law as the basic precondition for the successful achievement of the objectives it is designed to pursue. From a different perspective, however, the Convention on the Diversity of Cultural Expressions cannot take the blame as it recognizes to some degree the present level of organizational fragmentation that has captured the architecture of the international legal order as a whole. It remains to be seen, whether the said Convention on the Diversity of Cultural Expressions further contributes to the ongoing fragmentation not only of the two regimes governing culture and trade but also of international law in general.

4. TITLE I: OBJECTIVES AND GUIDING PRINCIPLES

Further clarifying the considerations laid down in the Preamble, Article 1 lists the principal objectives of the Convention on the Diversity of Cultural Expressions as subdividing into a total of nine *literae*. First and foremost, Article 1 makes clear, perhaps in order to avoid a basic misunderstanding, that the present Convention is neither about the protection or promotion of culture, nor about cultural diversity but instead about the diversity of cultural expressions, which it defines below as "expressions that result from the creativity

28 B. Hazucha, "Intellectual Property and Cultural Diversity: Two Views on the Relationship between Market and Culture", 26 *Intellectual Property Law and Policy Journal* 39, 90 (2010), *available at*: http://papers.ssrn.com//.cfm?abstract_id=1470103) (last visited 2 February 2012) (English version).

29 *See, e.g.*, P.K. Yu, "Traditional Knowledge, Intellectual Property, and Indigenous Culture: An Introduction", 11 *Cardozo J. Int'l & Comp. L.* 239 (2003); P.K. Yu, "Cultural Relics, Intellectual Property, and Intangible Heritage", 81 *Temp. L. Rev.* 433 (2008); V.J. Phillips, "Reflections on Intellectual Property, Traditional Knowledge and Cultural Expressions: Indigenous Rights to Traditional Knowledge and Cultural Expressions: Implementing the Millennium Development Goals", 3 *Intercultural Hum. Rts. L. Rev. 191* (2008); Valentina S. Vadi, "When Cultures Collide: Foreign Direct Investment, Natural Resources, and Indigenous Heritage in International Investment Law", 42 *Columbia Human Rights Law Review* 797, 868 (2011).

of individuals, groups and societies and that have cultural content".[30] Cultural content itself is defined as "the symbolic meaning, artistic dimension and cultural values that originate from express cultural identities".[31] The choice for the term "cultural expressions" appears thus as an attempt to narrow down the scope of the Convention on the Diversity of Cultural Expressions and demarcate it from the concept of "culture" and even from the one of "cultural diversity" which broadly refers to the "many ways in which the cultures of groups and societies find expression".[32]

The list of the residual objectives can be qualified as mentioning flanking measures accessory to the overall objective of protecting and promoting the diversity of cultural expressions. These accessory objectives comprise the encouragement of dialogue between cultures, that very interculturality rejecting explicitly the theory of a clash of cultures.[33] It also mentions the desire to promote respect and to raise awareness of the value of the diversity of cultural expressions at local, national and international levels. Article 1 also reiterates the importance of the link between culture and development for all countries. At this point, following the terms "for all countries", instead of emphasizing the special relevance for so-called "developing countries", it might have been helpful to introduce a new or more refined understanding of the distinction between "developed" and "developing countries".[34] Already highly questionable in the economic field,[35] such a distinction is particularly problematic in the cultural field, especially in light of the dynamism inherent in the concept of culture as recognized also in the Preamble, which acknowledges the principle of the equality of all cultures and the fact that culture takes diverse forms across time and space.[36] The two final objectives mentioned only reaffirm the sovereign

---

30 Convention on the Diversity of Cultural Expressions, *supra* note 2, Article 4(3).

31 Id., Article 4(2).

32 Id., Article 4(1).

33 *See* S.P. Huntington, "The Clash of Civilizations" 72 *Foreign Affairs* 22 (1993).

34 *See* R.J. Neuwirth, "A Constitutional Tribute to Global Governance: Overcoming the Chimera of the Developing-Developed Country Dichotomy" (European University Institute (EUI) Working Paper Law 2010/20 (2010)) (for a critique of the developing-developed country dichotomy).

35 *See, e.g.*, A. Sen, *Development as Freedom*, 1999; B. Frey and A. Stutzer, "What Can Economists Learn From Happiness Research?", 40 *Journal of Economic Literature* 402 (2002).

36 The principle of equality of cultures is a concomitant of the principle of equality of all states laid down in Article 2.1. UN Charter (*see* Charter of the United Nations, 24 October 1945, 1 UNTS XVI, Article 2.1.) and is, for example, restated in Article 1 of the 1966 *UNESCO Declaration of the Principles of International Cultural Co-operation* (*see* Declaration of Principles of International Cultural Co-operation, 4 November 1966, *available at* http://unesdoc.unesco.org/images/0011/001140/114048e.pdf#page=82 (last visited 2 February 2012), Paragraph 1 and 4 of the 1982 *Mexico City Declaration on Cultural Policies* (*see* Mexico City Declaration on Cultural Policies, 26 July – 6 Augustus 1982, *available at* http://portal.unesco.org/culture/en/files/35197/11919410061mexico_en.pdf/mexico_en.pdf (last visited 2 February 2012)), as well as implicitly recognzsed in the *Convention Concerning the Protection of the World Cultural and Natural Heritage* (*see* Convention Concerning the Protection of the World

rights of states in the adoption of cultural policies and the spirit of international cooperation and solidarity.

It must be noted that under *litera* (g) found hidden in between these residual flanking measures, is the objective "to give recognition to the distinctive nature of cultural activities, goods and services as vehicles of identity, values and meaning". Unlike the more programmatic flanking measures, this goal is at first sight susceptible to a more precise and less programmatic interpretation. It does not, however, clarify what kind of recognition is referred to and whether or not the recognition implies legal obligations.

More general information concerning the objectives is provided by Article 2, which lists the Guiding Principles of the Convention on the Diversity of Cultural Expressions. These principles include the following: the principle for respect of human rights and fundamental freedoms, the principle of sovereignty, the principle of equal dignity of and respect for all cultures, the principle of international solidarity and cooperation, the principle of the complementarity of economic and cultural aspects of development, the principle of sustainable development, the principle of equitable access (to a rich and diversified range of cultural expressions from all over the world), and the principle of openness and balance.

The brief explanations added to each of the principles are highly general in nature and therefore somehow repeat the basic considerations mentioned in the Preamble. They therefore unfortunately fail to elucidate and specify the obligations that Parties to the Convention will have to comply with once it has entered into force.

5. TITLE II: SCOPE OF APPLICATION

In Title II, the explanation given in Article 3 concerning the scope of application of the Convention on the Diversity of Cultural Expressions appears vague and of little significance when it states that "this Convention shall apply to the policies and measures adopted by the Parties relating to the protection and promotion of the diversity of cultural expressions". Article 3 can be regarded as superfluous.

6. TITLE III: DEFINITIONS

Article 4 provides definitions of the central concepts used throughout the Convention on the Diversity of Cultural Expressions, of which a few have been

Cultural and Natural Heritage, 16 November 1972, *available at* http://portal.unesco.org/en/ev.php-URL_ID=13055&URL_DO=DO_TOPIC&URL_SECTION =201.html (last visited 2 February 2012); *see*, *generally*, L. Galenskaya, "International Co-operation in Cultural Affairs", 198 *Rec. des Cours* 265 (1986).

quoted above. They merely summarize definitions formulated in previous related documents, such as the Cultural Diversity Declaration. Interesting to note, however, is the hierarchical order that can be read from the first five definitions (paragraphs 1–5), starting with "cultural diversity" as the principal concept of which "cultural content" and "cultural expressions" are important elements, and leading to "cultural activities, goods and services".

At the other end towards greater precision, the cultural industries, which are defined as "industries producing cultural goods and services" are, at least in legal terms and from a trade perspective, the most concrete concept. In contrast to the Preamble in Recital 18, Article 4 does not reiterate the dual nature underlying the cultural industries, which clearly marks their original *raison d'être* as the deliberate creation of an oxymoron.[37] The dual nature, both cultural and economic, is also one of the defining characteristics of these industries, to which the United States fiercely resisted and formally objected during the third session of the intergovernmental meeting.[38] This objection of the US comes somewhat as a surprise given that in 1998 the United States implicitly recognized this characteristic in a Communication to the WTO writing that:

> The United States wishes to join with the Secretariat in underscoring that audiovisual services reflect the social and cultural characteristics of a nation and its peoples, and in acknowledging the great social and political importance of these services – as a source of entertainment and education, as a means for helping to integrate a nation domestically, and in presenting to the rest of the world a nation's unique identity.[39]

Slightly further down the same Communication equally confirms that – fostered by technological innovation – the audiovisual sector possesses a special economic characteristic of high initial production but comparably low replication and distribution costs bringing about the tendency to strive towards audience maximization.[40]

This resistance during the negotiations perhaps helps to explain why the scope and meaning of the cultural industries is further concretized as it is, for instance, the case in the 1988 *Canada-United States Free Trade Agreement* ("CUSFTA"). In Article 2012, the CUSFTA broadly defines cultural industry as comprising any activity in the field of books, film, video and music recordings as

---

37 *See* Adorno, *supra* note 17, at 98.

38 *See* UNESCO, "Preliminary Report of the Director-General Setting out the Situation to be Regulated and the Possible Scope of the Regulating Action Proposed, Accompanied by the Preliminary Draft of a Convention on the Protection of the Diversity of Cultural Contents and Artistic Expressions", *33 C/23*, at 13 (4 August 2005).

39 *See* WTO, Council for Trade in Services, Communication from the United States, Audiovisual Services, *Doc. S/C/W/78*, §2 (8 December 1998).

40 *See* Id., §4.

well as broadcasting.[41] The advantage of not exhaustively defining the various sectors of goods and services is clearly its openness vis-à-vis new technological innovations and the resulting convergence between these sectors as well as the emergence of new ones, which cause new and difficult regulatory challenges to manifold legal regimes. For some guidance, the Convention could, however, have given a demonstrative list of some sectors belonging to the cultural industries.

The residual concepts defined are those of "cultural policies", "protection" and "interculturality", but do not give rise to further comments.

7. TITLE IV: "RIGHTS AND OBLIGATIONS OF PARTIES"

Generally, but also more specifically from a trade perspective, the next set of articles under Title IV contain some more significant provisions in terms of the application, implementation and possibly the overall success of the Convention. Their content was subject to intense negotiations, especially given that they laid down the basic rights and obligations of the Parties to the Convention on the Diversity of Cultural Expressions.[42]

Firstly, Article 5(1) restates as a general rule the Parties' rights and obligations, which reads as follows:

> The Parties, in conformity with the Charter of the United Nations, the principles of international law and universally recognized human rights instruments, reaffirm their sovereign right to formulate and implement their cultural policies and to adopt measures to protect and to promote the diversity of cultural expressions and to strengthen international cooperation to achieve the purposes of this Convention.

Especially the phrasing "sovereign right to formulate and implement cultural policies and to adopt measures" has been interpreted by critics of the Convention as an open invitation to a violation of other agreements and particularly obligations deriving from trade agreements. Yet, a closer look and more systematic interpretation undoubtedly required in a complex field like the one of cultural diversity, shows that such a position cannot be seriously sustained. This is because Article 5(1) explicitly requires the Parties to conform to some of the most important rules of international law. Moreover, it must be read in connection with Article 2(1) which specifies that "no one may invoke the

---

41 *See* Canada-United States Free-Trade Agreement, 4 October 1988, 27 *I.L.M.* 281 (1988); *See also* North American Free Trade Agreement between the Government of Canada, the Government of Mexico and the Government of the United States, 17 December 1992, 32 *I.L.M.* 605 (1993), Article 2106.

42 UNESCO, *supra* note 34, at 13.

provisions of this Convention in order to infringe human rights and fundamental freedoms". Finally, the scope of Article 5 is also limited by Article 20 which stipulates the Convention's relationship to other instruments.

In a more concrete way, Article 6 lists the Parties' rights and the measures they may adopt within the framework of cultural policies at a national level. By and large, these measures include regulatory means aimed at protecting and promoting diversity of cultural expressions. More specifically they equally include measures to provide opportunities for domestic activities, goods and services as well as those aimed at "providing domestic independent cultural industries and activities in the informal sector, effective access to the means of production, dissemination and distribution of cultural activities, goods and services". The mention not only of production but also of dissemination and distribution of cultural products corresponds to the numerous problems linked to the marketing of cultural products once they have been produced. These problems often appear in the form of "bottlenecks" where a few mostly large companies control and dominate the access to an efficient distribution network. Such control often comes from tendencies of production and distribution companies to minimize risks through vertical and horizontal integration and through recourse to unfair or anti-competitive practices. Such practices usually hit the independent and small producers hard, and unavoidably lead to a decrease in the diversity of products. In this context, Article 6(h) names measures aimed at enhancing diversity of the media, or, in other words, media pluralism, and explicitly emphasizes the role of public service broadcasting (PSB). The emphasis on PSB, however, should not be interpreted as an inherent criticism of private broadcasting companies, but instead read as a pledge for the creation of a dual system, *i.e.* a system in which private broadcasters can operate alongside their public counterparts. Other measures mentioned include the provision of public financial assistance, assistance to non-profit organizations, the establishment of public institutions and last but not least, "measures aimed at nurturing and supporting artists and others involved in the creation of cultural expressions".

A literal interpretation of Article 6, without systematically taking into account other relevant articles of the Convention on the Diversity of Cultural Expressions, may create the unfounded and false impression that as a result, Parties are allowed to take any kind of regulatory and other measures to support cultural expressions, such as subsidies, quotas, tax credits or content requirements, to mention but a few.[43] This, however, is only 'theoretical', since in fact, Article 20(2) on the relationship to other instruments, specifies that the Convention on the Diversity of Cultural Expressions does not modify the rights

---

43 *See, e.g.*, A. Castonguay, "151 Countries Support UNESCO's Draft Convention on the Diversity of Cultural Expressions. Only the U.S. and Israel Voted Against It.", *Le Devoir* (18 October 2005), *available at* www.ledevoir.com//10/18/92872.html (last visited 2 February 2012).

and obligations under any other treaties. This clearly has a restrictive effect on the scope of the rights enumerated in Article 6, but more on this will be said below in the context of Article 20. Finally, Article 6 also does not specify to what extent the use of the word "domestic" in the context of cultural activities or cultural industries means to distinguish between cultural products of foreign or of domestic origin.

Articles 7 and 8 then map out the framework for measures which, on the one hand, promote and, on the other, protect cultural expressions. This distinction, which also catches one's eye in the title of the Convention on the Diversity of Cultural Expressions, does not necessarily indicate a contradiction. Most importantly, protection is not identical to economic protectionism but instead is understood in the present context as the adoption of measures "aimed at the preservation, safeguarding and enhancement of the diversity of cultural expressions". Protection is then the complementary precondition for measures promoting the diversity of cultural expressions which according to Article 7(1) means the endeavour of Parties to create within their territory an environment that enhances the conditions and possibilities for individuals and social groups to create, disseminate, distribute and have access to their own cultural expressions. Paragraph 2 then extends the right of access to cultural expressions from other countries. Article 8 is a safeguard clause which allows a party to determine "the existence of special situations where cultural expressions on its territory are at risk of extinction, under serious threat, or otherwise in need of urgent safeguarding". Like Article 6, the safeguard clause of Article 8 fails to concretize the nature of such risks or threats and, in particular, whether these derive from domestic or from foreign cultural expressions.

Subsequently, Article 9 deals with information sharing and transparency and calls on the Parties to exchange information, to provide relevant information in their reports to UNESCO every four years, and to establish contact points responsible for information sharing.[44] Article 10 contains provisions aimed at fostering education and public awareness about the importance of the protection and promotion of the diversity of cultural expressions. Article 11 merely emphasises the fundamental role of civil society. In sum, these articles function as useful reminders but contain no legal obligations in a strict sense.

Articles 12 to 19 then refocus attention from the national level to cooperation at the international level, which the Convention on the Diversity of Cultural Diversity is set to promote. The various provisions oblige Parties to endeavour to strengthen their bilateral, regional and international cooperation for the creation of conditions conducive to the diversity of cultural expressions. Such obligations, as referred to in Article 12, include *inter alia* the facilitation of a dialogue among parties on cultural policy, the sharing of the most efficacious practices among

44 *See also* Convention on the Diversity of Cultural Expressions, *supra* note 2, Article 19 on "Exchange, analysis and dissemination of information" and Article 28 on "Points of contacts".

cultural institutions, the reinforcement of partnerships between civil society, NGOs and the private sector, the promotion of new technologies and the conclusion of co-production and co-distribution agreements. Article 13 explicitly calls on Parties:

> to integrate culture in their development policies at all levels for the creation of conditions conducive to sustainable development and, within this framework, foster aspects relating to the protection and promotion of the diversity of cultural expressions.

For this purpose, Article 14 then gives a demonstrative list of ways on how the support of the cooperation for sustainable development and poverty reduction can materialize. At this point, an interesting change of levels occurs because, generally in the field of development cooperation, the goals are relatively easy to define but extremely difficult to realize. The difficulty often stems from the lack of consensus on the means by which the goals may be best achieved. Thus what proves difficult is a smooth and sustainable transition from idea to reality, from theory to practice or from words to deeds. Article 14(1) therefore contains valuable information as it marks an attempt to carefully enter the 'world of deeds' by defining that such cooperation means the strengthening of the cultural industries. Unfortunately, here again the strengthening of the cultural industries is limited to the ill-termed concept of "developing countries", as if the cultural industries in so-called "developed countries" were already totally developed and need not be strengthened or protected from new threats.[45] Past and more recent experiences, however, show that especially the provision of culturally diverse, educative and informative as well as entertaining programmes of high quality is a difficult endeavour and battle which has to be won on a daily basis.[46] In the meantime we know that the mere increase in the number of television channels, publications and sound recordings, is no guarantee for a better and more diverse offer of content.

It's evident here that alignment with the new paradigm that the Convention on the Diversity of Cultural Expressions tries to introduce is lost. It is lost because it not only contradicts the principle of equality of all cultures and neglects the dynamic nature of the development of the human species, regardless of whether situated below or above the equator as emphasized in the Preamble, but it also violates an important premise of development understood as the freedom and capacity to lead "the kind of lives we have reason to value".[47] In other words, especially from the perspective of the diversity of cultural expressions, an individual's having a plasma wide-screen television connected to

---

45 *See, e.g.*, European Parliament Resolution on the Risks of Violation, in the EU and especially in Italy, of Freedom of Expression and Information (Article 11(2) of the Charter of Fundamental Rights), *P5_TA(2004)0373* (22 April 2004).

46 *See, e.g.*, A.E. Varona, "Changing Channels and Bridging Divides: The Failure and Redemption of American Broadcast Television Regulation" 6 *Minn. J.L. Sci. & Tech.* 1 (2004).

47 *See* Sen, *supra* note 31, at 18.

a satellite dish providing a selection of more than 300 channels is not superior to another individual's being able to contemplate the last sunrays of a sunset blanketing a green and well-cultivated valley.

Returning to the cultural industries mentioned in paragraph 1, Article 14 continues this flawed perception by calling on Parties to create and strengthen cultural production and distribution capacities in developing countries; to facilitate wider access to the global market and international distribution networks for their cultural activities, goods and services; to enable the emergence of viable local and regional markets; to facilitate access of cultural activities, goods and services to the territory of developing countries; and to support creative work and facilitate the mobility of artists from the developing world (lit. a to e). The last objective is repeated under Article 16, which obliges developed Parties to grant their developing counterparts preferential treatment with regard to artists and cultural goods and services. Only the last (lit. f), which calls on the Parties to foster cooperation between developed and developing countries in the relevant areas, such as music and film, is formulated neutrally in a sense that it does not start from the premise of a unilateral flow of benefits from the so-called "developed" to the "developing world". Finally, paragraphs 2 to 4 mention capacity building, transfer of technology and know-how, as well as financial support mainly through the International Fund for Cultural Diversity established by Article 18.

In sum, Article 14 as a whole as well as Article 16 can be characterized as carrying a number of trade aspects with particular relevance to the present multilateral trading regime, such as the degree of liberalization of trade in goods (GATT) and services (GATS), the treatment of emerging industries or facilitating the participation of developing countries (Article XVIII and XXXVI to XXXVIII GATT, Enabling Clause,[48] and Article IV GATS) the presence of natural persons of a Member in the territory of any other (WTO) Member (Mode 4; Article 1:2(d) GATS) and regionalism (Article XXIV GATT and Article V and V^{bis} GATS). References to "capacity building" and "technical assistance" also relate to technical assistance in the service sector (Article IV in connection with Article XXV GATS). Similarly, the envisaged support for the transfer of technology and know-how bears great relevance for the objective of the TRIPS Agreement.[49] The last paragraph on financial support, especially in combination

48 *See* Decision on Differential and More Favourable Treatment, Reciprocity and Fuller Participation of Developing Countries, 28 November 1979, *GATT Doc. L/4903*, *available at* www.wto.org/english/docs_e/legal_e/tokyo_enabling_e.pdf (last visited 2 February 2012).

49 *Cf.* Agreement on Trade-Related Aspects of Intellectual Property Rights, 15 April 1994, *LT/UR/A-1C/IP/1*, Article 7 [hereinafter "TRIPS Agreement"] (defining the objective of the TRIPS Agreement as follows: "The protection and enforcement of intellectual property rights should contribute to the promotion of technological innovation and to the transfer and dissemination of technology, to the mutual advantage of producers and users of technological knowledge and in a manner conducive to social and economic welfare, and to a balance of rights and obligations.").

with Article 18 establishing the International Fund for Cultural Diversity, raises rather general questions pertaining to the 'trade and development' problem, such as the coherence of economic policy making through the WTO, UNCTAD, the IMF and the World Bank.[50]

Article 15 contains obligations concerning the so-called "collaborative arrangements", and Article 17, which refers back to Article 8(1) calls for cooperation between the Parties in situations of "serious threat to cultural expressions". Unfortunately, Article 17 does not specify what embodies a serious threat and what measures Parties can or should take under such circumstances. In light of the significance of the cultural industries mentioned in Article 14 as well as their dual, *i.e.* economic and cultural, nature, this provision could not only have similarities but also implications for various safeguard or emergency actions described and authorized under the GATT (*e.g.* Articles VI, XII, XIX, XX and the Agreement on Subsidies and Countervailing Measures and Agreement on Implementation of Article VI of the General Agreement on Tariffs and Trade 1994)[51] and the GATS (*e.g.* Articles XII and XIV:a).[52]

8. TITLE V: "RELATIONSHIP TO OTHER INSTRUMENTS"

The previous comments on some specific articles of the Convention on the Diversity of Cultural Expressions suggest the existence of direct or indirect consequences for other areas of international law, in particular, international trade law. This impression, however, is ephemeral because it exists only as long as the text of the relevant article is interpreted literally and in strict isolation of the provisions laid down in Articles 20 and 21 under Title V of the Convention on the Diversity of Cultural Expressions. Title V, called "Relationship to Other Instruments", however, is crucial for the scope and objective of the Convention on the Diversity of Cultural Expressions since it draws the boundaries between

---

50 *Cf.* Memorandum of Understanding between the World Trade Organization and the United Nations Conference on Trade and Development, 16 April 2003, *available at* www.unctad.org/sections/press/docs/mou.pdf (last visited 2 February 2012); WTO, General Council, "Agreement between the WTO and the IMF and the World Bank", *WTO Doc. WT/L/194* (18 November1996) and its Addendum, *WT/L/194/Add.1* (18 November 1996); *See also* D. Ahn, "Linkages between International Financial and Trade Institutions – IMF, World Bank and WTO", 34 *J. World T.* 1 (2000).

51 *Cf.* Agreement on Implementation of Article VI of the General Agreement on Tariffs and Trade 1994 (Antidumping Agreement), 15 April 1994, 1868 *U.N.T.S.* 201, Annex 1A and Agreement on Subsidies and Countervailing Measures, 15 April 1994, *LT/UR/A-1A/9*, Articles 5 and 6.

52 With regard to Article XIV:a GATS, it should be noted that footnote 5 stipulates that "[t]he public order exception may be invoked only where a genuine and sufficiently serious threat is posed to one of the fundamental interests of society", *see* General Agreement on Trade in Services, 15 April 1994, *LT/UR/A-1B/S/1*, Article XIV:a, n. 5.

obligations and rights deriving from the present Convention and those deriving from other international agreements. Ultimately, it must be emphasized that this means that the articles of the Convention on the Diversity of Cultural Expressions, which are more than merely programmatic in character and, hence, contain more concrete rights and obligations, can only have their full effect within the boundaries drawn by Article 20 and, to a lesser extent by Article 21 of the Convention on the Diversity of Cultural Expressions. Together, Articles 20 and 21 must therefore be considered the central provisions of the Convention on the Diversity of Cultural Expressions because they either provide a point of contact for, or cut like a sharp razor blade through, the respective areas of culture and trade. The content of Articles 20 and 21 evaluates the success or failure of the Convention on the Diversity of Cultural Expressions through the creation of an appropriate regulatory setting for the cultural industries and, eventually, the diversity of cultural expressions with the aim of greater global cultural diversity.

The centrality of the enumerated articles is also reflected not only by the difficulty with which the text was drafted but also by the fierce battle that thereafter ensued. Both that difficulty and the battle signified a continuation of the primordial "agreement to disagree" over the treatment of cultural goods and services, reached during the Uruguay Round negotiations.[53] This time, the divergent views concerned not the legal treatment of this special category of goods and services but the initial intent and considerations that led to the decision to adopt a legally binding international instrument on cultural diversity. A divergence arose regarding the question of whether the Convention was aimed at clarifying the main aspects of the diversity of cultural expressions as an important aspect of cultural diversity, or whether it was designed to indirectly, and in disguise, change the trade rules established by the WTO, by securing special treatment for cultural goods and services under the aegis of UNESCO. On this last point it can be estimated that the main initiators of the Convention on the Diversity of Cultural Expressions probably considered it politically unrealistic to pursue this goal within the framework of the WTO.

Before turning to the content of Articles 20 and 21, their centrality indicates the necessity to look briefly at their drafting history.

8.1. THE EVOLUTION OF ARTICLE 20 OF THE CONVENTION ON THE DIVERSITY OF CULTURAL EXPRESSIONS

The difficulties concerning how to enhance the mutual supportiveness between the domains of culture and trade mentioned above are best reflected in the last

[53] *See* [this volume, introductory part] Kono and Van Uytsel, Section 2.4; [this volume, part IV] Neuwirth, Section 2.2.

draft proposal for Article 20 before the adoption of the Convention on the Diversity of Cultural Expressions, which reads as follows:

1. This Convention shall not affect the rights and obligations of Parties derived from other international agreements. Nor shall other international agreements affect the rights and obligations of Parties under this Convention.
2. When interpreting and applying other international instruments or when entering into other international obligations, Parties shall take into account the objectives and principles of the Convention.[54]

Obviously, the two sentences in paragraph 1 stand in clear opposition, not only contradicting each other but also creating a deadlock,which means that – literally as well as legally – the rights and obligations set forth in the Convention on the Diversity of Cultural Expressions add nothing useful to the objective of protecting and promoting the diversity of cultural expression. Thus any right or obligation mentioned in the Convention on the Diversity of Cultural Expressions is only authorized as long as it does not contradict a right or obligation deriving from any other international agreement. Considering the adage that "everything is allowed, unless it is prohibited", such a right already exists, even without the Convention on the Diversity of Cultural Expressions. This demonstrates why it adds little in legal terms, not only for consideration of greater cultural diversity but also for the entire area of international law, except perhaps for a further increase in the plethora of legal instruments and further fragmentation of international law.[55]

During the second session of the intergovernmental meeting, discussions among the delegations revealed a preference for a third way over the two proposed alternatives. During the third intergovernmental meeting, the issue of the relationship to other agreements was the subject of long and intense debate during which a new wording of the article was found and submitted to the Plenary. The United States and Australia formally objected to the article, while a few other delegations expressed reservations.

---

54 See UNESCO, "Preliminary Draft of a Convention on the Protection of the Diversity of Cultural Contents and Artistic Expressions", *171 EX/INF.18 Appendix 2*, at 15 (April 2005); for an even earlier version of Article 20 (then 19), *see* UNESCO, "*Preliminary Report of the Director-General Containing Two Preliminary Drafts of a Convention on the Protection of the Diversity of Cultural Contents and Artistic Expressions*", *CLT/CPD/2005/CONF.203/6*, at 36 (3 March 2005).

55 *See, e.g.*, B. Oppetit, "Les tendances régressives dans l'évolution du droit contemporain", in J.-F. Pillebout (ed.), *Mélanges dédiés à Dominique Holleaux*, 1990, 317; P.-M. Dupuy, "A Doctrinal Debate in the Globalization Era: On the "Fragmentation" of International Law", 1 *European Journal of Legal Studies* 1 (2007); G. Hafner, "Pros and Cons Ensuing from Fragmentation of International Law", 25 *Michigan Journal of International Law* 849 (2004) (discussing on the plethora of laws and fragmentation of international law).

At the end, the final version of Article 20 of the Convention on the Diversity of Cultural Expressions, which was adopted on October 20, 2005, read as follows:

1. Parties recognize that they shall perform in good faith their obligations under this Convention and all other treaties to which they are parties. Accordingly, without subordinating this Convention to any other treaty,
   (a) they shall foster mutual supportiveness between this Convention and the other treaties to which they are parties; and
   (b) when interpreting and applying the other treaties to which they are parties or when entering into other international obligations, Parties shall take into account the relevant provisions of this Convention.
2. Nothing in this Convention shall be interpreted as modifying rights and obligations of the Parties under any other treaties to which they are parties.

8.2. AN EVALUATION OF ARTICLE 20 OF THE CONVENTION ON THE DIVERSITY OF CULTURAL EXPRESSIONS

The first sentence of the culminating Article 20(1) merely restates the universally recognized principle of *pacta sunt servanda* as enshrined in Article 26 of the Vienna Convention on the Law of Treaties.[56] This principle means that once a convention has entered into force it is binding upon the parties to it and must be performed by them in good faith. The second sentence introduces the two subparagraphs by stating that Parties shall not subordinate the Convention on the Diversity of Cultural Expressions to any other treaty. Consequently subparagraph (a) calls on the Parties to "foster mutual supportiveness between this Convention and the other treaties to which they are parties". This can be read as a highly useful and necessary reminder of the need for greater coherence in global governance and international law. Such need is widely established not only for regulatory problems related to the multifaceted concept of cultural diversity but also to those of "cultural expressions" and "cultural industries", which have in common a demand for a more coherent relationship between the various existing and future legal instruments and their competent international organizations.[57] Ideally, this means an obligation to always consider possible

[56] *See* Vienna Convention, *supra* note 10.

[57] For the need of greater coherence, *see, e.g.*, M. Burri-Nenova, "Trade and Culture: Making the WTO Legal Framework Conducive to Cultural Considerations" 5 *Manchester Journal of International Economic Law* 2, 4 (2008); H. Ruiz Fabri, "Jeux dans la Fragmentation: la Convention sur la promotion et la protection de la diversité des expressions culturelles", 111 *Revue Générale de Droit International Public* 43 (2007); Graber, *supra* note 8, at 574, Tsai Yu Lin, "Exploring the Link Between Trade and Cultural Protection in the Context of Anti-Dumping", 42 *J. World T.* 563 (2008); C. Germann, "Diversité culturelle à l'OMC et l'UNESCO à l'example du cinéma", 2004 *Revue Internationale de Droit Économique* 325, 332;

linkages and implications between the Convention on the Diversity of Cultural Expressions and any other treaty. Subparagraph (b) then specifies that in addition to mutual supportiveness, Parties shall also bear in mind specific provisions of this Convention when they are interpreting and applying other treaties, or in the process of entering into other international obligations. As such, subparagraph (b) extends this duty to existing as well as future treaties.

Paragraph 2 then narrows the meaning and scope of paragraph 1 by clarifying that the Convention on the Diversity of Cultural Expressions shall not be interpreted as modifying existing rights and obligations. This restriction again limits not only the principle of non-subordination but also the margin of Parties to read greater mutual supportiveness in the relationship of, at least, existing treaties to which they are parties. The exact implication that paragraph 2 has for the first scenario mentioned in subparagraph (b) is also unclear because the modification of rights and obligations, which it sets out to prevent is opposite to the Parties' duty to take into account the Conventions' provisions when "interpreting and applying" other treaties. Article 20, however, is clear in the sense that it leaves no doubt as regards the due consideration, interpretation and application of the Convention's "spirit and letter" of the law to future obligations and treaties. It means that the Convention can only unfold legal effect *pro futuro* and by no means can have retroactive effects. This future-oriented approach is also reflected in Article 21, which commits Parties to "promote the objectives and principles of this Convention in other international forums".

In sum, it can be argued that Articles 20 and 21 bow to the legacy of Article IV GATT as previously noted, which has functioned as a political reminder of the actual link between culture and trade but equally of the strong need to rethink the mutual equilibrium between culture and trade in accordance with the respective societal and technological challenges posed at the time of consideration.

9. TITLE VI: ORGANS OF THE CONVENTION ON THE DIVERSITY OF CULTURAL EXPRESSIONS

The next title deals with the organs established by, and entrusted with the operation of the Convention on the Diversity of Cultural Expressions. Those organs include a Conference of Parties, as the plenary and supreme body of the Convention (Article 22) and an Intergovernmental Committee, to be composed of representatives of 18 States' Parties, elected by the Conference of Parties for a term of four years (Article 23). Only a subsidiary role was attributed to the UNESCO Secretariat, to assist the two principal organs of the Convention on the

R.J. Neuwirth, "The Cultural Industries and the Role of Article IV GATT: Reflections on Policy Options for Canada and the EU in the new WTO Round" (2002), *available at* http://papers.ssrn.com//.cfm?abstract_id=1352171 (last visited 2 February 2012).

Diversity of Cultural Expressions. Earlier ideas of setting up a Cultural Diversity Observatory and an Advisory Group were dropped based on the desire to avoid the creation of new bodies and concerns that the structures set up under the Convention on the Diversity of Cultural Expressions would be too burdensome.

10. TITLE VII: FINAL CLAUSES AND THE ANNEX

One of the central provisions of the final clauses is contained in Article 25, which in accordance with the procedure laid down in the Annex of the Convention on the Diversity of Cultural Expressions, regulates the *modus operandi* for the settlement of a conflict between Parties to this Convention. In the case of conflict, it first proposes a solution by negotiation. If this fails, the disputing Parties may seek good offices of, or request mediation by, a third party. If those attempts still fail, a Party may have recourse to the procedure laid down in the Annex of the Convention on the Diversity of Cultural Expressions. The Annex stipulates the creation of a so-called "Conciliation Commission", which under normal circumstances would be composed of five members, one of whom would be chosen to preside over the Commission. If the dispute involves more than two Parties, the Parties with shared interest can appoint their Commission members jointly. The Conciliation Commission shall then make its decision by a majority vote and render a proposal for the resolution of the dispute which the Parties shall consider in good faith. Given that there is no effective sanctioning mechanism, such as the one of the dispute settlement procedure of the Dispute Settlement Understanding ("DSU") under the WTO, it is highly questionable whether "good faith" alone will suffice to secure compliance with the award in the event of a serious conflict. Furthermore, the general and programmatic character of the Convention on the Diversity of Cultural Expressions leaves one wondering what kind of conflict may arise, particularly given that one of the most ardent critics of the Convention on the Diversity of Cultural Expressions is unlikely to ratify it.

The following clauses contain the usual provisions concerning the ratification, acceptance, or approval of, as well as accession to the Convention on the Diversity of Cultural Expressions (Articles 26 and 27). It is important to note that according to Article 27 paragraph 1, accession is open to all states that are Members of the United Nations, even those that are not members of UNESCO, on the sole condition that they are invited by the General Conference of UNESCO. Paragraph 2 contains special provisions for the membership of regional economic integration organizations, such as the European Union, which has made use of it. This specification was necessary since the Constitution of UNESCO does not foresee the Membership of Parties other than states.[58]

[58] *See* UNESCO Constitution, *supra* note 15, Article II.

Article 28 merely relates to the establishment of contact points as referred to in Article 9. Article 29 states that the Convention on the Diversity of Cultural Expressions shall enter into force three months after the date of deposit of the thirtieth instrument or ratification, acceptance, approval or accession but only with respect to those states or regional economic integration organizations that have deposited their instruments on or before that date. Any instrument deposited subsequently also enters into force with a delay of three months. Article 29 is therefore crucial because it means that the Convention on the Diversity of Cultural Expressions will have binding effect only between states party to the convention and not acquire the status of customary international law, at least for some time. This is an important aspect particularly with regard to the question of the relationship between the Convention on the Diversity of Cultural Expressions and other agreements and also with regard to the question of its applicability to the relationships between two or more states in other international bodies, such as the WTO DSB, if one of the states is a member of the Convention and the other is not.

Article 30 deals with the obligations of Parties deriving from the Convention and distinguishes between federal or unitary constitutional systems. Article 31 allows for the possibility of Parties to denounce the Convention through written notification.

Important from the perspective of dynamic development in the area of cultural expressions through rapid technological innovations in the industries supporting cultural expressions is Article 33, which foresees the possibility to amend the Convention on the Diversity of Cultural Expressions by a qualified majority of the Parties present and voting at the Conference of Parties.

Finally, Article 34 states that the authoritative languages of the text of Convention on the Diversity of Cultural Expressions are Arabic, Chinese, English, French, Russian and Spanish, and Article 35, which concludes the Convention on the Diversity of Cultural Expressions, lays down the registration of the convention with the Secretariat of the United Nations.

11. CONCLUDING REMARKS

The adoption of the Convention on the Diversity of Cultural Expressions was accompanied by great expectations as to the future reconciliation of culture and trade conflicts. In a total of 35 articles and one annex, the convention addresses a large number of concerns related to what is also known as "culture and trade problems". Despite some possible misunderstandings of a terminological nature caused by the title, the Convention provides some useful definitions and clarifications, notably regarding the concepts of cultural diversity, cultural content, and cultural industries, to mention but a few. In addition to clarifications as to its objectives and guiding principles, the Convention equally sets out to clarify the legal rights and obligations of parties both at the national and the international level. Some of the concepts used, however, fall short of the required hard legal nature so as to also assume full legally binding character. Otherwise, the Convention merely restates already existing legal concepts and principles. This is, for instance, the case with the principle of sovereignty and the corresponding explanation that it entails the right of each Party to "adopt measures aimed at protecting and promoting the diversity of cultural expressions within its territory" as laid down in Article 6(1) of the Convention on the Diversity of Cultural Expressions.

In sum, most provisions appear rather programmatic rather than strictly legal or normative in nature. This is perhaps best reflected in its failure to successfully address, let alone solve, the important legal issue of its relationship to other treaties as laid down in Article 20. Unfortunately, this failure includes not only questions of the relationship between the present Convention and trade agreements but even other cultural conventions, such as the Convention for the Safeguarding of Intangible Cultural Heritage. It also falls short in providing a convincing mechanism apt for the settlement of disputes should they arise from the Convention's interpretation or application by merely providing a conciliation procedure (Article 25 and Annex). At first glance, its greatest achievement consists, therefore, in the area of raising the public awareness of the issue of the diversity of cultural expressions and providing perhaps a useful glossary for future debates.

In sum, most provisions support the characterization of the Convention on the Diversity of Cultural Expressions as a "sheep in a wolf's clothing" or legally speaking as a "hard legal instrument" with a "soft legal content".[59] To what extent, its legal content has been and will be capable of influencing and steering future developments in international law in general, and towards a better reconciliation of cultural with commercial or trade concerns in international trade law in particular, therefore has and will have to be evaluated based on practice reflecting its reception by the international community.[60]

---

59 *See* A. Vlassis, "La mise en oeuvre de la Convention sur la diversité des expressions culturelles Portée et enjeux de l'interface entre le commerce et la culture", 42 *Revue Études internationales* 493, 495 (2011).

60 *See* [this volume, part IV] Neuwirth; [this volume, part IV] Voon.

THE IMPACT OF THE U.S. POSITION IN THE TRADE AND CULTURE DEBATE

Negotiation of the Convention on the Diversity of Cultural Expressions

Carol Balassa*, **

1. INTRODUCTION: THE DEBATE OVER APPLYING TRADE RULES TO MOTION PICTURES

Negotiation of the *Convention for the Promotion and Protection of Diversity of Cultural Expressions* (the "Convention on the Diversity of Cultural Expressions")[1] has been portrayed as but "the latest chapter in the longstanding debate over the relationship between trade and culture,"[2] a debate that pits two radically opposing views of cultural products against each other: "[o]ne approach sees cultural products as entertainment products that are similar, in commercial terms, to any other products and therefore completely subject to the rules of international trade. The other view is that cultural products are essential instruments of social communications which convey values, ideas and meaning, and thus contribute to fashioning the cultural identity. As such, they should be excluded from the reach of international trade agreements."[3]

Left undefined in the above description of the trade and culture debate is the term "cultural products." Is the term intended to encompass those artistic

---

* Carol Balassa has had a diverse career in the Office of the United States Trade Representative (1980 – 2007) where she led numerous trade negotiations on audiovisual, telecommunications, and energy services. Ms. Balassa served as a member of the U.S. delegation to UNESCO, where she brought a trade perspective to development of U.S. negotiating position on the Convention on the Diversity of Cultural Expressions.

** An earlier version of this chapter was published in J.P. Singh (ed.), *International Cultural Policies and Power*, 2010, Palgrave Macmillan.

1 *See* Convention on the Protection and Promotion of the Diversity of Cultural Expressions, 20 October 2005, *U.N. Doc. CLT-2005/CONVENTION DIVERSITE-CULT REV.* [hereinafter "Convention on the Diversity of Cultural Expressions"].

2 I. Bernier, "Trade and Culture" (Unpublished report on file with the author).

3 Id.

endeavours which, by their nature require the presence of an audience at a given site at a given time, are we talking about a broadly disseminated creative undertaking, which can be endlessly replicated at relatively little or no cost to a global audience, or are we talking about both simultaneously?

Given the language used above to describe the parameters of the trade and culture debate, it appears unlikely that "cultural products" refers to painting, sculpture, theatre or opera, whose value, to a greater or lesser degree, lies in its limited availability to audiences. Rather, "cultural products" refers to motion pictures, video discs, television programs, and sound recordings, the grouping of services which in the Uruguay Round were included under the heading of "audiovisual services," and which, as to be demonstrated in the discussion to follow, have been the focal point of the trade and culture debate in both the World Trade Organization (WTO) and the United Nations Economic and Social Organization (UNESCO). In this context, the U.S. position in the debate will be examined from the perspective of its most contentious, and most widely-discussed facet – trade in motion pictures.

It is the thesis of this chapter that the U.S. position on applying trade rules to motion pictures is today a complex and evolving balance of economic and cultural components which the U.S. has, for reasons that span both sides of the debate, been unable to realize in the GATT or its successor, the WTO, or in UNESCO. Despite the relative isolation of the U.S. on the issue, however, the fact that WTO trade disciplines apply to audiovisual services, as to virtually all services sectors, is of significant importance to the international trading system.

After Section 1, Introduction, the following four sections of the chapter trace evolution of the U.S. position in the trade and culture debate as follows: Section 2, Preparations to Negotiate Trade in Services (1980–1985); Section 3, The Uruguay Round (1986–1991)[4]; Section 4, The Doha Round (2000–2008); and Section 5, The UNESCO Convention on the Diversity of Cultural Expressions (2003–2005). The chapter concludes in Section 6 with an assessment on The Foundations and Influence of the U.S. Position in the Trade and Culture Debate.

2. PREPARATIONS TO NEGOTIATE TRADE IN SERVICES

2.1. THE UNITED STATES REPORT ON TRADE IN MOTION PICTURES

In the early 1980s, in preparation for upcoming negotiations of an agreement on trade in services in the Geneva-based GATT, the Office of the U.S. Trade

4 *See* C. Balassa, "International Cooperation to Improve Trade Rules", 6 (4) *North America Outlook* 25 (1998) (forming the inspirational basis for this section).

Representative (USTR) drafted a series of internal reports for different services sectors to determine whether GATT trade principles, such as most favoured nation (MFN), national treatment, market access, and transparency, would effectively address the problems that U.S. service providers encountered in their foreign operations.[5] The reports were also intended to determine whether GATT trade principles could be applied systematically across a broad range of different services sectors.[6]

The motion picture sector was one of twelve services sectors for which an internal report was drafted. The report, *Trade in Motion Picture Services* ("Motion Picture Report"),[7] provides a preliminary view of the U.S. position on applying international trade disciplines to the motion picture sector.

The starting point for the report is the dual nature of motion pictures. Pointing out that motion pictures is the only service sector to be covered by the GATT, the report explains that, as a tangible product, the feature film has been made subject to most GATT rules, but because the sector at the same time embodies a nation's cultural identity, it has been accorded special treatment. Article IV of the GATT, "Special Provisions Relating to Cinematographic Film," acknowledges, for example, that "government protection of a domestic film industry for cultural purposes is a legitimate social objective."[8] For this reason, the difficulty domestic film producers found in finding screen time to exhibit their films in the immediate post-World War II period was taken into account in drafting GATT Article IV, which permits countries to retain existing screen time quotas as long as they do not introduce new MFN discrimination. Article IV is the sole exception in the GATT to the principle of national treatment.[9]

2.2. THE TRADE ARGUMENT

The Motion Picture Report clearly makes the case that motion pictures are widely traded and face problems similar to those encountered by other traded

---

5 *See infra* note 7.

6 The reports included the following service sectors: telecommunications, data processing and information services, motion pictures, engineering and construction, maritime, banking and related financial services, insurance, professional services, advertising, travel and tourism, franchising, lodging, and aviation.

7 *See*, e.g., C. Balassa, "Trade Issues in the Motion Picture Industry" (unpublished report prepared for the Office of the United States Trade Representative (1981) (on file with the author); *See also* Office of the U.S. Trade Representative (ed.), "U.S. National Study on Trade in Services: A submission by the United States Government to the General Agreement on Tariffs and Trade – Motion Pictures", 1984, 154–9 (constituting an enlarged version of the original report provided by the U.S. Government Printing Office: 1984–464–694/20595).

8 Id, at 29.

9 *See* GATT, Group of Negotiations on Services, Working Group on Audiovisual Services, "Matters Relating to Trade in Audiovisual Services: Note by the Secretariat", *MTN. GNS/AUD/W/1* (4 October 1990).

goods and services. Based on extensive industry interviews with representatives from the Motion Picture Association of America (MPAA), its member companies, and independent film producers, the report lists numerous barriers encountered by U.S. motion picture exporters. Those barriers include, in addition to screen time quotas, import quotas, film rental price controls, dubbing taxes, tie-in arrangements, local work requirements, monopoly controls, discriminatory admission taxes, inappropriate customs valuation, restrictions on foreign remittances, unfavourable tax levies, limited exhibition possibilities, subsidies, piracy, and inadequate intellectual property protection.[10]

Linking the absence of trade barriers to the economic viability of the industry, the Motion Picture Report points out that motion pictures, like other traded goods and services, benefit significantly from international trade. In what came to be the economic cornerstone for the U.S. position on trade in motion pictures, the paper explains that "[t]he technology of the motion picture industry is such that nearly all the cost of making a film goes into the production of the first print. Once the original is completed, the cost of making additional prints is relatively small as compared to the initial cost of production, though rapidly rising copying and advertising costs are somewhat changing the picture. Nonetheless it is to the producer's interest to seek the widest possible market – both domestic and foreign – in order to maximize the return on his investment. Moreover, because the investment required to produce a feature film is substantial – $10 million on the average in the United States today [1980][11] – the motion picture industry is dependent on its export markets."[12]

The U.S. motion picture industry has often been accused of adopting a 'siege mentality' in its international negotiations, taking a position that no market, however small, is insignificant. Indirectly addressing this position, the Motion Picture Report explains that "[t]he realities of the motion picture business are such that, except in cases of blockbusters, the margin of profit on a film is often small. Consequently the loss of even a relatively small market may mean the difference between profits and loss which gives one company the edge over its competitor and provides the overall profit for a production. Such profits, in turn, permit the individual producer, engaged in both a commercial and artistic undertaking, to train talent, experiment, and undertake the risks intrinsic to his profession. Measures that reduce the producer's profits are therefore regarded as

10 *See* Balassa, *supra* note 7, at 7–18 (It is interesting to note that, in 1980, when the report was written, piracy issues were just emerging and appeared only at the end of a list of trade barriers that, at the time, appeared to be more important).

11 The average cost of producing a studio film in 2007 was about $75 million. *See* P. McClintock, "MPAA Specialty Films See Rising Costs", 2008 *Variety*, *available at* www.variety.com/article/VR1117981882.html?categoryid=13&cs=1 (last visited 2 August 2010).

12 Balassa, *supra* note 7, at 18.

a threat to the very features that are basic to a successful motion picture industry."[13]

Expanding the discussion to include the benefits of trade to smaller economies, the Motion Picture Report notes that, for the local movie industry, experience has shown that "contact with imported films serves to stimulate rather than to retard the production of high quality films. Countries with the healthiest film industries are the ones to have the least restrictive trade policies, for they understand the artistic stimulus and technical education that comes from contact with imported films."[14]

Importation of high quality films also benefits the local industry, the Motion Picture Report continues, by helping to develop a movie-going public "whose increased attendance at cinemas will provide an assured market and the stable conditions necessary to secure the investment for producing feature films."[15] Conversely, a restriction which delays importation of a film may prevent it from being shown during peak exploitation periods, creating uncertainty that "aggravates the financing problems of an industry that requires large investment and faces difficulties in obtaining financing at home."[16]

Given the importance of trade to the U.S. motion picture industry, it is not surprising that the U.S. was a leader in urging the creation of a multilateral discipline for trade in services that would include motion pictures. Because the motion picture sector was the only sector to be covered by GATT trade disciplines and at the same time share characteristics with service sectors, the U.S. regarded the motion picture sector as a model for the application of services trade rules. In addition, reflecting the convergence between developing technologies in the motion picture industry and other services sectors – notably telecommunications and advertising – the U.S. foresaw that extending trade rules to motion pictures "may help to assure an orderly expansion of economic relations in other dynamic services – and related merchandise areas too."[17]

2.3. THE CULTURE ARGUMENT

The Motion Picture Report balances discussion of trade benefits for the motion picture sector with recognition that governments often undertake restrictive trade measures "to foster a local film industry as a means to express a nation's cultural identity."[18] Turning its attention to the *Organization of European Cooperation and Development* (OECD) as well as the GATT, the report notes that

13 Id., at 19.
14 Id., at 26.
15 Id., at 27.
16 Id., at 21.
17 Id., at 6.
18 Id., 24.

in the GATT and the OECD, "protection of a local film [with screen time quotas] for cultural reasons is recognized as a legitimate social objective..."[19] while subsidies are permitted in the OECD as well.

Outlining a position it would largely abandon in the heat of the Uruguay Round negotiations,[20] the Motion Picture Report acknowledges that these two policy tools of screen time quotas and subsidies "permit governments to pursue legitimate social objectives without unnecessarily distorting international trade."[21] Citing industry sources, the Motion Picture Report states that "reasonable screen time quotas are a relatively straightforward and acceptable means of protecting a domestic film industry; subsidies, when paid for from general revenue (and not from box office receipts) have little impact on trade patterns."[22]

3. THE URUGUAY ROUND

3.1. CONFRONTATION WITH THE EU

In the Uruguay Round, the motion picture sector came to be subsumed in the audiovisual services sector, which, as noted above, also includes video tapes, television programs and sound recordings. Negotiations over audiovisual services became a bitterly contentious issue between the United States and the EU that came near to derailing the entire negotiation. The confrontation, often cast as a more general debate over 'culture', centred essentially around two major issues.

Firstly, arguing that audiovisual services were conveyors of a nation's unique cultural identity and so differed from other traded goods and services, the EU wanted to remove the audiovisual sector entirely from the framework of the new *General Agreement on Trade in Services* (GATS) so that the new trade rules for services would not apply to the audiovisual sector. This was the 'cultural exception' argument that the EU had taken up at France's insistence. According to one commentator, "[e]fforts to obtain a cultural exception reflected concern about multinational conglomerates' influence over cultural production and circulation, and a desire to ensure that countries can continue to make cultural policies and regulate their cultural markets without contravening commitments made as part of multilateral trade agreements..."[23] Secondly, the EU did not want to cap or remove its Television without Frontier Directive

19 Id., at 24.

20 *See infra* Section 3.

21 Balassa, *supra* note 7, at 35.

22 Id., at 35.

23 J. Smiers, "A Convention on Cultural Diversity: From WTO to UNESCO", 2004 *Media International Australia* 81 (Abstract), *available at* www.uq.edu.au/emsah/mia/issues/miacp111.html#smiers (last visited 2 February 2012).

[TWF Directive][24] limitation on the amount of foreign programming material that could be broadcast. It also did not agree to U.S. requests that it administer its generous system of film subsidies on a national treatment basis.

By contrast, the United States wanted the new GATS framework to include all service sectors and wanted the EU to make a specific commitment for audiovisual services that would remove the foreign content restrictions of the TWF Directive. The United States also sought to have the EU either cap its screen production subsidies or administer those subsidies, financed from box office taxes and blank tape levies imposed largely on U.S. content, on a national treatment basis.[25] At the time a number of U.S. filmmakers were making films in the EU and so were well-positioned to take advantage of guaranteed non-discriminatory access to EU film subsidies.

Further complicating negotiation of audiovisual services was the fact that the negotiations were also linked to other contentious issues in the Uruguay Round. "By the end of 1993," reports Luc Veron in a detailed study of the audiovisual negotiation, "both the US and the EU parties used the contentious audio-visual issue to try to extract concessions from the other party on other issues, like maritime transportation, or aircraft."[26]

3.2. FOCUS ON ECONOMIC ISSUES

Convinced that the EU's aggressive stance on audiovisual issues in the Uruguay Round had little to do with protecting a nation's cultural identity, but much to do with protecting its domestic industry, the U.S. hardened its position on audiovisual services. Persuaded that the EU's content quotas and cultural exception efforts posed serious threats to members of the MPAA, Jack Valenti warned:

---

24 *See* EC, Council of the European Communities, "Council Directive 89/552/EEC on the Coordination Certain Provisions laid Down by Law, Regulation or Administrative Action in Member States Concerning the Pursuit of Television Broadcasting Activities", *OJ L298* (3 October 1989), as amended by European Parliament and Council of European Union, "Directive 97/36/EC of the European Parliament and of the Council of 30 June 1997 amending Council Directive 89/552/EEC on the Coordination of Certain Provisions Laid Down by Law, Regulation or Administrative Action in Member States Concerning the Pursuit of Television Broadcasting Activities", *OJ L202* (30 July 1997). The two basic principles of the TWF Directive were to ensure the free movement of EU television programs within the EU market and to require EU television channels to reserve, "wherever practicable," a majority of their transmission time for European works.

25 *See* Press Release, Office of the United States Trade Representative, USTR Press Release on Special 301 Annual Review (1 May 1998) (on file with author) (indicating that the blank tape levy issue remained an ongoing problem for the U.S. motion picture industry).

26 L. Veron, "Hollywood and Europe: A Case of Trade in Cultural Industries, the 1993 GATT Dispute", at 3 (Columbia International Affairs Online, Working Papers CIAO Date 4/99), *available at* www.ciaonet.org/wps/ue/vel (last visited 2 February 2012).

> I don't want there to be any ambiguity. If those quotas exist, this is Armageddon time. In the United States, I'm on the Hill in a New York minute bringing out every Patriot missile, every F-16 in our armory, leading whatever legions we can find opposing this agreement ... Any GATT accord that allows the TV quota to stay in place would be totally unacceptable to us. I would fight it to the death.[27]

In the highly-charged atmosphere that characterized the Uruguay Round debate over audiovisual services, the U.S. focused almost exclusively on economic issues, refuting efforts to make the case for a cultural exception with the response that there is "nothing economically special about these products ...as justifying a repudiation of free trade premises."[28]

To press its case against the content quotas of the TWF Directive, the U.S. underscored that in the promising new areas of cable networks and direct satellite broadcasting services, quotas were as counterproductive for the EU as for the U.S.: "...imposing quotas on TV broadcast, cablecast, and direct satellite services...will have an immediate and devastating impact on the development of the new services just being developed in Europe, particularly new cable networks and direct satellite broadcasting," argued a U.S. negotiator, adding that "[n]o one can make television viewers watch what they do not want to watch."[29]

Elsewhere, in order to obtain support from EU broadcasters, U.S. negotiators pointed out that the low cost of U.S. programming would help broadcasters overcome the hurdle of relatively high start up costs: once established with the help of budget-priced American programs, so the U.S. argument went, EU broadcasters could then devote their limited resources to the development of local programming.

U.S. objections to a cultural exception from trade rules extended beyond concerns for its audiovisual services sector. While seriously concerned about the impact of a cultural exception relating to one of its most "lucrative areas of export,"[30] the U.S. was further concerned that, if an exception from WTO trade disciplines were granted to one sector considered sensitive by some, a precedent would be established for other countries to demand exceptions for sectors that they, too, considered sensitive. The result would be an unravelling of a services trade agreement whose economic benefits depended importantly on covering trade in essentially all service sectors.[31]

---

27 B. Stokes, "Tinseltown Trade War", 1991 *National Journal* 434, 438 (quoting Jack Valenti).

28 P. Sauvé and K. Steinfatt, "Towards Multilateral Rules on Trade and Commerce: Protective Regulation or Efficient Protection", in Productivity Commission (ed.), *Achieving Better Regulation of Services*, 2001, 323, 327, *available at* www.cid.harvard.edu/cidtrade/Papers/Sauve/sauveculture.pdf (last visited 2 February 2012).

29 "Suggested Remarks on EC Directive on Programming Quotas" (1989) (Internal U.S. document on file with the author).

30 K. Acheson and Ch. Maule, "International Agreements and the Cultural Industries", 6 *North American Outlook* 1, 12 (1995) (quoting from 51 (50) *Congressional Quarterly* 3463 (18 December 1993)).

31 *See, e.g.*, Balassa, *supra* note 7, at 23; the possible unraveling of a services agreement with sensitive sectors excluded is seen in: C. H. Farnsworth, "U.S. is Changing Its Tune on

3.3. OUTCOME OF THE URUGUAY ROUND

The Uruguay Round confrontation between the U.S. and the EU essentially ended in what was viewed at the time as a draw. The GATS agreement did not result in an EU commitment to modify the TWF Directive nor to cap the 51 per cent quota on non-European content programming as the U.S. had hoped. At the same time, however, the final GATS text did not contain language that provided a 'cultural exception', as the EU had desired.

As a result, no legal distinction was drawn between audiovisual services and any other service sectors – the general rules of the services agreement applied to the audiovisual sector as to all service sectors (with the exception of some civil aviation services). Relatively few countries scheduled commitments for audiovisual services however, and those commitments that were scheduled were, for the most part, seriously circumscribed. This meant that while general obligations of the GATS, such as MFN treatment and transparency, applied in principle to the audiovisual sector, only thirteen WTO members undertook specific market access and national treatment obligations for the sector. Moreover, a number of countries took an MFN exception for audiovisual services, in large part to cover co-production agreements, further limiting the impact of the general MFN obligation.[32]

Despite the apparent balancing of wins and losses in the audiovisual services negotiation, the bitterness and disappointment left by the negotiation was all too evident. Jack Valenti, for example, "express[ed] his frustration at the end of the GATT negotiations by declaring that culture was the European word for protectionism" while "President Mitterand had, a few months earlier, publicly asked "who could be blind today to the threat of a world gradually invaded by Anglo-Saxon culture, under the cover of economic liberalism."[33]

In retrospect, the U.S. came to realize that although the Uruguay Round may have ended in a draw between the U.S. and the EU, the U.S. hard-line position on audiovisual services had antagonized a number of countries, making future liberalization of the sector more difficult. Demands expressed on behalf of major U.S. film producers for non-discriminatory access to EU film subsidies, for example, are reported to have helped the European film lobby to mobilize "by arousing widespread fears that trade disciplines could be used to restrict the film subsidies on which most local film industries depended…"[34]

Liberalization of Trade", *New York Times* (29 October 1990), *available at* www.nytimes.com/1990/10/29/business/international-report-us-is-changing-itstune- (last visited 2 August 2010).

32 *See* WTO, Council for Trade in Services, "Audiovisual Services: Background Note by the Secretariat", *S/C/W/40*, at 8 (15 June 1998).

33 J. Sinclair, "Culture and Trade: Some Theoretical and Practical Considerations", in E.J. McAnany and K. T. Wilkinson (eds.), *Mass Media and Free Trade: NAFTA and the Cultural Industries*, 1997, 38 (quoting Jack Valenti).

34 Veron, *supra* note 26, at 4–5.

Further, some of the U.S. industry's strongest concerns over current and future application of the content quotas of the TWF Directive, for example, proved to be exaggerated. USTR reported in its 1998 *Foreign Trade Barriers Report*, for example, that "by the time an agreement was reached on a revised directive [in 1997], the divisive issue of strengthening European content quotas had fallen by the wayside despite the Parliament's protectionist line."[35]

4. THE DOHA DEVELOPMENT AGENDA AND THE AUDIOVISUAL SECTOR

4.1. THE AUDIOVISUAL OBJECTIVES PAPER

To prepare for the upcoming trade negotiation round, known as the Doha Development Agenda (Doha Round),[36] the WTO Group on Negotiating Services invited WTO members to table papers in December 2000 outlining their negotiating objectives for specific services sectors. In responding to this invitation, the United States included a number of sector specific papers, including one for audiovisual services, *Communication from the United States: Audiovisual and Related Service* ("Objectives Paper").[37]

The Objectives Paper for audiovisual services that the U.S. tabled at the WTO in 2000 represents a significant change in both tone and substance from the earlier U.S. position on audiovisual services. The change indicates serious concern on the part of both government and industry that its Uruguay Round position on content quotas and subsidies had hardened opposition to future liberalization commitments for the sector. The U.S. was also mindful at this time of ongoing discussions led by Canada and the EU to create a new international instrument to address cultural issues in UNESCO.[38] The threat of having the audiovisual sector removed entirely from multilateral trade rules was not taken lightly, either by U.S. Government officials or motion picture industry representatives, and the U.S. set about to improve its image on the issue.

---

35 U.S., Office of the United States Trade Representative, "Foreign Trade Barriers Report: Europe", 18 (1998), *available at* www.ustr.gov/assets/Document_Library/Reports_Publications/1998/1998_National_Trade_Estimate/asset_upload_file841_2758.pdf (last visited 2 February 2012); *See also* Veron, *supra* note 26, at 5.

36 *See, generally*, WTO, "Doha Development Agenda: Negotiations, Implementation and Development", *available at www.wto.org/english/tratop_e/dda_e/dda_e.htm* (last visited 2 February 2012).

37 WTO, Council for Trade in Services, "Communication from the United States: Audiovisual and Related Services", *S/CSS/W/21* (18 December 2000).

38 *See infra* Section 5.

4.2. CHANGE IN TONE

To remove recollections of its harsh stance on motion pictures in the Uruguay Round, the Objectives Paper sets out to place the forthcoming Doha Round negotiations of audiovisual services in a new light. "The audiovisual sector in 2000 is significantly different from the audiovisual sector of the Uruguay Round period when negotiations focused primarily on film production, film distribution, and terrestrial broadcasting of audiovisual goods and services,"[39] begins the paper. Whether or not this statement was strictly accurate turned out to be irrelevant. It was significant in that it signalled that the U.S. wanted to give a fresh start to audiovisual services negotiations.

Directly addressing the trade and culture debate that had characterized so much of the Uruguay Round discussion on the issue, the paper refutes the notion that the debate over the audiovisual sector in the WTO is an "'all-or-nothing' game" in which "the only available options were to exclude culture from the WTO or to liberalize completely all aspects of audiovisual and related services." Instead, in an effort to lay the groundwork for a constructive negotiation, the U.S. paper, recognizing "public concern for the preservation and promotion of cultural values and identity, outlines a proposal where preservation of national identity and liberalization of trade in audiovisual services may in fact "reinforce each other."[40]

To establish the link between trade and culture, the paper emphasizes that "[t]he ability to make and distribute audiovisual products both to domestic and foreign audiences is not independent of business and regulatory considerations." Pointing to the costly and uncertain nature of the audiovisual sector, there is, the Objectives Paper points out, "of necessity a commercial aspect to this artistic activity that will affect both the production and distribution of audiovisual product, which is widely traded internationally." For the motion picture industry, where timing is essential to successful distribution of a movie, "[p] redictable and clearly defined trade rules… [are required] to foster international exhibition and distribution opportunities and provide commercial benefits that audiovisual service providers must have to continue their artistic endeavors."[41]

The developmental objectives of the Doha Round are also served by liberalizing trade in motion pictures, the U.S. paper point out. "As part of the explosion in information technology that has taken place in the past decade … Audiovisual services, too, play their role in fostering a nation's economic development, both through the spread of information and ideas and by fostering investment in a nation's advanced communications infrastructure."[42]

---

39 WTO, Council for Trade in Services, *supra* note 37, at 1.

40 Id., at 3.

41 Id., at 2.

42 Id., at 1.

4.3. CHANGE IN SUBSTANCE

Turning to specific negotiating suggestions, the paper responds to criticisms that trade rules are too inflexible to address the special cultural qualities of audiovisual services. As examples of WTO flexibility on cultural issues, the paper points to the GATT national treatment exception for cinematic films and the flexibility that WTO rules offer countries in scheduling commitments for audiovisual, or any other, services sector "so long as the regulation is not administered in a way that represents an unexpected trade barrier."[43]

The audiovisual services request that the U.S. made to most of its trading partners in the Doha Round in fact exemplified the flexibility referenced in its Objectives Paper. It is to be recalled that in the GATS, liberalization of services trade is achieved largely through the request-offer process in which countries negotiate sector-specific liberalization requests of each other, many of which include requests for the removal or modification of trade restrictive measures or regulations.

By contrast to its Uruguay Round audiovisual request to the EU, which sought removal of content quotas and access to subsidies on a national treatment basis, in the Doha Round the U.S. made no rollback request, and asked instead that the EU inscribe in its schedule of commitments its current level of market openness for the sector. With a few notable exceptions, similar requests were made of most other WTO members.

Though the much softened U.S. audiovisual requests of the Doha Round were intended as a signal that the United States was seeking to change its earlier position on the issue. some recipients were quick to point out that the request was less benign than it appeared: The standstill commitment requested by the United States would in fact require a country to make a legally binding commitment not to impose any further restrictions in the potentially new and more lucrative technologies, such as video-on-demand and pay-per-view television. Few, if any, countries indicated a willingness to do so.

In a most notable shift away from its Uruguay Round stance, the U.S. in its Objectives Paper revised its position on subsidies. The issue was a dividing line between the U.S., which had no history of direct federal subsidies to its profit-making arts sector, and most of its trading partners, whose arts programs, including those for motion pictures, were heavily dependent on government funding.[44] Concern that WTO trade rules could restrict a government's ability to fund the arts, especially for motion pictures intended for commercial distribution, was a key factor in isolating the U.S. not only in WTO negotiations, but in the Convention on the Diversity of Cultural Expressions negotiations as well.[45]

---

43 Id., at 2.

44 *See* WTO, COUNCIL FOR TRADE IN SERVICES, *supra* note 32, at 6.

45 *See* C. BALASSA, "America's Image Abroad: The UNESCO Cultural Diversity Convention and U.S. Motion Picture Exports", at 20 (Paper Presented at a conference held in Washington, D.C. by the Curb Center for Art, Enterprise and Public Policy at Vanderbilt, on April 24, 2008).

Acknowledging that government funding of audiovisual services is "a sensitive issue for many Members where local theatrical film production is dependent on government support,"[46] the Objectives Paper states that "[t]he U.S. delegation is of the view that development of trade disciplines for the audiovisual sector need not necessarily restrict government subsidies for domestic film production and distribution, as long as subsidies are not derived from discriminatory practices."[47] The Objectives Paper concludes discussion of the issue with the suggestion that "[m]embers may also want to consider developing an understanding on subsidies that will respect each nation's need to foster its cultural identity by creating an environment to nurture local culture."[48] Negotiation of a subsidies code for motion picture was made contingent, however, on "negotiated commitments for audiovisual services."[49]

4.4. IMPACT

The negotiating tone for audiovisual services was far less confrontational in the Doha Round than in the Uruguay Round. While the conciliatory tone of the Objectives Paper contributed somewhat to the improved negotiating atmosphere, it is far more likely that other factors, both positive and negative, were responsible for the change in negotiating dynamics.

On the positive side, in the Doha Round the U.S. was no longer as completely isolated on the audiovisual issue as it had been in the Uruguay Round. Five other countries with significant motion picture export interests, namely Japan, Chinese Taipei, Hong Kong China, Singapore and Mexico, now came forward to join the United States in forming a *Friends Group for Audiovisual Services*, also known as the *Film Fans Club*.[50] The Friends Group for Audiovisual Services, like all other Friends groups, participated in the plurilateral negotiating process that was introduced in the Doha Round, preparing a plurilateral audiovisual request that it presented to a designated group of countries.

On the negative side, the absence of conflict over audiovisual services reflected not consensus, but unwillingness on the part of a number of countries, especially potential EU members, to discuss the issue in bilateral request-offer negotiations. The EU, for example, had made clear to prospective EU members that their membership in the EU would be compromised if they made any commitments for audiovisual services. Other countries justified their refusal to

46 WTO, Council for Trade in Services, *supra* note 37, at 2.

47 WTO, Council for Trade in Services, "Communications from the United States: Audiovisual Services", *S/C/W/78*, at 3 (8 December 1998).

48 WTO, Council for Trade in Services, *supra* note 37, at 3.

49 Id., at 3.

50 Each services sector had a friends group comprised of likeminded countries interested in working together to advance liberalization of the respective services sector.

discuss audiovisual services by referring to the ongoing UNESCO negotiation of the Convention on the Diversity of Cultural Expressions.[51]

So widespread was the apparent boycott of audiovisual services in the WTO that members of the Film Fans Club tabled a protest in the formal services negotiating group, the Group on Negotiating Services, complaining of efforts to create an automatic exclusion of the sector.[52] By the time the Doha Round ground to a halt in July 2008, little, if any, progress had been made in obtaining the standstill commitments the United States had requested for audiovisual services.

5. THE CONVENTION FOR THE PROTECTION OF THE DIVERSITY OF CULTURAL EXPRESSIONS

5.1. A DISGUISED TRADE NEGOTIATION WITHIN UNESCO

In the post-Uruguay Round period, beginning in 2001, France and Canada renewed their efforts to achieve the cultural exception they had unsuccessfully fought for in the Uruguay Round by establishing a new international instrument, which came to be known as Convention on the Promotion and Protection of the Diversity of Cultural Expressions. The chosen forum for negotiating the new instrument was the Paris-based UNESCO.[53]

To help coalesce support for the Convention on the Diversity of Cultural Expressions, France and Canada played on the dominant role of U.S. motion picture exports worldwide, viewed by many as responsible for the problems that domestic film industries encountered in their local, and international, markets. Exports of U.S. motion pictures in 2003, for example, accounted for 73% of box-office revenues in Europe.[54]

The anti-Hollywood undertone of the Convention on the Diversity of Cultural Expressions negotiations is seen, for example, in Canada's *Globe and*

---

51 *See infra* Section 5.

52 WTO, Council for Trade Services, "Audiovisual Services: Information Note by the Secretariat", *JOB(05)/192*, at 12 (19 September 2005). *See also* WTO, Council for Trade in Services, "Communication from Hong Kong China, Japan, Mexico, the Separate Customs Territory of Taiwan, Penghu, Kinmen and Matsu, and United States: Joint Statement on the Negotiations on Audiovisual Services", *TN/S/W/49* (30 June 2005).

53 *See, generally*, Balassa, *supra* note 45, at 16–8.

54 *See* G. H. Hanson and Ch. Xiang, "International Trade in Motion Picture Services", at 1 (January 2008), *available at* http://irpshome.ucsd.edu/faculty/gohanson/TradeinServicesNBER2008.PDF (last visited 2 February 2012) (mentioning in this respect a study of S. E. Siwek, *Engines of Growth: Economic Contributions of U.S. Intellectual Property Industries*, 2005, *available at* www.nbcuni.com/About_NBC_Universal/Intellectual_Property/pdf/Engines_of_Growth.pdf (last visited 2 August 2010).

Mail which, in the lead up to the final vote on the Convention, wrote that internationally, cultural diversity is "code for 'let's all get together and protect our national cultures against Hollywood.'"[55] Adding to the anti-Hollywood chorus, Brazil's Culture Minister said of the Convention "[w]e need to do something to avoid being suffocated by the unscrupulous presence of foreign [cultural] products in our countries."[56]

Though the U.S. originally attempted to support the broad objectives of the Convention on the Diversity of Cultural Expressions, subject to specific requests for language changes, its position gradually hardened in reaction to ever more troublesome language inserted into this Convention's text without consensus.[57] In the two-year period from October 2003 to October 2005, which overlapped with the ongoing WTO Doha Round of negotiations, the U.S. focused primarily on the Convention's implications for current and future multilateral and bilateral trade negotiations.[58] Relatively little attention was paid to the cultural issues that attracted broad support from many UNESCO delegations.

5.2. U.S. PERSPECTIVE ON TRADE IMPLICATIONS OF THE CONVENTION

As expressed in various statements by U.S. officials, U.S. concerns over the Convention on the Diversity of Cultural Expressions' possible impact on trade centred on the Convention's broad and vaguely defined scope, sweeping operational mandates, and ambiguous provisions outlining the relationship between the Convention and other international agreements.[59]

U.S. officials recognized that supporters of the Convention on the Diversity of Cultural Expressions were motivated in large part by the dominant position of American motion picture exports in most markets. The United States was concerned, however, that because the scope of the Convention on the Diversity of Cultural Expressions was broad and ill-defined, its provisions could be interpreted to extend far beyond motion pictures, touching on any service, good,

55 K. Taylor, "Our Sad Little Stand to Protect Canadian Culture", *Globe and Mail* (4 June 2005), *available at* www.friends.ca/news-item/3254 (last visited 4 April 2008).

56 A. Oppenheimer, "Cultural War is Taking Aim at Hollywood", *The Miami Herald*, at 16A (22 January 2006).

57 *See* Balassa, *supra* note 45, at 15 and 21–2 (the discussion is based on an author interview with Jane Cowley, Former Deputy Director for Office of UNESCO AFFAIRS, State Department, (4 February 2008)).

58 *See* Balassa, *supra* note 45, at 19.

59 *See* U.S. Department of State, Office of the Spokesman, "The Convention on the Protection and Promotion of the Diversity of Cultural Expressions" (11 October 2005) (referred to by Balassa, *supra* note 45, note 85).

or agricultural product that might be viewed as being related to cultural expression.[60]

Concerns over the broad and undefined scope of the Convention on the Diversity of Cultural Expressions were heightened by its sweeping provisions concerning implementation. Article 6 (1), for example, reads that "each Party may adopt measures aimed at protecting and promoting the diversity of cultural expressions within its territory."[61] So broadly cast was this language, some argued, that it could be misread as providing countries with broad authorization to impose an unlimited range of trade restrictive measures in the name of protecting cultural diversity.[62]

In an effort to explain the broad, unintended consequences of the Convention on the Diversity of Cultural Expressions to foreign officials, U.S. negotiators emphasized that the document could function as a double-edged sword. They pointed out that while the Convention on the Diversity of Cultural Expressions could give country A the right to restrict imports in the name of diversity of cultural expression, other countries could use the same justification under the Convention on the Diversity of Cultural Expressions to restrict exports from country A. To drive home this point, U.S. negotiators compiled a broad listing of goods, services and agricultural products that could be considered to represent cultural expressions.[63] The listing included textiles, magazines, books written in a foreign language, coffee, foie gras, new world wines, geographical indications (GIs), and a traditional farming way of life.

In addition to the broad and undefined scope of the Convention, U.S. negotiators were seriously concerned by the so-called 'Saving's Clause' of Article 20 of the Convention on the Diversity of Cultural Expressions,[64] a section that

---

60 *See* id.

61 Convention on the Diversity of Cultural Expressions, *supra* note 1, Article 6 (1).

62 *See* Balassa, *supra* note 45, at 16 (the discussion is based on U.S. Department of State, "The Convention on the Protection and Promotion of the Diversity of Cultural Expressions", *Fact Sheet* (11 October 2005), *available at* www.state.gov/r/pa/prs/ps/2005/54690.htm (last visited 2 August 2010).

63 *See, e.g.,* "UNESCO Overwhelmingly Approves Cultural Diversity Treaty", 9 (36) *BRIDGES Weekly Trade News Digest* (2005), *available at* http://ictsd.net/i/news/bridgesweekly/6211/ (last visited 2 February 2012); J. A. Smith and H. Dale, "Cultural Diversity and Freedom at Risk at UNESCO", *The Heritage Foundation Web Memo No. 885* (17 October 2005), *available at* www.heritage.org/Research/InternationalOrganizations/wm885.cfm (last visited 2 February 2012).

64 *See, e.g.,* A. R. Fullman, "Reconcilable Differences: The United States versus the Canadian Perspective Towards UNESCO's Convention on the Protection of the Diversity of Cultural Contents and Artistic Expressions", (Master's Thesis, George Mason University, December 2005), *available at* www.aimeefullman.com/Reconciliable_Differencespdf.pdf (last visited 2 February 2012) (based on interviews with selected U.S. delegation members to the UNESCO Convention on the Diversity of Cultural Expressions' negotiations, Fullman reports that they considered Article 20 to be by far the "most controversial element of the Convention." Id., at 72). *See also* Coalition Française pour la Diversité Culturelle, "The French Coalition Hail Successful Conclusion of UNESCO Negotiations for Treaty on Cultural

conveyed mixed signals about the relationship of the Convention on the Diversity of Cultural Expressions to other international agreements.[65] Article 20 first provides that the Convention on the Diversity of Cultural Expressions should not be interpreted as modifying rights and obligations under any other treaties. Confusing the situation, however, Article 20 also states that the Convention on the Diversity of Cultural Expressions is not subordinated to those other treaties and must be taken into account when interpreting and applying the provisions of other treaties. So unclear was Article 20 that the interpretation of the section "was disputed even among EU members, with the UK saying the provision 'did not permit the exclusion of cultural goods and services' and France saying that it did."[66]

According to statements by U.S. officials, Article 20's message on the relationship between the Convention on the Diversity of Cultural Expressions and other international agreements could "be misinterpreted as support for… major world markets to shut out goods and services from developing and other markets."[67] Further, the ambiguity of Article 20 could "impair rights and obligations under other international agreements [including the WTO] and adversely impact prospects for successful completion of the ongoing Doha Development Round of negotiations."[68]

Finally, U.S. trade officials also expressed concerns about Article 21 of the Convention on the Diversity of Cultural Expressions. This article obligates Parties to "promote the principles and objectives of this Convention in other international forums."[69] By making "consultation and coordination 'with other international forums' a key element in the application of Article 20," the U.S. argued, the article could be widely misunderstood as further justification for Parties to block or limit progress in future trade talks on any matters bearing on cultural goods and services.[70]

Diversity in spite of the Hostility of the United States, 8 June 2005", 5 (19) *The Diversity of Cultural Expressions Newsletter* (Archives) (20 June 2005), *available at* www.diversite-culturelle.qc.ca/index.php?id=110&L=1&tx_bulletinsirre_pi1[year]=2005&tx_bulletinsirre_pi1 [idbulletin]=32&cHash=be3338b4f4 (last visited 2 February 2012).

65 *See, e.g.*, T. Voon, "UNESCO and the WTO: A Clash of Cultures", 55 *ICLQ* 1, 2 (2006).

66 M. Petit, "UNESCO Approves the Convention on Cultural Diversity", *Broadcasting Regulation and Cultural Diversity*, 1 (4 November 2005) (referred to by Balassa, *supra* note 45). *See also* J. Pauwelyn, "The UNESCO Convention on Cultural Diversity, and the WTO: Diversity in International Law-Making?" *ASIL Insight* (15 November 2005), *available at* www.asil.org/insights/2005/11/insights051115.html (last visited 2 February 2012).

67 U.S. Department of State, Bureau of International Information Programs, "U.S. Opposed 'Deeply Flawed' U.N. Cultural Diversity Convention," (21 October 2005), *available at* www.america.gov/st/washfile-english/2005/October/20051020170821GLnesnoM3.670901e-02.html (last visited 2 February 2012).

68 Id.

69 Convention on the Diversity of Cultural Expressions, *supra* note 1, Article 21.

70 *See* A. Mattelart, "Cultural Diversity Belongs to Us All", *Le Monde Diplomatique* (15 November 2005), *available at* http://mondediplo.com/2005/11/15/15unesco (last visited 2 February 2012).

5.3. HUMAN RIGHTS IMPLICATIONS OF THE CONVENTION ON THE DIVERSITY OF CULTURAL EXPRESSIONS

In addition to its concerns over the possible trade implications of the Convention on the Diversity of Cultural Expressions, the United States focused on the possibility that its vague language could easily justify government-imposed restrictions on freedom of expression, including censorship and limitations on press freedom, and suppression of minority rights. If the Convention were, for example, to be used to restrict access to foreign or minority views in the name of protecting cultural diversity, then, the United States pointed out, the Convention could "undermine UNESCO's constitutional obligation to promote the free flow of ideas by word and image."[71]

Underlying U.S. comments on the Convention on the Diversity of Cultural Expressions' human rights implications was the message that the Convention was, in fact, more likely to restrict cultural diversity than promote it. Speaking to the General Conference Plenary Session after adoption of the Convention on the Diversity of Cultural Expressions, Ambassador Louise Oliver stated that "[t]he Convention, as now drafted, is aimed at reaffirming the rights of states to put in place policies that could be used or abused to control the cultural lives of their citizens – policies that a state might use to control what its citizen can see; what they can read; what they an listen to; and what they can do. We believe that all people have the right to make these decisions for themselves."[72]

The United States also linked the potential for human rights abuses to the Convention on the Diversity of Cultural Expressions' unstated trade agenda. In her address to the General Conference Plenary Session, Ambassador Oliver referred to "disturbing statements by some government leaders who have indicated a clear intention to use this Convention to control – not facilitate – the flow of goods, services, and ideas ..." By attempting "to block the import of agricultural and other products from the developing world and others," said Ambassador Oliver, "those leaders would extend the Convention's reach into trade matters, for which there is no justification ... The goal of the United States is to ensure the free flow of diversity in all its forms – cultural, informational, and trade."[73]

---

71 U.S. Department of State, *supra* note 67.

72 U.S., United States Mission to UNESCO, "UNESCO Convention Could Limit Freedom of Cultural Expressions and Trade" (20 October 2005), *available at* http://geneva.usmission.gov/Press2005/2010Oliver.htm (last visited 2 February 2012).

73 U.S. Department of State, *supra* note 67.

5.4. OUTCOME OF THE NEGOTIATION

On 20 October 2005, the UNESCO General Conference adopted the Convention on the Diversity of Cultural Expressions by a vote of 148 to 2. In a strongly worded statement of opposition, the United States, joined only by Israel, voted to oppose the Convention. Australia, Nicaragua, Honduras and Liberia abstained.[74]

The United States faced multiple challenges in attempting to build support to oppose or delay adoption of the Convention on the Diversity of Cultural Expressions. The United States arrived late to a negotiation that had started on an informal basis several years earlier, its return to UNESCO after a nineteen year absence was greeted with suspicion by a number of delegations, the UNESCO process was marred by serious procedural irregularities, and efforts to transmit concerns by some WTO delegations over the relationship between UNESCO and the WTO encountered serious procedural obstacles.

6. ASSESSMENT OF THE U.S. POSITION IN THE TRADE AND CULTURE DEBATE

Throughout the twenty-five year negotiating period involving motion picture trade issues discussed above, we have seen that the United States has consistently argued that motion pictures, along with video tapes, television programs and sound recordings, should be subject to the same trade disciplines imposed on other goods and services that enter into international trade. To characterize this position, as is often the case, as that of a "military and economic behemoth"[75] that sacrifices cultural values or beauty to crass commercialism is, however, a misreading of the U.S. position as expressed in recent negotiations and the historical forces that have shaped it.

First, while it is indeed correct that economic objectives are fundamental to the U.S. position; this is only a partial picture of the U.S. position on the issue. As the Objectives Paper stated, there is no inconsistency in applying trade disciplines to motion pictures to attain cultural, as well as, economic objectives, and indeed, the two goals may reinforce each other. "The economic approach," writes Tyler Cowan "holds a core of common sense at its centre. Art lovers sometimes write or talk as if economic costs do not matter,"[76] but unless a system of complete state subsidization of the arts exists, which is not the case in the United States, economic costs do indeed matter – a great deal.

Second, reliance on trade and trade disciplines for the motion picture sector, as for other goods and services, reflects a core belief in the social and political, as

74 Id.
75 Cowan, *Good and Plenty*, 2006, 3.
76 Id., at 8.

well as the economic, benefits of trade, unfettered by government-imposed trade barriers. Fundamental to the U.S. position in the trade and culture debate is longstanding suspicion of government involvement in the arts and in the production of content viewed by its citizens. In the United States, for example, the federal government has virtually no specific role in the production or distribution of cinematic motion pictures. There is no Ministry of Culture devoted to the development of the U.S. film sector, and there are no direct U.S. government subsidies to motion pictures intended for commercial distribution. Further, with the exception of obscenity, the federal government does not regulate or limit films imported into the United States and it is not in the business of distributing or exhibiting cinematic films.[77]

This policy is in part based on U.S. adherence to free trade principles. It is also based on the First Amendment guarantee of free speech that, holding that diversity of viewpoints and programming is valuable, extends to films and television programs. From a constitutional point of view, it appears unlikely that the federal government could limit the viewing choice of its citizens by restricting their access to programming based on its country of origin.[78] Along these lines, it is to be recalled that, in addition to trade concerns, a major U.S. objection to the Convention on the Diversity of Cultural Expressions was that its vague language could be misread to give governments the right to restrict imports of entertainment in the name of 'diversity'. After the Convention on the Diversity of Cultural Expressions' adoption, Ambassador Louise Oliver indicated that the Convention was more likely to restrict cultural diversity than promote it, stating that "The Convention…is aimed at reaffirming the rights of states to put in place policies that could be used or abused to control the cultural lives of their citizens…"[79]

Differences over subsidies to the motion picture industry have been one of the most divisive issues in both WTO trade and UNESCO Convention on the Diversity of Cultural Expressions negotiations, reflecting profound political and social differences between the United States and Europe in the way that the arts, and especially motion pictures, are funded.[80] The difference is explained in part by historical tradition, in part by reluctance to have the government become the arbiter of which arts projects should receive federal government funding.[81]

---

77 *See* Balassa, *supra* note 7, at 25.

78 *See* id., at 25–6.

79 Press Release, U.S. Mission to UNESCO, UNESCSO Convention Could Limit Freedom of Cultural Expressions and Trade (20 October 2005) (on file with the author).

80 WTO, Council for Trade in Services, *supra* note 51, at 12.

81 *See* B. Ivey, *Arts, Inc.*, 2008, 237–8 (pointing out that a direct per capita comparison between the budgets of European cultural ministries and the $130 million of the NEA is unrealistic, because European cultural ministries have responsibilities that far exceed those of the NEA, "often footing the bill for the operation of national and regional museums and performing arts centers while also financing the kind of trade and regulatory programs that lie totally outside the Endowment's portfolio." Nonetheless, correcting for this disparity by adding into

Unlike arts policy in Europe, which is based largely on direct subsidies, in the United States arts policy is financed largely though indirect subsidies, such as tax deductions for contributions and bequests to non-profits, and public support of universities that in turn foster the arts. "Commonly a German, French or Italian theatre, museum, or orchestra will receive 80 per cent or more of its budget directly from government," Cowan explains, pointing out that, "by contrast, in the United States, direct U.S. government support accounts for no more than 5 per cent of the total budget of non-profit arts organizations."[82]

Elaborating on the distinction between direct and indirect subsidies which underlies U.S.-EU differences in arts funding, Cowan further explains that the U.S. approach permits individual donors, and not the State, to decide which institution receive the funding. The neutrality of the tax deductions means that, in the United States, arts policy does not target any specific destination for the donation, and, in keeping with suspicion of government intervention in the arts, keeps the government out of the business of determining which arts are worth supporting.[83]

7. CONCLUSION: IMPACT OF THE U.S. POSITION ON THE CONVENTION ON THE DIVERSITY OF CULTURAL EXPRESSIONS IN INTERNATIONAL TRADE NEGOTIATIONS

This review of the U.S. position in trade and culture debates is striking in that, despite the fact that U.S. trading partners generally recognize the benefits of applying trade rules to goods and services, and the flexibility for audiovisual services that the U.S. signalled in its Objectives Paper, so few countries have come to support the U.S. position on applying trade disciplines to the audiovisual sector,

In the WTO, for example, to date only twenty-nine WTO Members have made commitments for audiovisual services out of a total membership of 153.[84] Of those twenty-nine commitments, many of which are severely circumscribed, thirteen were made at the conclusion of the Uruguay Round. Most of the

the NEA budget arts funding to other federal agencies and state and local arts commissions still leaves a major per capita disparity: In Europe, the per capita funding is between $60 to $80, while the adjusted NEA budget of $2.8 billion weighs in at just around $9 per American. Not taken into account in the adjusted NEA budget, however, are federal and state-level tax incentives, including the tax benefits that a number of states offer to attract film production).

82 Cowan, *supra* note 75, at 32.

83 *See* Id., at 39–41.

84 *See* WTO, "Member Sector/Matrix Report: Communications Services", *available at* http://tsdb.wto.org/matrixlist.aspx (last visited 2 February 2012); *See also* WTO, "Understanding the WTO: The Organization, Members and Observers" (23 July 2008), *available at* www.wto.org/english/theWTO_e/whatis_e/tif_e/org6_e.htm (last visited 2 February 2012).

remainder have been made by new WTO members, who, in order to meet U.S. demands for accession, were required to include some audiovisual services commitments in their accession schedule. In the Doha Round, of members making new or revised services offers, only seven included new or improved commitments for audiovisual services.[85]

Challenges that the U.S. has encountered in attempting to gain support for its position in the trade and culture debate are both self-inflicted and systemic. The dominant position of the U.S. motion picture industry worldwide has created suspicion that U.S. economic arguments in favour of trade rules is self-serving and intended only to assure continued U.S. global dominance of the sector. Frustrations encountered by foreign film producers attempting to have their films distributed in the U.S. have reinforced this position,[86] as did U.S. audiovisual demands for rollback of quotas and national treatment access to subsidies in the Uruguay Round.

Against this background of hostility and resentment, U.S. efforts to change the negotiating climate for audiovisual services in its Objectives Paper met with little success, as did U.S. efforts to press its trade case during negotiation of the Convention on the Diversity of Cultural Expressions in UNESCO. Perhaps most importantly, as the above discussion on subsidies illustrates, the trade and culture debate reflects a historic divide between the United States and most other countries on the issue of the government's role in cultural activities. Resolving such fundamental differences in a trade negotiation is difficult, though creative solutions might be considered to help bridge this gap: possible examples include development of a film distribution program to address the frustration of countries whose film producers lack the technical skills to distribute their films locally or internationally, negotiation of a special subsidies code for motion pictures as suggested in the Objectives Paper, development of an Audiovisual Services Annex that addresses in a trade forum the culture issues surrounding trade in motion pictures, or development a mechanism by which the U.S. Government enters into co-production agreements with its trading partners.

Despite the challenges the U.S. has encountered in the trade and culture debate, the United States has been successful on the critical issue of preventing a cultural carve out for audiovisual services from WTO disciplines, a not-insignificant victory with the following consequences for current and future international negotiations:

1. Supporting the application of trade disciplines to all services sectors has strengthened the WTO's institutional mandate to liberalize trade in all goods

---

[85] EC, Audiovisual and Media Policies, "The General Agreement on Trade in Services (GATS) and the Doha Development Agenda", *available at* http://ec.europa.eu/avpolicy/ext/multilateral/gats/index_en.htm (last visited 2 February 2012).

[86] *See* Balassa, *supra* note 45, at 4.

and service sectors. A 'cultural exception' could have led to a possible unravelling of a broad and unforeseen range of trade commitments and obligations in the WTO, undermining the stability of the organization;

2. Although few countries have made specific commitments for audiovisual services, general GATS rules, such as MFN treatment (unless specific exceptions are taken) and transparency apply to trade in this sector, helping both established and new motion picture exporters;
3. The WTO dispute settlement mechanism remains applicable to audiovisual and cultural-related activities, as it applies to all covered goods and services. This has been demonstrated in the 1997 case of *Canada–Periodicals*[87] (which prompted Canada to initiate the search for a new instrument to address 'cultural' issues) and the U.S.-China market access case involving copyright-intensive industries, recently resolved in favour of the United States;[88]
4. The Objectives Paper has helped to highlight the flexibility of WTO disciplines to accommodate the 'special cultural qualities' of audiovisual services, and has suggested avenues to explore in future WTO negotiations that could build a broader consensus to support liberalization of the sector, for example negotiating a special subsidies code for audiovisual services;
5. Applying trade disciplines to audiovisual services helps to stimulate the development of related service sectors such as telecommunications, which are dependent on obtaining quality audiovisual product through trade in order to attract investment in advanced telecommunications infrastructures;
6. Including audiovisual services within trade disciplines offers countries with emerging motion picture exporters or on-line content up loaders the opportunity to benefit from trade rules and the new technologies to which these trade rules apply. These are the countries most likely to benefit from application of WTO trade disciplines to the audiovisual sector (and the ones with the most to lose from the collapse of the Doha Round in July 2008).[89]

---

87 *See* Appellate Body Report, "Canada – Certain Measures Concerning Periodicals," *WT/DS31/AB/R* (30 June 1997); Panel Report, "Canada – Certain Measures Concerning Periodicals," WT/DS31/R (14 March 1997).

88 *See* WTO, "China – Measures Affecting Trading Rights and Distribution Services for Certain Publications and Audiovisual Entertainment Products: Request for Consultations by the United States", *WT/DS363/1, G/L/820, S/L/287* (16 April 2007) and Add. 1 (16 July 2007). *See also* E. Cody and A. Shin "WTO Ruling Could Further Open China to U.S. Entertianment Industry," *Washington Post* (13 August 2009), *available at* www.washingtonpost.com/wp-dyn/content/article/2009/08/12/AR2009081202971.html (last visited 2 February 2012); G. Szalai and P. Frater, "U.S. Prevails in WTO Case against China," *Hollywood Reporter* (12 August 2009), *available at* www.hollywoodreporter.com/news/prevails-wto-case-china-87591 (last visited 2 February 2012).

89 While WTO and member government officials have avoided officially announcing that the Doha Round has ended in failure, even its most optimistic supporters admit that it will take some time for it to start up again.

THE CONVENTION ON THE PROTECTION AND THE PROMOTION OF THE DIVERSITY OF CULTURAL EXPRESSIONS

A Cultural Analysis

Ivan Bernier

1. INTRODUCTION

Although the UNESCO *Convention on the Protection and Promotion of the Diversity of Cultural Expressions* (Convention on the Diversity of Cultural Expressions)[1] is quite clearly a cultural agreement negotiated in a cultural context and pursuing cultural objectives, it is strange to find that since its adoption in 2005, its legal analysis has been realized in a large measure by trade lawyers, as if the Convention was of interest essentially for its implication on the trade regime.[2] But this should not come entirely as a surprise, since the Convention on the Diversity of Cultural Expressions itself is intimately linked to the debate concerning the interface between culture and trade that was initiated in the 1920s (when European countries began resorting to screen quotas in order to protect their film industries from an influx of American films considered a threat to their cultures), that resurfaced after the Second World War in the

1 *See* Convention on the Protection and Promotion of the Diversity of Cultural Expressions, 20 October 2005, *U.N. Doc. CLT-2005/CONVENTION DIVERSITE-CULT REV.* [hereinafter "Convention on the Diversity of Cultural Expressions"].

2 *See, e.g.*, T. Voon, *Cultural Products and the World Trade Organization*, 2007; M. Hahn, "A Clash of Cultures? The UNESCO Diversity Convention and International Trade Law", 9 *J. Int. Econ. L.* 515–552 (2006); T. Voon, "UNESCO and the WTO: A Clash of Cultures?", 55 *ICLQ* 635–50 (2006); C. B. Graber, "The New UNESCO Convention on Cultural Diversity: A Counterbalance to the WTO", 9 *J. Int'l Econ. L.* 553–74 (2006); A. Khachaturian, "The New Cultural Diversity Convention and its Implications on the International Trade Regime: A critical Comparative Analysis," 42 *Texas Int. L. J.* 191–209 (2006); A. Bouder, "The UNESCO Convention on Cultural Diversity: Treacherous Treaty or Compassionate Compact", 18 *Pol. Papers on Transn. Econ. L.* 1–7 (2005); J. Pauwelyn, "The UNESCO Convention on Cultural Diversity, and the WTO: Diversity in International Law making?", *ASIL Insight* (November 15, 2005).

GATT negotiations (where it was considered important enough to justify a provision recognizing the cultural specificity of cinema). This debate evolved over the years, fuelled by a growing number of trade disputes regarding cultural goods and services and numerous articles and conferences bearing on the interface between commerce and culture.[3]

By the end of the 1990s, however, the debate had taken a new and broader dimension. Until the creation of the WTO, in 1995, it had essentially focused on exempting cultural products from international trade agreements. In the following years, a paradigm shift occurred. This shift coincided with a number of events such as the decision handed down in 1997 by the WTO Dispute Settlement Body in the case *Canada – Certain Measures Concerning Periodicals*,[4] the failure of the negotiations of the Organization for Economic Cooperation and Development (OECD) on a multilateral agreement on investments in October 1998[5] and the failure of the Seattle WTO Ministerial Conference in December 1999.[6] It is in this context that the idea of a new international instrument on cultural diversity gradually emerged, an instrument that would no longer consider the protection and promotion of cultural diversity as an impediment to trade to be addressed from a trade law perspective, but rather as a cultural problem in itself, to be addressed from a cultural perspective.

3 For a short history of the trade and culture debate, *see* I. Bernier, "Trade and Culture," in P.F.J. Macrory, A.E. Appleton, and M.G. Plummer (eds.), *The World Trade Organization. Legal, Economic and Political Analysis*, 2005, Vol. III, 747. The most recent example of a cultural dispute is that between China and the United States in '*China – Measures affecting trading rights and distribution services for certain publications and audiovisual entertainment products*', WTO, Request for the Establishment of a Panel by the United States, *Doc. WT/DS363/5* (11 October 2007), which has resulted in the Panel and Appellate Body report in 2009. *See* Panel Report, "China – Measures Affecting Trading Rights and Distribution Services for Certain Publications and Audiovisual Entertainment Products", *WT/DS 363/R* (12 Augustus 2009); Appellate Body Report, "China – Measures Affecting Trading Rights and Distribution Services for Certain Publications and Audiovisual Entertainment Products", *WT/DS363/AB/R* (21 December 2009).

4 *See* Panel Report, "Canada – Certain Measures Concerning Periodicals", *WTO Doc. WT/DS31/R* (14 March 1997); Appellate Body Report, "Canada – Certain Measures Concerning Periodicals", *WTO Doc. WT/DS31/AB/R* (30 June 1997).

5 During these negotiations, which began at the OECD in 1996, a number of countries spoke in favor of an exception for cultural industries and France formally proposed a draft clause to that effect. The negotiations in question, which were finally abandoned in 1998, prompted a strong reaction from cultural actors in many countries.

6 Fred Bergsten, former Assistant Secretary for International Affairs of the U.S. referring to the protests in Seattle, Davos, Bangkok and Washington, which he considered as a superficial manifestation of a very real problem, went so far as to declare in 2000 that "the world economy today faces a more fundamental set of challenges because the backlash against globalization is much more than economics. … There is also a huge cultural dimension which raises a mass of contentious and difficult issues of their own." C. F. Bergsten, "Speech before the Trilateral Commission: The Backlash against Globalization", (9 May 2000), *available at* www.petersoninstitute.org/publications/papers/paper.cfm?ResearchID=377 (last visited 2 February 2012).

A demand was formally submitted to UNESCO in February 2003[7] and the decision to move ahead with the negotiation of a convention regarding "the diversity of cultural contents and artistic expressions" was taken by the General Assembly in October 2003.[8] The Convention on the Diversity of Cultural Expressions was finally adopted by the General Assembly in October 2005, after three meetings of independent experts and three intergovernmental meetings of experts. In essence, the text begins by recognizing the "distinctive nature of cultural activities, goods and services as vehicles of identity, values and meaning,"[9] reaffirms the sovereign right of States "to maintain, adopt and implement policies and measures that they deem appropriate for the protection and promotion of the diversity of cultural expressions on their territory"[10] and proposes a program of action designed "to protect and promote the diversity of cultural expressions" and "to create the conditions for cultures to flourish and freely interact in a mutually beneficial manner."[11] With the entry into force of the Convention on the Diversity of Cultural Expressions on 18 March 2007, and the first meetings of the Conference of Parties and the Intergovernmental Committee having taken place in June and December 2007 respectively, the time appears ripe to consider its significance as a cultural instrument more closely.

This chapter will follow the terms of the *Vienna Convention on the Law of Treaties* ("Vienna Convention") of 1969[12] in attempting to assess the cultural significance of the Convention on the Diversity of Cultural Expressions, by considering not only "the terms of the treaty in their context and in the light of its object and purpose"[13] but also "the preparatory work of the treaty and the circumstances of its conclusion."[14] Three questions will be examined more closely. The first question concerns the purpose and scope of the Convention on the Diversity of Cultural Expressions (how it relates to other aspects of cultural diversity), the second the action plan of the Convention on the Diversity of

---

7 *See* Flash Info, "Cultural Diversity: 16 Ministers of Culture Received by the Director-General of UNESCO" (7 February 2003), *available at* http://portal.unesco.org/en/ev.php-URL_ID=9254&URL_DO=DO_TOPIC&URL_SECTION=201.html (last visited 2 February 2012). The demand that an item entitled "Development of an international convention on cultural diversity" be entered on the agenda of the hundred and sixty-sixth session of the Executive Council was made by Germany, Canada, France, Greece, Morocco, Mexico, Monaco and Senegal, all, except Germany, members of the International Network on Cultural Policy (INCP).

8 UNESCO, General Assembly, UNESCO, General Conference, "Desirability of Drawing Up an International Standard-Setting Instrument on Cultural Diversity", *Resolution 32 C/34* (13 October 2003), *available at* http://unesdoc.unesco.org/images/0013/001331/133171e.pdf (last visited 2 February 2012).

9 Convention on the Diversity of Cultural Expressions, *supra* note 1, Article 1(g).

10 Id., Article 1(h) and Article 5(1) (although in a slightly different language).

11 Id., Article 1(a) and (b).

12 Vienna Convention on the Law of Treaties, 23 May 1969, 1155 *UNTS* 331 [hereinafter "Vienna Convention].

13 Id., Article 31.

14 Id., Article 32.

Cultural Expressions (how it proposes to protect and promote the diversity of cultural expressions) and the third the approach of the Convention on the Diversity of Cultural Expressions in situations where trade considerations interfere with cultural considerations.

2. THE PURPOSE AND SCOPE OF THE CONVENTION ON THE DIVERSITY OF CULTURAL EXPRESSIONS

The General Conference decided in 2003 in *Resolution 32C34* "that the question of cultural diversity as regards the protection of the diversity of cultural contents and artistic expressions shall be the subject of an international convention."[15] Quite clearly, the purpose of the Convention envisaged was not the protection of cultural diversity in the broad sense of the term (including cultural heritage in all of its forms, cultural development, copyright, multiculturalism, cultural rights, the status of the artist and linguistic rights), but rather the protection of a specific aspect of cultural diversity, namely the diversity of cultural content and artistic expressions.[16] Later, in the course of the negotiations, the words "cultural [content] and artistic expressions" were replaced by "cultural expressions" for reasons of simplicity and clarity (to be known, cultural content must be expressed in one form or another, and artistic expressions are also cultural). In the Convention on the Diversity of Cultural Expressions as finally adopted, the overall purpose as expressed in the title and reiterated in Article 1(a) of the Convention on the Diversity of Cultural Expressions had become "the protection and promotion of the diversity of cultural expressions."

The concept of 'cultural expressions' occupies a central place in the Convention on the Diversity of Cultural Expressions, being mentioned more than forty times in the document. Article 3 of the Convention on the Diversity of Cultural Expressions, which determines the scope of the instrument, confirms this pre-eminence: "This Convention shall apply to the policies and measures adopted by the Parties related to the protection and promotion of the diversity of cultural expressions." The term "cultural expressions," as defined in Article 4(3),

---

15 UNESCO, *supra* note 8, at 64.

16 The Executive Council of UNESCO itself, before submitting Resolution 32C34 to the General Conference, had eliminated three options which had been identified in a preparatory document prepared by the Secretariat, namely 1) a new comprehensive agreement on cultural rights, 2) an instrument on the status of the artist and 3) a new protocol to the *Florence Agreement* of 1950, retaining the fourth option proposed which was that of an instrument on the protection of the diversity of cultural contents and artistic expressions. *See* UNESCO, Executive Board, "Preliminary Study on the Technical and Legal Aspects relating to the Desirability of a Standard-setting Instrument on Cultural Diversity", *166 EX/28* (12 March 2003).

refers to those expressions "that result from the creativity of individuals, groups and societies and that have cultural content." Cultural expressions are primarily embodied and conveyed in the "creation, production, dissemination, distribution of and access to cultural goods, services, and activities."[17] During the negotiations, the reference to the words "cultural goods and services" was the object of lengthy discussions, the United States opposing their use due to the view that they had an obvious trade connotation. But this appropriation of the words "cultural goods and services" exclusively for trade purposes was considered by the vast majority of States as not warranted.

The overall goal of the Convention on the Diversity of Cultural Expressions, as mentioned before, is to protect and promote the diversity of cultural expressions. In the preamble of the Convention on the Diversity of Cultural Expressions, it is made quite clear that the diversity of cultural expressions is under pressure. This led to the recognition in the 9th paragraph, of the need "to take measures to protect the diversity of cultural expressions, including their [content], especially in situations where cultural expressions may be threatened by the possibility of extinction or serious impairment." In the 19th paragraph, it is also noted "that while the processes of globalization, which have been facilitated by the rapid development of information and communication technologies, afford unprecedented conditions for enhanced interaction between cultures, they also represent a challenge for cultural diversity, namely in view of risks of imbalances between rich and poor countries." The use of the words "protect" and "protection" in this context was again strongly opposed by the United States. However, it was demonstrated during the debates on the use of these words that this usage conformed to prior UNESCO practice.[18] In the end, the word "protection" was defined in Article 4(7) as "the adoption of measures aimed at the preservation, safeguarding and enhancement of the diversity of cultural expressions" and the word "to protect" was defined as meaning "to adopt such measures."

The importance of cultural expressions for the protection of cultural diversity must not be underestimated. In Article 4(1) the Convention on the Diversity of Cultural Expressions makes the link between the two explicit when it states that:

> Cultural diversity is made manifest not only through the varied ways in which the cultural heritage of humanity is expressed, augmented and transmitted through the variety of cultural expressions, but also through diverse modes of artistic creation, production, dissemination, distribution and enjoyment, whatever the means and technologies used.

---

17 Convention on the Diversity of Cultural Expressions, *supra* note 1, Article 4(6).

18 The word "protection" is to be found in the title of three other UNESCO conventions, namely the Convention on the Protection of the Underwater Cultural Heritage of 2001, the Convention on the Protection of the World Cultural and Natural Heritage of 1972 and the Convention on the Protection of Cultural Property in the Event of Armed Conflict of 1954.

The fact is that cultural expression meets an essential need for every community. It is a key element in the adaptation of different cultures to the transformations imposed by globalization. The creators of culture and cultural stakeholders play a primary role in this regard in that they create a forum for critical confrontation between national and foreign values and between the values and behaviour of the past and perspectives for the future. In this sense, we can say that the preservation of cultural diversity can only occur through the preservation of cultural expressions. Furthermore, since the diversity of cultural expressions is "an important factor that allows individuals and peoples to express and to share with others their ideas and their values,"[19] it contributes by this very fact to public debate and constitutes a significant element of the democratic process. Thus, the protection and promotion of the diversity of cultural expressions, far from being a minor issue, is proving to be one of the major challenges of our time.

The fact that the Convention on the Diversity of Cultural Expressions limits itself to this specific aspect of cultural diversity does not lessen the importance of other aspects of cultural diversity. Indeed, a number of those aspects are already covered by other conventions (this is particularly the case for aspects related to the preservation of cultural heritage, cultural development, human rights, and intellectual property rights). Furthermore, the Convention on the Diversity of Cultural Expressions itself makes reference to some of those other aspects in its text, such as cultural heritage, human rights and fundamental freedoms, linguistic diversity, minorities and indigenous peoples, cultural development and intellectual property. These references, which are to be found in the preamble as well as in some of the articles of the Convention on the Diversity of Cultural Expressions, are intended to situate the Convention on the Diversity of Cultural Expressions with regard to these other preoccupations without treating them as specific objects of the Convention on the Diversity of Cultural Expressions.[20] Article 2(5), for instance, provides that "since culture is one of the mainsprings of development, the cultural aspects of development are as important as its economic aspects, which individuals and peoples have the fundamental right to participate in and to enjoy." This perspective is further developed in Article 13 which deals with the integration of culture in sustainable development.[21] Another example is linguistic diversity, which first appears in the preamble where the 14th paragraph recalls that "linguistic diversity is a

[19] Convention on the Diversity of Cultural Expressions, *supra* note 1, Preamble §13.

[20] The preamble refers in particular to such aspects as human rights and fundamental freedoms, linguistic diversity, minorities and indigenous peoples, and intellectual property rights.

[21] *See* Convention on the Diversity of Cultural Expressions, *supra* note 1, Article 13 (which reads as follows: "Parties should endeavour to integrate culture in their development policies at all levels for the creation of conditions conducive to sustainable development and, within this framework, foster aspects relating to the protection and promotion of the diversity of cultural expressions.").

fundamental, element of cultural diversity" and subsequently, in Article 6(2)(b), which mentions, among the measures that the Parties can take at the national level, those relating to the language used for cultural activities, goods and services. But the Convention on the Diversity of Cultural Expressions is not concerned with linguistic rights in areas of life others than those that relate to cultural expression, such as education, advertising or consumer protection. Finally, although the Convention on the Diversity of Cultural Expressions is practically silent on the issue of heritage preservation, the fact remains that cultural expressions and heritage are inseparable, since the cultural expression of the present is the cultural heritage of the future.

From what has been said so far concerning the purpose and scope of the Convention on the Diversity of Cultural Expressions, it will be understood also that it does not purport to protect cultures in a sociological and anthropological sense (referring to lifestyles, ways of living together, value systems, traditions and beliefs). But again, there is a close tie between the preservation of cultures in the sense of a community's cultural expression and the preservation of cultures in the sociological and anthropological sense. If globalization and the liberalization of trade lead to significant changes in cultures in the anthropological and sociological sense, it doesn't necessarily mean that such changes should be rejected because they affect the content of the cultures in question. Asserting the contrary would give a set meaning to notions of culture and cultural identity, a meaning that could only serve those desiring to use them as instruments of political control. In reality, any culture, if it is to survive, has to adapt over time to a variety of both internal and external changes. And this, as we have seen, is where cultural expression plays a particularly important role.

3. THE ACTION PLAN OF THE CONVENTION ON THE DIVERSITY OF CULTURAL EXPRESSIONS WITH REGARD TO THE PROTECTION AND PROMOTION OF THE DIVERSITY OF CULTURAL EXPRESSIONS

The plan of action of the Convention on the Diversity of Cultural Expressions with regard to the protection and promotion of the diversity of cultural expressions has two overall objectives. The first objective is to clearly establish the sovereign right of States "to maintain, adopt, and implement policies and measures that they deem appropriate for the protection and promotion of the diversity of cultural expressions on their territory."[22] This right is a prerequisite for the realization of the second objective, which is, broadly speaking, "to create

22 Id., Articles 1(h) and 5(1).

the conditions for cultures to flourish and to freely interact in a mutually beneficial manner."[23] This last objective can itself be subdivided into three distinct elements relating, successively, to the actions to be undertaken by the Parties within their territory to create an environment which encourages individuals and social groups to create, produce, distribute and have access to their own cultural expressions as well as to the cultural expressions of other countries of the world,[24] the actions to be undertaken by the Parties at the international level "to strengthen their bilateral, regional and international cooperation for the creation of conditions conducive to the promotion of the diversity of cultural expressions"[25] and finally the actions to be taken by the Parties "to support cooperation for sustainable development and poverty eradication, especially in relation to the specific needs of developing countries, in order to foster the emergence of a dynamic cultural sector."[26] This chapter deals with these various aspects of the plan of action in the Convention on the Diversity of Cultural Expressions in that order.

3.1. THE SOVEREIGN RIGHT OF STATES TO FORMULATE AND IMPLEMENT THEIR CULTURAL POLICIES AS A BASIS FOR CULTURAL ACTION

During the negotiations, many delegations expressed the view that the general rule on rights and obligations found in Article 5 was a pivotal element of the proposed convention.[27] In the final text, the importance of the statement concerning the sovereign right of States to formulate and implement their cultural policies in the Convention on the Diversity of Cultural Expressions was made as clear as possible. It appears in Article 1 as a goal of the Convention on the Diversity of Cultural Expressions, in Article 2 as a principle of the Convention on the Diversity of Cultural Expressions and again in Article 5, where it is more fully developed as a right reaffirmed by the Convention on the Diversity of Cultural Expressions. It is further confirmed in Article 6 which states in its first paragraph that within the framework of its cultural policies and measures, "each Party may adopt measures aimed at protecting and promoting the diversity of cultural expressions within its territory" and then goes on to provide in its second paragraph an illustrative list of such measures. In order to

23 Id., Article 1(b).
24 Id., Article 7.
25 Id., Article 12.
26 Id., Article 14.
27 *See* UNESCO, "Oral Report of the Rapporteur, Mr. Artur Wilczynski", at 5 (Closing Session of the First Intergovernmental Meeting of Experts on the Preliminary Draft Convention on the Protection of the Diversity of Cultural Contents and Artistic Expressions, 20–25 September 2004), *available at* www.unesco.org/culture/culturaldiversity/docs_pre_2007/oral_report_wilczynski_en_25092004.pdf (last visited 2 August 2010).

understand the significance of that right in the context of the Convention on the Diversity of Cultural Expressions, it is necessary to go back first to the sources mentioned in Article 5(1) Convention on the Diversity of Cultural Expressions, that is, the *Charter of the United Nations*, the principles of international law and universally recognized human rights instruments.

The right in question is not a new right created by the Convention on the Diversity of Cultural Expressions. It is part and parcel of one of the most basic principle of customary international law, that of State sovereignty, which was to become, after the Second World War, one of the pillars of the *Charter of the United Nations.*[28] State sovereignty involves the exclusive right to exercise the competence of a State, independence from other States, and the legal equality of States. The concept encompass all matters in which a State feels justified to intervene, including the choice of political, economic, social, and cultural systems and the formulation of foreign policy. However, the freedom of action of States in these matters is not absolute; it remains subject to State obligations under international law, including under treaties to which States are parties.[29]

The sovereign right of a State to formulate and implement its cultural policies is also related to another category of rights that have taken a particular significance in international law, that is to say, human rights. Article 5 of the UNESCO *Universal Declaration on Cultural Diversity* states in this regard:

> Cultural rights are an integral part of human rights, which are universal, indivisible and interdependent. The flourishing of creative diversity requires the full implementation of cultural rights as defined in Article 27 of the *Universal Declaration of Human Rights* and in Articles 13 and 15 of the *International Covenant on Economic, Social and Cultural Rights.*[30]

Article 27(1) of the *Universal Declaration on Human Rights* states that "[e] veryone has the right freely to participate in the cultural life of the community, to enjoy the arts and to share in scientific advancement and its benefits"[31] and Article 15 of the *International Covenant on Economic, Social and Cultural Rights* reproduces the same view in a slightly different form.[32] What these references to

---

28 See Charter of the United Nations, 26 June 1945, Article 2.1, *available at* www.un.org/en/documents/charter/intro.shtml (last visited 2 February 2012) (stating that [t]he Organization is based on the principle of the sovereign equality of all its Members).

29 *See* Permanent Court of International Justice, Case of the S.S. Wimbledon, Series A, No. 1 (1923).

30 *See* Universal Declaration on Cultural Diversity, 2 November 2001, Article 5, *available at* http://portal.unesco.org/en/ev.php-URL_ID=13179&URL_DO=DO_TOPIC&URL_SECTION =201.html (last visited on 2 February 2012).

31 Universal Declaration on Human Rights, 10 December 1948, Article 27(1), *available at* www.un.org/en/documents/udhr/ (last visited 2 February 2012).

32 *See* Covenant on Economic, Social and Cultural Rights, 16 December 1966, 993 *U.N.T.S.* 3, Article 15(1) (reading as follows: "The States Parties to the present Covenant recognize the right of everyone: (a) To take part in cultural life; (b) To enjoy the benefits of scientific

human rights imply, in the specific context of Article 5 of the Convention on the Diversity of Cultural Expressions, is that it is impossible to transpose into reality the right of individuals to participate in the cultural life of the community, in other words their right to cultural expression, without ensuring at the outset the sovereign right of States to adopt policies and measures to protect and promote the diversity of cultural expressions within their territory.

Generally speaking, there was an overwhelming consensus on Article 5.1 and its adoption raised few difficulties, presumably because the provision essentially reaffirmed an existing right. One might query whether it was necessary or useful to include such a provision. The answer, from a cultural perspective, is quite obvious. Article 5.1 was necessary, firstly because it is a reminder that unless States have voluntarily limited their capacity to act in the cultural field, they are totally free to formulate and implement their cultural policies and to adopt whatever measures they consider necessary to protect and promote the diversity of cultural expressions. By the same token, it is a reminder that before making new international commitments, States should take into account the impact on their capacity to formulate and implement their cultural policies. Secondly Article 5.1 is important because it conveys a strong message that Parties to the Convention on the Diversity of Cultural Expressions will not question measures adopted by other Parties in order to protect and promote the diversity of cultural expressions, provided such measures are consistent with the provisions of the Convention on the Diversity of Cultural Expressions as specified in Paragraph 2 of Article 5.[33]

The stipulation in Article 5(2) that "When a Party implement policies and takes measures to protect and promote the diversity of cultural expressions within its territory, its policies and measures shall be consistent with the provisions of the Convention on the Diversity of Cultural Expressions" must be read in conjunction with Article 2(8) (Principle of openness and balance). The principle in question reads as follows: "When States adopt measures to support the diversity of cultural expressions, they should seek to promote, in an appropriate manner, openness to other cultures of the world and to ensure that these measures are geared to the objectives pursued under the [Convention on the Diversity of Cultural Expressions]."[34] These two provisions, taken together, show quite clearly that the intent of Article 5 has to do essentially with culture

progress and its applications; (c) To benefit from the protection of the moral and material interests resulting from any scientific, literary or artistic production of which he is the author.").

33 In international law, States are always free to decide whether or not they will question the measures of another State that might be in breach of their rights.

34 The original version of Article 2(8) in a preliminary draft was more constraining, using the words "commit themselves to guaranteeing, in an appropriate manner, the openness..." *See* UNESCO, "Preliminary Draft of a Convention on the Protection of the Diversity of Cultural Contents and Artistic Expressions", *CLT/CPD/2004/CONF-201/2*, at 120 (July 2004) [hereinafter "Preliminary Draft Convention"].

and not with trade. A few Members of UNESCO expressed concerns during the negotiations regarding the possibility that Article 5(1) might result in conflict with other international treaties such as GATT and GATS and asked for the inclusion in Article 5(2) of the words "and consistent with their international obligations". This view was rejected by the majority who considered that the problem raised concerned the relationship between the Convention on the Diversity of Cultural Expressions and other international treaties, a question to be considered at a later stage. Following the adoption of Article 20 (Relationship to other treaties: supportiveness, complementarity and non-subordination) towards the end of the negotiations, it was decided that no changes to Article 5 were necessary. As we shall see later when discussing Article 20, there is a close relationship between that provision and Article 5.

Article 6 is essentially an illustrative list of measures that Parties may adopt in order to protect and promote the diversity of cultural expressions within their territory. The fact that the list is not restrictive can be seen from the use of the words "[s]uch measures may include" immediately before the list. The measures themselves are optional and there is no obligation on the Parties to have recourse to any of them. What is striking in the list is the variety itself of the measures that can be used in order to protect and promote the variety of cultural expressions. The obvious message is that protecting and promoting the diversity of cultural expressions is a complex matter and that there is more than one way of approaching this task, depending on the particular conditions and circumstances of each Party. During the negotiations, concerns were again raised by certain States concerning the fact that some of those measures, in particular those envisaged in Paragraphs 2(b) and (d), could conflict with existing trade agreements.[35] But as in the case of Article 5, the majority considered that the possibility of conflict between the Convention on the Diversity of Cultural Expressions and the WTO agreements was a matter to be considered at a later stage and that it was up for each party to decide what measures they would use in the full light of their cultural needs and existing international commitments.

3.2. CREATING THE CONDITIONS FOR CULTURAL EXPRESSIONS TO FLOURISH AND TO FREELY INTERACT IN A MUTUALLY BENEFICIAL MANNER

The second objective of the action plan of the Convention on the Diversity of Cultural Expressions is, in a sense, the counterpart of the first. The Parties, having had the sovereign right to formulate and implement their cultural

35 *See* Convention on the Diversity of Cultural Expressions, *supra* note 1, Article 2(b) and (d) (referring to quantitative restrictions and subsidies respectively).

policies confirmed, are expected to create the conditions for cultural expression to flourish and to freely interact in a mutually beneficial manner. This objective is truly at the heart of the Convention on the Diversity of Cultural Expressions and the success of the instrument will be assessed in future by reference to what it has achieved in this respect. As explained previously, this broad objective can be subdivided into three distinct elements.

3.2.1. Actions to be undertaken by the parties within their territory

There are basically five different types of actions that are to be undertaken by the Parties within their territory according to the Convention on the Diversity of Cultural Expressions. Two are directly related to the core objectives of the Convention on the Diversity of Cultural Expressions. They are found in Article 7 (Measures to promote cultural expressions) and in Article 8 (Measures to protect cultural expressions). The other three are more auxiliary in nature, concerning education and public awareness (Article 10), the participation of civil society (Article 11) and the integration of culture in sustainable development (Article 13).

Article 7 is much broader in scope than Article 8 and more positive in its approach, effectively projecting an overall picture of what the Convention on the Diversity of Cultural Expressions aims to achieve in future. It implicitly reflects the view that the best way of ensuring the diversity of cultural expressions in the long-term is to promote its development. Article 7 encompasses matters such as the creation, production, dissemination and distribution of the cultural expressions of the Parties with particular attention paid to the special needs and circumstances of women as well as various groups, including persons belonging to minorities and indigenous peoples, access to cultural expressions from other countries of the world and finally recognition of the important contribution of artists and others involved in the creative process, and their central role in the nurturing of the diversity of cultural expressions.[36] This is a vast program that will obviously require a great deal of conviction and effort to be realized. The obligation assumed by the Parties in this respect is one of 'best efforts.' This is very different from what was originally envisaged in Article 7 Preliminary Draft Convention, which imposed a strict obligation to promote the diversity of cultural expressions.[37] At the December 2004 session of the Drafting

[36] The reference to artists and creators can be read here in light of the UNESCO *Recommendation concerning the Status of the Artist* of 1980. *See* Recommendation concerning the Status of the Artist, 27 October 1980, *available at* http://unesdoc.unesco.org/images/0011/001140/114029e.pdf#page=144 (last visited 2 February 2012).

[37] *See* UNESCO, *supra* note 34, at 6 (Article 7.1 Preliminary Draft Convention read as follows: "States Parties shall provide all individuals in their territory with opportunities: (a) to create, produce disseminate, distribute, and have access to their own cultural expressions, goods and services, paying due attention to the special circumstances and needs of the various social groups, in particular minorities and indigenous peoples; (b) to have access to the cultural expressions, goods and services representing cultural diversity in other regions of the world.").

Committee which saw in-depth discussion on Article 7(1), a significant number of Committee members considered that the text should not create new rights, a view that was to prevail in the Plenary Session. What Article 7 says now is that the "Parties shall endeavour to create in their territory an environment which encourages individuals and social groups ..." which, in international law, is a good faith commitment to do their best.

Article 8, by comparison, deals with very specific situations that could be described as situations of urgency and the measures that it envisages can be described to some extent as safeguards. Under Article 8 of the Convention on the Diversity of Cultural Expressions, when a Party determines that there is a special situation within its territory such that cultural expressions are at risk, under serious threat, or otherwise in need of urgent safeguarding, it may take all appropriate measures to protect and preserve those cultural expressions in a manner consistent with the provisions of the Convention on the Diversity of Cultural Expressions. When it takes such measures, however, it is asked to report to the Intergovernmental Committee the measures taken to meet the particular exigency, and the Committee may make appropriate recommendations. In its original version, this article went much further, imposing a strict obligation on the Parties to take appropriate measures to protect vulnerable forms of cultural expressions and providing for actions by the intergovernmental Committee that could go as far as to require the relevant Party to take appropriate measures within a reasonable period of time. The original version was the subject of substantial modifications and in the final text it was made clear that Article 8 was not compulsory and that the intervention of the Committee would be limited to making recommendations. The duty to report measures to the Committee that remains in the text may still appear as a form of intervention in the internal affairs of the Party concerned, however the purpose of the article is far removed from that. What it attempts to do, in essence, is to put in place a procedure for providing help to those states that, by their own reckoning, are confronted with situations of the type described in Article 8. Article 8 should therefore be read in conjunction with Article 12, which asks that the Parties, when they develop bilateral, regional and international cooperation to create conditions conducive to the promotion of the diversity of cultural expressions, should take "particular account of the situations referred to in Articles 8 and 17," and in conjunction also with Article 17 of the Convention on the Diversity of Cultural Expressions which provides that "States shall cooperate in providing assistance to each other, and, in particular to developing countries, in situations referred to under Article 8." How this will work out in practice remains to be seen, but further developments may not be too long in waiting. The Conference of Parties, at its first ordinary session in June 2007, requested that the Intergovernmental Committee prepare operating guidelines, giving priority attention to Articles 7 and 8, 11 to 17 and 18 of the Convention on the Diversity of Cultural Expressions and to submit the results for consideration and approval at the second ordinary session of the Conference of Parties.[38]

A few words should be said about the other types of actions to be undertaken by the Parties within their territory. The first concerns education and public awareness (Article 10). The Parties are asked, among other things, to encourage and promote understanding of the importance of the protection and promotion of the diversity of cultural expressions and to encourage creativity and strengthen production capacities by setting up educational, training and exchange programs in the field of the cultural industries. Article 10 is not in the list of Articles designated for priority consideration for the purpose of developing operational guidelines and will therefore have to wait for the development of operational guidelines. Meanwhile, this does not prevent individual initiatives by the Parties to explain, for example, the importance of the protection and promotion of the diversity of cultural expressions or by the Secretariat to organize regional meetings to disseminate information about the content and the objectives of the Convention on the Diversity of Cultural Expressions.

The second type of actions concerns civil society. Article 11 acknowledges that civil society has an important role to play in protecting and promoting the diversity of cultural expressions and asks the Parties to encourage the participation of civil society in their efforts to achieve the objectives of the Convention on the Diversity of Cultural Expressions. The Intergovernmental Committee, at its first session in December 2007, examined the question of the role and participation of civil society in the implementation of the provisions of the Convention on the Diversity of Cultural Expressions,[39] as requested by the Conference of Parties. Following the debate on this issue, the Intergovernmental Committee invited the Secretariat to prepare draft operational guidelines that would include criteria for the accreditation of elements of civil society with interests and activities in the fields covered by the Convention on the Diversity of Cultural Expressions as well as modalities by which representatives of civil society can contribute to the Committee's work and implementation of the Convention on the Diversity of Cultural Expressions. It also requested that the Secretariat organize, with the full participation of all Parties to the Convention on the Diversity of Cultural Expressions, a session to exchange views with representatives of civil society, on the role and participation of civil society. The importance that the Committee gave to that issue and its decision to come back to it at an extraordinary session to be held in June 2008 augurs well for the future.

---

38 *See* UNESCO, Conference of the Parties, "Operational Guidelines" (June 2009), *available at* www.unesco.org/new/en/culture/themes/cultural-diversity/diversity-of-cultural-expressions/the-convention/operational-guidelines/ (last visited 2 February 2012).

39 *See* UNESCO, Intergovernmental Committee, "Role and participation of civil society in the implementation of the provisions of the Convention (Decision 1 IGC 5C)", *CE/07/1.IGC/Dec. Rev*, at 18 (13 December 2007), *available at* http://unesdoc.unesco.org/images/0015/001584/158430e.pdf (last visited 2 February 2012).

The third and last type of supportive actions concerns the integration of culture in sustainable development. Article 13 states that "[p]arties shall endeavour to integrate culture in their development policies at all levels for the creation of conditions conducive to sustainable development and, within this framework, foster aspects relating to the protection and promotion of the diversity of cultural expressions." The pertinence of that provision is not obvious at first sight but becomes clearer when read in conjunction with the principle of the complementarity of economic and cultural aspects of development (Article 2(5)) and with the principle of sustainable development (Article 2(6)) and, more importantly, in light of the historical involvement of UNESCO in the question of the contribution of culture to development. In 1970, UNESCO organized an Intergovernmental Conference on Institutional, Administrative and Financial Aspects of Cultural Policies in Venice that was the first of a series of regional conferences aimed at developing ideas on the issue of determining how cultural policies might be integrated into development strategies.[40] These activities led to the UN's declaration of the World Decade for Cultural Development 1988–1997, the mission of which was to place culture at the centre of development.[41] The primary achievement of the Decade was the creation of the independent World Commission on Culture and Development and the publication of the Commission's report, entitled *Our Creative Diversity*.[42] At the end of the World Decade for Cultural Development, UNESCO organized an important conference on *Cultural Policies for Development*, which was held in Stockholm in 1998. The primary objective of the conference was to transform the new ideas in the World Commission on Culture and Development Report into policies and practices.[43] The ideas expressed at this conference were further discussed during a conference jointly held by the World Bank and UNESCO in October 1999 in Florence, with the theme *Culture Counts: Financing, Resources and the Economics of Culture in Sustainable Development*,[44] and were also discussed by the Inter-American Development Bank.[45] Finally, in November 1999, a Round

40 *See* Katerine Sténou, *UNESCO and the Issue of Cultural Diversity: Review and Strategy, 1946–2004* (2004), revised version, *available at* www.unesco.org/culture/culturaldiversity/docs_pre_2007/unesco_diversity_review_strategy_1946_2004_en.pdf (last visited 2 February 2012).

41 *See* UNESCO, *Guide pratique de la Décennie mondiale du développement Culturel 1988–1997*, 17–8 (1987).

42 *See* World Commission on Culture and Development, *Our Creative Diversity: Report of the World Commission on Culture and Development*, 1995.

43 *See* UNESCO, "The Stockholm Conference", *available at* http://portal.unesco.org/culture/en/ev.php-URL_ID=18717&URL_DO=DO_TOPIC&URL_SECTION=201.html (last visited 2 February 2012).

44 *See* World Bank, "Culture Counts: Financing, Resources, and the Economics of Culture in Sustainable Development – Conference Proceedings" (2000), *available at* www-wds.worldbank.org/external/default/WDSContentServer/WDSP/IB/2000/11/17/000094946_00110405591265/Rendered/PDF/multi_page.pdf (last visited 2 February 2012).

45 *See* Press Release NR-60/99, Inter-American Development Bank, Forum on Development and Culture Stresses Role of Citizen Participation (13 March 1999).

Table of Ministers of Culture organized for the 30th session of the UNESCO General Conference examined the general theme of *Culture and Creativity in a Globalized World*.[46] The demand of Article 13 that culture be integrated in the development policies of the Parties at all levels should be seen as intervening in this context. Viewed in this way, Article 13 may be understood as a continuation of a trend, but with a particular emphasis on aspects relating to the protection and promotion of the diversity of cultural expressions. Interestingly, at its first regular session in December 2007, the Intergovernmental Committee invited Parties to the Convention on the Diversity of Cultural Expressions to make proposals by the end of June 2008 on modalities for implementing Article 13 regarding the integration of culture in sustainable development policies, with a view to the examination of proposals by the Committee at its session in December 2008.[47]

3.2.2 *The actions to be undertaken by the parties at the international level*

The actions envisaged here concern international cooperation in general (leaving aside cooperation for development) and are elaborated in Articles 9 (Information sharing and transparency), 12 (Promotion of international cooperation) and 19 (Exchange, analysis and dissemination of information). Since Article 12 is of a general character it will be considered first, turning then to examine Articles 9 and 19 together as they both deal with information.

Article 12 encourages the Parties to strengthen their bilateral, regional and international cooperation for the creation of conditions conducive to the promotion of the diversity of cultural expressions and draws up a list of specific goals to be pursued in those contexts. The list includes the facilitation of dialogue among Parties on cultural policy, professional and international cultural exchanges and sharing of best practices, the reinforcement of partnerships with and among elements of civil society, non-governmental organizations (NGOs) and the private sector, the promotion of the use of new technologies to enhance information sharing and the conclusion of co-production and co-distribution agreements. There are already a number of multilateral and regional organizations that pursue more or less similar objectives regarding the facilitation of dialogue on cultural policy and international cultural exchanges, such as UNESCO, the International Network on Cultural Policy, the International Organization of the Francophonie, the Council of Europe, the Convenio Andres Bello in Latin America and the Parties are impliedly to work with those networks to stimulate dialogue on issues that relate specifically to the

46 *See* UNESCO, "Reflections on Cultural Diversity – Conferences and Round Tables", *available at* http://portal.unesco.org/culture/en/ev.php-URL_ID=35258&URL_DO=DO_TOPIC&URL_SECTION=201.html (last visited 2 February 2012).

47 *See* UNESCO, Intergovernmental Committee, *supra* note 39, at 17 (International Cooperation – Decision 1 IGC 5B).

protection and preservation of the diversity of cultural expressions. The last goal mentioned in the list, the encouragement to conclude co-production and co-distribution agreements, is bound to raise some questions with regard to its compatibility with the WTO, but there again it is impossible to conclude from a trade law perspective that such a practice would be incompatible with existing trade commitments in all circumstances.[48] From a cultural perspective, however, there is no doubt that such agreements have played, and still play, an important role in the development of the cinema and television industry of developing countries. Article 12 will be on the agenda of the Intergovernmental Committee for consideration at its second regular session in December 2008.

Article 9 and 19 of the Convention on the Diversity of Cultural Expressions deal with an important aspect of the instrument, which is information gathering and sharing. It is interesting to point out in this respect that Article 9 is one of the few provisions of the Convention on the Diversity of Cultural Expressions which can be described as truly compulsory. It reads as follows:

> Parties shall:
>
> (a) provide appropriate information in their reports to UNESCO every four years on measures taken to protect and promote the diversity of cultural expressions within their territory and at the international level;
> (b) designate a point of contact responsible for information sharing in relation to this Convention;
> (c) share and exchange information relating to the protection and promotion of the diversity of cultural expressions.

The reports mentioned in Paragraph (a) are to be sent to the Intergovernmental Committee, which is responsible to transmit them to the Conference of Parties together with comments and a summary of their content.[49] According to Article 22(4)(b) the Conference itself is to receive and examine the reports in question.

Article 9 sets out the basic mechanism put in place by the Convention on the Diversity of Cultural Expressions for monitoring its implementation by the Parties. It offers an opportunity to each Party to take the measure of existing implementation by other Parties, to reflect on their own attainment of the Convention on the Diversity of Cultural Expressions objectives and to identify useful levers that could serve to protect and promote the diversity of cultural expressions. In this regard, Article 9 must be read in light of Article 19(1) of the Convention on the Diversity of Cultural Expressions which specifies that "[t]he Parties agree to exchange information and share expertise concerning data

48 *See* Hahn, *supra* note 2, 541–2.

49 *See* Convention on the Diversity of Cultural Expressions, *supra* note 1, Article 23(6)(c).

collection and statistics on the diversity of cultural expressions as well as on best practices for its protection and promotion." Cultural statistics play a particularly important role when the time comes to formulate and implement cultural policies and to adopt measures to protect and promote the diversity of cultural expressions. Unfortunately, cultural statistics are lacking in many countries, particularly in developing countries, and this may prove in time to be a serious impediment to the implementation of the Convention on the Diversity of Cultural Expressions. A serious effort will have to be made to correct this situation. Article 19 offers some hope in this respect when it calls on UNESCO to "facilitate, through the use of existing mechanisms within the Secretariat, the collection, analysis and dissemination of all relevant information, statistics and best practices (Paragraph 2) and, in order to facilitate the collection of data, to "pay particular attention to capacity-building and the strengthening of expertise for Parties that submit a request for such assistance" (Paragraph 4). But the financial and technical resources will have to be found and this is where actions of the Parties in support of cooperation for development become important. Meanwhile, considering the key role that the collection, exchange, analysis and dissemination of information will play in the implementation of the Convention on the Diversity of Cultural Expressions, it may be useful to start thinking immediately about the operational guidelines that will be necessary to implement the pertinent provisions of the Convention on the Diversity of Cultural Expressions, even if Article 9 and 19 are not among the articles that have been given priority attention by the Conference of Parties.

3.2.3. Actions in support of cooperation for development

Leaving aside Article 17, which simply asserts that the Parties shall cooperate in providing assistance to each other, in particular to developing countries, in situation of serious threat to cultural expressions, there are four articles in the Convention on the Diversity of Cultural Expressions that deal specifically with cooperation for development. These Articles must themselves be read in light of the principle of international solidarity and cooperation (Article 2(5)) which provides that "International cooperation and solidarity should be aimed at enabling countries, especially developing countries, to create and strengthen their means of cultural expressions, including their cultural industries, whether nascent or established, at the local, national and international levels."

The first such provision, Article 14, enumerates different means that Parties might use in order to foster the emergence of a dynamic cultural sector in developing countries. The means in question are grouped in four categories, which are: (a) the strengthening of the cultural industries in developing countries; (b) capacity-building; (c) technology transfer; and (d) financial support. For each category, various types of actions are proposed including, under (d)(i), the establishment of an International Fund for Cultural Diversity.

The list of means enumerated in Article 14 is characterized by a pragmatic approach to cultural development, closely reflecting the orientation suggested by the principle of international cooperation and solidarity in Article 1 of the Convention of on the Diversity of Cultural Expressions. The list in question, apart from guiding the actions of the Parties, contributes to delimiting the types of actions to be undertaken under Articles 15 (Collaborative arrangements) 16 (Preferential treatment for developing countries) and 18 (International Fund for Cultural Diversity), which are the three practical mechanisms envisaged by the Convention on the Diversity of Cultural Expressions for putting Article 14 into effect.[50]

Article 15 encourages "the development of partnerships, between and within the public and private sectors and non-profit organizations, in order to cooperate with developing countries in the enhancement of their capacities in the protection and promotion of the diversity of cultural expressions." The partnerships envisaged have something in common with those developed in the context of UNESCO's Global Alliance for Cultural Diversity and could certainly benefit from the experience gained in that context.[51] However, the narrower concerns of the Convention on the Diversity of Cultural Expressions and its focus on the development of cultural policies and measures as means of protecting and promoting the diversity of cultural expressions will no doubt require a certain degree of adaptation. The partnerships envisaged in Article 15 could benefit also from the resources of the International Fund for Cultural Diversity but, as we shall see in discussing the Fund, all decisions to this effect must remain the exclusive purview of the Intergovernmental Committee, deciding on the basis of guidelines determined by the Conference of Parties. At its December 2007 first ordinary session, the Intergovernmental Committee decided to put issues related to the elaboration of operational guidelines concerning matters including the concept of and modalities for partnerships on the agenda of an extraordinary session to take place in June 2008.[52]

The second mechanism envisaged by the Convention on the Diversity of Cultural Expressions is the granting of preferential treatment for developing countries (Article 16). This preferential treatment is to be granted, more specifically, to artists and other cultural professionals, as well as to cultural goods and services from developing countries. In the case of artists and other

---

50 At the extraordinary session of the Intergovernmental Committee of December 2007, it was decided that the question of the orientations on the use of the Fund (Article 18) would be examined together with that of cooperation for development (Article 14). *See* UNESCO, Intergovernmental Committee, *supra* note 39, at 20 (Dates and agenda of the future sessions of the Committee – Decision 1.IGC 7).

51 See UNESCO, "The Global Alliance on Cultural Diversity", *available at* http://portal.unesco.org/culture/en/ev.php-URL_ID=24468&URL_DO=DO_TOPIC&URL_SECTION=201.html (last visited 2 February 2012) (providing more information on the Global Alliance).

52 *See* UNESCO, Intergovernmental Committee, *supra* note 39.

professionals, the preferential treatment could apply either at the point of entry into the country (which could be problematic in view of the security questions that would inevitably be raised) or after entry (where the preferential treatment could more realistically apply, including to grants, admissions to school, colleges or universities). In the case of cultural goods and services, various options would be open but they would have to be considered in light of the rights and obligations of the Parties under other agreements, particularly trade agreements. The negotiators of Article 16 were rather circumspect from that point of view, qualifying the good faith commitment to grant preferential treatment with the words "through appropriate and legal frameworks". However the granting of preferential treatment to developing countries is not uncommon, particularly in the context of the WTO.[53] The possibility is there and could yield interesting results from a cultural perspective. The interest in and potential of Article 16 were considered important enough to justify the Intergovernmental Committee

> to invite the Secretariat to select in consultation with the Chair of the Committee, six qualified experts, representative of the different perspectives relating to preferential treatment (Article 16 of the [Convention on the Diversity of Cultural Expressions]) and coming from countries in different stages of economic development. Each of the experts will be tasked with preparing a factual document on this issue, enumerating definitions, regulations and existing practices, which will be submitted to the Committee for examination at its session in December 2008.[54]

The third and last mechanism envisaged by the Convention on the Diversity of Cultural Expressions is the International Fund for Cultural Diversity. As we have seen previously, cultural policies and measures play a crucial role in the protection and promotion of cultural expressions. The developed countries have understood this, and the vast majority of such countries have put in place an elaborate array of cultural policies and measures that substantially meet their needs. The developing countries also have cultural policies and measures, but these tend to be much less elaborate and may not be implemented for lack of sufficient funds. In this light, the Fund is seen as a concrete means of assistance.

The key provision concerning the Fund is the founding provision, Article 18. With the exception of the rules on funding, Article 18 is virtually identical to Article 25 of the 2003 *Convention for the Safeguarding of the Intangible Cultural Heritage* and Article 15 of the 1972 *Convention Concerning the Protection of the World Cultural and Natural Heritage*. With respect to funding, however, there is

---

53 The WTO agreements include numerous provisions giving developing and least-developed countries special rights or extra leniency – "special and differential treatment". Among these are provisions that allow developed countries to treat developing countries more favorably than other WTO members.

54 *See* UNESCO, Intergovernmental Committee, *supra* note 39, at 17 (International Cooperation – Decision 1.IGC 5 B).

a major difference. In the case of the *Convention on the Protection and Promotion of the Diversity of Cultural Expressions*, the parties are under no obligation to contribute to the Fund, whereas the opposite is true for the other two conventions. The decision to make Fund contributions by the Parties voluntary under this Convention on the Diversity of Cultural Expressions will undoubtedly have disadvantages. One very serious disadvantage is the resulting uncertainty about regular contributions to the Fund, and the subsequent challenges of developing a structured approach to assisting developing countries in the short and medium term. To remedy this situation, an effort will have to be made not only to encourage as many Parties as possible to contribute to the Fund on a regular basis, but also to identify alternative funding strategies based on the other funding modes mentioned in Article 18. To achieve this result, however, the funding issue will need active, ongoing attention.[55]

The first mention of the Fund in the Convention on the Diversity of Cultural Expressions, as we have seen previously, is in Article 14, which lists various means for fostering the emergence of a dynamic cultural sector in developing countries. The specific reference to the Fund as a means of financial support in the last paragraph of the article suggests that it be used in relation to the means of action envisaged in the preceding paragraphs. Article 18(5) stipulates that the Intergovernmental Committee may accept contributions and other forms of assistance for general and specific purposes relating to specific projects, provided that it has given these projects its approval. Article 18(6) mentions grounds for refusing contributions, namely that no political, economic, or other conditions incompatible with the objectives of the Convention on the Diversity of Cultural Expressions may be attached to contributions made to the Fund. Article 18(4) of the Convention on the Diversity of Cultural Expressions stipulates that the use of Fund resources shall be determined by the Intergovernmental Committee on the basis of guidelines set out by the Conference of Parties.

A lengthy discussion on that topic took place at the December 2007 session of the Intergovernmental Committee in response to the request of the Conference of Parties that the Committee submits draft guidelines on the use of the resources of the Fund to the Conference of Parties for approval at its second ordinary session in 2009. At the end of the discussion, it was decided to continue the preparation of the operational guidelines for further discussion at the second ordinary session of the Committee in December 2008 and a request was made to the Secretariat to prepare an interim report to be presented at the extraordinary session of June 2008 in light of the debates at the first session and written contributions to be submitted to the Secretariat before the end of February 2008.

---

55 *See* I. Bernier, "An Important Aspect of the Convention on the Protection and Promotion of the Diversity of Cultural Expressions: The International Fund for Cultural Diversity" (2007), *available at* www.mcc.gouv.qc.ca/diversiteculturelle/eng/pdf/fondsdiversiteculturelleeng (last visited 2 February 2012).

Quite clearly, there is a strong consensus among the Parties to the Convention on the Diversity of Cultural Expressions that the Fund should be made operational as quickly as possible. A number of the Parties have already announced their intention to make contributions and the amounts effectively pledged at the end of the December 2007 session of the Intergovernmental Committee exceeded USD 1 million.

4. THE POTENTIAL CONFLICTS BETWEEN THE CONVENTION ON THE DIVERSITY OF CULTURAL EXPRESSIONS AND OTHER AGREEMENTS

During the negotiations, the Convention on the Diversity of Cultural Expressions was characterized by certain States as intended to remove culture from trade agreements, a view that has also been picked up by some writers.[56] In support of that view, reference is made to specific provisions of the Convention on the Diversity of Cultural Expressions that allegedly have the potential to conflict with existing or future trade agreements, such as Articles 6(2)(b) and (d), Article 8 (Measures to protect cultural expressions), Article 12(e) on co-production and co-distribution agreements and Article 16 (Preferential treatment for developing countries). Such conflicts cannot be excluded entirely, but there is no certainty on the other hand that they will take place and that holds true even when the question is examined from a trade law perspective. Depending on the circumstances, those measures might be used without any contradiction with trade or other agreements. Many other conventions such as environmental conventions, health conventions or labour conventions also have the potential to conflict with trade agreements, but this has rarely, if ever, given raise to actual conflicts. Furthermore, it is important to point out that the possibility of conflicts between the Convention on the Diversity of Cultural Expressions and trade agreements will arise at the margins of the operation of the Convention on the Diversity of Cultural Expressions. As we have seen in the previous section, the essential thrust of the Convention on the Diversity of Cultural Expressions objectives is geared towards the development within the territory of the Parties of an environment encouraging individual and social

56 *See, e.g.*, HAHN, *supra* note 2, at 533 (where the author writes "[i]ts *raison d'être* is to create a safe haven for protectionist measures aimed at ensuring cultural diversity, read: For allowing WTO members to legally provide shelf-space for domestic productions in television programs and cinemas." But having said that, the author curiously continues: "The purpose to serve as an ersatz cultural exception is underlined by the almost complete lack of enforceable substantive provisions and a dispute settlement mechanism worth mentioning only as being reminiscent of the very early days of modern international law.").

groups to create, produce, distribute and have access to their own cultural expressions and to the cultural expressions of other countries of the world, something that can hardly be considered at first glance as threatening the WTO.

However, since the possibility of conflict cannot be ruled out, it had to be faced. From a cultural point of view, the solution reached was one that would make sure that cultural concerns were taken into consideration without undermining prior commitments of the Parties. This is precisely what Articles 20 and 21 of the Convention on the Diversity of Cultural Expressions purport to accomplish, however how they will operate is a matter for conjecture.

4.1. THE RELATIONSHIP BETWEEN THE CONVENTION ON THE DIVERSITY OF CULTURAL EXPRESSIONS AND OTHER TREATIES (ARTICLE 20)

Article 20 of the Convention on the Diversity of Cultural Expressions reads:

> 1. Parties recognize that they shall perform in good faith their obligations under this Convention and all other treaties to which they are parties. Accordingly, without subordinating this Convention to any other treaty,
>   (a) they shall foster mutual supportiveness between this Convention and the other treaties to which they are parties; and
>   (b) when interpreting and applying the other treaties to which they are parties or when entering into other international obligations, Parties shall take into account the relevant provisions of this Convention.
> 2. Nothing in this Convention shall be interpreted as modifying rights and obligations of the Parties under any other treaties to which they are parties.

It is only at the very end of the negotiations that Article 20 was finally adopted, after complex and lengthy discussions. For those who saw the Convention on the Diversity of Cultural Expressions as a disguised attempt to remove culture from the WTO, it had to be clearly stated that the Convention on the Diversity of Cultural Expressions would in no circumstances prevail over trade agreements. For the vast majority, however, cultural concerns had to find their place among other legitimate concerns and for that, it was necessary that the Convention on the Diversity of Cultural Expressions clearly assert the non-subordination of the instrument to other international agreements.

Those two seemingly contradictory views have found their way in the text finally adopted. An initial reading of Article 20 immediately reveals the tension between its first and second paragraphs. The first, in rather elaborate language, manifestly attempts to counterbalance the direct provisions of the second. Without entering into the details of the negotiations on Article 20, it is easy to see that, in general terms, Paragraph 2 is an answer to the trade concerns of the minority and that Paragraph 1 reflects the cultural concerns of the majority.

Since it is largely agreed that Paragraph 2 adequately protects the trade concerns of WTO members (stating that the Convention on the Diversity of Cultural Expressions cannot "be interpreted as modifying rights and obligations of the Parties under any other treaties to which they are parties" is another way of saying that it cannot prevail over those treaties),[57] we shall concentrate our attention here on the contribution of Paragraph 1 to the cultural concerns of the Parties to the Convention on the Diversity of Cultural Expressions.

The paragraph begins with a reminder that the parties shall perform their obligations under the Convention on the Diversity of Cultural Expressions and all other agreements to which they are parties in good faith. This is nothing more than a restatement of a basic principle of international law, that of good faith, but it is interesting to note that the obligation is applied equally to the Convention on the Diversity of Cultural Expressions and the other agreements. The paragraph goes on to elaborate on the type of conduct expected of Parties acting in good faith. There are three elements in the paragraph that can be considered as addressing specifically cultural concerns. The first is the statement regarding the non-subordination of the Convention on the Diversity of Cultural Expressions to other treaties, the second the reference to mutual supportiveness and the third the obligation imposed on the Parties to take the relevant provisions of the Convention on the Diversity of Cultural Expressions into account when they interpret or apply other treaties or when they enter into other international obligations. There is a common thread between these three elements: they convey the same message that protecting and promoting the diversity of cultural expressions is a concern that has to be taken into account on equal footing with other concerns.

This is obviously the message conveyed by the affirmation regarding the non-subordination of the Convention on the Diversity of Cultural Expressions. Article 30 of the Vienna Convention gives the following examples of situations where a treaty will be considered as subordinate to another treaty. This happens when a provision in a treaty explicitly envisages such a situation. Article 30(2) of the Vienna Convention states in this respect: "When a treaty specifies that it is subject to, or that it is not to be considered as incompatible with, an earlier or later treaty, the provisions of that other treaty will prevail." But this is not what Article 20(2) of the Convention on Diversity of Cultural Expressions says. It does not use the expressions 'subject to' and 'incompatible with' to describe the

57 Article 20(2) Convention on the Diversity of Cultural Expressions discards two possibilities regarding the impact of the *Convention* on other treaties. Firstly it eliminates the possibility of looking at the Convention on the Diversity of Cultural Expressions as an application of Vienna Convention, *supra* note 12, Article 41 (Agreement to modify multilateral treaties between certain of the parties only); secondly, it eliminates the possibility that the *Convention*, to the extent that it is considered as related to the same subject as the other treaties, modifies the right and obligations of other treaties that have entered into force at an earlier date (Vienna Convention, *supra* note 12, Article 30(3) and (4)).

relationship between the Convention on the Diversity of Cultural Expressions and other treaties. What it does instead is to proclaim in clear terms that the Convention on the Diversity of Cultural Expressions will not modify the rights and obligations of the Parties under any other treaties to which they are parties. In other words, it will not prevail over those other treaties. This is not the same as saying that the Convention on the Diversity of Cultural Expressions is subordinate to those other treaties as some writers affirm.[58] When both Paragraph 1 and Paragraph 2 are read together, it becomes clear that if the Convention on the Diversity of Cultural Expressions does not prevail over the other treaties, the other treaties themselves do not prevail over the Convention on the Diversity of Cultural Expressions. In other words, they stand on an equal footing.

But the Convention on the Diversity of Cultural Expressions is not satisfied with this neutral solution. It goes on to suggest positive ways of addressing the interface between trade and culture. It requires in Article 20(1)(a) that the Parties foster mutual supportiveness between the Convention on the Diversity of Cultural Expressions and other treaties. In other words, Parties should make efforts in good faith to accommodate both cultural concerns and trade concerns. This, however, is not to be an unilateral effort, as the word "mutual" clearly suggests. To the extent that the Parties are members of both the Convention on the Diversity of Cultural Expressions and of trade agreements, the effort to reconcile differences should be mutual. This is confirmed by the requirement, in Article 20(1)(b) that the Parties take into account the relevant provisions of the Convention on the Diversity of Cultural Expressions when they interpret and apply other treaties or when they enter into other international obligations.

The language of Article 20(1)(b), it must be noted, imposes a positive duty on the Parties to take the relevant provisions of the Convention on the Diversity of Cultural Expressions into account. The expression "to take into account" is sometimes seen as a weak obligation because it does not ensure a specific result. But this is a misunderstanding of the nature of the obligation, which is not a substantive obligation but a procedural obligation. It should be noted that procedural obligations are not insignificant.[59] Depending on the context, the failure to comply with an obligation to take into account may be sufficient to invalidate a process or a decision. The scope of an obligation of this type is normally clarified by decisions concerning on the one hand what is to be taken into account and on the other hand the circumstances that give rise to the obligation. Under Article 20(1)(b) of the Convention on the Diversity of Cultural Expressions what has to be taken into account is "the relevant provisions of the

58 *See* Hahn, *supra* note 2, at 546.

59 *See* Panel Report, "European Communities – Measures Affecting the Approval and Marketing of Biotech Products", *WT/DS291/R* (29 September 2006) (making this point with respect to the taking into account of the 1992 *Convention on Biological Diversity* and 2000 *Cartegena Protocol on Biosafety*).

Convention". This is rather vague and leaves much discretion to the Parties. But the circumstances which give rise to the obligation are much more specific: it is when Parties interpret or apply other treaties or when they enter into other international obligations. These circumstances are precise enough to facilitate inquiry as to whether, on a specific issue, the "taking into account" has taken place, which can be ascertained by looking at the practices of individual Parties. Apart from putting pressure on Parties to clarify their positions, this will not necessary yield concrete results as Parties are not individually in a position to influence the application or the interpretation of a treaty or, for that matter, the adoption of a new treaty. A more practical way of giving life to the obligation to "take into account" is that proposed in Article 21 which deals with international consultation and coordination to promote the objectives and principles of the Convention on the Diversity of Cultural Expressions in other international forums.

4.2. INTERNATIONAL CONSULTATION AND COORDINATION (ARTICLE 21)

According to Article 21, not only do the Parties undertake to promote the objectives and principles of the Convention on the Diversity of Cultural Expressions in other international forums but they shall also "consult each other, as appropriate, bearing in mind these objectives and principles." The original version of this article in the Preliminary Draft Convention provided that this consultation would take place within UNESCO.[60] During the negotiations, the reference to UNESCO was deleted, leaving it to the Parties to organize such consultation. But they were not left entirely at themselves. In the final text of the Convention on the Diversity of Cultural Expressions, a mandate is given to the Intergovernmental Committee to "establish procedures and other mechanisms for consultation aimed at promoting the objectives and principles of the Convention in other international forums."[61] It is difficult to tell at present when and how these procedures and mechanisms will be put in place. Article 21 was not among the provisions of the Convention on the Diversity of Cultural Expressions identified by the Conference of Parties for priority consideration by the Intergovernmental Committee.

Nevertheless, sooner or later, the matter will have to be considered and it is be interesting to consider what types of procedures or other mechanisms for consultation could be put in place. The easiest approach would be to build on the institutions put in place by the Convention on the Diversity of Cultural Expressions, that is the Conference of Parties and the Intergovernmental

60 Preliminary Draft Convention, *supra* note 34, Article 13.

61 Convention on the Diversity of Cultural Expressions, *supra* note 1, Article 23(6)(e).

Committee, and to proceed empirically, starting with problems that have already been identified by these institutions for consultation, such as the granting of preferential treatment to developing countries that is provided for in Article 16, or the integration of culture in sustainable development. Before proceeding with the consultations as such, it would appear necessary to prepare background material that would serve as a starting point for the consultations between the Parties. This is exactly what the Intergovernmental Committee has been asked to do at its first ordinary session with respect to Article 16 (preferential treatment for developing countries). Once an agreement has been reached on how to implement the provision in question, the Parties could undertake to promote their view on this specific subject in other international forums, including, in that case organizations such as the UNCTAD, the United Nations Development Program, the OECD, the WTO and regional agencies such as the Council of Europe. The experience gained could be used to refine the procedure and mechanisms and explore other subjects that relate either to the implementation of the Convention on the Diversity of Cultural Expressions or to developments that take place in other forums, including the WTO, regional arrangements and bilateral trade agreements. In this way, true mutual supportiveness could develop in a concrete manner between the Convention on the Diversity of Cultural Expressions and other treaties, in a true spirit of collaboration. This approach naturally does not exclude individual initiatives by the Parties who could always request that the question of consultation as envisaged in Article 21 be put on the agenda of either the Conference of Parties or the Intergovernmental Committee.

5. CONCLUSION

Ever since it was launched in 2003, the project of a new international convention on the protection of the diversity of cultural content and artistic expressions has received remarkable support from the Members of UNESCO and has been driven by an obvious desire to give recognition to the distinctive nature of cultural activities, goods and services as vehicles of identity, values and meaning, to protect and promote as a consequence the diversity of cultural expressions and to create the conditions for cultures to flourish and freely interact in a mutually beneficial manner. Unfortunately, the legal analysis of the Convention on the Diversity of Cultural Expressions has tended to concentrate so far on what it could not do from a trade law perspective (a bias that can be understood in view of the historical background of the Convention on the Diversity of Cultural Expressions) rather than on what it could do from a cultural perspective. To correct that situation, this chapter has concentrated on the instrument's significance as a cultural instrument, using analysis based on the actual text of the Convention on the Diversity of Cultural Expressions.

Three questions have attracted attention in this chapter. Firstly, regarding the purpose and scope of the Convention on the Diversity of Cultural Expressions, it is clear that, despite allegations to the contrary, the Convention on the Diversity of Cultural Expressions is essentially concerned with the protection and preservation of the diversity of cultural expressions, a focus which, far from being a minor issue, is proving to be one of the major challenges of our times. This chapter has also demonstrated that the fact that the Convention on the Diversity of Cultural Expressions limits itself to the protection and promotion of the diversity of cultural expressions does not diminish the importance of other aspects of cultural diversity in any way. Turning secondly to the plan of action in the Convention on the Diversity of Cultural Expressions for ensuring the protection and promotion of the diversity of cultural expressions, this chapter highlighted the plan's basic elements and reviewed the various types of actions envisaged, taking into account not only their background but also the work already done by the Conference of Parties and the Intergovernmental Committee in order to bring these actions to life. Finally, concerning the potential conflicts between the Convention on the Diversity of Cultural Expressions and other agreements, this chapter emphasized that such conflicts were bound to arise only in exceptional circumstances since the Convention on the Diversity of Cultural Expressions includes very few compulsory obligations, before noting that if conflicts were to arise, Article 20 ensures, as an opening position that the Convention on the Diversity of Cultural Expressions will not prevail over the commitments of the Parties under other treaties while at the same time it will also not be subordinated to other treaties. Then, moving beyond that neutral stand, Article 20 goes on to suggest that the Parties should make efforts to accommodate both cultural and other concerns, requiring, more particularly, that Parties take into account the relevant provisions of the Convention on the Diversity of Cultural Expressions when interpreting and applying other treaties or when entering into other international obligations. This could yield interesting results in the future, especially since the Parties are asked in Article 21 to consult each other in order to promote the objectives of the Convention on the Diversity of Cultural Expressions in other international forums.

The analysis of the Convention on the Diversity of Cultural Expressions in this chapter was intended to clarify its scope and to highlight its potential as a cultural instrument. This does not mean that it is without defects. It would be easy to point out that the Convention on the Diversity of Cultural Expressions, when compared to WTO agreements, has practically no compulsory obligations and no compulsory dispute settlement mechanism accompanied by sanctions[62]

62 But in the spirit of the Convention on the Diversity of Cultural Expressions, it was decided that a conciliation procedure could be activated upon the request of only one of the parties to the dispute, which means that if disputes actually arise, chances are that the conciliation procedure will be used. *See* Convention on the Diversity of Cultural Expressions, Article 25 Annex.

and to conclude that the best forum for resolving conflicts between culture and trade remains the WTO itself.[63] But two clarifications must be made in that respect. The first is that such a conclusion takes for granted that the WTO is the ultimate model for addressing important issues of international governance. Leaving aside, for the moment, the fact that the WTO has enough problems of its own, one may at least question from a global governance point of view the need to give a quasi-constitutional status to an organization that views reality from an exclusively commercial and economic view point. The second clarification is that constraint is not the only way to give life to a convention, especially in areas where it does not appear particularly suited, such as culture. If there is one lesson to learn from the process that has led to the adoption of the Convention on the Diversity of Cultural Expressions and to its prompt ratification, it is that a strong conviction shared by a very large number of States can go a long way in ensuring the success of a convention. One would be tempted to conclude from that point of view that a declining degree of conviction is perhaps what explains, at least in part, the present difficulties of the WTO.

63 This is the conclusion reached by Tania Voon in her 2007 book entitled *Cultural Products and the World Trade Organization*. *See* VOON, *supra* note 2, at 253 (2007). In the final analysis, her main argument for that conclusion is that the *Convention* could diminish the effectiveness of the WTO, which remains a one-sided view of what is at stake. Her own solution for dealing with the interface between commerce and culture in the context of the WTO, judging from the experience of the past, appears to be a remote possibility.

PART II

HERITAGE LAW & THE CONVENTION ON THE DIVERSITY OF CULTURAL EXPRESSIONS

THE 1972 WORLD HERITAGE CONVENTION AND THE CONVENTION ON THE DIVERSITY OF CULTURAL EXPRESSIONS

Federico LENZERINI*

1. INTRODUCTION

The recent expansion of international legal instruments dealing with different, but at the same time interrelated, aspects concerning the protection of culture and cultural heritage raises the question of whether and to what extent these instruments, in the real world, are suitable of interacting with each other while producing their effects.

This issue acquires special interest with respect to the interface between the *Convention on the Protection and Promotion of the Diversity of Cultural Expression* ("Convention on the Diversity of Cultural Expressions")[1] and the *Convention concerning the Protection of the World Cultural and Natural Heritage* ("World Heritage Convention").[2] In fact, certain cultural properties may be of significance under both these legal instruments, contextually incorporating different interests, defended by the two conventions, which in certain situations may even be at odds with each other.

The aim of the present chapter is to try to shed a light on the relationship between the aforementioned conventions, particularly in order to ascertain how they can be integrated with each other for ensuring better protection to cultural heritage (intended in its widest sense), as well as, on the other hand, how the potential conflicts between them may be settled. To this purpose, after providing

---

* Ph.D., International Law; Researcher and Professor of International Law and of European Union Law, University of Siena (Italy); Consultant to UNESCO.

1 *See* Convention on the Protection and Promotion of the Diversity of Cultural Expressions, 20 October 2005, *U.N. Doc. CLT-2005/CONVENTION DIVERSITE-CULT REV.* [hereinafter "Convention on the Diversity of Cultural Expressions"].

2 *See* Convention concerning the Protection of the World Cultural and Natural Heritage, 16 November 1972, *available at* http://portal.unesco.org/en/ev.php-URL_ID=13055&URL_DO=DO_TOPIC&URL_SECTION=201.html (last visited on 2 February 2012) [hereinafter "World Heritage Convention"].

a general assessment of the evolution of international law on cultural heritage and a summary review of the system set up by the World Heritage Convention, this chapter will be concentrated on the potential aspects of (positive and negative) interaction between the two conventions, with particular attention to their mutual supportiveness in interpretation, to their complementarity as well as, finally, to the latent aspects of conflict between them.

2. THE EVOLUTION OF INTERNATIONAL LAW ON CULTURE: FROM CULTURAL PROPERTY, THROUGH CULTURAL HERITAGE, TO A HOLISTIC VISION OF CULTURE

The Convention on the Diversity of Cultural Expressions may be plainly considered as representing the pinnacle of the evolution of the international community's perception concerning the safeguarding of cultural heritage and culture. This evolution has eventually been characterized by the drastic – although progressive – transformation, with respect to the earlier legal instruments, of the philosophy and legal rationale underlying the relevant actions of the international community.

In chronological terms, the first significant international provisions concerning the protection of cultural assets, which were included in the 1907 Hague Conventions on the laws and customs of war,[3] were in fact aimed at safeguarding cultural *property belonging* to a State from possible belligerent acts perpetrated against them by foreign armies. In substance, these provisions were finalized to protect an attribute of State sovereignty. The protected properties were conceived as national 'private' property, the legal significance of which was in no way determined by their intrinsic and objective value, but by the fact of representing a 'good' pertaining to the sovereign prerogatives of a given State. Destruction of or damage to the protected heritage, to the extent not justified by military necessity, was therefore considered to be an offence committed against the *private property* of another State, and this was the only rationale for the protected heritage falling within the scope of interest of international law at the time.

[3] *See* Convention (IV) Respecting the Laws and Customs of War on Land and its Annex: Regulations concerning the Laws and Customs of War on Land, 18 October 1907, 3 *Martens Nouveau Recueil (ser. 3)* 461, *available at* www.icrc.org/ihl.nsf (last visited on 2 February 2012) [hereinafter "Convention IV"](Article 27 of the Regulations annexed to the Convention IV established that "[i]n sieges and bombardments all necessary steps must be taken to spare, as far as possible, buildings dedicated to religion, art, science, or charitable purposes, historic monuments, hospitals, and places where the sick and wounded are collected, provided they are not being used at the time for military purposes."); *See also* Convention (IX) concerning Bombardment by Naval Forces in Time of War, 18 October 1907, 3 *Martens Nouveau Recueil (ser. 3)* 604, *available at* www.icrc.org/ihl.nsf (last visited on 2 February 2012) [hereinafter "Convention IX"] (Article 5 Convention IX expresses a similar principle).

The same rationale substantially shaped the 1954 Hague *Convention for the Protection of Cultural Property in the Event of Armed Conflict*,[4] but its Preamble marked the rise of a new international consciousness, which considered cultural heritage worth protecting for its inherent value, transcendent of national borders and interests. Although the operational aspects of the 1954 Convention retained a structure rooted in a system of reciprocal State relations based on the connotation of cultural assets as national property, the consciousness that 'the preservation of the cultural heritage is of great importance for all peoples of the world and that it is important that this heritage should receive international protection'[5] found explicit expression in the Preamble, which also proclaimed that 'damage to cultural property belonging to any people whatsoever means damage to the cultural heritage of all mankind, since each people makes its contribution to the culture of the world.'[6]

The new consciousness expressed in these statements constituted the *raison d'être* of the World Heritage Convention, adopted by the UNESCO General Conference on 16 November 1972, which is based on the conviction that the "deterioration or disappearance of any item of the cultural or natural heritage constitutes a harmful impoverishment of the heritage of all the nations of the world."[7] Founded on an eclectic approach, the World Heritage Convention combines the co-existing interests of single States in the protection of *their own* national heritage with the interest of the international community as a whole in the safeguarding of cultural and natural treasures, irrespective of their origin or location, as irreplaceable expressions of the beauty and variety of human genius and of the magnificence of the world. The adoption of the World Heritage Convention represented a crucial step in the evolution of a new legal approach for the protection of cultural heritage. This is particularly the case because the Convention set up a system of safeguards which in practice has proven actually capable of preserving the integrity of the most important expressions of the World Heritage, even against the adverse acts of States in which these expressions are located, thus leading in most cases to the effective prevalence of the global concerns of the international community over the parochial interests of territorial States.[8]

The next major step characterizing the evolution of the international legal action concerning cultural heritage was represented by its extension to the intangible expressions of such heritage. The deed for the safeguarding of intangible cultural heritage was eventually finalized in the adoption of the *Convention for the Safeguarding of Intangible Cultural Heritage* ("ICH

4 *See* Convention for the Protection of Cultural Property in the Event of Armed Conflict, 14 May 1954, 249 *UNTS* 240.

5 Id., Preamble §3.

6 Id., Preamble §2.

7 Id., Preamble §2.

8 *See infra* note 37 (corresponding text).

Convention") in 2003,[9] which considers this heritage to be "a mainspring of cultural diversity and a guarantee of sustainable development,"[10] deeply interrelated with "tangible cultural and natural heritage"[11] and providing groups and communities "with a sense of identity and continuity, thus promoting respect for cultural diversity and human creativity."[12] In this way, the perception of the international community has evolved toward an holistic and spiritual vision of culture, embracing not only the tangible and visually-outstanding manifestations of cultural heritage, but also those expressions which, although intangible in character, and thus inherently ephemeral in nature, are strictly intertwined with the very identity of human communities. The idea of *living culture* has consequently developed, conceived as the entirety of idiosyncratic emotional, spiritual and intellectual qualities characterizing any human group.

The richness and worth of living culture is particularly appreciable through understanding the value of diversity as a tool of mutual enrichment among peoples. It was for this reason that the ICH Convention was complemented by the Convention on the Diversity of Cultural Expressions in 2005. Leaving aside the trade-related implications which may have inspired and influenced the scope and content of the Convention, in objective terms it represents a significant step forward toward the affirmation of a humanized and dynamic vision of culture which is actually consistent with the basic values pursued today by the international community, particularly human rights and the rights of peoples. When cultural diversity is protected, the ultimate object that is safeguarded is in fact the cultural identity of the different peoples and communities of the world, since it is exactly the complex of all the cultural models making up humanity which actually shapes the realm of cultural diversity. This approach reflects the maturing consciousness of the international community concerning "the importance of cultural diversity for the full realization of human rights and

---

9 *See* Convention for the Safeguarding of the Intangible Cultural Heritage, 17 October 2003, *U.N. Doc. MISC/2003/CLT/CH/14* (2003) [hereinafter "ICH Convention"]. 'Intangible cultural heritage' is defined, by Article 2(1), as "the practices, representations, expressions, knowledge, skills – as well as the instruments, objects, artefacts and cultural spaces associated therewith – that communities, groups and, in some cases, individuals recognize as part of their cultural heritage. This intangible cultural heritage, transmitted from generation to generation, is constantly recreated by communities and groups in response to their environment, their interaction with nature and their history, and provides them with a sense of identity and continuity, thus promoting respect for cultural diversity and human creativity. For the purposes of this Convention, consideration will be given solely to such intangible cultural heritage as is compatible with existing international human rights instruments, as well as with the requirements of mutual respect among communities, groups and individuals, and of sustainable development."

10 Id., Preamble §2.

11 Id., Preamble §3.

12 Id.

fundamental freedoms,"[13] as well as the significance of cultural heritage for "the cultural identity of communities, groups and individuals, and [for] social cohesion, so that [if it is not adequately safeguarded] [...] adverse consequences on human dignity and human rights [may arise]."[14]

This portrayal of cultural diversity and of its significance for the international community clearly emerges from the text of the 2005 Convention, which defines 'cultural diversity' by referring to "the manifold ways in which the cultures of groups and societies find expression"[15] and solemnly affirms that "culture takes diverse forms across time and space" and that "[t]his diversity is embodied in the uniqueness and plurality of the identities and cultural expressions of the peoples and societies making up humanity."[16] Therefore, the dynamic and multifaceted concept of culture proclaimed by the 1982 *Mexico City Declaration on Cultural Policies*,[17] as "the whole complex of distinctive spiritual, material, intellectual and emotional features that characterize a society or social group [...] includ[ing] not only the arts and letters, but also modes of life, the fundamental rights of the human being, value systems, traditions and beliefs,"[18] has finally found concrete expression in the relevant treaty regime.

3. THE WORLD HERITAGE CONVENTION AND ITS SYSTEM OF IMPLEMENTATION

As noted in the previous section, one of the key moments in the evolution of the international action for safeguarding culture is represented by the adoption, in 1972, of the World Heritage Convention.[19] This Convention has the main purpose of creating an international scheme of protection for tangible and immovable manifestations of cultural and natural heritage of outstanding universal value. Since the very first years after its entry into force, the World Heritage Convention has been characterized by remarkable success, so that

13 Convention on the Diversity of Cultural Expressions, *supra* note 1, Preamble §5.

14 Declaration concerning the Intentional Destruction of Cultural Heritage, 17 October 2003, Preamble §5, *available at* http://portal.unesco.org/en/ev.php-URL_ID=17718&URL_DO=DO_TOPIC&URL_SECTION=201.html (last visited on 16 November 2011).

15 Convention on the Diversity of Cultural Expressions, *supra* note 1, Article 4(1).

16 Id., Preamble §7. This sentence reproduces the first part of Article 1 of the *Universal Declaration on Cultural Diversity*. *See* Universal Declaration on Cultural Diversity, 2 November 2001, *available at* http://portal.unesco.org/en/ev.php-URL_ID=13179&URL_DO=DO_TOPIC&URL_SECTION=201.html (last visited on 16 November 2011).

17 Mexico City Declaration on Cultural Policies, 26 July – 6 Augustus 1982, *available at* http://portal.unesco.org/culture/en/files/35197/11919410061mexico_en.pdf/mexico_en.pdf (last visited on 16 November 2011).

18 Id., at §6.

19 *See* F. Francioni (ed., with F. Lenzerini), *Commentary to the 1972 World Heritage Convention*, 2008 (providing an in-depth article-by-article analysis of the World Heritage Convention).

today it is one of the most ratified international treaties[20] and, due to its wide visibility among all sectors of civil society, is commonly seen as the foremost international instrument concerning the protection of culture.

The system set up by the World Heritage Convention is basically characterized by a double plan of safeguarding, represented by two schemes of protection to be implemented, respectively, at the national and at the international level. It is noteworthy, as an aside, that the scope of application of the Convention simultaneously covers cultural and natural heritage, on the condition that the property concerned is of "outstanding universal value,"[21] as prescribed by, respectively, Articles 1 (for cultural heritage) and 2 (for natural heritage).

The system of national protection contemplates a number of duties for States Parties, concerning in particular the identification, protection, conservation, presentation and transmission to future generations of the World Heritage situated in their own territories, as well as the adoption of appropriate measures to this end.[22] States Parties also undertake to cooperate in the protection of the World Heritage, as a "duty of the international community as a whole,"[23] as well as "not to take any deliberate measures which might damage directly or indirectly [such] heritage." This, however, is to be done through ensuring full respect for the "sovereignty of the States on whose territory the […] heritage [concerned] is situated."[24]

The scheme of international protection is much more specific and effective, representing, in essence, the concrete operation of the World Heritage Convention. It basically consists in the progressive formation and management of a list of the most notable tangible items of the cultural and natural heritage of humanity, which is defined as the *World Heritage List*.[25] The selection of the properties to be inscribed on this List is made by an *ad hoc* body, called the *World Heritage Committee*.[26] However, it is to be noted that no property may be included in the List without "the consent of the State concerned."[27] This reaffirmation of the principle of State sovereignty is apparently at odds with the philosophy and spirit of the Convention, which aims at safeguarding World

---

20 At the moment of writing, the Convention had been ratified by 189 States. *See* http://portal.unesco.org/la/convention.asp?KO=13055&language=E (last visited on 10 July 2012).

21 *See* F. Francioni, "Preamble", in Francioni (ed., with Lenzerini), *supra* note 19, 11; A. A. Yusuf, "Article 1: Definition of Cultural Heritage", in Francioni (ed., with Lenzerini), *supra* note 19, 23; C. Redgwell, "Article 2: Definition of Natural Heritage", in Francioni (ed., with Lenzerini), *supra* note 19, 63 (providing further information on the concept of outstanding universal value).

22 *See* World Heritage Convention, *supra* note 2, Articles 4–6.

23 Id., Article 6(1).

24 Id.

25 *See* T. Scovazzi, "Articles 8–11: World Heritage Committee and World Heritage List", in Francioni (ed., with Lenzerini), *supra* note 19, 148 (explaining different issues of the World Heritage List).

26 *See* World Heritage Convention, *supra* note 2, Article 8(1).

27 Id., Article 11(3).

Heritage in the interests of the international community as a whole, and clearly shows how an element of compromise permeates the entire Convention text. The World Heritage List is complemented by the *List of World Heritage in Danger*,[28] on which the properties already appearing on the World Heritage List for which "major operations are necessary and for which assistance has been requested"[29] are inscribed.

A special fund (the *World Heritage Fund*), formed for the most part by compulsory and voluntary contributions of State Parties, is established by Article 15 with the purpose of financing the activities carried out for the realization of the purposes of the Convention, particularly in view of ensuring adequate protection for the properties inscribed on the World Heritage List. The World Heritage Fund, in reality, covers only a minor part of the expenses necessary for the implementation of the Convention, which are primarily covered by funds from the budget of the UNESCO Regular Programme and, in particular, by extra-budgetary funds.[30] International assistance for properties inscribed on the World Heritage List (among which special attention is devoted to those inscribed on the List of World Heritage in Danger) is granted by the World Heritage Committee pursuant to the conditions and arrangements provided for by Articles 19–26 of the Convention.[31]

As already noted, the World Heritage Convention has emerged as an extremely successful and effective instrument for the protection of cultural (and natural) heritage of special interest to humanity. This success is reflected in the very large number of properties inscribed on the World Heritage List (962 after the 36th Session of the World Heritage Committee, held in Saint Petersburg from 24 June to 6 July 2012),[32] and paradoxically, in recent years has triggered concerns about the effective sustainability of the system of the Convention and the measures to be adopted in order to prevent its collapse.[33]

---

28 *See* G. P. Buzzini and L. Condorelli, "List of World Heritage in Danger", in Francioni (ed., with Lenzerini), *supra* note 19, 175 (elaborating on the List of World Heritage in Danger).

29 Article 11(4) World Heritage Convention (according to which the List of World Heritage in Danger "may include only such property forming part of the cultural and natural heritage as is threatened by serious and specific dangers, such as the threat of disappearance caused by accelerated deterioration, large-scale public or private projects or rapid urban or tourist development projects; destruction caused by changes in the use or ownership of the land; major alterations due to unknown causes; abandonment for any reason whatsoever; the outbreak or the threat of an armed conflict; calamities and cataclysms; serious fires, earthquakes, landslides; volcanic eruptions; changes in water level, floods, and tidal waves.").

30 *See* F. Lenzerini, "Articles 15–16: World Heritage Fund", in Francioni (ed., with Lenzerini), *supra* note 19, 269.

31 *See* A. Lemaistre and F. Lenzerini, "Articles 19–26: International Assistance", in Francioni (ed., with Lenzerini), *supra* note 19, 305.

32 *See World Heritage List, available at* http://whc.unesco.org/en/list (last visited on 10 July 2012).

33 Among these measures, the so-called *Cairns Decision* is worth mentioning, adopted by the World Heritage Committee at its 24th Session (Cairns, Australia, 27 November-2 December 2000), which limited the number of nominations that may be submitted to the Committee by

Apart from this problem of management, the World Heritage Convention is also marked by some notable shortcomings, mainly deriving from the hybrid characterization of its provisions as the result of compromise between the traditional idea of State sovereignty (which in the 1970s still permeated the generally-shared vision of international law) and the conception of cultural (and natural) properties as 'World Heritage.'[34] The recognition of the supreme sovereignty of States over the World Heritage located within their respective territories (irrespective of its 'outstanding universal value') is first of all reflected in the rigid requirement of the territorial State's consent to the inscription of a property on the World Heritage List.[35] This, in particular, prevents heritage sites from being included within the scope of operation of the Convention when the government concerned is, for whatever reason, unwilling to propose its inscription on the List or unable to comply with the logistic, administrative and organizational requirements to be fulfilled in order to make such an inscription possible. This inherent limit of the World Heritage Convention system appears quite unreasonable if viewed through the perspective of the *raison d'être* of the Convention itself, namely the goal of providing protection for heritage sites of outstanding universal value in the general interest of humanity, and not in the interest of the territorial State in which it is located. Equivalent considerations apply with respect to the rule set up by Article 19, according to which international assistance for a property inscribed on the World Heritage List (as well as on the List of World Heritage in Danger) may be provided *only* at the request of the territorial State in which the property is located. Also, the deference of the Convention to the principle of State sovereignty generally hinders the possibility of extending protection to sites over which sovereignty is claimed by more than one government or that are located in areas beyond State sovereignty.

In principle, the weight of the shortcomings just mentioned should be eased by the fact that, pursuant to the World Heritage Convention, the circumstance that a cultural or natural property is of outstanding universal value corresponds to an objective state qualifying the property for protection under the Convention, irrespective of whether it is inscribed on either of the two lists contemplated by article 11. This principle is expressly stated by Article 12, according to which "[t]he fact that a property belonging to the cultural or natural heritage has not been included in either of the two lists mentioned in paragraphs 2 and 4 of Article 11 shall in no way be construed to mean that it does not have an

a State party each year for inscription on the World Heritage List, recognizing a preferential treatment to those parties having no properties already inscribed on the List. See Scovazzi, *supra note* 25.

34 *See* F. Francioni and F. Lenzerini, "The Future of the World Heritage Convention: Problems and Prospects", in Francioni (ed., with Lenzerini), *supra* note 19, 401.

35 *See* F. Francioni, "Thirty Years On: Is the World Heritage Convention Ready for the 21st Century?", XII *Italian Yearbook of International Law* 13, 30 (2002).

outstanding universal value for purposes other than those resulting from inclusion in these lists." Nevertheless, this provision is virtually meaningless in practice, since its potential effects have been almost entirely nullified, so far, in the context of the implementation of the Convention, which has been characterized by the trend towards considering only properties inscribed on the World Heritage List as capable of benefiting of actual protection and international assistance.[36]

In any event, despite its shortcomings and the scarcity of effective State obligations in its text, which is characterized by a clear prevalence of rights and advantages over legal obligations in the technical sense of the term, and at least with respect to the properties inscribed on the World Heritage List, the World Heritage Convention has proven in the practice actually capable of pursuing its main goal, namely, to ensure the proper preservation of the integrity of such sites and to inhibit action by territorial governments potentially inconsistent with such a goal. Although, in fact, in most cases the advantages obtained by a State Party as a result of the inscription of a property on the List translate into huge benefits in terms of international visibility and economic profit, which greatly overcome the potentially adverse effects it may produce, there are important examples in the implementation of the Convention of development projects that certain countries have been forced to abandon due to possible negative consequences with respect to the integrity of a property inscribed on the World Heritage List.

In almost all such cases the World Heritage Committee has proven able to persuade the States concerned to give up their projects through reminding them of their obligations pursuant to the Convention and, especially, through threatening them with inscribing the relevant sites on the List of World Heritage in Danger (which may be catastrophic for a government in terms of international visibility when such an inscription is due to its own mismanagement of the property) in the event that such a project was carried out.[37] Only in two cases, taking place in 2007 and 2009 respectively, States Parties incurred in violations of the Convention so serious to persuade the Committee to delete properties

36 *See* F. Lenzerini, "Article 12: Protection of Properties Not Inscribed on the World Heritage List", in Francioni (ed., with Lenzerini), *supra* note 19, 201.

37 See, in particular, the long controversy over the Australian Kakadu National Park (concerning an expansive uranium mining project in a territory which, in addition of being inscribed on the World Heritage List, was considered sacred by the local Aboriginal communities) as well as the cases of Machu Picchu (where in 2001 the government of Peru had planned the construction of a cableway in order to facilitate access to the site by tourists) and of the Whale Sanctuary of El Vizcaino (which the Mexican government, in cooperation with the Japanese multinational corporation Mitsubishi, intended to use for the exploitation of salt mines). These cases are described in details by F. Lenzerini, "Lo'sfruttamento minerario sostenibile' come principio emergente nel diritto internazionale contemporaneo" ['Sustainable Mining' as Emerging Principle of Contemporary International Law], 1 *Rivista Giuridica dell'Ambiente* 165 (2004).

from the World Heritage List. The first of these decisions concerned the site of the Arabian Oryx Sanctuary, located in Oman, after the national government had decided to reduce the size of the protected area by 90 per cent with the purpose of developing hydrocarbon exploration activities within the original boundaries of the site, leading the property, in the view of the Committee, to "[deteriorate] to the extent [of loosing] its Outstanding Universal Value and integrity."[38] The other case related to the German Dresden Elbe Valley, which was delisted after a four-lane bridge was built in the heart of the area delimiting the property, also leading to the loss of its outstanding universal value.[39]

4. THE INTERACTION BETWEEN THE CONVENTION ON THE DIVERSITY OF CULTURAL EXPRESSIONS AND THE WORLD HERITAGE CONVENTION

Given the radically different aspects of culture addressed by the Convention on the Diversity of Cultural Expressions and the World Heritage Convention, it may *prima facie* appear that there are no significant elements of interaction between them. In reality, their co-existence in the international legal arena raises some interesting issues which deserve detailed analysis.

4.1. MUTUAL SUPPORTIVENESS IN INTERPRETATION

The first element of interaction between the Convention on the Diversity of Cultural Expressions and the World Heritage Convention lies in the mutual support provided by each of the two instruments with respect to the other in the context of the interpretation of their respective provisions, pursuant to Article 31(3)(c) of the *Vienna Convention on the Law of Treaties* ("Vienna Convention") of 1969.[40] According to this provision, in interpreting an international treaty 'any relevant rules of international law applicable in the relations between the parties' are to be taken into account, together with the context of the treaty itself. This is also consistent with Article 20(a) of the Convention on the Diversity of Cultural Expressions, which, in requesting States Parties to "foster mutual supportiveness between this Convention and the other treaties to which they are

38 UNESCO, World Heritage Committee, Decision 31 COM 7B.11, *WHC-07/31.COM/24* (31 July 2007).

39 *See* "Dresden is deleted from UNESCO's World Heritage List", 25 June 2009, *available at* http://whc.unesco.org/en/news/522 (last visited on 2 February 2012).

40 Vienna Convention on the Law of Treaties, 23 May 1969, 1155 *UNTS* 331.

parties," clearly refers to support to be provided, in essence, in the context of the interpretation of the treaties concerned.

In particular, the Convention on the Diversity of Cultural Expressions may be used as a tool for the evolutionary interpretation of the World Heritage Convention. Such an approach should lead to understanding the basic parameters of the World Heritage Convention, namely the 'outstanding universal value' of the manifestations of cultural heritage to be protected, as taking into account not only the 'objective' significance of a given cultural item according to standardized criteria, including those of aesthetic, artistic or architectural character, but also its value under a diversity-based perspective on culture, so as to include its spiritual and social significance for the specific groups and communities concerned. Such an approach should translate into a revision of the original conception of the parameters of outstanding universal value as based exclusively on the circumstance that a property is considered of great importance and significance by at least 'a large or significant segment of humanity,' as emphasized by the World Heritage Committee at its very first session.[41]

The recognition of the significance for the international community of the diversity of cultural expressions, epitomized by the Convention on the Diversity of Cultural Expressions, should lead to an acknowledgement that a property may be of outstanding universal value when it is of special importance for a given people or community as an essential part of its distinctive identity, although it is not immediately recognizable as such by the majority of the international community. In such a way, the value of cultural diversity would be effectively incorporated within the scope of the World Heritage Convention, which would prove sufficiently dynamic to respond to the evolution that has characterized the view of culture and cultural heritage in the international legal community in recent times. This would be feasible, in practice, through the adoption by the World Heritage Committee of a pluralistic and diversity-oriented approach, which is today actually facilitated by the presence in the *Operational Guidelines for the Implementation of the World Heritage Convention* of a criterion for inscription on the World Heritage List according to which the requirement of outstanding universal value is satisfied when the proposed property "bear[s] a unique or at least exceptional testimony to a cultural tradition or to a civilization which is living or which has disappeared."[42]

---

41 *See* UNESCO, World Heritage Committee, "Issues Arising in Connection with the Implementation of the World Heritage Convention", *Doc. CC-77/CONF.001/4*, §17 (9 June 1977), *available at* http://unesdoc.unesco.org/images/0003/000309/030934EB.pdf (last visited on 2 February 2012).

42 UNESCO, Intergovernmental Committee for the Protection of World Cultural and Natural Heritage, *Operational Guidelines for the Implementation of the World Heritage Convention*, §77(iii) (November 2011), *available at* http://whc.unesco.org/archive/opguide11-en.pdf (last visited on 2 February 2012).

It is to be noted that the above approach is demanded not only by the general rules of treaty interpretation provided for by the Vienna Convention, which reproduce corresponding obligations from customary international law, but also by the Convention on the Diversity of Cultural Expressions itself, which requires States Parties, "when interpreting and applying the other treaties to which they are parties or when entering into other international obligations, [to] take into account the relevant provisions of this Convention."[43] This rule is reinforced by the provision of Article 21, which requires Parties to "undertake to promote the objectives and principles of this Convention in other international forums."[44]

Needless to say that, in any event, an evolution in the interpretation of the World Heritage Convention carried out on the basis of the spirit and the rules of the Convention on the Diversity of Cultural Expressions may not in any way imply a modification of the rights and obligation ensuing for State Parties from the World Heritage Convention itself. This is also made clear by Article 20(2) of the Convention on the Diversity of Cultural Expressions, according to which "[n]othing in this Convention shall be interpreted as modifying rights and obligations of the Parties under any other treaties to which they are parties."[45]

The support the World Heritage Convention might provide for the interpretation of the Convention on the Diversity of Cultural Expressions is less evident. However, it is to be considered that, given the definition of the concept of 'cultural expressions' adopted by the latter Convention as "those expressions that result from the creativity of individuals, groups and societies, and that have cultural content,"[46] it is also possible that World Heritage sites are suitable for inclusion within the scope of this concept. When this happens, the provisions of the Convention on the Diversity of Cultural Expressions will be interpreted taking into full account the fact that the site concerned is protected by the World Heritage Convention in the general interest of humanity. As a consequence, the interests of the owners of such a site, viewed as a 'cultural expression' under the Convention on the Diversity of Cultural Expressions, will be balanced with the interests of the international community as a whole regarding the property, considered as World Heritage.

4.2. COMPLEMENTARITY

The way in which the Convention on the Diversity of Cultural Expressions complements the World Heritage Convention in finalizing the action of the

43 Convention on the Diversity of Cultural Expressions, *supra* note 1, Article 20(b).
44 Id., Article 21.
45 Id., Article 20(2).
46 Id., Article 4(3).

international community for the safeguarding of culture and cultural heritage, previously noted in Section 1, is also worth exploring in more detail.

Taking into account the various meanings that cultural heritage may have for humanity – considered not only in its whole, but also as the aggregation of an indefinite number of different groups and communities, all bearing different identities and cultural idiosyncrasies – the Convention on the Diversity of Cultural Expressions, together with the ICH Convention, fills a major gap in relevant law. In particular, the development of the idea of cultural diversity derives from the recognition that cultural heritage is of significance and worth safeguarding not only under an objective perspective, on the basis of standardized and, to a certain extent, stereotyped criteria, but also according to a subjective vision of culture evaluated in relation to the importance of a given cultural expression as a fundamental element of the identity of a community. This "subjective" approach is at the very heart of the Convention on the Diversity of Cultural Expressions, and permeates its whole text. It may first of all be detected in the Preamble, where the fact that "the diversity of cultural expressions [...] is an important factor that allows individuals and peoples to express and to share with others their ideas and values"[47] is recognized, as well as "the importance of the vitality of cultures, including for persons belonging to minorities and indigenous peoples, as manifested in their freedom to create, disseminate and distribute their traditional cultural expressions and to have access thereto, so as to benefit them for their own development."[48] It is also expressed in Article 1, where, among the objectives pursued by the Convention, the purpose of giving "recognition to the distinctive nature of cultural activities, goods and services as vehicles of *identity*, values and meaning"[49] is stressed. Also, as already noted,[50] this subjective approach clearly emerges from the accepted concept of 'cultural diversity,' defined by Article 4(1) as "the manifold ways in which the cultures of groups and societies find expression."[51] Last but not least, this approach finds expression in Article 7, where, among the measures aimed at promoting cultural expressions, it is recommended that States Parties create in their respective territories a favourable environment for encouraging 'individuals and social groups' to 'create, produce, disseminate, distribute and have access to *their own* cultural expressions.'[52]

The complementarity between the Convention on the Diversity of Cultural Expressions and the World Heritage Convention rests exactly on the circumstance that, taken together, the two instruments offer a comprehensive

47 Id., Preamble §13.
48 Id., Preamble §15.
49 Id., Article 1(g) [emphasis added].
50 *See supra* note 15 (corresponding text).
51 Convention on the Diversity of Cultural Expressions, *supra* note 1, Article 4(1).
52 Id., Article 7(1)(a) [emphasis added].

framework of protection covering both the global interests of humanity in tangible cultural heritage, evaluated on the basis of its 'objective' significance, as well as the 'subjective' value of living culture and cultural expressions for the groups and communities which reflect their own distinctive identity in these expressions.

4.3. POTENTIAL CONFLICTS

The description of the interaction of the Convention on the Diversity of Cultural Expressions with the World Heritage Convention should be followed by a consideration of the dark side of the coin. In fact, although no significant overlap seems to exist between the two conventions, there are potential points of conflict between them. This is due to the fact that, while the World Heritage Convention fosters a 'static' model of protection, aimed at preserving the original integrity of tangible cultural and natural items, the Convention on the Diversity of Cultural Expressions provides for a inherently dynamic form of safeguarding, in the context of which the manifestations of any culture are subject to change, in parallel with the natural evolution of the society of which they are an expression.

As previously noted, it is plain that a property inscribed on the World Heritage List may be included within the concept of cultural expressions, as defined by Article 4 of the Convention on the Diversity of Cultural Expressions.[53] When this happens, two opposing priorities may arise from the two conventions at issue: on the one hand, the World Heritage Convention is aimed at preserving the original integrity of the property concerned, presupposing the requirement that it be maintained unchanged according to its original physical status; on the other hand, the fact that such World Heritage property represents an essential element of a living culture may imply the need to allow it to be modified, so that it responds to the cultural evolution of the social groups it represents.

Many properties on the World Heritage List present themselves as the hybridised result of the various vicissitudes that have characterized their history. To illustrate, one may refer to the *Mezquita* of the Spanish city of Cordoba,[54] an outstanding combination of Islamic architecture and Christian art. It was constructed as a mosque by the Emir Abd ar-Rahman in 785 A.D. and was later complemented by a Christian cathedral, built inside the mosque in the 16th Century, after the end of the Islamic domination of Spain. The

53 See *supra* note 46 (corresponding text).

54 *See* "Historic Centre of Cordoba", *available at* http://whc.unesco.org/en/list/313 (last visited on 2 February 2012).

building of the cathedral inside the mosque was the natural result of the fact that the *Mezquita* had represented, since its construction, the very heart of the city, thus bearing a spiritual significance for the identity of all citizens of Cordoba. It would clearly have been illogical, at the relevant time, to take the view that the original integrity of the site, as a fundamental element of living culture of the place where it is located, was to be maintained unchanged, as it represented the vestiges of a foreign domination which no longer existed and was consequently extraneous to the identity of the people which were intended to take advantage of it.

What would the legal state of affairs be if a similar situation, or a less obvious case which would in some way require a physical modification of the site concerned, arose today with respect to a property inscribed on the World Heritage List? It is clear how in this event the requirement of preserving the integrity of a World Heritage property, provided for by the World Heritage Convention, could clash with the need to ensure its adjustment to the evolution of the groups whose cultural identity was reflected in the property concerned, which is implicitly endorsed by the Convention on the Diversity of Cultural Expressions (evidence for which includes Paragraph 16 of the Preamble, emphasizing "the vital role of cultural interaction and creativity, which nurture and *renew* cultural expressions"[55]).

Which value should be considered to take precedence over the other should such an eventuality occur? I would suggest that the evolution of the interpretation of the World Heritage Convention – in line with the consolidated development of international law on cultural heritage toward a 'holistic' vision of culture – would require that the obligation to ensure the 'preservation' of a World Heritage property should be viewed in a manner dynamic enough to allow minimal changes to its physical structure that are indispensable in order to adapt it to the cultural evolution of the communities whose identity is reflected by it, but do not lead to a drastic modification of its original connotation or to the loss of its outstanding value. When feasible in practice, this course of action would in no way result in a modification of the rights and obligations of States Parties under the World Heritage Convention (which, as previously noted, is explicitly prohibited by Article 20(2) of the Convention on the Diversity of Cultural Expressions), but would simply represent a reasonable balance between the two conventions as well as an interpretation of the World Heritage Convention in line with the rule expressed by Article 31(3)(c) of the Vienna Convention and by customary international law.[56]

---

55 Convention on the Diversity of Cultural Expressions, *supra* note 1, Preamble §16 [emphasis added].

56 *See, generally*, U. Linderfalk, *On the Interpretation of Treaties: The Modern International Law as Expressed in the 1969 Vienna Convention on the Law of Treaties*, 2007.

5. CONCLUSION

Cultural heritage represents an essential element of the life of any person. The identity of each of us is mirrored in the tangible and intangible elements of our personal culture, and our personality finds realization in the expressions in which our own cultural heritage is concretely translated. This significance of culture as an indispensable constituent for the personal realization of any human being connected with the fundamental values of human rights and dignity has been discovered by the international community only in recent times. In this respect, the idea that culture goes beyond a collection of buildings and other tangible objects which are considered as valuable according to 'objective' criteria has eventually been translated into the adoption in 2005 of the Convention on the Diversity of Cultural Expressions. This instrument represents a major triumph for the international community, but it is important to bear in mind that it is not to be evaluated and implemented in isolation from the other international instruments aimed at protecting cultural heritage. On the contrary, it is essential to remember that culture finds contextual expression both in the great treasures of human genius, which represent the union of the different peoples of the world under common pride in being part of humanity, and in the richness of the diverse cultural identities of all communities, each unique and inherently irreplaceable. It is especially in light of this twofold meaning of culture that the interaction between the Convention on the Diversity of Cultural Expressions and the World Heritage Convention is to be considered, bearing in mind the mutual complementarity of these instruments in ensuring the adequacy and effectiveness of actions taken by the international community for the protection of culture and cultural heritage, in light of the contemporary values pursued by the human family.

INTANGIBLE CULTURAL HERITAGE AND THE CONVENTION ON THE DIVERSITY OF CULTURAL EXPRESSIONS

Steven VAN UYTSEL* and Toshiyuki KONO**

1. INTRODUCTION

Immediately after the adoption of the Convention for the Safeguarding of Intangible Cultural Heritage ("ICH Convention")[1] in 2003, UNESCO faced a new challenge. UNESCO had to find an answer to the delicate issue of how to deal with the audiovisual sector within a globalizing world driven by a free trade orientated international regime. Within a time span of two years, UNESCO drafted a binding legal instrument to this end. The result was the Convention for the Promotion and the Protection of the Diversity of Cultural Expressions ("Convention on the Diversity of Cultural Expressions"),[2] adopted in 2005.

By focusing on expressions, the Convention on the Diversity of Cultural Expressions may well link with the ICH Convention. Indeed, intangible cultural heritage can manifest itself in *expressions* that communities, groups, and individuals have created in response to their environment, their interaction with nature, and their history, thus providing them with a sense of identity.[3] Furthermore, 'safeguarding' – the purpose of the ICH Convention – is also to be found in the Convention on the Diversity of Cultural Expressions. 'Protection', which is one of the aims of the Convention on the Diversity of Cultural Expressions, is defined as 'safeguarding'.[4]

---

* LL.B (1994) & LL.M. (1997) (University of Antwerp); LL.M (1998) & LL.D. (2005) Kyushu University. Associate Professor, Kyushu University Faculty of Law.

** Professor of Law, Kyushu University Faculty of Law.

1 *See* Convention for the Safeguarding of the Intangible Cultural Heritage, 17 October 2003, *U.N. Doc. MISC/2003/CLT/CH/14* [hereinafter "ICH Convention"].

2 *See* Convention on the Protection and Promotion of the Diversity of Cultural Expressions, 20 October 2005, *U.N. Doc. CLT-2005/CONVENTION DIVERSITE-CULT REV.* [hereinafter "Convention on the Diversity of Cultural Expressions"].

3 *See* ICH Convention, *supra* note 1, Article 2.

4 *See* Convention on the Diversity of Cultural Expressions, *supra* note 2, Article 4(7).

Considering that the Convention on the Diversity of Cultural Expressions has been conceptualized in such a way that its object and objectives could partially overlap with those of the ICH Convention, further study on how the two conventions relate to each other is warranted. Two main lines of arguments must be developed. First, on the presumption that the Convention on the Diversity of Cultural Expressions and the ICH Convention share some of their objects and objectives in common, the relationship on the operational level has to be analysed. Second, on the premise that both conventions are part of the whole body of public international law, to what extent each of these conventions can be used to interpret the other convention has to be investigated.

To develop these arguments, this Chapter will have two major parts. The first part will deal with the relationship between the conventions at the operational level. Within this part, we will analyse how the two conventions relate to each other in case the provisions of the conventions are mutually supportive. Further, we will also indicate what the solution is in case the conventions have conflicting provisions. The second part will elaborate on how the conventions relate to each other for interpretative purposes. Phrased differently, we will stipulate to what extent the Convention on the Diversity of Cultural Expressions can be used to interpret the ICH Convention and vice versa.

2. ESTABLISHING A COMMON FRAMEWORK

2.1. INTANGIBLE CULTURAL HERITAGE, CULTURAL EXPRESSIONS AND SAFEGUARDING

The ICH Convention states in Article 1(a) that its purpose is the safeguarding of intangible cultural heritage. Following the statement of purpose, the ICH Convention defines intangible cultural heritage as the "practices, representations, *expressions*, knowledge, skills ... that communities, groups and, in some cases, individuals recognize as part of their cultural heritage."[5] It is further important that the intangible cultural heritage is transmitted from generation to generation and constantly recreated by communities and groups in response to their environment, their interaction with nature, and their history in order to provide them with a sense of identity and continuity.[6]

The Convention on the Diversity of Cultural Expressions, after stipulating that the protection and promotion of the diversity of cultural expressions is one of its purposes, defines cultural expressions as "those *expressions* that result from the creativity of individuals, groups or societies, and that have cultural

---

5 ICH Convention, *supra* note 1, Article 2 (emphasis added).

6 *See* id.

content."[7] Comparing this part with the definition of intangible cultural heritage from the ICH Convention, it becomes obvious that the words 'expressions', 'individual' and 'group' are common to both conventions. At this point, it is worthwhile to indicate that the ICH Convention consistently uses 'community', whereas the Convention on the Diversity of Cultural Expressions refers to 'societies'. Further, it should be noted that the expressions must be created by these individuals, groups and communities or societies.

It is possible to argue that the definition of intangible cultural heritage in the ICH Convention is much more refined and that, therefore, the object of the ICH Convention is much more specific than the Convention on the Diversity of Cultural Expressions. Indeed, the ICH Convention has an idea of identity and continuity interwoven in its definition of intangible cultural heritage. By not only looking at the definition of cultural expressions, but also at other definitions in the Convention on the Diversity of Cultural Expressions, it may, however, be possible to construct similar ideas and attribute them to cultural expressions.[8] Taking into consideration the last part of the cultural expressions definition, specifically the reference to 'cultural content', the idea of identity can be brought within the scope of the Convention on the Diversity of Cultural Expressions. Indeed, it is required that the cultural expressions have a symbolic meaning, artistic dimension, and cultural values that originate from and express cultural identities.[9] Hence, the cultural expressions reflect the identity of the individuals, groups, or societies creating those expressions. The Convention on the Diversity of Cultural Expressions does not mention that the identity has to be the result of a response to the environment, an interaction with nature, or history.

The idea of continuity, reflected in the ICH Convention by references to the transmission and recreation of intangible cultural heritage, can be established in two different ways in the Convention on the Diversity of Cultural Expressions. First, the symbolic meaning, artistic dimension, and cultural values can originate from cultural identity.[10] What else could this mean than that some meaning, dimension, or value that existed within a cultural identity has been recreated as a response to some change? Second, the definition of cultural diversity explicitly indicates that the expressions are passed on within groups or societies. Undeniably, this will include the passing on through different generations within these groups and societies.[11]

Before concluding that there is a common object, as long as we are investigating how communities and societies relate to each other, there is yet another element that deserves some consideration. The common framework

7 Convention on the Diversity of Cultural Expressions, *supra* note 2, Article 4(3) (emphasis added).

8 *See* Convention on the Diversity of Cultural Expressions, *supra* note 2, Article 4(2) and (3).

9 *See* id., Article 4(2).

10 *See* id., Article 4(2).

11 *See* id., Article 4(1).

between the two conventions is not only created by a shared object, but also by a shared objective. Whereas the objective of the ICH Convention lies in safeguarding,[12] the Convention on the Diversity of Cultural Expressions aims at protecting and promoting.[13] At first sight, these objectives do not relate to each other. However, considering that the Convention on the Diversity of Cultural Expressions includes safeguarding within the definition of protection, it could be argued that both conventions share common objectives.

Arguing that the two conventions have shared objectives will inevitably lead us to the definition of safeguarding within the ICH Convention. 'Safeguarding' in the ICH Convention is conceptualized as being aimed at the viability of intangible cultural heritage. Even though such a definition is lacking in the Convention on the Diversity of Cultural Expressions, Article 8, which stipulates the reasons for taking protective measures, indicates that, among other risks, the risk of extinction justifies protection. As 'safeguarding' is part of the meaning of protection within the Convention on the Diversity of Cultural Expressions, no other conclusion could be drawn than that safeguarding in this Convention also aims at ensuring viability and survival.

2.2. COMMUNITIES: PART OF THE CONVENTION ON THE DIVERSITY OF CULTURAL EXPRESSIONS?

One of the important issues to be resolved in order to establish a common framework between the ICH Convention and the Convention on the Diversity of Cultural Expressions is the consistent divergence in the use of 'communities' and 'societies'. The central question regarding this issue is whether these concepts are mutually exclusive or whether one of them can encompass the other. In order to resolve this question, reference will be made to Ferdinand Tönnies, who extensively described the distinction between communities and societies in his famous work *Gemeinschaft und Gesellschaft*.[14]

Tönnies distinguishes *Gemeinschaft* (community) from *Gesellschaft* (society) by the intensity of the relationship. *Gemeinschaft*, or community, stems from a natural will among individuals to be linked together, which explains the loyalty of the individuals towards the community. The will to belong together is based on shared beliefs, places or kinship.[15] *Gesellschaft*, or society, on the contrary, is vested in more instrumental relations. Rational will of individuals is the driving force behind the larger group of individuals that is called society. Therefore,

12 *See* ICH Convention, *supra* note 1, Article 1.

13 *See* Convention on the Diversity of Cultural Expressions, *supra* note 2, Article 3.

14 *See* F. Tönnies, *Gemeinschaft und Gesellschaft: Grundbegriffe der reinen Soziologie* (Ch. P. Loomis, transl. & ed., Harper Torchbooks, 1957), 1887.

15 *See* id., at 33–95; *See also* B. Hazucha, "Community as a Holder of Intangible Cultural Heritage: A Broader Public Policy Perspective", in T. Kono (ed.), *Intangible Cultural Heritage and Intellectual Property: Communities, Cultural Diversity and Sustainable Development*, 2009, 227.

entering into a community and being part of a community as its representative will be much more difficult compared to a society.[16]

Given the differences between the two concepts, 'society' and 'community' cannot be used interchangeably. This does not mean, however, that the concepts in the real world are mutually exclusive. It is not that either a community or a society exists. Tönnies agrees that community characteristics can persist within a society, implying that several communities together could be part of a society. Within this societal structure, Tönnies predicts that the community characteristics will linger and decay. Eventually, this may lead to the disappearance of the community.[17]

Even though 'society' and 'community' do not mutually exclude each other's existence, these concepts have a different dimension. Therefore, cultural expressions from a society will not necessarily coincide with the ones from a community. Neither will cultural expressions from a community reflect the ones from a society as a whole. Does that mean that both conventions only share the same object in relation to groups and individuals? Phrased differently, and within the boundaries of this section, is the shared object between the ICH Convention and the Convention on the Diversity of Cultural Expressions extremely limited in scope?

To unravel the conundrum of whether the shared scope between the ICH Convention and the Convention on the Diversity of Cultural Expressions is limited or not, the scope of the Convention on the Diversity of Cultural Expressions could form a useful starting point. Looking at the inclusion of the word 'society' in various provisions defining cultural expressions,[18] the Convention on the Diversity of Cultural Expressions has indicated that its scope extends at least to a level beyond 'community'. What sense would it make for a convention to include various smaller units within a society, such as individuals and groups, and disregard others, like communities?

Communities, just like individuals and groups, could have expressions that they have created and that have given them a sense of identity. This is implied in the wording of the ICH Convention. By not mentioning communities in the Convention on the Diversity of Cultural Expressions, an impression is created that community expressions in particular are not worth protecting and promoting.

Yet, this would lead to a very awkward situation. On the one hand, we have a convention aiming at the diversity of cultural expressions, while on the other hand this convention would not care about certain cultural expressions. Such a stance would inherently be contrary to the aim of protecting and promoting diversity. Rather, diversity of expressions would be jeopardized by this

16 *See* Tönnies, *supra* note 14, at 33–95.

17 *See* id., at 223–59.

18 *See* Convention on the Diversity of Cultural Expressions, *supra* note 2, Article 4(1), (3), and (6).

interpretation of the Convention on the Diversity of Cultural Expressions. One way out of this conundrum would be to regard society not only as a reference to society as a whole, but also as a collective concept embracing all the different units it can comprise. This may well be so, especially since the Convention on the Diversity of Cultural Expressions replaces the word 'society' with 'social groups' elsewhere in the convention.[19]

3. INTERACTION AT THE OPERATIONAL LEVEL

3.1. MUTUALLY SUPPORTING OBLIGATIONS AND CONFLICTING ONES

States having expressions falling under both the ICH Convention and the Convention on the Diversity of Cultural Expressions will face the obligation to comply with both conventions. Two different scenarios are imaginable. The obligations under the ICH Convention and the Convention on the Diversity of Cultural Expressions may mutually support each other. It is perfectly possible for States to fulfil their duties under both conventions simultaneously. A different scenario will present itself if the obligations in the two conventions conflict with each other. A choice has to be made regarding which obligations have priority and thus must be complied with. Before turning to these issues, an overview will be provided of the different obligations within the two conventions and how they relate to each other.

The ICH Convention makes a distinction between obligations that are orientated at the national level[20] and ones that are directed at the international level.[21] Within the first category of obligations, taking safeguarding measures and setting up an inventory are the most strongly formulated ones.[22] The Convention on the Diversity of Cultural Expressions, without the strong language of 'shall' in its provisions,[23] encourages its Parties to promote or protect cultural expressions.[24] Whereas protection relates more to cultural expressions at risk of extinction, and is thus better discussed in relation to the ICH Convention's obligations at the international level, it is sufficient to indicate at this stage that the obligations under the Convention on the Diversity of Cultural

19 *See* id., Article 7.
20 *See* ICH Convention, *supra* note 1, Articles 11, 12, 13, 14, and 15.
21 *See* id., Articles 16, 17, and 18.
22 *See* id., Articles 11, 12, and 13.
23 *See* Convention on the Diversity of Cultural Expressions, *supra* note 2, Articles 6 and 7.
24 *See, e.g.*, R. Craufurd Smith, "The UNESCO Convention on the Protection and Promotion of the Diversity of Cultural Expressions: Building a New World Information and Communication Order?", 1 *International Journal of Communication* 24, 39 (2007).

Expressions align well with national level safeguarding and inventory-making under the ICH Convention.

At the international level, the focus is on the creation of a Representative List of Intangible Cultural Heritage of Humanity to ensure better visibility,[25] and a List of Intangible Cultural Heritage in Need of Urgent Safeguarding to deal with cases in which the viability of intangible cultural heritage is endangered.[26] Even though the Convention on the Diversity of Cultural Expressions does not aim at creating obligations at the international level, Article 8 encourages its Member States to take appropriate measures for cultural expressions that are at risk of extinction or facing any other serious threat. In this sense, the Convention on the Diversity of Cultural Expressions adds to the international obligations under the ICH Convention.

The ICH Convention and the Convention on the Diversity of Cultural Expressions do not always complement or support each other. One of the conflicts arises out of the definitions of intangible cultural heritage and cultural expressions. The ICH Convention emphasizes the role of the community in relation to safeguarding intangible cultural heritage,[27] while the Convention on the Diversity of Cultural Expressions consistently broadens it to society.[28] This distinction is further delineated by both conventions' handling of participation. The ICH Convention limits participation to groups and communities,[29] while the Convention on the Diversity of Cultural Expressions opens participation to civil society generally.[30]

Another point of divergence between the ICH Convention and the Convention on the Diversity of Cultural Expressions concerns the purpose of international cooperation. The ICH Convention aims at international cooperation for safeguarding purposes and thus the enhancement of the viability of intangible cultural heritage.[31] The Convention on the Diversity of Cultural Expressions envisages poverty eradication via international cooperation.[32] This divergence has been further articulated in the way the respective Intergovernmental Committees have conceptualized their funds. The Fund for the Safeguarding of the Intangible Cultural Heritage will be primarily used to facilitate international assistance.[33] The Fund for Cultural Diversity should support cooperation for sustainable development and poverty reduction in order to foster the emergence of a dynamic cultural sector in developing countries.[34]

25 *See* ICH Convention, *supra* note 1, Article 16.
26 *See* id., Article 17.
27 *See* id., Article 2.
28 *See* Convention on the Diversity of Cultural Expressions, *supra* note 2, Article 4(1), (3), and (6).
29 *See* ICH Convention, *supra* note 1, Article 15.
30 *See* Convention on the Diversity of Cultural Expressions, *supra* note 2, Article 11.
31 *See* ICH Convention, *supra* note 1, Article 20.
32 *See* Convention on the Diversity of Cultural Expressions, *supra* note 2, Article 14.
33 *See* ICH Convention, *supra* note 1, Article 25.
34 *See* Convention on the Diversity of Cultural Expressions, *supra* note 2, Article 18.

3.2. CONFLICT REGULATING PROVISIONS

The ICH Convention does not have any provisions stipulating its dealings with future treaties. The only provision dealing with other international instruments is the one found in Article 3, which relates to the World Heritage Convention,[35] intellectual property, and biological and ecological resources.[36] Hence, this article is not helpful in the context of this chapter.

The Convention on the Diversity of Cultural Expressions, on the other hand, contains a provision dealing with other instruments. The part of utmost importance within that particular provision is the one dealing with conflicts of obligations. In this respect, it is important to note that nothing that has been inscribed in the Convention on the Diversity of Cultural Expressions should be used to modify obligations that stem from other conventions.[37] Due to the fact that the Convention on the Diversity of Cultural Expressions cannot change the obligations under other conventions, it follows that in cases of conflicting obligations, supremacy should be given to the obligations under the other conventions.[38] Within the context of this chapter, this means that the obligations under the ICH Convention will prevail over the ones inscribed in the Convention on the Diversity of Cultural Expressions.

If conflicting obligations give rise to the supremacy of the Convention on the Diversity of Cultural Expressions, the non-subordination clause within this provision only applies to the non-conflicting obligations. Only when the obligations under both conventions mutually support each other must State Parties aim at implementing these obligations. In practice, this will mean that, unless the conventions stipulate identical obligations, a cumulative approach towards implementation has to be taken into consideration.

---

35 *See* ICH Convention, *supra* note 1, Article 3 (stating that nothing in the ICH Convention should be interpreted as "altering the status or diminishing the level of protection under the 1972 Convention concerning the Protection of the World Cultural and Natural Heritage of World Heritage properties with which an item of the intangible cultural heritage is directly associated").

36 *See* id. (providing that the ICH Convention cannot affect "the rights and obligations of States Parties deriving from any international instrument relating to intellectual property rights or to the use of biological and ecological resources to which they are parties").

37 *See* Convention on the Diversity of Cultural Expressions, *supra* note 2, Article 20(2) ("2. Nothing in this Convention shall be interpreted as modifying rights and obligations of the Parties under any other treaties to which they are parties.").

38 *See*, e.g., J. Wouters and B. De Meester, "Cultural Diversity and the WTO: David Versus Goliath", in H. Schneider and P. Van den Bossche (eds.), *Protection of Cultural Diversity from a European and International Perspective*, 2008, 128 (arguing that the conflict clause of the Convention on the Diversity of Cultural Expressions is unambiguous. The clause leaves little room for allowing policies that would go against provisions of other international conventions).

3.3. MUTUAL SUPPORTIVENESS BY IMPLEMENTING A DOUBLE SCHEME

Parties to the ICH Convention thus have to establish a national inventory for intangible cultural heritage. Expressions that qualify under the definition of intangible cultural heritage will have to be part of that inventory.[39] Some of these expressions may also qualify as cultural expressions under the Convention on the Diversity of Cultural Expressions. For these cultural expressions, the Convention on the Diversity of Cultural Expressions stipulates that an endeavour should be made to create an environment encouraging individuals and groups to create, produce, disseminate, and distribute cultural expressions.[40] Further, the Convention on the Diversity of Cultural Expressions emphasizes the need for serious endeavours to guarantee access to cultural expressions not only for the individuals or groups to which they belong, but also for anyone else.[41] It goes without saying that the obligations formulated in the Convention on the Diversity of Cultural Expressions nicely build upon the inventories of the ICH Convention. The soft language used in the Convention on the Diversity of Cultural Expressions in turn leaves enough space for Member States to give priority to the specificities of intangible cultural heritage.[42]

When cultural expressions are in need of safeguarding, the expressions can be listed on the List of Intangible Cultural Heritage in Need of Urgent Safeguarding.[43] This listing is connected to the obligation of taking appropriate safeguarding measures. As this obligation parallels a similar obligation under the Convention on the Diversity of Cultural Expressions, the ICH Convention's obligation seems to be reinforced by the former convention, at least for cultural expressions. The Convention on the Diversity of Cultural Expressions further requires a report from the State Party to be submitted to the Intergovernmental

---

39 *See* ICH Convention, *supra* note 1, Article 4. *See also* S. Van Uytsel and T. Kono, "Intangible Cultural Heritage Identified: Inventories as an Essential Part of the Safeguarding Process", in T. Kono (ed.), *Intangible Cultural Heritage and Intellectual Property: Communities, Cultural Diversity and Sustainable Development*, 2009, 46–7; N. Aikawa-Faure, "UNESCO Convention for the Safeguarding of Intangible Cultural Heritage – from its Adoption to the First Meeting of the Intergovernmental Committee", in Kokuritsu Binkazai Kikou, Tokyo Bunkazai Kenkyujo and Mukei Bunka Isanbu (eds.), *Safeguarding Intangible Cultural Heritage: International Cooperation and the Role of Japan*, 2008, 13, 21–5, *available at* www.tobunken.go.jp/~beino/pdf/sympo/07KeynoteSpeech2Aikawa.pdf (last visited 2 February 2012).

40 *See* Convention on the Diversity of Cultural Expressions, *supra* note 2, Articles 6 and 7.

41 *See* id., Article 7(b). It could be argued that the inventory-making process in the ICH Convention is also aimed at access. The question is how far the access should reach in the case of the ICH Convention. *See* S. Van Uytsel, "Inventory Making and Fairy Tales: Safeguarding of Intangible Cultural Heritage in Historical Perspective", in Kono, *supra* note 39, at 130–5.

42 Indeed, nothing obliges the State Parties to take specific actions. The Convention for the Diversity of Cultural Expressions only encourages State Parties to take appropriate actions.

43 *See* ICH Convention, *supra* note 1, Article 17.

Committee to explain all the measures taken to meet the exigencies of the situation.[44] This report could, among other things, contain information indicating that the respective cultural expressions have been put on the Urgent Safeguarding List under the ICH Convention.

3.4. THE ICH CONVENTION WILL TAKE PRIORITY IN CASES OF CONFLICT

3.4.1. The role of civil society

The emphasis that Article 11 of the Convention on the Diversity of Cultural Expressions puts on the participatory role of civil society for the protection and promotion of the diversity of cultural expressions may generate a potential conflict. The potential conflict lies in the fact that 'civil society' has been interpreted to mean non-governmental organizations. These non-governmental organizations are encouraged to actively participate in the protection and promotion of the diversity of cultural expressions.

Even though the ICH Convention does not mention the concept civil society, it refers to non-governmental organizations in some provisions.[45] Non-governmental organizations can be instrumental in the identification and definition of intangible cultural heritage.[46] In this sense, they can assist the State Parties. At the international level, they can contribute by advising the Intergovernmental Committee on matters related to the ICH Convention.[47] Civil

---

44 *See* Convention on the Diversity of Cultural Expressions, *supra* note 2, Articles 8(3) and 9(a). These reports have to be submitted to the Intergovernmental Committee and UNESCO. The former will transmit the reports to the Conference of the Parties. *See* id., Articles 8(3), 9(a), 22(4)(b), and 23(6)(c).

45 *See* ICH Convention, *supra* note 1, Article 11.

46 The role of non-governmental organizations in the ICH Convention was much contested during the drafting. Whereas some UNESCO Member States saw a participatory role for non-governmental organizations as essential, it was not welcomed by others. They saw their participation as eroding the sovereignty of the State to decide on the policies needed to safeguard intangible cultural heritage. As a result of these different views, Article 11 (b) of the ICH Convention was drafted as a consensus. *See* J. Blake, *Commentary on the UNESCO 2003 Convention on the Safeguarding of Intangible Cultural Heritage*, 2006, 62. *See also* Van Uytsel, *supra* note 41, at 128–9.

47 *See* ICH Convention, *supra* note 1, Article 9(1). *See also* UNESCO, General Assembly, *Operational Directives for the Implementation of the Convention for the Safeguarding of the Intangible Cultural Heritage*, Chapter III, 2, §96 (2008, as amended 2010), *available at* www.unesco.org/culture/ich/index.php?lg=en&pg=00026 (last visited 2 February 2012) [hereinafter "Operational Directives"] (according to these operational directives, the non-governmental organizations can be solicited for: a) nomination files for the List of Intangible Cultural Heritage in Need of Urgent Safeguarding; b) the programmes, projects and activities mentioned in Article 18 of the Convention; c) requests for international assistance; d) the effects of safeguarding plans for elements inscribed on the List of Intangible Cultural Heritage in Need of Urgent Safeguarding).

society has not been given an active role in the other processes of safeguarding intangible cultural heritage.[48]

By limiting the role of civil society to identifying and defining intangible cultural heritage at the national level, an argument could be made that the policies for safeguarding intangible cultural heritage should not focus on civil society as the driving force behind expressions that have once been created and transmitted within a community or a group at some time. Indeed, according to Article 2(1) of the ICH Convention, one can only speak of intangible cultural heritage if the expression is recognized by a community, group or individual. Once the recognition disappears, whatever the reason may be, the expression loses its status as intangible cultural heritage.

The Convention on the Diversity of Cultural Expressions, on the contrary, offers State Parties the possibility of designing policies in which a decisive role is given to civil society in relation to cultural expressions. These policies do not necessarily have to be limited to the identification or definition of these cultural expressions, but can be as extensive as the creation, production, dissemination or distribution of expressions, and even protection and preservation in cases where a cultural expression is seriously threatened.[49] Due to the different conceptualization of cultural expressions, in the sense that it only requires that these expressions have at some point been recognized by a group or a society as part of its values, the Convention on the Diversity of Cultural Expressions leaves much more room for the involvement of civil society in the protection and promotion of cultural expressions.

It is obvious that an active role for civil society may endanger the status of cultural expressions as intangible cultural heritage. Taking into consideration that the active participation of civil society is not an absolute obligation under the Convention on the Diversity of Cultural Expressions,[50] State Parties could reduce the role of civil society in the promotion and protection of cultural expressions that also qualify as intangible cultural heritage, and do this for the sake of the mutual supportiveness of the conventions. This kind of stance could be advocated by referring to the obligation of not using the Convention on the Diversity of Cultural Expressions to change obligations under other conventions, here the ICH Convention.[51]

The extensive role attributed to civil society in the Convention on the Diversity of Cultural Expressions could still play an important role for

48 *See* ICH Convention, *supra* note 1, Article 15 (only referring to communities, groups and individuals).

49 *See* Convention on the Diversity of Cultural Expressions, *supra* note 2, Article 11 (indicating that they can be involved in promotion and protection. Each of these activities are further defined in Article 6 and 7 of the Convention on the Diversity of Cultural Expressions).

50 *See* id. (including only the obligation of "shall encourage the active participation of civil society." This does not imply that their involvement is compulsory.).

51 *See* id., Article 20(2).

expressions that are dying out. Once vanished, the ICH Convention will cease to be applicable to these expressions. Nevertheless, the Convention on the Diversity of Cultural Expressions could then provide a framework in which these cultural expressions could remain vivid with the support of civil society.

3.4.2. Poverty eradication

To facilitate their operations, both conventions seek the establishment of a fund: the Fund for the Safeguarding of the Intangible Cultural Heritage ("ICH Fund")[52] and the Fund for Cultural Diversity.[53] Neither of the conventions stipulates how the respective funds are to be used. The conventions have deferred that decision to the Intergovernmental Committees.[54] The Operational Directives of the ICH Convention provide in Chapter 2 that the ICH Fund will be primarily used to facilitate international assistance.[55] For the Convention on the Diversity of Cultural Expressions, the Operational Guidelines state that the purpose of the Cultural Diversity Fund is to support cooperation for sustainable development and poverty reduction in order to foster the emergence of a dynamic cultural sector in developing countries.[56]

The aim of poverty reduction to foster the emergence of a dynamic cultural sector reveals one of the main incentives that have driven the adoption of the Convention on the Diversity of Cultural Expressions. The Convention on the Diversity of Cultural Expressions reflects the growing consciousness that cultural goods and services are not like any other form of merchandise. The challenges for these cultural goods and services have grown exponentially due to the process of globalization and rapid liberalization of trade in goods and services. More than ever, it was felt that the market for these cultural goods and services failed and that market interventions were necessary. The legal basis for state intervention was, however, lacking. The Convention on the Diversity of Cultural Expressions has been partly adopted to fill that gap.[57]

The ICH Convention has a completely different perspective. As a response to the failure of the World Heritage Convention to take intangible cultural heritage

---

52 *See* ICH Convention, *supra* note 1, Article 25.

53 *See* Convention on the Diversity of Cultural Expressions, *supra* note 2, Article 18.

54 *See* ICH Convention, *supra* note 1, Article 25(4); Convention on the Diversity of Cultural Expressions, *supra* note 2, Article 18(4).

55 *See* Operational Directives, *supra* note 46, Chapter II, 1, §66.

56 *See* UNESCO, Conference of the Parties, "Operational Guidelines on the Use of the Resources of the International Fund for Cultural Diversity (Article 18 of the Convention)" (June 2009), *available at* www.unesco.org/new/fileadmin/MULTIMEDIA/HQ/CLT/pdf/Conv2005_DO_Art_18_EN.pdf (last visited 2 February 2012).

57 *See* [this volume, introductory part] Kono and Van Uytsel. *See also* T. Kono, "The UNESCO Convention for the Protection and the Promotion of the Diversity of Cultural Expressions", in K. Alexander and M. Andenas (eds.), *The World Trade Organization and Trade in Services*, 2008, 894–8.

into consideration, the ICH Convention took on the challenge of ensuring that it is given a similar level of protection as is provided for tangible cultural and natural heritage, but in a form appropriate to intangible cultural heritage.[58] As it appears from the definition of intangible cultural heritage, the appropriate form for safeguarding intangible cultural heritage is one in which there is respect for involvement and continuity.

Involvement stems from the idea that people may value the intangible cultural heritage that their early ancestors have created, shaped, and re-created. Very often this has been a process in response to the outside world. Intangible cultural heritage, to which expressions belong, may thus have originated from contacts with the natural environment, such as nature, landscape, or climate.[59] Intangible cultural heritage may also be a reflection of their reaction to the social environment, including their history or interactions with other communities and cultures.[60] As the intangible cultural heritage shaped itself as a way to

---

58 *See* S. Van Uytsel, "Philosophies Behind the Intangible Cultural Heritage Convention: Equality in Heritage Protection, Community Recognition and Cultural Diversity" (2012), *available at* http://papers.ssrn.com/sol3/papers.cfm?abstract_id=2001835 (last visited 9 February 2012); *See also* T. Kono, "UNESCO and Intangible Cultural Heritage from the Viewpoint of Sustainable Development", in A.A. Yusuf (ed.), *Standard Setting in UNESCO: Normative Action in Education, Science and Culture*, 2007, 237–41; J. Blake, *Developing a New Standard-setting Instrument for the Safeguarding of Intangible Cultural Heritage: Elements for Consideration*, 2002; H. Deacon, *Legal and Financial Instruments for Safeguarding our Intangible Heritage*, *available at* www.international.icomos.org/victoriafalls2003/papers/C3-2%20-%20Deacon.pdf (last visited 2 February 2012).

59 The traditions of nomads significantly differ from those of communities that settled down and concentrated on agricultural use and exploitation of land. Similarly, the ways of traditional life in rainy forests considerably diverge from those of communities living in deserts, prairies or tundra. While the people living in deserts must learn how to survive in such conditions without water for a long time, those living in areas with rainy seasons must know when and how to plant crops in order to maximize their harvest. For discussion about various kinds of traditional knowledge, *see, e.g.*, W.E.A. van Beek and F. Jara, "'Granular Knowledge'" Cultural Problems with Intellectual Property and Protection", in F.W. Grosheide and J.J. Brinkhof (eds.), *Intellectual Property Law 2002: Articles on Cultural Expressions and Indigenous Knowledge*, 2002, 35–57.

60 In addition to the natural environment, communities also react through traditional cultural expressions and practices to their social environment, including their history and interactions with other communities and cultures. In territories where several communities live together, cross-cultural borrowings and communications occur on a daily basis. The result is that similar fairytales, legends, songs or fabric designs can be found in different communities living in such territories. Nowadays, the processes of cross-cultural borrowings and communications are even more magnified by recent social phenomena such as globalization, urbanization, modernization and the like, which have a crucial position in the globalizing world. For instance, the Javanese "classical" shadow theatre was on the edge of extinction despite several attempts to preserve it in the 1980s. All of them failed, until some performers came with new instruments and comic interludes, which were not used traditionally. Suddenly, this traditional cultural expression became popular and an integral part of modern Javanese culture. *See* L.J. Sears, "Comment", 43 *Current Anthropology* 147 (2002). Although some might criticize such a "modernization" of tradition cultural expressions, the only entities which can judge such modernizations are communities. Cultural expressions become traditions and parts of intangible cultural heritage only when they work, *i.e.* when they are

survive or to communicate, the ancestors have passed it down to future generations. As this process repeated itself, the intangible cultural heritage became associated with the communities.[61]

Even though the intangible cultural heritage links a community to its natural and socio-economic environment, it is also crucial to see that, due to its continued transmission, the intangible cultural heritage has provided communities with a sense of identity and continuity.[62] Indeed, it often reflects the spirit of a community.[63] Through its intangible cultural heritage, one community can distinguish itself from others and highlight its specialties and differences. Cultural expressions thus allow individuals to identify themselves with a particular community by showing how the traditions of other communities differ from theirs.[64] A community's self-esteem can thus be enhanced when its members appreciate the uniqueness of their traditions; intangible cultural heritage thus plays an important role in the processes of self-recognition and self-determination of communities.[65] The relationship between communities and their intangible cultural heritage is thus a two-way interaction. Communities not only shape and recreate their traditions, but at the same time, traditions contour and influence the affected communities and their members.

The fact that intangible cultural heritage is closely related to the identity of a community suggests that continuity of these expressions is indispensable. Without the intangible cultural heritage, the community loses at least a part of its identity. In the worst case, the community will cease to exist, as the

---

passed on through generations. *See* U. Kockel, "Reflexive Traditions and Heritage Production", in U. Kockel and M.N. Craith (eds.), *Cultural Heritages as Reflexive Traditions*, 2007, 28.

61 For a more profound analysis on how communities understand individual traditional cultural expressions as their belongings, *see* M.F. Brown, *Who Owns Native Culture?*, 2003. *See also* M. Rowlands, "Cultural Rights and Wrongs: Uses of the Concept of Property", in K. Verdery and C. Humphrey (eds.), *Property in Question: Value Transformation in the Global Economy*, 2004, 207–23 (analyzing the conflicts in cases where several communities claim proprietary interests in the same cultural heritage).

62 *Compare* R. Handler, "Who Owns the Past? History, Cultural Property, and the Logic of Possessive Individualism", in B. Williams (ed.), *The Politics of Culture*, 1991, 63–74, *with* E. Coleman, "Cultural Property and Collective Identity", in S. Herbrechter and M. Higgins (eds), *Returning (to) Communities: Theory, Culture and Political Practice of the Communal*, 2006, 161–71.

63 The origins might be found in the concept of *Volksgeist* as presented by J.G. Herder and G.W.F. Hegel. *Compare also* S. Hall, "Whose Heritage? Un-settling 'the Heritage', Re-Imaging the Post-Nation", in J. Littler and R. Naidoo (eds.), *The Politics of Heritage: The Legacies of 'Race'*, 2005, 25 (arguing that that "the nation slowly constructs for itself a sort of collective social memory" in a "discursive practice") with D. Scot, *Refashioning Futures: Criticism after Post-Coloniality*, 1999 (claiming that consensus and discord play an important role in this process).

64 N. Douglas, "Political Structures, Social Interaction and Identity Changes in Northern Ireland", in B. Graham (ed.), *In Search of Ireland: A Cultural Geography*, 1997, 151–2.

65 *See, e.g.*, Kockel, *supra* note 59 (describing how intangible cultural heritage is used in the formation of identity in the case of Ulster-Scots in Northern Ireland).

distinguishing characteristics will disappear together with the intangible cultural heritage.[66]

The emphasis that the ICH Convention places on a community creating its identity and passing it on to other generations is in no way envisaged to be a market-oriented legal instrument. This does not mean that intangible cultural heritage can generate economic remunerations for the community it belongs to. Nevertheless, it is not the purpose of the ICH Convention to set up structures so that each and every intangible cultural heritage can economically sustain its community. Rather, the ICH Convention has a much more limited aim of guaranteeing that a framework is set up for intangible cultural heritage to survive within a community and, if possible, letting the outside world know about the existence of the intangible cultural heritage.

The absence of any reference to poverty reduction and the difficulty of aligning this element with the purpose of the ICH Convention require State Parties to set up international cooperation structures, which are eventually financed by the respective funds, to carefully distinguish between the cultural expressions that also fall under the ICH Convention and the ones that do not. In order to avoid conflicts between the conventions, the cooperation structures established for the former should refrain from making reference to poverty reduction. For the same reasons as set out above, the Convention on the Diversity of Cultural Expressions should give priority to the ICH Convention. Again, this is possible since the Convention on the Diversity of Cultural Expressions integrates the poverty reduction requirement only as a soft obligation.

4. INTERACTION AT THE INTERPRETATION LEVEL

4.1. EXISTING INTERNATIONAL LAW FOR INTERPRETING NEW TREATIES

According to Article 31(3)(c) of the *Vienna Convention on the Law of Treaties* ("Vienna Convention"), "any relevant rules of international law applicable in the relations between the parties" can be used for the interpretation of another convention. The traditional view on this article is that any rule of international law that was applicable at the time of ratification of the new convention can be

66 G.J. Ashworth, B. Graham, and J.E. Tunbridge, *Pluralising Pasts: Heritage, Identity and Place in Multicultural Societies*, 2007, 8, 24–27, 73–76 (enquiring into the process of assimilation).

used to shed light on the provisions of the new convention.[67] This view still has validity. Transferred to the ICH Convention and the Convention on the Diversity of Cultural Expressions, the former can be used to interpret the latter.

'Safeguarding' is one of the concepts defined in the ICH Convention[68] but left unclear in the Convention on the Diversity of Cultural Expressions where the concept is incorporated in the definition of protection.[69] Hence, when the Convention on the Diversity of Cultural Expressions deals with measures protecting cultural expressions in Article 8, these measures could be understood as including identification, documentation, research, preservation, promotion, enhancement, transmission as well as revitalization of some aspects of the expressions.

Another concept that can be illuminated by looking at the ICH Convention is 'in need of urgent safeguarding'.[70] 'In need of urgent safeguarding' is one of the grounds justifying the adoption of protective measures. The concept is not further elaborated in the Convention on the Diversity of Cultural Expressions. Looking at the ICH Convention, a similar concept has been inscribed in the section dealing with international obligations. Article 17(2) of the ICH Convention provides that the Intergovernmental Committee shall point out in its Operational Directives when intangible cultural heritage, and thus also expression, are 'in need of urgent safeguarding.' The Operational Directives stipulate that such a situation will occur when the viability of the intangible cultural heritage is at risk. In extreme cases it may refer to the risk of non-survival of the intangible cultural heritage.[71]

Both Conventions put a lot of emphasis on the concept of sustainable development.[72] As the ICH Convention was one of the first legally binding instruments on culture to mention sustainable development, some further clarification could have been provided.[73] The lack of any indication as to how to interpret this concept reduces the relevance of the ICH Convention regarding the interpretation of this concept in the Convention on the Diversity of Cultural Expressions. Nevertheless, considering the call for mutual supportiveness, it would be advisable to develop this concept according to similar lines of thought in both conventions.

67 *See* U. Linderfalk, *On the Interpretation of Treaties: The Modern International Law as Expressed in the 1969 Vienna Convention on the Law of the Treaties*, 2007, 179.

68 *See* ICH Convention, *supra* note 1, Article 2(3).

69 *See* Convention on the Diversity of Cultural Expressions, *supra* note 2, Article 4(7).

70 *See* id., Article 8(1).

71 *See* Operational Directives, *supra* note 47, Chapter I, 1, §1.

72 *See* ICH Convention, *supra* note 1, Preamble Paragraph 2 and Article 2(1); Convention on the Diversity of Cultural Expressions, *supra* note 2, Preamble Paragraphs 3, 6, 8, 15 and 16 and Articles 1, 2(5), 2(6), 13, and 14.

73 *See* Kono, *supra* note 57, at 237 (making an attempt to link sustainable development with intangible cultural heritage).

4.2. LITTLE SPACE FOR EVOLUTIONARY INTERPRETATION BECAUSE OF SHARED PREMISES

The contemporary reading of Article 31(3)(c) of the Vienna Convention is more liberal. Rather than looking at the various points of ratification, this view allows for looking at all relevant rules of international law that are applicable at the time of interpretation.[74] Newly adopted conventions can therefore attribute meanings to already existing conventions and so trigger an evolution in the older legal instruments. Hence, the Convention on the Diversity of Cultural Expressions can in principle be used to interpret the ICH Convention.

Even though the possibility for evolutionary interpretation exists, the use of such an interpretation method may be minimal in the current case. The time span between the adoption of the ICH Convention and the Convention on the Diversity of Cultural Expressions has been relatively short. In fact, it was so short that the premises on which each of these conventions were built do not differ substantially. This was pointed out earlier in the section discussing the establishment of a common framework in relation to their object and objectives.[75]

If we look further at the level of action, a similar line is noticeable. The ICH Convention conceptualizes guarantees for the viability, transmission and respecting of intangible cultural heritage by promulgating safeguarding, respect, raising awareness, and cooperation and assistance in relation to intangible cultural heritage as the purposes of the convention.[76] Even though the purpose of the Convention on the Diversity of Cultural Expressions is more textually elaborated, its essence could be captured by similar concepts.[77] At the meta-level, the role of evolutionary interpretation may thus be less important.

---

74 *See* LINDERFALK, *supra* note 67, at 179.

75 *See supra* Section 2.

76 *See* ICH Convention, *supra* note 1, Article 1 ("(a) to safeguard the intangible cultural heritage; (b) to ensure respect for the intangible cultural heritage of the communities, groups and individuals concerned; (c) to raise awareness at the local, national and international levels of the importance of the intangible cultural heritage, and of ensuring mutual appreciation thereof; (d) to provide for international cooperation and assistance.").

77 *See* Convention on the Diversity of Cultural Expressions, *supra* note 2, Article 1 (the objectives are "(a) to protect and promote the diversity of cultural expressions; (b) to create the conditions for cultures to flourish and to freely interact in a mutually beneficial manner; (c) to encourage dialogue among cultures with a view to ensuring wider and balanced cultural exchanges in the world in favour of intercultural respect and a culture of peace; (d) to foster interculturality in order to develop cultural interaction in the spirit of building bridges among peoples; (e) to promote respect for the diversity of cultural expressions and raise awareness of its value at the local, national and international levels; (f) to reaffirm the importance of the link between culture and development for all countries, particularly for developing countries, and to support actions undertaken nationally and internationally to secure recognition of the true value of this link; (g) to give recognition to the distinctive nature of cultural activities, goods and services as vehicles of identity, values and meaning; (h) to reaffirm the sovereign rights of States to maintain, adopt and implement policies and

The importance of evolutionary interpretation has to be found in the refinements that the Convention on the Diversity of Cultural Expressions adds to vague concepts that are to be found in the ICH Convention. On this micro-level, the most obvious refinement that has been added is the need to take the aspect of diversity into consideration.[78] Whenever educational and awareness-raising programs are being set up, these programs should not only focus on the recognition of, the respect for and the enhancement of the expressions that are qualified as intangible cultural heritage, but at the same time, these programs need also to stress the understanding of the importance of having a diversity of expressions.

A similar line of thought can be followed for cooperation. International cooperation and assistance should not only be inspired by the safeguarding of a particular expression qualified as intangible cultural heritage, but also by the need to guarantee the diversity of expressions. This emphasis on the diversity of expressions will require international cooperation and assistance to pay particular attention to expressions in need of urgent safeguarding.

Another substantial refinement that could be transplanted to the ICH Convention by evolutionary interpretation is the pervasive emphasis on sustainable development. Sustainable development is not only put forward as a principle that has to be taken into account, similar to the ICH Convention, but has repeatedly been inscribed in several other provisions. One of them is the provision on cooperation, which demands that there should be an endeavour to support sustainable development with cooperation.

This idea of cooperation to achieve sustainable development again puts a very strong emphasis on the need to transcend the opportunities of the current generation. Indeed, sustainable development demands that the possibilities of the next generation in relation to cultural expressions should not be jeopardized.[79] Therefore, by incorporating the ethical demand of sustainable development into the cooperation programs, the most important object of cooperation again becomes cultural expressions in need of urgent safeguarding.

---

measures that they deem appropriate for the protection and promotion of the diversity of cultural expressions on their territory; (i) to strengthen international cooperation and solidarity in a spirit of partnership with a view, in particular, to enhancing the capacities of developing countries in order to protect and promote the diversity of cultural expressions.").

78 This does not imply that diversity for the sake of diversity has to be incorporated in the application of the ICH Convention. For example, diversity among the practices, representations, expressions, knowledge, and skills – as well as the instruments, objects, artifacts and cultural spaces associated therewith – should not be the aim when decisions are being made for inscribing in the list.

79 *See* World Commission on Environment and Development, *Our Common Future*, 1987, 47; *See also* A. Boyle and D. Freestone, "Introduction", in A. Boyle and D. Freestone (eds.), *International Law and Sustainable Development*, 1999, 12; *See* S. Anand and A. Sen, "*Sustainable Human Development: Concepts and Priorities*", *available at* www.undp.org.in/hdrc/APRI/Event/Colombo/resources/ppr/sustainable%20human%20development%20abstract.pdf (last visited 2 February 2012).

Of course, this does also imply the need to abstain from any cooperation activities that could mean the end of these expressions, even if they are not in need of urgent safeguarding.

5. CONCLUSION

The ICH Convention and the Convention on the Diversity of Cultural Expressions share a common object and objectives. Therefore, this Chapter has elaborated on how these two conventions interlink with each other. The main conclusion that can be drawn from the study is that the ICH Convention and the Convention on the Diversity of Cultural Expressions could nicely operate next to each other. The obligations stemming from the ICH Convention are further supported by the rights and obligations of the Convention on the Diversity of Cultural Expressions.

It is only on a few points that the ICH Convention and the Convention on the Diversity of Cultural Expressions diverge from each other, in which case the article on conflict resolution in the Convention on the Diversity of Cultural Expressions gives priority to the ICH Convention. Nevertheless, the soft language of the Convention on the Diversity of Cultural Expressions could already prevent many conflicts from happening.

Another point in which the ICH Convention and the Convention on the Diversity of Cultural Expressions could interact with each other is on the level of interpretation. The ICH Convention could help through the elaboration of concepts such as sustainable development, while the Convention on the Diversity of Cultural Expressions could emphasize the need for preserving diversity among intangible cultural heritages.

PART III

HUMAN RIGHTS & THE CONVENTION ON THE DIVERSITY OF CULTURAL EXPRESSIONS

CULTURAL RIGHTS AND THE CONVENTION ON THE DIVERSITY OF CULTURAL EXPRESSIONS

Included or Ignored?

Yvonne DONDERS*

1. INTRODUCTION

In 2001, the Universal Declaration on Cultural Diversity ("Cultural Diversity Declaration")[1] was adopted by the Member States of UNESCO. In this Declaration, cultural human rights were commended as an enabling environment for cultural diversity. After the Cultural Diversity Declaration, the Member States wished to adopt a legally binding instrument on cultural diversity. One of the options discussed was a new instrument on cultural rights. The Member States, however, opted for an instrument on cultural expressions and on 20 October 2005, the Convention on the Protection and Promotion of the Diversity of Cultural Expressions ("Convention on the Diversity of Cultural Expressions")[2] was adopted. Support for the Convention on the Diversity of Cultural Expressions was widespread: 148 States voted in favour, only 2 States voted against (the United States of America ("USA") and Israel) and 4 States abstained (Australia, Honduras, Liberia and Nicaragua). The Convention on the

* Prof. dr. Y.M. Donders is Professor International Human Rights and Cultural Diversity and Executive Director of the Amsterdam Center for International Law of the University of Amsterdam. At the time of the negotiations and adoption of the Convention, she worked at the Human Rights Division of the UNESCO Secretariat in Paris as Programme Specialist on Economic, Social and Cultural Rights.

1 *See* Universal Declaration on Cultural Diversity, 2 November 2001, *available at* http://portal.unesco.org/en/ev.php-URL_ID=13179&URL_DO=DO_TOPIC&URL_SECTION=201.html (last visited on 2 February 2012) [hereinafter "Cultural Diversity Declaration"].

2 *See* Convention on the Protection and Promotion of the Diversity of Cultural Expressions, 20 October 2005, *U.N. Doc. CLT-2005/CONVENTION DIVERSITE-CULT REV.* [hereinafter "Convention on the Diversity of Cultural Expressions"].

Diversity of Cultural Expressions entered into force in March 2007 and currently has 118 State Parties.[3]

The link between cultural diversity and human rights is clearly established in the Convention on the Diversity of Cultural Expressions. In Article 2(1) of the Convention on the Diversity of Cultural Expressions, it is stated that "…cultural diversity can be protected and promoted only if human rights and fundamental freedoms … are guaranteed." It is interesting to note that the Convention speaks of human rights in general, not of cultural rights. What happened to the important role of cultural rights as an 'enabling environment' for cultural diversity? What, if any at all, is the place of cultural rights in the Convention?

This Chapter will explore the role of cultural rights in the Convention on the Diversity of Cultural Expressions. In Section 2, it will first briefly outline what is meant by cultural rights, which is quite a discussion in itself. Then, in Section 3, several UNESCO instruments will be discussed to shed some light on the evolution of the debate on cultural rights in UNESCO. Finally, in Section 4, the drafting and adoption of the Convention on the Diversity of Cultural Expressions will be discussed in relation to the promotion and protection of cultural rights.

2. CULTURAL RIGHTS AS HUMAN RIGHTS

Although the division between the different categories of human rights – civil, political, economic, social and cultural – does not imply that one category of human rights is more important than another, practice shows that the different categories of human rights have not developed at an equal pace. Cultural rights have received less attention and are, therefore, less developed than civil, political, economic and social rights.[4] One of the main reasons for the underdevelopment of cultural rights and the lack of conceptualization of the field is the vagueness of the term 'culture'. Culture can refer to different things, varying from cultural products, such as arts and literature, to the cultural process or culture as a way of life. In between are the cultural institutions established to transfer culture, such as museums, educational institutions and the media. Accordingly, cultural rights can refer to various human rights and freedoms.

---

3 *See* UNESCO, "Diversity of Cultural Expressions", *available at* www.unesco.org/culture/en/diversity/convention (last visited 2 February 2012) (containing background information and information related to the status of ratifications).

4 *See, e.g.*, "Cultural Rights: An Underdeveloped Category of Human Rights. Conclusions of the Eighth Interdisciplinary Colloquium on Human Rights, organised by the University of Fribourg, 28–30 November 1991", 49 *The Review of the International Commission of Jurists* 51, 51–3 (1992); *See also* J. Symonides, "Cultural Rights", in J. Symonides (ed.), *Human Rights – Concepts and Standards*, 2000, 175, 175–6.

No international human rights instrument defines cultural rights as such and therefore different lists have been drawn up of legal provisions in international instruments that could be labelled 'cultural rights'. Which rights are included in a list of cultural rights depends on how broadly 'culture' is defined. As argued above, the concept of culture can vary from intellectual and artistic achievements, such as arts and literature, to culture in the anthropological sense, being the way of life of individuals and communities, as reflected in shared beliefs, language, traditions and customs. Accordingly, cultural rights could be rights concerning creativity, such as the rights to freedom of expression and artistic and intellectual freedom, as well as the rights related to the protection of producers of cultural products, including copyright. Cultural rights could also refer to the protection of cultural products and cultural expressions, including cultural heritage. Cultural rights in relation to the process of cultural development could include the right to self-determination, the rights to freedom of thought, religion and assembly and the right to education. Cultural rights can also concern 'the right to culture', in the sense of the right to preserve, develop and have access to culture.[5] In other words, the category of cultural rights could be very broad, and this means a more systematic approach is required.

2.1. CULTURAL RIGHTS IN THE NARROW AND IN THE BROAD SENSE

Drawing from universal human rights instruments,[6] a general distinction can be made between cultural rights in the narrow sense and cultural rights in the

5 *See, generally*, L. Prott, "Cultural Rights as Peoples' Rights in International Law", in J. Crawford (ed.), *The Rights of Peoples*, 1998, 93; P. Meyer-Bisch, Les Droits Culturels, Forment-Ils une Catégorie Spécifique de Droits de L'Homme?", in P. Meyer-Bisch (ed.), *Les Droits Culturels, une Catégorie Sous-Développée de Droits de L'Homme, Actes du VIIIe Colloque interdisciplinaire sur les droits de l'homme*, 1993, 18, 24; S. Marks,"Defining Cultural Rights", in M. Bergsmo (ed.), *Human Rights and Criminal Justice for the Downtrodden – Essays in Honour of Asbjorn Eide*, 2003, 293, 295.

6 The core UN human rights treaties are (in chronological order of adoption): Universal Declaration of Human Rights, 10 December 1948, GA Res. 217A (III), *UN Doc. A/810*, at 71 [hereinafter "UDHR"]; International Convention on the Elimination of All Forms of Racial Discrimination, 21 December 1965, 660 *UNTS* 195 [hereinafter "ICERD"]; International Covenant on Civil and Political Rights, 16 December 1966, 999 *UNTS* 171 [hereinafter "ICCPR"]; Covenant on Economic, Social and Cultural Rights, 16 December 1966, 993 U.N.T.S. 3 [hereinafter "ICESCR"]; International Convention on the Elimination of All Forms of Discrimination Against Women, 18 December 1979, 1249 *UNTS* 13 [hereinafter "CEDAW"]; Convention Against Torture and Other Cruel, Inhuman or Degrading Treatment or Punishment, 10 December 1984, 1465 *UNTS* 85; Convention on the Rights of the Child, 20 November 1989, *UN Doc. A/44/49* [hereinafter "CRC"]; International Convention on the Protection of the Rights of All Migrant Workers and Members of Their Families, 18 December 1990, GA Res. 45/158, *A/RES/45/158* [hereinafter "ICRMW"].

broad sense. The *group of cultural rights in the narrow sense* contains those provisions that explicitly refer to 'culture', such as the right to participate in cultural life,[7] or the right to equal participation in cultural activities.[8] Other cultural rights in the narrow sense include the right to enjoy culture for members of minorities,[9] the right to education for children with due respect for their cultural identity,[10] or the right of migrant workers to respect for their cultural identity and their right to maintain cultural links with their country of origin.[11]

The *group of cultural rights in the broad sense* includes the above-mentioned rights, but also other civil, economic, political or social rights that have a link with culture. It might be defensible to say that almost every human right has a link with culture, but the rights specifically meant here are: the right to self-determination,[12] the rights to freedom of thought and religion,[13] freedom of expression[14] and freedom of association[15] and the right to education.[16, 17]

2.2. THE CULTURAL DIMENSION OF HUMAN RIGHTS

Cultural rights may also refer to the cultural 'dimension' of human rights. Although some human rights, at first glance, may not have a direct link with culture, most of them have important cultural implications. The Committee on Economic, Social and Cultural Rights (Committee), supervising the implementation of the ICESCR, has acknowledged the cultural elements of, for instance, the rights to food, health and housing. For instance, it has determined that the right to adequate housing implies that the construction of houses, the building materials and the supporting policies "... must appropriately enable the expression of cultural identity and diversity of housing."[18] With regard to the right to health, the Committee has determined that "... all health facilities, goods

---

7 *See* ICESCR, *supra* note 6, Article 15(1)(a); CEDAW, *supra* note 6, Article 13; CRC, *supra* note 6, Article 31 and ICRMW, *supra* note 6, Article 43.

8 *See* ICERD, *supra* note 6, Article 5.

9 *See* ICCPR, *supra* note 6, Article 27.

10 *See* CRC, *supra* note 6, Article 29.

11 *See* ICRMW, *supra* note 6, Article 31.

12 *See* ICCPR, *supra* note 6, Article 1 and ICESCR, *supra* note 6, Article 1.

13 *See* ICCPR, *supra* note 6, Article 18 and ICRMW, *supra* note 6, Article 12.

14 *See* ICCPR, *supra* note 6, Article 19 and ICRMW, *supra* note 6, Article 13.

15 *See* ICCPR, *supra* note 6, Article 22 and ICRMW, *supra* note 6, Article 40.

16 *See* Article 13 and 14 ICESCR; Article 10 CEDAW and Article 30 ICRMW.

17 *See* Y.M. Donders, *Towards a Right to Cultural Identity?*, 2002, 65–92; Y. Donders, "The legal framework of the right to take part in cultural life", in Y. Donders and Vl. Volodin (eds.), *Human Rights in Education, Science and Culture: Legal Developments and Challenges*, 2007, 231, 232–6.

18 Committee on Economic, Social and Cultural Rights, "General Comment No. 4, The Right to Adequate Housing", *E/1992/23*, §8 (g) (1991).

and services must be...culturally appropriate, *i.e.*, respectful of the culture of individuals, minorities, peoples and communities..."[19] With regard to the right to adequate food, the Committee has stated that the guarantees provided should be culturally appropriate and acceptable.[20]

Several international judicial bodies, including the European Court of Human Rights ("European Court") and the Inter-American Court on Human Rights ("Inter-American Court"), have acknowledged the cultural dimension of 'classic' human rights provisions. The European Court has, for example, decided that the right to freedom of association[21] also protects cultural organizations.[22] It has further addressed the cultural dimension of the right to private life,[23] when it recognized that living in caravans is part of the traditional lifestyle of gypsies, and to be protected under this right.[24] The Inter-American Commission has issued several judgments on indigenous peoples and the protection of their culture under the right to life and the right to health.[25] It has also acknowledged the specific interpretation of the right to property to reflect the culture of indigenous peoples.[26]

In short, cultural rights include rights explicitly referring to culture, as well as rights that have a link with culture in the broad sense of the term. Apart from these cultural rights in the narrow and broad sense, the cultural dimension of human rights should be taken into account. The discussion below concerns other UNESCO instruments that have a link with cultural rights, followed by analysis as to which of these cultural rights can be found in the Convention on the Diversity of Cultural Expressions.

---

19 Committee on Economic, Social and Cultural Rights, "General Comment No. 14, The Right to the Highest Attainable Standard of Health", *E/C.12/2000/4*, §12 (c) (2000).

20 *See* Committee on Economic, Social and Cultural Rights, "General Comment No. 12, The Right to Adequate Food", *E/C.12/1999/5*, §7, 8 and 11 (1999).

21 *See* European Convention for the Protection of Human Rights and Fundamental Freedoms, 4 November 1950, *ETS* No. 5, Article 11 [hereinafter "ECHR"].

22 *See* European Court of Human Rights, *Sidiropoulos and others v. Greece*, 10 July 1998, no. 26695/95; European Court of Human Rights, *Stankov and the United Macedonian Organisation Ilinden v. Bulgaria*, 2 October 2001, nos. 29221/95 and 29225/95; European Court of Human Rights, *Gorzelik and others v. Poland*, 20 December 2001, no. 44158/98.

23 *See* ECHR, *supra* note 21, Article 8.

24 *See* European Court of Human Rights, *Chapman v. the United Kingdom*, 18 January 2001, no. 27238/95.

25 *See* Inter-American Court on Human Rights, *Yanomami Indians in OAS*, Inter-Am C.H. Res. No. 12/85, Case No. 7615 and in Annual Report of the Inter-American Commission of Human Rights (1984–85) OEA/Ser.L/V/II.66, doc. 10, rev. 1.

26 *See* Inter-American Court on Human Rights, *The Mayagna (Sumo) Indigenous Community of Awas Tingi v. the Republic of Nicaragua*, 31 August 2001, Inter-Am. C.H.R, Series C, No. 79; Inter-American Commission on Human Rights, *Maya Indigenous Communities and their Members v. Belize*, 5 October 2000, IACHR Report No. 78/00, case No. 12.053; Inter-American Commission on Human Rights, *Maya Indigenous Communities of the Toledo District Belize*, 12 October 2004, IACHR Report No. 40–04, case No. 12.053.

3. UNESCO AND CULTURAL RIGHTS

How have cultural rights been incorporated in UNESCO instruments? UNESCO is the prime international intergovernmental organization dealing with culture. UNESCO was set up in November 1945 as an autonomous UN organization or specialized agency under Article 57 of the UN Charter. Its main purpose is described in Article 1 of its Constitution: '... to contribute to peace and security by promoting collaboration among nations through education, science and culture in order to further universal respect for justice, for the rule of law and for the human rights and fundamental freedoms ... without distinction of race, sex, language or religion ...'

One of the tasks of UNESCO is the promotion and protection of human rights within its sphere of competence. These rights include the right to education,[27] the right to participate freely in cultural life and share in scientific advancement,[28] and the right to freedom of opinion and expression, including the right to seek, receive and impart information.[29] The Member States of UNESCO can, according to Article IV(4) of its Constitution, adopt conventions, which are binding upon the Member States, and recommendations, which are not legally binding, but do have a legal effect in that they should be implemented by States.[30] The possibility of adopting declarations and other non-binding instruments was added later by an amendment of the General Conference at its seventh session in 1952. It should be mentioned that in addition to standard-setting, UNESCO has played an important role in facilitating discussion and exchange between States and experts in order to improve cultural policies.

Although cultural rights are not specifically mentioned in the Constitution, the preparation of normative instruments in the field of culture is an important task of UNESCO. This is shown by the large number of instruments adopted by the Member States of UNESCO in the field of culture.[31] Some of these

---

27 *See* UDHR, *supra* note 6, Article 26 and ICESCR, *supra* note 6, Articles 13 and 14.

28 *See* UDHR, *supra* note 6, Article 27 and ICESCR, *supra* note 6, Article 15.

29 *See* UDHR, *supra* note 6, Article 19 and ICCPR, *supra* note 6, Article 19.

30 *See* Constitution of the United Nations Educational, Scientific and Cultural Organisation, 16 November 1945, 52 *UNTS* 275.

31 *See, generally,* Agreement on the Importation of Educational, Scientific and Cultural Materials, 17 June 1950, *available at* http://portal.unesco.org/en/ev.php-URL_ID=12074&URL_DO=DO_TOPIC&URL_SECTION=201.html (last visited 2 February 2012) (known as the *Florence Agreement*) and its *Nairobi Protocol* of 26 November 1976; Convention for the Protection of Cultural Property in the Event of Armed Conflict, 14 May 1954, 249 *UNTS* 240 (known as the *Hague Convention)* and its Protocol (1954); Convention on the Means of Prohibiting and Preventing the Illicit Import, Export and Transfer of Cultural Property, 14 November 1970, 823 *UNTS* 231; the Convention on the Exchange of Official Publications (1958); Universal Copyright Convention, 6 September 1952, 216 *UNTS* 133; the Recommendation on the Status of Scientific Researchers, 20 November 1974, *available at* http://unesdoc.unesco.org/images/0011/001140/114040e.pdf#page=166 [last visited 2 February 2012]; Recommendation concerning the Status of the Artist, 27 October 1980, *available at* http://portal.unesco.org/en/

instruments are dealt below in order to demonstrate the development of the link between culture and human rights in UNESCO's instruments, leading up to the adoption of the Cultural Diversity Declaration and the Convention on the Diversity of Cultural Expressions.

One of the first instruments adopted in the field of culture was the *Universal Copyright Convention*, adopted in 1952 and revised in 1971.[32] This Convention contains author's rights and the corresponding obligations of States to protect these rights. In this Convention, copyright was not addressed from a human rights, or cultural rights, perspective.

In November 1966 the General Conference of UNESCO adopted the *Declaration of Principles of International Cultural Co-operation* (Cultural Cooperation Declaration).[33] The Cultural Cooperation Declaration focuses on cooperation between States in the field of culture and the importance of such cooperation to maintain peace. Article 1 of the Cultural Cooperation Declaration reads as follows:

> 1. Each culture has a dignity and value which must be respected and preserved.
> 2. Every people has the right and the duty to develop its culture ...

While the first paragraph shows that the Member States consider culture to be a value that must be preserved and respected, the second paragraph contains a collective right and duty for peoples to develop cultures. No further clarification was given of the concepts 'people' and 'culture', which leaves their scope rather ambiguous. Since the Declaration was meant to encourage cooperation *between* States, it seems likely that it referred mainly to national cultures, probably in a narrow sense. The Cultural Cooperation Declaration is not legally binding. It therefore does not imply concrete State obligations, but reflects principles to be respected by States.

In November 1976 the General Conference adopted the *Recommendation on Participation by the People at Large in Cultural Life and their Contribution to It* (Recommendation).[34] The Recommendation is addressed to States and does not contain rights directly applicable to individuals or communities. In the

---

ev.php-URL_ID=13138&URL_DO=DO_TOPIC&URL_SECTION=201.html (last visited 2 February 2012); Recommendation on the Safeguarding of Traditional Culture and Folklore, 15 November 1989, *available at* http://portal.unesco.org/en/ev.php-URL_ID=13141&URL_DO=DO_TOPIC&URL_SECTION=201.html (last visited 2 February 2012).

32 *See* Universal Copyright Convention, 6 September 1952, 216 *UNTS* 133.

33 *See* Declaration of Principles of International Cultural Co-operation, 4 November 1966, *available at* http://unesdoc.unesco.org/images/0011/001140/114048e.pdf#page=82 (last visited 2 February 2012).

34 *See* Recommendation on Participation by the People at Large in Cultural Life and their Contribution to It, 26 November 1976, *available at* http://unesdoc.unesco.org/images/0011/001140/114038e.pdf#page=145 (last visited 2 February 2012) [hereinafter "Recommendation"].

Recommendation, however, participation in cultural life is clearly placed in a human rights framework, including references to universal human rights instruments.[35]

The Recommendation urges States to adopt legislation and regulations to ensure free access to national and world cultures without any form of discrimination, as well as encouraging free participation by all in the process of creating cultural values.[36] The States should also recognize the equality of cultures, including those of minorities and "... ensure that national minorities and foreign minorities have full opportunities for gaining access to and participating in the cultural life of the countries in which they find themselves in order to enrich it with their specific contributions, while safeguarding their right to preserve their cultural identity."[37] States should further protect and enhance all forms of cultural expressions, including national and regional languages and dialects.[38] Article 4 of the Recommendation also contains provisions concerning access to education, freedom of expression and communication, freedom of creation, the protection of cultural heritage and the role of the mass media in fostering mutual understanding. Attention is also paid to the possible negative aspects of cultural participation. It is stated that States should "... reject concepts which, under the guise of cultural action, are based on violence and aggression, domination, contempt and racial prejudice, as well as on debasing ideas or practices."[39]

The Recommendation emphasizes the broad meaning of culture, corresponding not only to cultural products and arts, but also to the way of life of communities and individuals, including issues such as education and communication. The Recommendation was developed to give communities and individuals the opportunity to have access to culture and to also actively participate in cultural life. This would imply that specific cultural policies are to be integrated in other policies in the fields of economics, social matters and education. Although individuals cannot invoke the Recommendation directly, because it is addressed to States, the instrument is a clear sign of the recognition of the importance of advancing cultural rights in the broad sense.

UNESCO is perhaps most famous for its activities concerning cultural heritage. The Member States of UNESCO have adopted several instruments on the protection of cultural heritage. The *Convention on the Protection of Natural and Cultural Heritage*, adopted in 1972, focuses on ways and means to protect cultural and natural heritage for future generations, but does not link cultural

35 The ICESCR, which includes in article 15(1) the right to take part in cultural life, came into force in the same year as the adoption of the Cultural Participation Recommendation. See Marks, *supra* note 5, at 304–6.

36 *See* Recommendation, *supra* note 34, Article 4(b).

37 Id., Article 4(f).

38 *See* id., Article 4(g).

39 Id., Article 4(s).

heritage to human rights or cultural rights.[40] The *Convention for the Safeguarding of the Intangible Cultural Heritage*, adopted in 2003, mentions human rights several times.[41] It is interesting to note that human rights are not referred to as rights to be enjoyed by individuals or communities, but as a safeguard against potentially harmful cultural practices. In the definition of 'intangible cultural heritage' it is stated that "[f]or the purposes of this Convention, consideration will be given solely to such intangible cultural heritage as is compatible with existing international human rights instruments, as well as with the requirements of mutual respect among communities, groups and individuals, and of sustainable development."[42]

In 1978, the General Conference of UNESCO adopted the *Declaration on Race and Racial Prejudice* (Declaration on Race), which emphasizes the value of differences.[43] Accordingly, the Declaration includes the right of individuals and groups to be different,[44] which, according to the Preamble, concerns the right not to be excluded, humiliated, exploited or forcibly assimilated. The Declaration on Race further contains a right for human beings to maintain cultural identity,[45] as well as the right of groups to their own cultural identity and the development of their distinctive cultural life.[46] With the Declaration on Race, States wished to recognize the diversity of cultures and to reaffirm that different communities should be able to decide on the development and expression of their cultures, thereby denouncing policies of forced assimilation of cultural communities.[47] The Declaration on Race contains several cultural rights in both the narrow and broad senses and reaffirms their significance. These rights cannot, however, be directly invoked by individuals and communities and the Declaration on Race is not legally-binding upon States.

The above-mentioned instruments show that many UNESCO instruments on culture reaffirm the importance of cultural rights, in both the narrow and broad senses. At the same time, only seldom do these instruments include cultural rights to be invoked by individuals or communities and those that do

---

40 *See* Convention concerning the Protection of the World Cultural and Natural Heritage, 16 November 1972, *available at* http://portal.unesco.org/en/ev.php-URL_ID=13055&URL_DO=DO_TOPIC&URL_SECTION=201.html (last visited 2 February 2012).

41 *See* Convention for the Safeguarding of the Intangible Cultural Heritage, 17 October 2003, *U.N. Doc. MISC/2003/CLT/CH/14.*

42 Id, Article 2(1).

43 *See* Declaration on Race and Racial Prejudice, 27 November 1978, *available at* http://portal.unesco.org/en/ev.php-URL_ID=13161&URL_DO=DO_TOPIC&URL_SECTION=201.html (last visited 2 February 2012).

44 *See* id., Article 1(2).

45 *See* id., Article 1(3).

46 *See* id., Article 5(1).

47 UNESCO, General Conference (20th session), "Draft Declaration on Race and Judicial Prejudice", *Doc. 20 C/18*, Annex, Explanatory Report, §5 (25 September 1978); UNESCO, "Working Paper of the Meeting of Government Representatives to Prepare a Draft Declaration on Race and Racial Prejudice", *Doc. SS-77/CONF.201/1*, at 18–9 (18 August 1977).

are not legally binding. Moreover, the concepts used in these instruments, such as 'culture' and 'participation' are not further clarified, thereby leaving concrete State measures or obligations rather vague. This shows that, although the promotion of human rights is included in its Constitution, UNESCO does not primarily adopt human rights instruments. UNESCO standards are generally not meant to directly provide substantive cultural rights to individuals or communities. Instead, the UNESCO instruments on culture aim to act as a catalyst for the cultural policies of States. The question is to what extent this is different for the UNESCO instruments on cultural diversity.

4. UNESCO UNIVERSAL DECLARATION ON CULTURAL DIVERSITY

The Member States of UNESCO adopted the Cultural Diversity Declaration at the General Conference in November 2001.[48] The Cultural Diversity Declaration aims to promote cultural diversity in the context of respect for human rights. It includes sections on identity, diversity and pluralism; cultural diversity and human rights; cultural diversity and creativity; and cultural diversity and international solidarity. The various provisions reflect the broad range of issues related to cultural diversity, among which are cultural rights.

Article 5 of the Cultural Diversity Declaration is entitled *cultural rights as an enabling environment for cultural diversity*. It reads as follows:

> Cultural rights are an integral part of human rights, which are universal, indivisible and interdependent. The flourishing of creative diversity requires the full implementation of cultural rights as defined in Article 27 of the Universal Declaration of Human Rights and in Articles 13 and 15 of the International Covenant on Economic, Social and Cultural Rights. All persons have therefore the right to express themselves and to create and disseminate their work in the language of their choice, and particularly in their mother tongue; all persons are entitled to quality education and training that fully respect their cultural identity; and all persons have the right to participate in the cultural life of their choice and conduct their own cultural practices, subject to respect for human rights and fundamental freedoms.

This provision stresses the importance of cultural rights for the promotion and protection of cultural diversity. It confirms that cultural diversity can only thrive if cultural rights are respected and implemented. It furthermore enumerates several cultural rights provisions from international human rights instruments, including cultural rights in the narrow sense (the right to participate in cultural life) and in the broad sense (freedom of expression and the right to education).

48 *See supra* note 1.

No reference is made to the right to freedom of religion or other human rights that form part of the category of cultural rights. The provision further deals with the limits to the enjoyment of cultural rights, in terms of the conduct of cultural practices that should be respectful to human rights. This provision, while confirming the importance of cultural rights, does not further clarify them in terms of normative content and State obligations.

The Cultural Diversity Declaration was adopted by consensus. It is not a legally binding instrument and mainly includes principles to be respected by the Member States. The States did, however, express their interest in elaborating further standard-setting instruments in the field of cultural diversity. In Article 12(c) of the Cultural Diversity Declaration it is stipulated that UNESCO should "pursue its activities in standard-setting ... in the areas related to the present Declaration ..." The *Main Lines of an Action Plan* (Action Plan) for the implementation of the Cultural Diversity Declaration confirm that Member States should deepen the international debate on cultural diversity. One of the recommendations was to make "... further headway in understanding and clarifying the content of cultural rights as an integral part of human rights."[49]

5. THE CONVENTION ON THE PROTECTION AND PROMOTION OF THE DIVERSITY OF CULTURAL EXPRESSIONS

Following the adoption of the Cultural Diversity Declaration the Member States discussed four possible instruments on cultural diversity, ranging from a new comprehensive instrument on cultural rights, over an instrument on the status of the artist, to a new Protocol to the Florence Agreement on Educational, Scientific and Cultural Materials or a new instrument on the protection of the diversity of cultural goods and artistic expressions.[50]

During the debate, two main approaches could be distinguished: some Member States approached cultural diversity from a human rights, or more specifically a cultural rights, perspective, while others approached it from a trade perspective. The Member States generally agreed on the importance of an international instrument on cultural rights, as this would improve consistency and understanding between States. It was maintained that cultural rights were not the subject of a single international instrument and were not as extensively

---

49 UNESCO, "Main Lines of an Action Plan for the Implementation of the UNESCO Declaration on Cultural Diversity", §§1 and 4 (2001), *available at* http://unesdoc.unesco.org/images/0012/001271/127160m.pdf (last visited 2 February 2012).

50 *See* UNESCO, Executive Board, "Preliminary Study on the Technical and Legal Aspects relating to the Desirability of a Standard-setting Instrument on Cultural Diversity", *166 EX/28*, §§20–23 (12 March 2003).

promoted as other human rights. It was stressed that "[g]iven the abundance of issues entailed by culture – issues that differ according to the approach adopted, whether anthropological or artistic – international law has yet to reach a clear-cut definition of cultural rights and their content."[51]

It was further maintained that international law does not determine exactly which rights fall into this category and provisions pertaining to cultural rights are dispersed in different international instruments.[52] In the end, however, Member States found the prospect of an international instrument on cultural rights "very remote,"[53] despite the Action Plan of the Cultural Diversity Declaration encouraging them to elaborate and clarify cultural rights. Instead the majority of Member States opted for the fourth option.[54] They preferred to draft a convention on cultural goods and expressions and to draft a culture-friendly trade agreement to overcome the negative effects of economic globalization on culture.[55]

After only two years of drafting and negotiations, the General Assembly of UNESCO adopted, the Convention on the Protection and Promotion of the Diversity of Cultural Expressions in October 2005, with a very large majority.

5.1. CULTURAL RIGHTS IN THE CONVENTION ON THE DIVERSITY OF CULTURAL EXPRESSIONS

The basic idea behind the Convention on the Diversity of Cultural Expressions is that "...cultural activities, goods and services have both an economic and a cultural nature, because they convey identities, values and meanings, and must therefore not be treated as solely having commercial value ..."[56] The purpose of the Convention on the Diversity of Cultural Expressions, as stipulated in Article 1, is to protect and promote the diversity of cultural expressions and "... to reaffirm the sovereign rights of States to maintain, adopt and implement policies and measures that they deem appropriate for the protection and promotion of the diversity of cultural expressions on their territory."[57]

As explained above, the Member States did not want to draft a cultural rights instrument. Accordingly, the Convention on the Diversity of Cultural

51 Id., §13.

52 *See* id., §20.

53 Id., §20.

54 UNESCO, "Preliminary Study on the Technical and Legal Aspects Relating to the Desirability of a Standard-Setting Instrument on Cultural Diversity," *32 C/52 No. 34*, at 64 (18 July 2003).

55 *See* UNESCO, Executive Board, *supra* note 50, §11; *See also* N. Obuljen, "From Our Creative Diversity to the Convention on Cultural Diversity", in N. Obuljen and J. Smiers (eds.), *UNESCO's Convention on the Protection and Promotion of the Diversity of Cultural Expressions: Making It Work*, 2006, 17, 19–20.

56 Convention on the Diversity of Cultural Expressions, *supra* note 2, Preamble §18.

57 Id., Article 1(h).

Expressions is not – and was not meant to be – a cultural rights instrument as such. It focuses on cultural goods and expressions and does not specifically aim at the promotion and protection of human rights or cultural rights by giving rights to States to develop their own policies. This is almost opposite to a human rights or cultural rights instrument, which would give rights to individuals and communities to be guaranteed by States. At the same time, however, several general references to human rights can be found in the Convention on the Diversity of Cultural Expressions. In the Preamble, for example, it is stated that cultural diversity is important for the full realization of human rights as proclaimed in the Cultural Diversity Declaration and other universal instruments. The Convention on the Diversity of Cultural Expressions further contains several 'guiding principles', among which Principle 1 concerns respect for human rights and fundamental freedoms.[58] It reads as follows:

> Cultural diversity can be protected and promoted only if human rights and fundamental freedoms, such as freedom of expression, information and communication, as well as the ability of individuals to choose cultural expressions, are guaranteed. No one may invoke the provisions of this Convention in order to infringe human rights and fundamental freedoms as enshrined in the Universal Declaration of Human Rights or guaranteed by international law or to limit the scope thereof.

This provision mainly confirms the importance of respect for human rights for the promotion and protection of cultural diversity. It enumerates several human rights specifically, although much less broadly than in the Cultural Diversity Declaration. Where this Declaration specifically mentions cultural rights in the narrow sense, such as the right to participate in cultural life and respect for cultural identity in education, the Convention on the Diversity of Cultural Expressions focuses on freedom of expression, including the right to information, two rights that belong to the broad meaning of cultural rights.

The drafting process shows that the issue of human rights was part of the debates on the Convention on the Diversity of Cultural Expressions from the very beginning. As argued above, some Member States wished to focus on the human rights dimension of cultural diversity. It is interesting to note that the Convention on the Diversity of Cultural Expressions speaks of 'human rights' and does not refer to 'cultural rights', as the Cultural Diversity Declaration does. Various persons involved in the drafting process explained that it was felt by many Member States that 'cultural rights' could be interpreted too narrowly, as referring mainly to the protection of cultural products or artists. The broader term was used because Member States preferred to place the Convention on the Diversity of Cultural Expressions in a broader human rights framework.

---

58 *See* id., Article 2(1).

While this may be a disappointment for those who would like the Convention on the Diversity of Cultural Expressions to contribute to the promotion of cultural rights, the choice to focus not only on cultural rights, but to opt for the more general approach using 'human rights', is not necessarily problematic. Although, as shown above, cultural rights is a very broad category of rights, if not clarified, the use of the term 'cultural rights' may indeed have been misleading or unnecessarily restrictive. The broad scope of cultural rights may not have been understood, or accepted, by all Member States.

There were, however, also States that actually feared that the Convention on the Diversity of Cultural Expressions could be misinterpreted as lacking respect for basic human rights. The main reason why the right to freedom of expression and information were specifically mentioned was because the United States, one of the crucial players in the negotiations, insisted on the importance of these rights for the Convention on the Diversity of Cultural Expressions. From the beginning of the negotiations the US was strongly opposed to the adoption of the Convention on the Diversity of Cultural Expressions. It disagreed with the idea of the dual nature – cultural and economic – of cultural goods and services. It was concerned that the definition of the word 'protection' would cause the Convention on the Diversity of Cultural Expressions to be a protectionist instrument, creating obstacles for the free exchange of goods and services, contrary to the idea of liberal trade at the bilateral or multilateral level. The US considered the sovereign right of States to take measures and formulate policies to promote and protect cultural diversity as an open invitation to violate other agreements and obligations, such as human rights and trade instruments.[59] The US continuously emphasized that UNESCO should promote the free flow of ideas by word and image.[60] It therefore insisted on the inclusion of freedom of expression and the free flow of information in the text of the Convention on the Diversity of Cultural Expressions. One cannot help but wonder, however, to what extent the US truly wished to protect these human rights, and whether it used these arguments as a pretext to protect its trade interests.

The Convention on the Diversity of Cultural Expressions also pays attention to the situation of minorities and indigenous peoples. For example, the Preamble refers to the importance of traditional knowledge systems, in particular of indigenous peoples, as a source of wealth. It also states that the vitality of

---

59 UNESCO, "Preliminary Report By the Director-General Setting Out the Situation to be Regulated and the Possible Scope of the Regulating Action Proposed, Accompanied by the Preliminary Draft of a Convention on the Protection of the Diversity of Cultural Contents and Artistic Expressions", *Doc. 33 C/23*, at 5–16 (4 August 2005); *See also* R.J. Neuwirth, "'United in Divergence': A Commentary on the UNESCO Convention on the Promotion and Protection of the Diversity of Cultural Expressions", 66/4 *Heidelberg Journal of International Law* 819, at 838–839 and 849 (2006).

60 UNESCO, "Draft Resolution submitted by the United States of America on the Desirability of drawing up an international standard-setting instrument on cultural diversity", *Doc. 32 C/COM.iv/DR.5 Paris* (2003).

cultures is taken into account, "… including for persons belonging to minorities and indigenous peoples, manifested in their freedom to create, disseminate and distribute their traditional cultural expressions and to have access thereto, so as to benefit from them for their own development."[61] Furthermore, Principle 3 as laid down in Article 2(1) Convention on the Diversity of Cultural Expressions recognizes the equal dignity of and respect for all cultures, including the cultures of persons belonging to minorities and indigenous peoples.

This leads to the question of the definition of cultural diversity. The title "Convention on the Diversity of Cultural Expressions" is in fact misleading. Although often referred to as such, including in this volume, in fact it is not, and was not meant to be a convention on the promotion and protection of cultural diversity in the broad and holistic sense of the concept. Draft texts proposed by networks outside UNESCO spoke of the promotion and protection of cultural diversity as such.[62] However, from the start of the negotiations, States deliberately chose to speak of the diversity of cultural expressions, not of cultural diversity as such, thereby narrowing the scope of the Convention on the Diversity of Cultural Expressions.

The Convention on the Diversity of Cultural Expressions includes a definition of cultural diversity in Article 4(1), which is "… the many ways in which the cultures of groups and societies find expression." This definition refers to the cultures of groups and societies. The Convention on the Diversity of Cultural Expressions further allows States to take measures to promote and protect the diversity of cultural expressions 'on their territory'.[63] The question is which cultural diversity it is that the Convention on the Diversity of Cultural Expressions tries to promote and protect. Is it merely the diversity *among* States, searching for a balance in the exchange of goods and services between States? Or would it also imply the diversity *within* States, which would imply the promotion and protection of the cultures of different communities within a society?

The Convention on the Diversity of Cultural Expressions leaves room for both perceptions. On the one hand, references can be found to national cultures as well as to cultures of minorities and indigenous peoples. On the other hand, however, the Convention on the Diversity of Cultural Expressions places a significant emphasis on the principle of the sovereignty of States through the sovereign right of States to take measures to promote and protect the diversity of cultural expressions. The emphasis on sovereignty may give the impression that mainly *national* cultures are to be promoted and protected. In this respect, it is

---

61 Convention on the Diversity of Cultural Expressions, *supra* note 2, Preamble §8.

62 *See, e.g.*, INCD, "Proposed Convention on Cultural Diversity" (2003), *available at* www.indc.net (last visited 2 February 2012); INCP, "Draft International Convention on Cultural Diversity by the Working Group on Cultural Diversity" (2003), *available at* www.incp-ripc.org (last visited 2 February 2012).

63 *See* Convention on the Diversity of Cultural Expressions, *supra* note 2, Articles 5(2), 6(1), 7(1), and 8(1).

interesting to note that one of the main supporters of the Convention on the Diversity of Cultural Expressions, namely France, does not officially recognize the existence of minorities on its territory.[64]

Although the Convention on the Diversity of Cultural Expressions does not contain substantive cultural rights for individuals or communities, several provisions speak of measures that *may* be taken by States to protect cultural diversity. These measures show significant similarities with measures that might possibly flow from cultural rights. For example, according to the Convention on the Diversity of Cultural Expressions, States may take measures that "… provide opportunities for … the creation, production, dissemination, distribution and enjoyment of such domestic cultural activities, goods and services, including provisions relating to the language used for such activities, goods and services."[65] This provision furthermore speaks of measures to establish and support public institutions, to support artists and others involved in the creation of cultural expressions, as well as measures to enhance the diversity of the media, including through public service broadcasting.[66] Such measures could also include public financial assistance.[67] States should furthermore encourage individuals and groups to create, produce, disseminate, distribute and have access to their own cultural expressions, "… paying due attention to the special circumstances and needs of women as well as various social groups, including persons belonging to minorities and indigenous peoples."[68]

6. CONCLUSION

The Convention on the Diversity of Cultural Expressions has encouraged an intense debate at the international level on the issue of cultural diversity. It codifies the right of States to implement cultural policies and it establishes a new foundation for future cooperation in the area of cultural diversity, with special attention for the needs of developing countries.

64 France has, for example, submitted a declaration under Article 27 ICCPR protecting the rights of members of minorities to enjoy their culture. The Declaration implies that, since the French Constitution prohibits all distinctions between citizens based on grounds of origin, race or religion, no minorities exist in France. Consequently, Article 27 is not regarded as being applicable to France. The French Constitutional Court has further declared that the Charter on Regional and Minority Languages (1992) and the Framework Convention on National Minorities (1995) of the Council of Europe are incompatible with the French Constitution on the basis of the same argument (Conseil d'Etat, avis No. 357466, 6 July 1995 and avis No. 359461, 24 September 1996).

65 Convention on the Diversity of Cultural Expressions, *supra* note 2, Article 6(b).

66 *See* id., Article 6(f), (g) and (h).

67 *See* id., Article 6(d).

68 Id., Article 7(a).

The importance of the Convention on the Diversity of Cultural Expressions lies in the fact that it confirms the value of cultural diversity and incorporates this concept in international law. Consequently, the Convention on the Diversity of Cultural Expressions has to be taken into account when States undertake new commitments in the cultural and other sectors at the bilateral or multilateral level. It may not imply many concrete commitments by States, but it is clearly an incentive for States to develop internal and international cultural policies. In developing these policies, States are to take human rights into account.

As argued above, the Convention on the Diversity of Cultural Expressions was not meant to be an instrument on human rights or cultural rights. In fact, it is an instrument containing mainly the rights of States, the very opposite of the idea of human rights, which are supposed to ensure that States guarantee human rights to be enjoyed by individuals and communities. In this regard, the Convention on the Diversity of Cultural Expressions confirms the position taken by the other UNESCO instruments on culture: they touch upon or even incorporate cultural rights, but are not primarily meant to promote and protect cultural rights as such.

In other words, for those who expected a new international instrument promoting and protecting cultural rights, the Convention on the Diversity of Cultural Expressions is clearly a disappointment. Although the human rights framework in relation to cultural diversity is recognized, cultural rights are not reaffirmed as the enabling environment for cultural diversity and are not further advanced. At the same time, the Convention on the Diversity of Cultural Expressions, together with the other UNESCO instruments on culture, confirms the importance of cultural rights as human rights. In this respect, the Convention on the Diversity of Cultural Expressions adds to the recent developments in the field of cultural rights. While for a number of years cultural rights formed a neglected category of human rights, they now have the full attention of scholars and States. There is an increasing number of studies conducted on cultural rights or on culture and human rights. Cultural rights are no longer seen as 'luxury rights' or rights that only matter after other human rights are implemented. Culture is recognized as an important aspect of human dignity that needs to be protected by human rights.

The political climate was, however, not ready to go further in adopting an international legal instrument on cultural rights. The question is whether this is so disappointing. An international instrument on cultural rights would improve their visibility and make them more well-known.[69] The fact is, however, that cultural rights provisions have been incorporated in existing international

69 A group of scholars, united in the Fribourg Group, has made a solid achievement in this respect in adopting a Declaration on Cultural Rights (May 2007). The aim of the Declaration was not to adopt a new legal instrument including a new set of rights, but to collect cultural rights provisions from existing international human rights instruments in order to enhance their visibility and coherence and to advance their realization. The Fribourg Declaration on

human rights instruments. Attention should be focused on further clarifying the normative content of these provisions, and on elaborating the cultural dimension of human rights. This could improve their advancement and implementation. Instruments such as the Convention on the Diversity of Cultural Expressions and other UNESCO instruments could certainly be helpful in this respect.

Cultural Rights has been translated in several languages, which can be found on www.unifr.ch/iiedh/fr/publications/declaration-de-fribourg (last visited 2 February 2012).

CIVIL AND POLITICAL RIGHTS AND THE CONVENTION ON THE DIVERSITY OF CULTURAL EXPRESSIONS

Eva BREMS*

1. INTRODUCTION

The UNESCO *Convention on the Protection and Promotion of the Diversity of Cultural Expressions* ("Convention on the Diversity of Cultural Expressions")[1] is not a human rights treaty. Yet as both its proponents and its opponents advance human rights arguments, it may be assumed that a human rights analysis of the Convention on the Diversity of Cultural Expressions has at least some relevance. Several human rights perspectives are possible, in particular that of cultural rights (including the right of cultural participation, and intellectual property rights as protected in Article 15 of the *Covenant on Economic, Social and Cultural Rights* ("CESCR"))[2], and that of minority rights. This chapter addresses the issue of civil and political rights. Two rights are specifically involved: the right to freedom of expression and the right of access to information.

The right to freedom of expression is protected in provisions including Article 19 of the *International Covenant on Civil and Political Rights* ("ICCPR"),[3] Article 10 of the *European Convention for the Protection of Human Rights and Fundamental Freedoms* ("ECHR")[4], Article 11 of the *Charter of Fundamental Rights of the European Union*,[5] Article 13 of the *American*

---

* Human Rights Centre, Ghent University, Belgium.

1 *See* Convention on the Protection and Promotion of the Diversity of Cultural Expressions, 20 October 2005, U.N. Doc. CLT-2005/CONVENTION DIVERSITE-CULT REV. [hereinafter "Convention on the Diversity of Cultural Expressions"].

2 *See* Covenant on Economic, Social and Cultural Rights, 16 December 1966, 993 *U.N.T.S.* 3 [hereinafter "CESCR"].

3 *See* International Covenant on Civil and Political Rights, 16 December 1966, 999 *U.N.T.S.* 171 [hereinafter "ICCPR"].

4 *See* European Convention for the Protection of Human Rights and Fundamental Freedoms, 4 November 1950, *ETS* No. 5 [hereinafter "ECHR"].

5 *See* Charter of Fundamental Rights of the European Union, 7 December 2000, *OJ 2000/C 364/01*.

Convention on Human Rights,[6] article 9 of the *African Charter on Human and Peoples' Rights*[7] and Article 13 of the *Convention on the Rights of the Child* ("CRC").[8] All of these provisions include within the right to freedom of expression the right to 'seek and receive' information and ideas.

In addition, the CRC has a specific provision on the child's right of access to information. Article 17 CRC emphasizes, on the one hand, the diversity of national and international sources of information, and on the other hand, the need to protect children against information or material that may be harmful to them and to encourage the dissemination of material that is beneficial for children.[9]

The human rights analysis below will firstly explore to what extent the Convention on the Diversity of Cultural Expressions furthers the right to freedom of expression and the right of access to information. In addition, it will examine possible restrictions of those rights by the Convention, and determine whether or not these constitute violations of human rights.

2. THE CONVENTION ON THE DIVERSITY OF CULTURAL EXPRESSIONS AS AN INSTRUMENT FURTHERING THE RIGHT TO FREEDOM OF EXPRESSION AND THE RIGHT OF ACCESS TO INFORMATION AND IDEAS

2.1. DRAFTING PROCESS

The resolution of the General Conference of UNESCO that spurred the drafting process of the Convention on the Diversity of Cultural Expressions emphasizes

6 *See* American Convention on Human Rights, 22 November 1969, 1144 *U.N.T.S.* 123.
7 *See* African Charter on Human and Peoples' Rights, 27 June 1981, 21 *I.L.M.* 58 (1982).
8 *See* Convention on the Rights of the Child, 20 November 1989, *UN Doc. A/44/49* [hereinafter "CRC"].
9 *See* Article 17 CRC:
'States Parties recognize the important function performed by the mass media and shall ensure that the child has access to information and material from a diversity of national and international sources, especially those aimed at the promotion of his or her social, spiritual and moral well-being and physical and mental health. To this end, States Parties shall:
(a) Encourage the mass media to disseminate information and material of social and cultural benefit to the child and in accordance with the spirit of article 29;
(b) Encourage international co-operation in the production, exchange and dissemination of such information and material from a diversity of cultural, national and international sources;
(c) Encourage the production and dissemination of children's books;
(d) Encourage the mass media to have particular regard to the linguistic needs of the child who belongs to a minority group or who is indigenous;
(e) Encourage the development of appropriate guidelines for the protection of the child from information and material injurious to his or her well-being, bearing in mind the provisions of articles 13 and 18.'

in its Preamble 'the importance of Article 19 of the Universal Declaration of Human Rights, which declares that everyone has the right to freedom of opinion and expression, including the freedom to seek, receive and impart information and ideas through any media and regardless of frontiers.'[10] Few further references to these freedoms are found in the reports of the meetings of the experts who drafted the Convention on the Diversity of Cultural Expressions. There is no indication that they served in any way as a guideline to the drafters.

Yet despite the absence of human rights language and of references to human rights provisions, the substance of the debates approached a human rights perspective in some respects. According to the report of the First Meeting of Experts, some experts emphasized the distinction between aims relating to the ultimate purpose of the Convention on the Diversity of Cultural Expressions and those relating to its implementation. With regard to the second category, "there was a broad convergence of views as to the two principles that should be promoted by a Convention: (a) access for all consumers and users to cultural products and artistic expressions that were rich and diversified, including in terms of geographical origin [...]; and (b) the participation of all creators in cultural life and their access to the widest possible means of dissemination."[11] The first of these aims is the translation of the right of access to information and ideas into the context of the Convention on the Diversity of Cultural Expressions; the second is an aspect of the right to freedom of expression in the sphere of cultural production. In addition, 'most experts also stressed that protection should imply "empowerment", particularly of those who had no means of expressing themselves and of becoming known nationally and internationally.'[12] Such an emphasis on individual empowerment rather than on the protection of collective or state interests is characteristic of a human rights approach. Despite the clear parallel between some of the Convention on the Diversity of Cultural Expressions goals on the one hand and human rights on the other, the report of the Third Meeting of Experts, the final meeting in the series, mentions that 'the experts felt that it was not desirable to give rise in this convention to new obligations relating to respect for human rights.'[13] It follows that whilst human

10 UNESCO, Intergovernmental Meeting of Experts, "Resolution 34: Desirability of Drawing Up an International Standard-Setting Instrument on Cultural Diversity", *CLT/CPD/2004/CONF.201/5* (17 October 2003), *available at* http://portal.unesco.org/culture/en/files/21974/10902326553Eng-Resolution32C34-conf.201-5.pdf/Eng-Resolution32C34-conf.201-5.pdf (last visited 2 February 2012).

11 UNESCO, First Meeting of Experts (category VI) on the First Draft of an International Convention on the Protection of the Diversity of Cultural Contents and Artistic Expressions, "Report", *CLT/CPD/2003-608/01*, at 3-4 (20 February 2004).

12 Id, at 4.

13 UNESCO, Third Meeting of Experts (category VI) on the First Draft of an International Convention on the Protection of the Diversity of Cultural Contents and Artistic Expressions, "Report", *CLT/CPD/2004/603/5*, at 4 (23 June 2004).

rights may have been 'the backdrop of the Convention,'[14] the drafters explicitly stated that they did not have the ambition of carrying human rights protection beyond what was already achieved by international law.

2.2. THE CONVENTION ON THE DIVERSITY OF CULTURAL EXPRESSIONS

Human rights are the rights of persons, and the Convention on the Diversity of Cultural Expressions creates rights and obligations only for State Parties. Yet human rights did achieve inclusion in the Convention on the Diversity of Cultural Expressions. The Preamble reaffirms that "freedom of thought, expression and information, as well as diversity of the media, enable cultural expressions to flourish within societies," suggesting that these human rights are instrumental to reaching the goals of the Convention on the Diversity of Cultural Expressions. The next paragraph recognizes "that the diversity of cultural expressions, including traditional cultural expressions, is an important factor that allows individuals and peoples to express and to share with others their ideas and values." This expresses the idea that the Convention on the Diversity of Cultural Expressions may be instrumental in realizing freedom of expression and of access to information.

More importantly, in the operative provisions of the Convention on the Diversity of Cultural Expressions, the 'principle of respect for human rights and fundamental freedoms' figures first among the 'guiding principles' of this Convention. Article 2(1) Convention on the Diversity of Cultural Expressions states: "Cultural diversity can be protected only if human rights and fundamental freedoms, such as freedom of expression, information and communication, as well as the ability of individuals to choose cultural expressions, are guaranteed. No one may invoke the provisions of the Convention on the Diversity of Cultural Expressions in order to infringe human rights and fundamental freedoms as enshrined in the *Universal Declaration of Human Rights* or guaranteed by international law, or to limit the scope thereof."[15] This confirms the instrumentalist, minimalist view of human rights described above. The elevation of human rights into a 'guiding principle' of the Convention on the Diversity of Cultural Expressions does not mean that this Convention is to be interpreted in the way that best furthers these rights, but rather that the Convention is not to be interpreted in any way that would allow a human rights violation or that would remove any situation from the sphere of human rights protection.

---

14 UNESCO, "Ten Keys to the Convention on the Protection and Promotion of the Diversity of Cultural Expressions", *CLT/CEI/DCE/2007/PI/32*, at 7 (2005).

15 Convention on the Diversity of Cultural Expressions, *supra* note 1, Article 2 (1).

To the extent that the Convention on the Diversity of Cultural Expressions imposes obligations on State Parties that benefit certain persons, it may be said that this Convention indirectly affirms rights in the sphere of civil and political rights. Most relevant in this respect is Article 7 Convention on the Diversity of Cultural Expressions. The state obligation in this provision is expressed in weak terms ('Parties shall endeavour to') and is by no means an obligation to achieve results. Yet this provision indirectly grants individuals and social groups a right to state efforts aimed at encouraging them "to create, produce, disseminate, distribute and have access to their own cultural expressions"[16] and "to have access to diverse cultural expressions from within their territory as well as from other countries of the world."[17] Moreover, it grants a right to women "as well as various social groups, including persons belonging to minorities and indigenous peoples"[18] for due attention to be paid to their special circumstances and needs in the context of State policies under Article 7. Finally, artists, others involved in the creative process, cultural communities, and organizations that support them may derive from the Convention on the Diversity of Cultural Expressions a right to state efforts to recognize their important contribution. In addition, under Article 11, members of civil society may claim a right to State action aimed at encouraging "the active participation of civil society in ... [the States] ... efforts to achieve the objectives of this Convention."[19]

Human rights, as a rule, entail three types of State obligations: obligations to respect human rights, namely to abstain from acts that constitute violations, obligations to protect human rights, namely to undertake action aimed at preventing or addressing violations by third parties, and obligations to fulfil human rights, namely to take action, including establishing legislation or policy, that is needed to realize human rights. As the Convention on the Diversity of Cultural Expressions is not drafted in human rights language, the use of the terms 'respect'[20] and 'protect'[21] cannot be understood as restricting the types of human rights obligations it confers.

Article 20(1) of the Convention on the Diversity of Cultural Expressions stipulates that State Parties have to "foster mutual supportiveness"[22] between the Convention and other treaties to which they are parties, and that "when interpreting and applying the other treaties to which they are parties or when entering into other international obligations, Parties shall take into account the

16 Id., Article 7(1)(a).
17 Id., Article 7(1)(b).
18 Id., Article 7(1)(a).
19 Id., Article 11.
20 *See, e.g.*, Article 2 (1) of the Convention on the Diversity of Cultural Expressions (titled "Principle of *respect for* human rights and fundamental freedoms" [emphasis added]).
21 *See, e.g.*, Article 8 of the Convention on the Diversity of Cultural Expressions (having as title "Measures to *protect* cultural expressions" [emphasis added]).
22 Convention on the Diversity of Cultural Expressions, *supra* note 1, Article 20 (1) (a).

relevant provisions of this Convention."[23] This supports an interpretation under which the commitments to further freedom of expression and information that States have undertaken in vague and general terms under human rights treaties are imbued with a degree of concrete content through being read jointly with the abovementioned provisions of the Convention on the Diversity of Cultural Expressions.

2.3. ANALYSIS

Viewed against the taxonomy of state human rights obligations above, the potential of the Convention on the Diversity of Cultural Expressions to further the right to freedom of expression and the right of access to information falls within state human rights obligations 'to fulfil human rights'. Translated in terms of civil and political human rights, the idea behind the Convention on the Diversity of Cultural Expressions is that in the cultural sphere, adequate protection of these rights may require state intervention.

2.3.1. Room for state discretion in the implementation of obligations to fulfil

A central objective of the Convention on the Diversity of Cultural Expressions is "to reaffirm the sovereign right of States to maintain, adopt and implement policies and measures that they deem appropriate for the protection and promotion of the diversity of cultural expressions on their territory."[24] Article 6 Convention on the Diversity of Cultural Expressions enumerates the types of measures that may be adopted under ordinary circumstances in this context. These are expressed in terms of supportive, rather than restrictive, measures, including financial assistance,[25] but are mostly formulated in very broad terms that may also encompass restrictive measures. For example, the formulation "regulatory measures aimed at protecting and promoting diversity of cultural expressions"[26] does not appear to exclude the imposition of quotas in the sphere of cultural goods and services. In "special situations where cultural expressions on its territory are at risk of extinction, under serious threat, or otherwise in need of urgent safeguarding," the restrictions, if any of the list in Article 6 of the Convention on the Diversity of Cultural Expressions do not apply and a State Party may take "all appropriate measures to protect and preserve cultural expressions."

---

23 Id., Article 20(1)(b).

24 Id., Article 1(h); *See also* Article 5(1) of the Convention on the Diversity of Cultural Expressions (stating that "[t]he Parties ... reaffirm their sovereign right to formulate and implement their cultural policies and to adopt measures to protect and promote the diversity of cultural expressions...").

25 *See* Convention on the Diversity of Cultural Expressions, *supra* note 1, Article 6(2)(d).

26 *See* id., Article 6(2)(a).

From a human rights perspective, these provisions *allowing* States to adopt measures that support the exercise of fundamental freedoms do not add anything new. Without the Convention on the Diversity of Cultural Expressions – and within the restrictions of other international obligations – States were already allowed to do so. It follows that the human rights impact of these provisions is chiefly a negative one, restricting States' options in the fulfilment of their positive obligations under the right to freedom of expression and the right of access to information in the cultural sphere. These restrictions are mostly of a procedural nature: States have to report on the protective measures they adopt[27] and States have to encourage the participation of civil society in their policies under the Convention on the Diversity of Cultural Expressions.[28]

Substantive restrictions may be found among the 'guiding principles' of the Convention in Article 2: the principle of respect for human rights and fundamental freedoms[29] and the principle of openness and balance.[30] To the extent that State Parties of the Convention on the Diversity of Cultural Expressions are parties to human rights conventions, the former does not add anything new. The latter obliges States to give policy support to the diversity of cultural expressions to "promote, in an appropriate manner, openness to other cultures of the world."[31] This is a significant restriction, as state policies will naturally tend to protect and promote domestic cultural expressions. The principle of openness and balance appears to exclude cultural policies that exclusively or excessively promote domestic cultural expressions to the detriment of other cultural expressions.

2.3.2. Mandatory measures to implement obligations to fulfil

Most of the obligations imposed by the Convention on the Diversity of Cultural Expressions on State Parties may be seen as mandatory measures requiring States to implement their 'obligations to fulfil' the right to freedom of expression and the right of access to information and ideas in the cultural sphere. The formulation in terms of an obligation to strive rather than an obligations to achieve results ('parties shall endeavour to …') is consistent with the nature of obligations to take steps towards fulfilment under civil and political human rights, and in that sense is comparable with positive obligations under economic, social and cultural human rights. The latter are usually formulated as progressive obligation,[32] obliging States to take steps leading toward the goal of complete

27 *See* id., Article 9.
28 *See* id., Artcile 11.
29 *See* id., Article 2(1).
30 *See* id., Article 2(8).
31 Id.
32 *See, e.g.*, Article 2(1) CESCR ("Each State Party to the present Covenant *undertakes to take steps*, individually and through international assistance and co-operation, especially

protection or fulfilment. Where state compliance with human rights obligations is generally evaluated by defining a bottom line that may not be crossed, 'obligations to fulfil' are oriented instead toward a horizon line of complete fulfilment and a state's compliance is measured by the steps it takes towards that horizon. The minimal level of state compliance is defined through 'core obligations'.[33] Progressive realisation as such is recognized only with respect to economic, social and cultural rights. Yet in practice, a similar device would be useful in the context of civil and political rights, in particular when 'obligations to fulfil' are concerned. A formulation such as that in the Convention on the Diversity of Cultural Expressions comes close, assuming that 'endeavour to' entails a requirement to take steps. The mandatory measures that are enumerated in the Convention on the Diversity of Cultural Expressions go beyond core obligations. They are not designed to express a minimum in human rights terms, but rather a list of what is required in the eyes of the drafters to reach the goals of the Convention on the Diversity of Cultural Expressions, which are not primarily human rights oriented.

Mandatory measures that may be seen as measures to fulfil the right to freedom of cultural expression and the right of access to cultural information and ideas include measures to create an environment that encourages cultural expressions and access thereto,[34] measures to recognize cultural contributions,[35] and specific types of measures supporting the cultural sector in developing countries.[36]

2.3.3. *The free marketplace of ideas*

The notion that state intervention in the area of freedom of expression may be necessary to correct a practical imbalance, in which non-dominant actors

---

economic and technical, to the maximum of its available resources, *with a view to achieving progressively the full realization of* the rights recognized in the present Covenant by all appropriate means, including particularly the adoption of legislative measures" [emphasis added]).

33 The Committee on Economic, Social and Cultural Rights [hereinafter "Committee"], responsible for monitoring the CESCR, enumerates core obligations in its General Comments on specific rights. *See, e.g.*, COMMITTEE, "General Comment 12: The Right to Adequate Food", *E/C.12/1999/5*, §8 (1999); COMMITTEE, "General Comment 13: The Right to Education", *E/C.12/1999/10*, §57 (1999); COMMITTEE, "General Comment 14: The Right to the Highest Attainable Standard of Health", *E/C.12/2000/4*, §§43–44 (2000); COMMITTEE, "General Comment 15: The Right to Water", *UN Doc. E/C.12/2002/11*, §37 (2002); COMMITTEE, "General Comment 17: The Right of Everyone to Benefit from the Protection of the Moral and Material Interests Resulting from any Scientific, Literary or Artistic Production of Which He or She is the Author", *UN Doc. E/C.12/GC/17*, §39 (2005); COMMITTEE, "General Comment 18: The Right to Work", *UN Doc. E/C.12/GC/18*, §31 (2006).

34 *See* Convention on the Diversity of Cultural Expressions, *supra* note 1, Article 7(1).

35 *See* id., Article 7(2).

36 *See* id., Articles 14 to 18.

experience unequal opportunities for access to communication channels, is a familiar one in human rights discourse. It is also a contested viewpoint.

The context in which this debate has been going on for decades, is that of the regulation of hate speech. Hate speech regulation is about the prohibition of certain types of speech on grounds of their harmful discriminatory effect on specific non-dominant groups. Restrictions on one fundamental right – the freedom of expression – are therefore based on the need to protect another fundamental right – the right to be free from discrimination. The argument made against hate speech regulation is that it is unnecessary state intervention that disturbs the free marketplace of ideas. It is said that the government should not restrict access to that marketplace, because the value of an idea will be most evident in its confrontation with other ideas, not in its confrontation with the law: speech is best met with counter-speech. Proponents of hate speech regulation argue that the free marketplace of ideas is a theoretical construct; in reality members of non-dominant groups do not enjoy equal opportunities for access to that marketplace. Hence the argument for government intervention is based on the need to create a 'level playing field'.

In the context of the Convention on the Diversity of Cultural Expressions, the assumption is that in an unregulated market of cultural expressions, some expressions will not reach their intended audience and that this is not simply the result of audience preference due to the quality of the cultural expression, but also to a large extent, the result of power imbalances. In this context, the 'marketplace of ideas' is not only a metaphor, but also an actual economic market, and the power imbalances that disturb the market are to a large extent related to economic power. Government interventions in the marketplace of ideas that may hamper the freedom of expression in this case are grounded in the desire to promote access to the market, or freedom of expression, for non-dominant actors, and the desire to promote the right of access to information and ideas by guaranteeing the availability of a wider and more diverse range of cultural products on the market.

It should be clear that compared to the debate around hate speech, there is much less reason for suspicion concerning government interventions in the free marketplace of ideas under the Convention on the Diversity of Cultural Expressions. As long as government measures remain short of a total ban on particular cultural expressions, while they may deprive some foreign cultural expressions of a share of their audience to the benefit of domestic cultural expressions, the interference with the right to freedom of expression and the right of access to information and ideas will be limited and the overall result for these rights will be positive. Active government support for the French film industry may mean that a Hollywood movie attracts a smaller audience in France than if that support had not been given, because a number of people will watch a French movie that would not have been produced without government support. Yet the Hollywood movie still has unhampered access to the French market and therefore loses little in terms of freedom of expression, and the freedom of choice of the French people in the area of cultural expressions remains intact. At the same time, the freedom of expression of French film makers is significantly enhanced, as is the right of the French people to have access to information and ideas, because of the broader choice offered to them. It follows that while hate speech regulation attempts to 'level the playing field' by removing certain expressions from the market, the Convention on the Diversity of Cultural Expressions does the opposite; it aims at broader access to the market for providers of cultural products.

Yet what if in reality, government support for the French film industry does not harm Hollywood, but instead reduces the market share of other non-dominant players, for example Spanish or Hungarian film makers? In that case, the human rights assessment is less positive, because the freedom of expression of these film makers suffers more serious interference, and because the right of the French people to have access to information and ideas is interfered with, as the range of cultural expressions available to them is more restricted and less diverse. Here, one can imagine that the principle of balance and openness may play a role in guiding the choice of government measures. For example, measures stimulating (e.g. through government subsidies) the production of French movies are likely to have a less exclusive effect than measures encouraging (e.g. through tax incentives) distributors or movie theatres to distribute or show French movies.

3. THE CONVENTION ON THE DIVERSITY OF CULTURAL EXPRESSIONS AS AN INSTRUMENT RESTRICTING THE RIGHT TO FREEDOM OF EXPRESSION AND THE RIGHT OF ACCESS TO INFORMATION AND IDEAS

3.1. THE CONVENTION ON THE DIVERSITY OF CULTURAL EXPRESSIONS AND ITS CRITICS

In contrast with the view of the Convention on the Diversity of Cultural Expressions as an instrument that furthers the rights to freedom of cultural expression and of access to cultural information and ideas, there is another view that considers the Convention on the Diversity of Cultural Expressions a threat to these same civil and political rights. The United States voted against the Convention on the Diversity of Cultural Expressions. In a statement outlining its position, the U.S. Department of State advanced two concerns: respect for free trade and respect for human rights and the free flow of information. On the latter topic, the statement claims that the text

> is ambiguous and contradictory in its treatment of the flow of cultural information and goods. Some paragraphs emphasize freedom of expression, information, and communication, while other paragraphs imply that there are acceptable government controls on such freedoms. For example, Article 8 of the draft authorizes State Parties to the Convention to take 'all appropriate measures' to protect and preserve cultural expressions under serious threat. The US believes that such an action-oriented provision needs to be carefully circumscribed to ensure that it could not be misinterpreted to justify measures that would interfere with human rights and fundamental freedoms. At a minimum, the Convention should be redrafted so that it cannot be misinterpreted to authorize "measures limiting freedom of expression or restricting the flow of information.[37]

Explaining her vote at a press conference, the U.S. Ambassador to UNESCO said that the Convention on the Diversity of Cultural Expressions "could be used by States to justify policies that could be used or abused to control the cultural lives of their citizens."[38]

The same risk was anticipated by the drafters of the Convention, who provided a guarantee against its occurrence by including a human rights oriented abuse clause: "No one may invoke the provisions of this Convention in order to infringe human rights and fundamental freedoms as enshrined in the *Universal Declaration of Human Rights* or guaranteed by international law, or to limit the scope thereof."[39] This applies regardless whether State Parties subscribe to relevant human rights conventions. To the extent that they do, an additional guarantee is found in Article 20(2) of the Convention on the Diversity of Cultural Expressions: "Nothing in this Convention shall be interpreted as modifying rights and obligations of the Parties under any other treaties to which they are parties." The principle of openness and balance in Article 2(8) of the Convention on the Diversity of Cultural Expressions provides further protection against the risk that the Convention might lead to censorship.[40]

---

[37] US Department of State, Office of the Spokesman, "The Convention on the Protection and Promotion of the Diversity of Cultural Expressions", (11 October 2005), *available at* www.state.gov/r/pa/prs/ps/2005/54690.htm (last visited 2 February 2012).

[38] J. Thomas, "US Deeply Disappointed by Vote on UNESCO Diversity Convention", *News Blaze*, 21 October 2005, *available at* http://newsblaze.com/story/20051021224840nnnn.nb/topstory.html (last visited 2 February 2012).

[39] *See* Convention on the Diversity of Cultural Expressions, *supra* note 1, Article 2(1).

[40] UNESCO, "30 Frequently Asked Questions Concerning the Convention on the Protection and Promotion of the Diversity of Cultural Expressions", *CLT/CEI/DCE/2007/PI/32*, at 13, *available at* http://unesdoc.unesco.org/images/0014/001495/149502E.pdf (last visited 2 February 2012).

3.2. ANALYSIS

3.2.1. Legitimate restrictions

Is the U.S.' fear that the UNESCO Convention may lead to restrictions of the right to freedom of expression and the right of access to information and ideas justified? It appears that restrictions may indeed occur. Yet under international human rights law it is crucial to distinguish between acceptable restrictions of human rights and unacceptable violations of human rights. Article 2(1) of the Convention on the Diversity of Cultural Expressions is cognizant of that distinction and protects only against the latter.

Article 19 ICCPR is a typical provision on the right to freedom of expression (including the right of access to information and ideas):

1. Everyone shall have the right to hold opinions without interference.
2. Everyone shall have the right to freedom of expression; this right shall include freedom to seek, receive and impart information and ideas of all kinds, regardless of frontiers, either orally, in writing or in print, in the form of art, or through any other media of his choice.
3. The exercise of the rights provided for in paragraph 2 of this article carries with it special duties and responsibilities. It may therefore be subject to certain restrictions, but these shall only be such as are provided by law and are necessary:
    1. For respect of the rights or reputations of others;
    2. For the protection of national security or of public order (*ordre public*), or of public health or morals.

The rights we are concerned with are formulated in the second paragraph. The third paragraph is a restriction clause, outlining the conditions under which those rights may legitimately be restricted. Apart from some exceptions, human rights are not absolute. They may well have priority over other collective or individual interests, but this does not mean that in any particular contest between a human rights claim and a claim based on another interest the former will necessarily prevail. What it does mean is that it is for the party invoking the other interest to justify the restriction of the human right in terms of international law. Article 19(3) ICCPR is a standard restriction clause, stipulating three conditions for a restriction to be acceptable. In the first place, it needs to be provided by law. This means that it has to be based on a general norm. In the second place, the restrictive measure has to pursue one of the aims enumerated in the clause. These relate either to general interests[41] or to the rights or reputations of others.[42] Finally, the restrictive measure had to be necessary for

[41] ICCPR, *supra* note 3, Article 19(3)(2).
[42] Id., Article 19 (3) (1).

the realisation of that aim. This implies a requirement of proportionality between means and ends.

When we apply this to restrictions of fundamental freedoms resulting from the application of the Convention on the Diversity of Cultural Expressions, the first requirement is automatically satisfied, as the Convention on the Diversity of Cultural Expressions provides the required legal basis. It should be noted though that this is not the case when measures that a state claims are based on the Convention on the Diversity of Cultural Expressions in fact rely on erroneous interpretations of its provisions. The practice of human rights monitoring bodies shows, moreover, that the second requirement, a legitimate aim for the restriction, is rarely a stumbling block. Under the Convention on the Diversity of Cultural Expressions, measures restricting the rights to freedom of expression or of access to information and ideas of some cultural providers or consumers will normally be justified by the "protection of the rights of others", in other words the protection of the same rights of other cultural providers or consumers. Accordingly, the pivotal question is that of proportionality. The scope and rights-restrictive effect of the measures should not go beyond what is necessary to achieve the aim. In the abstract, proportionality is hard to assess, however there is a significant body of case law in this area involving decisions of international human rights monitoring bodies, including the *UN Human Rights Committee*, the *European Court of Human Rights* and the *Inter-American Commission* and *Court of Human Rights*, that may serve to provide guidance.

It follows that, contrary to what the above-quoted U.S. government statement implies, some government controls of the rights to freedom of expression and access to information and ideas are acceptable under international law. Other government controls however will be unacceptable. Less restrictive measures are more likely to be held proportionate and therefore justifiable than more restrictive measures. Government subsidies for domestic European television and film industries may restrict citizens' access to U.S. products, but less so than quotas reserving, for example, a minimum percentage of broadcasting time for domestic products, and these in turn are less restrictive than measures that would impose an outright ban on certain products.

3.2.2. Conflicting rights

As explained above, restrictions of the rights to freedom of expression and of access to information and ideas under the Convention on the Diversity of Cultural Expressions may be justified on the ground of their necessity for the protection of these same rights of other persons. It follows that this is a situation of conflict between fundamental rights.[43] Human rights law does not, as yet,

---

[43] *See, generally*, E. Brems (ed.), *Conflicts Between Fundamental Rights*, 2008.

provide a specific methodology for approaching situations of conflicting rights. Yet it is immediately clear that restrictive measures that aim to guarantee human rights are less suspect than restrictive measures serving another purpose. The priority of human rights claims over other claims is not relevant in a situation where both sides invoke human rights. Finding the right balance between the conflicting rights is an enormous challenge for legislators and judges alike. Under international human rights law, the proportionality test in such situations will be applied loosely, leaving ample room for domestic decision makers to determine the right solution in a specific context.[44]

It has been argued that when the conflict involves, on the one hand, negative state obligations and on the other hand, positive state obligations, the former should normally prevail.[45] If that suggestion is accepted, it would mean that government measures under the Convention on the Diversity of Cultural Expressions become unacceptable as soon as they restrict the right to freedom of expression or the right of access to information and ideas. This is because the restrictive effect of these measures on rights would be evaluated under the State's obligation to respect human rights, which is a negative obligation, whereas the rights-enhancing effect of these measures would be assessed under the State's obligation to fulfil human rights, which is a positive obligation. The result would be even harsher than if a general interest were invoked as justification of the restrictive measures. It is therefore clear that the suggested rule giving negative state obligations priority over positive state obligations must be rejected for failing to take proper account of the fact that the restrictive measures serve a human rights purpose.

It may be useful to look at the individual and collective dimensions of the conflicting rights in addition to, or instead of, the distinction between positive and negative state obligations. The human rights concerned here are individual rights. The conflict concerned is one in which certain individuals claim that a particular government measure infringes their human rights, whereas other individuals claim that their human rights would be infringed in the absence of the same measure. It does not seem to be appropriate to determine the respective weight of each claim by counting the numbers of individuals affected on each side. But it may be relevant to look at the structural or collective stakes underlying the respective individual claims.

One such collective stake relates to the protection of cultural identity. It has been argued that

44 *See, e.g.*, European Court of Human Rights (Grand Chamber), Evans v. United Kingdom, 10 April 2007, *available at* www.echr.coe.int (last visited 2 February 2012).

45 *See* O. De Schutter and F. Tulkens, "Rights in Conflict: the European Court of Human Rights as a Pragmatic Institution", in Eva Brems (ed.), *Conflicts Between Fundamental Rights*, 2008, 169, 181–7.

> the definition of 'human rights' favoured by the US Department of State focuses primarily on the ability of individuals to freely 'express themselves.' UNESCO however, takes a broader view of human rights as the concept relates to the interest of those within a culture in its artistic traditions and the continued development and dissemination of its cultural products.[46]

When indigenous peoples are involved, the latter concern is recognized as a human right, which is collective in nature.[47] When, for example, the interest of the Portuguese people in the continuous development and dissemination of Portuguese cultural products is under discussion, it remains a concern that is very close to the hearts and minds of the people at large, including those who do not produce or consume Portuguese cultural products. Moreover, while this collective interest in itself does not carry human rights status, it is clear that ignoring it may threaten important human rights related to cultural identity.[48] On the other side of the equation, loss of a market share for Hollywood products does not in any similar way infringe a collective or structural interest. Potential loss of jobs in Hollywood, which is a threat to the right to work, due to protective cultural measures in Portugal would, in a global human rights balancing exercise, be outweighed by job creation in Portugal.

Another collective stake relates to the long-term structural preconditions of freedom of expression. From this perspective, the crucial value of policies under the Convention on the Diversity of Cultural Expressions lies in the fact that they expand the range of cultural products that are offered.

> The freedom to express one's opinion presupposes the freedom to form an opinion. Logically, the freedom to form an opinion would not be possible under circumstances where only a very limited choice regarding sources of information exists. Hence, freedom of expression presupposes a variety of sources of information. In modern societies characterized by mass communication, this ultimately presupposes media pluralism, which provides the basis for public discourse, thereby fostering free intellectual debate. Indeed, because the institutional aspect of the freedom of information is the precondition for the functioning of a democratic society, it can be viewed as overriding the individual aspect of this freedom.[49]

---

46 E. Brooks, Note, "Cultural Imperialism vs. Cultural Protectionism: Hollywood's Response to UNESCO Efforts to Promote Cultural Diversity", 5 *J. Int'l Bus. & L.* 112, 113 (2006).

47 *See* ILO Convention (No. 169) concerning Indigenous and Tribal Peoples in Independent Countries, 27 June 1989, 28 *I.L.M.* 1382, Articles 4, 5, 23; United Nations Declaration on the Rights of Indigenous Peoples, 13 December 2007, *A/RES/61/295*, Articles 5, 11, 16, 24, 26, 31.

48 The right to live according to one's traditional lifestyle has been recognized with respect to a minority lifestyle under Article 8 ECHR (right to protection of private life, family life and the home); *See also* European Court of Human Rights, Chapman v. United Kingdom, 18 January 2001, *available at* www.echr.coe.int (last visited 2 February 2012).

49 C.B. Graber, "The New UNESCO Convention on Cultural Diversity: a Counterbalance to the WTO?", 9 *J. Int'l Econ. L.* 553, 562 (2006).

3.2.3. *The risk of abuse*

The argument above presupposes governments acting in good faith. But what about the risk of governments abusing the room for rights-restrictive measures created by the Convention on the Diversity of Cultural Expressions to suppress the civil liberties of their people? A memo by the Heritage Foundation expresses the fear of abuse as follows:

> Imagine how much bolder such a convention will make countries like Burma, China, Iran, or Cuba, all of which are notorious for restricting freedoms, especially freedom of speech and of the press. China already forces Internet providers like Microsoft's MSN to restrict access to the words 'freedom' and 'democracy' if they want to do business there. Oppressive Islamic regimes that reject Western values, arts, and humanities could use the convention to restrict all sorts of goods they consider perverse. In Iran, teens have been arrested for dancing, and recently, the regime announced that women wearing their veils 'improperly' would be 'treated' like those who have no veil at all in public. Iran already goes to great lengths to 'protect and preserve' its oppressive definition of Iranian cultural expressions.[50]

Another U.S. opponent of the Convention on the Diversity of Cultural Expressions, Chairman of the National Endowment for the Arts Dana Gioia, expressed his fear that this Convention might legitimize "a potential situation where you have a permissible official culture and outsiders,"[51] that it might in other words create an obstacle for cultural change as well as for cultural diversity.

The fear that the Convention on the Diversity of Cultural Expressions would legitimize manifest violations of civil and political rights is not justified. States remain bound by their human rights obligations, by virtue of the human rights treaties and by virtue of several provisions in the Convention on the Diversity of Cultural Expressions, as explained above. Yet there is a broad grey zone in relation to which it is possible to discuss about whether or not a particular measure restricting the free flow of cultural products is a human rights violation. And as the overriding purpose of the Convention on the Diversity of Cultural Expressions can be interpreted as a beneficial one for civil and political rights, as explained above, restrictive measures falling within the scope of the Convention on the Diversity of Cultural Expressions are likely to be submitted to relatively light scrutiny.

It follows that the Convention on the Diversity of Cultural Expressions may provide governments with new arguments in support of controversial policies

---

50 J. A. Smith and H. Dale, "Cultural Diversity and Freedom at Risk at UNESCO" (17 October 2005), *available at* www.heritage.org/Research/InternationalOrganizations/wm885.cfm. (last visited 2 February 2012).

51 US Department of State, Foreign Press Center Roundtable, "UNESCO Cultural Diversity Convention: The US View" (27 September 2005), *available at* www.fpc.state.gov/fpc/54039.htm (last visited 2 February 2012).

that restrict free expression and access to information and ideas. In the grey zone mentioned above, some contestable measures might be more easily acceptable in the eyes of some in light of the Convention on the Diversity of Cultural Expressions than they would have been without the Convention on the Diversity of Cultural Expressions. This is unavoidable, as cultures, even in the narrow "artistic" meaning of the word, are heterogeneous and contested, and cultural policies are often closely intertwined with ideologies or party politics.

Any measure promoting or protecting Flemish culture in Belgium can be read as an ideological statement in a country in which communitarian strife between linguistic communities has been for decades the main political battlefield. At the same time such a measure will have to identify its scope not only by defining what is Flemish in opposition to what belongs to Francophone Belgium, but also by addressing the issue of cultural contributions of people from immigrant origin. It will therefore also be a statement in the political debate on multiculturalism, one of Europe's most divisive political topics. Surely it must be permissible to identify protected cultural products by their language? But if that is the case, can it be impermissible to identify them by reference to religion (*e.g.* Islam) or ideology (*e.g.* communism)? The cultural role and value of religion cannot be denied, and it seems that a good case can be made for the cultural role of ideologies such as communism, even though this may be contested. If Flanders can reserve a share of the media market for Flemish-language products, it makes sense that Iran would be able to reserve a share for Shi'a Islamic products, and Cuba to reserve a share for communist products. In both cases there would be strong arguments that the cultures are threatened, and such acts may actually be unproblematic. If Cuba and Iran were to reserve only a share of the market for communist and Islamic cultural products respectively, their citizens would have access to a much more diverse range of cultural products than they do today. On account of the principle of openness and balance as well as the principle of respect for human rights and fundamental freedoms, the Convention on the Diversity of Cultural Expressions does not allow for state censorship that would, for example, ban all cultural products that do not pass a test of conformity with Islam or with communism.

Revisiting the critical rhetoric cited above, the Convention on the Diversity of Cultural Expressions cannot justify Internet censorship in China or elsewhere, nor can it have anything to do with prohibitions on dancing or with the enforcement of Islamic dress rules. But it may support measures promoting and protecting Islam, and if communist culture is accepted as culture, it may also support measures protective of that culture. For those who consider anything related to Islam or communism or for that matter Flemish cultural nationalism as undesirable, the Convention on the Diversity of Cultural Expressions thus may have undesirable effects.

4. CONCLUSION

The Convention on the Diversity of Cultural Expressions is not a human rights treaty, yet it includes human rights language and indirectly affirms civil and political rights – the right to freedom of cultural expression and the right of access to cultural information and ideas – through the imposition of obligations on State Parties that benefit certain persons. While the Convention may protect some government policies that others find undesirable, the fear that the Convention itself might give rise to manifest human rights violations – creating an obstacle for cultural change as well as for cultural diversity – is not justified.

THE CONVENTION ON THE DIVERSITY OF CULTURAL EXPRESSIONS

What is Its Added Value for Minorities and Indigenous Peoples?

Anna MEIJKNECHT*

1. INTRODUCTION

Does the UNESCO *Convention on the Protection and Promotion of the Diversity of Cultural Expressions* ("Convention on the Diversity of Cultural Expressions")[1] protect minorities and indigenous peoples? Although the Convention on the Diversity of Cultural Expressions is not specifically devoted to the cultural expressions of minorities and indigenous peoples, it explicitly refers to minorities and indigenous peoples in some of its provisions. In its preamble, the Convention on the Diversity of Cultural Expressions underlines the importance of traditional forms of knowledge, particularly knowledge systems of indigenous peoples, as a source of intangible and material wealth and of the positive contribution of traditional knowledge to sustainable development. In Article 2(3), the Convention on the Diversity of Cultural Expressions affirms the principle of the equal dignity of and respect for all cultures, including the cultures of persons belonging to minorities and indigenous peoples. Finally, it calls on the Parties to the Convention to pay "due attention to the special circumstances and needs of women as well as various social groups, including persons belonging to minorities and indigenous peoples"[2] in order to encourage them to create, produce, disseminate, distribute and have access to their own cultural expressions.

* Dr A.K. Meijknecht is Assistant Professor of Public International Law at Tilburg University and Senior Researcher at the Center for Transboundary Legal Development.

1 *See* Convention on the Protection and Promotion of the Diversity of Cultural Expressions, 20 October 2005, *U.N. Doc. CLT-2005/CONVENTION DIVERSITE-CULT REV.* [hereinafter "Convention on the Diversity of Cultural Expressions"].

2 Id., Article 7(1)(a).

What do minorities and indigenous peoples gain from these and other provisions of the Convention? At first sight, it is difficult to discern the practical value of the Convention on the Diversity of Cultural Expressions. The references to minorities and indigenous peoples are few in number and perhaps disappointingly so, considering that these cultures are the main source of cultural diversity within most states. Moreover, the cultural identity and lifestyle of many a minority and indigenous people squarely depends on the protection of the diversity of cultural expressions. The purpose of this article is to consider the Convention on the Diversity of Cultural Expressions from a minorities' and indigenous peoples' perspective in order to see whether it offers them more than is immediately apparent.

Section 2 describes the emergence of the concept of cultural diversity in the existing UNESCO Conventions. Subsequently, section 3 examines the way in which the contribution of minorities and indigenous peoples to cultural diversity is reflected by the Convention on the Diversity of Cultural Expressions. Further, in section 4, the Convention on the Diversity of Cultural Expressions is placed in the context of the existing international legal instruments on minorities and indigenous peoples. Section 5 tries to grasp the added value of the Convention on the Diversity of Cultural Expressions form 5 different perspectives. Finally, section 6, conclusions are drawn with regard to the added value of the Convention on the Diversity of Cultural Expressions for minorities and indigenous peoples.

2. UNESCO AND CULTURAL DIVERSITY

The Convention on the Diversity of Cultural Expressions' s drafting process started in 2003. In the *Preliminary study on the technical and legal aspects relating to the desirability of a standard setting instrument on cultural diversity*,[3] it was concluded that "several aspects of cultural diversity are already governed by international standards, some binding, some non-binding."[4] Nevertheless, it was decided that a new instrument – in the form of a convention – was needed to protect the diversity of cultural contents and artistic expressions. The central purpose of the new convention would be

> to establish a link between the preservation of cultural diversity and the goals of development, notably through the promotion of creative activity and the cultural goods and services through which such activity is expressed … the goal is to define a set of general cultural policy principles in such a way as to ensure the necessary

[3] *See* UNESCO, Executive Board, "Preliminary Study on the Technical and Legal Aspects relating to the Desirability of a Standard-setting Instrument on Cultural Diversity", *166 EX/28* (12 March 2003).

[4] Id., at §17.

> autonomy in national policy while guaranteeing balanced international cooperation. In other words, the point is to ensure consistency between intra-State and inter-State policy. Under such circumstances, one might choose an instrument which placed particular emphasis on areas of cultural diversity in the context of globalization which do not yet enjoy adequate protection under existing conventions or recommendations.[5]

In the context of UNESCO, the development of the concept of cultural diversity and some related concepts had already started long before the adoption of the *Convention Concerning the Protection of the World Cultural and Natural Heritage* ("World Heritage Convention")[6] in 1972, and relatively recently, two other important documents followed: in 2001, the *Universal Declaration on Cultural Diversity* ("Cultural Diversity Declaration")[7], and, in 2003, the *Convention for the Safeguarding of the Intangible Cultural Heritage* ("ICH Convention").[8, 9] The Cultural Diversity Declaration can be seen as the closest predecessor of the Convention on the Diversity of Cultural Expressions. The Cultural Diversity

5 Id., at §§17–9.

6 *See* Convention concerning the Protection of the World Cultural and Natural Heritage, 16 November 1972, *available at* http://portal.unesco.org/en/ev.php-URL_ID=13055&URL_DO=DO_TOPIC&URL_SECTION=201.html (last visited 2 February 2012) [hereinafter "World Heritage Convention"].

7 *See* Universal Declaration on Cultural Diversity, 2 November 2001, *available at* http://portal.unesco.org/en/ev.php-URL_ID=13179&URL_DO=DO_TOPIC&URL_SECTION=201.html (last visited on 2 February 2012).

8 *See* Convention for the Safeguarding of the Intangible Cultural Heritage, 17 October 2003, *U.N. Doc. MISC/2003/CLT/CH/14* [hereinafter "ICH Convention"].

9 Other normative instruments developed by UNESCO and relevant in the area of cultural diversity include: the Convention on the Protection of the Underwater Cultural Heritage, 2 November 2001, *UNESCO Doc.MISC/2003/CLT/CH/4*; Convention on the Means of Prohibiting and Preventing the Illicit Import, Export and Transfer of Cultural Property, 14 November 1970, 823 *UNTS* 231; Convention for the Protection of Cultural Property in the Event of Armed Conflict, 14 May 1954, 249 *UNTS* 240; Universal Copyright Convention, 6 September 1952, 216 *UNTS* 133; Agreement on the Importation of Educational, Scientific and Cultural Materials, 17 June 1950, *available at* http://portal.unesco.org/en/ev.php-URL_ID=12074&URL_DO=DO_TOPIC&URL_SECTION=201.html (last visited 2 February 2012) (known as the *Florence Agreement*) and its *Nairobi Protocol* of 26 November 1976; Recommendation concerning the Promotion and Use of Multilingualism and Universal Access to Cyberspace, 2003, *available at* http://portal.unesco.org/ci/en/files/13475/10697584791Recommendation-Eng.pdf/Recommendation-Eng.pdf (last visited 2 February 2012); Recommendation on the Safeguarding of Traditional Culture and Folklore, 15 November 1989, *available at* http://portal.unesco.org/en/ev.php-URL_ID=13141&URL_DO=DO_TOPIC&URL_SECTION=201.html (last visited 2 February 2012); Recommendation concerning the Status of the Artist, 27 October 1980, *available at* http://unesdoc.unesco.org/images/0011/001140/114029e.pdf#page=144 (last visited 2 February 2012); and finally, Declaration on Race and Racial Prejudice, 27 November 1978, *available at* www2.ohchr.org/english/law/race.htm (last visited 2 February 2012) and Declaration of the Principles of International Cultural Co-operation, 4 November 1966, *available at* www.unhchr.ch/html/menu3/b/n_decl.htm (last visited 2 February 2012). *See also* UNESCO, EXECUTIVE BOARD, *supra* note 3, Annex.

Declaration and the Convention on the Diversity of Cultural Expressions are two different instruments, especially form a legal point of view; the former, as a legally non-binding declaration, is more generous and explicit in its provisions, whereas the latter, being a legally binding document, is more cautious. Nevertheless, it may be useful to read these Conventions as two complementary documents, especially where definitions are concerned.

In its preamble, the Cultural Diversity Declaration defines 'culture' as "the set of distinctive spiritual, material, intellectual and emotional features of society or a social group [encompassing,] in addition to art and literature, lifestyles, ways of living together, value systems, traditions and beliefs."[10] The Convention on the Diversity of Cultural Expressions does not define culture as such, but defines 'cultural expressions' as "those expressions that result from the creativity of individuals, groups and societies, and that have cultural content." 'Cultural content' refers to "the symbolic meaning, artistic dimension and cultural values that originate from or express cultural identities."[11] The Convention on the Diversity of Cultural Expressions refers to 'cultural diversity' as

> the manifold ways in which the cultures of groups and societies find expression. These expressions are passed on within and among groups and societies. Cultural diversity is made manifest not only through the varied ways in which the cultural heritage of humanity is expressed, augmented and transmitted through the variety of cultural expressions, but also through diverse modes of artistic creation, production, dissemination, distribution and enjoyment, whatever the means and technologies used.[12]

"Towards access for all to cultural diversity" is the heading of Article 6 Cultural Diversity Declaration. This article mentions the following guarantees of cultural diversity: freedom of expression, media pluralism, multilingualism, equal access to art and to scientific and technological knowledge, including in digital form, and the possibility for all cultures to have access to the means of expression and dissemination. Further, according to Article 4 Cultural Diversity Declaration, human rights are also guarantees of cultural diversity:

> The defence of cultural diversity is an ethical imperative, inseparable from respect for human dignity. It implies a commitment to human rights and fundamental freedoms, in particular the rights of persons belonging to minorities and those of indigenous peoples. No one may invoke cultural diversity to infringe upon human rights guaranteed by international law, nor to limit their scope.

10 Universal Declaration on Cultural Diversity, 2 November 2001, *CLT-2002/WS/9*, Preamble §5 (2002) [hereinafter "Cultural Diversity Declaration"].
11 Convention on the Diversity of Cultural Expressions, *supra* note 1, Article 4(2).
12 Id., Article 4(1).

The Convention on the Diversity of Cultural Expressions confirms this respect for human rights and fundamental freedoms, but omits the reference to minorities and indigenous peoples: it states that "cultural diversity can be protected and promoted only if human rights and fundamental freedoms, such as freedom of expression, information and communication, as well as the ability of individuals to choose cultural expressions, are guaranteed."[13]

3. MINORITIES, INDIGENOUS PEOPLES AND CULTURAL DIVERSITY

Minorities, indigenous peoples and cultural diversity are inextricably linked: cultural, linguistic, religious, and ethnic minorities and indigenous peoples are the main source of cultural diversity within most states. The existence of minorities and/or indigenous peoples within a state implies the existence of cultural diversity and vice versa. Cultural diversity relates, by definition, to the coexistence of majority and minority cultures. The necessity for this coexistence renders the promotion and protection of cultural diversity more fragile, more complicated and far from self-evident.

The link between cultural diversity, minorities and peace is not new. In the preamble to the 1995 Council of Europe *Framework Convention for the Protection of National Minorities* ("FCNM"), the signatories consider "that the creation of a climate of tolerance and dialogue is necessary to enable cultural diversity to be a source and a factor, not of division, but of enrichment for each society."[14] The possible tension between minority and majority cultures is also hinted at in the preamble of the 1992 *European Charter for Regional or Minority Languages* ("Languages Charter"): while 'the value of interculturalism and multilingualism' is stressed, the Languages Charter does caution that "the protection and encouragement of regional or minority languages should not be to the detriment of the official languages and the need to learn them."[15]

Tension is also palpable in the preamble to the Convention on the Diversity of Cultural Expressions. The parties to the Convention on the Diversity of Cultural Expressions are aware of the promise cultural diversity holds: "cultural diversity creates a rich and varied world, which increases the range of choices and nurtures human capacities and values, and therefore is a mainspring for sustainable development for communities, peoples and nations." At the same time, however, the parties acknowledge the vulnerability of cultural diversity.

---

13 Id., Article 2 (Guiding Principles).

14 Framework Convention for the Protection of National Minorities, 1 February 1995, *ETS 157*, Preamble §7 (1995) [hereinafter "FCNM"].

15 European Charter for Regional or Minority Languages, 5 November 1992, *ETS 148*, Preamble §5 (1992) [hereinafter "Languages Charter"].

They recall the indispensable framework in which cultural diversity can flourish and contribute to peace and security: this framework consists of democracy, tolerance, social justice and mutual respect between peoples and cultures. The Convention on the Diversity of Cultural Expressions further adds the principle of equal dignity of and respect for all cultures, which includes the cultures of persons belonging to minorities and indigenous peoples.[16] Without these conditions the protection and promotion of cultural diversity would become impossible and each attempt to promote diversity would turn into a source of tension or even conflict.

During the drafting process, little discussion seems to have been directed toward the way in which the Convention on the Diversity of Cultural Expressions would reflect the contribution of minorities and indigenous peoples to cultural diversity. The only discussion with regard to those groups boiled down to the debate between 'individual rights' and 'collective rights.' Several parties suggested the proper course would be "either to delete the reference to 'individuals' [in Article 7], or to delete the reference to 'minorities and indigenous peoples' and to 'social groups'."[17] Ultimately, a middle course was taken: 'minorities'[18] was replaced by 'persons belonging to minorities'[19], a solution that is in line with the 'extended' individual approach to minorities applied in other international minority right instruments.[20] Having been relegated to the level of 'cross-cutting issues,'[21] minorities and indigenous peoples appear only infrequently and at unexpected moments in the Convention on the Diversity of Cultural Expressions. A comparison of the final text with draft versions shows that minorities and indigenous peoples were more prominently present in earlier versions. For instance, one of the draft objectives and guiding principles was "to strengthen international cooperation and solidarity for the protection and promotion of cultural diversity, with the aim of developing effective skills training mechanisms that would enable societies and social groups in developing countries in particular, including individuals belonging to minorities and indigenous peoples, to protect and promote the diversity of cultural expressions."

16 Convention on the Diversity of Cultural Expressions, *supra* note 1, Article 2(3) (Guiding Principles).

17 UNESCO, "Preliminary Draft Convention on the Protection of the Diversity of Cultural Contents and Artistic Expressions", *CLT/CPD/2004/CONF.607/6*, at 120 (23 December 2004).

18 UNESCO, "Preliminary Report of the Director-General Containing Two Preliminary Drafts of a Convention on the Protection of the Diversity of Cultural Contents and Artistic Expressions", *CLT/CPD/2005/CONF.203/6*, at 34 (3 March 2005).

19 UNESCO, *supra* note 17, at 58–59.

20 *See*, for instance, the formulation chosen in Article 27 ICCPR and in Article 1.3 UN Declaration on the Rights of Persons Belonging to National or Ethnic, Religious and Linguistic Minorities.

21 *See* UNESCO, *supra* note 18, Appendix 1, at 13–14.

However, this option attracted limited support,[22] and in the final text, reference was merely made to "cultural industries, whether nascent or established." An amplified version of the principle of the respect of human rights also failed to qualify for the final text unimpaired: "No one may invoke the provisions of this Convention in order to infringe human rights of individuals belonging to minorities and indigenous peoples guaranteed by international law or to limit the scope thereof."[23] The inverse process also occurred in the drafting process: in the final version, the principle of equal dignity of all cultures includes reference to minorities and indigenous peoples, whereas a strongly supported earlier version read simply as follows: "The protection and promotion of the diversity of cultural expressions presupposes recognition of the equal dignity of all cultures."[24]

4. THE CONVENTION ON THE DIVERSITY OF CULTURAL EXPRESSIONS IN THE CONTEXT OF OTHER INSTRUMENTS ON MINORITIES AND INDIGENOUS PEOPLES

This section assesses the protection offered to minorities by the Convention on the Diversity of Cultural Expressions in the light of the most important international documents on the rights of minorities and indigenous peoples. As mentioned, minorities, indigenous peoples and cultural diversity are inextricably linked; minorities and indigenous peoples are the main source of cultural diversity within most states, and the successful promotion and protection of cultural diversity is directly linked to the position of minorities and indigenous peoples within a state.

Nevertheless, the Convention on the Diversity of Cultural Expressions refers to minorities and indigenous peoples more in passing than directly. It must be kept in mind that according to its explanatory report,[25] the Convention on the Diversity of Cultural Expressions is not primarily intended as an instrument for the protection of minorities and indigenous peoples. Such an intention would overlap with the existing instruments on the rights of minorities and indigenous peoples. During the Convention on the Diversity of Cultural Expressions' drafting process it was explicitly borne in mind that "when elaborating a new international standard-setting instrument it is essential to take account of

22 UNESCO, *supra* note 17, at 26 (Option 1).
23 Id., at 28 (Option 2).
24 Id., at 30–31 (Option 4).
25 UNESCO, "Ten Keys to the Convention on the Protection and Promotion of the Diversity of Cultural Expressions", *CLT/CEI/DCE/2007/PI/32* (2005).

existing international legal instruments."[26] The following short overview of universal and regional instruments will serve to give an impression of the protection of the cultural rights of minorities and indigenous peoples other than that offered by the Convention on the Diversity of Cultural Expressions:

Article 27 of the *International Covenant on Civil and Political Rights* ("ICCPR")[27] is the most widely accepted legally binding provision on minorities:

> In those States in which ethnic, religious or linguistic minorities exist, persons belonging to these minorities shall not be denied the right, in community with the other members of their group, to enjoy their own culture, to profess and practise their own religion, or to use their own language.

The Human Rights Committee observed that "this article establishes and recognizes a right which is conferred on individuals belonging to minority groups and which is distinct from, and additional to, all the other rights which, as individuals in common with everyone else, they are already entitled to enjoy under the [ICCPR]."[28]

In 1992, the General Assembly of the United Nations adopted the *Declaration on the Rights of Persons Belonging to National or Ethnic, Religious and Linguistic Minorities* ("UNDM").[29] The UNDM contains several rights of minorities, such as the right to enjoy their own culture, profess and practice their own religion, and use their own language freely in public and private, without any form of discrimination;[30] the right to participate effectively in cultural, religious, social, economic and public life;[31] and the right to participate effectively in decisions on the national and, where appropriate, regional level concerning their minority group or region.[32] The UNDM also formulates several obligations for states with regard to minorities, such as the obligation to protect their existence and their national or ethnic, cultural, religious and linguistic identity;[33] the obligation to create favourable conditions to enable the minorities to express their characteristics and to develop their culture, language, religion, traditions and customs;[34] the obligation to allow the minorities adequate opportunities to learn

---

26 UNESCO, "Preliminary Study on the Technical and Legal Aspects Relating to the Desirability of a Standard-Setting Instrument on Cultural Diversity", *32 C/52*, at 1 (18 July 2003).

27 *See* International Covenant on Civil and Political Rights, 16 December 1966, 999 *U.N.T.S.* 171 [hereinafter "ICCPR"].

28 Human Rights Committee, "General Comment 23, Article 27 (Fiftieth Session, 1994)", *Compilation of General Comments and General Recommendations Adopted by Human Rights Treaty Bodies, U.N. Doc. HRI/GEN/1/Rev.1*, at 38 (1994).

29 *See* Declaration on the Rights of Persons belonging to National or Ethnic, Religious and Linguistic Minorities, 18 December 1992, *Resolution 47/135* [hereinafter "UNDM"].

30 *See* id., Article 2(1).

31 *See* id., Article 2(2).

32 *See* id., Article 2(3).

33 *See* id., Article 1.

34 *See* id., Article 4(2).

their mother tongue or to have instruction in their mother tongue;[35] and the obligation to consider legitimate interests of minorities in developing national policies and programmes, as well as in planning and implementing programmes of cooperation and assistance.[36]

Convention No. 169 Concerning Indigenous and Tribal Peoples in Independent Countries ("ILO Convention No. 169"),[37] adopted by the International Labour Organization in 1989, is the most comprehensive binding international document dealing with indigenous peoples' rights. In its preamble, ILO Convention No. 169 calls attention to "the distinctive contributions of indigenous and tribal peoples to the cultural diversity and social and ecological harmony of humankind and the international co-operation and understanding."[38] Many provisions in ILO Convention No. 169 are aimed at national governments and contain obligations to take specific measures with regard to indigenous peoples.

The adoption of the *United Nations Declaration on the Rights of Indigenous Peoples* ("UNDRIP")[39] in 2007 was hailed as "a triumph for justice and human dignity following more than two decades of negotiations between governments and indigenous peoples' representatives."[40] The General Assembly of the United Nations affirms in the preamble that "all people contribute to the diversity and richness of civilizations and cultures, which constitute the common heritage of mankind" and is convinced that "control by indigenous peoples over developments affecting them and their lands, territories and resources will enable them to maintain and strengthen their institutions, cultures and traditions, and to promote their development in accordance with their aspirations and needs." The articles of the UNDRIP address both individual and collective rights and deal extensively with the cultural and identity rights of indigenous peoples, such as their rights to education, health, employment, and in relation to language. The UNDRIP also promotes the full and effective participation of indigenous peoples in all matters that concern them.

At the regional level, the main documents on minority rights are the following. The 1990 Document of the Copenhagen Meeting of the Conference on the Human Dimension of the Conference on Security and Co-operation in

---

35 *See* id., Article 4(3).

36 *See* id., Article 5.

37 *See* ILO Convention (No. 169) concerning Indigenous and Tribal Peoples in Independent Countries, 27 June 1989, 28 *I.L.M.* 1382 [hereinafter "ILO Convention"].

38 Id., Preamble §8.

39 *See* United Nations Declaration on the Rights of Indigenous Peoples, 13 December 2007, *A/RES/61/295.*

40 Office of the United Nations High Commissioner for Human Rights, "Declaration on the Rights of Indigenous Peoples", *available at* www.ohchr.org/english/issues/indigenous/declaration.htm (last visited 2 February 2012).

Europe (Copenhagen Document)[41] can be regarded as the first major international regional instrument on minority rights after the Second World War. The Copenhagen Document states that the persons belonging to a national minority have the right to freely express, preserve and develop their ethnic, cultural, linguistic or religious identity and to maintain and develop their culture in all its aspects, free of any attempts at assimilation against their will. Among the minorities' rights are the free use of their mother tongue in private and in public, and the establishment and maintenance of their own educational, cultural and religious institutions.

The 1992 Languages Charter[42] mentioned earlier stresses in its preamble 'the value of interculturalism and multilingualism' and has as its main purpose the protection and promotion of the historical regional or minority languages of Europe, some of which are in danger of eventual extinction. It tries to ensure the use of these languages in education and the mass media, also allowing their use in administrative, judicial, economic and social fields. Furthermore, Article 7 includes the following objectives and principles:

a. the recognition of the regional or minority languages as an expression of cultural wealth; ...
b. the need for resolute action to promote regional or minority languages in order to safeguard them;
c. the facilitation and/or encouragement of the use of regional or minority languages, in speech and writing, in public and private life; ...
d. the provision of appropriate forms and means for the teaching and study of regional or minority languages at all appropriate stages; ...
e. the promotion of study and research on regional or minority languages at universities or equivalent institutions; ...
f. the promotion of appropriate types of transnational exchanges, in the fields covered by this Charter, for regional or minority languages used in identical or similar form in two or more States.

The Council of Europe adopted the FCNM in 1995.[43] This legally binding convention consists mainly of programme-type provisions[44] concerning issues such as non-discrimination, education, cross-border contacts, full and effective

---

41 *See* Organization for Security and Co-operation in Europe, "Document of the Copenhagen Meeting of the Conference on the Human Dimension of the CSCE" (29 June 1990), *available at* www.osce.org/documents/odihr/2006/06/19392_en.pdf (last visited 2 February 2012).

42 *See supra* note 15.

43 *See supra* note 14.

44 *See* Council of Europe, "Explanatory Report to the Framework Convention for the Protection of National Minorities, Explanatory Report", §13, *available at* http://conventions.coe.int/Treaty/EN/Reports/Html/157.htm (last visited 2 February 2012).

equality, identity, association, religion, language, media and participation. The provisions of the convention leave the states concerned a measure of discretion in the implementation of the objectives and principles in order to enable them to take particular circumstances into account. The preamble of the FCNM declares that "a pluralist and genuinely democratic society should not only respect the ethnic, cultural, linguistic and religious identity of each person belonging to a national minority, but also create appropriate conditions enabling them to express, preserve and develop this identity."[45]

This short overview of the existing instruments in the field of the protection of minorities and indigenous peoples inevitably raises the question of what the added value of the Convention on the Diversity of Cultural Expressions is for minorities and indigenous peoples. An extensive comparison of the Convention on the Diversity of Cultural Expressions provisions explicitly mentioning minorities and indigenous peoples with substantively similar provisions in the other instruments may well cast the Convention on the Diversity of Cultural Expressions in a poor light: the level and the precision of the protection offered by the other instruments is much more advanced. A tentative conclusion might therefore be that the Convention on the Diversity of Cultural Expressions has little to add, especially, to the existing rights of indigenous peoples (as their rights are to a large extent dealt with in the ILO Convention No. 169 and the UNDRIP) and religious minorities[46] and a number of linguistic rights, such as the right to use minority languages in private and public;[47] to use one's name in minority languages; to display information of a private nature in minority languages, and to display topographical names in minority languages.[48] The protection of these rights depends on other conventions, especially the FCNM and the Languages Charter. However, both these instruments are regional instruments. The scope of the Convention on the Diversity of Cultural Expressions is universal and its ambition is to place "particular emphasis on areas of cultural diversity in the context of globalization which do not yet enjoy adequate protection under existing conventions or recommendations."[49] This justifies a closer look at the Convention on the Diversity of Cultural Expressions.

---

45 FCNM, *supra* note 14, Preamble §7.

46 *See* id., Articles 5 and 8.

47 *See* Languages Charter, *supra* note 15, Article 9; FCNM, *supra* note 14, Article 10.

48 FCNM, *supra* note 14, Article 11.

49 UNESCO, *supra* note 3, §§17–19.

5. LOOKING FOR THE ADDED VALUE OF THE CONVENTION ON THE DIVERSITY OF CULTURAL EXPRESSIONS

A quick look at the Convention on the Diversity of Cultural Expressions through the eyes of minorities and indigenous peoples reveals a positive feature of this document: it places their existence in the perspective of the diversity of cultural expressions. The Convention on the Diversity of Cultural Expressions puts the protection of the cultures of minorities and indigenous peoples in a positive light, as does the Cultural Diversity Declaration. The protection of their cultures is not primarily deemed necessary and inevitable to prevent conflicts or war, but is rather perceived as a valuable and positive contribution to society and to future generations. In its preamble, the Cultural Diversity Declaration takes into account "the importance of the vitality of cultures, including for persons belonging to minorities and indigenous peoples' and recognizes 'that the diversity of cultural expressions, including traditional cultural expressions, is an important factor that allows individuals and peoples to express and to share with others their ideas and values."

As pointed out, cultural diversity is inextricably linked with the existence of minorities and indigenous peoples. All the articles of the Convention on the Diversity of Cultural Expressions – and not only the articles explicitly mentioning minorities and indigenous peoples – may therefore be relevant to minorities and indigenous peoples. Firstly, the emphasis on culture and cultural diversity might be useful for cultural minorities. Secondly, the link between cultural diversity, on the one hand, and linguistic diversity and education, on the other hand, might offer some interesting insights into minorities and indigenous peoples. Thirdly, the explicit attention to the preservation of cultural diversity and the goals of development might be beneficial for some minorities and indigenous peoples in developing countries. Finally, the Convention on the Diversity of Cultural Expressions' emphasis on balanced international cooperation, namely "consistency between inter-State and intra-State policy"[50] opens up a new perspective for minorities and indigenous peoples within states (intra-state policy) and for transfrontier minorities and indigenous peoples (inter-state policy).

5.1. THE CULTURE OF MINORITIES AND INDIGENOUS PEOPLES

In the context of the Council of Europe, the Languages Charter gives a very extensive list of cultural activities and facilities, "especially libraries, video

---

[50] Id.

libraries, cultural centres, museums, archives, academies, theatres and cinemas, as well as literary work and film production, vernacular forms of cultural expression, festivals and the culture industries, including the use of new technologies", which are related to the protection and promotion of minority and regional languages and cultures.[51] The FCNM is less precise and states that the signatories "undertake to promote the conditions necessary for persons belonging to national minorities to maintain and develop their culture, and to preserve the essential elements of their identity, namely their religion, language, traditions and cultural heritage."[52] Both ILO Convention No. 169[53] and the UNDRIP contain several articles dealing with cultural rights. For instance, Articles 11 and 12 UNDRIP state that

> Indigenous peoples have the right to practice and revitalize their cultural traditions and customs. This includes the right to maintain, protect and develop the past, present and future manifestations of their cultures, such as archaeological and historical sites, artefacts, designs, ceremonies, technologies and visual and performing arts and literature...
> Indigenous peoples have the right to the dignity and diversity of their cultures, traditions, histories and aspirations which shall be appropriately reflected in education and public information.

In the context of UNESCO, the Convention on the Diversity of Cultural Expressions has many predecessors dealing with different aspects of cultural rights, including the 1972 World Heritage Convention, the Cultural Diversity Declaration of 2001 and, most recently, the ICH Convention of 2003. All three instruments are relevant to cultural minorities and indigenous peoples. The broad scope of the World Heritage Convention[54] offers protection to many of their cultural expressions. The Cultural Diversity Declaration is relevant, in particular, to linguistic and cultural minorities and indigenous peoples, because it underlines that

> all persons should be able to express themselves and to create and disseminate their work in the language of their choice, and particularly in their mother tongue; all

---

51 Languages Charter, *supra* note 15, Article 12.

52 FCNM, *supra* note 14, Article 5.

53 ILO Convention No. 169, *supra* note 37, Articles 4, 5, 13, 23, and 26–31.

54 *See, e.g.*, World Heritage Convention, Article 1 (describing 'cultural heritage' as "monuments: architectural works, works of monumental sculpture and painting, elements or structures of an archaeological nature, inscriptions, cave dwellings and combinations of features, which are of outstanding universal value from the point of view of history, art or science; groups of buildings: groups of separate or connected buildings which, because of their architecture, their homogeneity or their place in the landscape, are of outstanding universal value from the point of view of history, art or science"; and "sites" as "works of man or the combined works of nature and man, and areas including archaeological sites which are of outstanding universal value from the historical, aesthetic, ethnological or anthropological point of view").

> persons should be entitled to quality education and training that fully respect their cultural identity; and all persons have the right to participate in the cultural life of their choice and conduct their own cultural practices, subject to respect for human rights and fundamental freedoms.[55]

The ICH Convention is especially important for the preservation of the culture of minorities and indigenous peoples. Firstly, by ensuring matters such as "respect for the intangible cultural heritage of the communities, groups and individuals concerned"[56] the ICH Convention explicitly recognizes the group and community dimension of intangible culture. In its broad definition of 'intangible cultural heritage', the individual is presented as a mere exception: "the practices, representations, expressions, knowledge, skills – as well as the instruments, objects, artefacts and cultural spaces associated therewith – that communities, groups and, in some cases, individuals recognize as part of their cultural heritage." Another important feature of this Convention is its unmistakable 'match' with the culture of many minorities and indigenous peoples; the ICH Convention specifies that intangible cultural heritage is manifested in the following domains: "(a) oral traditions and expressions, including language as a vehicle of the intangible cultural heritage; (b) performing arts; (c) social practices, rituals and festive events; (d) knowledge and practices concerning nature and the universe; (e) traditional craftsmanship."[57]

Against the background of the two Council of Europe instruments, the two instruments on the rights of indigenous peoples, and, especially, the three comprehensive UNESCO conventions dealing with cultural rights and intangible and tangible cultural heritage, the preamble of the Convention on the Diversity of Cultural Expressions cannot but make do with "[c]*elebrating* the importance of cultural diversity for the full realization of human rights."[58] At the same time, the elusiveness of cultural diversity is acknowledged: "[C]ulture takes diverse forms across time and space and that this diversity is embodied in the uniqueness and plurality of the identities and cultural expressions of the peoples and societies making up humanity." However, in an attempt to be more concrete, the Convention on the Diversity of Cultural Expressions recognizes that there is a 'need to take measures to protect the diversity of cultural expressions, including their content, especially in situations where cultural expressions may be threatened by the possibility of extinction or serious impairment.'

The practical value of the Convention on the Diversity of Cultural Expressions for the protection of cultural expressions of minorities and indigenous peoples, will depend on the specific nature of the measures taken

---

55 Convention on the Diversity of Cultural Expressions, *supra* note 1, Article 5.

56 ICH Convention, *supra* note 8, Article 1.

57 Id., Article 2.

58 Id., Preamble §5 [emphasis added].

under this Convention, especially so in cases of extinction or serious impairment of minority or indigenous cultures.[59] Still, the practical value of the other UNESCO documents will probably remain much higher. The added value of the Convention on the Diversity of Cultural Expressions for cultural minorities and indigenous peoples must therefore be sought in its symbolic function: it brings the value of cultural diversity as such to the fore in an international sense. All existing documents deal with separate aspects of cultural diversity, some of them even in great detail. The Convention on the Diversity of Cultural Expressions, however, can be perceived as an overarching convention giving structure and direction to international developments in this field.

5.2. LINGUISTIC MINORITIES AND INDIGENOUS PEOPLES

In its preamble, the Convention on the Diversity of Cultural Expressions recalls that linguistic diversity is a fundamental element of cultural diversity. At first sight, it is difficult to point out exactly what the added value of the Convention on the Diversity of Cultural Expressions is with regard to linguistic diversity. The promotion of linguistic diversity has many different aspects and is the object of many international legal provisions and instruments.[60] For instance, at the universal level, Article 27 ICCPR affirms the right of persons belonging to a minority to use their own language. The ICH Convention has explained that this right is distinct from other language rights protected under the ICCPR, such as the general right to freedom of expression protected under Article 19.[61] Moreover, the parties to the UNDM[62] pledge to protect the existence of the linguistic identity of minorities within their respective territories and to encourage conditions for the promotion of that identity, including the possibility of learning their mother tongue or having instruction in their mother tongue (Articles 1 and 4). Article 13 UNDRIP gives indigenous peoples "the right to revitalize, use, develop and transmit to future generation their histories, languages, oral traditions, philosophies, writing systems and literatures, and to designate and retain their own names for communities, places and persons."

Regionally, the *Cultural Charter for Africa* ("Cultural Charter")[63] of the Organization of African Unity provides that the African states recognize the

59 Convention on the Diversity of Cultural Expressions, *supra* note 1, Articles 8 and 17.

60 *See* UNESCO, *supra* note 26, Appendix 4, at 3–5.

61 *See* Human Rights Committee, *supra* note 28, §5.3.

62 *See* United Nations, General Assembly, *supra* note 29.

63 *See* Cultural Charter for Africa, 5 July 1976, *available at* www.africa-union.org/root/au/Documents/Treaties/Text/Cultural_Charter_for_Africa.pdf (last visited 2 February 2012). This relatively unknown treaty entered into force on 19 September 1990 and is currently ratified by 43 States.

need to develop African languages, which will ensure their cultural advancement and accelerate their economic and social development, and to this end will endeavour to formulate a national policy in regard to languages. Furthermore, the Cultural Charter provides that African states should prepare and implement the reforms necessary for the introduction of African languages into education. To this end each state may choose one or more languages. The introduction of African languages at all levels of education should go hand in hand with literacy work among the people at large.[64] The Charter for African Cultural Renaissance[65], adopted in 2006 by the Organization of African Unity intends to replace the Cultural Charter. This document, which is clearly inspired by the Convention on the Diversity of Cultural Expressions, contains ambitious though still general provisions aiming, inter alia, "to encourage cultural co-operation among Member States with a view to the strengthening of African unity, through the use of African languages and the promotion of inter-cultural dialogue".[66] In this document African States perceive the need to develop African languages as a means to "to ensure their cultural advancement, and acceleration of their economic and social development." "To this end, they should endeavour to formulate and implement appropriate national language policies."[67] So far, this regional legal document which seems to have a rather instrumental approach to the protection of African languages, has been ratified by only 3 African States.

Within the context of the Organization for Security and Cooperation in Europe, the *Oslo Recommendation Regarding the Linguistic Rights of National Minorities*[68] of 1998 clarifies the definition of the linguistic rights of minorities.

Within the Council of Europe several instruments have been developed relating to linguistic diversity. In 1986, *Recommendation 1043 (1986) on Europe's Linguistic and Literary Heritage*[69] (Recommendation 1043) drew attention to the fact that Europe has developed as a cultural unity based on a diversity of interconnected languages and literary and cultural traditions; it encourages multilingualism in Europe, both in written material (whether in book or other form) and audiovisual media, and supports the development of the language

64 *See* id., Articles 17, 18 and 19.

65 *See* Charter for African Cultural Renaissance, 24 January 2006, *available at* www.au.int/en/sites/default/files/CHARTER_FOR_AFRICAN_CULTURAL_RENAISSANCE.pdf (last visited 2 February 2012).

66 *See* id., Article 3(f).

67 *See* id., Article 18.

68 *See* Organization for Security and Cooperation in Europe, "Oslo Recommendation Regarding the Linguistic Rights of National Minorities" (1 February 1998), *available at* www.osce.org/documents/hcnm/1998/02/2699_en.pdf (last visited 2 February 2012).

69 *See* Recommendation 1043 (1986) on Europe's Linguistic and Literary Heritage, 19 September 1986, *available at* http://assembly.coe.int/main.asp?Link=/documents/adoptedtext/ta86/erec1043.htm (last visited 2 February 2012).

industries with due respect for Europe's linguistic diversity.[70] The parties to the FCNM undertake to promote the conditions necessary for persons belonging to national minorities to maintain and develop their culture, and to preserve the essential elements of their identity, including their language, traditions and cultural heritage.[71] In Article 10 Recommendation 1043, these linguistic rights are elaborated in more detail. Articles 12, 13 and 14 Recommendation 1043 deal with different aspects of the right to education in and of minority languages and culture and the right of minorities to set up and to manage their own private educational and training establishments. This last right does not entail any financial obligation for the contracting parties. The Languages Charter, the most comprehensive instrument in this field, provides for the protection and promotion of the historical regional or minority languages of Europe. Article 8 Recommendation 1043 gives a set of rules which can be applied by states introducing, without prejudice to the teaching of the official language(s) of the state, education in regional or minority languages from the level of pre-school education up to university level.

As mentioned above, the Convention on the Diversity of Cultural Expressions sees linguistic diversity as a fundamental element of cultural diversity. The promotion of linguistic diversity as such, however, is not developed in a detailed and concrete way in its provisions. Unlike the FCNM and the Languages Charter, the Convention on the Diversity of Cultural Expressions does not focus on the right to education in or of the languages of minorities and indigenous peoples. The drafters of the Convention on the Diversity of Cultural Expressions may have come to the conclusion that detailed provisions on the promotion of linguistic diversity would constitute an overlap with the above international instruments.

Consistently with the educational purpose of UNESCO,[72] the Convention on the Diversity of Cultural Expressions emphasizes the role of educational and public awareness programmes in the international protection and promotion of the diversity of cultural expressions.[73] States are obliged to "endeavour to encourage creativity and strengthen production capacities by setting up educational, training and exchange programmes in the field of cultural

70 *See* id., Article 7(a) and (d).

71 FCNM, *supra* note 14, Article 5.

72 *See* Constitution of the United Nations Educational, Scientific and Cultural Organisation, 16 November 1945, 52 *UNTS* 275, Article I(1), *available at* http://portal.unesco.org/en/ev.php-URL_ID=15244&URL_DO=DO_TOPIC&URL_SECTION=201.html (last visited 2 February 2012) (stipulating that "[t]he purpose of the Organization is to contribute to peace and security by promoting collaboration among the nations through education, science and culture in order to further universal respect for justice, for the rule of law and for the human rights and fundamental freedoms which are affirmed for the peoples of the world, without distinction of race, sex, language or religion, by the Charter of the United Nations").

73 Convention on the Diversity of Cultural Expressions, *supra* note 1, Article 10(a) and (b).

industries" and "[t]hese measures should be implemented in a manner which does not have a negative impact on traditional forms of production."[74]

Linguistic minorities and indigenous peoples may well appreciate this latter sentence, but they may also likely be somewhat disappointed by the vague "endeavour to encourage" wording and abstract level of the educational commitments of states. The Convention on the Diversity of Cultural Expressions, in its aim of promoting and protecting the diversity of cultural expressions, appears to remain at a very abstract level, even for an international legal instrument; it is probably the only level on which this new instrument would not overlap with other UNESCO documents and other international instruments. This, however, is no accident: the drafters chose "an instrument which placed particular emphasis on areas of cultural diversity in the context of globalization which do not yet enjoy adequate protection under existing conventions or recommendations."[75]

5.3. MINORITIES AND INDIGENOUS PEOPLES IN DEVELOPING COUNTRIES

One of the most important purposes of the Convention on the Diversity of Cultural Expressions is to establish a link between the preservation of cultural diversity and the goals of development.[76] International promotion and cooperation, especially in the case of developing countries, are clearly at the heart of the Convention on the Diversity of Cultural Expressions.[77]

The link between cultural diversity and development had already been recognized in the Cultural Diversity Declaration: "Cultural diversity widens the range of options open to everyone; it is one of the roots of development, understood not simply in terms of economic growth, but also as a means to achieve a more satisfactory intellectual, emotional, moral and spiritual existence."[78] The link with globalization had also been established in the Cultural Diversity Declaration:

> In the face of current imbalances in flows and exchanges of cultural goods and services at the global level, it is necessary to reinforce international cooperation and solidarity aimed at enabling all countries, especially developing countries and countries in transition, to establish cultural industries that are viable and competitive at national and international level.[79]

---

74 Id., Article 10(c).
75 UNESCO, *supra* note 4, §§17–9.
76 *See* id., §§17–9.
77 *See* Convention on the Diversity of Cultural Expressions, *supra* note 1, Articles 12–19.
78 Cultural Diversity Declaration, *supra* note 10, Article 3.
79 Id., Article 10.

The Convention on the Diversity of Cultural Expressions confirms[80] and explicates these links particularly in Article 14: "Parties shall endeavour to support cooperation for sustainable development and poverty reduction ... in order to foster the emergence of a dynamic cultural sector." Subsequently, several means of achieving this goal are mentioned. Next to several economic measures to strengthen cultural industries in developing countries, measures are specified to provide support for creative work and facilitate the mobility of artists from the developing world. Contracting Parties will also encourage appropriate collaboration between developed and developing countries in areas such as music and film. Article 16 continues that "[d]eveloped countries shall facilitate cultural exchanges with developing countries by granting ... preferential treatment to artists and other cultural professionals and practitioners, as well as cultural goods and services from developing countries."

In contrast to other themes in the Convention on the Diversity of Cultural Expressions, the link with development is translated into relatively concrete measures. Moreover, the content of these measures is not covered by other conventions. It could therefore be said that the added value of the Convention on the Diversity of Cultural Expressions is to be found in Articles 12 to 19. Although minorities and indigenous peoples are not mentioned in these provisions, they may certainly benefit from the measures they contain. Increased mobility of artists and art between developing countries and developed countries may create artistic and political opportunities for artists belonging to minority or indigenous groups. This could enable them to break out of their generally marginalized position within their state and to draw attention to their specific culture and their often difficult political and social position.

5.4. INTRA-STATE POLICY: INTERACTION BETWEEN THE INDIVIDUAL AND INSTITUTIONAL STAKEHOLDERS

As mentioned in Section 2, one of the goals of the Convention on the Diversity of Cultural Expressions is "to define a set of general cultural policy principles in such a way as to ensure the necessary autonomy in national policy while guaranteeing balanced international cooperation. In other words, the point is to ensure consistency between intra-State and inter-State policy."[81] This "necessary autonomy in national policy"[82] is made concrete in the Convention on the Diversity of Cultural Expressions through the objective "to reaffirm *the sovereign rights of States to maintain, adopt and implement policies and measures that they*

80 Convention on the Diversity of Cultural Expressions, *supra* note 1, Preamble and Article 1.

81 UNESCO, *supra* note 3, §§17–9.

82 *See* Convention on the Diversity of Cultural Expressions, *supra* note 1, Articles 5 and 6 (1); *See also* Cultural Diversity Declaration, *supra* note 10, Article 9.

deem appropriate for the protection and promotion of the diversity of cultural expressions on their territory."[83]

There is inherent tension between this sovereign right of states and the aim to protect and promote cultural diversity. This tension is caused by the fact that the promotion and protection of cultural diversity also implies the protection and promotion of minority cultures. This raises a question with regard to any legal instrument on the protection of minorities and indigenous peoples: can a sovereign state which itself poses the greatest danger to minorities and indigenous peoples, be entrusted with their protection? The role allotted to the state in instruments on the protection of minorities and indigenous peoples should therefore be viewed with caution.

The explanatory report to the Convention on the Diversity of Cultural Expressions hastens to counter any impression of the Convention on the Diversity of Cultural Expressions creating a 'State monopoly', by the assurance that "the aim in reaffirming this right was not to establish a State monopoly but rather to put into practice cultural governance, i.e. interaction between individual and institutional stakeholders in sharing responsibility for the diversity of cultural expressions."[84]

This "interaction" takes shape in the Articles 6, 7 and 8 of the Convention on the Diversity of Cultural Expressions. Article 6(2) of the Convention on the Diversity of Cultural Expressions, for instance, lists a series of measures aimed at providing domestic independent cultural industries and activities in the informal sector with effective access to the means of production, dissemination and distribution of cultural activities, goods and services; measures aimed at providing public financial assistance; and measures encouraging non-profit organizations as well as public and private institutions and artists and other cultural professionals to develop and promote the free exchange and circulation of ideas, cultural expressions and cultural activities, goods and services.

In Article 7(1) of the Convention on the Diversity of Cultural Expressions, which contains measures to promote cultural expressions, the 'interaction' concept is muted and the role of the state increases:

> Parties shall endeavour to create in their territory an environment which encourages individuals and social groups: (a) to create, produce, disseminate, distribute and have access to their own cultural expressions, paying due attention to the special circumstances and needs of women as well as various social groups, including

83 Convention on the Diversity of Cultural Expressions, *supra* note 1, Article 1 (h) [emphasis added]; One of the questions raised by states during the drafting process was whether this right of a party to the Convention to protect and promote diversity "in its territory" is to be exercised for the benefit of "domestic" or "foreign" cultural expressions. *See* UNESCO, *supra* note 17, at 119.

84 UNESCO, *supra* note 25, at 6.

> persons belonging to minorities and indigenous peoples;[85] (b) to have access to diverse cultural expressions from within their territory as well as from other countries of the world.

Paragraph 2 of Article 7 of the Convention on the Diversity of Cultural Expressions stipulates that states "shall also endeavour to recognize the important contribution of artists, others involved in the creative process, cultural communities, and organizations that support their work, and their central role in nurturing the diversity of cultural expressions."

Article 8 of the Convention on the Diversity of Cultural Expressions contains measures to protect cultural expressions. Here the role of the state is crucial and the element of "interaction" has disappeared altogether: the state determines "the existence of special situations where cultural expressions on its territory are at risk of extinction, under serious threat, or otherwise in need of urgent safeguarding."[86]

It is interesting to compare this idea of "interaction" with the approach taken in other international instruments, such as the ICH Convention (see also Section 5.1) where the "interaction" between the state, individuals and groups is developed more convincingly.

According to Article 11 ICH Convention

> Each State Party shall: (a) take the necessary measures to ensure the safeguarding of the intangible cultural heritage present in its territory; (b) … identify and define the various elements of the intangible cultural heritage present in its territory, with the participation of communities, groups and relevant nongovernmental organizations.

Article 15 ICH Convention underlines once again that "[w]ithin the framework of its safeguarding activities of the intangible cultural heritage, each State Party shall endeavour to ensure the widest possible participation of communities, groups and, where appropriate, individuals that create, maintain and transmit such heritage, and to involve them actively in its management."

The right to participation is also a recurring theme in international legal documents on the rights of minorities and indigenous peoples. The ICH

---

85 A draft version of Article 8(7) Convention on the Diversity of Cultural Expressions was formulated as follows: "State Parties undertake to ensure in their territory … the protection of minority groups, particularly those regarded as threatened with extinction, and of their cultural contents and expressions." UNESCO, *supra* note 17, §62.

86 In a draft version of the Convention on the Diversity of Cultural Expressions, this Article 8 was formulated as follows: "If some cultural expressions, especially those of indigenous peoples and minorities, are deemed to be vulnerable to threatened by the possibility of extinction or serious curtailments, State Parties shall take appropriate measures to protect the diversity of cultural expressions within their territory." (…) UNESCO, *supra* note 17, §63 (Option 3).

Convention observed with regard to the exercise of the cultural rights protected under Article 27 ICCPR,

> that culture manifests itself in many forms, including a particular way of life associated with the use of land resources, especially in the case of indigenous peoples. That right may include such traditional activities as fishing or hunting and the right to live in reserves protected by law. The enjoyment of those rights may require positive legal measures of protection and measures to ensure the effective participation of members of minority communities in decisions which affect them.[87]

Articles 18 and 19 UNDRIP render the right to effective participation of indigenous peoples[88] in more specific terms:

> Indigenous peoples have the right to participate in decision-making in matters which could affect their rights, through representatives chosen by themselves in accordance with their own procedures, as well as to maintain and develop their own indigenous decision-making institutions.
> States shall consult and cooperate in good faith with the indigenous peoples concerned through their own representative institutions in order to obtain their free, prior and informed consent before adopting and implementing legislative or administrative measures that may affect them.

The added value of Articles 6, 7 and 8 of the Convention on the Diversity of Cultural Expressions for minorities and indigenous peoples depends on the level of their involvement and participation in decisions and measures affecting them. Unlike in other UNESCO and other international documents, in the Convention on the Diversity of Cultural Expressions this level of involvement and participation is inversely proportional to the gravity of the threat to cultural diversity. For that reason, the measures listed in Article 6 of the Convention on the Diversity of Cultural Expressions are likely to have the greatest relevance to minorities and indigenous peoples.

5.5. INTERNATIONAL COOPERATION AND THE RIGHTS OF TRANSFRONTIER MINORITIES AND INDIGENOUS PEOPLES

International cooperation and transnational contact are recurring themes in both the Convention on the Diversity of Cultural Expressions and other documents dealing with minorities and indigenous peoples. Nevertheless, due to

87 Human Rights Committee, *supra* note 28, at 38.
88 *See also* Article 6 ILO Convention No. 169.

its different aim or focus, reinforcement by the Convention on the Diversity of Cultural Expressions of existing rights in this field is not obvious.

On the one hand, international cooperation in the Convention on the Diversity of Cultural Expressions appears to be an essential tool to promote cultural diversity. According to the preamble of the Convention on the Diversity of Cultural Expressions, states are "aware that cultural diversity is strengthened by the free flow of ideas, and that it is nurtured by constant exchanges and interaction between cultures." Article 1 of the Convention on the Diversity of Cultural Expressions includes the objectives of "encouraging dialogue among cultures with a view to ensuring wider and balanced cultural exchanges in the world in favour of intercultural respect and a culture of peace"; and "foster[ing] interculturality in order to develop cultural interaction in the spirit of building bridges among peoples." These objectives are expressed in a slightly more concrete form in Article 12 of the Convention on the Diversity of Cultural Expressions:

> Parties shall endeavour to strengthen their bilateral, regional and international cooperation for the creation of conditions conducive to the promotion of the diversity of cultural expressions, … in order to: a) facilitate dialogue among Parties on cultural policy; … c) reinforce partnerships with and among civil society, non-governmental organizations and the private sector in fostering and promoting the diversity of cultural expressions; … e) encourage the conclusion of co-production and co-distribution agreements.

On the other hand, the aim of promoting minorities' and indigenous peoples' rights with regard to international contact and cooperation has a more natural character. In Article 2, paragraph 5 UDNM, persons belonging to minorities have the right to establish and maintain contact across frontiers with citizens of other states "to whom they are related by national or ethnic, religious or linguistic ties". In addition, the state is kept at a certain distance form this contact. With regard to transfrontier contact, Article 17 FCNM provides that:

> The parties undertake not to interfere with the right of persons belonging to national minorities to establish and maintain free and peaceful contacts across frontiers with persons lawfully staying in other states, in particular those with whom they share an ethnic, cultural, linguistic or religious identity, or a common cultural heritage.

Finally, official cooperation between states on questions relating to persons belonging to minorities[89] should be undertaken in moderation and only where necessary. For instance, Article 18 FCNM provides that:

> Parties shall endeavour to conclude, where necessary, bilateral and multilateral agreements with other States, in particular neighbouring States, in order to ensure

[89] UNDM, *supra* note 29, Article 6.

> the protection of persons belonging to the national minorities concerned. Where relevant, the Parties shall take measures to encourage transfrontier co-operation.[90]

The Languages Charter has among its principles the promotion of appropriate types of transnational exchanges for regional or minority languages used in identical or similar form in two or more states.[91]

In ILO Convention No. 169 and the UNDRIP a similar level of caution can be discerned with regard to the role of the state in the establishment of transnational contact for indigenous peoples. According to Article 32 ILO Convention No. 169 "[g]overnments shall take appropriate measures, including by means of international agreements, to facilitate contacts and co-operation between indigenous and tribal peoples across borders." Article 36 UNDRIP does not mention the state at all:

> Indigenous peoples, in particular those divided by international borders, have the right to maintain and develop contacts, relations and cooperation, including activities for spiritual, cultural, political, economic and social purposes, with their own members as well as other peoples across borders.

There is clearly a difference in how the tool of international cooperation is used between the Convention on the Diversity of Cultural Expressions, on the one hand, and the minority and indigenous rights instruments, on the other hand. Minorities and indigenous peoples wary of excessive state interference in their cultural rights and international contacts would no doubt express amazement at how the aim of international cooperation in the Convention on the Diversity of Cultural Expressions is promoted by 'constant exchanges' and 'interaction between cultures in favour of intercultural respect and a culture of peace' and 'interculturality'.[92] In contrast to these ambitions, which have a very open but also somewhat forced character, the corresponding minority and indigenous rights provisions evoke a sense of pragmatic moderation.

However, the Convention on the Diversity of Cultural Expressions might offer added value with regard to these rights in the "partnerships with and among civil society, non-governmental organizations and the private sector" mentioned in Article 12 Convention on the Diversity of Cultural Expressions. Once reinforced or established by the state, these partnerships might become an independent and useful tool facilitating contact across borders between minorities or indigenous peoples sharing an ethnic, cultural, linguistic or religious identity. Many minorities and indigenous peoples, who themselves are constitutive elements of cultural diversity within their State, often have difficulties preserving their own culture. For some of them, the imposition of

---

90 *See also* Languages Charter, *supra* note 15, Article 14.

91 Id., Article 7.

92 *See supra* Section 5.4.

extended cultural diversity in the name of 'the spirit of building bridges among peoples' might be 'a bridge too far'. For others, who might feel suffocated by their own culture, these new contacts with other cultures may be a welcome window of opportunity.

6. CONCLUSION

The Convention on the Diversity of Cultural Expressions is not chiefly intended as an instrument for the protection of minorities and indigenous peoples. Its scope is universal and its ambition is to emphasize areas of cultural diversity in the context of globalization which do not yet enjoy adequate protection under existing conventions or recommendations. The notion of cultural diversity, as introduced by the Convention on the Diversity of Cultural Expressions, can be perceived as an overarching notion. At a very abstract level, this notion covers all existing international legal instruments with regard to culture. Minorities and indigenous peoples are pillars of cultural diversity, but their position is complicated. They are inextricably linked with cultural diversity and one of its main sources, but their drive for a degree of cultural autonomy, their reserve with regard to their own state and their frequently uneasy social and cultural position make it sometimes difficult to match their needs with the somewhat vague and ambitious aims of the Convention on the Diversity of Cultural Expressions.

Perceived as pillars supporting the practical implementation of the abstract notion of cultural diversity, the existing instruments dealing with minorities' and indigenous peoples' rights differ in scope. For instance, linguistic diversity is presented as a fundamental element of cultural diversity in the Convention on the Diversity of Cultural Expressions, but the promotion of linguistic diversity is not developed in detail. The Languages Charter contains very concrete and detailed provisions with regard to the protection of regional and minority languages, and so buttresses the Convention on the Diversity of Cultural Expressions. The FCNM is a more slender pillar, because it is less detailed and leaves a large measure of discretion to states. The strength of this pillar depends on the degree of implementation by states. Article 27 ICCPR and the views of the HRC are also strong pillars of the Convention on the Diversity of Cultural Expressions, especially with regard to the development of cultural rights of indigenous peoples. In 2007, this pillar was further strengthened by the UNDRIP.

The purpose of this article has been to assess the added value of the Convention on the Diversity of Cultural Expressions for minorities and indigenous peoples. On first glance a comparison between the Convention on the Diversity of Cultural Expressions and international instruments on the rights of minorities and indigenous peoples casts the Convention on the

Diversity of Cultural Expressions in a poor light: the level and precision of the protection offered in other instruments is much more advanced, and the Convention on the Diversity of Cultural Expressions has little to add, especially, to the existing rights of religious and linguistic minorities. However, on closer inspection the aims of the Convention on the Diversity of Cultural Expressions reveal more positive conclusions.

Surprisingly, in addition to offering an abstract and symbolic interpretation of the Convention on the Diversity of Cultural Expressions, some provisions may be of great pragmatic value for minorities and indigenous. For instance, the aim of Articles 12 to 19 of the Convention on the Diversity of Cultural Expressions is to increase the mobility of artists and art between developing countries and developed countries. For minorities and indigenous peoples this may create unexpected artistic, social and even political opportunities to break out of their frequently marginalized position within their state and to draw attention to their specific culture and their often difficult political and social position.

In the main, however, the added value of the Convention on the Diversity of Cultural Expressions is in its symbolic function: it brings the value of cultural diversity as such to the fore in an international sense, and, as an overarching notion, it gives structure and direction to international developments in this field. From the point of view of legal scholars these are fascinating developments, which may result in a paradigm shift. Minorities and indigenous peoples, however, may be understandably sceptical of the abstract language of the Convention on the Diversity of Cultural Expressions when they are confronted with the very real prospect of the extinction or serious impairment of their culture.

PART IV

TRADE AND INTELLECTUAL PROPERTY & THE CONVENTION ON THE DIVERSITY OF CULTURAL EXPRESSIONS

THE CONVENTION ON THE DIVERSITY OF CULTURAL EXPRESSIONS AND ITS IMPACT ON THE "CULTURE AND TRADE DEBATE"

A Critical Evaluation after 5 Years

Rostam J. NEUWIRTH*

As variety is the spice of life,
so is it the spring of commerce.[1]
T.G. Williams, *The History of Commerce* (1926)

1. INTRODUCTION

On 18 March 2007 the UNESCO Convention on the Protection and Promotion of the Diversity of Cultural Expressions ("Convention on the Diversity of Cultural Expressions") entered into force following the deposit of the 30th instrument of ratification.[2] To briefly recall, the Convention on the Diversity of Cultural Expressions was adopted by the General Conference of the United Nations Education, Scientific and Cultural Organization ("UNESCO") at its 133rd meeting held in Paris on 20 October 2005, with 148 votes in favour, two opposed (United States of America and Israel) and four abstentions (Australia, Honduras, Nicaragua, and Liberia).[3] Immediately following the adoption, some commentators hailed the Convention on the Diversity of Cultural Expressions as a great success whereas others wanted to see it either not ratified or at least

* *Mag. iur.* (University of Graz), *LL.M.* (McGill), *Ph.D.* (EUI), Associate Professor at the Faculty of Law of the University of Macau; Email: rjn@umac.mo.

1 *See* T.G. WILLIAMS, *The History of Commerce*, 1926, 1.

2 *See* Convention on the Protection and Promotion of the Diversity of Cultural Expressions, 20 October 2005, *U.N. Doc. CLT-2005/CONVENTION DIVERSITE-CULT REV.* [hereinafter "Convention on the Diversity of Cultural Expressions"].

3 *See* A. RIDING, "U.S. all but alone in opposing Unesco cultural pact", *The New York Times* (20 October 2005), *available at* www.nytimes.com//10/20/world/americas/20iht-unesco.html.

revised.[4] Generally speaking, it came as no surprise that generally those supportive of the cause of a special clause for cultural products in the international trading regime established by the World Trade Organization ("WTO"), *i.e.* a so-called *"exception culturelle"* to use the French term, also supported the Convention on the Diversity of Cultural Expressions, whereas opponents to such special treatment of cultural products opposed it.

In other words, the culture and trade quandary, that characterized most of the 20th century and even previous centuries, was set to continue into the 21st century. As in former times, the quandary was manifested in a debate addressing the uncertainty about the nature and regulation of various cultural goods and services, such as cinematograph films, television programmes, video and sound recordings and publications. These categories of products, which are continuously being expanded by innovations and advances in digital and other technologies, generally fall under the rubric of cultural industries. It is the dual, *i.e.* cultural and economic, nature intrinsic to these cultural products that raises difficult questions about the mutual relationship between cultural and trade policies. Their special dual nature also evinced problems related to the institutional competence and the general fragmentation of international law in dealing with these products. In the run-up to the Convention on the Diversity of Cultural Expressions, it was discussed whether the WTO or UNESCO should be in charge of dealing with the issue of cultural diversity in the context of global trade liberalization. Although (or perhaps because) UNESCO does not present an efficient and legalistic regime the way the WTO does with its compulsory dispute settlement system,[5] it was decided to entrust UNESCO with the negotiation of an international instrument on cultural diversity instead of tackling the issue within the framework of the WTO.[6]

The problems that the drafters of the Convention on the Diversity of Cultural Expressions thus confronted were first how to define the cultural industries and delimit them from other ordinary products and second how to best respond to their special dual, cultural and economic, nature. As a third point, the drafters were equally called upon to try to close the institutional gap in the international

4 *See, e.g.*, J. Musitelli, "La Convention sur la diversité culturelle: anatomie d'un succès diplomatique" 62 *Revue internationale et stratégique* 10 (2006), *available at* www.diplomatie.gouv.fr//IMG/pdf/0701-MUSITELLI-EN.pdf (last visited 2 February 2012) (English version); *But see* the Fiche analytique du département d'État sur le project de convention de l'UNESCO, "Les É.-U. souhaitent la révision du projet de convention sur la diversité culturelle" (12 October 2005), *available at* www.mondialisations.org///.php?id=21122&lan=FR (last visited 2 February 2012).

5 *See also* J.-M. Djian, "Un laboratoire devitalise", *Le Monde Diplomatique* 26 (October 2005), *available at* www.monde-diplomatique.fr//10/DJIAN/12801; D.N. Palmeter and P.C. Mavroidis, *Dispute Settlement in the World Trade Organization: Practice and Procedure*, 2004.

6 *See also* G. Gagne (ed.), *La diversité culturelle: Vers une convention internationale effective?*, 2005, 11.

regulation of the cultural industries. This institutional gap emerged and has continued to widen since the adoption of the GATT 1947 as a result of the failure of the International Trade Organization ("ITO").[7] Hence expectations tied to the Convention on the Diversity of Cultural Expressions were high. In this respect it is noteworthy to mention that only a few weeks following the entry into force of the Convention on the Diversity of Cultural Expressions, namely on 10 April 2007, it was the United States ("US") that requested consultations with the People's Republic of China ("China") on a variety of Chinese measures relating to the regulation of the cultural industries.[8] In this case, which became known as *China – Measures Affecting Trading Rights and Distribution Services for Certain Publications and Audiovisual Entertainment Products* ("*China – Publications and Audiovisual Products*") a panel was eventually established and a panel report issued.[9] The panel report was appealed by both parties to the dispute and the Appellate Body issued its final report on 21 December 2009.[10] In summary, the *China Publications and Audiovisual Products* case picked up the culture and trade debate where the *Canada Periodicals* case ended.[11] The sole difference was that, in the meantime, the international community had adopted the Convention on the Diversity of Cultural Expressions.

It is therefore a good moment to briefly revisit the Convention on the Diversity of Cultural Expressions on its fifth anniversary in order to evaluate its legal impact on the culture and trade debate. To this end, Section 2 looks at selected "milestones" of "culture and trade conflicts" with a view to establishing a continuous thread between past conflicts and the most recent case. Section 3 offers a look at the state of the culture and trade debate following the adoption of the Convention on the Diversity of Cultural Expressions from the viewpoint of the scholarly debate and the work of the bodies established by the Convention. Finally, Section 4 brings some insights on the legal impact of the Convention on the Diversity of Cultural Expressions on the sphere of international trade law based on a ruling by the Appellate Body of the WTO, a judgment of the European Court of Justice ("ECJ") as well as insights gained from numerous

---

7 *See generally* R.J. Neuwirth, "The Cultural Industries and the Role of Article IV GATT: Reflections on Policy Options for Canada and the EU in the new WTO Round" (2002), *available at* http://papers.ssrn.com//.cfm?abstract_id=1352171 (last visited 2 February 2012).

8 *See* WTO, "Request for Consultations by the United States: China – Measures Affecting Trading Rights and Distribution Services for Certain Publications and Audiovisual Entertainment Products", *WT/DS363/1, G/L/820, S/L/287* (16 April 2007).

9 Panel Report, "China – Measures Affecting Trading Rights and Distribution Services for Certain Publications and Audiovisual Entertainment Products", *WT/DS 363/R* (12 August 2009).

10 Appellate Body Report, "China – Measures Affecting Trading Rights and Distribution Services for Certain Publications and Audiovisual Entertainment Products", *WT/DS363/AB/R* (21 December 2009).

11 Panel Report, "Canada – Certain Measures Concerning Periodicals", *WTO Doc. WT/DS31/R* (14 March 1997); Appellate Body Report, "Canada – Certain Measures Concerning Periodicals", *WTO Doc. WT/DS31/AB/R* (30 June 1997).

regional trade agreements ("RTAs") that became operative after the entry into force of the Convention on the Diversity of Cultural Expressions. The conclusion briefly summarizes the principal findings.

2. MILESTONES IN "CULTURE AND TRADE" CONFLICTS

2.1. THE NATURE OF "CULTURE AND TRADE CONFLICTS" AND THEIR PART IN THE "TRADE LINKAGE DEBATE"

In order to critically evaluate the impact of the new Convention on the multilateral trading rules as reviewed in Section 4, it is helpful to briefly outline the principal features of the debate surrounding culture and trade. To begin with, in 2000 a short publication by UNESCO, entitled *Culture, Trade and Globalization*, reaffirmed that "the issue of 'culture and trade' has now acquired prime strategic significance" and that when "culture is put on the table, it often prompts complex discussions on the relationship between the economic and non-economic value of things".[12] The problem of the precise relationship between economic and non-economic values is not limited to the sphere of culture but forms the core of several serious problems such as "trade and ... problems" otherwise referred to as the "trade linkage debate".[13] Such trade and ... problems usually appear in pairs, such as "trade and environment"[14], "trade and human rights"[15], "trade and development"[16], "trade and social, or labour standards"[17], "trade and migration"[18], "trade and security"[19], as well as "trade and education" to mention but a few.[20] Reality, however, suggests that each of the

---

12 UNESCO, *Culture, Trade and Globalization: Questions and Answers*, 2000, 9.

13 *See* J.P. Trachtman, "Trade and... Problems, Cost-Benefit Analysis and Subsidiarity", 9 *E.J.I.L.* 32 (1998).

14 *See, e.g.*, A. Fijalkowski and J. Cameron (eds.), *Trade and the Environment: Bridging the Gap*, 1998.

15 *See, e.g.*, S. Bal, "International Free Trade Agreements and Human Rights: Reinterpreting Article XX of the GATT", 10 *Minn. J. Global Trade* 62 (2001).

16 *See, e.g.*, V.N. Balasubramanyam (ed.), *Trade and Development: Essays in Honour of Jagdish Bhagwati*, 1996.

17 *See, e.g.*, R. Bhala, "Clarifying the Trade-Labor Link", 37 *Colum. J. Transnat'l L.* 11 (1998); E. Alben, "GATT and the Fair Wage: A Historical Perspective on the Labor-Trade Link", 101 *Colum. L. Rev.* 1410 (2001).

18 *See* R. Faini, J. de Melo, and K.F. Zimmermann, "Trade and migration: an introduction", in R. Faini and J. de Melo & K.F. Zimmermann (eds.), *Migration – The Controversies and the Evidence* 1 (1999).

19 *See, e.g.*, H.L. Schloemann and St. Ohlhoff, "'Constitutionalization'and Dispute Settlement in the WTO: National Security as an Issue of Competence", 93 *A.J.I.L.* 424 (1999).

20 *See, e.g.*, J. Knight, "Trade in Higher Education Services: *The Implications of GATS*", *The Observatory on Borderless Education* (March 2002), *available at* http://firgoa.usc.es//files/.pdf (last visited 2 February 2012).

individual pairs is part of a larger complex whole that could be described by reference to the trade linkage debate in the context of the debate about the governance of global affairs in the 21st century.[21]

Within the broader trade linkage debate the "culture and trade problem" certainly holds a privileged position.[22] Considering the breadth and elasticity of both the term "culture" and that of "trade" or "commerce", which fortunately, due to intrinsic dynamism, have so far proven legally indefinable, it can also be argued that, in a wider sense, the "culture and trade debate" is about a certain "culture" in trade. Such a "cultured" approach to trade is reflected in the Preamble to the WTO Agreement and consists of efforts to enhance international trade by entering into "reciprocal and mutually advantageous arrangements".[23] Such qualification of the culture and trade debate also resonates in the following statement:

> Unless trade people can deal with the cultural issue, how do you expect them to deal with environmental issues, labor issues, or social standards?[24]

Thus, through its etymological origin, found in the cultivation of the Gods, the Earth and later the mind,[25] the term "culture" also connotes concern for the improvement and proper cultivation of the environment, advancement of human rights, and of many more values essential to human life. This means that the organization of human life has progressively increased in complexity up to now. This process of "complexification", as used by Pierre Teilhard de Chardin in *Le phénomène humain* (1955), when applied to the context of global governance can be read to mean that any single policy can only be dealt with successfully by considering the entirety of other policies simultaneously.

As for trade and commerce, the evolution of the GATT regime over the past fifty years has shown the creeping extension of trade from goods to services, to investment, subsidies, and intellectual property rights ("IPRs"). Closely related to this expansion is the issue of what kind of "culture" or what form of "trade" commentators are talking about. Usually there exists less disagreement when it comes to questions on the general relationship between "culture" and "trade", yet

21 *See, e.g.*, J.N. Rosenau, "Governance in the 21st Century", 1 *Global Governance* 13 (1995).

22 *See* M.E. Footer & C.B. Graber, "Trade Liberalization and Cultural Policy" 3 *J.I.E.L.* 115 (2000); *See also* B. de Witte, "Trade in Culture: International Legal Regimes and EU Constitutional Values", in G. de Búrca and J. Scott (eds.), *The EU and the WTO – Legal and Constitutional Issues*, 2001, 237.

23 *See* Marrakesh Agreement Establishing the World Trade Organization, 15 April 1994, *LT/UR/A/2*, Preamble items 1 and 3 [hereinafter "Marrakesh Agreement"].

24 *See* K.C.C. Stein, "The Management and Resolution of Cross Border Disputes as Canada/U.S. Enter the 21st Century: Telecommunications and Culture: Transborder Freedom of Information or Cultural Identity?", 26 *Can.-U.S. L.J.* 313, 314 (2000).

25 *Cf.* the concepts "*cultus deorum*", "*cultura agris*" and "*cultura mentis*", in A.L. Kroeber and C. Kluckhohn, *Culture – A Critical Review of Concepts and Definitions*, 1952, 15; J. Rundell and St. Mennell (eds.), *Classical Readings in Culture and Civilization*, 1998, 12.

friction is likely to increase when it comes to more specific questions concerning cultural taste, cultural contents, the nature of cultural products in the sphere of culture, or the form of trade liberalization, such as whether to include services or the free movement of persons in the sphere of trade. As a further element to the debate, one can identify a tendency to confuse ideological disagreements with disagreements over the nature of a new phenomenon and the appropriate regulatory response to it. As a result, the quandary concerning the optimal regulatory response may persist with regard to each separate policy field, a quandary which only intensifies when two or more different fields are treated simultaneously. The resulting complexity means a challenge for which most governments, public authorities, institutions and international organizations not only lack the political will but also the adequate structure in institutional or organizational terms. The structural inadequacy usually stems from the underlying division of competences, hierarchical structures and strong compartmentalization. While one aspect of the culture and trade conflict concerns questions about the right architecture of the legal framework governing their interaction, another aspect concerns the subjection of certain phenomena under their respective rules. With regard to the second aspect, aside from the cultural industries, cases have shown that practically every product, such as meat,[26] spaghetti,[27] cheese,[28] alcoholic drinks including beer, wine and *shochu*,[29] and even toasters with or without pictures,[30] do bear some cultural traits and even conform to certain cultural stereotypes though to a varying degree. This degree depends on the extent of cultural content, which in turn depends on several distinct factors, such as the products' origin, quantity, quality, or their service life, and particularly the way they are manufactured, reproduced, transported and consumed.

---

26 *See* Israel-United States Free Trade Area Agreement, 19 August 1985, *24 I.L.M. 657*, Article 8 [Special Exception for Kashruth] (which stipulates that "This Agreement shall not preclude the adoption or enforcement by either Party of measures relating to prohibitions on religious or ritual grounds provided that they are applied in accordance with the principle of national treatment"); *See also* Canada-Israel Free Trade Agreement, 1 January 1997, Annex 4.1. (Exceptions to Article 4.1. National Treatment) Section B §1(c), *available at* www.international.gc.ca/trade-agreements-accords-commerciaux/agr-acc/israel/toc-tdm.aspx?lang=eng&view=d (last visited 2 February 2012); Appellate Body Report, "European Communities – Measures Concerning Meat and Meat Products (Hormones)", *WT/DS48/AB/R* (16 January 1998).

27 *See* Case 407/85, *3 Glocken GmbH and Gertraud Kritzinger v USL Centro-Sud and Provincia autonoma di Bolzano*, [1988] E.C.R. 4233.

28 *See* Case 286/86, *Ministère public v Gérard Deserbais*, [1988] E.C.R. 4907.

29 *See, e.g.*, Case 178/84, *Commission v. Germany*, [1987] E.C.R. 1227; Case 170/78, *Commission of the European Communities v United Kingdom of Great Britain and Northern Ireland*, [1983] E.C.R. 2265; *Japan – Taxes on Alcoholic beverages, WT/DS1/AB/R, WT/DS10/AB/R, WT/DS22/AB/R* (October 4, 1996).

30 C.R. Sunstein, "Television and the Public Interest", 88 *Calif. L. Rev.* 499, at 507 n. 36 (2000) (quoting former FCC Chairman Mark Fowler, who is reported to have called television "just an other appliance", a "toaster with pictures").

Considering these factors, it is argued that the core of most culture and trade conflicts is best exemplified by the category of various cultural goods and services as summarized in the term "cultural industries". Looking at the legal definition in the NAFTA, the cultural industries include various cultural goods and services such as books, magazines, film, video and music recordings as well as radio-communications and broadcasting.[31] These and other categories (*e.g.* video games) following the broad trend of convergence through digitization and other technologies are characterized by their strong dependence on technological progress, innovation, creative input and on copyright protection, partly due to the combined characteristics of goods and services, of public and private goods attributes, and mostly to their dual, economic and cultural nature. Additionally, the cultural industries bear specific traits with regard to their production, reproduction, and distribution before their final consumption. Such specificity of the industry is found, for instance, in the initial investment risk caused by high production costs and dependence on volatile consumer taste and relatively low unit costs which may be compensated by the comparably very low reproduction and distribution costs. These elements often attract producers to different kinds of competitive as well as anti-competitive business practices, such as vertical and horizontal integration, or concerted practices (*e.g.* star system, prototypes, block booking, zoning) in order to minimize risks yet at the same time maximize sales in the greatest number of markets (transnational market imperative) so as to generate the highest possible revenues (profit maximization). Based on their modes of consumption, which usually rely on cognitive processes, another unique feature is found in their secondary promotional effect on other ordinary goods and services, warranting them the categorization as "trade getters" or "silent salesmen".[32] Equally, they have been identified, both negatively as a threat to,[33] and positively as the foundation of a democratic society.[34]

---

31 *Cf.* Article 2107 NAFTA; North American Free Trade Agreement between the Government of Canada, the Government of Mexico and the Government of the United States, 17 December 1992, 32 *I.L.M.* 605 (1993).

32 *See* F.A. Tichenor, "Motion Pictures as Trade Getters", 128 *Annals Am. Acad. Pol. & Soc. Sci.* 84 (1926); J. Klein, "What are Motion Pictures doing for Industry?", 128 *Annals Am. Acad. Pol. & Soc. Sci.* 79 (1926).

33 *See, e.g.* G. Orwell, *Nineteen Eighty-Four*, 2000, 185 (summing up the various subsectors of the cultural industries as follows: "The invention of print, however, made it easier to manipulate public opinion, and the film and the radio carried the process further. With the development of television, and the technical advance which made it possible to receive and transmit simultaneously on the same instrument, private life came to an end".).

34 *See, e.g.*, European Parliament Resolution on Cultural Industries, 4 September 2003, *P5_TA-PROV(2003)0382,* Recital P (recognizing "the importance of television and other mass media services for the democratic opinion-forming process, with a view to ensuring and enhancing diversity of opinion and pluralism"); *see also* N. Weinstock Netanel, "Asserting Copyright's Democratic Principles in the Global Arena", 51 *Vand. L. Rev.* 217, 329 (1998) (writing that: "A democratic culture, supported by the widespread dissemination of information and opinion, an independent and pluralist media, and a belief in the efficacy of individual contributions to public discourse, is central to that process of democratization.").

Finally, to give but one last example, another central role of cultural industries has been confirmed in the field of development.[35]

In short, the cultural industries, therefore, qualify as the most complex category of products falling within the culture and trade quandary, not because they are situated at the extremity of each concept, but because they oscillate between the two, thereby creating a centre of gravity drawing everything else without mercy into their gravitational field.

2.2. 'CULTURE AND TRADE CONFLICTS' FROM THE PAST TO THE ADOPTION OF THE CONVENTION ON THE DIVERSITY OF CULTURAL EXPRESSIONS

The assumption that the cultural industries are from a legal point of view the most important operational field for culture and trade conflicts is also supported by records from the historical past. There are records of legal problems, suggesting that already in the early days of human history the question arose as to whether all things can be subject to trade and commerce or whether there are certain categories of products that should be exempted due to some special, videlicet cultural, features.[36] Aside from these precedents, the conflicts underlying the present global culture and trade debate are very much phenomena of the twentieth century. The reason for their relatively recent emergence is a combination of the appearance of important technological inventions, such as cinematograph and radio-communication technology on a global scale, which in turn led to the gradual introduction of modes of mass production and mass distribution into the cultural field. The various consequences of these inventions for the cultural field and, notably, the work of art are well presented and analysed in the famous article "*Das Kunstwerk im Zeitalter seiner technischen Reproduzierbarkeit*" published by Walter Benjamin in 1936.[37] His analysis was soon complemented by a conceptual innovation introduced by Theodor W. Adorno and Max Horkheimer by way of the term "*Kulturindustrie*" or "culture

[35] *See, e.g.*, G. Pagniet, "Industries de la culture et développement", 194 *Le Courrier ACP* 42 (2002) (characterising the role of the cultural industries as follows: "Phénomène social aux caractéristiques très diverses et aux multiples ramifications, les industries culturelles doivent être étudiées à travers les divers sous-secteurs qui les composent. Au fil du temps, une prise de conscience de plus en plus forte des enjeux liés aux "industries culturelles" a abouti à l'idée que culture et développement sont intimement lies.").

[36] The Roman lawyer *Gaius* (130–180 BCE), for instance, identified in his *Institutiones* certain categories of things, such as things subject to divine dominion like statues, altars or cultic objects, which cannot be the object of exchange or of any legal commercial transaction (*res extra commercium* or *res quarum commercium non est*); *See* M. Kaser, *Römisches Privatrecht*, 15th ed., 1989, 90–1.

[37] "The Work of Art in the Age of Mechanical Reproduction"; *See* W. Benjamin, "Das Kunstwerk im Zeitalter seiner technischen Reproduzierbarkeit", in R. Tiedemann and H. Schweppenhäuser (eds.), *Walter Benjamin – Gesammelte Schriften*, Vol. I, 2nd ed., 1978, 436.

industry".[38] The culture industry was first designed to contrast two apparently contradictory terms but gradually evolved into a special category of cultural goods and services. A remnant from its philosophical origin is its role as a paradoxical riddle, something we are – most probably – still trying still to resolve today.

Such technological and philosophical innovations were soon accompanied by respective legal responses, for which the predecessor of UNESCO, the International Committee for Intellectual Cooperation ("ICIC"), established by the League of Nations in 1922 and four years later transformed into the International Institute of Intellectual Cooperation ("IICI"), provided the proper link.[39] Confronted with the new phenomenon of mass media, particularly films and broadcasting, the IICI was involved in the drafting of two early relevant international conventions, the 1933 *Convention for Facilitating the International Circulation of Films of an Educational Character* and the 1936 *International Convention Concerning the Use of Broadcasting in the Cause of Peace*.[40] The two conventions were designed to respectively contribute to international peace and security through the exemption of all customs duties and accessory charges for films with international educational aims in order to encourage moral disarmament, to ensure physical, intellectual and moral progress and to prevent broadcasting from being used in a manner prejudicial to good international understanding. Their major intent was to utilize the possibilities offered by this medium of intercommunication for better mutual understanding between peoples.

The next legal milestone in the culture and trade quandary was the adoption of Article IV on "cinematograph films" in the GATT 1947, which is still in force today.[41] Its text was based on Article 19 of the Havana Charter for an International Trade Organization ("ITO")[42] and was inspired by a similar provision in the so-called "*Blum-Byrnes Agreement*", concluded between the United States of America and the Provisional Government of the French Republic in 1946.[43] In regulatory terms, Article IV GATT effectively stipulates that if GATT Contracting Parties and, now WTO Members, want to establish or maintain internal quantitative regulations relating to exposed cinematograph

38 *See* Th.W. Adorno and M. Horkheimer, *Dialectic of Enlightenment*, 1997; *see also* Th.W. Adorno, *The Culture Industry*, 1991, 98.

39 *See generally* H. Bonnet, "L'œuvre de l'institut international de coopération intellectuelle", 61 *Rec. des Cours* 457 (1937).

40 *See* the Convention for Facilitating the International Circulation of Films of an Educational Character, 11 October 1933, 1 *L.N.T.S.* 333; International Convention concerning the Use of Broadcasting in the Cause of Peace, 23 September 1936, 186 *L.N.T.S.* 301.

41 *See* General Agreement on Tariffs and Trade, 30 October 1947, 55 *U.N.T.S.* 187.

42 *See* UN Conference on Trade and Employment, "Havana Charter for an International Trade Organization and Final Act and Related Documents", *UN Doc ICITO/1/4/1948* (Havana November 21, 1947 to March 24, 1948).

43 *See especially* Declaration by the Government of the United States of America and the Provisional Government of the French Republic on Commercial Policy and Related Matters, 28 May 1946, 418 *U.S.T. LEXIS* 1, at 69 *et seq.*

films, *i.e.* movies, then such regulations shall take the form of screen quotas. According to John H. Jackson the rationale for the introduction of Article IV GATT was the closer regulatory connection of films to domestic cultural policies rather than to economics and trade.[44] Such an approach still reflects the then predominant separation of cultural issues from commercial ones on the basis of the old legal adage *expressio unius est exclusio alterius* (the choice of one part excludes the other), at a time when the economic features of a good or service could still be regarded separate from its cultural features.[45] Moreover, it shows only the gradual awareness of the dual, *i.e.* both economic and cultural, dimension of cinematograph films and other cultural goods and services.[46] Since then, Article IV GATT can be considered as the most important legal recognition of the cultural specificity of certain categories of cultural goods and services now commonly referred to as the cultural industries in the international trading regime.[47] Even if its legal significance and use has decreased over the years due to extremely dynamic technological innovations, it is still a powerful political reminder of a clear contact point between culture and trade.[48]

Soon after the entry into force of the GATT in 1948, another important reminder of the close relationship between culture and trade was seen in the adoption of two agreements under the aegis of UNESCO, the 1948 *Agreement for Facilitating the International Circulation of Visual and Auditory Materials of an Educational, Scientific and Cultural Character* ("Beirut Agreement")[49] and the 1950 *Agreement on the Importation of Educational, Scientific and Cultural Materials* ("Florence Agreement").[50] Both agreements aimed at removing economic obstacles to the free circulation of ideas based on rapid technological progress. It is important to note that, as an interesting precedent of comity between international organizations, UNESCO submitted the draft Florence

44 *See* J.H. Jackson, *World Trade and the Law of GATT*, 1969, 293; *see also* D.A. Irwin, P.C. Mavroidis and A.O. Sykes, *The Genesis of the GATT*, 2008, 140 (mentioning the example of the New Zealand film hire tax as another reason to support the exemption of cinematograph films from national treatment).

45 *See, generally,* H. Mosler, "General Principles of Law", in R. Bernhardt (ed.), *Encyclopaedia of Public International Law*, Vol. 7, 1984, 89 and (mainly) 92–3.

46 An early account of the dual nature of films is given in the statement "*par ailleurs, le cinéma est une industrie*"; *see* A. Malraux, *L'esquisse d'une psychologie du cinéma*, 1939.

47 *See, e.g.*, T. Cottier, "Die völkerrechtlichen Rahmenbedingungen der Filmförderung in der neuen Welthandelsorganization WTO-GATT", 38 *Z.U.M.* 749, 751 (1994).

48 *See* Neuwirth, *supra* note 7; *See also* D. Beppu, "When Cultural Value Justifies Protectionism: Interpreting the Language of the GATT to Find a Limited Cultural Exception to the National Treatment Principle", 29 *Cardozo L. Rev.* 1765 (2008).

49 Agreement for Facilitating the International Circulation of Visual and Auditory Materials of an Educational, Scientific and Cultural Character, 10 December 1948, 197 *U.N.T.S.* 3.

50 Agreement on the Importation of Educational, Scientific and Cultural Materials, with Annexes A, B, C, D and E and Protocol annexed, 22 November 1950, 131 *U.N.T.S.* 25 (1952); see also the Protocol to the Agreement on the Importation of Educational, Scientific and Cultural Materials, 26 November 1976, 1259 *U.N.T.S.* 3 (1982).

Agreement for comments and revision to a working group of the Contracting Parties of the GATT.[51]

The confirmation of the ever continuing tension between dynamic technological innovations on the one hand, and culture and trade conflicts exemplified in Article IV GATT as a tentative regulatory effort to reconcile culture and trade concerns on the other, occurred with the worldwide rise of international television programmes through satellite broadcasting. The central question was whether television fell within the scope of Article IV GATT and thus whether it must be qualified as a good, or as a service, falling outside the scope of the GATT regime. For this purpose, a working group was established in which the United States, advocating the applicability of the GATT to television programmes, faced resistance from France and other Contracting Parties.[52] In the end, no agreement was reached and the problem was merely left for a later date in the history of culture and trade conflicts.

The conflict over the treatment of television programmes and audiovisual services arose again during the final phase of the Uruguay Round negotiations (1986–93) and was centred on the idea of an *exception culturelle*, advocated mainly by France, the European Union and Canada and radically opposed by the United States. The controversy arose with regard to the former disagreement between the United States and Canada during the negotiations for *the Canada-United States Free Trade Agreement* ("CUSFTA"),[53] and the United States and the European Union with the adoption of the *Television Without Frontiers Directive* in 1989.[54] Altogether, the difference in the position of these countries almost derailed the successful creation of the World Trade Organization (WTO) in 1994.[55] Ultimately, the successful creation of the WTO was only made possible by a compromise, known as the so-called "agreement to disagree".[56] The

51 *See* UNESCO, *A Guide to the Operation of the Agreement on the Importation of Educational, Scientific and Cultural Material*, 4th ed., 1969, 5.

52 GATT, "Application of GATT to International Trade in Television Programmes", *L/1615* (16 November 1961); GATT, "Application of GATT to International Trade in Television Programmes", *L/1646* (21 November 1961); GATT, "Working Party on Application of GATT to International Trade in Television Programmes", *L/1686* (18 December 1961); GATT, "Application of GATT to International Trade in Television Programmes – Report of the Working Party", *L/1741* (13 March 1962); GATT, "Application of GATT to International Trade in Television Programmes – Revised United States Draft Recommendation", *L/1908* (10 November 1962); GATT, "Application of GATT to International Trade in Television Programmes – Proposal by the Government of the United States", *L/2120* (18 March 1964).

53 *See* Canada-United States Free-Trade Agreement, 4 October 1988, 27 *I.L.M.* 281.

54 *See* Council Directive 89/552/EEC on the Coordination of Certain Provisions Laid Down by Law, Regulation or Administrative Action in Member States Concerning the Pursuit of Television Broadcasting Activities, 3 October 1989, *OJ 1989 L 298/23.*

55 *See, e.g.*, J. Croome, *Reshaping the World Trading System: A History of the Uruguay Round*, 1995, 376; I. Bernier, "Cultural Goods and Services in International Trade Law", in D. Browne, ed., *The Culture/Trade Quandary – Canada's Policy Options*, 1998, 108, 127.

56 "Agreement to disagree" is an expression apparently used by both the trade representatives of the US (Mickey Kantor) and of the EU (Sir Leon Brittan) in a joint press conference in the final

compromise allowed WTO Members greater flexibility with regard to their sectoral commitments under the newly established *General Agreement on Trade in Services* ("GATS").[57]

The truce in the form of this "agreement to disagree" only lasted for a few years and new fuel was added to the flames with the Panel Report rendered in the *Canada Periodicals Case*, *i.e.* a trade dispute between the US and Canada over Canadian measures affecting the importation of split-run periodicals into Canada.[58] In its ruling, the Panel, which was later confirmed by the Appellate Body, held Canada responsible for an infringement of its trade obligations based on domestic measures aimed at supporting Canada's magazine industry, with a view to safeguarding and promoting its cultural identity. *En passant*, the Panel also noted that "cultural identity was not at issue here".[59] Although the Panel's statement was widely consistent with trade rules established under the WTO, the ruling did very little to address the central problem of the present trading regime, namely its general incapability to address various trade-related concerns, such as cultural or other concerns raised under the so-called "trade linkage debate". The ruling in the *Canada Periodicals* case is therefore crucial for culture and trade conflicts because it established a global precedent displaying the felt vulnerability of WTO Member's national measures aimed at cultural identity and cultural diversity. In this way, as later protests against a *Multilateral Agreement on Investment* ("MAI") as well as ministerial meetings in Seattle and Cancun confirmed, it nurtured a growing resistance in the world against a form of globalization which is perceived as predominantly focusing on trade liberalization (negative integration) without introducing the adequate accompanying measures in order to account for potential structural problems and financial losses (positive integration).[60]

Following the ruling in the *Canada Periodicals* case, awareness of and efforts to advocate for greater cultural diversity intensified around the globe. As a result, a series of documents addressing the issue were prepared which, by and large, promoted the adoption of a legally binding document for cultural diversity.[61]

---

stages of the Uruguay Round negotiations; *see* L. Elliott and E. Luce, "US and Europe Clear Obstacles to GATT Deal", *The Guardian (London)* 1 (15 December 1993); E. Luce, "The Deal: High Price of Accord in Services Package", *The Guardian (London)* 12 (15 December 1993).

57 General Agreement on Trade in Services,15 April 1994, 33 *I.L.M.* 1168, Annex 1B.

58 Panel Report, *supra* note 9.

59 Id., §5.45.

60 *See generally* R. Dattu, "A Journey from Havana to Paris: The Fifty-Year Quest for the Elusive Multilateral Agreement on Investment", 24 *Fordham International Law Journal* 275 (2000); D.K. Das, "Debacle at Seattle: *The Way the Cookie Crumbled*", 34 *J. World T.* 181 (2000); F. Roche, "Que reste-t-il de l'exception culturelle après Seattle?", 258 *Regards sur l'actualité* 13, 13–5 (2000).

61 *See, e.g.*, International Network for Cultural Diversity, "Draft Convention on Cultural Diversity", *available at* www.incd.net/.html (last visited 2 February 2012); *See* Universal Declaration on Cultural Diversity, 2 November 2001, *available at* http://portal.unesco.org/en/ev.php-URL_ID=13179&URL_DO=DO_TOPIC&URL_SECTION=201.html

An important matter regarding the feasibility of such an instrument was the question of finding a competent international organization for its negotiation, adoption and administration. Proposals included UNESCO and the WTO as well as a possible third way, consisting either of a combined approach of mutual cooperation between the two, or the creation of an entirely new international body.[62] Even within the WTO, in light of the imminent services negotiations, a background note and several communications dealt with this question.[63] Their content and the better preparation of the complex issue of cultural goods and services raised expectations that – in contrast to the Uruguay Round – the next round would lead to a fruitful and mutually acceptable solution of the conflict. Nonetheless, despite the debate within the WTO and good reasons for the involvement of the WTO, arguments tipped in favour of UNESCO, as the competent organization to address the problem. Hence, following the adoption of a non-legally binding *Universal Declaration on Cultural Diversity* ("Cultural Diversity Declaration") in 2001, the General Conference of UNESCO decided in October 2003 based on a preliminary study[64] that "the question of cultural diversity as regards the protection of the diversity of contents and artistic expressions shall be the subject of an international convention".[65]

(last visited on 2 February 2012); The Cultural Industries Sectoral Advisory Group on International Trade (SAGIT), "An International Agreement on Cultural Diversity – A Model for Discussion" (September 2002), *available at* www.international.gc.ca/trade-agreements-accords-commerciaux/assets/pdfs/sagit_eg.pdf (last visited 2 February 2012).

62 *See, e.g.*, C. Carmody, "When 'Cultural Identity was not at Issue': Thinking About Canada – Certain Measures Concerning Periodicals", 30 *Law & Pol'y Int'l Bus.* 231 (1999); T. Voon, *Cultural Products and the World Trade Organization*, 2007; R.J. Neuwirth, *The Cultural Industries in International Trade Law: Insights from the NAFTA, the WTO, and the EU*, 2006.

63 *See* WTO, Council for Trade in Service, "Audiovisual Services: Background Note by the Secretariat", *S/C/W/40* (15 June 1998); WTO, Council for Trade in Service, "Communication from the United States: Audiovisual Services", *S/C/W/78* (8 December 1998); WTO, Council for Trade in Service, "Communication from Israel: Review of Article II Exemptions / Replies to Questions Posed on Israel's MFN Exemptions in the Area of Audiovisual Services in the Course of the Review of MFN Exemptions", *S/C/W/158* (10 July 2000); WTO, Council for Trade in Service, "Communication from the United States: Audiovisual and Related Services", *S/CSS/W/21* (18 December 2000); WTO, Council for Trade in Service, "Communication from Japan: The Negotiations on Trade in Services", *S/CSS/W/42* (22 December 2000); WTO, Council for Trade in Service, "Communication from Canada: Canadian Initial GATS Sectoral/Modal/Horizontal Negotiating Proposals", *S/CSS/W/46* (14 March 2001); WTO, Council for Trade in Service, "Communication from Switzerland: GATS 2000, Audio-visual Services", *S/CSS/W/74* (4 May 2001); WTO, Council for Trade in Service, "Communication from Brazil: Audiovisual Services", *S/CSS/W/99* (9 July 2001).

64 UNESCO, Executive Board, "Preliminary Study on the Technical and Legal Aspects Relating to the Desirability of a Standard-Setting Instrument on Cultural Diversity", *166 EX/28* (12 March 2003).

65 *See* UNESCO, General Conference, "Desirability of Drawing Up an International Standard-Setting Instrument on Cultural Diversity", *Resolution 32 C/34* (19 September – 17 October 2003). *See also* UNESCO, General Conference, "Opportunité de l'elaboration d'un instrument normatif international concernant la diversité culturelle", *32 C/52* (18 July 2003).

After two years of negotiations the Convention on the Diversity of Cultural Expressions was adopted by the General Conference of UNESCO on 20 October 2005 in Paris.[66] On 9 December 2005 the then Director-General of UNESCO, Koïchiro Matsuura, and the then President of the General Conference, Ambassador Musa Bin Jaafar Bin Hassan, signed the text of the Convention on the Diversity of Cultural Expressions which certifies the six language versions of the Convention, thus opening the path for its ratification by Member States. The Convention on the Diversity of Cultural Expressions finally entered into force on 18 March 2007, following the deposit of the 30th instrument of ratification. Generally, the entry into force of the new Convention sparked new hopes and expectations that finally the culture and trade debate had entered a new era. In trying to assess to what extent such expectations were fulfilled, it is thus helpful to turn to subsequent developments in relation to the Convention on the Diversity of Cultural Expressions.

3. THE 'CULTURE AND TRADE DEBATE' AFTER THE ADOPTION OF THE CONVENTION ON THE DIVERSITY OF CULTURAL EXPRESSIONS

3.1. ELEMENTS OF CRITICISM OF THE CONVENTION ON THE DIVERSITY OF CULTURAL EXPRESSIONS

The brief chronology of milestones in the culture and trade debate has shown that the debate's main legal focus before the adoption of the Convention on the Diversity of Cultural Expressions was on the question in which forum the issue could be best dealt with and, closely related to that, through which legal instruments the principal objectives could be best achieved.[67] Finally, it was decided that UNESCO would be the competent forum to negotiate an international instrument on cultural diversity. During the negotiations, the strongest scepticism and fierce resistance came from the US Government. Such resistance even led some observers to the conclusion that the US only joined UNESCO again after almost two decades of absence in order to either water it down to a 'non-paper' or to prevent its adoption from the outset.[68] In addition

66 The various stages in the negotiation history of the Convention are well documented. *See, e.g.*, UNESCO, Executive Board, "Report of the Director-General on the Progress Achieved During the Third Session of the Intergovernmental Meeting of Experts on the Preliminary Draft Convention on the Protection of the Diversity of Cultural Contents and Artistic Expressions", *172 EX/20* (11 August 2005).

67 *See especially* Voon, *supra* note 62; Neuwirth, *supra* note 62.

68 *See, e.g.*, "A Madrid, une Convention réaffirme la spécificité des biens culturels", *Le Monde* (June 12, 2005) (writing that: "les Etat's Unis crient au protectionnisme et ne manqueront pas, selon plusieurs représentants, de tenter d'amender la convention ou d'en atténuer les effets

to the resistance within UNESCO, the then US Secretary of State, Condoleezza Rice, circulated a letter to member governments expressing her "deep concern" with the draft convention, denouncing its "ambiguous language", and urging other Parties to postpone its adoption because it would, in her eyes, allow Parties to block further progress towards the global liberalization of trade and could be used by certain governments to restrict the free flow of information and suppress minority viewpoints.[69] The US Government's main criticism was made publicly accessible in an Analytical Sheet of the State Department, which recommended the revision of the draft text because it argued that it was hastily drafted, bearing the potential for an abusive interpretation with regard to the creation of new obstacles for the free exchange of goods, services and even agricultural products, which are susceptible of being considered linked to cultural expressions.[70] Shortly before the adoption of the Convention on the Diversity of Cultural Expressions, the US also proposed a list of proposals for amendments, which reflects similar concerns principally regarding the relationship to other agreements.[71] More precisely still, the US Ambassador to UNESCO, Louise V. Oliver, explaining the negative vote cast by the US, regarded the Convention on the Diversity of Cultural Expressions as "hastily drafted", "deeply flawed" and expressed concern that it could be "misinterpreted, hindering the free flow of ideas by word and image and also affecting other areas, notably trade".[72] Objectively, the US criticism of the Convention on the Diversity of Cultural Expressions, according to which the vagueness and ambiguity of the text literally invites governments to neglect due respect for human rights through the restriction of the free flow of information, the suppression of minority viewpoints and freedom of expression, must be dismissed as lacking substance. To view the Convention on the Diversity of Cultural Expressions as an invitation to such abusive practices requires indeed, as one journalist observed, a considerable dose of "bad faith".[73] Moreover, it must be remembered here that in

juridiques, réfutant sa non-subordination a l'Organization mondiale du commerce (OMC)"); J. Altwegg, "Artenschutz für Schönes: Die Unesco spricht: Kultureller Protektionismus soll erlaubt sein", *Frankfurter Allgemeine Zeitung* 35 (9 June 2005) (reporting that "Amerika war nach neunzehn Jahren Abwesenheit der Unesco wohl nur deshalb wieder beigetreten, weil es die Charta zu Fall bringen will").

69 *See* A. Riding, "Next lone U.S. dissent: Cultural diversity pact", *The New York Times*, E3 (12 October 2005).

70 *See* Fiche analytique du département d'État sur le project de convention de l'UNESCO, *supra* note 4.

71 *See* Projét de Résolution (presenté par les États-Unis d'Amérique), *33C/COM.IV/DR.4* (13 October 2005).

72 *Explanation of Vote of the United States on the UNESCO Convention on the Protection and Promotion of the Diversity of Cultural Expressions* – Statement by the US Ambassador to UNESCO, Louise V. Oliver, in U.S. Embassy Ottawa, Information Resource Center, Washington File (October 20, 2005) (on file with the author).

73 *See* J. Boileau, "Baroud d'honneur", *Le Devoir* (12 October 2005), *available at* www.ledevoir.com//10//92377.html (last visited 2 February 2012).

bad faith most laws and international legal texts can be misinterpreted and applied in a way to deprive them from their intended meaning and purpose. Therefore, it appeared more likely that the US opposition against the Convention on the Diversity of Cultural Expressions seemed to be driven by the fear of its implications for international trade in various goods and services, a topic to which we shall now turn.

3.2. THE IMPACT ON INTERNATIONAL TRADE

The hopes and expectations raised by the Convention's entry into force met with more critical views of scholars who, based on a legal analysis of its legal text, had predicted a limited legal role of the Convention in the regulation of international trade.[74] Most comments concurred in expressing serious concerns for the consistency of the international legal framework henceforth governing the regulation of cultural products. With titles like "Clash of Cultures", "Counterbalance" or "United in Divergency", the articles' titles reflected serious concerns about an ongoing bifurcation in the regulation of cultural products based on the division of competences between the separate regimes of UNESCO and the WTO.[75] A closer look at single provisions of the Convention on the Diversity of Cultural Expressions, such as, notably, those on the relationship to other instruments (Articles 20–21), but also on the Dispute Settlement procedure provided by the Convention on the Diversity of Cultural Expressions (Article 25) in contrast to the WTO's dispute settlement system, inevitably led to the conclusion that the Convention on the Diversity of Cultural Expressions would add little to mitigate the negative effects caused by the widening gap in the international regulation of cultural products. Even some of the most optimistic evaluations of the future of the Convention on the Diversity of Cultural Expressions merely concluded that it may only develop a legal value with regard to future trade negotiations, such as in the negotiation of regional trade

[74] *See, generally,* M. Hahn, "A Clash of Cultures? The UNESCO Diversity Convention and International Trade Law", 9 *Journal of International Economic Law* 515 (2006); R.J. Neuwirth, "United in Divergency"*supra* note 59, 830 et seq.; T. Voon, "UNESCO and the WTO: A Clash of Cultures?", 55 *International and Comparative Law Quarterly* 635 (2006); C.B. Graber, "The New UNESCO Convention on Cultural Diversity: A Counterbalance to the WTO?", 9 *J.I.E.L.* 553 (2006); E. Brooks, "Cultural Imperialism vs. Cultural Protectionism: Hollywood's Response to UNESCO Efforts to Promote Cultural Diversity", 5 *J. Int'l Bus. & L.* 112 (2006); A. Khachaturian, "The New Cultural Diversity Convention and its Implications on the WTO International Trade Regime: A Critical Comparative Analysis", 42 *Tex. International Law Journal* 191 (2006); *see also* J.H.B. Pauwelyn, "The UNESCO Convention on Cultural Diversity, and the WTO: Diversity in International Law-Making?", *ASIL Insight* (2005), *available at* www.asil.org/insights/2005/11/insights051115.html (last visited 2 February 2012).

[75] Id.

agreements.[76] Most authors agreed that its actual value would be symbolic and that its potential value lay in awareness building and influencing the political will of governments so as to render them more sensitive towards the issue of cultural diversity. Related publications focused on the negotiation history of the Convention on the Diversity of Cultural Expressions,[77] and especially its role in the further fragmentation of international law.[78] In other articles fears about the potential restrictive impact of the Convention on the Diversity of Cultural Expressions on trade in general and on the cross-border flow of cultural products in particular were voiced.[79] Additional publications widely replicated or further supported the arguments of the initial comments and concerns.[80] In sum, the various comments seemed to confirm, that – to use the words of Professor Hahn – the Convention on the Diversity of Cultural Expressions had by no means put the debate to an end but had rather "re-started it".[81] Or in the words of Bruner, even after the adoption of the Convention on the Diversity of Cultural

---

76 *See, e.g.*, Neuwirth, *supra* note 59, at 846 (writing that due to Article 20, the Convention will only unfold legal effect *pro futuro* and will by no means have retroactive effects); *but see* Voon, *supra* note 74, at 16 (writing on the basis of general international law rules on successive treaties that the "UNESCO Convention could not modify rights or obligations of WTO Members under future WTO agreements"); *see also* L. Richieri-Hanania, *Diversité culturelle et droit international du commerce*, 2009, 325–31 (seeing the possibility that even in the case that both parties to a dispute before the WTO are parties to the Convention, the probability is high that the convention is not taking into account or that commercial considerations will prevails over cultural ones).

77 *See* Y. Donders, "The History of the UNESCO Convention on the Protection and Promotion of the Diversity of Cultural Expressions", in H. Schneider and P. Van den Bossche (eds.), *Protection of Cultural Diversity from a European and International Perspective*, 2008, 1–30.

78 *See* J. Wouters and B. de Meester, "The UNESCO Convention on Cultural Diversity and WTO Law: A Case Study in Fragmentation of International Law", 42 *J. World T.* 205 (2008); H. Ruiz Fabri, "Jeux dans la Fragmentation: la Convention sur la promotion et la protection de la diversité des expressions culturelles" 111 *Revue Générale de Droit International Public* 43 (2007).

79 *See* E.H. Chiang, "The UNESCO Convention on the Protection and Promotion of the Diversity of Cultural Expressions: A Look at the Convention and Its Potential Impact on the American Movie Industry", 6 *Wash. U. Global Stud. L. Rev.* 379 (2007); C. Balassa, "America's Image Abroad: The UNESCO Cultural Diversity Convention and U.S. Motion Picture Exports", at 16–8 (Paper Presented at a conference held in Washington, D.C. by the Curb Center for Art, Enterprise and Public Policy at Vanderbilt, on 24 April 2008).

80 *Cf.* C.M. Bruner, "Culture, Sovereignty, an Hollywood: UNESCO and the Future of Trade in Cultural Products", 40 *New York University Journal of International Law and Politics* 351 (2008); M. Burri-Nenova, "Trade and Culture: Making the WTO Legal Framework Conducive to Cultural Considerations", 5 *Manchester Journal of International Economic Law* 2 (2008); C. Wright, "Reconciling Cultural Diversity and Free Trade in the Digital Age: A Cultural Analysis of the International Trade in Content Items", 41 *Akron Law Review* 399 (2008); I. Bernier, "The Unesco Convention on the Protection and Promotion of the Diversity of Cultural Expressions: A Cultural Instrument at the Junction of Law and Politics" (2008), *available at* www.diversite-culturelle.qc.ca//documents//du-droit_eng.pdf (last visited 2 February 2012); R. Craufurd Smith, "The UNESCO Convention on the Protection and Promotion of the Diversity of Cultural Expressions: Building a New World Information and Communication Order?", 1 *International Journal of Communication* 24 (2007).

81 M. Hahn, *supra* note 74, at 552.

Expressions it was still appropriate to state that "pro-trade and protectionist voices in the trade and culture debate essentially speak past one another".[82] Even the most recent publications, already building on interesting insights in the early stages of the Convention's implementation process, suggest that the latest culture and trade conflicts caused mixed feelings of either "amnesia" or "déjà vu"[83], or qualified the Convention on the Diversity of Cultural Expressions as a "hard legal instrument" with a "soft legal content".[84] In total, even though the adoption of the Convention on the Diversity of Cultural Expressions outside the WTO framework could be considered to have provided the "second best choice", it was still capable of providing an opportunity as much as a mandate to undertake efforts of developing "better institutional ties with the WTO in order to increase the coherence between cultural and trade policies".[85] To what extent, however, such optimistic appraisal, according to which a window of opportunity has opened "for the Convention to be used as a point of reference when the definition of boundaries between trade and culture is discussed in future WTO trade negotiations or dispute settlement procedures",[86] became true must finally be evaluated in view of recent developments in the area of international trade law. Before turning to these events, however, the work of the main bodies of the Convention on the Diversity of Cultural Expressions shall be briefly reviewed.

3.3. THE WORK OF UNESCO AND THE MAIN BODIES OF THE CONVENTION ON THE DIVERSITY OF CULTURAL EXPRESSIONS

Since its entry into force, the principal question relating to the Convention on the Diversity of Cultural Expressions has evolved and now focuses on the legal value of the Convention and its ability to lastingly influence the understanding and the legal governance of the relationship between culture and trade.[87] In this respect, one indicator is the wide support that the Convention on the Diversity of Cultural Expressions received first in the vote of adoption.[88] This trend

---

82 *See* Bruner, *supra* note 80, at 365.

83 *See* R.J. Neuwirth, "The 'Culture and Trade Debate' Continues: The UNESCO Convention in Light of the WTO Reports in China – Publications and Audiovisual Products: Between Amnesia or Déjà Vu?", 44 *J. World T.* 1333 (2010).

84 *See* A. Vlassis, "La mise en oeuvre de la Convention sur la diversité des expressions culturelles Portée et enjeux de l'interface entre le commerce et la culture", 42 *Revue Études internationales* 493, 495 (2011).

85 *See* R.J. Neuwirth, *The Cultural Industries, supra* note 68, at 513; Neuwirth, "'United in Divergency'", *supra* note 59, at 862.

86 *See* Graber, *supra* note 74, at 574.

87 *See, e.g.*, G.C. Shaffer and M.A. Pollack, "Hard vs. Soft Law: Alternatives, Complements, and Antagonists in International Governance", 94 *Minnesota Law Review* 706, 767–773 (2010); Vlassis, *supra* note 84.

88 *See supra* note 3.

continued in the support the Convention on the Diversity of Cultural Expressions received following its adoption, which is reflected in the relatively short time period between the date of adoption of the Convention on the Diversity of Cultural Expressions on 20 October 2005 to its entry into force three months after the date of deposit of the 30th instrument of ratification which was on 18 March 2007. As of 1 January 2012 the Convention on the Diversity of Cultural Expressions has been ratified (or accepted, accessed or approved) by a total number of 118 states plus the European Union as the only regional economic integration organization.[89] It is interesting to note that Australia and Nicaragua, which originally voted against or abstained from the vote, have in the meantime acceded to or ratified the Convention on the Diversity of Cultural Expressions. The large number of ratifications indicates a generally strong support for the Convention on the Diversity of Cultural Expressions except for a few countries like the United States, Japan, and Russia, in terms of size, and for the Arab and Asian region, in terms of a balanced geographical support. It is reported that at present five more Member States (Bahrain, Colombia, Indonesia, Thailand and Turkey) are pursuing the ratification of the Convention on the Diversity of Cultural Expressions but the goal is to attract a minimum of 140 parties to the Convention on the Diversity of Cultural Expressions by the end of 2013.[90] The existing strong support, however, may be misleading in terms of being an indicator for a convergence between cultural and trade-related concerns. This is often because policy coherence within national governments, especially such as between the respective ministries of trade and commerce, on the one hand and cultural affairs on the other, is lacking. Moreover, policy initiatives in this field are often more based on the dedication of one individual rather than being the focus of a formal policy objective supported by the respective ministry or government. In the short term, it will be interesting to observe how newly admitted WTO Members, notably such as the Russian Federation, bringing WTO Membership to 157 countries,[91] will address the Convention on the Diversity of Cultural Expressions and eventually influence or enhance the coherence between cultural and trade policies in the long term.[92]

---

89 UNESCO, "The Convention for the Protection and Promotion of the Diversity of Cultural Expressions", *available at* http://portal.unesco.org//.asp?=31038&=E (last visited 2 February 2012) (proving a list of the parties to the convention).

90 UNESCO, Intergovernmental Committee, "Secretariat's Report of Activities 2011", *CE/11/5.IGC/213/INF.3*, at 2 (27 November 2011).

91 Pending the respective ratification procedures, the most recent accessions to the WTO include Samoa, Montenegro, and the Russian Federation; *see* WTO Press Release, "Ministerial Conference approves Russia's WTO membership" (16 December 2011), *available at* www.wto.org//_e/_e/_rus_16dec11_e.htm (last visited 2 February 2012); WTO Press Release, "WTO membership of Montenegro and Samoa approved" (17 December 2011), *available at* www.wto.org//_e/_e/_wsm_17dec11_e.htm (last visited 2 February 2012).

92 As of 1 January 2012, only Montenegro is a Member of the UNESCO Convention. As for the future practice of the Russian Federation, see, as a possible indicator, the Address by H.E. Ms Eleonora Valentinovna Mitrofanova, Chairperson of the Executive Board of UNESCO,

As a second criterion, it is useful to look at the work of UNESCO as the host organization and the central bodies created by the Convention on the Diversity of Cultural Expressions. Until now the Conference of Parties (*i.e.* the plenary body of the Convention) has met in three ordinary sessions which were mainly devoted largely to procedural or organizational issues, such as the adoption of the rules of procedure, the distribution of seats and the election of the members of the Intergovernmental Committee (IGC).[93] So far, the IGC, which is composed of 24 State Party members, elected for four years by the Conference of Parties, has met in five ordinary and two extraordinary sessions.[94] The centre of activities of these bodies can be described as being devoted to procedural issues and increasing the visibility of the Convention. In terms of visibility, the Convention on the Diversity of Cultural Expressions has triggered several initiatives, such as the organization of the U-40 World Forum by the German Commission for UNESCO.[95] Generally initiatives aimed at raising the visibility of the Convention on the Diversity of Cultural Expressions are in principal laudable, but as was feared, it is in accordance with the institutional rift between culture and trade at the national as well as international level that their impact is limited in terms of mainly reaching out to the cultural epistemic communities while not extending to their trade-related counterparts. Or else, the growing awareness about the diversity of cultural expressions in international law has perhaps even had the effect of strengthening divergent positions rather than mediating between them.

Permanent Delegate of the Russian Federation to UNESCO, at the occasion of the Celebration of the Tenth Anniversary of the Universal Declaration on Cultural Diversity on 2 November 2011, stressing the active role the Russian Federation played among other partners in making a substantive contribution to the elaboration and implementation of the principles of the Declaration on Cultural Diversity; *See* Permanent Delegation of the Russian Federation with UNESCO, "Address by H.E. Ms Eleonora Valentinovna Mitrofanova, Chairperson of the Executive Board of UNESCO, Permanent Delegate of the Russian Federation to UNESCO" (2 November 2011), *available at* www.unesco.mid.ru/pr_e_73.html (last visited 2 February 2012).

93 *See* UNESCO, "Conference of Parties", *available at* www.unesco.org//en/culture//cultural-diversity/cultural-expressions/meetings/conference-of-parties/ (last visited 2 February 2012) (providing links to the Conference of Parties 1st Ordinary Session (18–20 June 2007), 2nd Ordinary Session (15–16 June 2009), and 3rd Ordinary Session (14–15 June 2011)).

94 *See* UNESCO, "Intergovernmental Committee", *available at* www.unesco.org//en/culture// cultural-diversity/expressions/// (last visited 2 February 2012), providing links to the 1st Ordinary Session (10–13 December 2007); 2nd Ordinary Session (8–12 December 2008); 3rd Ordinary Session (7–11 December 2009); 4th Ordinary Session (29 November – 3 December 2010); 5th Ordinary Session (5–7 December 2011); 1st Extraordinary Session (24–27 June 2008); 2nd Extraordinary Session (23–25 March 2009).

95 *See* German Commission for UNESCO, "U40-World Forum 'Cultural Diversity 2030'", *available at* www.unesco.de/.html?&L=1 (last visited 2 February 2012). *See also* A. Sekhar and A. Steinkamp (eds.), *Mapping Cultural Diversity – Good Practices from Around the Globe: A Contribution to the Debate in the Implementation of the UNESCO Convention on the Protection and Promotion of the Diversity of Cultural Expressions*, 2009, *available at* www.unesco.it/_filesDIVERSITAculturale/_DUK.pdf (last visited 2 February 2012).

In line with the framework provided by the Convention on the Diversity of Cultural Expressions, so far UNESCO and the convention's central bodies have hardly produced any substantive and concrete legal results which may contribute to open questions concerning the future treatment of the cultural industries and the protection and promotion of the diversity of cultural expressions. For UNESCO as a whole this means that there still appears to reign internal confusion concerning its own work and in particular the legal links between the various conventions adopted under its aegis, notably such as between the Convention on the Diversity of Cultural Expressions, the 2003 Convention for the Safeguarding of the Intangible Cultural Heritage and the 1972 the World Cultural Heritage Convention.[96] More generally still, it appears that in its administrative practice, UNESCO is still clinging to an understanding of international law and relations which – driven by a great number of technological, societal as well as geopolitical changes – has become widely obsolete.[97] As far as the bodies of the Convention on the Diversity of Cultural Expressions are concerned, the only concrete results that are noteworthy are the adoption of operational guidelines. As the terminology states, these guidelines provide an interpretative tool and serve to put the Convention and its content into practice and action. Nonetheless, the precise legal status of these guidelines and their exact legal effect on the parties to the Convention remain unclear.[98] So far, guidelines have been adopted for measures to promote and protect cultural expressions (Articles 7, 8, and 17), for information sharing and transparency (Article 9), for education and public awareness (Article 10), on the role and participation of civil society (Article 11), on the integration of culture in sustainable development (Article 13), on cooperation for development (Article 14), on partnerships between and within the public and private sectors and non-profit organizations (Article 15), on preferential treatment for developing countries (Article 16), on the use of the resources of the International Fund for Cultural Diversity ("IFCD") (Article 18) and the exchange, analysis and dissemination of information (Article 19).[99] The Conference of Parties has also

---

96 My question in this regard posed to Ms. Galia Saouma-Forero (Director of the Division of Cultural Expressions and Creative Industries, UNESCO), on 12 June 2009, in the context of the U40-World Forum 2009 organized by the German UNESCO Commission, remained unanswered.

97 *See, e.g.*, the "Text of Statement by U.S. on its Withdrawal from UNESCO", *The New York Times*, A10 (20 December 1984); EU-Position on the reform and development of UNESCO, 15 December 1999, *available at* www.unesco.org////eu_reform_en.shtml (last visited 2 February 2012) (providing some early criticism of UNESCO).

98 Most likely, these operational guidelines can be considered as soft law instruments which have a limited binding effect on the subjects adopting or declaring them. In the present context, however, their legal effect is even more limited since most of the provisions of the (legally binding) Convention, which they serve to clarify, are equally devoid of "hard" legal rights and obligations. Thanks are due to Yvonne Donders for pointing this question out.

99 *See* UNESCO, Conference of the Parties, *Operational Guidelines* (June 2009), *available at* www.unesco.org/new/en/culture/themes/cultural-diversity/diversity-of-cultural-expressions/the-convention/operational-guidelines/ (last visited 2 February 2012).

explicitly decided not to adopt such guidelines on international cooperation (Article 12).[100] It is also noteworthy that no operational guideline has been adopted on Articles 20 and 21 of the Convention on the Diversity of Cultural Expressions. Since these articles deal with the relationship to other instruments and especially to other treaties, they must be considered as the most important provisions of the Convention on the Diversity of Cultural Expressions vis-à-vis the realm of international trade. For this reason it is highly regrettable that yet another opportunity to clarify the opaque legal relationship between the Convention on the Diversity of Cultural Expressions and the agreements administered by the WTO was missed. Instead, the IGC asked the Secretariat to prepare preliminary draft operational guidelines governing the use of an emblem to be designed for the Convention on the Diversity of Cultural Expressions.[101]

Generally, these guidelines are certainly useful in clarifying the meaning of some of the provisions laid down in the Convention on the Diversity of Cultural Expressions, but do little to make concrete the legal aspects of the steps to be taken. The sole exception here is perhaps the International Fund for Cultural Diversity, which has so far received about $5 million USD.[102] The amount may appear generous considering that contributions are voluntary. In relation to the overall revenues generated by the cultural industries or only some of its sectors in world trade,[103] or the box office results of a single movie, such as Avatar,[104] it must, however, be dismissed as irrelevant for being capable of mitigating some negative consequences associated with global trade in cultural products. In spite of the fact that so far the Intergovernmental Committee approved 17 projects to be implemented in 17 developing countries for a total of $1.3 million USD in

---

100 *See* UNESCO, Conference of Parties, "Approval of the Operational Guidelines for the Implementation of the Convention and Future Activities of the Committee", *CE/09/2 CP/210/7*, at 3 §5 (30 March 2009), 3(5), *available at* http://unesdoc.unesco.org//0018/001826/182661E.pdf (last visited 2 February 2012).

101 See UNESCO, Intergovernmental Committee, "Fifth Ordinary Session – Decisions", *CE/11/5.IGC/213/Dec.*, at 9 (7 December 2011).

102 As of January 1, 2012, the total amount of contributions to the International Fund for Cultural Diversity (IFCD) received is US$ 5,137,957.41. *See, available at* UNESCO, "Contributions to the IFCD", *available at* www.unesco.org/new//culture//diversity/expressions// (last visited 2 February 2012).

103 The Motion Picture Association of America (MPAA) reports "that worldwide box office for all films released in each country around the world reached $31.8 billion in 2010, up 8% over 2009's total, boosted by box office increases in markets outside the U.S./Canada". *See* MPAA, "Theatrical Market Statistics 2010", 3, *available at* www.mpaa.org//93bbeb16–0e4d-4b7e-b085–3f41c459f9ac.pdf (last visited 2 February 2012).

104 *See, e.g.*, E. Smith, "'Avatar' Opens Strongly, in Test for Industry – James Cameron's 3-D Sci-Fi Movie, a Costly Bet on New Film-Making Technology, Takes in $232.2 Million Globally", *Wall Street Journal (Eastern edition)* B.6 (21 December 2009) (reporting that the film "Avatar" grossed $73 million on its opening weekend in North America alone).

funding,[105] it is in view of the disparity between the volume of the film industry and the donations to the fund that it remains unlikely that the Fund will play a significant role in supporting "cooperation for sustainable development and poverty reduction in order to foster the emergence of a dynamic cultural sector in developing countries" as set forth by the guidelines.[106] Unfortunately, this is also likely to hold true for the residual objectives or actions mentioned in the guidelines, such as the one on partnerships between and within the public and private sectors and non-profit organizations.

The only truly trade-related guideline is the one on preferential treatment (Article 16), which lays out the following objective:

> Developed countries shall facilitate cultural exchanges with developing countries by granting, through the appropriate institutional and legal frameworks, preferential treatment to artists and other cultural professionals and practitioners, as well as cultural goods and services from developing countries.[107]

The issue of preferential treatment for developing countries or "special and differential treatment" as it is known in WTO jargon, however, is the subject of a great number of detailed provisions in the agreements covered by the WTO.[108] It is therefore clearly a so-called "trade matter" falling within the competence of the WTO which is also explained by the operational guidelines' emphasis on its "trade dimension" which is set out as follows:

> 3.4.1 Multilateral, regional and bilateral frameworks and mechanisms belonging to the field of trade can be used by Parties to implement preferential treatment in the field of culture.
> 3.4.2 Parties to the Convention that have concluded multilateral, regional and/or bilateral trade agreements may take into account the provisions of these agreements and the respective mechanisms provided by them with a view to offering preferential treatment in favour of developing countries within the meaning of Article 16.

---

105 *See* UNESCO, "17 New Projects Get Funding From the IFCD", *available at* www.unesco.org//en///diversity/expressions/international-fund/ (last visited 2 February 2012).

106 *See* UNESCO, Conference of the Parties, Operational Guidelines on the Use of the Resources of the International Fund for Cultural Diversity (Article 18 of the Convention) (June 2009), *available at* www.unesco.org/new/fileadmin/MULTIMEDIA/HQ/CLT/pdf/Conv2005_DO_Art_18_EN.pdf (last visited 2 February 2012).

107 *See* Convention on the Diversity of Cultural Expressions, *supra* note 2, Article 16. This article is further developed in UNESCO, Conference of the Parties, Operational Guidelines on Preferential Treatment for Developing Countries (Article 16 of the Convention) (June 2009), *available at* www.unesco.org/new/fileadmin/MULTIMEDIA/HQ/CLT/pdf/Conv2005_DO_Art_16_EN.pdf (last visited 2 February 2012).

108 *See* WTO, Committee on Trade and Development, "Implementation of Special and Differential Treatment Provisions in WTO Agreements and Decisions", *WT/COMTD/W/77* (25 October 2000).

> 3.4.3 When making use of such frameworks and provisions for preferential treatment, Parties shall take into account the relevant provisions of the Convention, pursuant to its Article 20.

The reference to Article 20 of the Convention on the Diversity of Cultural Expressions in the last paragraph shows again that legally, the provision on preferential treatment is at its best the expression of political will and bears no relevance for the regulation of trade in cultural products between developing and developed countries. Generally and as mentioned before, the adequacy of the developing-developed country terminology to address the problems underlying the culture and trade debate is more than questionable, both from a cultural perspective as well as from an economic perspective.[109] Even from a merely economic perspective, the distinction needs to be better operationalized.[110] Certainly, the recognition of the combination of trade and cultural dimensions in this context is more useful, which the operational guidelines describe as follows:

> 3.5.1 Parties may develop and implement specific agreements bringing together trade and cultural dimensions which concern notably cultural goods and services, and/or artists and other cultural professionals and practitioners (*e.g.* Florence Agreement and its Nairobi Protocol).

The recognition of the dual nature of cultural products in this place, however, is merely the repetition of the content of the Convention on the Diversity of Cultural Expressions and brings no additional clarity on the question of how to implement this recognition in the regulatory framework. In sum, the activities of UNESCO and the bodies created by the Convention on the Diversity of Cultural Expressions merely clarify further the provisions contained in the text of the Convention. From a legal perspective, they change or make concrete little or nothing due to the failure to create "hard" legal instruments and remedies. It appears, even, that the debate in UNESCO disregards some crucial points raised in the debate by scholars, to which we shall now turn for further insights into the value of the Convention on the Diversity of Cultural Expressions.

---

109 *See* R.J. Neuwirth, "A Constitutional Tribute to Global Governance: Overcoming the Chimera of the Developing-Developed Country Dichotomy", *European University Institute (EUI) Working Paper LAW* 2010/20 (2010).

110 *See* A. Mitchell and T. Voon, "Operationalizing Special and Differential Treatment in the WTO: Game Over?", 15 *Global Governance* 343 (2009).

4. "MOMENTS OF TRUTH": THE CONVENTION ON THE DIVERSITY OF CULTURAL EXPRESSIONS PUT INTO PRACTICE

4.1. THE WTO DISPUTE SETTLEMENT BODY AND *CHINA – AUDIOVISUAL ENTERTAINMENT PRODUCTS*

A first important indicator for possible progress made in the culture and trade debate was provided by the emergence of two related disputes brought before the WTO Dispute Settlement System by the U.S. Government against China. Before panels were formally established, predictions on the possible legal impact of the Convention on the Diversity of Cultural Expressions on trade disputes were based on speculations drawn from the legal analysis of the text of the Convention on the Diversity of Cultural Expressions, and in particular its Articles 20 and 21.[111] The time of uncertainty was finally over when in *China – Measures Affecting Trading Rights and Distribution Services for Certain Publications and Audiovisual Entertainment Products* (*China – Publications and Audiovisual Products*), a WTO Panel and later the Appellate Body were called to decide on the consistency of a wide range of Chinese laws and regulations with China's obligations under the WTO agreements and its Accession Protocol.[112] Thus, the case established an important legal precedent, primarily because it was the first prominent "culture and trade case" since the *Canada Periodicals* case.[113] Secondly, it is important from a regulatory perspective because the case covered not only a single sector of the cultural industries but combined almost all of them. This confirmed the continuous trend of the convergence of the various sectors of the cultural industries in the past as well as an overall increase in the complexity of trade regulation. Third, it is also interesting because it involves China, one of the largest trading powers, a recent WTO Member, and the world's most populated country with great cultural diversity, and one of the world's oldest civilizations.[114] This is important as the context in which the case is set also

---

111 *See also* H. Gao, "The Mighty Pen, the Almighty Dollar, and the Holy Hammer and Sickle: An examination of the conflict between trade liberalization and domestic cultural policy with special regard to the recent dispute between the US and China on restrictions on certain cultural products", 2 *Asian Journal of WTO & International Health Law and Policy* 313, at 337 (2007) (predicting that the "Convention might not be of much use to China after all").

112 *See* Panel Report, *supra* note 9; Appellate Body Report, *supra* note 10.

113 *See* Panel Report, *supra* note 11; Appellate Body Report, *supra* note 11; *See also* Japan – Measures Concerning Sound Recordings, "Notification of a Mutually-Agreed Solution", *WT/DS28/4 – IP/D/1/Add.1* (5 February 1997) and *WT/DS42/4-IP/D/4/Add.1* (17 November 1997); Turkey – Taxation of Foreign Film Revenues, "Notification of Mutually Agreed Solution", *WT/DS43/3-G/L/177* (24 July 1997).

114 *See generally* Heng Wang, "What do Trading Rights and General Exceptions Mean for China? Some Observations of China-Audiovisual Services", 12 *Gonzaga Journal of International Law* 3 (2009).

has some critical repercussions for the debate. Most important of all, it is the first major case in international trade dealing with cultural products since the entry into force of the Convention on the Diversity of Cultural Expressions.

To briefly lay out the context and background of the case, China entered the WTO on 11 December 2001 and, unlike the U.S., it also ratified the Convention on the Diversity of Cultural Expressions as the 44th country to do so on 30 January 2007. The background of the dispute was found in both fierce competition but also a close economic interconnection between the two countries, which is characterized by a soaring trade deficit on the side of the U.S. The escalating U.S. trade deficit[115] in general and with China in particular is linked to the fact that the cultural industries are one of the top sources for revenue for the U.S. This link helps to explain the reason for the simultaneous request for the establishment of a Panel in this and in a second dispute (*China – Intellectual Property Rights*) in 2007.[116] Both cases contain complaints by the U.S. against a content review system established by China. The first case concerns barriers to trade in cultural products throughout the customs territory of China while the second was set in the context of copyright protection and enforcement. The U.S. motivation in both cases appears to have been driven by the calculus that the contested measures were responsible for huge financial losses to the involved U.S. industries. The second case was decided first, namely in January 2009 and resulted in the Panel's finding that Chinese copyright law was indeed inconsistent with China's international trade obligations.[117] It was particularly a provision in the Chinese copyright law which "denied works, the publication and/or dissemination of which are prohibited by law" the protection of copyright that was found to be inconsistent.[118] According to the Panel, this included the class of works that failed content review and, to the extent that they constituted copyright works, the deleted portions of works edited to satisfy content review but not works that were never submitted due to awaiting results of content review in China.[119] With regard to content review, which in contrast to the economic right of copyright protection pursues a cultural objective, the Panel emphasised that "the United States' claim did not challenge China's right to conduct content review" and that "the Panel's findings do not affect China's right

115 *See, e.g.*, D.M. Dickson, "September trade gap widened 18.2 percent", *The Washington Times* 1 (14 November 2009) (reporting that the "trade deficit with China is on track to exceed $200 billion this year for the fifth year in a row").

116 Panel Report, "China – Measures Affecting the Protection and Enforcement of Intellectual Property Rights", *WT/DS 362/R* (26 January 2009); *see also* R.J. Neuwirth, "Der WTO-Bericht zu China – Measures Affecting the Protection and Enforcement on Intellectual Property Rights: ein Kommentar" 58 *Gewerblicher Rechtsschutz und Urheberrecht, Internationaler Teil* 367 (2009).

117 Panel Report, *supra* note 116, §8.1.

118 Id., §7.1.

119 Id., §7.103.

to conduct content review".[120] For the residual claims relating to customs measures and thresholds in its criminal law, the Panel cleared China from allegations of inconsistency.[121] In this case, no mention of or reference to the Convention on the Diversity of Cultural Expressions was made. On 19 March 2010, China notified that it had implemented the recommendations made by the DSB and since then no compliance proceedings have been initiated.[122]

The *China – Publications and Audiovisual Products* case was closely connected to the first case as it concerned the cultural industries as the major copyright industries and, in particular, certain Chinese measures affecting the market access and distribution.[123] It also featured a tension between the economic impact of certain measures in relation to the public interest and cultural goals. Although consultations were requested simultaneously, the *China – Publications and Audiovisual Products* case took considerably longer to decide (apparently due to problems related to the translation of the Chinese laws as well as their volume reflected in the 500 page total). The case was also appealed by both parties.[124] In sum, the US claimed the inconsistency of a total of 17 Chinese measures regulating activities relating to the importation and distribution of various cultural industries, such as reading materials (for example, books, newspapers, periodicals, electronic publications); audiovisual home entertainment ("AVHE") products (for example, videocassettes, video compact discs, digital video discs (DVDs)); sound recordings (for example, recorded audio tapes); and films for theatrical release.[125] The alleged inconsistencies were based on China's obligations under the WTO Accession Protocol, Article III:4 GATT and Article XVI and XVII GATS.

During the proceedings before the Panel, China emphasised the special, *i.e.* dual nature of cultural goods, and tried to justify the contested measures by invoking the Convention on the Diversity of Cultural Expressions as well as the Cultural Diversity Declaration.[126] In the view of the Panel, however, China failed to note that the Convention on the Diversity of Cultural Expressions expressly provides the following:

> Nothing in this Convention shall be interpreted as modifying the rights and obligations of the parties under any other treaties to which they are parties." In any event, nothing in the text of the WTO Agreement provides an exception from WTO

---

120 Id., §7.144.

121 Id., §§8.1 and 8.2.

122 WTO, "Understanding between China and the United States Regarding Procedures under Articles 21 and 22 of the DSU", *WT/DS362/15* (13 April 2010).

123 *See* T. Voon, "China – Measures Affecting Trading Rights and Distribution Services for Certain Publications and Audiovisual Entertainment Products", 103 *American Journal of International Law* 710 (2009).

124 *See*, *infra* note 138.

125 Appellate Body Report, *supra* note 10, §1.

126 Panel Report, *supra* note 9, §§4.108 and 4.207.

> disciplines in terms of "cultural goods," and China's Accession Protocol likewise contains no such exception.[127]

The same views were purported by Australia and Korea, which based on Article 20(2) of the Convention on the Diversity of Cultural Expressions and the respective article of the DSU denied the Convention on the Diversity of Cultural Expressions any legal relevance in the case at issue.[128] At a later stage, China also tried to rely on the public morals exemption of Article XX(a) GATT by invoking both the Convention on the Diversity of Cultural Expressions and Cultural Diversity Declaration.[129] The mention of this declaration was probably due to the fact that the US has not ratified the Convention on the Diversity of Cultural Expressions and the hope that the Cultural Diversity Declaration may have assumed some kind of status under customary international law. Nonetheless, in reply to the arguments of China, the Panel, evading a closer inquiry into the Cultural Diversity Declaration's content and legal nature, stated as follows:

> We note China's reference to the UNESCO Declaration on Cultural Diversity. We observe in this respect that China has not invoked the Declaration as a defence to its breaches of trading rights commitments under the Accession Protocol. Rather, China has referred to the Declaration as support for the general proposition that the importation of products of the type at issue in this case could, depending on their content, have a negative impact on public morals in China. We have no difficulty accepting this general proposition, but note, as indicated, that we need to focus more specifically on the types of content that are actually prohibited under China's relevant measures.[130]

The Panel hence avoided a closer look into the legal nature of the two UNESCO instruments, and rather, spent some considerable time on the question of the nature of cultural products with regard to their goods or service characteristics. In this context also Article IV GATT on "Special Provisions relating to Cinematograph Films" was discussed for the first time in a GATT/WTO dispute.[131] In this regard, China argued that films for theatrical release are not goods but services because China in its GATS Schedule of Commitments had limited the number of motion pictures for theatrical release on a revenue-sharing basis to 20 on an annual basis.[132] However, based on Article IV GATT which treats cinematograph films as goods, the Panel concluded that the relevant Chinese measures fall under its trading rights commitments in the Accession

---

127 Id., §4.207.
128 Id., §§5.13 and 5.61.
129 Id., §7.751.
130 Id., §7.756 n. 538.
131 Id., §§4.199, 4.307, 4.420–2, 4.515, 7.506, and 7.517–9.
132 Id., §§4.184 and 7.758.

Protocol.[133] The Panel's statement has helped to clarify some doubts regarding the legal characterization of cinematograph films but has left other questions, such as whether audiovisual products in purely electronic form are also subject to the GATT, unanswered.[134] Thus, the uncertainty concerning the application of the GATT and the GATS to cultural products still prevails and the question of their mutual relationship remains unresolved.

In summary, the Panel found most Chinese measures regulating the cultural industries in China inconsistent with its international trade obligations and only occasionally exercised judicial economy or dismissed single claims of the US.[135] It also found all inconsistent measures to be unjustifiable under the public morals exception of Article XX(a) GATT, except for the "state plan requirement" laid down in Article 42 of the *Publications Regulation* which stipulates that "the approval of publication import entities conform to China's State plan for the total number, structure, and distribution of publication import entities".[136] The Panel hence established for the inconsistent Chinese measures that they nullified or impaired the benefits accruing to the US from the relevant agreements and, accordingly, recommended to bring them into conformity with the law of the WTO.[137]

Only shortly after the Panel report was circulated, both parties to the dispute notified their intent to appeal the case to the Appellate Body (AB).[138] China's appeal concerned, in particular, its trading rights commitments under the WTO Accession Protocol, the Panel's necessity analysis, as well as the findings that various measures at issue are not "necessary" within the meaning of Article XX(a) of the GATT 1994 to protect public morals in China and that "Sound recording distribution services" in its GATS Schedule also encompasses the distribution of sound recordings through electronic means.[139] The US, on the other hand, asked the AB to uphold the contested Panel's findings but to reverse the Panel's intermediate finding that the state plan requirement can be characterized as "necessary" to protect public morals in China within the

133 Id., §7. 560.

134 *See* Voon, *supra* note 123, at 716.

135 Panel Report, *supra* note 9, §§8.1–8.2.

136 Id., §7.836.

137 Id., §8.3–8.4.

138 WTO, "China – Measures Affecting Trading Rights and Distribution Services for Certain Publications and Audiovisual Entertainment Products: Notification of an Appeal by China under Article 16.4 and Article 17 of the Understanding on Rules and Procedures Governing the Settlement of Disputes (DSU), and under Rule 20(1) of the Working Procedures for Appellate Review", *WT/DS363/10* (23 September 2009); WTO, "China – Measures Affecting Trading Rights and Distribution Services for Certain Publications and Audiovisual Entertainment Products: Notification of an Other Appeal by the United States under Article 16.4 and Article 17 of the Understanding on Rules and Procedures Governing the Settlement of Disputes (DSU), and under Rule 23(1) of the Working Procedures for Appellate Review", *WT/DS363/11* (6 October 2009).

139 Appellate Body Report, *supra* note 10, §14 and §§15–53.

meaning of Article XX(a) of the GATT 1994.[140] In its findings, the Appellate Body finally upheld most findings of the Panel and only reversed the finding that the state plan requirement is "necessary" to protect public morals in China.[141] This means that China was practically defeated in all points. In its deliberations, the AB also briefly reiterated China's references to both the UNESCO Cultural Diversity Declaration and the Convention on the Diversity of Cultural Expressions but did not enter a closer analysis of it.[142]

In sum, the case in *China – Publications and Audiovisual Products* disproves claims of a direct legal relevance of the Convention on the Diversity of Cultural Expressions for the outcome of the dispute. As said before, a reading of the ruling by the WTO DSB reads more like the repetition of previous arguments and can be considered "amnesic" to changes in the legal context.[143] This was also due to the fact that only one of the two parties to the dispute, namely China, had ratified the Convention on the Diversity of Cultural Expressions; for obvious reasons mentioned above, the U.S. decided (so far) not to ratify it. Even if both parties to the dispute had been members of the Convention on the Diversity of Cultural Expressions, it would still have remained doubtful whether the WTO DSB would have decided differently.[144] Hence, the Convention on the Diversity of Cultural Expressions has, at its best, helped to clarify the terminology and nature of cultural products. The clarification notwithstanding, the case displays the ongoing fragmentation of international law in the areas of culture and trade. Furthermore, the case also illustrates the fragmentation within the WTO administered agreements, notably such as in the mutual relation of the agreements on trade in goods (GATT), services (GATS) and trade-related aspects of intellectual property rights (TRIPS). This is evident from the fact that it was decided in isolation from the *China – Intellectual Property Rights* case which arose at the same time. Last but not least, a simultaneously waged controversy over the treatment and actions of Google in China also shows the disparities between the governance of economic and political affairs, as well as the divide between public and private international law. This divide causes the exclusion of private subjects from the realm of public international law to continue.[145]

---

140 Id., §91.

141 Id., §§414–416.

142 Id., §§25 and 141 n 238.

143 *See* Neuwirth, *supra* note 83.

144 *See* ECJ Case C-222/07, *Unión de Televisiones Comerciales Asociadas (UTECA) v Administración General del Estado*, [2009] E.C.R. I-01407.

145 *See, e.g.*, "Google, don't be evil?", *Xinhuanet* (29 January 2010), *available at* http://news.xinhuanet.com///2010-01/29/c_13155970.htm (last visited 2 February 2012); M. Wines, "China Issues Sharp Rebuke to U.S. Calls for an Investigation on Google Attacks", *The New York Times* 6 (26 January 2010); M. Landler and W. Wong, "China Says Clinton Harms Relations With Criticism of Internet Censorship", *The New York Times* 4 (23 January 2010) (on Google's alleged copyright violations in China, attacks on its business activities and implications in the political realm).

4.2. THE EUROPEAN COURT OF JUSTICE

In yet another example of international dispute settlement, the Convention on the Diversity of Cultural Expressions was also briefly cited in one case brought before the European Court of Justice in a preliminary ruling at the request of a court in Spain. The case concerned the content rules laid down in the 1989 Television Without Frontiers Directive in relation to the European Union's rules on state aid (former Article 87 TEC; now Article 107 TFEU) and non-discrimination (former Article 12 TEC; now Article 18 TFEU).[146] More concretely, the Court was asked to decide whether a measure adopted by a Member State which "requires television operators to earmark 5% of their operating revenue for the pre-funding of European cinematograph films and films made for television and, more specifically, to reserve 60% of that 5% for the production of works of which the original language is one of the official languages of that Member State" is inconsistent with European Union Law.[147] Second it had to decide whether the same measure constitutes prohibited State aid in favour of the cinematograph industry of the Member State in question. The Court answered both questions in the negative and hence ruled in favour of a cultural and linguistic consideration for a policy measure. In its considerations, the Court also referred to the Convention on the Diversity of Cultural Expressions by pointing out the intrinsic link between language and culture and cited paragraph 14 of the Preamble of the Convention on the Diversity of Cultural Expressions.[148] In this case, the Convention on the Diversity of Cultural Expressions was equally indecisive on the ruling of the Court but was used as a reference for the clarification of the meaning of linguistic diversity. It is an example of the indirect legal impact of the Convention on the interpretation of international (or supranational) law.

4.3. THE UNESCO CONVENTION AND REGIONAL TRADE AGREEMENTS (RTAS): THE CASE OF KOREA (AND WHY THE US MIGHT WANT TO JOIN THE UNESCO CONVENTION)

Last but not least, another means to evaluate the legal value of the Convention on the Diversity of Cultural Expressions consists in trying to assess its impact on

---

[146] The Consolidated Version of the Treaty on the Functioning of the European Union, *O.J. 2008/C 115/47, available at* www.ecb.int/ecb/legal/pdf/fxac08115enc_002.pdf (last visited 2 February 2012).

[147] ECJ Case C-222/07, *Unión de Televisiones Comerciales Asociadas (UTECA) v Administración General del Estado, supra* note 144.

[148] Id., §33; *See also* ECJ, Opinion of Advocate General Kokott, Case C-222/07, [2009] E.C.R. I-0140 at §§13–19, 95, 98–99 (providing a more elaborate discussion of the Convention on the Diversity of Cultural Expressions).

the negotiation of international agreements and notably on regional trade agreements ("RTAs") subsequent its entry into force five years ago. In the past two decades, regionalism is increasingly becoming an important levelling base for trade liberalization and cultural diversity, in particular in view of the stagnating conditions at the multilateral level.[149] The Convention's potential impact on trade agreements negotiated after its entry into force derives from Article 20(1)(b) in connection with Article 21 of the Convention on the Diversity of Cultural Expressions, according to which parties shall take into account the relevant provisions of the Convention "when entering into other international obligations" and equally "undertake to promote the objectives and principles of this Convention in other international forums". In practical terms, this means that, following the entry into force of the Convention on the Diversity of Cultural Expressions on 18 March 2007, 60 RTAs have been notified to the WTO to have entered into force.[150] However, the negotiation of some of these RTAs had been initiated before the Convention on the Diversity of Cultural Expressions materialized into hard law, which may have minimized its effect on the final outcome. Additionally, there are currently about 39 RTAs under negotiation for which a potential impact of the Convention on the Diversity of Cultural Expressions will have to be assessed at a later moment.[151] Generally, these statistics underline the growing importance of RTAs in the past two decades against the backdrop of a crisis of multilateralism as expressed in the staggering progress of the Doha Round negotiations.[152] Nonetheless, a brief look at a selected number of RTAs promises to provide some interesting insights into the actual role and legal impact of the Convention on the Diversity of Cultural Expressions on international trade regulation and perhaps allows for some comments on future trends.

In this context, two sets of questions are of particular interest in evaluating the actual impact and future trends: first whether the new RTAs provide evidence of a change in a country's policy *vis-à-vis* culture and trade, and, second, whether there has been a change also in the regulatory technique or

---

149 *See* S. Formentini and L. Iapadre, "Cultural Diversity and Regional Trade Agreements: The Case of Audiovisual Services" (2006), *available at* www.etsg.org///.pdf (last visited 2 February 2012).

150 *See* WTO, "Regional Trade Agreements Notified to the GATT/WTO and in Force: By Date of Entry into Force", *available at* http://rtais.wto.org/UI/PublicPreDefRepByEIF.aspx (last visited 2 February 2012).

151 *See* WTO, "List of All Early Announcements Made to WTO", *available at* http://rtais.wto.org/UI/PublicEARTAList.aspx (last visited 2 February 2012).

152 *See* WTO, "Regional Trade Agreements", *available at* www.wto.org//_e/region_e/region_e.htm (last visited 2 February 2012) (the RTA Database available on the WTO Homepage reports that "The surge in RTAs has continued unabated since the early 1990s. As of 15 November 2011, some 505 RTAs, counting goods and services notifications separately, have been notified to the GATT/WTO. Of these, 367 RTAs were notified under Article XXIV of the GATT 1947 or GATT 1994; 36 under the Enabling Clause; and 102 under Article V of the GATS. At that same date, 313 agreements were in force".).

regulatory approach to the "culture and trade quandary". In this regard, it is noteworthy that out of a total number of 47 participating states (including regional economic integration organizations ("REIO") or custom territories("CT")) in these RTAs, the list of countries having concluded most RTAs during the time period from 18 March 2007 until 1 January 2012 is led by Japan (9 RTAs), followed by the EU (and former EC) and Chile (each 8 RTAs), Peru, India, and the EFTA states (each 7 RTAs), Turkey (6 RTAs), Korea, China and ASEAN (each 4 RTAs), Canada (3) and the U.S. (2 RTAs).[153] Among these participating parties, Japan, Brunei Daroussalam, Colombia, El Salvador, Fiji, Hong Kong (China), Malaysia, Nepal, Pakistan, Papua New Guinea, Philippines, Taiwan (Chinese Taipei), Singapore, Thailand, Turkey, the respective regional economic integration organizations in the sense of Article 27 of the Convention on the Diversity of Cultural Expressions (to the exception of the EU/EC), and, last but not least, the U.S. have not yet become members of the Convention on the Diversity of Cultural Expressions. Generally, it can be stated that the different legal types of RTAs are concluded by the equally distinctive nature of contracting parties often characterized by widely divergent political, legal, economic, and cultural backgrounds, which is why it is hard to determine a general trend. Even the various RTAs signed by one party with other parties may differ considerably and not only in terms of scope. For example, the various RTAs concluded by China, differ in their nature from RTAs concluded by the US and the EU,[154] usually containing no special reference to culture, cultural diversity or cultural cooperation.[155] The Peru-China FTA, however, exempts "cultural industries" from most-favoured nation (MFN) treatment and the China-NZ contains a special reference concerning the illicit import of cultural property.[156]

From a general perspective, a brief survey of these RTAs seems to suggest that trading partners have not altered their regulatory approach to the 'culture and trade conundrum' or, from a legal perspective, applied new regulatory techniques. Even Canada, for instance, as the main driving force behind the Convention's adoption, continues its former practice and uses a general exception for the cultural industries as already incorporated in the 1988 CUSFTA and 1994 NAFTA.[157] However, Canadian RTAs recognize that "states

---

153 *See* WTO, "List of all RTAs", *available at* http://rtais.wto.org//.aspx (last visited 2 February 2012).

154 *See* P.K. Yu, "Sinic Trade Agreements", 44 *U.C. Davis L. Rev.* 953 (2011).

155 *Cf.* Peru-China (FTA & EIA); China-Singapore (FTA & EIA); China-New Zealand (FTA & EIA); Pakistan-China (FTA & EIA); *available at* http://rtais.wto.org/UI/PublicAllRTAList.aspx (last visited 2 February 2012).

156 *See* Peru-China (FTA & EIA), Article 131(3)(b); China-New Zealand FTA, Article 200(4). *See also* the Peru-Chile (FTA & EIA) with respect to "*industrias culturales*"; and the Chile Colombia (FTA & EIA) with regard to "*industrias y actividades culturales*".

157 *Compare* CUSFTA Article 2012 and NAFTA Article 2106 *with* Canada-Colombia (FTA & EIA) Article 2206, Peru-Canada (FTA & EIA) Article 2205, and EFTA-Canada (FTA) Article 23 and Annex J.

must maintain the ability to preserve, develop and implement their cultural policies for the purpose of strengthening cultural diversity, given the essential role that cultural goods and services play in the identity and diversity of societies and the lives of individuals" or to express the commitment to "co-operate in promoting recognition that States must maintain the ability to preserve, develop and implement their cultural policies for the purpose of strengthening cultural diversity".[158] Otherwise and to the exception of the agreements concluded by the EU,[159] few RTAs contain special references to cultural policies or related issues. A few agreements mention intangible cultural heritage, or cultural development, most frequently in the context of provisions on intellectual property rights.[160] The majority of agreements simply incorporate the general exceptions enshrined in the GATT and GATS respectively, or use similar wordings, thus maintaining a regulatory technique exempting cultural or other "non-trade" issues (*e.g.* national treasures possessing artistic, historic or archaeological value) from the realm of trade as it was already used in 1947.[161] In this respect, it is interesting to

158 *See* the Preambles of the Canada-Colombia (FTA & EIA), the Peru-Canada (FTA & EIA), and the EFTA-Canada (FTA).

159 *See, e.g.*, the Protocol on Cultural Cooperation of the Korea-EU (FTA & EIA); EU Serbia Stabilization Agreement (SAA), signed on 29 April 2008 (not yet entered into force), Articles 103–107, *available at* http://ec.europa.eu////_document/_en.pdf (last visited 2 February 2012); EC-Montenegro (FTA & EIA), Articles 103–107; Preamble EC-Cameroon (FTA); EU-Papua New Guinea-Fiji (FTA), Article 3(2)(A); EC-CARIFORUM (FTA & EIA), Article 3(2)(a); however, no references to cultural aspects are made in the Côte d'Ivoire (FTA) and the EC-Bosnia and Herzegovina (FTA).

160 *See* Peru-China (FTA & EIA), Article 131(3)(b); China-New Zealand FTA, Article 200(4); Japan-Indonesia (FTA-EIA), Article 123(c); Hong Kong-New Zealand FTA, Chapter 11 Articles 1 and 8 (on intellectual property rights stipulates as its objectives to "promote the importance of intellectual property rights in fostering trade in goods and services, innovation, and economic, social and cultural development" and also authorizes parties to take appropriate measures to protect genetic resources, traditional knowledge and traditional cultural expressions or folklore"). *See also* Nicaragua-Taiwan (FTA & EIA), Articles 17.17 – 17.19 (featuring provisions on the protection of traditional knowledge, folklore and genetic resources, with the specific focus on a special system to register, promote and market the rights of indigenous peoples and local and ethnic communities with a view to "emphasize the autochthonous sociological and cultural values of the indigenous people and the local and ethnic communities and to bring them social justice").

161 *See, e.g.* Egypt-EFTA (FTA), Articles 21 and 22; India-Chile (PTA), Article XIX; Chile-Japan (FTA & EIA), Articles 192 and 193; Japan-Thailand (FTA & EIA), Article 10; Nicaragua-Taiwan (FTA & EIA), Articles 32.01 – 23.02; Pakistan-Malaysia (FTA & EIA), Article 126; Taiwan-Honduras-El Salvador (FTA & EIA), Article 16.02–16.03; Panama-Chile (FTA & EIA), Articles 14.1–14.2; EFTA-SACU (FTA), Articles 23–24; Turkey-Albania (FTA), Articles 30 and 31; Japan-Indonesia (FTA-EIA), Article 11; Chile-Honduras (FTA & EIA), Articles 20.02–20.03; Brunei Darussalam-Japan (FTA & EIA), Article 8; China-New Zealand (FTA & EIA), Articles 200 and 201; Article 16 Turkey-Georgia (FTA); Panama-Costa Rica (FTA & EIA), Articles 21.02–21.03; ASEAN-Japan (FTA & EIA), Articles 7–8; Japan-Philippines (FTA & EIA), Article 23; Article 105–106 China-Singapore (FTA & EIA); US-Oman (FTA & EIA), Article 21.1–21.2; Panama-Honduras (FTA & EIA), Articles 21.02–21.03; US-Peru (FTA & EIA), Articles 22.1–22.2; Peru-Chile (FTA & EIA), Articles 17.1.-17.2; Australia-Chile (FTA & EIA), Articles 22.1–22.2; Chile-Colombia (FTA & EIA), Articles 21.1.-

note that the ASEAN-Australian-NZ RTA also exempts measures referred to in Article XX(f) of GATT 1994 and defines them so as to include "measures necessary to protect national treasures or specific sites of historical or archaeological value, or measures necessary to support creative arts of national value".[162] In a footnote, it also clarifies the meaning of "Creative arts" as follows:

> Creative arts include the performing arts – including theatre, dance and music – visual arts and craft, literature, film and video, language arts, creative on-line content, indigenous traditional practice and contemporary cultural expression, and digital interactive media and hybrid art work, including those that use new technologies to transcend discrete art form divisions. The term encompasses those activities involved in the presentation, execution and interpretation of the arts, and the study and technical development of these art forms and activities.[163]

In practice, this interpretative extension of the scope of Article XX(f) from national treasures to various cultural industries beyond the effect of the present RTA remains dubious.[164] In the end, an even closer look at regionalism following the entry into force of the Convention on the Diversity of Cultural Expressions suggests a modest impact on the culture and trade link as far as its legal aspects are concerned. In other words, as if caught on some kind of path dependency, most countries follow their previous practices, appearing more likely to alter in accordance with internal changes (though in an interconnected world, change may be triggered by external factors). This can be compared to the change in practice of the European Communities before the creation of the European Union.[165]

Put briefly, the Convention's impact after its entry into force on the negotiation of international trade agreements must – despite the steadily growing number of ratifications – still be evaluated as limited as most states continue their past practices in the area of international trade. This means that

---

21.2; MERCOSUR-India (PTA), Article 9; EFTA-Canada (FTA), Article 22; Peru-Singapore (FTA & EIA), Articles 18.1–18.2; Article 22 Japan-Switzerland (FTA & EIA); ASEAN-India Framework Agreement (FTA), Article 10; ASEAN-Australia-New Zealand (FTA & EIA), Chapter 15; Korea-India (FTA & EIA), Article 2.9; Peru-China (FTA & EIA), Articles 193 and 194; Turkey-Serbia (FTA), Article 32; EFTA-Serbia (FTA), Articles 22–23; EFTA-Albania (FTA), Article 21–22; Hong Kong-New Zealand (FTA & EIA), Chapter 19 Articles 1–2; Chile-Turkey (FTA), Article 56–57; India-Malaysia (FTA & EIA), Chapter 12; EFTA-Peru (FTA), Articles 2.19–2.20; Peru-Korea (FTA & EIA); Peru-Korea (FTA & EIA), Articles 24.1–24.2; India-Japan (FTA & EIA), Articles 11 and 109; Article 2201–2202 Canada-Colombia (FTA & EIA); These FTA, EIA and PTA are available at http://rtais.wto.org//cAllRTAList.aspx (last visited 2 February 2012); see also Gilbert Gagné, "Free Trade and Cultural Policies: Evidence from Three US Agreements", 45 Journal of World Trade 1267–1284, at 1270 (2011).

162 *See* ASEAN-Australian-NZ (FTA & EIA), Chapter 15 Article 1(3).

163 *See* id.

164 *See* Neuwirth, supra note 62, 169–83 (providing a discussion Article XX:f GATT).

165 *See* R.J. Neuwirth, "The European Union and the Culture Industries: From the Common Market to a 'Common Sense'", in D. Ward (ed.), *The European Union & the Culture Industries: Regulation and the Public Interest*, 2008, 241.

countries in favour of cultural diversity continue to support it, while those against it, express their dismay or try to fight it. More often though, this practice consists still in a wide separation of culture from trade, or even of trade from (what is ill termed) "non-trade issues" (and should be at least called "trade-related" issues instead).[166] This practice reflects some important conceptual, legal, and institutional problems allowing for the establishment of a more coherent policy approach. These problems persist at the global level (notably between the WTO and UNESCO), at the regional level (*e.g.* between the 27 EU Member States and the EU institutions, between the EU institutions themselves, or even within one EU institution, such as the various Commission Directorates) and nationally as well as locally between the different ministries or competent authorities. In this regard, the US Government, by defying any linkages, has acted most consistently in the past decades. However, in its continuous suspicion against the Convention, it may have overlooked some of the changing conditions and their legal implications.

In this regard, the recent bilateral agreements concluded by Korea with the EU, which was signed on 6 October 2010 and has entered into force on 1 July 2011, and with the U.S., which was signed on 30 July 2007 and still awaits entry into force, are of special interest to peruse as being indicative of future trends.[167] The special interest of these agreements derives first from the fact that, accused of "cultural protectionism" in the past, Korea has been an interesting playing field for the culture and trade conundrum and for the debate about an *exception culturelle* as it has been experimenting rather successfully with cultural policies in the audiovisual sector based on the screen quotas for cinematograph films as authorized in Article IV GATT.[168] Korea has also ratified the Convention on the Diversity of Cultural Expressions on 1 April 2010, that is to say after the signing of the FTA with the US but before the signing of the FTA with the EU. Secondly, it is therefore interesting to look at the bilateral negotiations between Korea with one "country" (or more precisely a *sui generis* regional organization), which has ratified the Convention on the Diversity of Cultural Expressions and another country (the US), which has consistently opposed and thus not ratified the Convention on the Diversity of Cultural Expressions. Perhaps the two bilateral agreements concluded by Korea are thus indicative of the legal or general value of the Convention for the issue of cultural diversity in the realm of international trade.

---

166 *See, e.g.*, Canada-Colombia (FTA & EIA), Articles 1801 and 1802 (for the scope of cooperation in "trade-related issues").

167 *See generally* D. Ahn, "Legal and Institutional Issues of Korea-EU FTA: New Model for Post-NAFTA FTAs?" *GEM Policy Brief* (October 2010), *available at* http://gem.sciences-po.fr////_KOREU%20FTA%20201010.pdf (last visited 2 February 2012).

168 *See* J. Kim, "The Viability of Screen Quotas in Korea: The Cultural Exception under the International Trade Regime", 26 *Korean J. of Int'l & Comp. L.* 199 (1998).

To begin with the earlier of the two agreements, the KORUS FTA exploratory talks started in 2004 and negotiations were resumed in 2006.[169] The agreement's text was finally signed on 30 July 2007 and slightly revised in 2010. At the time of the writing of this article, it has still not entered into force and is currently in the process of ratification in both countries despite ongoing protests.[170] Legally, the final outcome shows that the only time the word "culture" or "cultural" are mentioned in the FTA is in the list of central governmental entities on Korea's government procurement schedule, namely its Ministry of Culture and Tourism as well as the Cultural Heritage Administration.[171] Thus the U.S. consistently negotiated the agreement with culture being "America's blind spot".[172] This means that for Americans, cultural products are regarded like any other product, as is reflected in famous American statements in the debate, such as those by former FCC Chairman Mark Fowler, who was reported as having said that television equals a "toaster with pictures"[173], and former USTR Carla Hill's advising the French that if they make their films as good as their cheese, they will also sell them.[174] Back to the KORUS FTA, in the words of its Preamble, the main focus is on the desire "to raise living standards, promote economic growth and stability, create new employment opportunities, and improve the general welfare in their territories by liberalizing and expanding trade and investment between their territories".[175] In substantive terms, Korea apparently found no reasons to insist on a different or more culture-sensitive terminology despite having in the meantime ratified the Convention on the Diversity of Cultural Expressions. Instead, Korea appears to have opted for a more defensive position, namely by exempting several areas of cultural products from its commitments. In this respect, Annex I of Korea's services schedule lists some of the existing measures which do not comply with the agreement's basic obligations. As one of the most contentious issues and exceptions to the agreement's performance

169 *See* J.J. Schott, S.C. Bradford and T. Moll, "Negotiating the Korea–United States Free Trade Agreement", 4 *Policy Briefs in International Economics* 1 (2006), *available at* www.iie.com/publications/pb/pb06–4.pdf (last visited 2 February 2012).

170 Recently, President Obama signed the implementing bill while the Korean National Assembly passed the ratification bill on November 22, 2011 in spite of continuous protests and even tear gas thrown by an opposition member in the assembly. *See, e.g.*, Choe Sang-Hun, "As Surprised Opponents Protest, South Korea Pushes U.S. Trade Pact Through Parliament", *The New York Times* 10 (23 November 2011).

171 *See* United States-Korea Free Trade Agreement, 30 June 2007, Annex 17a "Government Procurement", *available at* www.ustr.gov/agreements/trade-agreements/fta/final-text (last visited 2 February 2012) [hereinafter "KORUS FTA"].

172 *See* J. Bhagwati, "Culture and Trade: America's Blindspot", in J. Bhagwati (ed.), *The Wind of the Hundred Days: How Washington Mismanaged Globalization*, 2002, 209.

173 Quoted in C.R. Sunstein, "Television and the Public Interest", 88 *Calif. L. Rev.* 499, 507 (2000).

174 *See* T.M. Murray, "The U.S.-French Dispute over GATT Treatment of Audiovisual Products and the Limits of Public Choice Theory: How an Efficient Market Solution was 'Rent-seeking'", 21 *Md. J. Int'l L. & Trade* 203, 209 (1997).

175 KORUS FTA, *supra* note 172, Preamble Recital 3.

requirements and market access obligations, Korea still maintained that in the projection of motion picture services, "cinema operators must project Korean motion pictures for at least 73 days per year at each screen in Korea".[176] Existing plus possible future new or more restrictive non-conforming measures are laid down in Annex II. In this category and as exceptions to national treatment, most-favoured-nation treatment, performance requirements, and local presence obligations, Korea also reserved for itself the right "to adopt or maintain any measure with respect to motion picture promotion, advertising, or postproduction services".[177] Similarly, Korea also reserved for itself the right "to adopt or maintain any measure with respect to the conservation and restoration of cultural heritage and properties, including the excavation, appraisal, or dealing of cultural heritage and properties".[178] Korean screen quotas have been a controversial issue long before the negotiation of the KORUS FTA. A first controversial issue regarding the screen quota is in fact related to their actual effectiveness or possible role in the emergence of a viable Korean audiovisual industry. Based on the box office performance of Korean films, it has been argued that it may not have played a significant role, even though the data fail to discuss how a viable film industry in Korea emerged in the first place.[179] By contrast, arguments were also advanced according to which the quota could be abolished and replaced by subsidies on the following grounds:

> Korea's screen quota should be repealed because it encourages the Korean film industry to produce films of poor quality that are not commercially viable. Moreover, the quota only requires that Korean companies make the films, not that the films reflect Korean culture. As a result, despite the fact that the screen quota has been in existence for more than thirty years, the Korean domestic film industry continues to be dominated by foreign films.
> Government subsidies linked to film quality, cultural content, and commercial viability would encourage the Korean film industry to produce quality films that reflect Korean culture and values.[180]

As a matter of fact, the Korean screen quotas have long been such a thorny issue in U.S.-Korea relations that they already derailed the negotiation of a bilateral investment treaty in the 1990s.[181] In fact, upon pressure of the U.S. Government, the Korean government even cut the existing level of screen quota time reserved

176 KORUS FTA, *supra* note 172, Annex I-Korea-60.

177 Id., Annex II-Korea-41.

178 Id., Annex II-Korea-42.

179 *See* S. Y. Lee, E.-M. Kim and Y. I. Kim, "The Effect of the Korean Screen Quota System on Box Office Performance", 42 *J. World T.* 335 (2008).

180 *See* C. H.-K. Kim, "Building the Korean Film Industry's Competitiveness: Abolish the Screen Quota and Subsidize the Film Industry", 9 *Pac. Rim L. & Pol'y* 353, 378 (2000).

181 *See* W.H. Cooper (coordinator), "The U.S.-South Korea Free Trade Agreement (KORUS FTA): Provisions and Implications", *CRS Report for Congress* 41 (30 November 2011), *available at* http://fpc.state.gov///.pdf.

for Korean films in half (from 146 to 73 per year) before the negotiations for the KORUS FTA were officially launched in 2006.[182] The same number of days has been reserved in the KORUS FTA. Thus, in the present case, the Convention on the Diversity of Cultural Expressions had no direct influence on the negotiations as the question of the screen quotas was already unilaterally addressed by the Korean Government before the Convention entered into force, before Korea became a member, and even before the negotiations were officially launched. It therefore amounts to mere speculation when one asks if the screen quota level would have remained the same had the Convention already entered into force at that time. What is more interesting at this stage is to look at the actual development of the Korean audiovisual industry once the KORUS FTA enters into force. Legally, however, an interesting development deriving from the KORUS FTA is the question of the possible conflict between Article IV GATT and provisions of the Convention on the Diversity of Cultural Expressions (notably Articles 6 and 8 of the Convention on the Diversity of Cultural Expressions) as raised by Korean Professor Won-Mog Choi.[183] A possible conflict between them could emerge if domestic screen quotas adopted based on Article IV GATT were understood as preventing domestic consumers from enjoying the diversity of cultural expressions provided by the global production of foreign cultural products. Such conflict is indeed possible as the Convention on the Diversity of Cultural Expressions fails to specify in Articles 6 and 8 whether the protection and promotion of the diversity of cultural expressions is understood to only address imported or also domestically produced products. In other words, it does not specify whether the Convention is inward or outward looking only, or, if in fact corresponding to national treatment and most-favoured nations treatment, it aims at establishing a balance not only between domestic and foreign produced films but also between the variety of foreign produced films. In conjunction with Article 8, Article 6 of the Convention on the Diversity of Cultural Expressions could hence be read to mean that if a domestic market is strongly dominated by domestic productions, foreign (*i.e.* imported) cultural products would have to be promoted. Such a reading could also benefit the U.S. and constitute an argument for it to ratify the Convention in the sense that Articles 6 and 8 of the Convention on the Diversity of Cultural Expressions may be used as a means to ask other governments to abolish screen quotas so as to enhance the diversity of cultural content offered in a given market that is

---

182 Y.-S. Lee, J. Lee and K.H. Sohn, "The United States – Korea Free Trade Agreement: Path to Common Economic Prosperity or False Promise?", 6 *U. of Pennsylvania East Asia Law Review* 112, 124 (2011); Y. Sohn and M. G. Koo, "Securitizing trade: the case of the Korea-US Free Trade Agreement", 11 *International Relations of the Asia-Pacific* 433, 444 n. 10 (2011).

183 W.-M. Choi, "Screen Quota and Cultural Diversity: Debates in Korea-US FTA Talks and Convention on Cultural Diversity", 2 *Asian J. WTO & Int'l Health L & Pol'y* 267, 272–83 (2007).

largely dominated by domestic productions.[184] In turn, however, it might also be used by other countries to pressure the U.S. Government to diversify the cultural content offered to the U.S. audience by encouraging the distribution of foreign films (and not merely increasing the number of U.S. remakes of foreign movies). Given that in the U.S. market the "foreign film" was compared to an "endangered species",[185] the safeguard of Article 8 of the Convention on the Diversity of Cultural Expressions, aimed at protecting cultural expressions at risk of extinction", appears to be a viable legal argument in a realistic scenario.

Ultimately, such reading of Articles 6 and 8 of the Convention on the Diversity of Cultural Expressions would indeed signify a strong paradox in the relation between Article IV GATT and the Convention on the Diversity of Cultural Expressions. This is because Article IV GATT was and continues to be the sole exception of the cultural industries enshrined in the GATT/WTO system, which allowed GATT/WTO Members some freedom in adopting cultural policies. Historically, it provided the seed from which the Convention on the Diversity of Cultural Expressions eventually germinated. In the end and akin to the Freudian notion of parricide, such a reading would finally mean that – because of the Convention on the Diversity of Cultural Expressions – Article IV GATT has over time turned from a norm favouring the protection of domestic cultural policies into a tool for opening foreign cultural markets to foster trade liberalization in cultural products.

In view of this interesting paradox, it is interesting to look at some aspects of the negotiations between Korea and the EU. By contrast, the Korea-EU FTA was being negotiated since May 2007 and was signed on 6 October 2010, before being provisionally applied since 1 July 2011. In substantive terms, it differs considerably from the KORUS FTA when it comes to the approach to cultural aspects of trade. As to the difference from the latter, the Korea-EU FTA includes a Protocol on Cultural Cooperation (PCC).[186] The Preamble of the PCC opens with a reference to the ratification of the Convention on the Diversity of Cultural Expressions by both parties and recognizes the "importance of the cultural industries and the multi-faceted nature of cultural goods and services as activities of cultural, economic and social value".[187] In terms of its objectives, it "sets up the framework within which the Parties shall cooperate for facilitating exchanges regarding cultural activities, goods and services, including inter alia,

184 *See* K. Scully, "The Most Dangerous Game: U.S. Opposition to the Cultural Exception", 36 *Brooklyn J. Int'l L.* 1183 (2011).

185 *See* A. Kaufman, "Is Foreign Film the New Endangered Species?", *The New York Times* 23 (22 January 2006).

186 *See* Protocol on Cultural Cooperation, [2011] *O.J. L 127/1418* [hereinafter "PCC"].

187 Id., Preamble Recital 2 (note that the German version features the incorrect translation of "cultural industries" (*Kulturindustrien*) to "*Kulturwirtschaft*" (*i.e.* cultural economy), which will further erode a shared understanding and unitary debate on the issue of cultural diversity in a broad sense).

in the audiovisual sector".[188] The PCC also incorporates the meaning of the principal terms, such as cultural diversity, cultural content, cultural expressions, cultural activities, goods and services, and cultural industries, as defined in the Convention on the Diversity of Cultural Expressions.[189]

As a major substantive issue and difference from the KORUS FTA, the Korea-EU FTA stipulates that under certain conditions, co-produced audiovisual works shall be entitled to benefit from both the EU Party and Korean schemes for the promotion of local/regional cultural content.[190] In practice, this means that the PCC makes it possible for co-productions meeting these conditions to be defined as "European works" in the EU market and as "Korean works" in the Korean market and to hence benefit from the local content requirements or screen quotas reserved for "domestic productions". This provision of the PCC has been criticized in view of Article 16 of the Convention on the Diversity of Cultural Expressions whereby preferential treatment should be awarded only to developing countries and not developed ones, such as Korea.[191] As in the context of the KORUS FTA, it is also unclear to what extent the relevant provisions of the Convention on the Diversity of Cultural Expressions mean to cover measures to protect and promote a "balanced global" diversity of cultural expressions available in the respective domestic market. It also recalls practical questions about the criteria for establishing the criteria for "domestic works", whether it suffices that the director or main actor are "European", "Canadian", or "Korean".[192]

In institutional terms, the PCC also sets up a Committee on Cultural Cooperation and excludes the Trade Committee set up by the Korea-EU FTA from exercising jurisdiction over this Protocol.[193] The same separation also persists in the context of the settlement of disputes.[194] Thus, this institutional separation again divides the issue of culture from the one of trade and reflects the problems of reconciling culture and trade in line with the dual nature of cultural products. The separation also reflects the ongoing internal conflict of the division of competences between the EU Member States and the European institutions.[195] The compartmentalized nature of EU policy making, which is

[188] Id., Article 1.

[189] Id., Article 1(4).

[190] Id., Article 5.

[191] See J. Loisen and F. De Ville, "The EU-Korea Protocol on Cultural Cooperation: Toward Cultural Diversity or Cultural Deficit?", 5 *International Journal of Communication* 254, 262 (2011).

[192] *See also* J. Filipek, "'Culture Quotas': The Trade Controversy Over the European Community's Broadcasting Directive", 28 *Stan. J. Int'l L.* 323, 334 (1992); Kim, *supra* note 168; K. Acheson and C. Maule, "Canadian Content Rules: A Time for Reconsideration" 16 *Canadian Public Policy* 284, 285–88 (1990).

[193] *See* Korea-EU-FTA, Article 2.16; *See also* PCC, *supra* note 186, Article 3(3).

[194] *See* Korea-EU-FTA, Article 14.2.

[195] *See* Loisen and De Ville, *supra* note 192, at 257–9.

found duplicated at the MS level, further aggravates the separation between cultural and trade policies.[196]

In sum, the legal and institutional problems confronted in both regional trade agreements concluded by Korea point to a deeper conceptual problem in dealing with apparently antagonistic concepts, such as not only culture or trade but also municipal and international law, developing and developed countries to mention but a few. At the stage of this preliminary evaluation, it is too early to tell what the two agreements, between Korea and the EU on the one hand, and between Korea and the U.S. on the other, mean for other RTAs and what these developments will bring for the future regulation of trade and culture at the global level. At present, it is safe to say that the regulatory approaches to culture and to trade have not significantly altered and still largely rely on the regulatory tools of general or special exceptions. Moreover, single countries still act in line with their traditional approach to the relationship between culture and trade, either denying the special character of so-called "cultural products" due to their dual nature or overemphasizing either their cultural or their commercial aspects. In this regard, the US approach that treats cultural products like other ordinary products appears more consistent, but usually, the denial of a cultural discourse appears to increase fears on behalf of actual or potential negotiation partners. In this regard, the EU's practice appears to be less consistent, as the EU itself is internally divided over culture and trade, but at least assists in minimizing fears. It is equally certain that the proliferation of RTAs will further compartmentalize, fragment and complicate the interpretation and application of rules governing culture and trade related issues. This ultimately brings up an old problem, which consists of the lack of a proper conceptual approach capable of tackling the challenges deriving from the dual nature of cultural products, thus inevitably leading to a lack of policy coherence and the likely emergence of future conflicts.

5. CONCLUSION

Around five years after the entry into force of the Convention on the Diversity of Cultural Expressions, a critical review of the state of the art of the culture and trade debate revealed no major changes or major progress towards an enhanced understanding and improved governance of the two closely related areas of culture and trade. Initially, it was hoped that the adoption of the Convention on the Diversity of Cultural Expressions would help to mitigate these culture and trade conflicts and to make the regulatory regime for the cultural industries more consistent and more sensitive to the dual, that is to say economic and cultural, nature of cultural products. It was also associated with concerns about the unity of the international legal order and the objective of improving the

196 Id., at 266.

policy coherence in global governance in general and between cultural policies governed by UNESCO and trade policies formulated in the WTO in particular.

As the previous sections show, these expectations were clearly not met. Already in the wake of the adoption of the Convention on the Diversity of Cultural Expressions, critical comments from scholars expressed serious doubts as to the possibility that the Convention on the Diversity of Cultural Expressions could have an impact on international law. Furthermore, it was feared that the Convention on the Diversity of Cultural Expressions rather re-started the culture and trade debate as similar questions almost derailed the successful conclusion of the Uruguay Round negotiations in the early 1980s. Still today, more than half a century after the adoption of Article IV GATT 1947 on cinematograph films, the realms of culture and of trade remain widely separated both in terms of substantive law and in terms of the competency of international organizations. Moreover, trade policy makers and cultural policy makers still speak past one another at both the national as well as international level. This situation means that the issue of cultural diversity in the era of economic globalization is subject to a large degree of legal uncertainty. It is also a situation which is totally inadequate to deal with the existing business practices and technological possibilities, let alone of embracing new ones.

The doubts expressed by legal experts about the limited impact of the Convention on the Diversity of Cultural Expressions on the realm of international trade were eventually confirmed in December 2009 when the WTO Appellate Body issued its final ruling in the *China – Publications and Audiovisual Products* case. This case was of great interest because it was the first case decided by the WTO dispute settlement system after the entry into force of the Convention on the Diversity of Cultural Expressions and it therefore allowed for a first test of its legal impact on the realm of international trade law. In this case, it must be mentioned, only one of the parties to the dispute, namely China, had ratified the Convention on the Diversity of Cultural Expressions. Judging from the content of the Convention and from a case decided before the European Court of Justice, however, it is believed that the Convention would not have made a bigger impact, even had the U.S. ratified the Convention on the Diversity of Cultural Expressions. The only area where an increased activity can be detected is in the negotiation of regional trade agreements (RTAs). From the entry into force of the Convention on the Diversity of Cultural Expressions until early 2012, 60 new RTAs have entered into force and 39 are currently being negotiated. More RTAs will follow. Several factors, such as the fact that negotiations were often launched before the Convention's entry into force or that negotiations were held behind closed doors, make it difficult to assess the Convention's actual impact on the outcome. Based on the letter of the law only, as exemplified in the case of Korea having negotiated in parallel an FTA with the U.S. and with the EU, many countries still pursue their traditional approach to the issue of culture and trade or even adapt in relation to their negotiation partners. Legally, the overall regulatory practice, namely one of separating the area of culture from the one of trade by virtue of general or special exceptions, has therefore not considerably changed. Having said this, it will be interesting to observe the application of existing RTAs and negotiation of future ones to arrive at future trends. Considering that Article IV GATT was inspired by a bilateral trade agreement between the U.S. and France, it will also be interesting to try to assess the medium term impact of the proliferation of RTAs on the negotiation of multilateral agreements once they receive new momentum.

For these reasons, it can be concluded that the Convention on the Diversity of Cultural Expressions has indeed done little to enhance the legal coherence between cultural and trade policies or to improve the regulatory situation of the cultural industries. Largely as a reminder or through its symbolic value, it may have contributed to some greater awareness about the importance of cultural diversity in public debates, as visible in some of the arguments raised during the negotiation of RTAs. At the same time, it failed to address problems related to changes in the current business practices or to help to prepare the international community for future challenges deriving from the changes caused by rapidly shortening cycles of technological innovations and their subsequent impact on cultural diversity. For this, however, the Convention on the Diversity of Cultural Expressions is not alone to blame. To have a long lasting impact and to improve the regulatory situation of global trade while at the same time respecting the diversity of cultural expressions, a much more fundamental reform of the architecture of the international legal system presently in place is required. Such reform, the culture and trade debate mandates, should also take into account a much wider area of policy issues. For this, the recent international financial crisis could have provided a good example as well as a starting point, but it must be feared that even in this area the initial momentum that was gained, has been lost. Nonetheless, in the near future and to avoid the impression that nothing has been learned from history, the culture and trade debate will have to broaden in scope to better encompass trade rules in relation to other areas, such as competition rules, intellectual property rights, financial and fiscal rules, to mention but a few, while at the same time strengthening its institutional framework so as to better coordinate and balance between them. The debate will equally have to rethink the concept of "cultural diversity" and "diversity of cultural expressions" in terms of discarding the distinction between domestic and foreign produced cultural products. In a steadily globalizing world, diversity of cultural expressions must be read to mean a local availability of a well-balanced and diverse offer of globally as well as locally produced cultural products. In the pursuit of this important cultural policy objective, the basic regulatory tools of international trade, namely the most-favoured nation clause and the national treatment principle, provide some useful guidance.

SUBSTANTIVE WTO LAW AND THE CONVENTION ON THE DIVERSITY OF CULTURAL EXPRESSIONS

Tania VOON*

1. INTRODUCTION

The World Trade Organization ("WTO") affects culture in myriad ways. At a broad level, liberalizing trade necessarily influences cultures across the globe by facilitating the influx of foreign products, services, and even people, while modifying the conditions of competition and therefore the way of life of local workers and communities. More specifically, from a legal perspective, the agreements reached among WTO Members touch on numerous aspects of culture, leading to an extensive overlap between the WTO and the *Convention on the Protection and Promotion of the Diversity of Cultural Expressions* ("Convention on the Diversity of Cultural Expressions") that was adopted by the General Conference of the United Nations Educational, Scientific and Cultural Organisation ("UNESCO") on 20 October 2005 and entered into force on 18 March 2007.[1] In this chapter, I outline key WTO rules that affect culture and so create a potential clash with the Convention on the Diversity of Cultural Expressions. I leave to one side the question of how to resolve an actual clash.[2]

The possible conflict between the Convention on the Diversity of Cultural Expressions and the WTO agreements is emblematic of the larger, complex relationship between culture and trade, which has long been the subject of

* Ph.D. (Cambridge), LL.M. (Harvard), Grad. Dip. Int'l L. (Melb), LL.B. (Hons) (Melb), B.Sc. (Melb), A.Mus.A. Associate Professor, Melbourne Law School, University of Melbourne; Former Legal Officer, Appellate Body Secretariat, WTO; Fellow, Tim Fischer Centre for Global Trade & Finance, Bond University. Email: <tania.voon@unimelb.edu.au>. I am grateful to Timothy Lau for helpful research and editorial assistance.

1 Convention on the Protection and Promotion of the Diversity of Cultural Expressions, 20 October 2005, *U.N. Doc. CLT-2005/CONVENTION DIVERSITE-CULT REV.* [hereinafter "Convention on the Diversity of Cultural Expressions"].

2 *See, e.g.*, T. VOON, "UNESCO and the WTO: A Clash of Cultures?" 55 *ICLQ* 635, 642–645 and 647–650 (2006) (discussing the issue of resolving conflicts between the Convention on the Diversity of Cultural Expressions and WTO law).

academic and political debate.[3] In the context of the Convention on the Diversity of Cultural Expressions and the WTO agreements, the possibility of conflict begins with the very objectives of these treaties and their underlying organizations. The purpose of UNESCO includes "promoting collaboration among the nations through … *culture*".[4] In comparison, the Preamble to the treaty establishing the WTO recognizes objectives including "expanding the production of and *trade* in goods and services" and proposes "contributing to these objectives by entering into reciprocal and mutually advantageous arrangements directed to the substantial reduction of tariffs and other barriers to trade and to the elimination of discriminatory treatment in international trade relations."[5] One might therefore perceive a contradiction between UNESCO and the WTO: the first aims to promote regulatory cultural measures, and the second to prevent them where they would impede trade.

However, even at this most basic level, the two organizations share certain goals and recognize a more nuanced relationship between culture and trade than one might expect. Both may be seen as prioritizing global peace and security[6] as well as human rights (expressly in the case of UNESCO and by implication through reference to 'raising standards of living', among other things, in the case of the WTO).[7] The Convention on the Diversity of Cultural Expressions itself exposes specific ways in which promoting cultural diversity may require not only protection and preservation but also interaction and exchange of culture. Thus, although the Convention on the Diversity of Cultural Expressions declares States' "sovereign right to adopt measures and policies to protect and promote the diversity of cultural expressions within their territory,"[8] it also calls on Members to do so while "seek[ing] to promote … openness to other cultures of the world."[9] Trade is one way of supporting this approach. Conversely, as detailed further in this chapter, the WTO framework acknowledges that some

---

3 *See, generally,* T. Voon, *Cultural Products and the World Trade Organization*, 2007; R.J. Neuwirth, *The Cultural Industries in International Trade Law: Insights from the NAFTA, the WTO, and the EU*, 2006; C. Graber, *Handel und Kultur im Audiovisionsrecht der WTO: Völkerrechtliche, ökonomische und kulturpolitische Grundlagen einer globalen Medienordnung*, 2003; D. Throsby, *Economics and Culture*, 2001; R. Towse (ed.), *A Handbook of Cultural Economics*, 2003; UNESCO, *Culture, Trade and Globalization: Questions and Answers*, 2000; Cultural Industries Sectoral Advisory Group on International Trade, *Canadian Culture in a Global World: New Strategies for Culture and Trade*, 1999.

4 Constitution of the United Nations Educational, Scientific and Cultural Organisation, 16 November 1945, 52 *UNTS* 275, Article I(1) [hereinafter "UNESCO Constitution"] [emphasis added].

5 Marrakesh Agreement Establishing the World Trade Organization, 15 April 1994, LT/UR/A/2, Preamble [hereinafter "Marrakesh Agreement"] [emphasis added].

6 *See* UNESCO Constitution, *supra* note 4, Article I(1); WTO, *10 Benefits of the WTO Trading System*, 2007, 2.

7 *See* UNESCO Constitution, *supra* note 4, Article I(1); Marrakesh Agreement, *supra* note 5, Preamble.

8 Convention on the Diversity of Cultural Expressions, *supra* note 1, Article 2(2).

9 Id., Article 2(8).

domestic regulatory objectives such as promoting culture may justify exceptions to prevailing obligations or 'disciplines' imposed on WTO Members in certain circumstances.

In the following sections, I examine some of the main ways in which culture and trade intersect in the WTO agreements, noting differences with the Convention on the Diversity of Cultural Expressions where relevant. I first address the key WTO disciplines affecting trade in goods and services that could conflict with certain cultural policy measures that a WTO Member might wish to impose (whether pursuant to Convention on the Diversity of Cultural Expressions provisions or otherwise), before turning to WTO 'exceptions' that may provide sufficient flexibility to allow such measures even where they would ordinarily violate the general disciplines. In this context, I am primarily examining the *General Agreement on Tariffs and Trade 1994* ("GATT 1994")[10] and the *General Agreement on Trade in Services* ("GATS"),[11] although I also mention the *Agreement on Subsidies and Countervailing Measures* ("SCM Agreement"),[12] the *Agreement on Agriculture*,[13] and the *Agreement on Safeguards*.[14] Other WTO agreements (not covered in this chapter) may also affect the relationship between trade and culture, including the *Agreement on Trade-Related Aspects of Intellectual Property Rights* ("TRIPS Agreement")[15] and the *Agreement on the Application of Sanitary and Phytosanitary Measures* ("SPS Agreement").[16]

This review demonstrates the many areas in which the Convention on the Diversity of Cultural Expressions and the WTO agreements overlap, in either conflicting or harmonious ways. The often complicated connections between the

---

10 *See* General Agreement on Tariffs and Trade 1994, 15 April 1995, *LT/UR/A-1A/1/GATT/1* [hereinafter "GATT 1994"].

11 *See* General Agreement on Trade in Services, 15 April 1994, *LT/UR/A-1B/S/1* [hereinafter "GATS"].

12 *See* Agreement on Subsidies and Countervailing Measures, 15 April 1994, *LT/UR/A-1A/9* [hereinafter "SCM Agreement"].

13 *See* Agreement on Agriculture, 15 April 1994, *LT/UR/A-1A/2.*

14 *See* Agreement on Safeguards, 15 April 1994, *LT/UR/A-1A/8.*

15 *See* Agreement on Trade-Related Aspects of Intellectual Property Rights, 15 April 1994, *LT/UR/A-1C/IP/1.* On this issue, *see, e.g.*, R. Coombe, "Protecting Cultural Industries to Promote Cultural Diversity: Dilemmas for International Policymaking Posed by the Recognition of Traditional Knowledge", in K. Maskus and J. Reichman (eds.), *International Public Goods and Transfer of Technology Under a Globalized Intellectual Property Regime*, 2005, 599; T. Broude, "Conflict and Complementarity in Trade, Cultural Diversity and Intellectual Property Rights", 2 *Asian Journal of WTO & International Health Law and Policy* 345 (2007); WTO, Council for Trade-Related Aspects of Intellectual Property Rights, "The Protection of Traditional Knowledge and Folklore: Summary of Issues Raised and Points Made – Note by the Secretariat (Revision)", *P/C/W/370/Rev.1* (9 March 2006); T. Broude, "Taking 'Trade and Culture' Seriously: Geographical Indications and Cultural Protection in WTO Law", 26 *University of Pennsylvania Journal of International Economic Law* 623 (2005).

16 *See* Agreement on the Application of Sanitary and Phytosanitary Measures, 15 April 1994, *LT/UR/A-1A/12.* On this issue, *see* M. Echols, *Food Safety and the WTO: The Interplay of Culture, Science and Technology*, 2001.

substantive rules of the two agreements would need to be untangled to determine whether a particular "cultural policy measure" proposed under the Convention on the Diversity of Cultural Expressions was consistent with the WTO agreements. Although it may be impossible to determine the outcome of such an exercise in advance, the wording under both treaties may be broad enough to prevent conflicts in most cases.

2. THE POTENTIAL CLASH REGARDING CULTURAL GOODS AND SERVICES

2.1. THE CULTURAL CHARACTER OF GOODS AND SERVICES

The Convention on the Diversity of Cultural Expressions defines '[c]ultural activities, goods and services' as those that "embody or convey cultural expressions, irrespective of the commercial value they may have."[17] This is an expansive definition, given that cultural expressions are defined by reference to cultural content, which "refers to the symbolic meaning, artistic dimension and cultural values that originate from or express cultural identities."[18] Evidently, no clear guideline determines whether a given good or service that might be traded subject to WTO rules is 'cultural' or not.[19] However, one might contend that GATT 1994 governs trade in tangible goods that embody or expose culture such as works of art, televisions, CDs, and books, as well as more mundane reflections of culture in the form of products such as food items and motor vehicles.[20] At the same time, the Agreement on Agriculture covers agricultural products that may be seen as protecting culture through, for example, the rural landscape or national staples. GATS regulates trade in cultural services such as film production, libraries, tourism and sports,[21] including (to a limited extent) the common practice of subsidizing these services. Disputes between WTO Members concerning goods or services that might be characterized as 'cultural'

---

17 Convention on the Diversity of Cultural Expressions, *supra* note 1, Article 4(4).

18 Id., Articles 4(2) and (3).

19 In addition, the categories of 'goods' and 'services' are sometimes vague and overlapping.

20 Goods are classified according to the nomenclature set out in the *International Convention on the Harmonized Commodity Description and Coding System*, 14 June 1983, 1503 *UNTS* 167, Annex.

21 Services are frequently classified according to the GATT Uruguay Round Group of Negotiations on Services. *See* WTO, Secretariat, "Services Sectoral Classification List – Note by the Secretariat", *MTN.GNS/W/120* (10 July 1991) (see especially sectors 1.F.r, 2.D, 9, 10) and its cross-references to UNITED NATIONS, "Central Product Classification Version 1.1", *Statistical Papers, Series M, No. 77* (2004).

have included *Canada – Periodicals*,[22] *Japan – Alcoholic Beverages II*,[23] and, more recently, *China – Publications and Audiovisual Products*.[24]

Below, I consider three key WTO disciplines under GATT 1994 and GATS that could create a potential clash with the Convention on the Diversity of Cultural Expressions: national treatment, most favoured nation (MFN) treatment, and market access.

2.2. NATIONAL TREATMENT

Non-discrimination is a central principle of WTO law, comprising two main prongs: national treatment and MFN treatment. National treatment is the obligation that could most obviously conflict with WTO Members' cultural policy measures. This essentially requires Members to treat other Members' products as well as their own. Under GATT 1994, Members should not apply internal taxes or charges to imports from other Members in excess of those applied to like domestic products.[25] Members must also accord such imports treatment no less favourable than that accorded to like domestic products.[26] Similarly, under GATS (in sectors where a Member has made commitments to provide national treatment), Members must accord services and service suppliers of other Members treatment no less favourable than that accorded to its own like services and service suppliers in respect of all measures affecting the supply of services.[27] This obligation aims to reduce market distortion and ensure that foreign and domestic production compete on an equal footing.

The WTO obligation to provide national treatment may clash with some WTO Members' desires to protect their domestic 'cultural' industries or products, as exhibited in the Convention on the Diversity of Cultural Expressions. Article 6(2) of the Convention on the Diversity of Cultural Expressions, for example, suggests that parties may wish to adopt measures that "provide opportunities … for the creation, production … and enjoyment of … domestic cultural activities, goods and services," that "provide domestic

22 *See* Appellate Body Report, "Canada – Certain Measures Concerning Periodicals", *WT/DS31/AB/R* (30 June 1997); Panel Report, "Canada – Certain Measures Concerning Periodicals", *WT/DS31/R* (14 March 1997).

23 *See* Appellate Body Report, "Japan – Taxes on Alcoholic Beverages", *WT/DS10/AB/R, WT/DS11/AB/R, WT/DS8/AB/R* (4 October 1996); Panel Report, "Japan – Taxes on Alcoholic Beverages", *WT/DS10/R, WT/DS11/R, WT/DS8/R* (11 July 1996).

24 *See* Appellate Body Report, "China – Measures Affecting Trading Rights and Distribution Services for Certain Publications and Audiovisual Entertainment Products", *WT/DS363/AB/R* (21 December 2009); Panel Report, "China – Measures Affecting Trading Rights and Distribution Services for Certain Publications and Audiovisual Entertainment Products", *WT/DS363/R* (12 August 2009).

25 *See* GATT 1994, *supra* note 10, Article III:2 (first sentence).

26 *See* id., Article III:4.

27 *See* GATS, *supra* note 11, Article XVII:1.

independent cultural industries… effective access to… means of production," or that are "aimed at nurturing and supporting artists and others." In the negotiations leading to GATS, many WTO Members apparently recognized the potential clash between cultural policy and WTO rules, at least in the context of audiovisual services, such that few made national treatment commitments in this sector.[28] Other exceptions exist under the WTO rules, such as a specific provision regarding cinematograph films and allowances for some subsidies, as discussed further below.

2.3. MOST FAVOURED NATION TREATMENT

MFN treatment plays a crucial role in the WTO system[29] because it essentially prevents Members from treating some Members better than others (or non-Members better than Members) in the context of trade. Under GATT 1994, where a Member grants a particular advantage to an import from, or export to, one country with respect to customs duties or regulations regarding importation or exportation, it must grant the same advantage to all other Members.[30] Under GATS, with respect to measures affecting trade in services, each Member must accord to services and service suppliers of all other Members treatment no less favourable than that it accords to like services and service suppliers of any other country (subject to any MFN exemptions it has specifically listed in its schedule).[31] In principle, the MFN rule means that even the smallest, poorest and weakest WTO Members reap the benefits of agreements reached through negotiations among the biggest, richest and strongest WTO Members.

The WTO obligation to provide MFN treatment may conflict with some Members' desires to promote culture through cooperative arrangements with other countries. The Convention on the Diversity of Cultural Expressions reflects this desire in Articles 12 to 16, which highlight the need for cross-border cooperation, especially in relation to developing countries. Under Article 12, parties agree to "endeavour to strengthen their bilateral, regional and international cooperation for the creation of conditions conducive to the promotion of the diversity of cultural expressions," and under Article 13 they

28 *See* WTO, Council for Trade in Services, "Audiovisual Services: Background Note by the Secretariat", *S/C/W/40*, §24 (15 June 1998). *See also* M. Roy, "Beyond the Main Screen: Audiovisual Services in PTAs", in J. A. Marchetti and M. Roy (eds.), *Opening Markets for Trade in Services: Countries and Sectors in Bilateral and WTO Negotiations*, 2009, 340.

29 *See, e.g.*, Appellate Body Report, "Canada – Certain Measures Affecting the Automotive Industry", *WT/DS139/AB/R, WT/DS142/AB/R*, §69 (19 June 2000); WTO, Consultative Board, "The Future of the WTO: Addressing Institutional Challenges in the New Millennium", 59 (2004), *available at* www.wto.org/english/thewto_e/10anniv_e/future_wto_e.pdf (last visited 2 February 2012).

30 *See* GATT 1994, *supra* note 10, Article I:1.

31 *See* GATS, *supra* note 11, Articles II:1 and II:2.

agree to "endeavour to integrate culture in their development policies." WTO Members seeking to comply with these kinds of provisions might face difficulties where this would mean providing trade benefits to one or more countries but not all WTO Members. Some WTO Members already dealt with this problem in negotiations leading to GATS, as shown (for example) by references to co-production agreements in some Members' list of MFN exemptions.[32] The other primary means of dealing with this potential conflict pursuant to the WTO rules are the exceptions for preferential trade agreements and tariff preferences for developing countries, as discussed further below.

2.4. MARKET ACCESS

The concept of market access in the WTO differs according to the context, but in general it refers to the ease with which a foreign product is able to enter the market or markets of another Member to compete with domestic products. In relation to goods, two of the most significant market barriers that the WTO rules address are tariffs (customs duties on imports) and quantitative restrictions (for example, export licences or maximum quotas on the number of imports of a particular product allowed in a given period). Under GATT 1994, each Member's Schedule includes extensive tariff 'bindings', representing the maximum tariff that that Member may apply to a particular type of good.[33] Broadly speaking, quantitative restrictions are prohibited under GATT 1994,[34] having been converted to tariffs during the Uruguay Round to increase transparency and predictability for commercial operators. The process of 'tariffication' was also designed to facilitate comparisons between different Members' levels of market access and to enable increasing market access through tariff reductions negotiated in the future.[35]

Tariffs are not generally applicable to services, due to technological limitations and the fact that services do not tend to cross the border in the same way as goods.[36] However, GATS contains a provision on market access that is broadly comparable to the GATT 1994 prohibition on quantitative restrictions. Under GATS Article XVI, where a Member has made a commitment to provide

32 *See, e.g.*, WTO, "India – Final List of Article II (MFN) Exemptions", *GATS/EL/42* (15 April 1994); WTO, "Canada – Final List of Article II (MFN) Exemptions", *GATS/EL/16* (15 April 1994).

33 *See* GATT 1994, *supra* note 10, Article II:1 (a).

34 *See* id., Article XI:1.

35 *See* B. Hoekman and M. Kostecki, *The Political Economy of the World Trading System: The WTO and Beyond*, 2nd ed., 2001, 148; J. Jackson, *The World Trading System: Law and Policy of International Economic Relations*, 2nd ed., 1997, 140.

36 *See* WTO Secretariat, *A Handbook on the GATS Agreement*, 2005, 17; A. Mattoo, "National Treatment in the GATS: Corner-Stone or Pandora's Box?", 31 *Journal of World Trade* 107, 113 (1997).

market access in a given sector, it must not maintain measures such as maximum quotas on the number of service suppliers, limitations on the total number of natural persons that may be employed in a particular service sector, or limitations on the participation of foreign capital in terms of maximum percentage limits on foreign shareholding.[37] In addition, GATS Article VI on 'domestic regulation' may also be viewed as governing market access, particularly given the major impact that regulations may have on the supply of services. For instance, Article VI imposes obligations on Members concerning the fair administration of "measures of general application affecting trade in services,"[38] the provision of tribunals for review of "administrative decisions affecting trade in services,"[39] and the application of "qualification requirements and procedures, technical standards and licensing requirements."[40] If unchecked, these kinds of measures (or their absence) could create barriers to trade, preventing services or service suppliers from entering the market.

As foreshadowed above, the Convention on the Diversity of Cultural Expressions includes as one of its 'guiding principles' the 'principle of equitable access', which recognises that "[e]quitable access to a rich and diversified range of cultural expressions from all over the world" is an "important elemen[t] for enhancing cultural diversity."[41] This principle suggests that Parties to the Convention on the Diversity of Cultural Expressions need not and should not hinder market access in order to promote cultural goals. On the other hand, the Convention on the Diversity of Cultural Expressions also hints at the possibility of *too much* market access, leading to a flood of cultural imports threatening the local culture. For example, under Article 8 of the Convention on the Diversity of Cultural Expressions, in "special situations where cultural expressions on its territory are at risk of extinction, under serious threat, or otherwise in need of urgent safeguarding," a Party may take "all appropriate measures to protect and preserve cultural expressions" consistent with the Convention on the Diversity of Cultural Expressions. In striving for cultural diversity, these different provisions demonstrate the difficulty in finding a middle ground between too much foreign culture and too little. Parties may therefore need to protect local cultural elements from foreign dominance while allowing sufficient intercultural dialogue for cultural development. If they choose to limit market access for cultural goods or services, they may face conflicts with their WTO obligations.

---

37 GATS Article XVI:2 lists these and other measures that a Member may not maintain where they have made a market access commitment, unless otherwise specified in its Schedule. Debate exists as to whether Article XVI:2 contains an exhaustive or non-exhaustive list. *See* Appellate Body Report, "United States – Measures Affecting the Cross-Border Supply of Gambling and Betting Services", *WT/DS267/AB/R*, §256 (3 March 2005).

38 GATS, *supra* note 11, Article VI:1.

39 Id., Article VI:2.

40 Id., Articles VI:4 and VI:5.

41 Convention on the Diversity of Cultural Expressions, *supra* note 1, Article 2 (7). *See also* id., Article 7 (1) (b).

3. MANAGING THE CLASH REGARDING CULTURAL GOODS AND SERVICES

Other parts of this book examine how to deal with a 'real' conflict between WTO law and the Convention on the Diversity of Cultural Expressions, relying in particular on Article 20 of the Convention and various rules of public international law. However, the presence of explicit exceptions in WTO law to the disciplines detailed in the previous section may resolve several potential clashes between the WTO agreements and the Convention on the Diversity of Cultural Expressions, avoiding the need to resort to Article 20 or other rules. In particular, this includes the allowance under WTO law for certain kinds of subsidies (often used in the cultural sector) and safeguards. In addition, the screen quotas exception under GATT 1994 and the general exceptions, development exceptions, and exceptions for preferential trade agreements under GATT 1994 and GATS may provide shelter for cultural policy measures taken pursuant to the Convention on the Diversity of Cultural Expressions. I discuss these exceptions in turn below.

3.1. SUBSIDIES

For many countries, subsidising local culture and the arts is an important means of promoting cultural diversity and development. This would ordinarily violate the obligation of national treatment, assuming that imported products are not subsidised (and are therefore treated less favourably than domestic products). However, many Members have long used subsidies in a range of industries, not just cultural, and the WTO rules reflect this. Under Article III:8(b) of GATT 1994, the national treatment obligation does not prevent Members from paying subsidies "exclusively to domestic producers." However, Members paying subsidies must comply with other detailed obligations under the SCM Agreement.[42] In particular, a general prohibition is imposed on export subsidies (i.e., subsidies contingent on export performance) and import substitution subsidies (i.e., subsidies contingent on the use of domestic over imported goods).[43] Members may also face dispute settlement challenges or countervailing duties where their 'specific'[44] subsidies cause certain adverse effects to other Members or their industries.[45]

---

42 Subsidies disciplines also apply under the Agreement on Agriculture with respect to certain products.

43 *See* SCM Agreement, *supra* note 12, Article 3.1.

44 *See* id., Article 2 (that is, specific to an enterprise or industry or a group of them).

45 *See* id., Articles 5 and 15.

In the context of services, the 'exception' for subsidies is less clear. GATS contains no equivalent to Article III:8(b), meaning that where a Member has made a national treatment commitment in a given sector it must provide subsidies in that sector on a non-discriminatory basis (to its own services and service suppliers and to the services and service suppliers of other Members alike), unless otherwise indicated in its Schedule.[46] GATS Article XV provides for the WTO Members to negotiate to develop disciplines on services subsidies (which might include an explicit exemption from the national treatment obligation under certain conditions), but the Members have not yet reached agreement in this area.[47]

Article 6(2)(d) of the Convention on the Diversity of Cultural Expressions mentions "measures aimed at providing public financial assistance" as an example of the kinds of measures that a Party may wish to adopt in order to protect and promote "the diversity of cultural expressions within its territory."[48] In the case of goods, such measures would not violate the national treatment obligation even if provided to local producers only, but they would still need to comply with the SCM Agreement assuming that they fell within the definition of a subsidy in that agreement.[49] Subsidies for agricultural production would need to comply with the Agreement on Agriculture in addition to the SCM Agreement. This means that the 'exception' for subsidies under GATT 1994 does not give a Convention on the Diversity of Cultural Expressions Party that is also a WTO Member free rein to subsidise in the name of culture. In the case of services, no such exception even exists, so a Party wishing to subsidise only its own services would need to rely on any relevant national treatment limitations in its Schedule or the absence of a national treatment commitment in the relevant sector.

3.2. SAFEGUARDS

Article XIX of GATT 1994 and the Agreement on Safeguards allow Members to impose increased tariffs or quantitative restrictions on imports of particular products from all countries[50] where they are being imported "in such increased

[46] *See* GATT, Uruguay Round Group of Negotiations on Services, "Scheduling of Initial Commitments in Trade in Services: Explanatory Note", *MTN.GNS/W/164*, §9 (3 September 1993); WTO, Council for Trade in Services, "Guidelines for the Scheduling of Specific Commitments under the General Agreement on Trade in Services (GATS): Adopted by the Council for Trade in Services on 23 March 2001", *S/L/92*, §16 (28 March 2001).

[47] *See* WTO, Working Party on GATS Rules, "Report of the Meeting of 22 June 2011: Note by the Secretariat", *S/WPGR/M/74*, at 21–43 (19 July 2011); WTO, Working Party on GATS Rules, "Report of the Meeting of 17 September 2007: Note by the Secretariat", *S/WPGR/M/59*, §§9–15 (2 October 2007).

[48] Convention on the Diversity of Cultural Expressions, *supra* note 1, Article 6(1).

[49] *See* SCM Agreement, *supra* note 12, Article 1.1.

[50] *See* Agreement on Safeguards, *supra* note 14, Article 2.2.

quantities... and under such conditions as to cause or threaten to cause serious injury to the domestic industry that produces like or directly competitive products."[51] In order to rely on this exception to the tariff bindings and the prohibition on quantitative restrictions mentioned above, the Member must conduct a thorough investigation in accordance with specific WTO rules. No such exception exists in the current GATS, although Article X foreshadows negotiations on this issue, which are still continuing after four years.[52]

The term 'safeguard' calls to mind Article 8 of the Convention on the Diversity of Cultural Expressions, as already mentioned above. A Party to the Convention on the Diversity of Cultural Expressions might wish to impose safeguards on the basis that a flood of imports was injuring a domestic cultural industry and thereby threatening local culture. Although the WTO agreements provide some flexibility in relation to safeguards, the WTO rules are quite stringent and the Party (if also a WTO Member) would need to take considerable care to avoid violating them.

In the services context, the Party would need to rely on some other WTO exception, since 'safeguards' as understood in WTO parlance are not yet available. In the goods context, Members and commentators alike have criticised the way in which the Appellate Body has interpreted the WTO rules, such that Members find it extremely difficult to comply with their obligations when imposing safeguards.[53] In particular, the Appellate Body has held that Members must comply not only with the Agreement on Safeguards but also with Article XIX of GATT 1994, including by demonstrating that the increase in imports results from "unforeseen developments."[54] Therefore, it would not be sufficient to point to an unexpected surge in cultural imports without identifying some separate unforeseen development leading to that surge. Perhaps an unforeseen change in consumer preferences or a technological development (for instance, making it easier to access cultural products remotely) could qualify. In addition,

51 Id., Article 2.1.

52 *See, e.g.*, WTO, Working Party on GATS Rules, "Report of the Meeting of 22 June 2011: Note by the Secretariat", *S/WPGR/M/74*, at 2–17 (19 July 2011); WTO, Working Party on GATS Rules, "Report of the Meeting of 17 September 2007: Note by the Secretariat", *S/WPGR/M/59*, at 2–5 (2 October 2007). Some Members seem doubtful, however, as to the feasibility of an ESM for services: *see* WTO, Working Party on GATS Rules, "Report of the Meeting of 10 November 2009: Note by the Secretariat", *S/WPGR/M/66*, at 8 (25 January 2010).

53 *See, e.g.*, WTO, Dispute Settlement Body, "Minutes of Meeting Held in the Centre William Rappard on 10 December 2003", *WT/DSB/M/160*, at 32–3 (27 January 2004); G. Grossman and A. Sykes, "United States – Definitive Safeguard Measures on Imports of Certain Steel Products", 6 *World Trade Review* 89, 119–22 (2007).

54 *See* Panel Report, "Argentina – Definitive Safeguard Measure on Imports of Preserved Peaches", *WT/DS238/R*, §7.13 (14 February 2003); Appellate Body Report, "United States – Safeguard Measures on Imports of Fresh, Chilled or Frozen Lamb Meat from New Zealand and Australia", *WT/DS177/AB/R*, *WT/DS178/AB/R*, §68 (1 May 2001); Appellate Body Report, "Argentina – Safeguard Measures on Imports of Footwear (EC)", *WT/DS121/AB/R*, §90 (14 December 1999).

although safeguards constitute 'emergency' action under Article XIX of GATT 1994, Members are generally expected to examine trends in data covering a period of preceding years in determining whether safeguards are available and appropriate.[55] This might make safeguards ineffective in responding to the 'urgent' kinds of situations foreseen in Article 8 of the Convention on the Diversity of Cultural Expressions.

3.3. ARTICLE IV(A) OF GATT 1994

GATT 1994 and GATS contain a range of other exceptions that might enable Members to adopt cultural policy measures pursuant to the Convention on the Diversity of Cultural Expressions without violating their WTO obligations, even where the measures would otherwise conflict with the disciplines described above. Most of these exceptions are not specifically 'cultural', but some are, notably Article IV(a) of GATT 1994, which allows Members to impose minimum quotas on the exhibition of "cinematograph films of national origin", contrary to the national treatment obligation.[56] GATS contains no analogous exception, although the inherent flexibility of GATS (under which Members may choose to make national treatment and market access commitments in particular sectors) may make an Article IV(a) equivalent less necessary.

Nevertheless, this difference between GATT 1994 and GATS creates much uncertainty. For instance, if a Member that had made a national treatment commitment under GATS in respect of audiovisual services imposed a screen quota falling within Article IV(a) of GATT 1994, would GATT 1994 and GATS apply independently (resulting in a GATS violation but no GATT 1994 violation), or would Article IV(a) imply no violation of either agreement, or would the GATS commitment supersede Article IV(a) to create a violation under both?[57] These questions exacerbate the difficulties arising from the difference between goods and services,[58] the application of Article IV to television as opposed to cinema,[59] and the broader relationship between the Convention on the Diversity

55 *See* Appellate Body Report, "Argentina – Safeguard Measures on Imports of Footwear (EC)", *WT/DS121/AB/R*, §129–131 (14 December 1999). *See also* Appellate Body Report, "United States – Definitive Safeguard Measures on Imports of Certain Steel Products", *WT/DS248/AB/R, WT/DS249/AB/R, WT/DS251/AB/R, WT/DS252/AB/R, WT/DS253/AB/R, WT/DS254/AB/R, WT/DS258/AB/R, WT/DS259/AB/R*, §346 and §§354–355 (10 November 2003).

56 GATT 1994 Article IV(c) provides a limited exception for screen quotas for films from other countries, contrary to the MFN obligation.

57 P. Mavroidis, *The General Agreement on Tariffs and Trade: A Commentary*, 2005, 278 (suggesting that Article IV of GATT 1994 "should have been superseded by the advent of the GATS").

58 See Voon, *supra* note 3, at 70–5.

59 GATT, "Application of GATT to International Trade in Television Programmes: Report of the Working Party", *L/1741*, Annex 1 (13 March 1962); B. de Witte, "Trade in Culture: International Legal Regimes and EU Constitutional Values", in G. de Búrca and J. Scott (eds.),

of Cultural Expressions and WTO law. As a result, a Member wishing to impose a screen quota in order to promote the values of the Convention on the Diversity of Cultural Expressions could not be sure how a WTO Panel or the Appellate Body would approach it.

3.4. GENERAL EXCEPTIONS

GATT 1994 and GATS both contain a list of 'general exceptions', some of which might apply to cultural policy measures. These include, in particular:

- Article XX(f) of GATT 1994 (for measures imposed "for the protection of national treasures of artistic, historic or archaeological value");
- Article XX(a) of GATT 1994 (for measures "necessary to protect public morals") and Article XIV(a) of GATS (for measures "necessary to protect public morals" or "to maintain public order");
- Article XX(b) of GATT 1994 and Article XIV(b) of GATS (for measures "necessary to protect human, animal or plant life or health"); and
- Article XX(d) of GATT 1994 and Article XIV(c) of GATS (for measures "necessary to secure compliance with laws or regulations which are not inconsistent with the provisions of this Agreement").

Paragraph (f) of Article XX of GATT 1994 may be too limited to justify cultural policy measures relating to contemporary creative productions, such as films or television programs. In addition, the absence of a corresponding provision in GATS means that services aspects of cultural products could not be protected as national treasures.

A more useful exception for cultural goods may be Article XX(a) of GATT 1994. In *China – Publications and Audiovisual Products*,[60] China sought to justify various restrictive and discriminatory measures imposed on foreign publications and audiovisual products by invoking GATT 1994 Article XX(a).[61] China argued that "reading materials and finished audiovisual products are ... cultural goods" and these are "of a unique kind with a potentially serious negative impact on public morals".[62] The Panel and Appellate Body found that the

The EU and the WTO: Legal and Constitutional Issues, 2001, 237, 245–46. For further general discussion of Article IV of GATT 1994, *see* L. Ehring, "GATT Article IV", in R. Wolfrum and P.-T. Stoll (eds.), *Max Planck Commentaries on World Trade Law*, Vol. 5, 2009.

60 *See* T. Voon, "China and Cultural Products at the WTO", 37(3) *Legal Issues of Economic Integration* 253 (2010).

61 Unusually, China invoked GATT Article XX(a) to justify violations of its Accession Protocol rather than violations of GATT 1994.

62 Panel Report, "China – Measures Affecting Trading Rights and Distribution Services for Certain Publications and Audiovisual Entertainment Products", *WT/DS363/R*, §7.751 (12 August 2009).

relevant measures were not justified under this exception in the circumstances because they did not meet the necessity test in Article XX(a).[63] Nevertheless, significantly from the perspective of cultural policy, the Panel held, and the Appellate Body did not question, that monitoring the content of cultural products and preventing their importation if they contain prohibited content are measures to protect public morals.[64]

The Convention on the Diversity of Cultural Expressions recognises the relationship between cultural diversity and human rights, including "freedom of expression, information and communication, as well as the ability of individuals to choose cultural expressions."[65] Paragraphs (a) and (b) of Article XX of GATT 1994 and of Article XIV of GATS are more likely to cover cultural policy measures if these provisions are seen as promoting human rights, and cultural rights in particular. This would be consistent with a 'human rights' approach to interpreting WTO rules, which several international bodies have proposed.[66] The exceptions regarding securing compliance with other laws may assist where cultural policy measures enforce intellectual property laws protecting cultural property, as discussed further below. However, a Member wishing to rely on any of these general exceptions would need to establish not only that their cultural policy measure fell within the relevant paragraph, but also that it met the stringent requirements of the introductory paragraph (the so-called 'chapeau') of Article XX of GATT 1994 or Article XIV of GATS,[67] as the case may be. This makes it harder to predict whether a given cultural policy measure would be saved under these provisions.

---

63 Appellate Body Report, "China – Measures Affecting Trading Rights and Distribution Services for Certain Publications and Audiovisual Entertainment Products", *WT/DS363/AB/R*, §415(e) (21 December 2009); Panel Report, "China – Measures Affecting Trading Rights and Distribution Services for Certain Publications and Audiovisual Entertainment Products", *WT/DS363/R*, §7.913 (12 August 2009).

64 Panel Report, "China – Measures Affecting Trading Rights and Distribution Services for Certain Publications and Audiovisual Entertainment Products", *WT/DS363/R*, §7.766 (12 August 2009).

65 Convention on the Diversity of Cultural Expressions, *supra* note 1, Article 2(1).

66 *See, e.g.*, UN, Commission on Human Rights, "Globalization and its Impact on the Full Enjoyment of Human Rights: Report of the High Commissioner for Human Rights Submitted in Accordance with Commission on Human Rights Resolution 2001/32", *E/CN.4/2002/54*, §10 (15 January 2002); UN, International Law Commission, "Fragmentation of International Law: Difficulties Arising from the Diversification and Expansion of International Law – Report of the Study Group – Finalized by Martti Koskenniemi", *A/CN.4/L.682*, §170 (13 April 2006). *See also* G. Marceau, "WTO Dispute Settlement and Human Rights", 13(4) *European Journal of International Law* 753, 779 (2002).

67 *See, e.g.*, Appellate Body Report, "United States – Import Prohibition of Certain Shrimp and Shrimp Products", *WT/DS58/AB/R*, §§148–151 and §§156–159 (12 October 1998); Appellate Body Report, "Brazil – Measures Affecting Imports of Retreaded Tyres", *WT/DS332/AB/R*, §§224–232 (3 December 2007).

3.5. SPECIAL AND DIFFERENTIAL TREATMENT

In numerous provisions, the Convention on the Diversity of Cultural Expressions highlights the need to pay special attention to developing countries. For example, its objectives include "to reaffirm the importance of the link between culture and development for all countries, particularly for developing countries" and "to strengthen international cooperation... with a view... to enhancing the capacities of developing countries in order to protect and promote the diversity of cultural expressions."[68] Similarly, the WTO agreements reflect a principle of 'special and differential treatment' for developing countries,[69] in recognition of the "need for positive efforts designed to ensure that developing countries, and especially the least developed among them, secure a share in the growth in international trade commensurate with the needs of their economic development."[70] Accordingly, several WTO provisions provide greater flexibility to developing country Members in complying with WTO disciplines or allow Members to accord preferential treatment to developing country Members contrary to the MFN obligation.[71]

Unfortunately, this common spirit of the two agreements would not necessarily translate into uniform treatment of a given measure. This is primarily because special and differential treatment in the WTO is often limited and unenforceable (which is why Members continue to negotiate on this issue).[72] Where, for instance, a Convention on the Diversity of Cultural Expressions Party wished to assist a developing country to strengthen its cultural industries in accordance with Article 14(a) by providing "preferential treatment to ... cultural goods and services from developing countries,"[73] if this violated the MFN obligation the Party would need to point to a specific special and differential treatment provision (assuming no other exception was available) in order to justify its conduct. But such provisions cover only specific areas and might not be relevant to the kinds of measures the Party wished to adopt. Their applicability might also depend on the extent to which WTO Panels and the

68 Convention on the Diversity of Cultural Expressions, *supra* note 1, Articles 1(f) and 1(i).

69 *See, generally*, A. Mitchell, "A Legal Principle of Special & Differential Treatment for WTO Disputes?" 5 *World Trade Review* 445 (2006).

70 Marrakesh Agreement, *supra* note 5, Preamble.

71 *See, e.g.*, SCM Agreement, *supra* note 12, Article 27; WTO, "Decision on Differential and More Favourable Treatment, Reciprocity, and Fuller Participation of Developing Countries", *L/4903, BISD 26S/203* (28 November 1979) (known as the 'Enabling Clause').

72 WTO, Ministerial Conference, "Ministerial Declaration adopted on 14 November 2001", *WT/MIN(01)/DEC/1*, §44 (20 November 2001); WTO, Ministerial Conference, "Implementation-Related Issues and Concerns – Decision of 14 November 2001", *WT/MIN (01) 17*, §12.1 (i) (20 November 2001); WTO, General Council, "Decision Adopted by the General Council on 1 August 2004", *WT/L/579*, §1(d) (2 August 2004); WTO, Ministerial Conference, "Doha Work Programme: Ministerial Declaration Adopted on 18 December 2005", *WT/MIN(05)/DEC* §§35–8 (22 December 2005).

73 Convention on the Diversity of Cultural Expressions, *supra* note 1, Article 16.

Appellate Body were prepared to interpret 'development' as involving cultural aspects, in the way suggested by the Convention on the Diversity of Cultural Expressions.[74]

3.6. PREFERENTIAL TRADE AGREEMENTS

Just as a Convention on the Diversity of Cultural Expressions Party might wish to collaborate with a developing country for cultural purposes associated with development,[75] so too might a Party wish to collaborate with any Member or country to promote cultural diversity and exchange in accordance with the Convention on the Diversity of Cultural Expressions principles (for example, by providing tax incentives for co-produced films).[76] Again, this might violate the MFN obligation under WTO law. Collaboration of this kind might be justified if the Party had scheduled a relevant MFN exemption under Article II:2 of GATS or if it fell within the exception for preferential trade agreements (PTAs) under GATT 1994[77] or GATS.[78] However, little jurisprudence exists on the meaning of the PTA exceptions,[79] and the cultural aims of these projects are unlikely to affect their analysis under these provisions, rendering their WTO-consistency uncertain.

4. CONCLUSION

In explaining just some of the commonalities and discrepancies between the Convention on the Diversity of Cultural Expressions and the WTO agreements, this chapter has revealed the close and complex relationship between these two treaties. Although, at a conceptual level, both recognise the need for balance

---

[74] For instance, the Appellate Body has read the Enabling Clause as allowing Members to differentiate between beneficiaries of their "Generalized System of Preferences (GSP)" schemes (that is, to provide more favorable tariff treatment to certain products from certain beneficiaries) in order to respond positively to particular development, financial or trade needs: Appellate Body Report, "European Commission – Conditions for Granting Tariff Preferences to Developing Countries", *WT/DS246/AB/R* §§160–4 (7 April 2004). Cultural needs could fall within the notion of development needs in this context.

[75] *See* Convention on the Diversity of Cultural Expressions, *supra* note 1, Article 14(a)(vi).

[76] *See* id., Article 12(e).

[77] GATT 1994, *supra* note 10, Article XXIV.

[78] GATS, *supra* note 11, Article V:1.

[79] *But see* Appellate Body Report, "Turkey – Restrictions on Imports of Textiles and Other Clothing Products", *WT/DS34/AB/R*, §58 (22 October 1999); Panel Report, "Brazil – Measures Affecting Imports of Retreaded Tyres", *WT/DS332/R*, §7.274 and §7.284 (12 June 2007). *See also* N. Lockhart and A. Mitchell, "Regional Trade Agreements under GATT 1994: An Exception and its Limits", in A. Mitchell (ed.), *Challenges and Prospects for the WTO*, 2005, 217.

between trade and exchange on the one hand, and social policies and goals such as cultural diversity on the other hand, the more concrete provisions are difficult to reconcile. A WTO Member that is also a Party to the Convention on the Diversity of Cultural Expressions would face considerable uncertainty in attempting to further the priorities of the Convention on the Diversity of Cultural Expressions without acting inconsistently with WTO law. This uncertainty stems in large part from the ambiguity of many WTO provisions, as well as the absence of clear interpretations of those provisions from either the WTO's 'judicial' arm (Panels and the Appellate Body) or its 'parliamentary' arm (the General Council and Ministerial Conference).[80] Nevertheless, the substantive rules of the Convention on the Diversity of Cultural Expressions and the WTO agreements certainly do not stand in clear conflict. Ultimately, the vague boundaries of these treaties' provisions may enable States to navigate successfully through their rights and obligations under both at the same time.

80 Under Marrakesh Agreement Article IX:2, the General Council and the Ministerial Conference have exclusive authority to adopt interpretations of the WTO agreements. However, in practice, Panels and the Appellate Body interpret WTO law in applying it to cases that come before them, and their reports have some precedential weight.

INTELLECTUAL PROPERTY AND CULTURAL DIVERSITY

Two Views on the Relationship between Market and Culture

Branislav HAZUCHA*

1. INTRODUCTION

The relationship between intellectual property and cultural diversity is as controversial as defining and measuring cultural diversity.[1] The actual place of copyright[2] and other intellectual property policies in cultural policy is the issue

---

* LL.M. 1999 (Comenius University); Dr. jur. 2002 (Trnava University); LL.D. 2005 (Kyushu University); Associate Professor, Hokkaido University School of Law. The author would like to acknowledge, with thanks, the insights and comments of Yoshiyuki Tamura, Nobuko Kawashima and other participants of Global COE Symposium on "Proprietary versus Shared Creativity in Hybrid Economy: The Role of Intellectual Property in Cultural Policy" organised by the Hokkaido University Research Institute for Information Law & Policy. All the remaining shortcomings and omissions are of the author's sole responsibility. The research upon which this Chapter is based has been generously supported by the Matsushita International Foundation Research Grant No. 09–016.

1 Convention on the Protection and Promotion of the Diversity of Cultural Expressions, Article 4(1), 20 October 2005, U.N. Doc. CLT-2005/CONVENTION DIVERSITE-CULT REV., *available at* http://unesdoc.unesco.org/images/0014/001429/142919e.pdf (last visited 2 February 2012) [hereinafter "Convention on the Diversity of Cultural Expressions"] (defining 'cultural diversity' as "the manifold ways in which the cultures of groups and societies find expression"). For discussions on defining and measuring cultural diversity, *see*, *e.g.*, F. BENHAMOU, R.G. FLÔRES JR. and S. PELTIER, "The Use of Diversity in Cultural Economics: Theoretical and Applied Considerations" (11–13 December 2008) (paper presented at "Conference on Models of Cultural Dynamics and Diversity", Paris School of Economics, Paris, France), *available at* www.cepr.org/meets/wkcn/2/2393/papers/Benhamou.pdf (last visited 2 February 2012); UNESCO INSTITUTE FOR STATISTICS, *Measuring the Diversity of Cultural Expressions: Applying the Stirling Model of Diversity in Culture*, 2011, *available at* www.uis.unesco.org/Library/Documents/tp6-11.pdf (last visited 2 February 2012); H. RANAIVOSON, "Measuring Cultural Diversity: A Review of Existing Definitions" (2007), *available at* www.uis.unesco.org/culture/Documents/Ranaivoson.pdf (last visited 2 February 2012); F. BENHAMOU and S. PELTIER, "How Should Cultural Diversity Be Measured? An Application Using the French Publishing Industry", 31 *J. Cult. Econ.* 85 (2007).

2 For the purposes of this Chapter, the term 'copyright' is used in a broad sense as used in common law countries, where it covers economic rights of authors, performers, phonogram

where many scholars and countries diverge in their approaches to the role of intellectual property rights as a means for the protection and promotion of cultural diversity. In general, these approaches can be divided into two groups pursuant to the importance and role of the market and state interventions in the production of cultural goods and services.[3] This divide is also reflected in individual countries' position towards the *2005 UNESCO Convention on the Protection and Promotion of the Diversity of Cultural Expressions* ("Convention on the Diversity of Cultural Expressions").[4] On the one side, the group of countries led by the United States advocates a free market approach without any state intervention. On the other side, the remaining countries, among them France and Canada, search for some form of protecting their domestic cultural industries[5] against the dominance of foreign multinational enterprises in their national markets.

This Chapter scrutinises both of the abovementioned approaches to the role of intellectual property as a means of protection and promotion of cultural diversity in order to check their efficiency and impact on cultural diversity on the local, regional and global level. Its main aim is to draw attention to the sometimes overlooked drawbacks of each currently advocated solution. By identifying the weak points of both approaches, the Chapter attempts to point out their innate shortcomings and the necessity of preventing their negative consequences in order to efficiently achieve the adequate protection and promotion of cultural diversity.

Section 1 identifies possible tensions which may occur during the implementation of the Convention on the Diversity of Cultural Expressions in the event that it clashes with some international intellectual property treaties. To properly understand such tensions and frictions, it is essential to look at how the position of intellectual property in protecting and promoting cultural diversity changed during the drafting of the Convention, and to what extent this change can affect its implementation.

---

producers and broadcasting organisations. Accordingly, it covers the exclusive economic rights of author's rights and neighbouring rights as classified in civil law countries.

3 Due to the focus of this Chapter on the role of intellectual property as a means for the protection and promotion of cultural diversity, the term 'cultural goods and services' is used in a narrow sense covering the goods, the production and distribution of which rely on intellectual property protection. For discussion on defining 'cultural goods', *see, e.g.*, R. McCain, "Defining Cultural and Artistic Goods", in V.A. Ginsburgh and D. Throsby (eds.), *Handbook of the Economics of Art and Culture*, 2006, 147.

4 Convention on the Diversity of Cultural Expressions, *supra* note 1.

5 In literature, the terms 'cultural industries' and 'creative industries' are used as interchangeable or partially overlapping notions. For discussion on defining one or the other term; *see, e.g.*, D. Throsby, "Modelling the Cultural Industries", 14 *Int'l J. Cult. Pol'y* 217 (2008); J. Hartley, "Creative Industries", in J. Hartley (ed.), *Creative Industries*, 2005, 1; A.C. Pratt, "Cultural Industries and Public Policy: An Oxymoron", 11 *Int'l J. Cult. Pol'y* 31 (2005); N. Garnham, "Afterword: The Cultural Commodity and Cultural Policy", in S. Selwood (ed.), *The UK Cultural Sector: Profile and Policy Issues*, 2001, 445; J. O'Connor, "The Definition of the Cultural Industries", 2(3) *Eur. J. Arts Educ.* 15 (2000).

Sections 2 and 3 then sketch in more details the two contravening approaches towards the role of intellectual property in protecting and promoting cultural diversity. Section 2 scrutinises the so-called 'pure market' approach. It also examines the critique of intellectual property regimes expressed by the opponents of this approach, who lay stress on the incompatibility of their operation with cultural diversity. In order to partially or completely rebut such critiques, it is crucial to analyse the individual features of intellectual property regimes to see whether they can play any role in the protection and promotion of cultural diversity.

Section 3 focuses on the various state interventions aiming to support local cultural industries. In order to enquire into the efficiency of such protection measures, it is vital to properly understand the reasons for U.S. dominance in the international trade of cultural goods and services, because it is the flooding of local markets with foreign, often U.S. cultural production,[6] which commonly triggers the adoption of protectionist measures by affected countries. Among other protectionist measures, many national intellectual property regimes embody several mechanisms and schemes, which aim at moderating the inefficiencies of, and the perceived distributive injustices caused by, intellectual property regimes either by collecting and redistributing certain funds to individual authors, performers and other artists, or by providing public funds to support local cultural production. This Section thus scrutinises the efficiency of such redistributive mechanisms and schemes. It also tests the possibility of accommodating the claims for providing cultural traditions with sufficient protection against their misappropriation within intellectual property regimes as a part of achieving the efficient protection and promotion of cultural diversity.

This Chapter concludes by stressing the importance of striking an appropriate and adequate balance between granting individual intellectual property rights on the one side and state interventions, such as screen quotas, taxes, subsides or other types of redistributive mechanisms and schemes, on the other, in searching for an efficient cultural policy to protect and promote cultural diversity on the local, regional and international level.

2. INTELLECTUAL PROPERTY AND THE CONVENTION ON THE DIVERSITY OF CULTURAL EXPRESSIONS

The current discussions on the relationship between intellectual property and cultural diversity circle around three main premises expressed in Article 8 of the

---

6 For the purposes of this Chapter, the term 'cultural production' is used in a narrow sense covering mainly the production of cultural goods and services which relies on intellectual property protection.

2001 UNESCO Universal Declaration on Cultural Diversity.[7] First, there is an urgent need to achieve sufficient "diversity of the supply of creative works".[8] Second, cultural goods and services should not "be treated as mere commodities or consumer goods" due to their "specificity".[9] Third, particular attention should also be paid to the "due recognition of the rights of authors and artists".[10] While the countries mainly exporting cultural goods and services stress the third premise and suggest that this measure is crucial and sufficient for achieving cultural diversity worldwide, countries flooded by foreign cultural production draw attention to the first two premises and see the solution in the adoption of measures protecting their local industries.

The former so-called 'pure market' approach heavily relies on the operation of the free market without any state intervention beyond setting up the rules of the game, including the adoption of intellectual property legislation. Granting some intellectual property rights, such as copyright, but not others (*e.g.*, *droit de suite* or geographical indications),[11] is supposed to be essential and satisfactory for the protection and promotion of cultural diversity.[12] Any other state intervention which would moderate the operation of the market is seen as causing only detrimental market distortions. The supporters of this approach thus warn against any form of state intervention, such as screen quotas, subsidies or taxes.[13] They criticise state protectionism for overprotection of local

7 *See* Universal Declaration on Cultural Diversity, 2 November 2001, 41 *I.L.M.* 57 (2001).

8 *See* id., Article 8.

9 Id.

10 Id.

11 While geographical indications or *droit de suite* (resale right) are recognised within the European Union, there has been considerable opposition against their adoption in the United States. For instance, during negotiations on the TRIPS Agreement, *infra* note 51, a considerable divide occurred between the United States and European countries with regard to the protection of geographical indications and its scope; *see, e.g.*, S.K. Sell, *Private Power, Public Law: The Globalization of Intellectual Property Rights*, 2003, 112. *Droit de suite* is even more controversial. Its adoption was and is still contentious in many countries, especially in those which have a significant stake in art auctions, such as the United States and United Kingdom; *see, e.g.*, M.E. Price, "Government Policy and Economic Security for Artists: The Case for the Droit de Suite", 77 *Yale L.J.* 1333 (1968); S. Perlmutter, "Resale Royalties for Artists: An Analysis of the Register of Copyright's Report", 16 *Colum.-VLA J.L. & Arts* 395 (1993); M.B. Reddy, "The Droit de Suite: Why American Fine Artists Should Have the Right to a Resale Royalty", 15 *Loy. L.A. Ent. L. Rev.* 59 (1995). For more detailed analysis of *droit de suite, see, e.g.*, N. Kawashima, "The Artist's Resale Right Revisited: A New Perspective", 14 *Int'l J. Cult. Pol'y* 299 (2008); J.H. Merryman, "The Proposed Generalisation of the Droit de Suite in the European Communities", 1 *I.P.Q.* 16 (1997).

12 For the role of copyright in protecting and promoting cultural diversity, *see* H. Wager, "Copyright and the Promotion of Cultural Diversity", in H. Schneider and P. Van den Bossche (eds.), *Protection of Cultural Diversity from a European and International Perspective*, 2008, 193 (analysing the relation between trade and culture, and the current treatment of cultural products within the World Trade Organisation regime).

13 *See* General Agreement on Tariffs and Trade, Article IV, 30 October 1947, 55 *U.N.T.S.* 194 (1947) [hereinafter "GATT"] (allowing screen quotas for cinematograph films); Convention on the Diversity of Cultural Expressions, *supra* note 1, Articles 5–8 (allowing states to adopt

industries, which is not deemed to be helping local production in any way. Conversely, state protection is considered only as causing harm to local industries by having a considerable negative impact on their incentives to compete with foreign competitors. Heavily subsidised entrepreneurs rarely have any sufficient motivation to behave competitively due to state paternalism and a lack of exposure to competition in markets distorted in that way.[14] The critics of state protectionism therefore emphasise that at the end of the day, the consumers are not able to benefit from the higher cultural diversity supposedly stimulated by state protectionism, since they are provided only with a variety of low quality cultural goods and services, which are unable to compete with cultural production supplied by other unsubsidised competitors.[15]

On the other hand, the approach supported by countries flooded with foreign cultural production is the critique of solutions based only on granting intellectual property rights to cultural goods and services, and merely relying upon the free market to guarantee a sufficient assortment of cultural production to satisfy consumers' demands for product variety. Its advocates blame intellectual property regimes for the current state of copyright and other intellectual property industries,[16] be they record labels, studios or broadcasting networks.[17] Due to the high degree of worldwide horizontal and vertical integration, a handful of multinational enterprises control substantial portions of international trade in sound recordings and audiovisual cultural products and services.[18] The considerable decline of market shares held by local artists,

various measures aiming to protect and promote cultural diversity and local cultural expressions). *See also generally* R.J. Neuwirth, *The Cultural Industries in International Trade Law: Insights from the NAFTA, the WTO and the EU*, 2006; T. Voon, *Cultural Products and the World Trade Organization*, 2007; L.R. Hanania, *Diversité culturelle et droit international du commerce*, 2009.

14 *See, e.g.*, T. Cowen, "French Kiss-Off: How Protectionism Has Hurt French Films", *Reason*, July 1998, *available at* www.reason.com/news/show/30691.html (last visited 2 February 2012) (suggesting that "[i]f Europeans treat their films as weak, those films will become permanently weak"); J. Buchsbaum, "'The *Exception Culturelle* is Dead.' Long Live Cultural Diversity: French Cinema and the New Resistance", 47 *Framework: The Journal of Cinema and Media* 5 (2006) (analysing and criticising the situation in the French movie industry); S.A. Pager, "Beyond Culture vs. Commerce: Decentralizing Cultural Protection to Promote Diversity Through Trade", 31 *NW. J. Int'l L. & Bus.* 63, 75–97 (2011) (criticising European state patronage).

15 *See, e.g.*, Cowen, *supra* note 14.

16 As the terms 'cultural industries' or 'creative industries' also cover industries, the business models of which are not directly built on copyrights or other types of intellectual property rights, the term 'copyright industries' or 'intellectual property industries' will be used for the purposes of this Chapter. This term refers to various entertainment and media industries which heavily rely on the commercial use of copyrighted works, such as newspapers, journals, books, sound recordings, movies or video games, and of other types of intellectual property.

17 *See, e.g.*, F. Macmillan, "The UNESCO Convention as a New Incentive to Protect Cultural Diversity", in Schneider and Van den Bossche, *supra* note 12, 163, 169–73.

18 For an excellent outline of horizontal and vertical integration, *see* C. Wright, "Reconciling Cultural Diversity and Free Trade in the Digital Age: A Cultural Analysis of the International Trade in Content Items", 41 *Akron L. Rev.* 399 (2008).

performers, directors or producers has led many countries to adopt several forms of protection measures against the dominance of foreign production on their domestic markets.[19] Some opponents of pure market solutions even go further and argue that intellectual property is apt to negatively affect cultural diversity, whether due to its predisposition for industry concentration[20] or due to its operation inherently tending towards homogenisation of cultural production based on intellectual property.[21]

The above-described differences in views on how to strike an appropriate and adequate balance between *economic* and *cultural values*[22] of cultural production cause the divergences and tensions between individual countries' approaches to cultural diversity. These divergences and tensions were fully manifested during the drafting process of Convention on the Diversity of Cultural Expressions and are apparent in its final, adopted text. While its *Preliminary Draft*,[23] published on July 2004, contained several explicit references to intellectual property in a number of places, the adopted version seems to intentionally neglect controversial issues related to intellectual property rights as a means of protecting and promoting cultural diversity. Except for Article 20 of the

---

19 Individual protection schemes and regimes have already raised several trade disputes between the United States and the concerned countries. For example, the Canadian regime requiring Canadian-oriented advertising to be published in Canadian magazines led to WTO dispute settlement proceedings; *see* WTO Report of the Appellate Body, *Canada – Certain Measures Concerning Periodicals*, 30 June 1997, WT/DS31/AB/R, *available at* www.wto.org/english/tratop_e/dispu_e/cases_e/ds31_e.htm (last visited 2 February 2012). *See also* K. Scully, "The Most Dangerous Game: U.S. Opposition to the Cultural Exception", 36 *Brooklyn J. Int'l L.* 1183, 1199–1206 (2011) (discussing US-China trade dispute on audividual products); C.M. Bruner, "Culture, Sovereignty, and Hollywood: UNESCO and the Future of Trade in Cultural Products", 40 *N.Y.U. J. Int'l L. & Pol.* 351, at 384–93 (2008) (discussing the situation in Canada, France and the European Union); K.A. Kish, "Protectionism to Promote Culture: South Korea and Japan, a Case Study", 22 *U. Pa. J. Int'l Econ. L.* 153 (2001) (discussing the situation in South Korea and Japan); G.A. Gottselig, "Canada and Culture: Can Current Cultural Policies Be Sustained in the Global Trade Regime?", 5 *Int'l J. Comm. L. & Pol'y* 1 (2000) (discussing the situation in Canada); T. Magder, "Franchising the Candy Store: Split-Run Magazines and a New International Regime for Trade in Culture", *Canadian-American Public Policy* No. 34 (1998) (discussing the situation in Canada); J.D. Donaldson, "'Television Without Frontier': The Continuing Tension Between Liberal Free Trade and European Cultural Integrity", 20 *Fordham Int'l L.J.* 90 (1996) (discussing the situation in European Union).

20 *See* R. Towse, "Why Has Cultural Economics Ignored Copyright?" 32 *J. Cult. Econ.* 243, 252 (2008).

21 *See, e.g.*, E.C. Baker, "International Trade in Media Products", in N. Elkin-Koren and N.W. Netanel (eds.), *The Commodification of Information*, 2002, 267; Y. Benkler, "Intellectual Property and the Organization of Information Production", 22 *Int'l Rev. L. & Econ.* 81 (2002).

22 For discussions on values of cultural goods and services, *see, e.g.*, D. Throsby, *Economics and Culture*, 2001, 19–41; A. Klamer, "Cultural Goods Are Good for More than Their Economic Value", in V. Rao and M. Walton (eds.), *Culture and Public Action*, 2004, 138 (presenting discussions on values of cultural goods and services).

23 UNESCO, "Preliminary Draft of a Convention on the Protection of the Diversity of Cultural Contents and Artistic Expressions", *CPL/CPD/2004/CONF-201/2* (July 2004) [hereinafter "Preliminary Draft"].

Convention on the Diversity of Cultural Expressions which governs the relationship between the Convention on the Diversity of Cultural Expressions and other international treaties, only its Preamble expressly recognises the importance of intellectual property rights for cultural diversity by pointing to their "importance ... in sustaining those involved in cultural creativity".[24] However, it is only a moderated version of the originally proposed provision in the Preliminary Draft which stressed the need to endow the works of authorship "with appropriate intellectual property rights".[25]

The change in the approach toward the role of intellectual property in protecting and promoting cultural diversity is also mirrored in the main text of the Convention on the Diversity of Cultural Expressions, where several express references to intellectual property, present in the Preliminary Draft, were omitted. The current definition of 'cultural activities, goods and services' does not state anymore that they are those goods, services and activities which "generate, or may generate, intellectual property, whether or not they are protected under existing intellectual property legislation."[26] The adopted text also avoids imposing explicitly on the contracting parties the duty to ensure "that intellectual property rights are fully respected and enforced according to existing international instruments, particularly through the development or strengthening of measures against piracy."[27]

On the contrary, Article 5(1) of the Convention on the Diversity of Cultural Expressions reaffirms the "sovereign right [of contracting parties] to formulate and implement their cultural policies and to adopt measures to protect and promote the diversity of cultural expressions".[28] The measures which the contracting parties may adopt are only demonstratively listed in Article 6(2).[29] Each contracting party is allowed under Article 8(1) and (2) to take "all appropriate measures to protect and preserve cultural expressions in situations"[30] "where cultural expressions on its territory are at risk of extinction, under serious threat, or otherwise in need of urgent safeguarding."[31] Although such measures must be taken "in a manner consistent with the provisions of this Convention",[32] it is left upon individual contracting parties to "determine the existence of [such] special situations".[33] At the same time, the concerned parties

24 Convention on the Diversity of Cultural Expressions, *supra* note 1, Preamble §17.
25 Preliminary Draft, *supra* note 23, Preamble, §9.
26 *Compare* id., Article 4(4)(c), *with* Convention on the Diversity of Cultural Expressions, *supra* note 1, Article 4(4).
27 Preliminary Draft, *supra* note 23, Article 7(2)(b).
28 Convention on the Diversity of Cultural Expressions, *supra* note 1, Article 5(1).
29 Id., Article 6(2).
30 Id., Article 8(2).
31 Id., Article 8(1).
32 Id., Article 8(2).
33 Id., Article 8(1).

are obliged to report all the measures to the Intergovernmental Committee, which "may [only] make appropriate recommendations."[34]

The vagueness, or say open-endedness, of the Convention on the Diversity of Cultural Expressions leads Willem Grosheide to conclude that "the [Convention on the Diversity of Cultural Expressions] is a policy-oriented international legal instrument which does not contain any material substantive law rules or means of enforcement, leaving it up to the parties to the convention to apply and introduce whatever legal instruments they may consider to be useful for the realisation of the conventional objectives".[35] For the same reason, the United States has heavily criticised the adopted text of the Convention, since they worry that some countries may use the Convention as an excuse for raising trade barriers in the audiovisual sector.[36]

Accordingly, a question arises as to how to solve the situation where measures adopted by contracting parties to implement the Convention on the Diversity of Cultural Expressions clash with other international treaties, especially the World Trade Organisation ("WTO") regime and international intellectual property treaties. Pursuant to Article 30(3) of *1969 Vienna Convention on the Law of Treaties*,[37] any treaty modifies the previously concluded treaties between the concerned parties so that "the earlier treaty applies only to the extent that its provisions are compatible with those of the later treaty."[38] An exception is "[w] hen a treaty specifies that it is subject to, or that it is not to be considered as incompatible with, an earlier or later treaty".[39] In such a case, "the provisions of that other treaty prevail."[40]

To prevent a situation that the Convention on the Diversity of Cultural Expressions would modify the duties and obligation under previously concluded treaties, the Preliminary Draft proposed that the relationship of the Convention to other treaties would be based on the prevalence of existing international intellectual property treaties to the Convention.[41] However, the proposed text

34 Id., Article 8(3).

35 F.W. Grosheide, "Cultural Diversity and Copyright Law: Between Good Intentions and Better Functioning", 5 (6–7 October 2008) (paper presented at the "2008 ALAI Conference on Cultural Diversity: Its Effects on Authors and Performers in the Context of Globalisation", Dubrovnik, Croatia), *available at* www2.law.uu.nl/priv/cier/Documenten/Worddoceng/ALAICONFERENCE2008DUBROVNIKCROATIA22%20final.doc (last visited 2 February 2012).

36 *See, e.g.*, Bruner, *supra* note 19, at 398–403 (describing the U.S. opposition against the Convention on the Diversity of Cultural Expressions, *supra* note 1, in various stages of its drafting and after its adoption).

37 Vienna Convention on the Law of Treaties, 23 May 1969, 1155 *U.N.T.S.* 331 (1969).

38 Id., Article 30(3).

39 Id., Article 30(2).

40 Id.

41 Preliminary Draft, *supra* note 23, Version A, Article 19(1) ("Nothing in this Convention may be interpreted as affecting the rights and obligations of the States Parties under any existing international instrument relating to intellectual property rights to which they are parties.").

was substituted by current provision of Article 20(1) of the Convention on the Diversity of Cultural Expressions, which contains the following three main principles on the relationship between the Convention and other international treaties: mutual supportiveness, complementarity and non-subordination. To put it more bluntly, the contracting parties are to "foster mutual supportiveness between this Convention and the other treaties to which they are parties",[42] and "to take into account the relevant provisions of this Convention"[43] "when interpreting and applying the other treaties to which they are parties or when entering into other international obligations".[44] When they do so, they are obliged to "perform in good faith their obligations under this Convention and all other treaties to which they are parties."[45]

Although Article 20(1) might seem to be an elegant solution to the relationship between the Convention on the Diversity of Cultural Expressions and other international treaties, its actual implementation can be hampered by Article 20(2) of the Convention on the Diversity of Cultural Expressions. Article 20(2) clarifies the relationship between previously existing treaties and the Convention on the Diversity of Cultural Expressions so that "[n]othing in [the latter] shall be interpreted as modifying rights and obligations of the Parties under any other treaties to which they are parties."[46] This provision has caused severe criticism, since it "seems to envisage no conflict"[47] between the Convention and other international treaties, especially the WTO regime. Conversely, many commentators suggest that such conflicts can simply occur. For instance, Fiona Macmillan foresees them quite apparently as "an issue of systemic governance, or more simply, politics".[48] She suggests that "[t]he clash, if there is one, is some sort of overall systemic conflict where two systems, viewed in their entirety, produce results that cannot co-exist with any comfort."[49] If any dispute occurs, it is highly probable that the party which will claim the violation of a particular provision under the WTO regime will seek to settle the respective trade dispute through the WTO dispute settlement proceedings, under which it may be in a much better position than in the conciliation proceedings under the Convention on the Diversity of Cultural Expressions.[50]

---

42 Convention on the Diversity of Cultural Expressions, *supra* note 1, Article 20(1)(a).

43 Id., Article 20(1)(b).

44 Id.

45 Id., Article 20(1).

46 Id., Article 20(2).

47 Macmillan, *supra* note 17, at 185.

48 *See* id., at 186.

49 *See* id.

50 *Compare* Understanding on Rules and Procedures Governing the Settlement of Disputes, 15 April 1994, Marrakesh Agreement Establishing the World Trade Organization, Annex 2, Legal Instruments – Results of the Uruguay Round, 33 *I.L.M.* 1125 (1994) *with* Convention on the Diversity of Cultural Expressions, *supra* note 1, Article 25 and Annex (containing procedures for settling disputes between individual parties to the Convention on the Diversity of Cultural Expressions).

Article 20(2) may then lead the WTO panel or Appellate Body to conclusion that the Convention on the Diversity of Cultural Expressions has no relevance in relation to the *Agreement on Trade-Related Aspects of Intellectual Property Rights*[51] or other international intellectual property law agreements, since it does not modify any rights or obligations of the contracting parties acquired under those treaties pursuant to the provision of this Article. It may thus allow an easy circumvention of the three main principles provided by Article 20(1) of the Convention on the Diversity of Cultural Expressions.

As shown above, the tensions concerning the role of intellectual property in protecting and promoting cultural diversity during the drafting of the Convention on the Diversity of Cultural Expressions considerably affected its finally adopted text. One may suggest that the Convention intentionally avoids express references to intellectual property in order to prevent situations where overemphasis could be given to the importance of intellectual property regimes in the protection and promotion of cultural diversity during implementation or interpretation of the Convention. Accordingly, while many celebrate its adoption as an important step to achieve sufficient diversity of cultural expressions[52] on the local, regional and global level, others, including the United States, condemn it for its ambiguity towards intellectual property regimes and for its potential to be used as an excuse for raising trade barriers in the audiovisual sector.[53] To cut the Gordian knot concerning the role of intellectual property in protecting and promoting cultural diversity, it is essential to carefully scrutinise the advantages and drawbacks of individual solutions based on the free market or state interventions.

3. CULTURE, FREE MARKET AND INTELLECTUAL PROPERTY

The advocates of the 'pure market' solution argue that granting intellectual property rights and relying upon the free market is the best way to create the necessary environment for sufficient cultural production and product variety. It goes in line with the conventional view that intellectual property regimes are the result of a public bargain.[54] On the one side, the exclusive proprietary rights to

51 Agreement on Trade-Related Aspects of Intellectual Property Rights, 15 April 1994, Marrakesh Agreement Establishing the World Trade Organization, Annex 1C, Legal Instruments – Results of the Uruguay Round, 33 *I.L.M.* 1125 (1994) [hereinafter "TRIPS Agreement"].

52 Convention on the Diversity of Cultural Expressions, *supra* note 1, Article 4(3) (defining the term 'cultural expression' as "those expressions that result from the creativity of individuals, groups and societies, and that have cultural content").

53 *See, e.g.*, BRUNER, *supra* note 19, at 399 n. 203 (quoting the U.S. Ambassador Louise V. Oliver's intervention at the 33rd UNESCO General Conference).

54 There are also other theories justifying intellectual property regimes. For a thorough outline of various justifications; *See, e.g.*, P. DRAHOS, *A Philosophy of Intellectual Property*, 1996; W.J.

some results[55] of intellectual creative human labour are granted to their authors, creators, inventors or other stakeholders for a limited period of time as a reward for the investment of their time, money and labour, as well as an incentive to stimulate further creative and innovative activities. On the other side, the public is provided with access to an ample variety of diverse intangibles, including cultural goods and services, which are the results of such stimulated activities. The question is whether intellectual property rights actually play so important, or indeed any, role in protecting and promoting cultural diversity. Many opponents of pure market solution condemn the current intellectual property regimes for harming or even diminishing cultural diversity as a result of the high degree of horizontal and vertical concentration in the intellectual property and communication industries. This Section thus examines the foundations of this criticism and especially whether some intellectual property regimes, in particular a copyright regime which is closely related to cultural production, contain any features or mechanisms indispensable for supporting and promoting a variety of cultural expressions.

3.1. INCENTIVES AND REWARDS

There is an array of diverse reasons why individual authors create new intangible goods, including cultural expressions. Although there is some part of the population which does not expect any return from providing others with access to the results of their intellectual creative labour, they are often exceptions rather than the rule. As Samuel Johnson, the eighteenth century English author, essayist and critic, noted tersely, "[n]o man but a blockhead ever wrote, except for money."[56] Some authors therefore create since they need to earn money for living by selling the results of their intellectual creative activities.[57] Others indulge in creative and innovative activities in order to obtain prestige, fame or other forms of public acknowledgement.[58] Even in many cases where no tangible benefits for the concerned creators are obviously visible there are hidden reasons of satisfying some internal human needs or desires of creators, such as personal pleasure or self-satisfaction by helping, satisfying needs of, or just causing pleasure to, others.[59]

Gordon, "A Property Right in Self Expression: Equality and Individualism in the Natural Law of Intellectual Property", 102 *Yale L.J.* 1533 (1993); J. Hughes, "The Philosophy of Intellectual Property", 77 *Geo. L.J.* 287 (1988).

55 *See* the text accompanying note 74.

56 J. Boswell, *Boswell's Life of Johnson*, Ch.G. Osgood (ed.), 1917 (quoting Samuel Johnson), *available at* www.gutenberg.org/files/1564/1564-h/1564-h.htm (last visited 2 February 2012).

57 *See, e.g.*, W.M. Landes and R.A. Posner, *The Economic Structure of Intellectual Property Law*, 2003, 38 (referring to "authors who actually live on their royalties").

58 *See* id., at 48 (discussing as one of the factors that would limit copying even in the absence of copyright law the situation where "authors derive substantial benefits from publication that are over and beyond any royalties", such as "self-advertisements and self-promotion").

59 Many individuals do so because they expect reciprocity from others under the same or similar conditions.

To create any intangible good, including literary and artistic works,[60] public performances, sound recordings and broadcastings,[61] requires the consumption of limited resources, such as time, money and human intellectual creative labour. But the willingness to spend privately held limited resources on the creation of cultural goods or the provision of cultural services can be considerably reduced due to the 'public goods'[62] character of such goods and services if sufficient legal protection is not provided to protect it.

Public goods are characterised by two main features: *non-excludability* and *non-rival consumption*. When public goods are accessible by one person, it is hard to exclude the access of others. For instance, once the result of certain artistic or scientific activity is presented publicly, such as a song is sung, the story is told or dance is danced publicly, anyone can sing, retell or dance the same song, story or dance again at any time afterwards. Simultaneously, the consumption of public goods by one person does not act in rivalry with their consumption by another person, in contrast to the case with tangible goods. When a slice of bread is eaten by someone, another person cannot consume that slice anymore, but when someone sings a song or reads a book, another person can sing the same song or can read the copy of the same book at the same or different time somewhere else.

Hence, the main feature of public goods is that their nature allows some of their users or consumers not to internalise their original production costs, *i.e.* public goods lack natural barriers which could prevent the free riding of others on someone's activities.[63] To express it differently, in the case of cultural production without sufficient legal protection, the second comers can benefit from substantial advantages against the entrepreneur who spent a considerable amount of money to find a niche market with a particular cultural good or service, when they can swiftly produce or provide identical or very similar goods or services which have comparable quality for a substantially lower price and

---

60 Berne Convention for the Protection of Literary and Artistic Works, Article 2(1), 9 September 1886, 828 *U.N.T.S.* 211 (last revised at Paris, 24 July 1971) ("The expression 'literary and artistic works' shall include every production in the literary, scientific and artistic domain, whatever may be the mode or form of its expression, such as books, pamphlets and other writings; lectures, addresses, sermons and other works of the same nature; dramatic or dramatico-musical works; choreographic works and entertainments in dumb show; musical compositions with or without words; cinematographic works to which are assimilated works expressed by a process analogous to cinematography; works of drawing, painting, architecture, sculpture, engraving and lithography; photographic works to which are assimilated works expressed by a process analogous to photography; works of applied art; illustrations, maps, plans, sketches and three-dimensional works relative to geography, topography, architecture or science.").

61 International Convention for the Protection of Performers, Producers of Phonograms and Broadcasting Organisations, Article 3, 26 October 1961, 496 *U.N.T.S.* 44 (1961) (defining terms such as 'performers', 'phonograms' and 'broadcasting').

62 *See* H. Demsetz, "The Private Production of Public Goods", 13 *J. L. & Econ.* 293 (1970).

63 In many case, the first mover will benefit from a lead time. However, new digital technologies have reduced the advantages of lead time almost to a minimum.

which are thus perfect substitutes for the copied original ones.[64] The introduction of numerous reproduction and distribution technologies, such as the printing press, movie camera, photocopier, sound or video cassette recorder, or DVD burner,[65] over and over again, has significantly reduced reproduction and distribution costs.[66] Going even further, new digital and networking technologies allow millions of their users to freely access an array of cultural goods and services and to make high quality copies of copyrighted works immediately for almost no cost.[67] The reduction of reproduction and distribution costs thus causes many producers of cultural goods or providers of cultural services to be unable to recoup their initial investment in their creations. This has a negative impact on the entrepreneurs' incentives to start with new creative cultural production. At the end of the day, it leads to underproduction or even non-production of affected cultural goods and services on a commercial basis, unless the expected benefits from the initial investment in someone's intellectual creative human labour can be obtained by the first mover in some way.

Consequently, it is deemed as indispensable to provide authors, artists, inventors and other entities with some form of protection or support of their intellectual creative activities that result in the production of cultural goods or the provision of cultural services. There are several ways to do so which have developed through centuries of human civilisation, such as patronage, public subsidies and intellectual property protection. However, the individual solutions should not be taken independently and separately. Rather, they should be considered as a spectrum where the extremes are represented by a situation in which private or public funds are used to subsidise cultural production in some way. While government employs mechanisms based on taxes, quotas or subsidies financed from public funds, private entities do so through patronage or sponsorship. Somewhere in between state and private interventions are located

---

64 *See, e.g.*, Landes and Posner, *supra* note 57, at 13.

65 For an excellent historical overview of the development of copyright doctrines as a reaction to the introduction of numerous reproduction and distribution technologies, *see* P. Goldstein, *Copyright's Highway: From Gutenberg to the Celestial Jukebox*, 2003 (rev. ed.); S. Vaidhyanathan, *Copyrights and Copywrongs: The Rise of Intellectual Property and How It Threatens Creativity*, 2003.

66 The consequences of reduced reproduction and distribution costs caused by the introduction of new technologies do not directly affect the production of artistic works valued for their genuineness and authenticity, such as paintings and sculptures. *See, e.g.*, Landes and Posner, *supra* note 57, at 41.

67 The situations where an unlimited number of people have access to limited resources often lead to attempts to reap private benefits by too many people from such limited resources held in commons. The result is that overuse of limited resources causes their destruction. In literature, the term "tragedy of commons" is used to describe such a situation; *see* G. Hardin, "The Tragedy of the Commons", 162 *Science* 1243 (1968). However, it occurs only where there are no social norms inducing cooperative behaviour between particular individuals. For cases where resources held in commons were not depleted due to the existence of social norms between members of society; *see* E. Olstrom, *Governing the Commons: The Evolution of Institutions for Collective Action*, 1990, 18–21.

approaches which rely on granting proprietary rights to some intangible goods and relying upon the market to decide the extent of funds which should be used for supporting individual cultural production.

At this point, it should be stressed that each of these solutions has its cons and pros. The advantage of state intervention is that the public is often provided with a higher quantity of certain products which are protected by specifically designed taxes or quotas, or with free access to the results of creative and innovative activities financed by public funds. Its disadvantage is that the quality of many protected and subsidised goods and services is rarely adequate. Furthermore, public funds are habitually limited. As governmental officers are to decide which creative activity should be supported, the government is allowed to censor creative activities by determining which art is proper for obtaining support from public funds and which should be restricted or discriminated against by refusing to provide it with sufficient funds.[68] At the same time, governmental power is akin to corruption. There is always enough room for bribery or abuse of public funds in regimes based on state intervention in the operation of the market.[69] Finally, public funds are often limited and insufficient to finance satisfactorily the necessary scope and size of cultural production. As the solutions anchored in state intervention are dealt with in more detail below,[70] we put them aside for now and focus mainly on solutions relying on private funds and the free market.

In the case of private intervention, private funds are used pursuant to the will and taste of individuals who control the concerned funds. While private administration reduces the possibility of wasting limited resources due to corruption and inefficient public administration, it does not prevent the limited funds from being overused in some areas and not allocated at all in others.[71] In addition, individuals and foundations controlling private funds often follow their private interests and seldom fully take into account public interests.[72]

---

68 *See, e.g.*, Y. Benkler, "Through the Looking Glass: Alice and the Constitutional Foundations of the Public Domain", 66 *Law & Contemp. Prob.* 173, 183 (2003) ("[D]ependence of government largesse or patronage tends to require authors, media, and others to be solicitous to those who pay the piper.").

69 *See, e.g.*, T. Frye and A. Shleifer, "The Invisible Hand and the Grabbing Hand", 87 *Am. Econ. Rev.* 354 (1997) (distinguishing three models of government with regard to corruption: the 'invisible-hand' model, the 'helping-hand' model and the 'grabbing-hand' model); J.R. Macey, "New Theories of the Regulatory Statecynicism and Trust in Politics and Constitutional Theory", 87 *Cornell L. Rev.* 280, 287 (2002) (arguing that "all three models [of Frye-Shleifer taxonomy] operate simultaneously" in case of a modern welfare state).

70 Pros and cons of state intervention, such as taxes, quotas or subsidies, are analysed in details in Section Four below.

71 *See, e.g.*, N.W. Netanel, "Copyright and a Democratic Civil Society", 106 *Yale L.J.* 283, 353 (1996) (describing the patronage systems prior to the first modern copyright regimes adopted in the eighteenth century).

72 *See* id., at 353 (criticising artists' dependency on their patrons for undermining "expressive autonomy and thwart[ing] the development of a vital, freethinking intelligentsia") and at 358 (stating that "in a world with neither copyright nor massive state subsidy, authors would

Accordingly, the free market proponents present the granting of intellectual property rights as a middle road that avoids the disadvantages of state or private interventions which allow the distortion and control of cultural production by a limited number of people who have access to public or private funds. Thomas B. Macaulay put it tersely in his 1841 speech to the House of Commons: "I can conceive no system more fatal to the integrity and independence of literary men than one under which they should be taught to look for their daily bread to the favour of ministers and nobles."[73] By granting them the exclusive proprietary rights to the results of their creative intellectual labour,[74] some authors and other creators are protected against copying or other types of slavish imitation of their works. Intellectual property rights thus give them an incentive to create new intellectual works on a commercial basis. This foundation and justification of intellectual property rights is succinctly expressed in Article 1, Section 8, of the *1787 U.S. Constitution*[75] which empowers the U.S. Congress to adopt laws "[t]o promote the progress of science and useful arts, by securing for limited times to authors and inventors the exclusive right to their respective writings and discoveries".[76]

The positive outcomes of the granting of strong intellectual property rights are seen by their proponents in relying on the market to decide which works should be created and which creators should need to search for support in the form of private funding, such as patronage or sponsorship. In this way, the market is considered the best medium to communicate the demands and tastes of consumers to creators and intellectual property industries.[77]

3.2. CRITIQUE OF INTELLECTUAL PROPERTY REGIMES

Although it seems that granting intellectual property rights, and especially copyrights, is essential for providing individual writers, composers, actors,

---

likely rely heavily on private patronage, forcing them to cater to the tastes, interests, and political agenda of the wealthy").

73 T.B. Macaulay, *The Life and Works of Lord Macaulay: Complete in Ten Volumes*, Edinburgh ed., 1896, Vol. VIII, 198 (containing the speech delivered in the House of Commons on 5 February 1841).

74 It should be made clear that the creators are not granted with the respective intellectual property rights to the results of someone's creative intellectual human labour in any case of creative or innovative activities. For example, once disclosed new scientific theory, whatever its importance for humankind can be, is not protected by any intellectual property law, unless it is expressed in some tangible form or it can have practical application in industry. Even in those cases, the intellectual property protection does not directly concern the scientific theory, but its expression or the invention based upon the theory, respectively.

75 U.S. Constitution, 17 September 1787.

76 *See* id., Article 1, §8. *See also* J. Hughes, "Copyright and Incomplete Historiographies: Of Piracy, Propertization, and Thomas Jefferson", 79 *S. Cal. L. Rev.* 993, at 1021–26 (2006) (analysing the drafting process of the Copyright Clause in the U.S. Constitution, *supra* note 75).

77 For the criticism of this argument pointing to its flaws and shortcomings, *see* the text accompanying notes 127–30.

singers and other artists with adequate incentive to continue in creative artistic activities on a commercial basis, empirical studies show that copyright regimes do not provide authors and other artists sufficiently with the expected rewards.[78] In reality, average artists need to search for other sources of income, such as public performances, sales of original copies of their works or even non-artistic activities.[79] Only a few authors and artists can support their living merely from revenues obtained from the exploitation of their copyrighted works.[80] Most of them are superstars[81] for whom the income from copyright royalties is not actually essential. They earn substantial revenues from other sources, such as public performances and marketing of their popularity through advertisement campaigns or other commercial activities. Despite the lack of significant financial rewards obtained by the majority of artists from copyright sources, Ruth Towse points out that the artists greatly value "the intrinsic reward of legal protection through copyright law, which they perceive as giving them status."[82] As some superstars and artists with market power benefit financially from copyright protection and the others at least immaterially by obtaining their social status, she concludes that "copyright law is an institutional incentive that combines intrinsic and extrinsic incentives and rewards for creativity."[83]

A further criticism of intellectual property law stresses the substantial diminishing of variety in the case of cultural production. It is based on a severe critique of the current situation in intellectual property industries which are often characterised by a high degree of horizontal and vertical concentration.[84] There are just a handful of multinational enterprises (approx. four or five in each

---

78 *See* M. Taylor and R. Towse, "The Value of Performers' rights: An Economic Approach", 20 *Media, Culture & Society* 631 (1998); R. Towse, "Copyright and Economic Incentives: An Application to Performers' Rights in the Music Industry", 54 *KYKLOS* 369 (2001) (examining musical performers' remuneration from the public performance right in Denmark, Sweden and the United Kingdom); R. Towse, *Creativity, Incentive and Reward: An Economic Analysis of Copyright and Culture in the Information Age*, 2001, 164–66; S. Matsumoto, "Performers in the Digital Era: Empirical Evidence from Japan", in R. Towse (ed.), *Copyright in the Cultural Industries*, 2002, 196 (studying the situation of music performers in Japan); Towse, *supra* note 20, at 251 (referring to other studies on the impact of copyright law on authors, composers, performers and other artists in different countries).

79 *See* Throsby, *supra* note 22, at 98–102 (outlining the following "three ways in which income might be entered into [his] model of the creative process": (a) as a constraint; (b) as a joint maximand and (c) as a sole maximand).

80 The term 'copyrighted work' is used, in the broad sense, to any work which is an eligible subject matter of copyright in common law countries or author's rights and neighbouring rights in civil law jurisdictions.

81 *See* R. Towse, "Partly for the Money: Rewards and Incentive to Artists", 54 *KYKLOS* 473, 480 (2001) ("Superstar authors and performers with market power can do very well from royalty earnings".).

82 *See* id., at 481.

83 *See* id.

84 *See, e.g.*, Macmillan, *supra* note 17, at 171; G. Pessach, "Copyright Law as a Silencing Restriction on Noninfringing Materials: Unveiling the Scope of Copyright's Diversity Externalities", 76 *S. Cal. L. Rev.* 1067, 1087–91 (2003); J.S. Curtis, "Culture and the Digital

field, *i.e.* record labels, studios as well as broadcasting networks)[85] which controls a major amount of respective cultural production worldwide. In some fields, they even control more than two thirds of the world market sales in question.[86] In addition to the concentration within a particular segment of cultural production, the media conglomerates belong to groups which also control various channels for distributing their production, such as chains of movie theatres and broadcasting networks, where their production can be promoted on news channels and also played on movie channels or radio stations.[87] Additionally some of these groups own, or are controlled by, related technology providers, such as consumer electronic producers[88] or internet service providers.[89] Accordingly, some companies providing copyrighted content have very close links to those allowing access to content either through numerous distribution channels or by providing consumers with necessary technologies.[90]

Due to its substantial reduction of reproduction and distribution costs, horizontal and vertical concentration has two negative impacts on a range of cultural production. On the one side, it creates market entrance barriers for new entrants and puts independent producers into a detrimental position. As independent producers and creators cannot benefit from lower costs of efficient distribution networks available to media conglomerates, it is more difficult for them to compete with the media conglomerates' production. The same problem also has to be faced by new entrants to whom it amounts to a considerable barrier to entering the market.[91]

On the other hand, the production concentration also affects the variety of cultural goods and services provided by media conglomerates. Guy Pessach,

---

Copyright Chimera: Assessing the International Regulatory System of the Music Industry in Relation to Cultural Diversity", 13 *Int'l J. Cult. Prop.* 59, 64 and 79 (2006).

85 For an overview of current situation in copyright industries, *see, e.g.*, R.V. Bettig, "Concentration in the Copyright Industries", in P.K. Yu (ed.), *Intellectual Property and Information Wealth: Issues and Practices in the Digital Age*, Vol. I (Copyright and Related Rights), 2007, 361; Wright, *supra* note 18.

86 *See, e.g.*, Wright, *supra* note 18, at 430–33 (describing the situation on the global content markets in movies, television programmes and sound recordings) and at 502–3 (providing data on revenues from theatre box office receipts from different countries, which are attributable to movies originating in the United States).

87 *See, e.g.*, A.D. Lotz, *The Television Will Be Revolutionized*, 2007 (discusing production and distribution models in the U.S. television broadcasting industry).

88 The Sony Group is composed of, *inter alia*, Sony Corporation, a leading manufacturer of consumer electronics, and of many important content providers, such as Sony Music Entertainment, Sony Pictures Entertainment and Sony Computer Entertainment.

89 In addition to major content providers, such as Warner Bros. Entertainment, Inc., Time Inc. and Turner Broadcasting System, Inc., which are subsidiaries of Time Warner Inc., one of world's largest media and entertainment conglomerates, AOL (formerly America Online), a leading Internet service provider, is also its subsidiary. On 9 December 2009, Time Warner Inc. spinned off AOL into a separate public company.

90 For more details on vertical and horizontal concentration of copyright industries, *see* Bettig, *supra* note 85; Wright, *supra* note 18, at 423–25 and 486–501.

91 *See* Pessach, *supra* note 84, at 1090.

amongst others, observes that "the economics of reduced copying and distribution costs strengthen corporate media's incentive toward producing content that is relatively homogenous and not unique."[92] As the product variety divides the group of customers and increases the per-person costs of production, concentrated cultural production focuses on the topics, genres and styles attracting mass audiences. Concurrently, it shows a heavy bias against minority tastes and preferences.[93] The result is that while a considerable amount of funds is overinvested in the mainstream market, customers' demands for other cultural products and services significantly diverging from mainstream tastes and production are not satisfied due to the lack of investment in those niche markets, since the media conglomerates do not consider them to be sufficiently profitable.

The empirical studies confirm this lamentable situation. The more concentrated the industry is, the lower the product variability is.[94] The negative impact of industry concentration on variability of supplied cultural goods and provided cultural services can be partially moderated by decentralising cultural production through its partial or complete outsourcing, *i.e.* subcontracting independent production companies or directly groups of artists to produce the respective cultural goods and services.[95] However, it should be made clear that the moderating effect of decentralised production occurs only when subcontracted companies have enough room for their creative and artistic decision making.

Many see the cause of concentrated cultural production and the current unsatisfactory situation in intellectual property industries in copyright and other intellectual property laws.[96] For instance, Macmillan expresses it quite tersely: "[S]omething has gone wrong and we need to look very carefully again at the shape of copyright law and consider whether there are parts that we might want to jettison or change dramatically".[97] Some even go further and suggest that there is an inherent tendency in copyright and other intellectual property rights to lead to horizontal and sometimes even vertical concentration.[98] The

92 Id., at 1089.

93 *See* id.

94 *See* P.J. Alexander, "Product Variety and Market Structure: A New Measure and a Simple Test", 32 *J. Econ. Behav. & Organ.* 207 (1997) (studying the U.S. recording industry between 1955 and 1988 by using entropy to generate a measure of product variety).

95 *See* T.J. Dowd, "Concentration and Diversity Revisited: Production Logics and the U.S. Mainstream Recording Market, 1940–1990", 82 *Social Forces* 1411 (2004) (studying the recording industry in the U.S. between 1940 and 1990).

96 *See, e.g.*, Macmillan, *supra* note 17, at 171; Pessach, *supra* note 84, at 1087–91; Curtis, *supra* note 84, at 64 and 79.

97 Macmillan, *supra* note 17, at 184.

98 *See, e.g.*, Macmillan, *supra* note 17, at 170 (stating that "[c]opyright law has contributed to, augmented, or created a range of market features that have resulted in a high degree of global concentration in the ownership of intellectual property in cultural goods and services"); Curtis, *supra* note 84, at 79 ("By giving monopoly rights over content to an ever-decreasing and ever-consolidating group of cultural conglomerates, those companies can consume the

more copyrighted and other proprietary works a company has in its portfolio, the more valuable target of future acquisition it is.[99] Similarly, the more efficiently the media group can distribute its copyrighted works, the more profitable and valuable its portfolio is.

Nevertheless, the problem of horizontal and vertical concentration is not faced only by intellectual property industries. It is not the specific problem of intellectual property laws. Similar problems occur in other industries and relates to the transaction costs of dealing with customers and other competitors. The decision of competitors as to whether they will compete with their rivals or acquire them is often based on a cost-benefit analysis.[100] Consequently, it is the responsibility of antitrust law and its enforcement authorities to set up the appropriate and adequate measures to prevent industry concentration which will harm other competitors and customers.[101] In this endeavour, the empirical studies on the impact of industry and production concentration can assist the respective authorities to properly strike a balance in allowing mergers and acquisitions in intellectual property industries.

3.3. INTELLECTUAL PROPERTY AS A MEANS FOR CULTURAL DIVERSITY

Although the critiques of intellectual property law, especially copyright law, for the current concentration of concerned industries and for its failure to provide sufficient remuneration to individual authors and other artists are severe, some scholars argue that intellectual property laws provide a platform necessary for creating an environment that allows authors, performers and other artists to place the results of their intellectual creative labour on the market.[102] To put it in other words, by guarantying that corporate intermediaries, such as publishing

---

market by pushing independent music labels, self-produced artists, and others out of the market for recorded music."); PESSACH, *supra* note 84, at 1103–4.

99 *See, e.g.*, TOWSE, *supra* note 20, at 252 (suggesting as a hypothesis to be tested the following premise: "copyright creates assets for firms, which make them amenable to mergers and acquisitions, thus enabling the build up of the giant international oligopolies that we know control the record, film, publishing and broadcasting industries").

100 *See, e.g.*, L. PEEPERKORN and V. VEROUDEN, "The Economics of Competition", in J. FAULL and A. NIKPAY (eds.), *The EC Law of Competition*, 2007, 3, 7 and 14–16.

101 *See, e.g.*, P. RÉGIBEAU and K. ROCKETT, "The Relationship Between Intellectual Property Law and Competition Law: An Economic Approach", in S.D. ANDERMANN (ed.), *The Interface Between Intellectual Property Rights and Competition Policy*, 2007, 505, 541 (arguing that "copyright-based market power will usually stem from a significant concentration of copyrighted materials" and that "[m]ergers between firms that hold significant intellectual property portfolios should carefully consider the potential effects of an increase in the concentration of ownership of copyrighted material"); N.W. NETANEL, "Copyright and 'Market Power' in the Marketplace of Ideas", in F. LÉVÊQUE and H. SHELANSKI (eds.), *Antitrust, Patents and Copyright: EU and US Perspectives*, 2005, 149.

102 *See, e.g.*, TOWSE, *supra* note 81, at 478–80; TOWSE, *supra* note 20, at 252.

houses, record labels, studios and other intellectual property industries, can actually recoup with a profit their investment in publishing a book, journal or other literary work, recording a CD or producing a movie, the protection of their intellectual property gives them the necessary incentives to search for cultural goods and services demanded by the public. It thus allows intellectual property industries to spend their private funds to provide the public with the cultural goods and services it demands and to promote individual cultural expressions in order to attract the attention of targeted consumers. On the other hand, an optimally operating free market guarantees that individual consumers are provided with an ample product variety to satisfy, if not completely then at least partially, their needs and demands. Copyright and other intellectual property laws therefore create an environment indispensable for achieving a certain degree and variety of cultural production. As cultural industries heavily rely on copyright law, we put other intellectual property laws aside for now and the following analysis in this Section concentrates mainly on copyright law.[103]

Copyright law has several features which are indispensable for creating an environment for stimulating the diversity of copyrighted works. One of its key features is that copyright law protects only expressions and not the ideas embodied in them. In many countries, the courts have established tests by which they can determine the point between what is protected expression and what is unprotected idea.[104] The courts are traditionally very cautious when they have to decide whether a particular work infringes the copyright of another work. The higher and the stricter the threshold is, the more numerous the product variety on a particular theme, style and genre can be. Simultaneously, the 'hard to infringe' standard can lead to crowding in a particular market niche, while the variety of cultural goods and services offered in other segments of the market can be much lower or even missing. Nevertheless, the actual variety of offered products heavily depends on the particular degree of concentration and the way

---

103 For the importance of some other intellectual property regimes for cultural diversity, *see* Sections 4.2. and 4.3. below.

104 *See, e.g., Nichols v. Universal Pictures Corp.*, 45 F.2d 119, 121 (2d Cir. 1930) ("Upon any work, and especially upon a play, a great number of patterns of increasing generality will fit equally well, as more and more of the incident is left out. That last may perhaps be no more than the most general statement of what the play is about, and at times might consist only of its title; but there is a point in this series of abstractions where they are no longer protected, since otherwise the playwright could prevent the use of his 'idea' to which, apart from their expression, his property is never extended."). *See also* P. Goldstein, *International Copyright: Principles, Law, and Practice*, 2001, 184–85 (analysing the idea-expression dichotomy under the Berne Convention, *supra* note 60); R.E. Schechter and J.R. Thomas, *Intellectual Property: The Law of Copyrights, Patents and Trademarks*, 2003, 31–36 (analysing the idea-expression dichotomy under the U.S. copyright law); A. Lucas and H.-J. Lucas, *Traité de la propriété littéraire et artistique*, 3rd ed., 2006, 59–62 (analysing the idea-expression dichotomy under the French copyright law); Y. Tamura, *Chosakukenho gaisetsu [Copyright Law]*, 2nd ed., 2001, 15–22 (analysing the idea-expression dichotomy under the Japanese copyright law).

cultural production is concentrated and organised.[105] Empirical studies show that "high and low levels of concentration result in lessened variety, and maximum variety is promoted by a moderately concentrated structure."[106]

Another way of protecting and promoting cultural diversity is to avoid discrimination against particular cultural expressions. The exclusive proprietary rights are thus granted to any expression of idea if it satisfies the basic requirements for its copyrightability.[107] To be copyrightable, the expression of an idea conventionally needs to be original, creative and fixed in some form.[108] Although not any expression of idea is copyrightable, the threshold in many jurisdictions is usually set very low. It is sufficient when the expression is neither a copy of another person's work nor a result of mundane and routine labour.[109] No artistic value of the work is required and evaluated before the exclusive proprietary rights to the work are granted to its creator. If the artistic value of a work was essential for granting copyright,[110] it would allow discrimination against some forms of cultural expressions. This is the reason why the courts in many countries refuse to indulge in value judgements that allow the evaluation of cultural expressions according to the tastes and views held by a particular social group.[111]

In some jurisdictions, especially those influenced by the French copyright law, this approach is extended to the entire 'art' in a broad sense through the 'unity of art' doctrine.[112] The copyright laws of these countries go so far that they provide any result of intellectual creative human labour with copyright protection regardless of whether it is in the field of human activities which are

---

105 *See* the text accompanying notes 94 and 95 above.

106 Alexander, *supra* note 94, at 207.

107 The requirements of copyrightability diverge to a minor extent from one country to another; *See, e.g.*, Goldstein, *supra* note 104, at 157–203.

108 The civil law countries do not require fixation in a tangible medium of expression; *see* id., at 196–97.

109 The copyrightability requirements are extremely low in the United Kingdom (the 'skill, judgment and labour' requirement); *see, e.g.*, W. Cornish and D. Llewelyn, *Intellectual Property: Patents, Copyright, Trade Marks and Allied Rights*, 7th ed., 2010, 441–61; L. Bently and B. Sherman, *Intellectual Property Law*, 3rd ed., 2009, 91–118.

110 *See* Towse, *supra* note 20, at 249 (considering as one of "three drawbacks to copyright as an incentive to artistic creation from the point of view of cultural policy" the fact that copyright "is indiscriminate and does not attempt to encourage or reward higher quality or innovative work").

111 *See, e.g.*, *Bleistein v. Donaldson Lithographing Co.*, 188 U.S. 239, 251–52 (1903) ("It would be a dangerous undertaking for persons trained only to the law to constitute themselves final judges of the worth of pictorial illustrations, outside of the narrowest and most obvious limits. At one extreme some works of genius would be sure to miss appreciation. Their very novelty would make them repulsive until the public had learned the new language in which their author spoke. It may be more than doubted, for instance, whether the etchings of Goya or the paintings of Manet would have been sure of protection when seen for the first time. At the other end, copyright would be denied to pictures which appealed to a public less educated than the judge … [T]he taste of any public is not to be treated with contempt.").

112 *See, e.g.*, Lucas and Lucas, *supra* note 104, 69–71.

traditionally considered as copyrightable, such as a novel, poem, song, opera, statute, painting or carving. In this way, the exclusion of some types of creative intellectual human endeavours, such as perfumes, fashion and designs, from copyright protection is prevented. For instance, the Dutch courts have recently extended copyright protection also to perfumes,[113] and the French law traditionally protects any kind of fashion under the condition that they reflect the author's personality.[114] However, it should be pointed out that in many countries which have not adopted such a broad approach towards copyrightability, their laws provide other forms of equivalent or comparable protection against the slavish copying or imitation of the respective results of such intellectual creative activities.[115] Hence, the fact that a domestic law grants or does not grant copyright protection to a particular type of intellectual creative human endeavour can sometimes be misleading when the broader legal framework is not taken into consideration.

Copyright law also contains several other key features,[116] which are important for supporting or promoting diverse literary and artistic creative activities, but the detailed analysis of which goes beyond the scope of this Chapter. To mention just some of them, copyright law limits the scope of granted exclusive rights in order to create the necessary environment for further creativity and diversity of cultural expressions. In this regard, an important role is played by numerous exceptions, which allow criticism, reporting of current events, parody, collage and other types of creative borrowings.[117] The copyright exceptions permit creators to borrow from pre-existing copyrighted works in their intellectual creative endeavours. It allows a broadening of the variety of works around certain topics, styles, items, features and information.

Consequently, it is undoubted that the idea of cultural diversity is in the core of copyright law. Many copyright and other intellectual property doctrines and rules[118] are essential for the protection and promotion of cultural diversity, although they were not originally designed mainly for this purpose or were not expressly presented in this context. Adolf Dietz, amongst others,[119] utters it succinctly: "For a long time the cultural dimension of

---

113 *See, e.g.*, C. Seville, "Copyright in Perfumes: Smelling a Rat", 66 *Cambridge L. J.* 49 (2007).

114 *See* Lucas and Lucas, *supra* note 104, at 66–67 and 107–10.

115 *See, e.g.*, S. Scafidi, "Intellectual Property and Fashion Design", in Yu, *supra* note 85, at 115 (analysing different ways of protecting fashion design under the U.S. law).

116 For more details, *see, e.g.*, Wager, *supra* note 12 (analysing several key features of copyright law, such as idea-expression dichotomy, time limited protection, various exceptions allowing parody, reporting of current events, criticism, borrowings and *collage*).

117 For an excellent comparative analysis of copyright limitations, *see* L.C.R. Guibault, *Copyright Limitations and Contracts: An Analysis of the Contractual Overridability of Limitations on Copyright*, 2002, 15–90.

118 For an analysis of some other intellectual property doctrines and rules, *see* Sections 4.2. and 4.3. below.

119 *See, e.g.*, Grosheide, *supra* note 35, at 5 (similarly putting forward that "policy-driven, time and place-bound cultural objectives have always been part of international copyright law,

copyright law, if always present in legal doctrine, very rarely was made explicit in legal texts".[120]

At the same time, it should still be kept in mind that policy makers should be very cautious with designing an appropriate and adequate cultural policy. The free market approach based only on granting intellectual property rights to the results of intellectual creative human labour can achieve a certain degree and variety of cultural production, but it may fail to work for the tastes and demands of minority and marginal groups. Such market failures occur especially, when cultural production is heavily concentrated and centralised. Guaranteeing satisfactory conditions for a variety of cultural production is thus a task for the government to accomplish by employing various measures either within copyright law (*e.g.*, redistribution of fees and levies collected for various forms of private copying or using of copyrighted works based upon blanket licences)[121] or outside copyright law (*e.g.*, grants, subsidies, taxes or screen quotas).[122] It is the task of each government to properly and adequately balance diverse forms of incentives and supports within national cultural policy so that the public has access to a sufficient variety of cultural expressions. The following analysis enquires into the advantages and drawbacks of such redistribution mechanisms and schemes.

4. CULTURE, PROTECTIONISM AND REDISTRIBUTIVE JUSTICE

So far, the analysis has mainly focused on the operation of the market and the role of intellectual property as a means for protecting and promoting cultural diversity within national borders. International trade with cultural goods and services, however, brings new tensions in relation to the operation of the free market and intellectual property regimes, and its implications for cultural diversity. The issue is even more contentious when we take into account that the international trade in this field is currently heavily dominated by a single country, the United States, which is then regionally followed by some other developed countries, such as Japan or South Korea within the East Asia region,

---

although this is rarely made explicit in any legal texts"); H. Wager, *supra* note 12, at 195 (stating that "[c]ultural objectives have always been element underlying multilateral copyright law").

120 A. Dietz, "Cultural Diversity and Copyright", 16 *Les Cahiers de propriété intellectuelle (Hors série)* 109, 116 (2004).

121 *See* the text accompanying notes 145–51.

122 As this Chapter examines the relation between intellectual property and cultural diversity, the redistribution and state protectionist mechanisms and schemes which are not built in intellectual property regimes are partially omitted here. For a detailed analysis of such protectionist measures, *see, e.g.*, Voon, *supra* note 13.

and Germany, France and Spain in countries where people speak French, German or Spanish, respectively.[123] Looking at the situation in many developed and developing countries, the U.S. cultural production often holds an overwhelming share in numerous national markets. The lamentable prospects of local cultural production in competition with cultural goods supplied and cultural services provided by global media conglomerates have brought many countries to adopt a number of protection measures for local industries. To properly and adequately understand the issue, it is essential to examine the reasons for the U.S. dominance in the international trade of cultural goods and services, and the efficiency of protectionist policies and mechanisms aiming to moderate the negative consequences of distorted international trade in this field and to achieve cultural diversity on a local, regional and international level.

4.1. DISTORTED INTERNATIONAL MARKET AND LIBERALISED TRADE

The reasons of the U.S. dominance in the international trade in sound recordings, movies and television programmes are severalfold. They relate to the economies of scale and scope. The higher the investment in production and promotion is, the higher the probability is that the products or services will attract a mass audience. The bigger the size of the market is, the higher the chance is to recoup the higher production, distribution and promotion costs.

To attract consumers in different countries with diverse cultures, media conglomerates focus on content which can be easily translatable from one culture to another. Hence, they concentrate on the production of cultural goods and the provision of services which are not closely linked to a particular culture. According to C. Edwin Baker who relies on Eli Noam's threefold categorisation of cultural content,[124] customers prefer 'domestic content' to 'universal content' or 'foreign content'.[125] While domestic and foreign contents have closer cultural links to a specific culture through employing distinctive humour, mentality, stereotypes, nuances or connotations,[126] universal content lacks cultural

---

123 *See, e.g.*, W.W. Fu and C. Sim, "Examining International Country-to-Country Flow of Theatrical Films", 60 *J. Comm.* 120, 138 (2010) (an empirical study indentifying factors affecting the flow of theatrical films in the international trade).

124 Eli Noam distinguishes between 'domestic content', 'foreign content' and 'universal content'; *see* E. Noam, *Television in Europe*, 1991, 18.

125 *See* Baker, *supra* note 21, at 279–80.

126 *See* Fu and C. Sim, *supra* note 123, at 132–38 (proving that the low cultural distance and sharing the same language have positive effect on the ability to export and import theatrical movies); W.W. Fu, "Concentration and Homogenization of International Movie Sources: Examining Foreign Film Import Profiles", 56 *J. Comm.* 813, 826–27 (2006) (similar findings with regard to sharing the same language).

markers and is "easily translatable, understandable or appealing for people of widely varying local cultures and political circumstances."[127]

In addition to the content homogenisation and universalization which are so characteristic for cultural production of global media conglomerates, there are also other aspects which considerably affect the marketability of their cultural goods and services. Contrary to Baker's premise of customers' inclination to domestic content, it should be noted that individuals diverge in their personal preferences and tastes. While there are customers who are inclined towards domestic content, there are also customers who favour U.S. goods and services, because they consider those goods and services to have higher quality than products provided by local industries. The fame of Hollywood actors, singers, musicians, directors or other types of artists also plays its role in affecting the customers' choice of cultural goods and services. A considerable group of customers bases their decision to watch a particular movie on whether they like the directors, casted actors or actresses, used soundtracks and their singers, or whether the movie is produced by a studio established in a specific country. For this group of people, the quality and attractiveness of a movie is proved by the pure fact that their favourite director directed the movie, their favourite actor or actress plays a role in it or the movie was produced in a particular country.

Major Hollywood stars and studios are well-known worldwide compared to the movie stars and studios of other countries which are known regionally or sometimes only locally. For instance, the Spanish or French actress can be recognised in Spain, France or also in other European countries. However, when she wants to become famous worldwide, it is crucial for her to break through in Hollywood. It also applies to other regions, *e.g.* to Chinese, Korean or Japanese celebrities and their popularity within the Far East region.[128] The fact that a non-U.S. or non-English speaking celebrity becomes famous in Hollywood often guarantees that she will become marketable worldwide.

A further aspect which needs to be taken into account is the flexibility of consumers' preferences which can be affected by numerous internal and external factors.[129] For the purposes of this Chapter, it is important to point out that media conglomerates can effectively shape consumers' decision-making in various ways. They can do so either through public or institutionalised channels, such as news, commercials and other forms of promotion and marketing, or through informal channels, such as opinions, suggestions and recommendations

127 *See* id., at 280.

128 *See, e.g.*, S.Y. Lee, E-M Kim and S.H. Jun, "On the Exportability of Korean Movies", 13 *Rev. Dev. Econ.* 28 (2009) (explaining the popularity of Korean movies and television programmes in Far East Asia, so-called *Hallyu* or Korean Wave, partially through the popularity of individual Korean actors and actresses in the region).

129 For the purpose of this Chapter, the following analysis focuses mainly on external factors. However, it should be underscored that both types and their interrelationships are important for understanding of consumers' purchase preferences.

obtained by consumers within numerous social groups and networks of which they are members, *e.g.* amongst friends, relatives or co-workers. The influence of social groups and networks is especially considerable and often more efficient in influencing consumers' preferences for specific cultural goods and services than promotion made through institutionalised channels.[130] However, both types of information channels should not be viewed in isolation from each other or working in a vacuum. The converse is true. Their various forms mutually interact and have diverse synergic effects in different social groups and networks.[131] Consequently, through the targeted promotion which can efficiently affect the consumers' preferences, the media conglomerates can create cultural lock-ins,[132] *i.e.* customers' stable preferences for a specific type of cultural expressions.

On the other hand, the higher investment in the production and promotion of U.S. blockbusters and television programmes requires a bigger size of the market to recoup the high initial investment. If the actors, directors or other artists are famous only locally or regionally, the size of the market where they are marketable does not allow for the recouping of the higher production investment into projects in which they are involved. As the marketability of Hollywood movies and U.S. television programmes is worldwide, the investors can obtain more revenues from them than those who invest in movies produced in other regions.[133] Accordingly, the United States has a comparative advantage in cultural production compared to other countries. Only a few audiovisual goods and services from other countries[134] can be marketed worldwide and are thus able to obtain more investment for their production with the guarantee that the investors will get their money back with adequate profit.

To understand how the U.S. copyright and other intellectual property industries gained their power, it is important to look also at the size of the U.S. domestic market.[135] Although the size of E.U. market is bigger than the U.S. one, its disadvantage is that it is multilingual and multicultural. Additionally, the strong national feelings and preferences for local cultural production also play an import role on the E.U. market. The production from one E.U. country thus has to compete with the U.S. goods and services in local markets in other European countries. Furthermore, many cultural goods produced and cultural

---

130 *See, e.g.*, M.B. Holbrook and M. Addis, "Art Versus Commerce in the Movie Industry: A Two-Path Model of Motion-Picture Success", 32 *J. Cult. Econ.* 87 (2008).

131 *See id.*, at 100–1.

132 *See* Pessach, *supra* note 84, at 1086.

133 For statistics concerning world movie market trends in between 2005 and 2009, *see, e.g.*, European Audiovisual Observatory, *Focus 2010: World Film Market Trends*, www.obs.coe.int/online_publication/reports/focus2010.pdf (last visited 2 February 2012).

134 Several examples of such products are *manga* (comics), *anime* (cartoons) and video games.

135 *See* Fu and C. Sim, *supra* note 123, at 132 (proving that the size of economy and the level of cinema attendance at the domestic market have positive effect on the ability to export theatrical movies); Fu, *supra* note 126 (studying the impact of the market size of exporting and importing countries on their shares of the market with theatrical movies).

services provided by the E.U. industries are often closely linked to a particular culture of the country where the product was produced. Their close cultural linkage may be an advantage on their domestic markets, but at the same time a disadvantage on foreign markets against the universal content provided by the global media conglomerates.

A further advantage of U.S. cultural goods and services is that individual foreign local markets are only derivative or ancillary markets for many multinational enterprises besides their main U.S. market, while the foreign local markets are the initial and often the only markets for many local independent producers.[136] Although the costs of U.S. production are often recouped on the U.S. market or divided between the U.S. and several other main foreign markets, the local markets flooded by the U.S. cultural goods and services are essential markets for many local producers with regard to collecting their revenues.

Accordingly, as shown above, the international market is considerably distorted and frequently it is very difficult for many local independent producers to compete with the production of global media conglomerates. However, the logic of liberalised international trade is that countries should not protect their local industries against foreign competitors. If a country is unable to compete with other countries in one area of production, it should focus on the area in which it has comparative advantage. In practice, this would lead to the situation where, for instance, country A should focus on agricultural production, country B on cultural industries and country C on technological innovations.

In the view supported by the United States, the approach based on complete liberalisation of international trade will lead to more competition in the field of cultural production and thus the consumers will be supplied with a variety of diverse cultural expressions with high quality. Its supporters depict cultural diversity so that each country is represented by one colour. By allowing free trade of cultural products and services without any local corrections or interventions, the expected result should be that each country will not be represented by a single colour anymore. It will be represented by the colour indicating the local culture and various colours assigned to cultural goods and services imported from other countries. Accordingly, the more intense the international trade is, the more culturally diverse the individual countries can be.

Nonetheless, the actual consequences of liberalised distorted international trade on local industries may completely change the above-outlined picture. As shown previously, it is often quite hard for local industries to compete in domestic or regional markets with the cultural production of global media conglomerates, especially due to the popularity of Hollywood and other U.S. celebrities, the promotion of U.S. production, cultural lock-ins and barriers to

136 *See* Pessach, *supra* note 84, at 1095.

entry. All these factors can drive many independent local firms out of business[137] and induce further global concentration in the respective industries. The model based upon assigning colours to individual cultures may then actually look completely different, especially when each country is seen from the beginning as a mixture of different colours representing local diversity of cultural expressions. Through liberalised distorted international trade, the situation in individual national markets may change so dramatically that a considerable part of each national market would be represented by goods produced or services provided by media conglomerates from certain countries, especially the United States and in particular regions followed by some other developed countries. Hence, the market remaining for originally diverse local cultural production would significantly shrink or would even be completely marginalised.

To sum up, the approach based upon liberalised trade and stressing the comparable advantages of individual countries is highly questionable and controversial in the field of cultural production. This is particularly so when it leads to the situation where the countries with a comparative advantage in cultural fields are only exporting countries and the other countries are simply consumers of foreign cultural production. Furthermore, it would have a considerably negative impact not only on cultural diversity in the countries which would be net importers of foreign cultural goods and services, but also on cultural diversity in the exporting countries as well and on cultural diversity worldwide. When media conglomerates concentrate on production which can be placed on the global market, they tend to produce content to satisfy the tastes and demands of mass audiences worldwide. In order to be easily translatable from one culture to another, such cultural production misses close cultural links to any specific local culture. This causes its cultural distinctiveness to slowly, but steadily diminish. The stress and focus on universal content is therefore clearly at the expense of local cultural expressions, be they cultural expressions of countries purely exporting or importing cultural goods and services.

4.2. INTELLECTUAL PROPERTY AND REDISTRIBUTIVE JUSTICE

To support a sufficient amount and variety of cultural production on a local, regional and international level, many perceived that the negative outcomes of purely liberalised trade with cultural content should in some way be prevented in cases where the international market is distorted. Many countries, the markets of which are flooded by cultural goods and services from abroad, thus

---

137 *See, e.g.*, Curtis, *supra* note 84, at 79; M.S. Nadel, "How Current Copyright Law Discourages Creative Output: The Overlooked Impact of Marketing", 19 *Berkeley Tech. L.J.* 785, 797–810 (2004).

search for efficient protective measures in favour of local cultural production which could allow local cultures to survive at least in domestic markets. They attempt to reduce or even completely diminish the disadvantages of local cultural industries, which have sometimes almost no chance to compete with imported cultural production. Such state protectionism is met by severe criticism from the U.S. based media conglomerates supported by the U.S. government. The opponents of state protectionism claim that the negative impact of liberalised international trade on local cultural production is just temporary and the consumers' preferences in favour of local content would lead to a new equilibrium between local and foreign cultural production, where the former will regain its position.[138] But this scenario is based upon the premise that local production will still have an access to efficient channels to get to consumers. This can become quite difficult if the global media conglomerates gain complete control over the local distribution channels in the meantime.

From the beginning it should be made clear that this clash of views on state intervention in the market and international trade of cultural goods and services mainly applies to popular culture. When it concerns the 'Culture' or put otherwise 'high culture',[139] *i.e.* the art, the intervention either from the public or private sector is deemed necessary on both sides of the Atlantic. As Towse puts it succinctly, "[i]n most countries the arts and heritage are supported by some form of government intervention, whether state provision, government subsidy or indirect support via tax breaks and the like, depending on cultural policy."[140]

The clash occurs when it comes to culture or so-called 'low', mass-produced culture,[141] especially with regard to state protectionism of domestic copyright industries, such as publishing houses, record labels, studios and broadcasting networks.[142] Although approaches to so-called "traditional" creative and performing arts, such as visual arts, literature, music, dance, opera or drama,[143] also diverge from one country to another, the supports to individual authors, performers and other artists are not as contentious as state protectionism of corporate entrepreneurs. The latter is the area where the main frictions occur, particularly due to the position of U.S. industries in the international trade of cultural goods and services.

Although the detailed analysis of screen quotas, taxes, subsidies or other protection measures goes beyond the scope of the Chapter,[144] the several points

---

138 *See, e.g.*, Cowen, *supra* note 14.

139 *See* R. Towse, "Copyright and Cultural Policy for the Creative Industries", in O. Granstand (ed.), *Economic, Law and Intellectual Property: Seeking Strategies for Research and Teaching in a Developing Field*, 2003, 419, 421 and 423.

140 Id., at 424.

141 Id., at 421 and 423.

142 Id., at 423–24.

143 Id., at 423.

144 *See* the text accompanying note 122.

should be raised in this regard. The protection measures does not have only positive impacts on the protection and promotion of cultural diversity, but can also have negative ones. The governments therefore have to be cautious in the implementation of such measures, since they can considerably distort affected markets and can reduce incentives of heavily subsidised local industries to behave competitively. Accordingly, the screen quotas should be set up so that they will reflect the actual size and potential of local industries. Otherwise, local industries may mainly focus on quantity in order to fill the quotas, disregarding the consumers' demands for quality of cultural production.[145] Similarly, the subsidies are to be designed so that they will not allow directing funds abroad to pockets of foreign multinational enterprises without benefiting local cultural production.[146] At the same time the successful local producers should not be 'penalised' in any way for their success through the operation of protection measures, *e.g.* taxes imposed in order to support other local competitors.[147]

In addition to the abovementioned protectionist measures, in many jurisdictions copyright laws also contain several mechanisms which aim to support local creative activities and to strike a fair and just balance between individual creators and corporate entrepreneurs. The former are frequently implemented within the regimes designed for collective management of copyrights and neighbouring (related) rights through special organisations established either by law or agreement between copyright holders. The collecting societies allow commercial exploitations of managed rights through licences, including blanket licences, and manage collected levies imposed on reproduction technologies, blank media and commercial activities leading to private copying of copyrighted and other protected works. Some jurisdictions require a part of the collected funds[148] not to be distributed directly amongst copyright and neighbouring right holders, but to be used for 'collective purposes', such as the

---

145 For cases where local industries concentrate rather on quantity of produced audiovisual works than on their quality, *see, e.g.*, B.M. Yecies, "Parleying Culture Against Trade: Holywood's Affairs with Korea's Screen Quotas", 38 *Korea Observer* 1 (2007), *available at* http://ro.uow.edu.au/cgi/viewcontent.cgi?article=1119&context=artspapers (last visited 2 February 2012) (discussing cases from South Korea); Cowen, *supra* note 14 (criticising the situation in France).

146 *See, e.g.*, Buchsbaum, *supra* note 14, at 16–17 (presenting a case in France).

147 *See, e.g.*, Cowen, *supra* note 14 (criticising the situation in France).

148 The exact figure varies from one country to another, *e.g.* Belgium (up to 30%), Denmark (1/3), France (25%) and Spain (20%); *See, e.g.*, P.B. Hugenholtz, L. Guibault and S. van Geffen, *The Future of Levies in a Digital Environment*, 2003, 20–21 (referring to Belgium, France and Spain), *available at* www.ivir.nl/publications/other/DRM&levies-report.pdf (last visited 2 February 2012); D.J. Gervais, "Collective Management of Copyright and Neighbouring Rights in Canada: An International Perspective", 1(2) *Can. J. L. & Tech.* 21, 34 (2002) (referring to Denmark); N. Piaskowski, "Collective Management in France", *in* D.J. Gervais (ed.), *Collective Management of Copyright and Related Rights*, 2006, 153, 176 (presenting the respective provisions of French law).

promotion of creation,[149] aid programs for the diffusion of live shows[150] and the training of authors and artists,[151] or promotion of other activities and services to the benefit of its members.[152] Although the allocation of such funds in various forms to promote creativity is an important mechanism, it should also be made clear that the actual size of the allocated funds is very limited.[153] In addition, collecting societies spend a considerable part of collected funds for their administrative and operational purposes.[154]

Many national copyright laws also have other redistribution mechanisms which attempt to strike a fair and just balance between authors, artists and other creators on the one side and corporate entrepreneurs to which individuals habitually assign the copyrights to their works either by an assignment agreement or through the operation of made-for-hire doctrine. The authors, artists and other individual creators are thus allowed to get back their copyrights under certain conditions, *e.g.* automatically,[155] by asking the concerned copyright holder to transfer them back after the expiry of a certain period,[156] or when the assignee does not commercially exploit the assigned copyrighted works, *i.e.* the concerned work is not available on the market for a certain time period.[157] In some countries, such redistribution mechanisms are even built into the redistribution schemes of some levies collected for private copying. For instance, the share of collected levies allocated in Germany for the works that are out of print are not divided between authors and publishers, but are distributed only amongst the authors.[158]

---

149 *See, e.g.*, HUGENHOLTZ, GUIBAULT and VAN GEFFEN, *supra* note 148, at 20–21 (referring to Belgium and France).

150 *See* id., at 21 (referring to France).

151 *See* id., at 21 (referring to France and Spain).

152 *See* id. (referring to Spain).

153 In the European Union, the funds allocated to special cultural purposes equal to 23% of collected levies for private copying, or, to put it otherwise, to 3.7% of total income of collecting societies; *See* CAP GEMINI, "Music in Europe: Sound or Silence?" (2004), *available at* www.soundorsilence.nl/cg_rapport_buma-stemra.pdf (last visited 2 February 2012); EUROPEAN COMMISSION, "Fair Compensation for Acts of Private Copying", at 10–11 (14 February 2008), *available at* http://ec.europa.eu/internal_market/copyright/docs/levy_reform/background_en.pdf (last visited 2 February 2012).

154 The administration fees charged by collecting societies amount approximately up to 10 percents of collected and administered funds. This figure varies from one country to another and also amongst individual collecting societies.

155 *See, e.g.*, GOLDSTEIN, *supra* 102, at 223 (referring (i) to Article 122 of Italian Copyright Act of 1941, as amended, which "imposes a twenty-year ceiling on publishing contracts"; and (ii) to Section 14(1) of Canadian Copyright Act of 1921, as amended, which "provides for a nonwaivable reversion to the author's estate, twenty-five years after the author's death, of any copyrights transferred by the author in his lifetime").

156 *See, e.g.*, U.S. Copyright Act, §§203 and 304(c) and (d), 19 October 1976, Pub. L. No. 94–553, 90 Stat. 2541 (1976), as amended. *See also* SCHECHTER and THOMAS, *supra* note 104, at 159–65.

157 *See, e.g.*, GOLDSTEIN, *supra* note 104, at 223 (referring to Article 41 of German Copyright Act of 1965, as amended).

158 *See, e.g.*, HUGENHOLTZ, GUIBAULT and VAN GEFFEN, *supra* note 148, at 20.

Another redistribution mechanism is presented by the artist's resale right (*droit de suite*) regimes, which have been introduced in several countries, such as California and within European Union.[159] The opponents of resale rights argue that the resale right regimes cause more harm than benefit to living artists. While a few estates and heirs of famous dead artists benefit a lot from such regimes, the opponents put forward that the majority of living artists are mainly harmed by them, since the resale right regimes can considerably reduce the amount of funds available on the primary market either (i) by switching the collectors' demand preferences to markets with other collectibles such as paintings and other art unaffected by the resale right regime, antiquities or manuscripts; or (ii) by transferring limited funds available for supporting young artists from galleries and dealers to heirs of few famous artists.[160] At the same time, the opponents suppose that the primary market is not distorted and the prices of art are market prices. Moreover, they underline that the increase of the price of art at secondary market depends on numerous factors and art world players (*e.g.*, critics, galleries, museums, collectors, dealers and auction houses), and not exclusively only on the artists.[161]

However, several empirical studies show that the case is not as clear as drawn by the opponents of resale rights. The art dealers often set up the prices on primary market below the actual value of individual works in order to maximize their value in the future.[162] The artists also habitually sell their art to museums and galleries below the price for which it is normally sold. On the other hand, public presentation of art in museums and galleries adds the value to the artists' art mainly on the secondary market and partially on the primary one where the actual prices increase more slowly.[163] Accordingly, the resale right reduces this 'inter-temporal unfairness'. By reducing profit made by reselling art, the incentive for speculations on art market are also slightly reduced in this way, since the individuals actually interested in the artistic value of art do not collect the art with the main object to immediately resell it for gaining profit.[164]

---

159 *See, e.g.*, Reddy, *supra* note 11, at 515–25 (analysing the situation in several countries all around the world); H. Vanhees, "Directive 2001/84/EC – Directive on the Resale Right for the Benefit of the Author of an Original Work of Art", in T. Dreier and B. Hugenholtz (eds.), *Concise European Copyright Law*, 2006, 405–521 (commentary of Directive 2001/84/EC of the European Parliament and of the Council on the resale right for the benefit of the author of an original work of art); K. Lubina and H. Schneider, "The Implementation of Droit de Suite – Inventory and Reflection in the Light of the Community's Cultural Competence", in Schneider and Van den Bossche, *supra* note 12, at 317 (analysing the implementation of Directive 2001/84/EC in several Member States of European Union).

160 *See, e.g.*, Merryman, *supra* note 11, at 27–28.

161 *See* id., at 23–24.

162 *See, e.g.*, O. Velthuis, *Talking Prices: Symbolic Meanings of Prices on the Market for Contemporary Art*, 2005, 124 and 163; U. Klein, *The Business of Art Unveiled: New York Art Dealers Speak Up*, 1994, 27, 81 and 243.

163 *See, e.g.*, Klein, *supra* note 162, at 116; Kawashima, *supra* note 11, at 309.

164 *See, e.g.*, Kawashima, *supra* note 11, at 310.

Another argument supporting the resale right is that it repairs 'inter-disciplinary unfairness' and allows the artists to participate on the profits from their artistic works gained by the seller,[165] contrary to other areas where the copyright holders benefit whenever a copy of their work is sold to the public.

In addition to the abovementioned measures, several scholars suggest various other possible schemes and mechanisms to stimulate creative intellectual activities, *e.g.* prizes, awards or government subsidies, which are proposed as alternatives or complements to the current intellectual property regimes.[166] Although some of them believe that creativity can be actively stimulated by those measures, Towse, amongst others, categorically rejects such views. She puts it tersely: "We simply do not know how to stimulate creativity."[167] As there might be some way to influence creative output through education,[168] Towse suggests that "success on the labour market and productivity can be enhanced by investment in schooling, resulting in human formation."[169] She also puts forward, as another option of supporting creative intellectual activities, the establishment of funds "to loan creators the capital to exploit their own work, loans which can be paid back out of royalty income."[170]

Although several abovementioned alternative regimes for supporting cultural activities seem very promising in protecting and promoting cultural diversity, some scholars are extremely cautious to support the idea that any of them can completely substitute copyright and other intellectual property regimes, since the proposed alternatives also have their own innate deficiencies. Towse utters it firmly: "I do not believe we should abandon copyright law for one reason alone: the proposed alternatives – government subsidies to artists vetted by Arts Councils and Academies, prizes and awards presided over by other artists and the arts establishment – as we know from cultural economics are no better and probably worse."[171]

As shown above, intellectual property policy (and especially copyright policy) is an important, but not the only, part of cultural policy. In many countries, this is the reason why the institutions responsible for cultural policy are also responsible for copyright policy. For instance, in Japan it is the Agency

---

165 *See* id., at 307.

166 For an excellent outline of various proposed and applied schemes and mechanisms, *see* S.J. Liebowitz and R. Watt, "How To Best Ensure Remuneration for Creators in the Market for Music?: Copyright and Its Alternatives", 20 *J. Econ. Surv.* 513, 525–37 (2006); R. Towse, "Copyright and Artists: A View from Cultural Economics", 20 *J. Econ. Surv.* 567, 568–72 (2006).

167 *See* R. Towse, "Copyright and Creativity: An Application of Cultural Economics", 3 *Rev. Econ. Res. on Copyright Issues* 83, at 89 (2006).

168 *See id.*, at 88–89; R. Towse, "Human Capital and Artists' Labour Markets", in V. Ginsburgh and D. Throsby (eds.), *Handbook of the Economics of the Arts and Culture*, 2006, 865.

169 *See* Towse, *supra* note 167, at 89.

170 *See* id., at 90.

171 *See* id.

for Cultural Affairs which is responsible for various aspects of cultural policy, including copyright policy and the promotion of cultural activities.[172] There are still countries where this is not the case. In some of them, initial changes in this direction can be observed. The close relationship between cultural industries and the arts in the United Kingdom resulted in the cultural industries being transferred from the authority of the Department of Trade and Industry, which was previously responsible for designing policy in the commercial cultural industries, to the remit of the Department for Culture, Media and Sport.[173] But copyright is still dealt with by the U.K. Intellectual Property Office under the Department for Business, Innovation and Skills.[174] There are also countries where different independent institutions are responsible for industrial property policy, copyright policy and cultural policy.[175] However, it should be pointed out that the fact that a single institution is responsible for designing intellectual property policy and cultural policy can be sometimes misleading. Although the institutional design of governmental agencies can have considerable impact on the designing of individual cultural policies, it should still be kept in mind that the actual design, interrelation and synergic impact of individual cultural policies on cultural diversity is what matters.

4.3. INTELLECTUAL PROPERTY AND INTANGIBLE CULTURAL HERITAGE

A further critique of intellectual property regimes with regard to cultural diversity emphasises that they do not satisfactorily reflect the needs of non-Western cultures.[176] Attention is especially drawn to the fact that they conventionally fail to sufficiently protect traditional knowledge and traditional

---

172 For the actual scope of activities within the remit of the Japanese Agency for Cultural Affairs, *see* Agency for Cultural Affairs, "Administration of Cultural Affairs in Japan – Fiscal 2011", *available at* www.bunka.go.jp/english/index.html (last visited 2 February 2012).

173 For the actual scope of activities within the remit of U.K. Department for Culture, Media and Sport, *see* Department for Culture, Media and Sport, *Department for Culture, Media and Sport, available at* www.culture.gov.uk/ (last visited 2 February 2012).

174 For the actual scope of activities within the remit of U.K. Intellectual Property Office, *see* Intellectual Property Office, "Our Mission", *available at* www.ipo.gov.uk/about/whatwedo.htm (last visited 2 February 2012).

175 An example of such country is the United States.

176 For analyses of problems concerning the clashes between intellectual property regimes and protection of cultural traditions, *see* M.F. Brown, *Who Owns Native Culture?*, 2003; G. Dutfield, *Intellectual Property, Biogenetic Resources and Traditional Knowledge*, 2004; J. Gibson, *Community Resources: Intellectual Property, International Trade and Protection of Traditional Knowledge*, 2005; S. von Lewinski (ed.), *Indigenous Heritage and Intellectual Property: Genetic Resources, Traditional Knowledge and Folklore*, 2nd ed., 2008; B. Hazucha, "Community as a Holder of Intangible Cultural Heritage: A Broader Public Policy Perspective", in T. Kono (ed.), *Intangible Cultural Heritage and Intellectual Property: Communities, Cultural Diversity and Sustainable Development*, 2009, 223.

cultural expressions.[177] The severity of this critique is even more overwhelming when we take into account that cultural traditions are crucial for cultural diversity,[178] since cultural heritage, be it tangible or intangible,[179] provides the respective cultural communities with a sense of identity and continuity[180] which is then reflected in individual cultural expressions.[181]

The main problem with calls for protection of traditional knowledge and cultural expressions is the diversity and heterogeneity of individual proposals and forms of cultural traditions.[182] Some rituals, habits or customs forming the intangible cultural heritage[183] of indigenous, traditional or other local communities are considered as sacred. They can be used only for spiritual purposes. Their use for other purposes, and especially for commercial ones, is perceived to be incompatible with their sacred and spiritual character. The advocates of protecting cultural traditions by law therefore campaign for empowering the affected communities with efficient legal instruments and mechanisms to keep such traditional cultural expressions secret.

---

177 The terms 'traditional knowledge' and 'traditional cultural expressions' are used consistently with their definitions by currently drafted international instruments for their protection under the auspices of the World Intellectual Property Organisation (WIPO); *see* WIPO, Intergovernmental Committee on Intellectual Property and Genetic Resources, Traditional Knowledge and Folklore, "The Protection of Traditional Knowledge: Draft Objectives and Principles", Annex, Article 3(2), *WIPO/GRTKF/IC/10/5* (2 October 2006), *available at* www.wipo.int/edocs/mdocs/tk/en/wipo_grtkf_ic_10/wipo_grtkf_ic_10_5.pdf (last visited 2 February 2012); WIPO, Intergovernmental Committee on Intellectual Property and Genetic Resources, Traditional Knowledge and Folklore, "The Protection of Traditional Cultural Expressions/Expressions of Folklore: Draft Objectives and Principles", Annex, Article 1(a), *WIPO/GRTKF/IC/10/4* (2 October 2006), *available at* www.wipo.int/edocs/mdocs/tk/en/wipo_grtkf_ic_10/wipo_grtkf_ic_10_4.pdf (last visited 2 February 2012).

178 *See, e.g.*, Convention for the Safeguarding of the Intangible Cultural Heritage, Article 2(1), 17 October 2003, U.N. Doc. MISC/2003/CLT/CH/14 (2003), *available at* http://unesdoc.unesco.org/images/0013/001325/132540e.pdf (last visited 2 February 2012) [hereinafter "ICH Convention"].

179 For the issues related to the protection of cultural heritage; *see, e.g.*, P. Seitel (ed.), *Safeguarding Traditional Cultures: A Global Assessment*, 2001; B.T. Hoffman (ed.), *Art and Cultural Heritage: Law, Policy and Practice*, 2005; J.H. Merryman, A.E. Elsen and S.K. Urice, *Law, Ethics, and the Visual Arts*, 5th ed., 2007; Kono, *supra* note 176.

180 ICH Convention, *supra* note 178, Article 2(1).

181 Convention on the Diversity of Cultural Expressions, *supra* note 1, Article 4(2) ("'Cultural content' refers to the symbolic meaning, artistic dimension and cultural values that originate from or express cultural identities.") and Article 4(3) ("'Cultural expressions' are those expressions that result from the creativity of individuals, groups and societies, and that have cultural content.").

182 *See, e.g.*, W.E.A. van Beek and F. Jara, "'Granular Knowledge': Cultural Problems with Intellectual Property and Protection", in F.W. Grosheide and J.J. Brinkhof (eds.), *Intellectual Property Law 2002: Articles on Cultural Expressions and Indigenous Knowledge*, 2002, 35, 48–49 (describing three-layer social organization in Kapsiki society in relation to the access to medicinal information); B. Hazucha and T. Kono, "Conceptualization of Community as a Holder of Intangible Cultural Heritage", in T. Kono (ed.), *supra* note 176, 145, 151–52.

183 ICH Convention, *supra* note 1, Article 2(1) (defining the term 'intangible cultural heritage').

While the concerned groups and communities want to exclude outsiders from any access to this type of cultural tradition, intellectual property regimes mainly concentrate on trading with intangible goods by creating the necessary environment for producing and selling the protected intangible goods to the public and thus making them publicly accessible. The exception is trade secrets, but trade secrets are essentially used in commercial activities of their holders. Hence, the use of trade secrets to this type of cultural traditions would go against their sacred character. In general, the grant of intellectual property rights is thus not a sufficient measure for protecting such cultural traditions. The way intellectual property law can be partially ameliorated towards respecting sacred and other important cultural traditions is to establish a mechanism for rejecting granting intellectual property rights to the objects which are identical or similar to specific traditional cultural expressions. In many countries, some intellectual property regimes, especially trademark laws, respect culturally sensitive content by excluding such content from eligible subject matter of trademarks.[184]

On the other hand, the commercial exploitation of other traditional knowledge or cultural expressions does not cause problems as to its commercial character. Such exploitation is considered unjust only when prior informed consent is not obtained from concerned indigenous, traditional or other local community and the obtained profit is not fairly shared with its members,[185] when such production substitutes the cultural goods produced or cultural services provided by members of respective communities,[186] or when particular cultural traditions are used inappropriately by non-members of concerned community.[187] But it should be underlined again that many conventional intellectual property rights do not fit very well to traditional knowledge and cultural expressions for several reasons, especially due to the subject matter of protection which is often only indirectly related to cultural traditions in questions, time limitation of intellectual property rights and the requirement of originality, novelty or distinctiveness.[188]

---

184 *See, e.g.*, A. Kur and R. Knaak, "Protection of Traditional Names and Designations", in von Lewinski, *supra* note 176, at 293, 318–322 (describing the protection of Native American Tribes in the United States by rejecting the registration of offensive marks on the one side and native insignia compiled in a database of Native American insignia on the other by the U.S. Patent and Trademark Office, and the protection of Maori signs, including Maori text and imagery, in New Zealand by establishing the Advisory Committee which is to examine all the trademark applications containing or deriving from a Maori sign).

185 *See, e.g.*, P-T. Stoll and A. von Hahn, "Indigenous Peoples, Indigenous Knowledge and Indigenous Resources in International Law", in von Lewinski, *supra* note 176, at 7, 46–48; A. Taubman, "Genetic Resources", in von Lewinski, *supra* note 176, 181, 259–262.

186 *See, e.g.*, S. von Lewinski, "Final Considerations", in von Lewinski, *supra* note 176, at 507, 513–15.

187 *See, e.g.*, Kur and Knaak, *supra* note 184, at 293–96 (describing several such cases).

188 *See* id., at 301; Hazucha, *supra* note 176, at 240–42; R.K. Paterson and D.S. Karjala, "Looking Beyond Intellectual Property in Resolving Protection of the Intangible Cultural Heritage of Indigenous Peoples", 11 *Cardozo J. Int'l & Comp. L.* 633, 646–52 (2003).

While conventional copyright laws can provide limited protection to some indigenous and traditional artists and performers which recreate traditional motives, themes and styles in new original and creative works of authorship,[189] the claims for indefinite communal rights to cultural traditions go against the spirit of such laws. To moderate conventional copyright laws to traditional cultural expressions, the levy systems for the use of traditional cultural expressions were introduced in several countries.[190] Under such systems, the levy is imposed for any commercial use of traditional cultural expressions. The funds collected for the use of such parts of the public domain (*domain payant*) are then used for the protection and promotion of traditional cultural expressions or to satisfy other public interests of the concerned indigenous, traditional or other local communities.[191] Due to the lack of necessary data on their actual operation, it is hard to evaluate to which extent the regimes are actually able to collect any sufficient funds and the efficiency of their redistribution. However, the criticism made previously to the administration of collected funds by collecting societies also applies to the administration and distribution of these funds.[192]

Another possible strategy for protection of cultural traditions is the adoption of some regime guaranteeing authenticity of product containing traditional knowledge or cultural expression either as to its producer or the geographical area from which it originates. It can be done through conventional trademarks,[193] community collective trademarks[194] or geographical indications.[195] Individual regimes can differ in particular requirements for obtaining protection for the respective mark or geographical indication, such as the requirement of registration, distinctiveness of mark[196] or link to a particular geographical

189 *See, e.g.*, von Lewinski, *supra* note 186, at 513; Hazucha, *supra* note 176, at 238–39.

190 *See, e.g.*, A. Lucas-Schloetter, "Folklore", in von Lewinski, *supra* note 176, at 339, 364–68, 372–73, 445–47.

191 *See* id., at 372–73.

192 *See also, e.g.*, Hazucha, *supra* note 176, at 243–44; von Lewinski, *supra* note 186, at 526.

193 *See, e.g.*, www.arcticinuksuk.com/index.php?option=com_content&view=article&id=9&Itemid=8 (last visited 2 February 2012) (providing information on "Igloo Tag" regime certifying authenticity of Inuit Art in Canada); www.toiiho.com/ (last visited 2 February 2012) (providing information on "toi iho" registered trade mark for Maori arts and crafts in New Zealand).

194 For instance, Council Regulation (EC) No. 40/94 of 20 December 1993 on the Community Trade Mark, Articles 64–72, OJ L 11 of 14 January 1994, p. 1, as amended; Japanese Trademark Act, Article 7*bis*, 13 April 1959, Law No. 127 (1959), as amended. *See also, e.g.*, Kur and Knaak, *supra* note 184, at 312–13; M. Hirao, *Shouhyouhou [Trademark Law]*, 1st rev. ed., 2006, 29–39.

195 For instance, Council Regulation (EC) No. 509/2006 of 20 March 2006 on Agricultural Products and Foodstuffs as Traditional Specialities Guaranteed, OJ L 93 of 31 March 2006, p. 1; Council Regulation (EC) No. 510/2006 of 20 March 2006 on the Protection of Geographical Indications and Designations of Origin for Agricultural Products and Foodstuffs, OJ L 93 of 31 March 2006, p. 12, as amended. *See also, e.g.*, Kur and Knaak, *supra* note 184, at 301–8, 310–12, 328–330.

196 In case of community collective trademarks, the requirement of distinctiveness of mark is often lower than in case of conventional trademarks.

location.[197] Nevertheless, the main deficiency of these regimes is that they protect only the use of mark or geographic indication in relation to particular products and services, and not directly traditional knowledge or cultural expressions embodied in the concerned product. In addition, they require that a community applying for registration or claiming for the respective right has to be socially organized or geographically concentrated in a certain degree. This can cause considerable problems as to the applicability of such protection measures to some indigenous, traditional or other local communities.[198]

As outlined above and shown in more details elsewhere,[199] intellectual property regimes can play an important role in the protection and promotion of intangible cultural heritage to a certain degree. At the same time, it should be taken into account that they can sometimes present considerable obstacles to the efforts to achieve its appropriate and efficient protection and promotion.

5. CONCLUSION

Although intellectual property laws and their application are frequently criticized for harming and reducing cultural diversity in the globalised world, many branches of modern intellectual property laws contain means and mechanisms for the protection and promotion of cultural diversity under certain conditions. Consequently, intellectual property policies are an important, but not the only part of cultural policy. A close relationship between intellectual property policies and other cultural policies is evident in many jurisdictions, but they are still often considered as two independent policies. Their frequent separate handling can cause inconsistencies amongst individual cultural policies and negative consequences of their operation on cultural diversity. Intellectual property policies as well as state protectionist policies relying on quotas, taxes, subsidies or other types of redistributive mechanisms and schemes can therefore have expected positive effects on cultural diversity, as well as inadvertent negative implications, *i.e.* either directly harming or insufficiently protecting and promoting cultural diversity. Furthermore, the differences in understanding cultural diversity often lead not only to a diverse combination of cultural policies in individual countries, but also to clashes and trade disputes between some of them, especially those which mainly export cultural goods and services on the one side and those which are largely consumers of foreign cultural production on the other.

---

197 *See, e.g.*, Kur and Knaak, *supra* note 184.

198 *See, e.g.*, S. Frankel, "Trademarks and Traditional Knowledge and Cultural Intellectual Property", in G.B. Dinwoodie and M.D. Janis (eds.), *Trademark Law and Theory: A Handbook of Contemporary Research*, 2008, 433, 453.

199 *See, e.g.*, Gibson, *supra* note 176; von Lewinski, *supra* note 176; Hazucha, *supra* note 176; Paterson and Karjala, *supra* note 188.

To smooth tensions and frictions in the field of cultural production, it is essential that the institutions responsible for cultural affairs and intellectual property policies understand that the only way to achieve efficient protection and promotion of cultural diversity on the local, regional and global level is to strike an appropriate and adequate balance between individual cultural policies, *i.e.* intellectual property and other cultural policies. The Convention on the Diversity of Cultural Expressions can assist the contracting parties to achieve a balance between individual policies and to calibrate an adequate role for intellectual property regimes as means of protecting and promoting a diversity of cultural expressions. For this reason, Grosheide praises the Convention for "stimulating participating states to provide the best possible societal environment for the act of creating, and as a consequence for the production of cultural goods and services."[200] However, the Convention also allows different ways for its implementation. Hence, individual countries have to be extremely vigilant in adopting any particular cultural policy in order to implement it and their actual implications on cultural diversity on the local, regional and global level have to be carefully studied.

[200] Grosheide, *supra* note 35, at 5.

PART V

DEVELOPMENT & THE CONVENTION ON THE DIVERSITY OF CULTURAL EXPRESSIONS

INTERNATIONAL COOPERATION ON DEVELOPMENT AND THE CONVENTION ON THE DIVERSITY OF CULTURAL EXPRESSIONS

Lilian Richieri Hanania* and Hélène Ruiz Fabri**

1. INTRODUCTION

Cultural industries face major economic risks both in national and international markets, stemming particularly from the specific economic features of cultural goods. In the first place, the appreciation of the quality of these goods is in most cases entirely subject to the experience and subjectivity of people, which means that the value which will be attributed to them is, most of the time, uncertain at the time of their production. Further, they are what may be called 'imitation goods', since, in order to reduce this value uncertainty, consumers tend to look for products that have been recommended or have sold well. This creates a kind of 'social contagion', which arises frequently and easily through massive marketing investments by cultural conglomerates. Aiming at attenuating risks resulting from these features, cultural industries tend to form large-scale economies, where a reduced number of big companies invest massively in the marketing and distribution of a few universally attractive cultural works. As a consequence, the exchange of cultural goods and services becomes quite unbalanced. Such imbalance is especially perceptible when the market share of cultural goods and services coming from developing States is compared to that of those coming from developed countries.

The starting point of this article is that cultural goods and services contain not only an 'entertainment' component, but also, and notably, an important

* Dr. Lilian Hanania is an Attorney (São Paulo and Paris) and an Associate researcher at the University of Paris I – Panthéon, Sorbonne. Her PhD thesis (University of Paris I, 2007) and recent works address International Economic Law and Cultural Diversity. She worked at the French Ministry of Foreign and European Affairs from 2009 to 2011 and currently works as Legal Counsel in a law firm in Houston, TX, USA.

** Professor Hélène Ruiz Fabri is dean of the Sorbonne Law School (University of Paris I – Panthéon, Sorbonne) and director of the Joint Institute of Comparative Law.

cultural element. They are therefore particularly relevant to social cohesion in modern multicultural societies. Consequently, if cultural industries of developing countries face difficulties in introducing their cultural products in either the national or international market, they may arguably suffer not only economic but also social harm. In fact, in spite of a marked deficiency in statistical data regarding developing countries' markets, the existing data shows a regrettable situation when it comes to the participation of developing countries in the global cultural market.[1] Data on the audiovisual and music markets provides useful information.

If it is true that some audiovisual industries originating from developing countries have attempted to significantly impact neighbouring countries' markets (for instance India and Hong Kong's films in relation to Pakistan and Bangladesh, or Mexico, Brazil and Argentina's television productions in relation to other Latin American countries), the cultural markets of developing countries are mostly taken by American audiovisual production. The cultural exports of developing countries today mainly concern equipment relating to cultural production.[2] Cinematographic production is limited by restricted financial capacity. National distribution sectors are normally very weak (cinema) or very concentrated (radio and television) and particularly import oriented.[3] This situation becomes all the more problematic since the hegemonic position of a few industries in the cultural sector appears not only in the international market but also inside national borders, where large national companies reproduce the features of international conglomerates. When it comes to the music sector, in most cases large international companies control production and, notably, distribution in developing countries through local affiliates. In 2003, for example, the major companies in the music sector represented 80% of the European and North American markets, 75% of the Latin America market and 62% of the Asian market (except for Japan).[4] In the African market, the same major companies are present only in South Africa, but in other African countries the independent music industry stands for informal, unsophisticated and unstructured production.[5]

As governments in developing countries generally have more urgent matters to deal with, relating for instance to fundamental infrastructure, they are often unable to invest in national cultural production and distribution in order to

1 *See, e.g,* UNESCO, "Tendances des Marchés Audiovisuels: – Perspectives Régionales – Vues du Sud", *CI/COM/2006/PUB/10*, at 122 (2006); L. Richieri Hanania, *Diversité culturelle et droit international du commerce*, 2009, 480.

2 C. Van Grasstek, "Le Traitement des Biens et des Services Culturels dans les Accords Commerciaux Internationaux", in UNESCO, *supra* note 1, at 122.

3 E. Cocq and F. Lévy, "Les Marchés Audiovisuels Dans les Pays en Développement. Bilan Statistique Centré Sur 11 pays – Chine, Corée du Sud, Inde, Philippines, Thaïlande, Costa Rica, Mexique, Salvador, Burkina Faso, Sénégal, Nigeria", in UNESCO, *supra* note 1, at 50, 54 and 64.

4 *See* id., at 83.

5 *See* id., at 84–86.

redress weaknesses of their cultural industries. Most of the time, such weaknesses and the resultant imbalance in the cultural sector may be simply explained by a lack of equipment and technology capable of assuring the birth of a viable industry. Certainly Internet and digital technology represent great potential in this sense. Yet the digital and technology gap faced by developing countries will probably still prevent their contribution to the cultural market for some time and the consequences of such a state of things are quite concerning. They imply that a large number of national cultural expressions, incapable of reaching the global cultural market (and often not even national markets), do not have the necessary incentive for production. The lack of diversity of cultural expressions has in fact become a significant problem in most of these countries. Cooperation on development in the cultural sector becomes absolutely necessary in order to correct that situation.

The need for cooperation to promote cultural exchanges was already recognised in the 1950 Agreement on the Importation of Educational, Scientific and Cultural Materials (Florence Agreement) and especially in its 1976 Nairobi Protocol. Cooperation between parties to the Florence Agreement is advocated in the Preamble to the Agreement. The Nairobi Protocol is more expressive, prescribing in Article VI(8) that "[t]he contracting States undertake (...) (b) to encourage through appropriate measures the free flow and distribution of educational, scientific and cultural objects and materials produced in the developing countries," which means that the concern with the balance of cultural exchanges expressed within UNESCO in the 1970s was clearly taken into consideration in that text. Nevertheless, no precise measure aiming at attaining 'encouragement' in favour of developing countries was foreseen.

The concern with special circumstances surrounding developing countries is also manifest in Article VII(10) of the Nairobi Protocol. According to this provision, "developing countries (...) may suspend or limit the obligations under this protocol relating to importation of any object or material if such importation causes or threatens to cause serious injury to the nascent indigenous industry in that developing country." A rebalancing of cultural exchanges in favour of the cultural industries of developing countries for the specific products covered by the Florence Agreement and its Nairobi Protocol would accordingly seem quite simply and clearly legitimated by such a provision. However, the implementation of this clause is challenged today by the need to respect trade liberalisation commitments contracted by the World Trade Organisation ("WTO") Members.

The same difficulty appears regarding a much more recent international law instrument, the *Convention on the Protection and Promotion of the Diversity of Cultural Expressions* ("Convention on the Diversity of Cultural Expressions")[6],

6 *See* Convention on the Protection and Promotion of the Diversity of Cultural Expressions, 20 October 2005, *U.N. Doc. CLT-2005/CONVENTION DIVERSITE-CULT REV.* [hereinafter "Convention on the Diversity of Cultural Expressions"].

which has tried to establish a legal counterbalance to international trade rules that tend to consider cultural goods and services as the same as any other merchandise. It aims at reaffirming the sovereign right of every State to intervene in favour of cultural expressions within its territory, in order to support every culture to express itself and, therefore, contribute to the rebalancing of the exchange of cultural goods and services and the achievement of cultural diversity. By legitimising the intervention of each State in favour of cultural expressions, the Convention on the Diversity of Cultural Expressions allows its Parties, if not in contradiction with the commitments they have already assumed within the WTO and other international agreements, to resort, for instance, to screen, radio and television quotas, as well as to subsidies in favour of national cultural production. In addition, attaining the richness resulting from the diversity of cultural expressions also requires balanced international exchanges of these expressions and, therefore, cooperative international action and in some cases preferential provisions in favour of the cultural industries of developing countries. Accordingly, the Convention on the Diversity of Cultural Expressions attempts to offer a new legal framework aiming at supporting cooperation for development in the cultural sector.

A question arises however on how this international cooperation framework interacts with international trade provisions. In order to respond to this question, some WTO provisions on trade and development will firstly be examined in Section 2. Section 3 will further present the main provisions of the Convention on the Diversity of Cultural Expressions provisions dealing with cooperation for development and their potential contribution to developing countries' needs.

2. DEVELOPMENT AND INTERNATIONAL TRADE PROVISIONS

In a nutshell, WTO Agreements are based on the non-discrimination principle. Products and services coming from different countries must be treated alike (most-favoured-nation treatment), and national products and services must not be treated more favourably than foreign products and services (national treatment). Measures tending to discriminate in favour of developing countries' industries may therefore be prohibited, according to the commitments assumed by each Member. Yet trade provisions in favour of developing countries and least-developed countries have been introduced in the international trade law system since 1947.[7] They clearly demonstrate the recognition by Members of

---

7 *See* WTO, Committee on Trade and Development, "Special and Differential Treatment for Least-Developed Countries", *WT/COMTD/W/135* (5 October 2004); WTO, Committee on Trade and Development, "Implementation of Special and Differential Treatment Provisions in WTO Agreements and Decisions", *WT/COMTD/W/77* (25 October 2000);

the need to take into account the particular development situation of each country when trade liberalization commitments are undertaken and to establish preferential provisions to support developing and least developed countries.

In this sense, Article XXVIII *bis*, paragraph 3, of the 1947 General Agreement on Tariffs and Trade ("GATT") states that

> [n]egotiations shall be conducted on a basis which affords adequate opportunity to take into account: (...) (b) the needs of less-developed countries for a more flexible use of tariff protection *to assist their economic development* and the special needs of these countries to maintain tariffs for revenue purposes and (c) all other relevant circumstances, including the *fiscal, developmental, strategic and other needs* of the contracting parties concerned [emphasis added].

According to this provision, relations with developing and least-developed countries should be governed by the principle of non-reciprocity and preferential treatment, which was reinforced in the 1960s by the introduction of Part IV of the GATT, entitled 'Trade and Development'.

The consolidation of more favourable treatment for developing and least-developed countries was accomplished by the Generalized System of Preferences ("GSP"), adopted in 1971 through a decision taken by the Contracting Parties to the GATT.[8] This decision allowed developed Parties, during ten years, to derogate from Article I of the GATT (most-favoured-nation treatment)[9] in order to grant a more favourable and non-reciprocal treatment exclusively to certain developing countries selected by them and to particular goods originating from those countries. Nevertheless, there has been frequent criticism of the efficiency of this system, since it implies that relations between developed and developing countries depend totally on the goodwill of developed States.[10]

WTO Secretariat, "Summary of the Provisions contained in the Uruguay Round Agreements for the Differential and More Favourable Treatment of Developing and Least Developed Countries", *available at* www.wto.org/english/tratop_e/devel_e/anexii_e.doc. (last visited 2 February 2012).

8 GATT Decision of 25 June 1971, "Generalized System of Preferences", *BISD18S/24* (28 June 1971).

9 The most-favoured-nation clause, inscribed in Article I GATT, requires that "any advantage, favour, privilege or immunity granted by any contracting party to any product originating in or destined for any other country shall be accorded immediately and unconditionally to the like product originating in or destined for the territories of all other contracting parties". In the GATS (General Agreement on Trade in Services), article II establishes this same treatment in the services sector: "With respect to any measure covered by this Agreement, each Member shall accord immediately and unconditionally to services and service suppliers of any other Member treatment no less favourable than that it accords to like services and service suppliers of any other country".

10 See J. McMillan, "A Game-Theoretic View of International Trade Negotiations: Implications for the Developing Countries", in K. Anderson and B. Hoekman, *The Global Trading System*, Vol. 2, 2002, 184–97 (defending the idea that developing countries' interests would be better protected if reciprocity was applied to them in its entirety, because of the greater certainty it

On November 28, 1979, a new decision was adopted, entitled 'Decision on Differential and More Favourable Treatment, Reciprocity and Fuller Participation of Developing Countries' and often called the 'Enabling Clause'.[11] It legally embraces the GSP in its paragraph 2(a) and states, in paragraph 5, that '[t]he developed countries do not expect reciprocity for commitments made by them in trade negotiations to reduce or remove tariffs and other barriers to the trade of developing countries, i.e., the developed countries do not expect the developing countries, in the course of trade negotiations, to make contributions which are inconsistent with their individual development, financial and trade needs. Developed contracting parties shall therefore not seek, neither shall less-developed contracting parties be required to make concessions that are inconsistent with the latter's development, financial and trade needs.' Such a clause clearly aims at benefiting developing and least-developed countries during trade negotiations and great flexibility is indeed given to contracting parties. However, no legal guarantee is given to developing and least-developed countries and no precise measure of more favourable treatment is defined.

The same reasoning exists under the General Agreement on Trade in Services ("GATS"). Article IV GATS, entitled 'Increasing Participation of Developing Countries', states that

> The increasing participation of developing country Members in world trade shall be facilitated through negotiated specific commitments, by different Members pursuant to Parts III and IV of this Agreement, relating to:
> (a) the strengthening of their domestic services capacity and its efficiency and competitiveness, inter alia through access to technology on a commercial basis;
> (b) the improvement of their access to distribution channels and information networks; and
> (c) the liberalization of market access in sectors and modes of supply of export interest to them.

Paragraph 3 further requires that "special priority" be given in these cases to least-developed countries.[12] In theory, Article IV covers a wide range of ways to help developing countries' industries by increasing their trade opportunities. However, it is limited to the framework of 'negotiated specific commitments' and implies logically that "liberalization of market access in sectors and modes of

---

would provide); *See also* P. Sutherland *et al.*, "The Future of WTO: Addressing Institutional Challenges in the New Millennium", at 12 and 24–5 (2004), *available at* www.wto.org/english/thewto_e/10anniv_e/future_wto_e.pdf (last visited 2 February 2012).

11 GATT Decision of 28 November 1979, "Differential and more favourable treatment reciprocity and fuller participation of developing countries", *L/4903* (3 December 1979).

12 *See* GATS Article IV, Paragraph 3 (stating that "account shall be taken of the serious difficulty of the least-developed countries in accepting negotiated specific commitments in view of their special economic situation and their development, trade and financial need").

supply of export interest to developing countries" shall be extended to every other WTO Member, in respect of the most-favoured-nation treatment.

Furthermore, the differential treatment foreseen by the GATS is also completely dependent on the will of developed countries, which may choose, according to their own interests, the sectors they wish to liberalize and their level of commitment. Article XIX:2 GATS reinforces this rationale, when it stipulates that "[t]he process of liberalization shall take place with due respect for national policy objectives and the level of development of individual Members, both overall and in individual sectors. There shall be appropriate flexibility for individual developing country Members for opening fewer sectors, liberalizing fewer types of transactions, progressively extending market access in line with their development situation and, when making access to their markets available to foreign service suppliers, attaching to such access conditions aimed at achieving the objectives referred to in Article IV." Again, no real obligation is imposed on developed countries and, in practice, commitments are always conditional on the negotiating power of each Member.

The WTO General Council, in its Decision of 1 August 2004 (the 'July Package')[13], showed special concern in relation to this matter and decided that special and differential treatment provisions should be re-examined, strengthened and arranged so as to become more precise, effective and operational. The importance of technical assistance and capacity building for developing and least-developed countries was also reiterated. Nevertheless, and once more, no specific binding provision was adopted in favour of development, even if the General Council's Decision might well be used by Members to increase their negotiating pressure on developed Members.

The consciousness of the insufficiencies of such a situation clearly appears in a Submission to the WTO Committee on Trade and Development from Argentina, Brazil, India, Indonesia, Namibia, Pakistan, Philippines, South Africa and Venezuela dated 1 December 2005[14], which highlights, *inter alia* and along with the 1979 Enabling Clause, that "[d]eveloping countries cannot be expected to pay for the much needed reforms in the agriculture sectors of developed countries (…), by overly ambitious requests of them in industrial tariffs that do not take into account the realities of their levels of economic development and their adjustment needs." Moreover, concessions from developing countries should "be commensurate with their levels of development in a full expression of the principle of special differential treatment" and "the principle of less than full reciprocity" (paragraph 14).

Since developing countries tend to make liberalization offers in economically weaker sectors and bearing in mind that their cultural industries are often not

---

13 WTO, General Council, "Doha Work Programme", *WT/L/579* (2 August 2004).

14 WTO, Committee on Trade and Development, "Reclaiming Development in the WTO Doha Development Round", *WT/COMTD/W/145* (1 December 2005).

very profitable, the reasons why developing Members (and especially those having recently acceded to the WTO) decide to liberalize their cultural services sector, in exchange for concessions in sectors where they possess more competitive industries, become quite understandable. Non-reciprocal and more favourable treatment in favour of development therefore becomes fundamental in order to safeguard the capacity of developing and least-developed countries to culturally express themselves and participate in the cultural global market. The Convention on the Diversity of Cultural Expressions provisions could arguably reinforce WTO Members' bargaining power in trade negotiations.

3. COOPERATION ON DEVELOPMENT IN FAVOUR OF CULTURAL DIVERSITY

As stressed above, developing countries are often unable to implement cultural subsidies and the existing cultural market structure frequently prevents those countries from introducing their goods and services in the national and international market. The Convention on the Diversity of Cultural Expressions endeavours to offer an answer to these two specific difficulties through international cooperation for development and the strengthening of the cultural industries of developing countries.

In Article 2.4, the Convention on the Diversity of Cultural Expressions establishes a 'principle of international solidarity and cooperation': "International cooperation and solidarity should be aimed at enabling countries, especially developing countries, to create and strengthen their means of cultural expression, including their cultural industries, whether nascent or established, at the local, national and international levels." Further on, the Convention on the Diversity of Cultural Expressions contains a series of practical provisions which aims at encouraging international cooperation between its Parties. Some of these provisions promote stronger cooperation specifically designed to overcome developing countries' difficulties in the cultural sector.

3.1. GENERAL COOPERATION MODALITIES

Most of the provisions of the Convention on the Diversity of Cultural Expressions establishing general terms of cooperation between States Parties are not binding and not precise enough to contradict existing international obligations of Parties and they rarely concern market access. It follows that their implementation will hardly impact international trade obligations.

In fact, the sole true obligation imposed by the Convention on the Diversity of Cultural Expressions relates to the duty of contracting Parties to provide, every four years, within their national reports to UNESCO, information on the measures taken in favour of the protection and promotion of the diversity of cultural expressions at the national and international level (Article 9(a)). The same provision requires that Parties share and exchange information relating to the protection and promotion of the diversity of cultural expressions and that information sharing be carried out through points of contact selected by each contracting party. Such a provision may become remarkably useful in the future, since it has the potential of filling the gap in uniform data on the cultural markets of developing countries. A greater amount of information on the positive practices of States with different cultural market situations and the exchange of such information may not only legitimise those practices, but also help other States (and especially developing countries) find solutions to the specific problems of their cultural industries.

This information sharing obligation is strictly linked to Article 19 of the Convention on the Diversity of Cultural Expressions, entitled "Exchange, analysis and dissemination of information," which states, *inter alia*, that

1. Parties agree to exchange information and share expertise concerning data collection and statistics on the diversity of cultural expressions as well as on best practices for its protection and promotion.
2. UNESCO shall facilitate, through the use of existing mechanisms within the Secretariat, the collection, analysis and dissemination of all relevant information, statistics and best practices.
3. UNESCO shall also establish and update a data bank on different sectors and governmental, private and non-profit organizations involved in the area of cultural expressions.

Complementing Article 9 of the Convention on the Diversity of Cultural Expressions, this provision acknowledges the importance of the centralisation of information on cultural markets and the recourse by States Parties to such information. To some degree, it goes along with the proposal of some authors[15] and of some delegations at the beginning of the negotiations on the Convention in favour of the creation of an observatory of the cultural market. The idea of an 'Observatory of cultural diversity' was nevertheless finally set aside. However, the UNESCO Institute for Statistics and the UNESCO Secretariat will have a relevant role to play in the years to come, by gathering information and promoting its circulation among the States Parties to the Convention.

International cooperation pursuant to the Convention on the Diversity of Cultural Expressions is also sought for education and public awareness (Article 10(a)) about the importance of cultural policies designed to protect and promote

15 *See, e.g.*, J. Smiers, *Arts under Pressure – Promoting Cultural Diversity in the Age of Globalization*, 2003, 201 (proposing that an independent 'observatory of cultural life' should be created, in order to follow up developments and changes in cultural policy).

the diversity of cultural expressions. The development of this kind of consciousness may represent an important gain for developing countries, where most of the time the large part of the population is unable to have access to cultural expressions coming from diverse origins. Article 10(c) of the Convention on the Diversity of Cultural Expressions adds that Parties shall "endeavour to encourage creativity and strengthen production capacities by setting up educational, training and exchange programmes in the field of cultural industries." In spite of the weakness of the term 'endeavour' and the lack of precision on the type of measures to be adopted, this article covers not only governmental action limited to the territory of one single Party, but also cooperative action aimed at strengthening cultural production capacities.[16] When applied, this provision may embrace a large range of exchange and cooperation measures. The latter should, moreover, "be implemented in a manner which does not have a negative impact on traditional forms of production." Such precision attempts to respond to developing countries' concerns about traditional local cultural expressions.

Another general non-binding cooperation provision is established at Article 12 of the Convention on the Diversity of Cultural Expressions: "Parties shall endeavour to strengthen their bilateral, regional and international cooperation for the creation of conditions conducive to the promotion of the diversity of cultural expressions, taking particular account of the situations referred to in Articles 8 and 17." The latter refers to special situations where cultural expressions are at risk of extinction, under serious threat, or otherwise in need of urgent safeguarding, and concerns particularly developing countries, as clearly stated by Article 17 of the Convention on the Diversity of Cultural Expressions: "Parties shall cooperate in providing assistance to each other, and, in particular to developing countries, in situations referred to under Article 8."[17] The large extension of such cooperation (at the bilateral, regional and international levels) seems to be a useful means of attaining diversity, openness and exchange among the Parties to the Convention on the Diversity of Cultural Expressions, including and especially for the benefit of developing States.[18] Cooperation should be promoted on a North-South but also on a South-South basis.

---

16 *See* UNESCO, Conference of the Parties, "Operational Guidelines on Education and Public Awareness (Article 10 of the Convention)", in particular paragraphs 10 and 11 (June 2009), *available at* www.unesco.org/new/fileadmin/MULTIMEDIA/HQ/CLT/pdf/Conv2005_DO_Art_10_EN.pdf (last visited 2 February 2012).

17 *See* L. Richieri Hanania and H. Ruiz Fabri, "Comment on Article 8" and "Comment on Article 17", in S. Von Shorlemer and P.-T. Stoll (eds.), *The UNESCO Convention on the Protection and Promotion of the Diversity of Cultural Expressions: Explanatory Notes* (2012).

18 A. Salambéré, "Attentes des Pays du Sud à l'Égard d'une Convention sur la Diversité des Expressions Culturelles", at 3 (speech held at 'Le Dix-Huitièmes Entretiens' du Centre Jacques Cartier – Rhône-Alpes: Le Combat pour la Diversité Culturelle) (5 December 2005), *available at* www.diversite-culturelle.qc.ca/fileadmin/documents/pdf/salambere.pdf (last visited 2 February 2012) (advocates the necessity of regional and international cooperation in order for African States to assure the survival of their cultural expressions); *See also* Smiers, *supra* note 15, 204 (also recommending the relevance of regional cooperation).

According to Article 12 of the Convention on the Diversity of Cultural Expressions, cooperation at all levels should 'notably' (and thus not exclusively) aim at the following objectives: dialogue among Parties on cultural policy, information sharing and cultural understanding, strengthening of the public sector strategic and management capacities in cultural public sector institutions, promotion of partnerships[19], use of new technologies, and the conclusion of co-production and co-distribution agreements. Among these many goals, the last objective is the only one which may be in contradiction with a trade obligation (the most-favoured-nation treatment), depending on the commitments adopted by each State in trade agreements. The other objectives come within what may be called "pure cultural cooperation", with no market access impact. The explicit reference to co-production agreements implies the acknowledgement of these instruments as a helpful tool in favour of cultural diversity. Even if experience shows, as highlighted by some authors[20], that most of these agreements are signed with countries whose markets are beforehand considered promising, and not with those that actually need support, these agreements are doubtless a source of cultural cooperation between States and play an especially important role in favour of developing countries, as they generally allow for the cultural works of one State to benefit from the measures of another State in favour of its national works. The reference to co-production contained in Article 12 might arguably support the refusal of the Parties to the Convention on the Diversity of Cultural Expressions to eliminate, within WTO negotiations, their exemptions to Article II GATS (most-favoured-nation treatment). In fact, most of the Article II exemptions in the audiovisual services sector refer to co-production agreements, as they naturally establish discriminatory treatment between foreign countries. Their explicit inclusion in each Member's list allows Members to keep such measures. Even if it is the case that exemptions to the most-favoured-nation clause were supposed to be wiped out by WTO Members in 2005 and that a lot of pressure has been brought to bear by certain WTO Members in order to oblige other Members to eliminate such exemptions, they are still in force and subject to review by the Council for Trade in services, which takes into account their utility and necessity. Within

19 As a result of State disengagement in the cultural sector, partnerships with civil society, non-governmental organizations and the private sector may become a practical solution for the promotion of cultural industries in contemporary times. Article 15 of the Convention on the Diversity of Cultural Expressions provides greater precision on the matter when it advocates the recourse to 'collaborative arrangements' designed specifically to favour developing countries.

20 *See* S. Von Shorlemer, "Promoting International North-South Cooperation in the Framework of the UNESCO Convention on the Protection and Promotion of the Diversity of Cultural Expressions: First Steps 2007–2010" (document prepared for the conference on Cultural Diversity – Europe's Wealth. Bringing the UNESCO Convention to Life, 26–28 April 2007, Essen), *available at* www.unesco.org/culture/culturaldiversity/Schorlemer_essen_20070427_en.pdf (last visited 2 February 2012).

the third review of Article II exemptions, which started in June 2010, many WTO Members highlighted the importance of co-productions in the audiovisual sector for cultural diversity, key social and cultural objectives, as well as cultural exchanges and cooperation.[21] Article 12 of the Convention on the Diversity of Cultural Expressions may serve to reinforce WTO Members' arguments for keeping such exemptions in their lists. Since developing countries are often disadvantaged in relation to developed States in trade bargaining, even the mild support given by this provision might be of help. The same kind of support for trade negotiations may result from other provisions directly designed to favour development through cooperation.

3.2. COOPERATION IN FAVOUR OF DEVELOPMENT

International cooperation aiming particularly at responding to the needs of developing countries is defined in Article 14 of the Convention on the Diversity of Cultural Expressions, entitled 'Cooperation for development'. According to this provision, "[p]arties shall endeavour to support cooperation for sustainable development and poverty reduction, especially in relation to the specific needs of developing countries, in order to foster the emergence of a dynamic cultural sector." Contrary to many provisions of the Convention on the Diversity of Cultural Expressions in which objectives are defined without an indication of the precise means necessary to achieve them, Article 14 of the Convention on the Diversity of Cultural Expressions establishes a non-exhaustive list of ways to promote cooperation and the 'emergence of a dynamic cultural sector'[22], which

---

21 When reviewing Article II exemptions, the Council for Trade in Services examines "whether the conditions which created the need for the exemption still prevail" (GATS, Annex on Article II Exemptions, article 4). The third review of Article II Exemptions started in June 2010 and ended in May 2011. The next review should be held no later than 2016. *See* Report of the meeting held on 17 November 2010 of the Council for Trade in Services (S/C/M/102, presenting the views expressed by Members like Canada, India, Brazil, Australia, European Union on the importance of keeping an exemption for co-production agreements in the audiovisual sector and the opinion of Hong Kong, "doubtful whether co-production agreements were the only effective way to pursue cultural policy objectives") and Report of the meeting held on 2 May 2011 of the Council for Trade in Services (S/C/M/105).

22 These means are the following: "(a) the strengthening of the cultural industries in developing countries through: (i) creating and strengthening cultural production and distribution capacities in developing countries; (ii) facilitating wider access to the global market and international distribution networks for their cultural activities, goods and services; (iii) enabling the emergence of viable local and regional markets; (iv) adopting, where possible, appropriate measures in developed countries with a view to facilitating access to their territory for the cultural activities, goods and services of developing countries; (v) providing support for creative work and facilitating the mobility, to the extent possible, of artists from the developing world; (vi) encouraging appropriate collaboration between developed and developing countries in the areas, inter alia, of music and film; (b) capacity-building through the exchange of information, experience and expertise, as well as the training of human resources in developing countries, in the public and private sector relating to, inter alia,

is to a certain degree reminiscent of the prescriptions of Article IV GATS in favour of developing and least-developed countries: strengthening of the capacity of developing countries, access to distribution channels and information networks, and access to developed countries' markets.

Similarly to Article IV GATS, the implementation of Article 14 of the Convention on the Diversity of Cultural Expressions depends on the political will of the Parties to this Convention. Indeed the wording used by Article 14 is "endeavour to support cooperation" and the means prescribed are not very precise, even if operational guidelines have been approved by the Conference of Parties on this article in June 2009.[23] Besides that, every positive discrimination in favour of developing countries must be in accordance with existing international trade provisions.

In fact, certain articles of the Convention on the Diversity of Cultural Expressions were the subject of particular criticism from some delegations during negotiations on the Convention. The main reason for this disapproval was the possibility of contradiction between such clauses and international trade agreements, and especially those established in the framework of the WTO. In the following portion of this chapter, three provisions of the Convention on the Diversity of Cultural Expressions will be examined, which detail some of the matters covered by Article 14: preferential treatment, financial assistance and collaborative arrangements in favour of developing countries.

3.2.1. Preferential treatment

Access to global and national markets, as well as to international distribution networks represents a stumbling block for the cultural goods and services of developing countries. Article 16 Convention on the Diversity of Cultural Expressions brings clarification to the practical ways access could be achieved, stating that "[d]eveloped countries shall facilitate cultural exchanges with developing countries by granting, through the appropriate institutional and legal frameworks, preferential treatment to artists and other cultural professionals

---

strategic and management capacities, policy development and implementation, promotion and distribution of cultural expressions, small-, medium- and micro-enterprise development, the use of technology, and skills development and transfer; (c) technology transfer through the introduction of appropriate incentive measures for the transfer of technology and know-how, especially in the areas of cultural industries and enterprises; (d) financial support through: (i) the establishment of an International Fund for Cultural Diversity as provided in Article 18; (ii) the provision of official development assistance, as appropriate, including technical assistance, to stimulate and support creativity; (iii) other forms of financial assistance such as low interest loans, grants and other funding mechanisms."

23 *See* UNESCO, Conference of the Parties, "Operational Guidelines on Cooperation for Development (Article 14 of the Convention)" (June 2009), *available at* www.unesco.org/new/fileadmin/MULTIMEDIA/HQ/CLT/pdf/Conv2005_DO_Art_14_EN.pdf (last visited 2 February 2012).

and practitioners, as well as cultural goods and services from developing countries." The means prescribed by this article to attain cultural diversity consist in preferential treatment to cultural goods and services coming from developing countries. Nevertheless, the term 'facilitate' implies only a 'best efforts' obligation, which depends on the will of each State for implementation. Moreover, the level of facilitation granted by developed States is not precise and the mobility of artists and other cultural professionals and practitioners is limited to what is established in 'appropriate institutional and legal frameworks.'[24] Operational guidelines on Article 16 state that "[p]referential treatment as defined by Article 16 is wider than the narrow trade meaning. It is to be understood as having both a cultural and a trade component."[25]

Since the Convention cannot modify existing WTO obligations or obligations contained in other trade agreements,[26] developed countries will have to respect their contracted trade commitments when applying article 16 in order to avoid being subjected to the WTO Dispute Settlement Body or other dispute settlement mechanisms. Granting preferential treatment to goods and services of some countries may be incompatible with the non-discrimination principle established under WTO Agreements. However, Article 16 of the Convention on the Diversity of Cultural Expressions seems to be covered by the special and differential treatment provisions of the WTO. These may in fact provide Parties to the Convention with a justification for putting Article 16 into practice, on the condition that this preferential treatment is granted according to precise and reasonable criteria and in a non-discriminatory manner with respect to other developing countries in the same circumstances. In this sense, Article 16 might be seen as a translation of the special and differential treatment established in the WTO into the cultural sector.[27] In practical terms, such preferential

---

24 Such a limitation goes along with article 14 (v), prescribing the facilitation 'to the extent possible' of mobility of artists from developing countries. See on this matter Von Schorlemer, *supra* note 17, 170.

25 *See* UNESCO, Conference of the Parties, "Operational Guidelines on Preferential Treatment for Developing Countries (Article 16 of the Convention)" (June 2009), *available at* www.unesco.org/new/fileadmin/MULTIMEDIA/HQ/CLT/pdf/Conv2005_DO_Art_16_EN.pdf (last visited 2 February 2012) [hereinafter "Operational Guidelines on Article 16"].

26 *See* Convention on the Diversity of Cultural Expressions, *supra* note 7, Articles 20 and 21 (establishing the rules governing the articulation between the Convention and other international obligations and notably a relationship of equality between the Convention and other international instruments); *See also* Richieri Hanania, *supra* note 1, at 304 and following.

27 *See* H. Ruiz Fabri, "Culture seized by globalization: can international law be of any help? Reflections on possible future legal implications of the UNESCO Convention on the protection and promotion of the diversity of cultural expressions", in A. Reinish and U. Kriebaum (eds.), *The Law of International Relations: Liber Amicorum Neuhold*, 2007, 299; *See also* H. Ruiz Fabri, "Analyse et Commentaire Critique de l'Avant-Projet de Convention sur la Protection de la Diversité des Contenus Culturels et des Expressions Artistiques dans la Version Soumise pour Commentaires et Observations aux Gouvernements des Etats Membres de l'UNESCO", 29 (2004), *available at* www.francophonie.org/IMG/pdf/Analyse_

treatment could be expressed, for instance, in an organised framework for co-production arrangements and technical assistance in favour of developing countries.

However, two remarks deserve to be made at this point. Firstly, as already mentioned, WTO rules on special and differential treatment are often not effectively applied. Secondly, the manner in which the preferential treatment for developing countries under the Convention should be brought to fruition within the WTO is not very clear. For example, it could be proposed that developed countries accept market access or national treatment requests from developing countries in the cultural services sector and inscribe the same on their GATS Schedules. Nevertheless, such a path would not be adequate in a system where most- favoured-nation treatment exists. In fact, if a developed WTO Member (*e.g.*, the European Union) opens its market for developing countries' cultural services, it will be obliged to extend such a treatment to other Members, including to those already well-established in the market. This would probably strengthen the economic conditions of the few already existing hegemonic agents,[28] without benefiting the industries of developing countries.

An alternative means found by the European Commission was to negotiate Protocols on Cultural Cooperation attached to trade agreements with developing countries according to which a preferential treatment shall be granted in the European market to co-produced audio-visual works respecting certain conditions. The first Protocol on Cultural Cooperation was negotiated in the framework of the EU-Cariforum Economic Partnership Agreement. In spite of much criticism expressed against such protocols when such practice was extended to developed trade partners of the European Union[29], their value for developing countries and the possible ways to improve them in order to better respond to the needs of those countries deserve to be explored.

---

et_commentaire_av-projet_convention_protection_div_contenus_cult_et_expr_artistiques.pdf (last visited October 24, 2011); *See also* J. Wouters and B. De Meester, "UNESCO's Convention on Cultural Diversity WTO Law: Complementary or Contradictory?", 22 (Institute for International Law, Working Paper No. 73, 2005) (quoting the WTO Appellate Body Report *EC – Conditions for the Granting of Tariff Preferences to Developing Countries* (DS246)). I. Bernier, "La première réunion d'experts gouvernementaux sur l'avant-projet de convention sur la protection de la diversité des contenus culturels et des expressions artistiques de l'UNESCO: Les implications pour la suite de la négociation", 14 (2004), *available at* www.diversite-culturelle.qc.ca/fileadmin/documents/pdf/chronique04–12.pdf (last visited 2 February 2012).

30 *See* J. Guerrier, "Négociations commerciales: la position de l'Union Européenne quant aux services audiovisuels", in C.B. Graber, M. Girsberger and M. Nenova (eds.), *Free Trade versus Cultural Diversity*, 2004, 132.

29 *See* Communication by France, "For a new European Union external cultural strategy" (December 2009), *available at* www.diplomatie.gouv.fr/fr/IMG/pdf/2009-12-21_Communication_France_Strategie_culturelle_exterieure_ENG.pdf (last visited 2 February 2012).

3.2.2. *Financial assistance*

Another tool foreseen by Article 14 of the Convention on the Diversity of Cultural Expressions which was the subject of frequent discussion during negotiations is financial support for developing countries, which may be envisaged in two ways: (a) assistance through the Convention's international fund and (b) general financial assistance.

A. Assistance in the framework of Article 18 of the Convention on the Diversity of Cultural Expressions

Article 18 of the Convention on the Diversity of Cultural Expressions envisages the creation and the financing of an International Fund for Cultural Diversity. Similar provisions were inserted in the 2003 Convention for the Safeguarding of the Intangible Cultural Heritage (Articles 25 to 28 ICH Convention; establishing a 'Fund for the Safeguarding of the Intangible Cultural Heritage'), as well as in the 1972 Convention concerning the Protection of the World Cultural and Natural Heritage (Article 15 World Heritage Convention; creating a 'Fund for the Protection of the World Cultural and Natural Heritage') and the 1999 Second Protocol to the 1954 Hague Convention for the Protection of Cultural Property in the Event of Armed Conflict (Article 29 Hague Convention; establishing a 'Fund for the Protection of Cultural Property in the Event of Armed Conflict').

The International Fund for Cultural Diversity was created by the first Conference of Parties held in Paris from 18 to 20 June 2007 and represents the outcome of the strong attachment of developing countries to financial mechanisms capable of gathering funds in favour of their cultural industries. However, as with most of the provisions of the Convention, Article 18 does not create a real obligation for Parties. Again, its use will be subordinated to the political will of developed countries.

Although the potential for financing the Fund is quite extensive, no obligatory contribution from the Parties to the Convention is prescribed. Indeed, Paragraph 3 of Article 18 of the Convention on the Diversity of Cultural Expressions states that the resources of the Fund shall come from: voluntary contributions (unlike the Fund for the Safeguarding of the Intangible Cultural Heritage or the Fund for the Protection of the World Cultural and Natural Heritage); funds appropriated by the General Conference of UNESCO; contributions, gifts or bequests by States, organizations, programmes, public and private bodies or individuals; the interest due on Fund resources; collections and receipts from events organized for the benefit of the Fund; and any other resources authorized by the Fund's regulations.[30] On the other hand, paragraph

[30] *See* I. Bernier, "An Important Aspect of the Implementation of the Convention on the Protection and Promotion of the Diversity of Cultural Expressions: the International Fund

7 determines only that "Parties *shall endeavour to* provide voluntary contributions on a regular basis towards the implementation of this Convention."[31]

As for the practical use of the Fund, Article 18 of the Convention on the Diversity of Cultural Expressions establishes general directions. Some guarantees of objectivity are prescribed, as well as the competence of the Intergovernmental Committee to decide on the use of the Fund, according to the guidelines of the Conference of Parties (paragraph 4). Moreover, "no political, economic or other conditions that are incompatible with the objectives of this Convention may be attached to contributions made to the Fund" (paragraph 6). Operational guidelines on Article 18 were adopted by the Conference of Parties in June 2009.[32]

When it comes to the compatibility of the Fund with WTO Agreements, it should be noted that the Fund aims at benefiting cultural diversity in general, according to specific and isolated decisions of an international body, the Intergovernmental Committee. Article 18 of the Convention on the Diversity of Cultural Expressions does not establish a discriminatory rule against free trade, even if it may favour specific developing WTO Members. Therefore, there seems to be no contradiction between this provision and the WTO non-discrimination principle.

However, other kinds of problems may arise in relation to Article 18 of the Convention on the Diversity of Cultural Expressions, relating to the complexity of developing countries' needs in the cultural sector and the difficulty in finding appropriate responses to them. For instance, a condition may be imposed by a contributing Party on the specific use of contributions to the Fund. Paragraph 5 of Article 18 of the Convention on the Diversity of Cultural Expressions states

for Cultural Diversity", 18 (2007), *available at* www.diversite-culturelle.qc.ca/fileadmin/documents/pdf/fonds-diversite-culturelle-eng.pdf (last visited 2 February 2012) (providing commentaries on these different resources and a comparison with other instruments).

31 *See* Convention on the Diversity of Cultural Expressions, *supra* note 7, Article 18, §7 [emphasis added] (note that the Spanish official version of the Convention contains more binding wording, even if the contributions are still considered voluntary: 'Las Partes *aportarán* contribuciones voluntarias periódicas para la aplicación de la presente Convención' (The Parties shall provide… – free translation). The French and the English versions (both the negotiating languages) confirm a less binding interpretation, but according to Article 34 of the Convention, the texts in Arabic, Chinese, English, French, Russian and Spanish are all equally authoritative. As Article 33 of the Vienna Convention on the Law of Treaties prescribes, a difference of meaning among authentic texts in different languages should be interpreted in the way '*which best reconciles the texts, having regard to the object and purpose of the treaty*'. Differences among the six versions of the 2005 Convention might thus create interpretation difficulties in the future.

32 *See* UNESCO, Intergovernmental Committee for the Promotion and Protection of the Diversity of Cultural Expressions, "Preparation of Guidelines on the Use of the Resources of the International Fund for Cultural Diversity", *CE/07/1.IGC/6* (25 October 2007), *available at* www.unesco.org/culture/culturaldiversity/december07/igc1_6_en.pdf (last visited October 24, 2011); *See also* Operational Guidelines on Article 16, *supra* note 25.

indeed that "[t]he Intergovernmental Committee may accept contributions and other forms of assistance for general and specific purposes relating to specific projects, provided that those projects have been approved by it." Contributions may thus be made in favour of particular projects, at the expense of a global strategy in favour of cultural diversity in developing countries.[33] In addition, the Fund could be used by developed countries instead of other more appropriate tools foreseen by the Convention, like Article 16 of the Convention on the Diversity of Cultural Expressions. The Fund could also become an ineffective tool, serving the interests of developed countries or, according to some authors, even a kind of 'cultural imperialism' instrument.[34] Moreover, it is not impossible that the advantages flowing from the Fund might discourage developing countries from working hard to develop their cultural industries. The Fund could arguably create an 'attitude of dependency', often pointed out by certain developed countries like the United States as a negative consequence of governmental subsidies in favour of cultural goods and services. All these risks might nevertheless be set aside if effective political monitoring is carried out and the recent experience with the use of the Fund seems to show that the most important problem faced by it relates rather to the lack of resources.

Still regular contributions and the financing of the Fund seem to be a very important way of legitimising and giving credibility to the Convention on the Diversity of Cultural Expressions as a whole among the international community, and especially developing countries, which would find it appealing to also become Parties. In fact, the Fund could progressively respond to the lack of resources which generally prevents developing countries from having recourse to cultural policy measures, including those foreseen by the Convention itself, notably in Articles 5 to 13 of the Convention on the Diversity of Cultural Expressions. Eventually, it may respond to legitimate expectations of developing countries which gave their support for the adoption of the Convention.[35]

Finally, it should be noted that nothing in the Convention prevents Parties from obtaining financial support independently of the Fund. In fact, the Convention aims at encouraging the creation, production and distribution of cultural expressions through avenues that are both various and flexible.

B. General financial assistance

As a distinctive tool among the mechanisms created in 2005, the effective use of the Fund may certainly lead to a greater credibility for the Convention compared

---

33 *See, e.g.*, Bernier, *supra* note 30, at 12.

34 C. Germann, "Towards a *Global Cultural Contract* to Counter Trade Related Cultural Discrimination", in N. Obuljen and J. Smiers (ed.), *The UNESCO Convention on the Promotion and Protection of the Diversity of Cultural Expressions: Making it work*, 2006, 286.

35 *See* H. Ruiz Fabri, "Reflections on Possible Future Legal Implications of the Convention", in Obuljen and Smiers (ed.), *supra* note 34, at 82.

to other means of financial help. However, all avenues for financial support of developing countries' cultural industries other than the Fund are covered by Article 14 Convention on the Diversity of Cultural Expressions, which acknowledges the relevance of 'other forms of financial assistance' in favour of the diversity of cultural expressions. In order to reinforce the political weight of the Convention on the Diversity of Cultural Expressions, Parties that would prefer not to contribute through Article 18 should nonetheless refer to the Convention as a basis for their actions when according financial support.

In any case, it should be noted that support on a North-South basis, outside the Fund, might entail the risk that the Convention on the Diversity of Cultural Expressions is seen as an "Eurocentric protectionist instrument".[36] Financial contributions to the Fund would therefore be preferable, since they would rather reflect international solidarity.

3.2.3. Collaborative agreements

Article 15 of the Convention on the Diversity of Cultural Expressions, which concerns collaborative partnership arrangements,[37] is also directly related to cooperation to promote the capacity of developing countries. A good example of a partnership to promote reading is that promoted by the 'Organisation Internationale de la Francophonie' (OIF) through the 213 'Centres de lecture et d'animation culturelle' (CLAC) established since 1986 in 18 countries in Africa, the Indian Ocean, the Caribbean and the Middle East.[38] Another interesting partnership initiative has been the creation of international broadcasting channels by groups of States, like *Telesur*, which commenced broadcasting on 24 July 2005 and involves Venezuela (51% of the company's assets), Cuba (19%), Uruguay (10%) and Argentina (20%). This kind of initiative may contribute to the development of national capacity by providing national television with a complementary channel for the broadcasting of national cultural works.[39]

Those kinds of arrangements would generally not be contested in the framework of WTO and other trade agreements, notably because they would

---

36 *See* Von Shorlemer, *supra* note 17, at 166.

37 *See* Convention on the Diversity of Cultural Expressions, *supra* note 7, Article 15 (this article reads as follows: "Parties shall encourage the development of partnerships, between and within the public and private sectors and non-profit organizations, in order to cooperate with developing countries in the enhancement of their capacities in the protection and promotion of the diversity of cultural expressions. These innovative partnerships shall, according to the practical needs of developing countries, emphasize the further development of infrastructure, human resources and policies, as well as the exchange of cultural activities, goods and services").

38 *See* Organisation International de la Francophonie, "Centre de lecture et d'animation culturelle: 20 ans d'expérience dans le pays francophone", *available at* www.francophonie.org/IMG/pdf/CLAC_Francais-2.pdf (last visited 2 February 2012).

39 *See* G. Rey, "Les Tendances et Perspectives du Marché Audiovisuel en Colombie, au Pérou et au Venezuela", *in* UNESCO, *supra* note 1, at 179–80.

hardly be considered as a threat to trade in the cultural sector. However, Article 15 of the Convention on the Diversity of Cultural Expressions may raise some important issues when it mentions, as a relevant aspect of cooperation for development, the objective of 'further development of infrastructure'. This joins up with the need for the transfer of technology and know-how acknowledged in Article 14 of the Convention on the Diversity of Cultural Expressions and the relevance of the balanced implementation of intellectual property provisions to benefit developing countries. The intellectual property aspects of cultural expressions could not be given detailed treatment by the negotiating Parties to the Convention on the Diversity of Cultural Expressions, but are certainly a central topic in serious discussions about the protection and the promotion of cultural diversity.[40] The Convention on the Diversity of Cultural Expressions limits itself to recognising in its Preamble "the importance of intellectual property rights in sustaining those involved in cultural creativity."[41] Every other reference to intellectual property rights was eventually been pushed aside from the negotiations, since some delegations and some actors of civil society feared that ambiguities in the text could weaken existing provisions on the subject.[42]

4. CONCLUSION

In the light of the above, it seems that the Convention on the Diversity of Cultural Expressions may help to create an environment of healthy cooperation for the exchange of cultural expressions. Its provisions on international cooperation for development do not, in essence, contradict the international trade obligations of its Parties. It should be reminded that the Convention remains a legally weak instrument, depending generally on the political will of its Parties, its primary contribution being to raise consciousness of the importance of cultural policy and cooperation in attaining cultural diversity, and to lead countries to act to promote cultural diversity.

---

40 *See* Richieri Hanania, *supra* note 1, at 386 and following.

41 Convention on the Diversity of Cultural Expressions, *supra* note 7, Preamble §17.

42 *See* S. Regourd, "Le Projet de Convention sur la Diversité Culturelle: Vers une Victoire à la Pyrrhus...", 226 *Légipresse* 115, 118 (2005).

SUSTAINABLE DEVELOPMENT AND THE CONVENTION ON THE DIVERSITY OF CULTURAL EXPRESSIONS

David THROSBY*

1. INTRODUCTION

The potential for fostering links between culture and sustainable development was one of the key drivers of moves towards the formulation of an international instrument promoting cultural diversity that evolved during the late 1990s and early 2000s. Sustainability had been explicitly mentioned in the resolutions arising from the 1998 Stockholm Conference on Cultural Policies for Development[1]; the Conference proposed that governments should recognise culture in such a way that cultural policies would "become one of the key components of endogenous and sustainable development".[2] The importance of sustainability also underlay the provisions of the 2001 Universal Declaration on Cultural Diversity,[3] which initiated the process that led eventually to the Convention for the Protection and Promotion of the Diversity of Cultural Expressions (hereinafter "Convention on the Diversity of Cultural Expressions").[4]

The concept of sustainable development was duly introduced into the Convention on the Diversity of Cultural Expressions in two of its Articles, and

* Professor of Economics, Macquarie University, Sydney.

1 *See* UNESCO, Intergovernmental Conference on Cultural Policies for Development (Stockholm, 30 March – 2 April, 1998), *available at* http://portal.unesco.org/culture/en/ev.php-URL_ID=18717&URL_DO=DO_TOPIC&URL_SECTION=201.html (last visited 2 February 2012).

2 UNESCO, "The Final Report on the Intergovernmental Conference on Cultural Policies" 13, CLT-98/Conf.210/5 (31 August 1998), *available at* unesdoc.unesco.org/images/0011/001139/113935eo.pdf (last visited 2 February 2012).

3 *See* Universal Declaration on Cultural Diversity, 2 November 2001, *available at* http://portal.unesco.org/en/ev.php-URL_ID=13179&URL_DO=DO_TOPIC&URL_SECTION=201.html (last visited on 2 February 2012).

4 *See* Convention on the Protection and Promotion of the Diversity of Cultural Expressions, 20 October 2005, *U.N. Doc. CLT-2005/CONVENTION DIVERSITE-CULT REV.*

guidelines for interpreting these Articles have been put together during the implementation process following the Convention's entry into force in March 2007. This Chapter examines the links between cultural diversity and sustainable development and discusses the contribution the Convention on the Diversity of Cultural Expressions can or should make to encouraging and exploiting these linkages. We begin in Section 2 by briefly examining the evolution of the concept of sustainable development and its implications for culture. Section 3 turns to the issue of diversity as an element in sustainable development. We then draw these strands together by asking how successful the Convention on the Diversity of Cultural Expressions has been or is likely to be in connecting diversity and sustainability in a policy-relevant way. The paper concludes with some observations on further developments.

2. SUSTAINABLE DEVELOPMENT

Sustainability as a way of characterising desirable properties of a national or global development path grew up in the second half of the twentieth century with the concerns being expressed about a relentless concentration on increases in real GDP per capita as the sole objective of development policy. Not only did economists begin to broaden their ideas about economic progress to take on board wider aspects of human development, there was also a growing understanding of the serious environmental costs being imposed on society by pursuit of untrammelled economic growth. These two discourses were brought together under the explicit rubric of sustainable development by the work of the UN World Commission on Environment and Development (The Brundtland Commission).[5] The Commission's report, *Our Common Future*, published in 1987, put forward what has become an accepted definition of sustainable development as "development that meets the needs of the present without compromising the ability of future generations to meet their own needs".[6]

The Brundtland Report's definition encompasses the core ideas of sustainability as implying long-term viability. Thus sustainable development strategies will focus not on short-term results but on outcomes that will last and be in some sense self-reinforcing. In economics this proposition is cast in terms of intergenerational equity, or fairness in the distribution of benefits from the allocation of resources between this generation and those to come.

The concern of the Brundtland Commission was with problems caused by exploitative resource use in industrialised countries that was threatening the air, land and water systems of the planet and was a direct contributor to problems of poverty and lack of development in the developing world. As such, the

5 *See* World Commission on Environment and Development, *Our Common Future*, 1987.
6 Id., at 47.

Commission's primary focus was on environmentally or ecologically sustainable development. Over the years since the publication of the Commission's report, a number of efforts have been made to broaden the concept, especially by incorporating social values into the assessment of sustainable development paths.[7] One particular area of interest has been the application of sustainability principles to culture.

The role of culture in development was brought into focus by a successor to the Brundtland Commission, the UN World Commission on Culture and Development, chaired by Javier Pérez de Cuéllar. The title of the WCCD's report, *Our Creative Diversity*, published in 1995, echoed that of its predecessor.[8] The Pérez de Cuéllar Commission stopped short of identifying a specific concept of culturally sustainable development, although the concept had been suggested to the Commission in a background paper.[9] Nevertheless, the broad notion of sustainability permeated its report, and was given further elaboration in the two *World Culture Reports* published by UNESCO in 1998 and 2000.[10]

During the first decade of the new millennium, the links between culture and development have been further explored, particularly in the context of the creative or cultural industries. These industries see traditional knowledge and distinctive cultural practices -- the songs, the dances, the poetry, the stories, the images and symbols that are the unique heritage of the land and its people -- as fundamental resources that are kept alive by written, oral, musical and pictorial transmission of cultural traditions from one generation to the next. They do not stay still, but are constantly interpreted, reinterpreted, added to, and adapted to new formats. They are accessed by the people in many different ways, serving as a rich cultural resource from which can be derived a wide variety of creative expressions. The essential feature of the creative industries which link traditional knowledge at one end of the chain with the ultimate consumer at the other end is their capacity to serve both cultural and economic objectives in the development process. In this regard the creative industries can be seen as consistent with the sustainable development paradigm for policy formulation in the developing

7 *See, e.g.*, V.E. Udo and P.M. Jansson, "Bridging the Gaps for Global Sustainable Development: A Quantitative Analysis", 90 *Journal of Environmental Management* 3700 (2009); V. Mauerhofer, "3-D Sustainability: An Approach for Priority Setting in Situation of Conflicting Interests Towards Sustainable Development", 64 *Ecological Economics* 496 (2008); C. Sneddon, R.B. Howarth, and R.B. Norgaard, "Sustainable Development in a Post-Brundtland World, 57 *Ecological Economics* 253 (2006) (for some recent contributions to this discussion).

8 *See* World Commission on Culture and Development, *Our Creative Diversity: Report of the World Commission on Culture and Development*, 1995.

9 *See* D. Throsby, *Linking Culture and Development Models: Towards a Workable Concept of Culturally Sustainable Development*, 1994; D. Throsby, "Culture, Economics and Sustainability", 19 *Journal of Cultural Economics* 199 (1995) (containing the substance of the background paper).

10 *See* UNESCO, *World Culture Report 2000: Cultural Diversity, Conflict and Pluralism*, 2000; UNESCO, *World Culture Report 1998: Culture, Creativity and Markets*, 1998.

world, because these industries bring together economic and cultural dimensions of development within a holistic policy framework.

The notion of *culturally sustainable development* mentioned above can now be stated more formally, by adapting the general principles on which sustainability depends to reflect the specific parameters applicable to culture. Following Throsby we can suggest the following propositions[11]:

- *intergenerational equity*: development must take a long-term view and not be such as to compromise the capacities of future generations to access cultural resources and meet their cultural needs; this requires particular concern for protecting and enhancing a nation's tangible and intangible cultural capital.
- *intragenerational equity*: development must provide equity in access to cultural production, participation and enjoyment to all members of the community on a fair and non-discriminatory basis; in particular, attention must be paid to the poorest members of society to ensure that development is consistent with the objectives of poverty alleviation.
- *importance of diversity*: just as sustainable development requires the protection of biodiversity, so also should account be taken of the value of cultural diversity to the processes of economic, social and cultural development.
- *precautionary principle*: when facing decisions with irreversible consequences such as the destruction of cultural heritage or the extinction of valued cultural practices, a risk-averse position must be adopted.
- *interconnectedness*: economic, social, cultural and environmental systems should not be seen in isolation; rather, a holistic approach is required, i.e. one that recognises interconnectedness, particularly between economic and cultural development.

This set of principles comprises not so much a definition of culturally sustainable development as a checklist against which any particular development strategy can be judged in order to assess the extent to which it can be regarded as culturally sustainable.

3. CULTURAL DIVERSITY

The link between culturally sustainable development and cultural diversity is seen in the third of the principles listed above, which draws the parallel between biodiversity and the diversity of cultural expressions.[12] This parallel is part of a

[11] *See* D. Throsby, *The Economics of Cultural Policy*, 2010, 195.

[12] *See* further J. Pretty et al., "The Intersections of Biological Diversity and Cultural Diversity: Towards Integration", 7 *Conservation and Society* 100 (2009). *See also* D. Throsby, "Linking Cultural and Ecological Sustainability", 8 *International Journal of Diversity in Organisations,*

wider juxtaposition between natural capital and cultural capital that has been put forward in cultural economics. The former type of capital is defined as comprising natural resources (both exhaustible and renewable), biological ecosystems and biodiversity. Cultural capital in its economic interpretation entails assets which embody or give rise to cultural value, and includes cultural resources (both tangible and intangible), cultural ecosystems and cultural diversity.

The parallel continues when questions of valuation are addressed. It can be suggested that cultural diversity is valued for reasons that are congruent with the basis on which society places a value on biodiversity.[13] These sources of value can be described as follows:

- the variety of cultures and cultural expressions that comprise cultural diversity are seen as important *per se*, and as having qualities that are valued as a part of the "human mosaic"; in economic terms these sources of value are public goods deriving from the existence value of the diversity in question – people gain benefit from the knowledge that cultural diversity in all its richness is simply there;
- cultures do not exist in isolation, and the webs of relationships and interconnectedness that characterise what are known as "cultural ecosystems" are valuable because they support economic activity; the invisible networks and relationships that hold cultures together and give meaning to people's lives are important in underpinning the economic processes of production, consumption and exchange; and
- it is possible that certain cultural manifestations may have both economic and cultural value that is not yet evident; hence cultural diversity is valuable because it keeps options open for the future.

These sources of value are likely to be realised by society on a continuing basis over the long term. It is thus apparent that a concern for cultural diversity must be added to that for biodiversity as an essential component of sustainable development.

We can conclude that the creation, maintenance and enhancement of cultural capital assets in both developing and industrialised countries will be a significant ingredient in any sustainable development policy package, especially because of the fact that cultural capital contains diversity as one of its important elements.[14]

Communities and Nations 15 (2008) (discussing a broader view of the links between cultural and ecological sustainability).

13 *But see* D. Heyd, "Cultural Diversity and Biodiversity: A Tempting Analogy", 13 *Critical Review of International Social and Political Philosophy* 159 (2010) (warning that the analogy between cultural and biological diversity may contain "fallacies and dangers" if pressed too far).

14 *See* P. Dalziel and C. Saunders, *Sustainable Development and Cultural Capital*, 2009 (for further discussion on the relationship between cultural capital and sustainable development).

4. THE CONVENTION ON THE DIVERSITY OF CULTURAL EXPRESSIONS

As noted in the Introduction to this paper, the Convention on the Diversity of Cultural Expressions addresses the issue of sustainable development in two places. The first is as a principle in Article 2:

> **Article 2 Para 6 – Principle of sustainable development:** Cultural diversity is a rich asset for individuals and societies. The protection, promotion and maintenance of cultural diversity are an essential requirement for sustainable development for the benefit of present and future generations.

The wording of this principle enshrines the concept of cultural capital through its description of cultural diversity as a "rich asset", and through its reference to future generations. It may be noted that this principle is stated not as a contestable proposition, but as an axiom that is self-evidently true.

The second and most significant allusion to sustainable development in the Convention on the Diversity of Cultural Expressions occurs in Article 13:

> **Article 13 – Integration of culture in sustainable development:** Parties shall endeavour to integrate culture in their development policies at all levels for the creation of conditions conducive to sustainable development and, within this framework, foster aspects relating to the protection and promotion of the diversity of cultural expressions.

It is important to observe that the opening words of this Article widen the scope of the Convention on the Diversity of Cultural Expressions from being an instrument specifically about cultural diversity to one that relates to culture more generally. Furthermore, the requirement that States Parties endeavour to integrate culture into their development policies could be read in two ways. On the one hand, this phrase could be interpreted as seeing culture not as a direct contributor to sustainable development but as a pre-condition for the successful pursuit of sustainable development, where the latter is intended in its standard interpretation as relating only to economic and environmental sustainability. On the other hand, the intention could be to promulgate the importance of looking to the sustainability of culture itself, in other words to embrace culturally sustainable development as discussed above.

Indeed the final clause of Article 13 does enjoin States Parties to "foster aspects" of their development policies that will protect and promote cultural diversity within a sustainable development framework. This injunction opens the way to a range of cultural development strategies, including providing support for the cultural industries and other measures that will contribute to both economic and cultural advancement in line with the principles of culturally sustainable development.

In the period since the Convention's entry into force in 2007, the Intergovernmental Committee has been developing operational guidelines to assist States Parties in their efforts to implement the Convention's various provisions.[15] One set of guidelines relates specifically to Article 13. A document commissioned to assist the Committee in its consideration of this Article[16] suggested a set of practical guidelines for policy formulation aimed at integrating culture into sustainable development, conditional on the principles for culturally sustainable development. The following idealised set of guidelines was suggested in the document:

- No single policy prescription or instrument will deliver culturally sustainable development; rather, a package of policy measures will be required whose components will differ in emphasis in different countries depending on particular needs.
- For this reason policy formulation will not be the responsibility of a single ministry, but will require collaboration and cooperation across a range of government instrumentalities and agencies concerned with economic, social and cultural development.
- Recognising the economic potential of the cultural industries provides a practical way for introducing culture into a broader economic development agenda. At the same time the responsibilities of policy to deliver cultural as well as economic benefits must be recognised; this requires a clear distinction to be maintained between economic value and cultural value in the deliverables from the cultural sector of the economy.
- In line with the previous requirement, an essential element of any culturally sustainable development policy, regardless of the national context, will be attention to the needs of creative artists and arts organisations and a strong policy stance in regard to the conservation of tangible and intangible cultural heritage.
- Attention should be paid to long-term investment in infrastructure[17] including: *physical* infrastructure to support cultural production, distribution and consumption; *institutional* infrastructure such as public

15 *See* UNESCO, Intergovernmental Committee for the Protection and Promotion of the Diversity of Cultural Expressions, *Operational Guidelines* (June 2009), *available at* www.unesco.org/new/en/culture/themes/cultural-diversity/diversity-of-cultural-expressions/the-convention/operational-guidelines/ (last visited 2 February 2012).

16 See D. Throsby, "Culture in Sustainable Development: Insights for the Future Implementation of Art. 13", *CE/08/Throsby/Art.13* (14 January 2008), *available at* http://unesdoc.unesco.org/images/0015/001572/157287e.pdf (last visited 2 February 2012).

17 *See* A. Du Plessis and C. Rautenbach, "Legal Perspectives on the Role of Culture in Sustainable Development" 13 *Potchefstroom Electronic Law Journal* 26 (2010) (stipulating that sound infrastructure is a necessary prerequisite for good cultural governance).

cultural instrumentalities and agencies; *legal* and *regulatory* infrastructure such as an effective copyright regime; and *financial* infrastructure to provide a sound basis for provision of financial services.
- Given that ultimately the processes of culturally sustainable development are played out within communities, it is important that long-term capacity-building at local level be undertaken, so that decision making and resource allocation for culture can be devolved as far as possible to local levels.
- Any package of policy measures put together in accordance with these guidelines should be assessed against the principles for culturally sustainable development specified above in order to ensure the essential requirements for sustainability are met.

Most of the above points appear in one way or another in the final Guidelines for the Implementation of Article 13 as approved at the Conference of Parties in June 2009. The standard definition of sustainable development is accepted and the protection and promotion of cultural diversity is seen as an essential component of sustainable development policies aimed at strengthening identity and social cohesion, building inclusive societies and achieving human development goals, notably poverty reduction. The Guidelines argue particularly that integration of culture into development policies will help in realising the full potential of the cultural industries to accelerate economic growth and promote a good quality of life. It is noted in the Guidelines that sustainable development policies will implicate a number of different policy areas, and will require awareness-raising across a range of decision-makers. The Guidelines acknowledge in particular the importance of education, the needs of women and the prospects for use of new technologies in policy implementation.

The Guidelines go on to suggest a variety of measures that will facilitate the integration of cultural diversity into sustainable development policies. The range of measures proposed covers the operations of artists and cultural practitioners, small- to medium-enterprises in the cultural industries, public authorities, local stakeholders, civil society and so on. Governments are encouraged to adopt policies to facilitate investment in infrastructure, to raise awareness, to build local capacity, to promote access and to improve financing provisions for the creation, production, distribution and dissemination of cultural activities, goods and services. Altogether the wide-ranging nature of these policy recommendations reinforces the view that although the Convention on the Diversity of Cultural Expressions is ostensibly about cultural diversity, it can be seen to have a wider reach, to the point where it might be better labelled a Cultural Policy Convention rather than one dealing simply with the diversity of cultural expressions.

5. CONCLUSION

This paper has discussed the relationships between the concepts of sustainable development and cultural diversity as represented in the Convention on the Diversity of Cultural Expressions. We have outlined how the sustainable development paradigm has evolved and how it has been adapted to yield the more specific notion of culturally sustainable development. Likewise the interpretation of cultural diversity itself has evolved, in particular through its incorporation as an element of cultural capital, in parallel with the inclusion of biodiversity in natural capital. The 2005 Convention brings these concepts together by seeing diversity as a cultural capital asset whose maintenance is essential for achieving conditions conducive to sustainable development.

Since cultural diversity is valued as a phenomenon in its own right, an increase in levels of diversity *per se* will presumably add to the sum of human welfare, other things being equal; such an outcome would be consistent with the principles of sustainable development. But although the Convention on the Diversity of Cultural Expressions is couched in terms of the desirable properties of cultural diversity, it does not seek directly to increase diversity *per se* so much as to facilitate, protect and promote the quantity and quality of cultural expressions whose beneficial expansion may or may not give rise to increased levels of diversity as a consequence. Thus the sorts of benefits listed above as being derived from diversity itself that may be generated by the operations of the Convention on the Diversity of Cultural Expressions are, if they exist at all, likely to be overshadowed by the much more substantial benefits flowing from all the good outcomes that the Convention hopes to achieve, such as raising the profile of culture in national and international policy agendas; facilitating the production, distribution and consumption of cultural goods and services; supporting the activities of creative artists; encouraging intercultural dialogue; and, last but by no means least, integrating cultural policy into States Parties' sustainable development strategies.

PART VI

IMPLEMENTATION OF AND VIEWS ON THE CONVENTION ON THE DIVERSITY OF CULTURAL EXPRESSIONS

THE CONVENTION ON THE DIVERSITY OF CULTURAL EXPRESSIONS AND THE EUROPEAN UNION

The Quest for Competence and Implementation

Evangelia Psychogiopoulou*

1. INTRODUCTION

On 20 October 2005, the General Conference of the United Nations Educational, Scientific and Cultural Organisation (UNESCO) adopted the *UNESCO Convention on the Protection and Promotion of the Diversity of Cultural Expressions* ("Convention on the Diversity of Cultural Expressions").[1] The Convention entered into force on 18 March 2007, three months after the date of deposit of the instruments of ratification of twelve of the Member States of the European Union ("EU" or the "Union")[2] and the instrument of accession of the European Community, now replaced and succeeded by the EU as a result of the entry into force of the Treaty of Lisbon on 1 December 2009.[3] By allowing the minimum threshold of thirty ratifications required by Article 29 of the Convention on the Diversity of Cultural Expressions to be reached, the EU and its Member States contributed to the critical mass of countries resolved to

* Research Fellow, Hellenic Foundation for European and Foreign Policy (ELIAMEP).

1 *See* Convention on the Protection and Promotion of the Diversity of Cultural Expressions, 20 October 2005, *U.N. Doc. CLT-2005/CONVENTION DIVERSITE-CULT REV.* [hereinafter "Convention on the Diversity of Cultural Expressions"].

2 Finland, Austria, France, Spain, Sweden, Denmark, Slovenia, Estonia, Slovakia, Luxembourg, Lithuania and Malta ratified the Convention on 18 December 2006. Romania, which became an EU Member State on 1 January 2007, had deposited its instrument of accession on 20 July 2006.

3 *See* Treaty of Lisbon amending the Treaty on European Union and the Treaty establishing the European Community, 13 December 2007, *OJ C 306/1* (17 December 2007).

establish the Convention as an international binding treaty in the field of cultural diversity.

Complementary to a variety of international and regional instruments with a cultural component, the Convention on the Diversity of Cultural Expressions has been greeted by many as a landmark achievement for the preservation and enhancement of cultural distinctiveness.[4] The Convention acknowledges the dual nature of cultural goods, services and activities as vehicles of cultural and commercial value, and espouses the purpose of creating conditions for cultures to flourish and to freely interact in a mutually beneficial manner. According to Article 3 of the Convention, "the Convention shall apply to the policies and measures adopted by the Parties related to the protection and promotion of the diversity of cultural expressions". These are broadly defined in Article 4 as "those policies and measures relating to culture, whether at the local, national, regional or international level that are either focused on culture as such or are designed to have a direct effect on cultural expressions of individuals, groups or societies, including on the creation, production, dissemination, distribution of and access to cultural activities, goods and services".

The rights and obligations of the parties to the Convention are subdivided into three main pillars: a) Articles 5 and 6 enshrining in international law the states' sovereign right to adopt and implement cultural policies; b) Articles 7–11 concerning the protection and promotion of the diversity of cultural expressions in the territory of the parties to the Convention; and c) Articles 12–19 on the parties' cooperation.[5]

The provisions of the first pillar safeguard and foster state capacity for cultural policy-making. They acknowledge the sovereign right of states to formulate and implement cultural policies both at the national and the international levels and provide a non-exhaustive list of the measures that the parties may adopt in order to protect and promote the diversity of cultural expressions within their territory, including regulatory, institutional and financial measures. The second pillar recognises the parties' right to take action in order to protect cultural expressions that are at risk of extinction, under serious threat, or otherwise in need of urgent safeguarding on their territory. It also stipulates that the parties can formulate measures to promote an environment that encourages individuals and social groups to create, disseminate, distribute and have access to their own cultural

---

4 *See, e.g.*, R. Craufurd Smith, "The UNESCO Convention on the Protection and Promotion of the Diversity of Cultural Expressions: Building a New World Information and Communication Order?", 1 *International Journal of Communication* 24 (2007); M. Hahn, "A Clash of Cultures? The UNESCO Diversity Convention and International Trade Law", 9 *J. Int'l Econ. L.* 515 (2006); H. Ruiz-Fabri, "Reflections on Possible Future Legal Implications of the Convention", in N. Obuljen and J. Smiers (eds.), *UNESCO's Convention on the Protection and Promotion of the Diversity of Cultural Expressions: Making It Work*, 2006, 73.

5 *See* C. B. Graber, "Substantive Rights and Obligations under the UNESCO Convention on Cultural Diversity", in H. Schneider and P. Van den Bossche (eds.), *Protection of Cultural Diversity from a European and International Perspective*, 2008, 141, 146.

expressions, as well as diverse cultural expressions from within their territory and from other countries of the world. An obligation of information sharing and transparency is imposed, while provisions pertaining to the protection and promotion of the diversity of cultural expressions through education, public awareness programmes, and the active participation of civil society are set forth. Under the third pillar, the parties commit to endeavour to integrate culture into sustainable development and reinforce international cooperation,[6] in particular in support of developing countries, through recourse to a variety of means, including technology transfers, capacity building, financial assistance and the strengthening of domestic cultural industries. Also, the Convention on the Diversity of Cultural Expressions features innovative wording, which specifically requires developed countries to provide preferential treatment to artists and other cultural professionals and practitioners, as well as cultural goods and services, from developing countries in order to facilitate and widen cultural exchanges.[7] Collaborative arrangements between and within the public and private sectors and non-profit organisations for the enhancement of developing countries' cultural capacities are to be encouraged, and an International Fund for Cultural Diversity created. The parties further undertake to exchange information and share expertise concerning data collection and statistics on the diversity of cultural expressions as well as on best practices for its protection and promotion.

Notably, most of the provisions of the Convention on the Diversity of Cultural Expressions place the emphasis on rights rather than obligations. The wording employed by the Convention (parties "may" rather than parties "shall") shows that for the most part the Convention contains good faith declarations. This non-compulsory element of the Convention is also evident in the procedure laid down in Article 25 for the settlement of disputes between parties to the Convention concerning its interpretation or application. First, a solution by negotiation is to be sought, which in case of non-agreement, can lead to parties seeking the good offices of, or mediation by, a third party. Should no settlement be reached, parties can resort to the so-called Conciliation Commission, whose decision however does not bind the parties to the dispute.[8]

The Convention on the Diversity of Cultural Expressions is the final outcome of a two-fold preparatory venture.[9] Between December 2003 and May 2004, three meetings of independent experts were held, culminating in the production

6 *See* Convention on the Diversity of Cultural Expressions, *supra* note 1, Article 17 (including in situations of serious threat to cultural expressions).

7 *See* id., Article 16.

8 Parties are to consider "in good faith" the proposal made by the Conciliation Commission for the resolution of the dispute. Interestingly, the Convention also contains an opt-out clause, enabling each party to decide, at the time of ratification, acceptance, approval of, or accession to the Convention, that it does not recognise the conciliation procedure.

9 *See* N. Obuljen, "From 'Our Creative Diversity' to the Convention on Cultural Diversity: Introduction to the Debate", in Obuljen and Smiers (eds.), *supra* note 4, at 31.

of a preliminary draft text.[10] Subsequently, between September 2004 and June 2005, three sessions of intergovernmental negotiations took place, resulting in a revised preliminary draft convention.[11] As per the mandate conferred by the Council of the European Union ("the Council") in November 2004, the European Commission ("the Commission") participated actively in the negotiations of the Convention.[12] Article 27 of the final text agreed upon made accession by regional economic integration organisations possible. Since prior to the entry into force of the Treaty of Lisbon, the Treaty on European Union did not contain any provisions on the EU's legal personality, it was the European Community ("Community") which became party to the Convention on the Diversity of Cultural Expressions because its respective Treaty expressly declared it to have legal personality and thus the power to conclude and adhere to international agreements.[13]

Most often identified with processes of economic integration, the dynamic role played by the EU in working towards an international standard-setting instrument on cultural diversity has come under close scrutiny, with criticism levelled at the curtailment of Member States' cultural autonomy. Clearly, the Community did prove an ardent proponent of UNESCO's noble objective to defend cultural wealth and to bolster dialogue amongst cultures. Not only did it negotiate the Convention on the Diversity of Cultural Expressions, a true novelty given its UNESCO 'observer' seat, but it also rapidly adhered to the Convention on the Diversity of Cultural Expressions, accepting being bound by its provisions. But was it competent to assume such a central position in the establishment of an international legal framework supportive of cultural richness and interaction? Moreover, were the requirements of the Convention on

---

10 *See* UNESCO, "Preliminary Draft of a Convention on the Protection of the Diversity of Cultural Contents and Artistic Expressions", *CLT/CPD/2004/CONF-201/2* (July 2004), *available at* www.incd.net/docs/UNESCOdraft04.pdf (last visited 2 February 2012).

11 *See* UNESCO, "Preliminary Report by the Director-General Setting out the Situation to be Regulated and the Possible Scope of the Regulating Action Proposed, Accompanied by the Preliminary Draft of a Convention on the Protection of the Diversity of Cultural Contents and Artistic Expressions", *33 C/23* (4 August 2005), *available at* http://portal.unesco.org/culture/en/files/28182/1124818579333C23_Eng.pdf/33C23_Eng.pdf (last visited 2 February 2012).

12 *See* Council of the European Union, Press Release: 2616th Council Meeting, Education, Youth and Culture, *14380/04 (Presse 310)* (15–16 November 2004), *available at* www.consilium.europa.eu/ueDocs/cms_Data/docs/pressData/en/educ/82679.pdf (last visited 2 February 2012); Council of the European Union, "Draft Council Decision Authorising the Commission to Participate, on behalf of the Community, in the Negotiations within UNESCO on the Convention on the Protection of the Diversity of Cultural Contents and Artistic Expressions", *13840/04 CULT 103* (29 October 2004), *available at* http://register.consilium.eu.int/pdf/en/04/st13/st13840.en04.pdf (last visited 2 February 2012).

13 *See* Consolidated Versions of the Treaty on European Union and of the Treaty establishing the European Community, Article 281, *available at* http://eur-lex.europa.eu/LexUriServ/LexUriServ.do?uri=OJ:C:2006:321E:0001:0331:EN:pdf (last visited 2 February 2012).

the Diversity of Cultural Expressions translated into concrete action, once the Convention entered into force?

The purpose of this chapter is to reach a better understanding of the European Union's contribution to the adoption and implementation of the Convention on the Diversity of Cultural Expressions. Section 2 explores the principal features of the cultural competence enjoyed by the EU. This is to serve as a backdrop for gauging the real impact, in section 4, of the powers bestowed on the EU that enabled it to embrace and nurture the UNESCO initiative, following a brief discussion in section 3 of the way in which the European Community negotiated and acceded to the Convention on the Diversity of Cultural Expressions. The focus then shifts in part 5 to the implementation of the Convention on the Diversity of Cultural Expressions, examining whether the agreement entered into has served to invigorate the delivery of culture-friendly policies at the EU level. A short epilogue follows in section 6, with an overall assessment of the EU's conduct in relation to the Convention on the Diversity of Cultural Expressions.

2. EUROPEAN UNION CULTURAL COMPETENCES: DELINEATION AND EXERCISE

With the Treaty establishing the European Community ("the EC Treaty"), the Community tasks laid down in Article 3 EC were expanded to comprise a "contribution ... to the flowering of the cultures of the Member States."[14] The introduction of Article 151 EC – now Article 167 of the Treaty on the Functioning of the European Union ("TFEU")[15] – signalled a resolve to bring culture formally within the spectrum of EU activity. This marked a significant disjuncture from previous piecemeal intervention in the cultural domain, mainly as part of the drive towards establishing a common market in which cultural goods, persons and services could also circulate unhindered.[16] Article 151 EC created a concrete legal basis for the undertaking of culture-specific action at the EU level.[17] At the same time, it assigned a carefully delineated cultural mandate to the European institutions. A merely complementary

14 *See* id.

15 *See* Consolidated Versions of the Treaty on European Union and the Treaty on the Functioning of the European Union, *OJ 2008/ C 115/1* [hereinafter "TEU" and "TFEU" respectively].

16 *See, generally*, B. De Witte, "The Cultural Dimension of Community Law", in *Collected Courses of the Academy of European Law*, Vol. IV-1, 1993, 229; R. Craufurd Smith, "Community Intervention in the Cultural Field: Continuity or Change?", in R. Craufurd Smith (ed.), *Culture and European Union Law*, 2004, 19, 28; J.M.E. Loman et al., *Culture and Community Law: Before and After Maastricht*, 1992, 14.

17 *See* E. Psychogiopoulou, *The Integration of Cultural Considerations in EU Law and Policies*, 2008, 24; R.B.F. Lévy, *Les compétences culturelles de la Communauté Européenne*, 2004, 275; Craufurd Smith, *supra* note 16, at 49; N.N. Shuibhne, *EC Law and Minority Language*

competence, firmly based on respect for cultural diversity and the principle of subsidiarity, was conferred on the Community, with the Member States maintaining primary responsibility for cultural affairs.

The Treaty of Lisbon, which abolished the pillar system, did not alter the nature of the cultural competence enjoyed by the EU. Article 6 TFEU incorporates culture among the policy areas in which "the Union shall have competence to carry out actions to support, coordinate or supplement the actions of the Member States". Article 2(5) TFEU further specifies that EU action in the field may not supersede Member States' competence. Article 167 TFEU has generally maintained the wording of Article 151 EC. Paragraph 1 of Article 167 TFEU stipulates that "the Union shall contribute to the flowering of the cultures of the Member States, while respecting their national and regional diversity and at the same time bringing the common cultural heritage to the fore." Framed in broad terms, with no attempt to define the concept of "culture", the provision makes clear, as does its precursor, that the role of the EU is essentially one of stimulating the cultural systems of the Member States. Article 167(2) TFEU provides that EU action aims to encourage cooperation between the Member States, and, if necessary, support and supplement their activity in specifically defined areas: improving the knowledge and dissemination of the culture and history of the European peoples; the conservation and safeguarding of cultural heritage of European significance; non-commercial cultural exchanges; and artistic and literary creation, including in the audiovisual sector. Article 167(3) TFEU centres on the external dimension of EU cultural activity, requiring the Union (together with the Member States) to foster cooperation with third countries and the competent international organisations in the sphere of culture.

The legal instruments through which pursuit of EU cultural objectives may be sought continue to be restricted to incentive measures and recommendations. Nevertheless, the Treaty of Lisbon has erased previous Council voting safeguards requiring unanimity. Incentive measures are to be adopted under the co-decision procedure – now renamed "ordinary legislative procedure" – but decision-making in the Council must rest on qualified majority voting. The expansion of qualified majority voting in the field of culture might facilitate decision-making, reducing the risk of national veto in cultural affairs. Quite importantly, however, any harmonisation of the laws and regulations of the Member States remains excluded. This indicates the high level of national sensitivity in the area, which is also reflected in Article 3(3) of the Treaty on European Union that states that the Union "shall respect its rich cultural and linguistic diversity, and shall ensure that Europe's cultural heritage is safeguarded and enhanced,"[18] as well as Article 207(4) TFEU concerning the EU's common commercial policy. The latter

Policy: Culture, Citizenship and Fundamental Rights, 2002, 107 and 126; De Witte, *supra* note 16, at 291; J.M.E. Loman, *supra* note 16, at 192.

18 TFEU, *supra* note 15, Article 3.

stipulates among others that the Council shall act unanimously for the negotiation and conclusion of agreements with one or more third countries or international organisations "in the field of trade in cultural and audiovisual services, where these agreements risk prejudicing the Union's cultural and linguistic diversity".[19]

The fact that Article 167(5) TFEU does not allow for the adoption of harmonising measures in the field of culture merits attention. Article 167(4) TFEU (formerly Article 151(4) EC) is enlightening in this regard.[20] Affirming that 'the Union shall take cultural aspects into account in its action under other provisions of the Treaties, in particular in order to respect and to promote the diversity of its cultures', Article 167(4) TFEU discloses that EU measures with a cultural component may be founded on a legal basis other than Article 167(5) TFEU. Article 167(4) TFEU requires the Union to heed the cultural repercussions of the activities developed in other policy areas within its purview, and thus allows for the adoption of measures which pursue cultural objectives alongside other legitimate EU policy goals.[21] Seen from this angle, Article 167(4) TFEU is important in acknowledging that culture interconnects with a series of EU policies. But beyond this, it also serves to endow the European institutions with a set of *implicit* powers to attain cultural policy goals in support of cultural diversity when exercising the competences they enjoy in other policy fields, some of which might allow for harmonisation.[22] In exercising such powers, the European legislator must of course establish a clear link between the measure adopted and the policy objectives that the legal basis on which the measure is founded seeks to attain. By default, resort to provisions other than Article 167(5) TFEU for the adoption of what are essentially cultural measures would amount to a circumvention of Article 167(5) TFEU.

The margin of discretion left to the European institutions by means of Article 167(4) TFEU has resulted in dispersed "cultural mainstreaming" efforts for years.[23] Conversely, Article 167(5) TFEU (formerly Article 151(5) EC) has given rise to a series of cultural funding tools, devised to foster cultural creation and encourage diffusion of cultural content. Moving from a first generation of

---

19 Note that according to Article 207(4) TFEU, the Council shall also act unanimously for the negotiation and conclusion of agreements concerning the commercial aspects of intellectual property where such agreements include provisions for which unanimity is required for the adoption of internal rules.

20 *See, generally*, C.B. Cunningham, "In Defense of Member States Culture: The Unrealised Potential of Article 151(4) of the EC Treaty and the Consequences for EC Cultural Policy", 34 *Cornell Int'l L. J.* 119 (2001); E. Psychogiopoulou, "The Cultural Mainstreaming Clause of Article 151(4) EC: Protection and Promotion of Cultural Diversity or Hidden Cultural Agenda?", 12 *European Law Journal* 575 (2006).

21 *See* B. De Witte, "Non-Market Values in Internal Market Legislation", in N.N. Shuibhne (ed.), *Regulating the Internal Market*, 2006, 61, 69.

22 *See* Psychogiopoulou, *supra* note 17, at 54.

23 *See* id., at 337.

sectoral programmes to a single financing and programming instrument, the EU has offered financial assistance to various cultural cooperation projects.[24] *Culture (2007–2013)*, the successor to *Culture 2000*, presently provides for three levels of intervention: support for cultural actions of variable length and scale, support for highly specialised bodies active in the field of culture, and support for research, analysis and sharing of experience in relation to European cultural cooperation and European cultural policy development.[25]

EU cultural action seems to have entered a new era with the *Communication on a European Agenda for Culture in a Globalising World*, published by the Commission in May 2007 (the "Agenda Communication").[26] The Agenda Communication suggested a set of interrelated objectives to guide the cultural action of the EU, and envisaged new working methods for the development of cultural partnerships between the European institutions, the Member States and cultural stakeholders. Promotion of cultural diversity and intercultural dialogue, promotion of culture as a catalyst for creativity in the framework of the Lisbon strategy, and promotion of culture as a vital element of the EU's international relations were identified as overarching goals of EU cultural activity. The Commission emphasised the importance of engaging in structured dialogue with the cultural sector, advocated increased attention to "cultural mainstreaming" and argued for the acquisition of evidence-based information for the conduct of EU cultural policy. Crucially, it also anticipated use of the open method of coordination, an attempt to rejuvenate EU cultural action through the exchange of best practices and the fostering of mutual learning between the Member States. The Agenda Communication was endorsed by the Council on 16 November 2007[27] and has since then served as the main policy document driving the cultural activity of the EU forward, including the implementation of the Convention on the Diversity of Cultural Expressions, as will be explained further below.

---

24 *See* id., at 40; R. Craufurd Smith, "From Heritage Conservation to European Identity: Article 151 EC and the Multi-faceted Nature of Community Cultural Policy", 32 *Eur. Law Rev.* 48, 60 (2007).

25 *See* Decision 1855/2006/EC of the European Parliament and of the Council of 12 December 2006 establishing the Culture Programme (2007–2013), *OJ 2006 L 372/1*; Decision 508/2000/EC of the European Parliament and of the Council of 14 February 2000 establishing the Culture 2000 Programme, *OJ 2000 L 63/1*.

26 *See* Communication from the Commission to the European Parliament, the Council, the European Economic and Social Committee and the Committee of the Regions, "On a European Agenda for Culture in a Globalising World", *COM (2007) 242* (10 May 2007).

27 *See* Resolution of the Council on a European Agenda for Culture, 16 November 2007, *OJ 2007 C 287/1*.

3. THE CONVENTION ON THE DIVERSITY OF CULTURAL EXPRESSIONS AND THE EU'S INVOLVEMENT IN ITS DRAFTING

The interest of the EU in the Convention on the Diversity of Cultural Expressions can be traced back to the early days of discussions on the desirability of an international legal instrument on cultural diversity. In the wake of the *Universal Declaration on Cultural Diversity* and its supporting *Action Plan*, which invited UNESCO Member States to consider "the advisability of an international legal instrument on cultural diversity,"[28] the Commission produced a Communication, entitled '*Towards an International Instrument on Cultural Diversity*', addressed to the Council and the European Parliament.[29] The Commission expressed full support for a legally binding document, designed to consolidate certain cultural rights, commit parties to international cooperation, create a forum for debate on cultural policies and establish a global monitoring mechanism on the state of cultural diversity worldwide.[30] Taking note of the intention of the General Conference of UNESCO to decide on the feasibility and nature of a standard-setting instrument at its 32nd session, the Commission declared that it would cooperate with the EU Member States in order to ensure convergence in stance.[31] Should the General Conference result in the launch of negotiations on an international instrument on cultural diversity, the Commission announced that it would propose a recommendation to the Council for a decision to authorise the Commission to negotiate in UNESCO.

---

28 *See* Universal Declaration on Cultural Diversity, 2 November 2001, Article 1, *available at* http://portal.unesco.org/en/ev.php-URL_ID=13179&URL_DO=DO_TOPIC&URL_SECTION =201.html (last visited on 25 November 2011).

29 *See* Communication from the Commission to the Council and the European Parliament, "Towards an International Instrument on Cultural Diversity", *COM (2003) 520* (27 August 2003).

30 *See* id., at 6–7 (in the Commission's view, the envisaged instrument ought primarily to focus on: a) promoting cultural diversity; b) contributing to the dialogue between cultures and to mutual understanding and respect; c) developing international cultural cooperation, aimed at boosting the exchanges of cultural goods and services, including those in provenance of developing countries; d) favouring the development of cultural policies and instruments at the national, regional and international level; e) providing a focal point and a forum for members to discuss and debate cultural policies; f) providing technical assistance and expertise to members; and g) establishing an institutional framework to monitor the state of cultural diversity in the world, at the same time engaging in the elaboration and definition of indicators and international standards in the field of cultural diversity).

31 *See* id., at 10 (an annexure to the Communication, titled *Initial Elements for a Declaration on Behalf of the European Community and its Member States with a View to the Presentation of a Common Position on the Issue Related to the Drawing-Up of a Standard-Setting Instrument on Cultural Diversity, for the Forthcoming UNESCO General Conference*, contained the initial elements of a declaration on behalf of the Community and its Member States regarding the instrument that UNESCO would negotiate).

Negotiations would be conducted on behalf of the then fully functional European Community *and* the Member States.

Welcoming the unanimous decision of the General Conference to open negotiations on the drawing-up of a convention, the European Parliament underlined that due weight should be accorded to recognising the distinct nature of cultural products and services, enshrining in international law the legitimate right of any state or group of states to freely determine their cultural policies, and strengthening international cultural cooperation and solidarity.[32] Advocating unity, the Parliament advised Member States to entrust the Commission with the conduct of negotiations, and demanded close collaboration between the EU Presidency and the Commission.

The Commission's recommendation to the Council was issued on 1 September 2004.[33] Notably, the Commission did not request an authorisation to negotiate on behalf of the Community *and* the Member States. It rather called for a mandate that would allow it to negotiate on behalf of the Community, in consultation with a special committee appointed by the Council for that purpose. The main argument advanced to justify involvement in the negotiations was that the preliminary draft convention, produced by a group of independent experts and transmitted to the members of UNESCO on 16 July 2004,[34] would affect the *acquis communautaire*.

For the Commission, the implicated EU policies did not simply relate to cultural activity deriving from what was then Article 151 EC (now Article 167 TFEU); they also involved policies and measures, which though non culture-specific, could exert a significant influence on cultural affairs. The provisions of the preliminary draft convention regarding matters such as artists' and creators' mobility, the facilitation of access to global markets for works from developing countries, intellectual property, and international cooperation and coordination were closely connected to EC Treaty provisions on free movement, immigration, external trade, the customs union, and development cooperation. In the Commission's view, the preliminary draft convention could seriously impinge

---

32 *See* Resolution on Preserving and Promoting Cultural Diversity: The Role of the European Regions and International Organisations such as UNESCO and the Council of Europe, 14 January 2004, *OJ 2005 C 92E/322*, §31; *See also* Resolution on Working towards a Convention on the Protection of the Diversity of Cultural Content and Artistic Expression, 14 April 2005, *OJ 2006 C33E/591*. With the latter, the Parliament instructed Member States to deploy every effort for the coordination of positions among themselves and with the Community, noting that lack of unity could undermine the Community's credibility in the negotiations.

33 *See* Recommendation from the Commission to the Council to Authorise the Commission to Participate, on behalf of the Community, in the Negotiations within UNESCO on the Convention on the Protection of the Diversity of Cultural Contents and Artistic Expressions, 1 September 2004, *SEC (2004) 1062*, *available at* http://ec.europa.eu/avpolicy/docs/ext/mandat_en.pdf (last visited 2 February 2012).

34 *See* UNESCO, *supra* note 10.

on existing policy instruments and circumscribe capacity for policy-making at the EU level.

In response to the remarks of the Commission, and following a set of initial comments submitted by the Dutch Presidency to UNESCO on behalf of both the Community and the Member States,[35] the Council, at its 2616th meeting, adopted a Decision authorising the Commission to participate in the negotiations on behalf of the Community.[36] Under the Negotiating Directives, laid down in an annexure to the Decision, the Commission was given permission to conduct negotiations with regard to matters falling within the scope of Community competence. The Commission was specifically instructed to ensure consistency between the UNESCO Convention and the *acquis*, maintaining the Community's and Member States' "capacity to define and implement their cultural and audiovisual policies for the purpose of preserving their cultural diversity."[37] It was also charged with securing the inclusion of provisions in the Convention that would enable the Community to become a contracting party to it and would guarantee the primacy of Community law over the Convention in Member States' mutual relations. The Council clarified that the Commission would negotiate *alongside* the Member States in negotiating areas concerning matters of shared competence, securing Member States' prior common accord for any position expressed. The Council's Cultural Affairs Committee would be kept informed of the progress of negotiations.

To coordinate interventions, a code of conduct was issued, assigning specific duties to the Presidency and the Commission.[38] Underlining that, in conformity with the principle of attribution of powers, the distribution of tasks "cannot be read as affecting in any way the respective competences of the Community and the Member States,"[39] the code of conduct required the Presidency to negotiate and express, on behalf of the Member States, common positions reached in the coordination process on aspects of domestic cultural policies, public awareness and education, human rights, international cultural cooperation (in particular with developing countries but without covering trade-related issues), follow-up bodies and mechanisms, and any other matter falling

35 *See* Communication of the European Community and its Member States to UNESCO, "On the Preliminary Draft UNESCO Convention on the Protection of the Diversity of Cultural Contents and Artistic Expressions", (15 November 2004), *available at* http://trade.ec.europa.eu/doclib/docs/2004/december/tradoc_120449.pdf (last visited 2 February 2012).

36 *See* Council of the European Union, *supra* note 12.

37 *See* id., point 1.

38 *See* Council of the European Union, "Code of Conduct between the Council, the Member States and the Commission on the UNESCO Negotiations on the Draft Convention on the Protection of the Diversity of Cultural Contents and Artistic Expressions", *5768/05 CULT 4* (31 January 2005), *available at* http://register.consilium.europa.eu/pdf/en/05/st05/st05768.en05.pdf (last visited 2 February 2012).

39 *See* id., at 1.

exclusively or primarily within the competence of the Member States.[40] The Commission, for its part, was required to negotiate on behalf of the Community and express Community positions in relation to free movement of goods, persons, services and capital, the common rules on competition with a special focus on state aids, the internal market, Community measures introduced in the sphere of intellectual property and development cooperation, legislative action taken on the basis of Title IV of the EC Treaty on visas, asylum and immigration, the common commercial policy, and any other matter falling exclusively or primarily within Community competence. Where these competences proved inextricably linked, the Presidency and the Commission were to agree as to which would deliver any statement on behalf of the Community and the Member States. The code of conduct mandated best endeavours in the search for common positions. If no agreement could be reached, and provided that the matter had been referred to the Cultural Affairs Committee, Member States could express, if necessary, their point of view on the matters falling exclusively or primarily within their competence.

Appearing as a single entity and speaking with two voices during negotiations, that of the Commission and that of the Presidency, depending on the subject under discussion, the EU and its Member States succeeded in having most of their suggestions included in the final text. Two months after the adoption of the Convention on the Diversity of Cultural Expressions, the Commission published a proposal for a Council Decision on the conclusion of the Convention on the Diversity of Cultural Expressions by the Community.[41] The proposal claimed the procedural legal basis of Article 300(2) and (3) EC (now, as amended, Article 218 TFEU), and the sectoral legal bases of Articles 89 (state aids), 133 (common commercial policy), 151 (culture), 181 (development cooperation) and 181a (economic, financial and technical cooperation with third countries) EC (now Articles 109, 207, 167, 211 and 212 TFEU). Ascertaining that the Convention on the Diversity of Cultural Expressions is intended to "fill a legal vacuum in world governance by establishing a series of rights and obligations, at both national and international levels, with a view to the protection and promotion of cultural diversity,"[42] the Commission declared consistency with Community policies, Article 151(4) EC (now Article 167(4) TFEU) and the *Charter of Fundamental Rights of the European Union*, in

---

40 The Presidency was asked to convene, on its own initiative or at the request of the Commission or a Member State, coordination meetings in Paris before, during and after each negotiating session.

41 *See* Commission of the European Communities, "Proposal for a Council Decision on the Conclusion of the UNESCO Convention on the Protection and Promotion of the Diversity of Cultural Expressions", *COM (2005)* 678 (7 December 2005).

42 *See* id., at 3.

particular Article 22, which proclaims that "the Union shall respect cultural, religious and linguistic diversity."[43]

On 18 May 2006, pronouncing that the "UNESCO Convention constitutes a relevant and effective pillar for promoting cultural diversity and cultural exchanges, to which both the Community, as reflected in Article 151(4) of the EC Treaty (now Article 167(4) TFEU), and its Member States, attach the greatest importance," the Council adopted *Council Decision 2006/515/EC*, approving the Convention on the Diversity of Cultural Expressions on behalf of the Community.[44] The Council stressed that both the Community and its Member States had competence in the fields covered by the Convention on the Diversity of Cultural Expressions, and urged Member States to become contracting parties to it, "so that together with the Community they can fulfil the obligations laid down by the UNESCO Convention and exercise the rights invested in them by it, in situations of mixed competence in a coherent manner."[45]

4. THE CONVENTION ON THE DIVERSITY OF CULTURAL EXPRESSIONS AS A TEST-BED FOR THE DEMARCATION OF CULTURAL POWERS BETWEEN THE EUROPEAN UNION AND ITS MEMBER STATES

Evidently, the participation of the European Community in the negotiations of the Convention on the Diversity of Cultural Expressions was striking to many, and formed the object of lengthy debates within UNESCO itself.[46] The Community was granted "enhanced observer status", and was allowed to take part in the preparation of the Convention on the Diversity of Cultural Expressions, with the right to speak, to reply, to put forward proposals and amendments, and to participate in committees, working groups, and formal or informal meetings with its own nameplate. The tactics employed to ensure the active engagement of the Community in the process, as well as the way in which

43 *See* Charter of Fundamental Rights of the European Union, 7 December 2000, *OJ 2000/C 364/1.*

44 *See* Council Decision 2006/5/5/EC on the Conclusion of the Convention on the Protection and Promotion of the Diversity of Cultural Expressions, 18 May 2006, *OJ 2006 L 201/15.*

45 *See* id., §5.

46 *See, in particular,* UNESCO, Executive Board, "Participation of the European Commission in the Intergovernmental Meeting of Experts (Category II) on the Preliminary Draft Convention on the Protection of the Diversity of Cultural Contents and Artistic Expressions", *170 EX/37* (12 September 2004); UNESCO, Executive Board, "Participation of the European Community in the Intergovernmental Meeting of Experts (Category II) on the Preliminary Draft Convention on the Protection of the Diversity of Cultural Contents and Artistic Expressions", *171 EX/47* (17 March 2005).

the Community negotiated the Convention on the Diversity of Cultural Expressions, have fuelled discourse about national cultural sovereignty and its erosion through a widening of EU competences in the cultural field.[47] The argument has been made that the appearance of the EU as a single actor negotiating a binding legal instrument on cultural diversity provides evidence of an incremental absorption of national cultural competences by the European institutions. Did the Convention on the Diversity of Cultural Expressions serve to produce such a *de facto* reallocation of cultural powers? In other words, was the European Community competent to negotiate the Convention on the Diversity of Cultural Expressions and become party to it?

The Convention on the Diversity of Cultural Expressions is beyond dispute a cultural agreement. It is designed to protect and promote the diversity of cultural expressions, acknowledging that cultural diversity forms the common heritage of humanity that should be cherished and preserved for the benefit of all. But, although a cultural agreement "par excellence", the Convention on the Diversity of Cultural Expressions does not address culture in "a vacuum". Attentive to culture's transverse nature, it adopts an open-ended approach to its subject matter, recognising and affirming that protection and promotion of the diversity of cultural expressions rests on a variety of measures and instruments, which do not necessarily come within the scope of what one may call "cultural policy" in the strict sense. As a matter of fact, from the standpoint of the Convention on the Diversity of Cultural Expressions, "cultural policies and measures", defined in Article 4, not only cover policies and measures regarding culture as such; they similarly encompass policies and measures with an impact in the cultural sphere.

From this perspective, the EU had arguably little choice but to intervene in the process. With such a broad scope of application, the Convention on the Diversity of Cultural Expressions was to affect EU prerogatives and influence the future design of EU policies that are of importance and relevance to culture. The assortment of treaty articles which form the sectoral legal basis of *Council Decision 2006/515/EC*, approving the Convention on the Diversity of Cultural Expressions on behalf of the Community, confirms this position. Annex 1(b) to the Council's Decision is particularly illustrative. The Annex contains a Declaration by the European Community, in application of Article 27(3)(c) of the Convention on the Diversity of Cultural Expressions,[48] indicating the

[47] See International Network for Cultural Diversity, "Statement on the Position of the European Union in the negotiations on the Convention on the Protection of the Diversity of Cultural Contents and Artistic Expressions", *available at* www.incd.net/docs/Europeanposition.htm (last visited 2 February 2012); D. Ferri, "EU Participation in the UNESCO Convention on the Protection and Promotion of the Diversity of Cultural Expressions: Some Constitutional Remarks", 3 *European Diversity and Autonomy Papers – EDAP* (2005), *available at* www.eurac.edu/documents/edap/2005_edap03.pdf (last visited 2 February 2012).

[48] Convention on the Diversity of Cultural Expressions, *supra* note 1, Article 27(3)(c), according to which "a regional economic integration organisation and its Member State or States which

competences, in the areas covered by the Convention on the Diversity of Cultural Expressions, that were transferred to the Community by the Member States under the EC Treaty (now to the European Union following the entry into force of the Treaty of Lisbon).[49] Accordingly,

> The Community [now the Union] has exclusive competence for the common commercial policy (Articles 131–134 of the Treaty) [now, as amended, Articles 206–207 TFEU], except for the commercial aspects of intellectual property and trade in services in those areas set out in Article 133(5) and (6) of the Treaty [now, as amended, Article 207(4)-(6) TFEU] (in particular, in this context, trade in cultural and audiovisual services) where responsibility is shared between the Community [now the Union] and the Member States. It conducts a development cooperation policy (Articles 177–181 of the Treaty) [now, as amended, Articles 208–211 TFEU] and a policy of cooperation with industrialised countries (Article 181a of the Treaty) [now, as amended, Articles 212–213 TFEU] without prejudice to the respective competences of the Member States. It has shared competence as regards the free movement of goods, persons, services and capital (Articles 23–31 and 39–60 of the Treaty) [now, as amended, Articles 28–37 and 45–59 TFEU], competition (Articles 81–89 of the Treaty) [now Articles 101–109 TFEU] and the internal market, including intellectual property (Articles 94–97 of the Treaty) [now Articles 114–117 TFEU]. Pursuant to Article 151 of the Treaty [now Article 167 TFEU], in particular paragraph 4 thereof, the Community [now the Union] takes cultural aspects into account in its action under other provisions of the Treaty [now the Treaties, that is, the Treaty on European Union and the Treaty on the Functioning of the European Union], in particular in order to respect and to promote the diversity of its cultures.

---

have agreed on a distribution of responsibilities … shall inform the Parties of any such proposed distribution of responsibilities in the following manner: (i) in their instrument of accession, such organisation shall declare with specificity, the distribution of their responsibilities with respect to matters governed by the Convention; (ii) in the event of any later modification of their respective responsibilities, the regional economic integration organisation shall inform the depositary of any such proposed modification of their respective responsibilities; the depositary shall in turn inform the Parties of such modification".

49 *See* Council Decision, *supra* note 44, Annex 1 (b), "Declaration of the European Community in Application of Article 27(3)(c) of the Convention on the Protection and Promotion of the Diversity of Cultural Expressions" (The Annex also contains a list of acts, attesting to the exercise of EU competences which are touched on by the Convention on the Diversity of Cultural Expressions. The list builds on a variety of instruments, ranging from *Culture 2000* and the *Television without Frontiers Directive* to the signing of the *Cotonou Agreement* and the conclusion of the agreements reached in the multilateral negotiations of the Uruguay Round. Emphasising that the exercise of EU competences is by its nature subject to continuous development, the Community reserved "the right to notify other future declarations regarding the distribution of competences between the European Community [now the European Union] and the Member States." According to Article 27(3)(d) of the Convention on the Diversity of Cultural Expressions, the Member States are presumed to retain competence over all matters in respect of which no mention is made in the declaration).

The excerpt selected shows unequivocally that the spectrum of EU competences bore heavily on the decision to negotiate and finally conclude the Convention on the Diversity of Cultural Expressions. The fact that deep coordination was required between the European institutions and the Member States in order to present coherent positions should not come as a surprise. The Court of Justice of the European Union (CJEU) has clarified on several occasions that Article 10 of the EC Treaty (now Article 4(3) of the Treaty on European Union), which lays down the general principle of loyal cooperation, requires the Member States to facilitate the achievement of the Community's (now the Union's) tasks and to abstain from any measure which may jeopardise the attainment of Community (now Union) objectives.[50] More conspicuously, the CJEU has held that "where it is apparent that the subject-matter of an agreement or convention falls in part within the competence of the Community [now the Union] and in part within that of the Member States, it is essential to ensure close cooperation between the Member States and the Community [now the Union] institutions, both in the process of negotiation and conclusion and in the fulfilment of the commitments entered into."[51] This 'duty of cooperation' that binds the EU and the Member States in the process of the negotiation, conclusion and implementation of international agreements stems from the general principle of loyal cooperation, enshrined in Article 4(3) of the Treaty on European Union.[52] This somewhat explains two Commission statements, incorporated in the code of conduct and insisting on the exceptional nature of individual Member States taking the floor

---

50 Court of Justice of the European Union, Opinion 2/91, Convention N° 170 of the International Labour Organisation concerning Safety in the Use of Chemicals at Work [1993] *ECR I-1061*, §10.

51 Court of Justice of the European Union, Opinion 1/94, Competence of the Community to Conclude International Agreements concerning Services and the Protection of Intellectual Property [1994] *ECR I-5267*, §108. *See also* Opinion 2/91, *supra* note 50, §12.

52 The Court has also stated that 'the duty of cooperation ... results from the requirement of unity in the international representation of the Community' [now the Union] (see Court of Justice of the European Union, Opinion 2/91, *supra* note 50, §36). However, it has ultimately confirmed that the foundation of the 'duty of cooperation' is located in the general principle of loyal cooperation rather than in the 'requirement of unity' (see Court of Justice of the European Union, C-459/03, Commission v Ireland (MOX Plant) [2006] *ECR I-4635*, §§174–175). On the 'duty of cooperation' see in detail, P. Eeckhout, *External Relations of the European Union – Legal and Constitutional Foundations*, 2004, 241; M. Cremona, "Defending the Community Interest: The Duties of Cooperation and Compliance", in M. Cremona and B. de Witte (eds.), *EU Foreign Relations Law – Constitutional Fundamentals*, 2008, 125; C. Hillion, "Mixity and Coherence in EU External Relations: The Significance of the 'Duty of Cooperation'" (Centre for the Law of EU External Relations, CLEER Working Papers 2009/2); C. Hillion, "Mixity and Coherence in EU External Relations: The Significance of the Duty of Cooperation", in C. Hillion and P. Koutrakos (eds.), *Mixed Agreements Revisited: The EU and its Member States in the World*, 2010, 87.

either to support common positions or to express views on matters falling within their competence.[53]

In light of the preceding analysis, rather than creating momentum for undue accretion of EU cultural powers, the Convention on the Diversity of Cultural Expressions illustrated the fact that culture stretches across the broader EU policy agenda. That said, the inclusion of former Article 151 EC (now Article 167 TFEU) among the sectoral legal bases of the Commission's proposal for a Council Decision approving the Convention on the Diversity of Cultural Expressions, and the final Decision adopted by the Council for that purpose, elucidates that for both the Commission and the Council, the conclusion of the Convention on the Diversity of Cultural Expressions lay within the scope of the EU's explicit cultural competence as well. Should Article 167 TFEU be construed as enabling the European institutions to conclude agreements with third countries or international organisations in the field of culture? Guidance may be sought from Article 167(3) TFEU.

Article 167(3) TFEU calls on the Union, in conjunction with the Member States, to foster cooperation with third countries and international organisations in the sphere of culture. Although it does not expressly refer to any treaty-making powers, it should be possible for the European institutions to enter into agreements for the purpose of cultural cooperation, as it is difficult to envisage how they could otherwise give effect to the role assigned to them by this provision. A decisive factor for the inclusion of what is now Article 167 TFEU among the legal bases of *Council Decision 2006/515/EC* appears, in fact, to have been Article 12 of the Convention on the Diversity of Cultural Expressions, which invites parties to strengthen bilateral, regional and international cooperation for the creation of conditions conducive to the promotion of the diversity of cultural expressions. Obviously, one could counter-argue that, were the EU to accept international obligations in the field of culture, this could lead to circumvention of the prohibition of harmonisation contained in Article 167(5) TFEU.[54] The provisions of the Convention on the Diversity of Cultural Expressions seem to exclude such a scenario. The undemanding, 'best efforts' language used in Article 12 of the Convention on the Diversity of Cultural Expressions does not match the concept of 'harmonisation' within the meaning of EU law.

---

53 *See* Council of the European Union, "Code of Conduct between the Council, the Member States and the Commission on the UNESCO Negotiations on the Draft Convention on the Protection of the Diversity of Cultural Contents and Artistic Expressions", *supra* note 38, §§5 and 7.

54 *See* P. Eeckhout, *supra* note 52, at 95.

5. IMPLEMENTING THE CONVENTION ON THE DIVERSITY OF CULTURAL EXPRESSIONS: THE WAY AHEAD

As principal actor behind the preparation and drafting of the Convention on the Diversity of Cultural Expressions, the European Community, by approving the final text adopted, became bound by its provisions. A priority written question submitted by the European Parliament regarding the implications of the Convention on the Diversity of Cultural Expressions for Community law and practice provided the opportunity for a clear statement on behalf of the Commission concerning the status of the Convention: the Convention was binding on the European Community and formed part of Community law.[55] Following the Lisbon Treaty and the succession of the European Community by the European Union, the Convention on the Diversity of Cultural Expressions is binding on the EU and forms part of EU law.

One may wonder what were the reasons that prompted the European Parliament to raise a question that for the EU law scholar has an obvious answer. Article 216(2) TFEU (formerly Article 300(7) EC) states that "agreements concluded by the Union are binding upon the institutions of the Union and on its Member States." The issue has also been settled for good by the CJEU. In a judgment of 30 April 1974, *R. & V. Haegeman v the Belgian state*, the Court affirmed that an agreement concluded by the Council is an act of one of the institutions of the Community (now the Union) and therefore from its coming into force, forms an integral part of Community (now Union) law.[56] It seems therefore that, rather than seeking a genuine answer on behalf of the Commission, the European Parliament sought to raise awareness of the Convention on the Diversity of Cultural Expressions and alert the European institutions, especially the Commission, about the need to implement it in a prompt and smooth manner.

The recognition that the Convention on the Diversity of Cultural Expressions forms part of EU law entails significant consequences for the design and implementation of EU policies. The EU is duty-bound to conform to and implement the provisions of the Convention on the Diversity of Cultural Expressions when exercising the competences it enjoys in the areas covered by the Convention. According to the Code of Conduct between the Council, the Member States and the Commission, adopted on 1 February 2007, for the

---

55 *See* Parliamentary Questions, "Written Question by Ruth Hieronymi (PPE-DE) to the Commission, "UNESCO Convention on the Protection and Promotion of the Diversity of Cultural Expressions", P-554/07 (8 November 2007), *available at* www.europarl.europa.eu/sides/getDoc.do?pubRef=-//EP//TEXT+WQ+P-2007–5554+0+DOC+XML+V0//EN (last visited on 2 November 2011).

56 Court of Justice of the European Union, Case C-181/73, *R.&V. Haegeman v the Belgian State,* [1974] E.C.R. 449, §§4–5.

participation of the Community (now the Union) and its Member States in the meetings organised within the framework of UNESCO for the implementation of the Convention,[57] these competences encompass free movement of goods, persons, services and capital (Articles 23–31 and 39–60 EC) (now, as amended, Articles 28–37 and 45–59 TFEU); competition, in particular as regards state aids (Articles 81–89 EC) (now Articles 101–109 TFEU); the internal market (Articles 94–97 EC) (now Articles 114–117 TFEU); intellectual property (Articles 95 and 308) (now Articles 114 and 352 TFEU); the common commercial policy (Articles 131 to 134 EC) (now, as amended, Articles 206–207 TFEU); visas, asylum and immigration (Articles 61–69 EC) (now, as amended, Articles 67, 72, 74, 77–79 and 81 TFEU); development cooperation (Articles 177 to 181 EC) (now, as amended, Articles 208–211 TFEU) and cooperation with industrialised countries (Article 181a EC) (now, as amended, Articles 212–213 TFEU) without prejudice to Member States' national competence; and any other matter falling exclusively or primarily within EU competence.[58] It is therefore useful, in what follows, to disentangle the influence that the Convention on the Diversity of Cultural Expressions has so far exerted on EU law and policy by looking first at the impact of the Convention on internal EU policies, in particular free movement, the single market and competition law, and then at the impact of the Convention on external EU policies.

5.1. FREE MOVEMENT, THE INTERNAL MARKET AND THE CONVENTION ON THE DIVERSITY OF CULTURAL EXPRESSIONS

An essentially declaratory instrument with few positive obligations and many "promotion", "facilitation" and "encouragement" requirements imposed on its parties, the Convention on the Diversity of Cultural Expressions has not yet become the object of systematic consideration by the European institutions when developing action to ensure the smooth functioning of the internal market. Recent internal market harmonisation instruments with ramifications in the cultural field do not offer any evidence to suggest that the Convention on the

[57] *See* Council of the European Union, "Code of Conduct between the Council, the Member States and the Commission for the participation of the Community and its Member States in meetings regarding the implementation of the Convention on the Protection and Promotion of the Diversity of Cultural Expressions", *5914/07*, point 3 (1 February 2007), *available at* http://ec.europa.eu/culture/documents/pdf/code_conduct_council_en.pdf (last visited 2 February 2012).

[58] The Member States, for their part, are required to abide by and implement the Convention in the areas under their powers, namely, with regard to aspects of cultural policies within their competence; public awareness and education; international cooperation in the field of culture, in particular with developing countries (except for trade related issues); human rights; follow-up bodies and mechanisms; and any other matters falling exclusively or primarily within their competence. *See* id., point 2.

Diversity of Cultural Expressions has influenced EU decision-making and policy practice in a substantive way. Mention could be made, for example, to Directive 2011/77/EU, which amended Directive 2006/16/EC on the term of protection of copyright and certain related rights.[59] This Directive extends the term of protection for performers from 50 to 70 years but contains no reference to the Convention on the Diversity of Cultural Expressions and its implications, if any, for the revised legal framework. In addition, a number of policy documents that have been issued in the field of intellectual property following the entry into force of the Convention, give no consideration to it. This was the case, for instance, with the Commission's Green Paper on the online distribution of audiovisual works, which launched a process of reflection on the existing copyright licensing framework and the challenges and opportunities it creates for cross-border availability of online audiovisual services in the EU.[60] A concrete reference to the Convention on the Diversity of Cultural Expressions can be found in the Audiovisual Media Services (AVMS) Directive.[61] However, the Directive does no more than simply state in recital 7 that it respects the principles of the Convention.

The absence of systematic attention afforded to the Convention on the Diversity of Cultural Expressions in the field of *positive integration*, that is, the harmonisation of the rules of the Member States to the extent necessary for the proper functioning of the internal market (also known as *policy integration*) and its preparatory documents might indicate that, for the European institutions, the Convention adds nothing to previously established policy-making patterns. Some consideration is expected to be given to the cultural ramifications of the measures adopted anyway. In the field of *market integration*, which requires national measures restricting free movement to be abolished (also known as *negative integration*), things might be different. The case law of the CJEU is enlightening in this respect. In *UTECA*,[62] a judgment issued on 5 March 2009, the issue of the relevance of the Convention on the Diversity of Cultural Expressions arose as part of the broader question whether cultural considerations can be accepted as a ground for preserving regulatory barriers to free movement.

59 Directive 2011/77/EC of the European Parliament and of the Council of 27 September 2011 amending Directive 2006/116/EC on the term of protection of copyright and certain related rights, 11 October 2011, *OJ 2011 L 265/1*.

60 European Commission, "Green Paper on the online distribution of audiovisual works", *COM (2011) 427* (13 July 2011).

61 Directive 2007/65/EC of the European Parliament and of the Council amending Council Directive 89/552/EEC on the Coordination of Certain Provisions Laid Down by Law, Regulation or Administrative Action in Member States Concerning the Pursuit of Television Broadcasting Activities, 11 December 2007, *OJ 2007 L 332/27* [hereinafter "Amended Directive 89/552/EEC"].

62 Court of Justice of the European Union, Case C-222/07, *Unión de Televisiones Comerciales Asociadas (UTECA) v Administración General del Estado*, [2009] E.C.R. I-01407.

The case originated in a dispute, referred for a preliminary ruling, concerning the compatibility of legal provisions in Spain with EU primary law as well as the Television without Frontiers (TWF) Directive,[63] the precursor of the AVMS Directive. Spanish legislation required broadcasters to earmark at least 5% of their operating revenue for the production of European cinematographic films and films made for television. 60% of that funding had to be reserved for productions whose original language was one of the official languages of Spain. The Court took the position that the TWF Directive did not preclude Spain from enacting such legislation. It then examined the conformity of the Spanish rules with EU fundamental freedoms and found that the obligation imposed on Spanish broadcasters to allocate 60% of the 5% of their operating revenue reserved for the production of European audiovisual works to the production of films in one of the official languages of Spain contravened several fundamental freedoms, in particular, freedom to provide services, freedom of establishment, free movement of capital and free movement of workers. The Spanish government argued that the disputed measure pursued a cultural policy objective: its aim was to promote Spanish multilingualism. The Court agreed, noting that such an objective had already been found in earlier jurisprudence to constitute an overriding reason in the public interest that could justify restrictions on free movement.[64] The Court held that the measure was appropriate and proportional to the goal pursued and concluded that the Spanish legislation was compatible with EU law.

Interestingly, in order to examine whether the Spanish measure went beyond what was necessary to achieve the cultural objective pursued, the Court drew directly upon the Convention on the Diversity of Cultural Expressions. According to the Commission, the Spanish legislation did not meet the proportionality requirement because the Spanish authorities had not laid down precise criteria in order to ensure that only audiovisual productions of cultural value – and not audiovisual productions in general – would form the object of investment. The Court rejected the argument. Noting that the Convention on the Diversity of Cultural Expressions recognises linguistic diversity as "a fundamental element of cultural diversity",[65] the Court stated that "language and culture are intrinsically linked".[66] Protecting and promoting one or several of the official languages of Spain through investment in audiovisual works, and thus Spanish culture, should not necessarily be accompanied by

---

63 Council Directive 89/552/EEC on the Coordination of Certain Provisions Laid Down by Law, Regulation or Administrative Action in Member States Concerning the Pursuit of Television Broadcasting Activities, 3 October 1989, *OJ 1989 L 298/23*.

64 See in particular Court of Justice of the European Union, Cases C-379/87, *Groener*, [1989] E.C.R. 3967 and C-250/06, *United Pan-Europe Communications Belgium and Others*, [2007] E.C.R. I-11135.

65 *See* Directive 2011/77/EC, *supra* note 62, §33.

66 *See* id.

additional cultural criteria regarding such works in order to justify a restriction on free movement.[67]

In her opinion on the UTECA case,[68] Advocate General Kokott gave consideration to the Convention on the Diversity of Cultural Expressions when examining whether the objective pursued by the Spanish legislation – a language policy goal – was legitimate in the first place. Her reasoning was based on the argument that "the Community [now the Union] and the Member States that are Contracting States to the UNESCO Convention have undertaken to take that Convention into account when interpreting and applying other treaties, that is to say inter alia when interpreting and applying the EC Treaty [now the TFEU Treaty]"[69] and its free movement provisions. The Advocate General emphasised that the Convention acknowledges the sovereign right of states to adopt measures for the protection and promotion of the diversity of cultural expressions, including those in the cultural services sector,[70] and noted that the Convention expressly allows contracting states to adopt measures regarding the language of such services.[71]

5.2. COMPETITION LAW AND THE CONVENTION ON THE DIVERSITY OF CULTURAL EXPRESSIONS

Public assistance to cultural activities comes within the scope of the EU competition rules and in particular the state aid provisions of the Treaty on the Functioning of the European Union. In accordance with Article 107(1) TFEU, any aid granted by a Member State or through state resources, which distorts or threatens to distort competition by favouring certain undertakings or the production of certain goods, is incompatible with the internal market insofar as it affects trade between the Member States. However, the Treaty also specifies in Article 107(3)(d) TFEU that "aid to promote culture and heritage conservation" may be considered to be compatible with the internal market "where such aid does not affect trading conditions and competition in the Union to an extent that is contrary to the common interest". This provision has served on several occasions as the basis for the authorisation of Member States' cultural support schemes by the Commission, which is entrusted with the exclusive task of

---

67 *See* id.

68 Opinion of Advocate General Kokott delivered on 4 September 2008, Case C-222/07, Unión de Televisiones Comerciales Asociadas (UTECA), *available at* www.curia.eu.int (last visited 2 February 2012) [hereinafter Opinion of Advocate General Kokott"].

69 *See* id., at §99; *See also* Convention on the Diversity of Cultural Expressions, *supra* note 1, Article 20(1)(b).

70 *See* Opinion of Advocate General Kokott, *supra* note 68, §98; *See also* Convention on the Diversity of Cultural Expressions, *supra* note 1, Articles 1(h), 2 (20), 5, 6(1) and (2)(a).

71 *See* Opinion of Advocate General Kokott, *supra* note 68, §98; *See also* Convention on the Diversity of Cultural Expressions, *supra* note 1, Article 6(2)(b).

scrutinizing Member States' aid measures and their compliance with the Treaty rules.

In a series of culture-related state aid cases, the Commission has taken into account the Convention on the Diversity of Cultural Expressions when evaluating, under Article 107(3)(d) TFEU, the nature of the objective pursued by the aid under examination. For instance, in a case concerning the provision of state resources through direct grants for the renovation of the grandstand of the Leipzig racecourse in Germany, the Commission expressly noted that the aid sought to "strengthen culture and the conservation of the cultural heritage, both in terms of Article 167 TFEU and the UNESCO Convention on the Protection and Promotion of the Diversity of Cultural Expressions".[72] Similar statements were made in relation to aid granted by the Ministry of Interior of the Republic of Hungary in order to cover the operational costs of the Danube Art Ensemble and the Danube Symphony Orchestra,[73] and aid provided by the *Centre national du cinema et de l'image animée* in France for the creation, development and production of audiovisual works intended for multi-platform distribution.[74]

In another set of cases, the Commission underlined that its state aid evaluation gave due consideration to the Convention on the Diversity of Cultural Expressions. This was the case, for instance, concerning the award of grants targeting the promotion of various museum activities in the Basque region in Spain;[75] aid for the construction of a shellfish museum in Limfjorden (Denmark);[76] aid in the form of direct grants for the production and promotion of dance, music, poetry, theatre and circus performances in Spain and abroad;[77] and aid for the promotion of the use of the Basque language in social life[78] and at the workplace.[79] However, the Commission did not explain what the

72 European Commission, Decision of 24 August 2010 on State Aid N 164/2010, Germany, Leipziger Reit- und Rennverein Scheibenholz, §11.

73 *See* European Commission, Decision of 13 December 2010 on State Aid N 122/2010, Hungary, Danube Cultural Palace, §3.

74 *See* European Commission, Decision of 23 February 2011 on State Aid N 446/2010, France, Aide aux projects pour les nouveaux médias.

75 Such as the organisation of art exhibitions, conferences and seminars, the development of publications and educational material, the creation of inventories of works of art and the digitalisation of museum collections. *See* European Commission, Decision of 11 May 2011 on State Aid 32643 (2011/N), Spain, State aid to Basque museums, §23.

76 *See* European Commission, Decision on State Aid 30649 (N 2011), Denmark, State aid to the Danish Shellfish Centre, 11 May 2011, §23.

77 *See* European Commission, Decision of 4 April 2011 on State Aid 32144 (N 2011), Spain, State aid to dance, theatre and poetry, §1; European Commission, Decision of 4 April 2011 on State Aid SA.32119 (2011/N), Spain, State aid to activities in the theatre and circus sectors, §16.

78 *See* European Commission, Decision of 19 April 2011 on State Aid 32549 (N 2011), Espagne, Subventions pour le développement de l'usage de la langue basque dans la vie sociale.

79 *See* European Commission, Decision of 19 April 2011 on State Aid 32266 (N 2011), Spain, Aid for the promotion of the Basque language at the workplace, §26.

precise contribution of the Convention was in state aid evaluation under Article 107(3)(d) TFEU. At the same time, it should be noted that in a handful of cases dealing with support measures that were similar to those mentioned above, no explicit reference was made to the Convention. It may thus be queried whether the Commission affords substantive and systematic consideration to the Convention on the Diversity of Cultural Expressions when evaluating Member States' aid schemes that promote culture and heritage protection. The same also applies for the assessment of state aid measures that, though not culture-specific – and therefore assessed on the basis of other state aid derogations of the Treaty on the Functioning of the European Union – may support culture and cultural diversity in an indirect manner.

One of the rare cases in which the Commission has concretely used the Convention on the Diversity of Cultural Expressions to justify its stance is *Commission Decision 2008/354/EC*.[80] The case concerned a French state aid scheme in the form of a tax credit for the creation of video games. According to the information provided by the French authorities, to be eligible for the tax credit, video games should inter alia adapt an existing work from Europe's cultural heritage in a scenario written in French or enjoy a concept of high quality and originality and contribute to expressing Europe's cultural diversity and creation. The Commission raised doubts as to whether the measure under review could be authorised on the basis of the cultural state aid derogation of Article 107(3)(d) TFEU. While recognising that certain video games could be regarded as cultural products, the Commission considered that the criteria laid down to determine eligible video games could be subject to broad interpretation and therefore did not guarantee that the selected video games would have a cultural dimension. In response to the Commission's concerns, the French authorities substantially amended the scheme and introduced a points-based system in order to determine aid eligibility. To become eligible for funding, video games should gather 14 points out of a total of 22 points from five different sections of the test: section 1 on "heritage", section 2 on "original creation", section 3 on "cultural content", section 4 on "European location of expenditure and nationality of creative collaborators", and section 5 on "editorial and technological innovation".

Maintaining its initial position that video games do not constitute cultural products in general but rather serve to provide interactive entertainment, the Commission examined whether the scheme as amended could secure access to funding for video games containing cultural content. Such an examination involved identifying the different criteria of the selection test that guaranteed that the content of the video games receiving aid would be cultural and

[80] *See* European Commission, Decision of 11 December 2007 on State Aid C 47/06 (ex N 648/05), Tax credit introduced by France for the creation of video games (2008/354/EC), *OJ 2007 L 118/16*.

certifying that a sufficient number of points were allocated to them. Among others, the second part of the test ("original creation") awarded up to two points to video games displaying originality on the basis of the scenario and the creativity of their graphic and sound environment. Accepting the cultural dimension of this criterion, the Commission noted that creativity is an essential part of the definition of "cultural expressions" given in the Convention on the Diversity of Cultural Expressions.[81] The Convention was also used in the assessment of one of the criteria listed under section 3 of the test ("cultural content"), namely that artistic expenditure should account for more than 50% of the production budget.[82] Artistic expenditure covered the personnel costs for the producer, the assistant producer, the artistic director and the persons responsible for the scenario, the animation and the sound environment of the video games. Noting that the Convention on the Diversity of Cultural Expressions refers to the artistic dimension when defining "cultural content", the Commission took the position that the artistic expenditure criterion indicated the importance attached by the aid scheme to the design, scenario, dialogue and music of the funded video games, and hence to video games with cultural content (as opposed to more "technical" video games, such as sports games or games of pure simulation).

Undoubtedly, during the last few years, the Commission has systematically required Member States to authenticate the cultural content of the works and services that they support in order to benefit from the cultural state aid derogation under Article 107(3)(d) TFEU. According to the Cinema Communication on state aid schemes targeting the production of cinematographic and audiovisual works in particular, Member States may benefit from the derogation of Article 107(3)(d) TFEU if they ensure that the content of the audiovisual production receiving aid is cultural according to "verifiable" national criteria.[83] In the video games case, the Commission applied the same principle and used the Convention on the Diversity of Cultural Expressions in order to evaluate the cultural relevance of some of the eligibility criteria devised by the French authorities. In another case, concerning an Austrian aid scheme for the production of feature films and documentaries, the Commission similarly took the Convention on the Diversity of Cultural Expressions into account when examining whether the Austrian authorities had

81 *See* id., §70. *See also* Convention on the Diversity of Cultural Expressions, *supra* note 1, Article 4(3).

82 *See* European Commission, *supra* note 80, §72. *See also* Convention on the Diversity of Cultural Expressions, *supra* note 1, Article 4(2).

83 *See* European Commission, "Communication to the Council, the European Parliament, the Economic and Social Committee and the Committee of Regions on Certain Legal Aspects relating to Cinematographic and Other Audiovisual Works", *COM (2001) 534* (26 September 2011). *See also* E. Psychogiopoulou, "The 'Cultural' Criterion in the European Commission's Assessment of State Aids to the Audio-Visual Sector" 37 *Legal Issues of Economic Integration* 273 (2010).

designed "verifiable" national criteria to guarantee the cultural content of the productions receiving aid.[84]

5.3. EXTERNAL RELATIONS AND THE CONVENTION ON THE DIVERSITY OF CULTURAL EXPRESSIONS

Perhaps greater awareness of the need to implement the Convention on the Diversity of Cultural Expressions in a systematic way can be observed through dialogues launched with partner countries and regions around the world. The Agenda Communication of the Commission was clear in this respect. It noted that "the rapid entry into force of the UNESCO Convention on the Protection and Promotion of the Diversity of Cultural Expressions illustrates the new role of cultural diversity at the international level".[85] The Communication went on to explain that, as parties to the Convention on the Diversity of Cultural Expressions, the Community (now the Union) and the Member States "have reaffirmed their commitment to developing a new and more pro-active cultural role for Europe in the context of Europe's international relations and to integrating the cultural dimension as a vital element in Europe's dealings with partner countries and regions".[86]

The promotion of the Convention on the Diversity of Cultural Expressions and its implementation in the context of the EU's external relations figured prominently among the priority areas and topics for action determined by the Council's work plan for culture for the periods 2008–2010 and 2011–2014.[87] As a result, in addition to consistently promoting the ratification of the Convention on the Diversity of Cultural Expressions by third states,[88] the EU has increasingly mobilised resources for cultural cooperation in the context of the European Neighbourhood Policy, the EU enlargement and development cooperation policies, the Eastern Partnership, the policies supporting the Union

84 *See* European Commission, Decision of 31 August 2010 on State Aid N 96/2010, Austria, Austrian film support scheme, §36.

85 *See* Agenda Communication, *supra* note 26, at 7.

86 *See* id., 11.

87 *See* Conclusions of the Council and of the Representatives of the Governments of the Member States, meeting within the Council, on the Work Plan for Culture 2008–2010, *OJ 2008 C 143/9* (10 June 2008); Conclusions of the Council and of the Representatives of the Governments of the Member States, meeting within the Council, on the Work Plan for Culture 2011–2014, *OJ 2010 C 325/1* (2 December 2010).

88 *See, e.g.*, Council Decision 2008/211/EC on the Principles, Priorities and Conditions contained in the European Partnership with Bosnia and Herzegovina and Repealing Decision 2006/55/EC, 18 February 2008, *OJ 2008 L 80/18*, at 24; Communication to the Council and to the European Parliament, "On the General Approach to Enable ENP Partner Countries to Participate in Community Agencies and Community Programmes", *COM (2006) 724*, at 8 (4 December 2006) (where it is mentioned that the Convention's ratification is a prerequisite for participation in the MEDIA 2007 programme).

for the Mediterranean, and bilateral partnerships with developed and emerging partner countries.[89] Moreover, in the field of trade relations, a template protocol on cultural cooperation was drafted by the Commission, following intensive inter-service consultation, to serve as a basis for discussion in ongoing and future trade negotiations with third countries and regional state groupings. The *Protocol*, properly adjusted, was included in the economic partnership agreement concluded with the Caribbean Forum of ACP States (the "Cariforum").[90]

The *Protocol* makes explicit reference to the Convention on the Diversity of Cultural Expressions, and calls on the parties to "cooperate within the framework of its implementation, building on the principles of the Convention and developing actions in line with its provisions."[91] Recognising the multi-faceted nature of cultural goods and services, the *Protocol* stresses the importance of fostering cultural cooperation between the parties, taking into account, on a case by case basis, "the degree of development of their cultural industries, the level and structural imbalances of cultural exchanges and the existence of preferential schemes for the promotion of local and regional cultural content."[92] The parties "endeavour" to facilitate the entry and temporary stay of artists and other cultural professionals and practitioners in their territory, and to bolster training opportunities and contacts. They are also to exchange best practices and information, and provide counselling for the elaboration of policies, the drafting of legislation, and the usage and transfer of technologies and know-how. The *Protocol* draws special attention to audiovisual and cinematographic cooperation, as well as to cooperation in the fields of performing arts, heritage protection, literature and publications. With regard to audiovisual cooperation in particular, the parties are encouraged to negotiate (and implement existing) co-production agreements, promote interoperability of

---

89 European Commission Report to the European Parliament, the Council, the European Economic and Social Committee and the Committee of the Regions on the implementation of the European Agenda for Culture, *COM (2010) 390*, at 6 (19 July 2010).

90 *See* Protocol III (on Cultural Cooperation) to the Economic Partnership Agreement between the CARIFORUM States and the European Community and its Member States, *available at* http://ec.europa.eu/culture/our-policy-development/doc/cultural_cooperation_protocol.pdf (last visited 2 February 2012).

91 Id., Preamble §§1 and 2 (in particular, the Protocol focuses on Articles 14 (cooperation for development), 15 (collaborative arrangements) and 16 (preferential treatment for developing countries) of the Convention on the Diversity of Cultural Expressions).

92 As explained in a recent Commission Staff Working Paper (*see* European Commission, "Staff Working Paper on the External Dimension of Audiovisual Policy", *SEC (2009) 1033*, at 17–20 (14 July 2009)), opportunities for the conclusion of cultural cooperation protocols with third counties must be assessed on a case by case basis, with careful consideration of the mechanisms involved, so as to take into account the different situations and characteristics of the partners with whom the EU enters into negotiations. The objective of fostering wider and more balanced cultural exchanges as part of the implementation of the Convention on the Diversity of Cultural Expressions is equally valid vis-à-vis partners which have a level of development comparable to that of the EU. However, in such instances, strict reciprocity of the advantages earned from cooperation is likely to be demanded.

audiovisual technologies, enable temporary importation of the technical material and equipment necessary for the shooting of audiovisual works, and facilitate market access for co-productions, including through the granting of preferential treatment. Of no lesser importance, co-produced audiovisual works may qualify as "European works" in accordance with Article 1(n)(i) of the TWF Directive, as amended by the AVMS Directive,[93] and benefit from the "European content quotas" laid down in Articles 3i(1) and 4(1) of the Directive.[94]

Drafted with the aim of preserving and enhancing domestic capacity to determine and develop cultural policies, the *Protocol* implements the Convention on the Diversity of Cultural Expressions in a concerted and succinct manner. Certain of its provisions are remarkably innovative. Article 3, for example, which invites parties to assist the entry and temporary stay of artists and other cultural professionals and practitioners in their territory, targets situations that do not come within the meaning of service supply and, as such, fall outside the scope of the "Investment, Trade in Services and E-Commerce" Title of the agreement. This provision is of interest to operators who do not provide a cultural "service", yet engage in activities supportive of cultural interaction. Attending a literary festival or participating in an audition are some of the activities that could be envisaged under Article 3. On the other hand, arrangements are made to ensure that the cooperation channels established do not undermine EU Member States' production capacity and thus the projection and radiation of "European" cultures. The conditions that need to be fulfilled for the "European quota rules" to cover EU-Cariforum co-productions are a case in point.[95] Access to

---

93 *See* Amended Directive 89/552/EEC, *supra* note 61, Article 1(n)(i) (according to which "European works" cover, among others, works co-produced within the framework of agreements related to the audiovisual sector concluded between the Community [now the Union] and third countries, and fulfilling the conditions defined in each of those agreements.

94 *See* id., Article 3i(1) of *Directive* 89/552/EEC (stipulating that the Member States need to ensure that on-demand audiovisual media services provided by media service providers under their jurisdiction promote, where practicable and by appropriate means, the production of and access to "European works". Such promotion may relate *inter alia* to the financial contribution made by such services to the production and rights acquisition of European works or to the share and/or prominence of European works in the catalogue of programmes offered by the on-demand audiovisual media service); Amended Directive 89/552/EEC, *supra* note 61, Article 4(1) (pursuant to which Member States shall ensure, where practicable and by appropriate means, that broadcasters reserve for European works, a majority proportion of their transmission time, excluding the time appointed to news, sports events, games, advertising, teletext services and teleshopping).

95 For co-productions to qualify as European works, the following conditions must be met: a) the co-produced audiovisual works must be realised between undertakings which are owned and continue to be owned, whether directly or by majority participation, by a Member State of the European Union or a signatory CARIFORUM state and/or by nationals of a Member State of the European Union or nationals of a signatory CARIFORUM state; b) the representative director(s) or manager(s) of the co-producing undertakings must have the nationality of a Member State of the European Union and/or of a signatory CARIFORUM state; c) the total financial contributions of one or several producers of the EC party (taken together), and the total financial contributions of one or several producers of signatory

European screens is carefully circumscribed, so that audiovisual works of limited European financial participation may not take advantage of the regime introduced.

6. CONCLUDING REMARKS

Recent developments in the struggle towards protecting and promoting cultural diversity have brought EU competences enjoyed in the cultural field to centre stage. The negotiation and conclusion of the Convention on the Diversity of Cultural Expressions has triggered processes at the EU level that vividly document the vast array of powers the European Union has at its disposal for the development of cultural activity. EU cultural action does not simply derive from Article 167 TFEU; it also originates in other provisions of the Treaty on the Functioning of the European Union that can be used for the attainment of cultural objectives, combined with other legitimate EU policy goals.

But beyond this, the fervent support offered by the EU to the Convention on the Diversity of Cultural Expressions unveils the ambitious agenda developed by the European institutions with regard to culture in recent years. The result of a long process of progressive affirmation of cultural diversity at the international level, the Convention on the Diversity of Cultural Expressions recognises the significance of public policies for safeguarding and promoting cultural diversity, and underlines the importance of international cultural cooperation in order to foster cultural exchanges worldwide. Through the Convention on the Diversity of Cultural Expressions, the EU aspires to portray itself as a staunch promoter of Member States' cultural diversity and a world actor in favour of cultural rapprochement.

At the same time, the implementation record of the EU does not allow one to argue that the EU has systematically integrated the prescriptions of the Convention on the Diversity of Cultural Expressions in its various activities. The preceding analysis discloses asymmetrical implementation. Overall, there seems to be genuine attention afforded to the Convention on the Diversity of Cultural Expressions in the context of the EU external policies and piecemeal consideration given to the Convention on the Diversity of Cultural Expressions in the context of the EU internal policies, although there are important exceptions that should not be neglected. On this basis, it seems that the challenge for the European institutions is to prevent a patchwork approach and adopt a holistic strategy for the implementation of the Convention that ensures the development of a broad range of innovative culture-friendly EU policies. Ultimately, the key question revolves around the tenor of the Convention on the

CARIFORUM states (taken together) must not be less than 20 percent and not more than 80 percent of the total production cost.

Diversity of Cultural Expressions itself. As an inherently weak instrument that creates hortatory rather than strict obligations, can the Convention on the Diversity of Cultural Expressions become firmly entrenched in the EU legal order and take a prominent position in EU policy thinking? To put it another way, can the Convention on the Diversity of Cultural Expressions enjoy "effective" implementation? These are the issues the European institutions (and other parties to the Convention on the Diversity of Cultural Expressions) will have to cope with in the years to come.

IMPLEMENTATION OF THE CONVENTION ON THE DIVERSITY OF CULTURAL EXPRESSIONS IN SOUTH AFRICA

Perspectives from a 'Developing Country'

Christa RAUTENBACH*

Our Convention – and I need to reiterate this – is based on respect; respect for the diversity of all cultures, respect for the dignity of each of us and acknowledgment of our common humanity. These are the values of my own South African Constitution. These are the values of what we call ubuntu, the profound tenet of African philosophy, which holds that one is only fully human when recognising the humanity of others.[1]

1. INTRODUCTION

South Africa[2] is located at the most southern tip of Africa with an estimated population of fifty million made up of diverse origins,[3]

---

* Prof. Dr. C. Rautenbach is a Professor of Law at the North-West University of Potchefstroom, South Africa. She is also an alumnus of the Alexander von Humboldt foundation and a member of the Civil Society Working Group on the Convention.

1 K. ASMAL, "What the Convention Means to Me", in N. OBULJEN and J. SMIERS (eds.), *UNESCO's Convention on the Protection and Promotion of the Diversity of Cultural Expressions*, 2006, 353, 356.

2 *See* SOUTH AFRICAN GOVERNMENT INFORMATION, "About SA", *available at* www.info.gov.za/aboutsa/index.htm (last visited 2 February 2012) (providing information about South Africa and its people).

3 *See* D. BURGER (ed.), *The South African Yearbook 2007/08*, 2008, 2–3 (indicating that one part of the African (or black) population, such as the Zulu, Xhosas, Bapedis and Venda groups, is unique to South Africa. Other groups (the Basotho, Tswana, Swazi, Ndebele and Shangaan groups) are descendants of South Africa's neighbours. The white population is descended from various European countries, including the Netherlands, United Kingdom, Germany, France and Portugal. A number of South Africans also originated in India and other parts of Asia).

cultures,[4] languages[5] and religions.[6] For many years, racial conflict was the order of the day as a result of the former government's policy of separate development based on racial segregation.[7] This policy became notoriously known as 'apartheid', a term which has been directly absorbed into the English language without translation from the Afrikaans language.[8] After a long and sometimes violent struggle on the national and international levels South Africa's transition from apartheid to constitutional democracy commenced with the removal of apartheid laws in 1991, the implementation of the *Constitution of the Republic of South Africa*[9] (the "Interim Constitution") in 1994, and finally the coming into effect of the *Constitution of the Republic of South Africa* (the "Constitution")[10] in 1996.

---

4 *See* Statistics South Africa, "Mid-Year Population Estimates 2011", 4 (2011), *available at* www.statssa.gov.za/publications/P0302/P03022011.pdf (last visited 2 February 2012) (describing that demographically, the South African population can broadly be divided into the following population groups: Africans almost 79.4%, Coloreds 8.9%, Indian/Asian 2.6% and Whites 9.1%. These groups can be subdivided even further depending on the ethnicity, language, religion or origins of a particular group. The term "Colored" is one of the remnants of the classification system of South Africa and is used to describe the mixed-race people of South Africa. It also includes the Khoisan people who is regarded as truly indigenous to South Africa).

5 *See* Constitution of the Republic of South Africa, Section 6 (Act of 1996) [hereinafter "Constitution"] (stipulating in Section 6(1) that there are 11 official languages, namely Sepedi, Sesotho, Setswana, siSwati, Tshivenda, Xitsonga, Afrikaans, English, isiNdebele, isiXhosa and isiZulu. At least two of these languages must be used in official documents, but there is a tendency to use English as the common denominator at official meetings. According to the 2001 census, isiZulu is the mother tongue of 23.8% of the population, followed by isiXhosa (17.6%), Afrikaans (13.3%), Sesotho (9.4%), and English and Setswana (8.2% each). The least-spoken indigenous language in South Africa is isiNdebele, which is spoken by 1.6% of the population. In addition to the 11 official languages, several local and foreign dialects are also spoken in South Africa. *See* Statistics South Africa, "Census 2001: Primary Tables South Africa: Census 96 and 2001 Compared", at 8–12 (2004), *available at* www.statssa.gov.za/publications/Report-03-02-04/Report-03-02-042001.pdf (last visited 2 February 2012).

6 *See* Statistics South Africa, *supra* note 5, at 24 (clarifying that in terms of religious affiliation, about two-thirds (79%) of South Africans are Christian, mainly Protestant. They belong to a variety of churches, including many that synthesize Christian and traditional African beliefs. Other noteworthy religions are Islam, Hinduism and Judaism. About 15% of the population practices no religion at all). *See also* South Africa.info, "South Africa: Fast Facts", *available at* www.southafrica.info/about/facts.htm (last visited 2 February 2012).

7 The former National Party commenced with its policy of separate development in 1948, followed by racial segregation laws such as the Separate Representation of Voter's Act (Act No. 46 of 1951) and the Population Registration Act (Act No. 30 of 1950). For an overview on the historical development of apartheid in South Africa, *see* S. Woolman and J. Swanepoel, "Constitutional History", in S. Woolman and M. Bishop (eds.), *Constitutional Law of South Africa*, 2010, 2.15–2.34.

8 For example, A.S. Hornby, *Oxford Advanced Learner's Dictionary,* 2010, 55 describes "apartheid" as "the former political system in South Africa in which only white people had full political rights and other people, especially black people, were forced to live away from white people, go to separate schools, etc."

9 *See* Constitution of the Republic of South Africa (Act No. 200 of 1993) [hereinafter "Interim Constitution"].

10 *See* Constitution, *supra* note 5.

At long last, South Africa made a peaceful transition from a system of parliamentary sovereignty which excluded the involvement of certain racial groups from parliament, to a democratic, constitutional state where everyone could participate in the political processes. This transition remains one of the most amazing political achievements of modern times.[11] The new South Africa, even though politically united as a country, consists of a pluralistic society, a fact which is constitutionally recognized[12] and politically endorsed by South African leaders.[13] Although the apartheid system has been abolished, South Africa is still burdened by its legacy in certain respects; communities previously divided along racial lines still live apart although the legal restraints which forcibly kept them apart no longer exist. Although this tendency is slowly changing, the grouping of people together in racial or cultural terms strengthens cultural and religious identities, which makes it difficult for the South African government to create "a single South African identity without marginalizing culture."[14]

Previous interventions of the international community were instrumental in South Africa's transition from an apartheid state to a democratic state, and it is envisaged that the international norms contained in the *Convention on the Protection and Promotion of the Diversity of Cultural Expressions* 2005 (the "Convention on the Diversity of Cultural Expressions")[15] will assist South Africa to advance its cultural policies on a national and international level and to reconcile commercial and cultural perspectives whilst dealing with cultural diversity issues. As one of the leaders on the African continent, South Africa has a pre-eminent role to play in the advancement of a new economic world order based on more equitable practices, as well as towards the minimizing of the impact of globalism on the African continent.[16]

---

11 For modern readings on the political transformation of South Africa, *see, generally*, W. Beinhart, *Twentieth-Century South Africa*, 2001; J. Barber, *South Africa in the Twentieth Century: A Political History – In search of a Nation State*, 1999; H. Giliomee and B. Mbenga, *New History of South Africa*, 2007.

12 The Preamble to the Constitution reads: "... united in our diversity...", whilst various other provisions protect rights associated with culture or religion. *See* Section 9 Constitution (equality), Section 15 Constitution (freedom of religion), Section 30 Constitution (language and culture), Section 31 Constitution (cultural, religious and linguistic communities) and Section 211 Constitution (customary law).

13 The expression "Rainbow Nation" was originally used by Archbishop Desmond Tutu, and later by Nelson Mandela. It has become a well-known slogan which explains South Africa's newly developing multicultural diversity after apartheid.

14 W. du Plessis, "South Africa", in R. Blanpain (ed.), *International Encyclopaedia of Laws*, 2006, 13.

15 *See* Convention on the Protection and Promotion of the Diversity of Cultural Expressions, 20 October 2005, *U.N. Doc. CLT-2005/CONVENTION DIVERSITE-CULT REV.* [hereinafter "Convention on the Diversity of Cultural Expressions"].

16 *See* South Africa, Department of Foreign Affairs, "South African Foreign Policy", *available at* www.info.gov.za/greenpapers/1996/forafl.htm (last visited 2 February 2012).

This chapter deals with the scope and application of the Convention on the Diversity of Cultural Expressions from the viewpoint of a 'developing country',[17] namely South Africa, beginning with the role of the country leading up to the implementation of the Convention on the Diversity of Cultural Expressions. The chapter then turns to the principles applicable to the application of the Convention on the Diversity of Cultural Expressions in South Africa, in the process examining South Africa's expectations in terms of the Convention and role as a developing country. Finally, this chapter focuses on the practical application of the Convention on the Diversity of Cultural Expressions in South Africa and the role of civil society in its implementation, concluding with a few general remarks on the future role of the Convention in the country.

2. SOUTH AFRICA'S ROLE LEADING UP TO THE CONVENTION ON THE DIVERSITY OF CULTURAL EXPRESSIONS

South Africa played a significant role in the creation of the Convention on the Diversity of Cultural Expressions.[18] Being a member country of the International Network on Cultural Policy (INCP),[19] South Africa formed part of a group of Ministers of Culture who agreed to make a submission to UNESCO supporting the development of an international instrument on cultural diversity. In 2002 South Africa assumed the chair of the INCP and also hosted the Fifth Annual Meeting in Cape Town in the same year in order to discuss, amongst other matters, issues pertaining to cultural diversity in developing countries and the challenges of globalization, as well as a draft text for an

17 There are conflicting viewpoints as to whether South Africa can still be regarded as a developing country or not. *See infra* Paragraph 3.3 for further discussion.

18 The historical events leading up to the adoption of the Convention on the Diversity of Cultural Expressions are set out in N. Obuljen, "From Our Creative Diversity to the Convention on Cultural Diversity: Introduction to the Debate", in Obuljen and Smiers (eds.), *supra* note 1, 17–35.

19 *See* International Network on Cultural Policy, "Welcome to the INCP", *available at* www.incp-ripc.org/index_e.shtml (last visited 2 February 2012) (the INCP is an informal international forum through which culture ministers can explore and exchange views on new and emerging cultural policy issues and develop strategies to promote cultural diversity). The idea of cultural diversity has been part and parcel of the international arena for a very long time and awareness of some of the issues can be attributed to a report *Our Creative Diversity* compiled by the World Commission for Culture and Development. This commission, founded by UNESCO and the UN, started its work in 1993. *See* World Commission on Culture and Development, *Our Creative Diversity: Report of the World Commission on Culture and Development*, 1995.

international instrument on cultural diversity.[20] One of the outcomes of the meeting was the decision to engage in talks with UNESCO with a view to discussing the option of UNESCO hosting the proposed international instrument on cultural diversity. In February 2003 the Ministers of Culture associated with the INCP had a meeting with UNESCO's Director General to discuss the implementation of the Convention on the Diversity of Cultural Expressions under the auspices of UNESCO, thereby setting the events in motion for the drafting of the Convention on the Diversity of Cultural Expressions.[21]

South Africa recognized the importance of an international agreement which addresses all the concerns of African countries, and during November 2004 the

---

20 *See* International Network on Cultural Policy, "Annual Ministerial Meeting: Fifth Annual Ministerial Meeting – Cape Town, South Africa October 14 to 16, 2002", *available at* www.incp-ripc.org/meetings/2002/index_e.shtml (last visited 2 February 2012). The idea of an international instrument to promote cultural diversity was raised for the first time at the Third Annual Ministerial Meeting which was held in Greece in September 2000. During the Fourth Annual Ministerial Meeting in Lucerne in September 2001, the ministers endorsed the report and advice of the Working Group on Cultural Diversity and Globalization on the scope and framework of an International Instrument on Cultural Diversity and mandated the Working Group to draft such an international instrument over a period of two years. *See* International Network on Cultural Policy, "Annual Ministerial Meeting: Lucerne Statement", *available at* www.incp-ripc.org/meetings/2001/statement_e.shtml (last visited 2 February 2012). The Working Group presented three documents for discussion at the Fifth Annual Ministerial Meeting of the INCP in Cape Town, including a Draft Text of an International Instrument on Cultural Diversity. *See* International Network on Cultural Policy, "Annual Ministerial Meeting: An International Instrument on Cultural Diversity", *available at* www.incp-ripc.org/meetings/2002/instrument_e.shtml (last visited 2 February 2012). During the Fifth Annual Ministerial Meeting held in Cape Town during October 2002 it was resolved to expedite the work on the international instrument on cultural diversity by putting it on the agenda of key international institutions such as UNESCO, the United Nations Conference on Trade and Development (UNCTAD), the African, Caribbean and Pacific Group of States (ACP), the World Bank, Francophonie, New Partnership for Africa's Development (NEPAD) and the African Union (AU), and to encourage public distribution and discussion. *See* International Network on Cultural Policy, "Annual Ministerial Meeting: Cape Town Statement", *available at* www.incp-ripc.org/meetings/2002/statement_e.shtml (last visited 2 February 2012).

21 During the 166th session of the Executive Board of UNESCO, an item entitled *Preliminary Study on the Technical and Legal Aspects relating to the Desirability of a Standard-setting Instrument on Cultural Diversity* was placed on the agenda. *See* UNESCO, Executive Board, "Preliminary Study on the Technical and Legal Aspects relating to the Desirability of a Standard-setting Instrument on Cultural Diversity", *166 EX/28* (12 March 2003). On the basis of the recommendation of the Executive Board, the General Conference of UNESCO requested that the Director-General submit a Preliminary Report accompanied by a Preliminary Draft of a Convention on the Protection of the Diversity of Cultural Contents and Artistic Expressions at the October 2005 session. *See* UNESCO, Intergovernmental Meeting of Experts, 'Resolution 32C/34: Desirability of Drawing up an International Standard-Setting Instrument on Cultural Diversity", *CLT/CPD/2004/CONF.201/5* (27 October 2003). *See also* UNESCO, "Historical Background of the 2005 Convention", *available at* www.unesco.org/new/en/culture/themes/cultural-diversity/cultural-expressions/the-convention/historical-background/ (last visited 2 February 2012) (providing an overview of the historical background of the Convention on the Diversity of Cultural Expressions).

Department of Arts and Culture (DAC) in partnership with the University of South Africa (UNISA) and UNESCO hosted a national conference on the "Protection of the Diversity of Cultural Contents and Artistic Expression and the Role of Cultural Diversity in the New Partnership for Africa's Development (NEPAD)"[22] with its main objectives being to identify the importance, implications and challenges of an international cultural policy and to formulate a national position on cultural diversity in a South African context.

Also in 2004, a South African, the late Kader Asmal,[23] was elected as the president of the Inter-governmental Committee of Experts mandated to draft the proposed Convention on the Diversity of Cultural Expressions. A Drafting Committee comprising of the usual regional representatives was set up but the Committee could not reach consensus and consequently it was decided that Asmal would prepare a presidential draft, this taking place at a Cape Town meeting. This draft formed the basis of the final Convention on the Diversity of Cultural Expressions which was adopted in October 2005.[24]

In 2007, Asmal was elected as chairperson of the Conference of Parties (COP) to the Convention at its first ordinary session.[25] During this meeting, South Africa was elected as a member of the Inter-governmental Committee (IGC) sharing with four other Member States in Group V(a), namely Burkina Faso,

---

22 *See* South Africa, Department of Arts and Culture, "South Africa Takes a Leading Role on the Protection of Cultural Diversity – To Host a Conference" (2004), *available at* www.info.gov.za/speeches/2004/04110812451002.htm (last visited 2 February 2012); *See further* NEPAD, "About NEPAD", *available at* www.nepad.org/about (last visited 2 February 2012) (NEPAD is "a radically new intervention, spearheaded by African leaders, to address critical challenges facing the continent: poverty, development and Africa's marginalisation internationally.").

23 *See* Asmal, *supra* note 96, at 354–55. Kader Asmal was a former member of the South African parliament. His reasons for participating in the drafting of the Convention on the Diversity of Cultural Expressions also reflect the fears and expectations of other developing countries. His viewpoints on the convention are reflected in the addresses delivered during his chairmanship of the Inter-governmental Committee of Experts. These addresses can be consulted via the UNESCO website. *See* UNESCO, "Intergovernmental Meeting of Experts", *available at* www.unesco.org/new/en/culture/themes/cultural-diversity/cultural-expressions/the-convention/historical-background/intergovernmental-meetings-of-experts/ (last visited 2 February 2012). Today, Asmal is regarded as the founding father of the convention. He passed away on 22 June 2011 at the age of 76 years. *See* UNESCO, "Prof. Kader Asmal, founding father of the Convention, passes away", *available at* www.unesco.org/new/en/culture/themes/cultural-diversity/cultural-expressions/the-convention/historical-background/tribute-to-asmal/ (last visited 2 February 2012).

24 *See* UNESCO, General Conference, "Preliminary Report by the Director-General on the Progress Achieved During the Third Session of the Intergovernmental Meetings of Experts on the Preliminary Draft Convention on the Protection of the Diversity of Cultural Contents and Artistic Expressions", *33C/23* (11 August 2005).

25 *See* UNESCO, Conference of Parties, "Resolutions", *CE/07/1.CP/CONF/209/Resolutions* (21 June 2007), *available at www.*unesco.org/fileadmin/MULTIMEDIA/HQ/CLT/diversity/pdf/convention_2005/CoP/cp1_resolutions_en.pdf (last visited 2 February 2012). *See further* Convention on the Diversity of Cultural Expressions, *supra* note 15, Article 22 (indicating that the COP is one of the organs of the Convention on the Diversity of Cultural Expressions).

Mali, Mauritius and Senegal.[26]The First Ordinary Session of the IGC took place in Canada. South Africa was elected, together with India, Lithuania and Tunisia, as vice-chairperson of the first session of the committee.[27] One of the objectives of the IGC was to prepare the operational guidelines for the implementation and application of the provisions of the Convention on the Diversity of Cultural Expressions and it was obviously in South Africa's interest to actively participate in the drafting of these guidelines in order to ensure that its agenda on cultural diversity for the country and the African region reaches its fullest potential. To date, South Africa has participated in all of the sessions of the IGC. At the first session of the IGC the IGC invited the Secretariat[28] to select, in consultation with the Chairperson of the IGC, six qualified experts, representative of both the different perspectives relating to preferential treatment in terms of Article 16 of the Convention on the Diversity of Cultural Expressions and countries in different stages of economic development.[29] The selection took place and the experts were tasked with preparing a factual report on this issue, establishing definitions, regulations and existing practices. These documents were submitted to the IGC for examination at its second ordinary session in December 2008.[30] South Africa's proposed expert was one of the experts chosen to prepare a factual report and he submitted his report in line with the distinctive needs of a developing country, amongst others, that the focus should be on research, capacity building, cooperation and development.[31]

---

26 *See* Convention on the Diversity of Cultural Expressions, *supra* note 15, Article 23 (specifying that the IGC is another organ of the Convention on the Diversity of Cultural Expressions).

27 *See* UNESCO, Intergovernmental Committee, "Decisions", *CE/07/1.IGC/Dec.Rev*, *available at* http://unesdoc.unesco.org/images/0015/001584/158430E.pdf (last visited 2 February 2012). During this session, the IGP had to prepare, *inter alia*, preliminary draft guidelines on the use of the resources of the International Fund. South Africa was one of 27 parties that expressed an opinion on the use of the Fund's resources. *See also* UNESCO, Intergovernmental Committee, "Interim report on the use of the resources of the International Fund for Cultural Diversity", *CE/07/1.IGC/6* (4 October 2007) *available at* www.unesco.org/culture/culturaldiversity/doc/6_en.doc (last visited 2 February 2012).

28 *See* Convention on the Diversity of Cultural Expressions, *supra* note 15, Article 24 (explaining that the Secretariat is responsible for assisting the COP and the IGC); *See also* Rule 39 of the Rules of Procedure of the Intergovernmental Committee for the Protection and Promotion of the Diversity of Cultural Expressions.

29 *See* UNESCO, Intergovernmental Committee, "Decision 1.IGC 5B", *CE/07/1.IGC/Dec. Rev.*, *available at* http://unesdoc.unesco.org/images/0015/001584/158430E.pdf (last visited 2 February 2012).

30 *See* UNESCO, Intergovernmental Committee, "Second Ordinary Session", *Doc. CE/08/2. IGC/8* (17 September 2008), *available at* http://unesdoc.unesco.org/images/0017/001779/177924E.pdf (last visited 2 February 2012).

31 South Africa's initial appointed expert was Eugene Mthetwa, Chairman of the Association of Independent Record Companies (AIRCO), which is a non-profit National Music Industry Association. However, Mthetwa withdrew from the process in July 2008. He was replaced by two other experts including one from India and one from South Africa, Professor Mandlenkosi Stanley Makhanya, the Principal and Vice-Chancellor of the University of South Africa. He is also the Deputy Chair of the South African National Commission for UNESCO and the Chair of the Culture Sector of the South African National Commission for

South Africa has to ensure its active participation in mapping out the scope and application of the Convention on the Diversity of Cultural Expressions in the next few years through its continued membership of international organisations, such as the IGC and UNESCO. It follows that South Africa is responsible, both domestically and in terms of the African continent to ensure that the wishes of the African countries, especially those qualifying as developing countries, are heard.

3. APPLICATION OF THE CONVENTION ON THE DIVERSITY OF CULTURAL EXPRESSIONS IN SOUTH AFRICA

3.1. APPLICATION OF THE CONVENTION ON THE DIVERSITY OF CULTURAL EXPRESSIONS IN GENERAL

The DAC,[32] the main government department responsible for the implementation of the Convention on the Diversity of Cultural Expressions, understands the Convention on the Diversity of Cultural Expressions to be an internationally legally-binding international agreement[33] that (a) confirms the right of Member States to intervene in the global cultural market; and (b) gives Member States the opportunity to take protective and promotional measures deemed necessary to ensure the prosperity of the diversity of cultural expressions.[34] Moreover, the Convention on the Diversity of Cultural Expressions is deemed to be of importance for the developing world, because it envisages measures to correct imbalances in the cultural trade

UNESCO. *See* UNESCO, Intergovernmental Committee, "First Extraordinary Session", *CE/08/1.EXT.IGC/7, available at* http://unesdoc.unesco.org/images/0015/001598/159842E.pdf (last visited 2 February 2012). Makhanya's report was published as part of a UNESCO document containing the expert reports. *See* M. S. Makhanya, "Expert Reports on Preferential Treatment for Developing Countries – Article 16 of the Convention on the Protection and Promotion of the Diversity of Cultural Expressions", *CE/08/2.IGC/8* (17 September 2008), *available at* http://unesdoc.unesco.org/images/0017/001779/177924E.pdf (last visited 2 February 2012).

32 The vision of the DAC is to develop and preserve South African culture to ensure social cohesion and nation-building. *See* South Africa, Department of Arts and Culture, "Departmental Vision and Mission", *available* at www.dac.gov.za/vision_mission.htm (last visited 2 February 2012).

33 South Africa uses the term "international agreement" instead of the more common term "treaty". The general point of view, though, is that the two terms are synonymous. *See* J. Dugard, *International Law: A South African Perspective*, 2005, 63.

34 *See* T. Wakashe, "Post Ratification Strategy," (Presentation at the Arts and Culture Portfolio Committee, 12 February 2008), *available at* www.pmg.org.za/files/docs/080212prs.ppt (last visited 2 February 2012).

market,[35] and it establishes financial support and capacity building for cultural industries.[36]

Nonetheless, the Convention on the Diversity of Cultural Expressions has not been incorporated by an act of Parliament into South African domestic law to date and the question remains as to whether any direct effect can be given to its provisions. South African follows a 'dualist' approach as regards the application of international agreements. Prior to 1994 the common law[37] prescribed the rules pertaining to the applicability of international agreements. The power to enter into agreements was entrusted to the executive, whilst the power to transform the treaties into domestic law was assigned to the legislature.[38] For an interim period of two years, the Interim Constitution changed the common law situation somewhat: the President[39] obtained the power to enter into agreements (negotiate and sign), whilst parliament, consisting of the National Assembly and the Senate, had to agree to the ratification of or accession to agreements, and also had the power to transform an agreement into domestic law by means of a mere resolution.[40]

However, since 1996 the situation has more or less returned to the pre-1994 position pertaining to the transformation of international agreements, while still providing for parliamentary ratification of an agreement under certain circumstances.[41] The negotiating and signing of agreements remain the

35 Statistics compiled by UNESCO during 2003 show that South Africa is the only country in sub-Saharan Africa to play a prominent role in the trade of core cultural goods. South Africa exported almost 40% of its goods to other sub-Saharan African countries in 2003, and almost 20% to the USA. On the other hand, almost 60% of the South African imports of cultural goods originated from developed countries such as the United Kingdom and the USA. *See* UNESCO, Institute for Statistics and Sector for Culture, *International Flows of Selected Cultural Goods and Services, 1994–2003: Defining and Capturing the Flows of Global Cultural Trade,* 2005, 32–3, *available at* http://unesdoc.unesco.org/images/0014/001428/142812e.pdf (last visited 2 February 2012).

36 *See* Parliamentary Monitoring Group, "Minutes: UNESCO Convention on Protection and Promotion of Diversity of Cultural Expressions" (20 November 2006), *available at* www.pmg.org.za/print/8540 (last visited 2 February 2012).

37 The common law of South Africa is an uncodified system of law based on Roman-Dutch law and influenced by English law, which can be found in the writings of the old Roman-Dutch authorities, legislation, precedents (court decisions), custom, customary law (indigenous law) and the writings of modern writers.

38 *See* Dugard, *supra* note 33, at 49–50; *Pan American World Airways Incorporated* v. *SA Fire and Accident Insurance Co Ltd* 1965 3 SA 150 (A) 161C-D.

39 *See* Interim Constitution, *supra* note 9, Section 82(1)(i) (reading that "[t]he President shall be competent to exercise and perform the following powers and functions, namely- … (i) to negotiate and sign international agreements.").

40 *See* id., Section 231(2) (empowering parliament to agree to the ratification of or accession to an international agreements negotiated and signed in terms of Section 82(1)(i). The purpose of the Interim Constitution was to smooth the progress of the incorporation of international documents into domestic law, although this objective was not realized); *See* Dugard, *supra* note 33, at 59.

41 *See* Constitution, *supra* note 5, Section 231(3) (providing that "(3) Where Parliament agrees to the ratification of or accession to an international agreement under sub-s. (2), such

responsibility of the executive[42] and an international agreement becomes binding only after parliamentary approval,[43] except if it is an international agreement of a technical, administrative or executive nature or an agreement that does not require ratification or accession. In the latter case, the agreement will be binding without the approval of the two houses of parliament.[44]

The transformation of international agreements into the domestic law of South Africa is dealt with in Schedule 231(4) of the Constitution:[45] On the one hand it affirms the pre-1994 common law position which required an international agreement to be enacted into law by national legislation,[46] and on the other, it creates an exception in that a self-executing provision in an international agreement approved by parliament becomes part of domestic law without the enactment of national legislation, provided that it is not inconsistent with the Constitution or an act of parliament.[47]

Both houses of parliament approved the Convention on the Diversity of Cultural Expressions and consequently South Africa ratified the Convention on the Diversity of Cultural Expressions on 21 December 2006.[48] To date, the

---

international agreement shall be binding on the Republic and shall form part of the law of the Republic, provided Parliament expressly so provides and such agreement is not inconsistent with this Constitution.").

42 *See* id., Section 231(1) (reading as follows: "The negotiating and signing of all international agreements is the responsibility of the national executive").

43 *See* id., Section 231(2) (stipulating that: "An international agreement binds the Republic only after it has been approved by resolution in both the National Assembly and the National Council of Provinces, unless it is an agreement referred to in subsection (3)").

44 *See* id., Section 231(3) (containing the following: "An international agreement of a technical, administrative or executive nature, or an agreement which does not require either ratification or accession, entered into by the national executive, binds the Republic without approval by the National Assembly and the National Council of Provinces, but must be tabled in the Assembly and the Council within a reasonable time."). Dugard points out that it would be a matter of interpretation to decide whether treaties fall in this category or not. *See* Dugard, *supra* note 33, at 56.

45 *See* Constitution, *supra* note 5, Section 231(4) (providing that: "Any international agreement becomes law in the Republic when it is enacted into law by national legislation; but a self-executing provision of an agreement that has been approved by Parliament is law in the Republic unless it is inconsistent with the Constitution or an Act of Parliament").

46 There are three legislative methods of incorporation of international agreements: (a) the provisions of an international agreement may be embodied in the text of an act; (b) the international agreement may be included as a schedule to an act; and (c) an act of parliament may give the executive the power to bring a treaty into effect by means of proclamation or notice in the *Government Gazette*. *See* Dugard, *supra* note 33, at 61. *See also supra* note 41.

47 The concept of self-executing agreements is a fairly new introduction into South African law. For a discussion of the concept in the context of extradition agreements, *see President of the Republic of South Africa v. Quagliani* 2009 (2) SA 466 (CC). *See* Dugard, *supra* note 33, at 58–62 (discussing self-executing agreements); *See also* M. Olivier, "Informal Agreements under the 1996 Constitution", 22 *SAYIL* 63–75 (1997).

48 The legal implications of the Convention on the Diversity of Cultural Expressions were considered by the State Law Advisor and the Department of Foreign Affairs, before the DAC proceeded with its campaign to have the Convention on the Diversity of Cultural Expressions ratified by South Africa. *See* Parliamentary Monitoring Group, "UNESCO Convention

Convention on the Diversity of Cultural Expressions has not been transformed into law by national legislation. Nevertheless, the fact that South Africa ratified the Convention on the Diversity of Cultural Expressions makes it binding on South Africa on an international level, irrespective of whether it has been incorporated into domestic law or not. Failure to comply with the provisions of the Convention on the Diversity of Cultural Expressions may result in South Africa laying itself open to liability towards the other Member States.[49]

While the incorporation of the Convention on the Diversity of Cultural Expressions into the domestic law of South Africa is still outstanding, its value in terms of judicial interpretation is not. Schedule 39(1)(b) of the Constitution declares that a court must consider international law when interpreting the Bill of Rights, whilst Schedule 233 of the Constitution specifically states that in interpreting any legislation an interpretation consistent with international law is to be preferred.[50] So far it seems that the attitude of the courts is to construe its mandate in this regard widely rather than restrictively. In its second judgment the Constitutional Court already emphasized the interpretive value of international law, where Chaskalson P stated in *S* v. *Makwanyane*:[51]

> … public international law would include non-binding as well as binding law. They may both be used under the *section* as tools of interpretation. International agreements and customary international law accordingly provide a framework within which [the *Bill of Rights*] can be evaluated and understood, and for that purpose, decisions of tribunals dealing with comparable instruments … may provide guidance as to the correct interpretation of particular provisions of [the *Bill of Rights*].[52]

At this moment, the Convention on the Diversity of Cultural Expressions is of importance for South Africa for two reasons. To begin with, it provides an international framework wherein all future development of cultural diversity issues must be formulated, and secondly, it is a valuable tool for the judicial interpretation of cultural diversity issues.

---

on Protection and Promotion of Diversity of Cultural Expressions: Policy & Legislative Review" (14 November 2006), *available at* www.pmg.org.za/print/8511 (last visited 2 February 2012).

49 *See* Dugard, supra note 33, at 62.

50 *See* E. De Wet, "The 'Friendly but Cautious' Reception of International Law in the Jurisprudence of the South African Constitutional Court: Some Critical Remarks", 28 *FILJ* 1529–65 (2005) (for an exposition of the South African court's dealings with international law).

51 *See S.* v. *Makwanyane* 1995 3 SA 391 (CC) (although this case deals with the place of international law in the context of the Interim Constitution and its Bill of Rights, the same argument and principles are applicable with regard to the new Constitution and its Bill of Rights).

52 Id., Paragraph 35.

3.2. SOUTH AFRICA'S EXPECTATIONS IN TERMS OF THE CONVENTION ON THE DIVERSITY OF CULTURAL EXPRESSIONS

In line with most developing countries' expectations, South Africa had certain expectations before the negotiation process pertaining to the Convention on the Diversity of Cultural Expressions began in earnest. Almost certainly its most important expectation deals with the challenges of globalization on cultural diversity in developing countries. On the one hand, globalization presents various opportunities for the expansion of the cultural sector and the development of cultural policies. Cultural diversity is seen as a strategic resource for developing countries.[53] It has the potential: (a) to increase cultural industries by encouraging local artistic production and by generating job opportunities; (b) to enrich national heritage; (c) to develop national identity and social unity; and (d) to increase revenues from the tourism industry.

On the other hand, globalization can have a negative impact on the cultural sectors of developing countries, especially their cultural policies. The product of globalization in the cultural sphere is often one of cultural homogenization. In this manner it inhibits cultural diversity.[54] Also, another problem is the unequal relationships between stronger and weaker economies that result in the monopolization of the cultural markets by the former to the detriment of the latter.[55] The Convention on the Diversity of Cultural Expressions is expected to reconcile the objects of the World Trade Organization (WTO) agreements with the expectations of developing countries. As another writer points out:

> Globalisation has raised the issue of cultural diversity to a new level. Cultural-ethnic and religious communities have become acutely aware of the threat to their identities by an engulfing, mainly western driven, economic globalisation. The question is increasingly being raised. How can we reconcile these identities and cultural practices, which diverge in many essential ways with the idea of international standards? How can we enforce such standards, especially when major powers such as the United States, literary reject the whole idea of an international law and decide unilaterally to engage in what they have decided to call 'pre-emptive intervention' and engage in wars that are not approved by international law?[56]

---

53 *See* South Africa, Department of Arts and Culture, "Cultural Diversity in Developing Countries: The Challenges of Globalisation", 9 (October 2002), *available at* www.incp-ripc.org/meetings/2002/challenges_e.pdf (last visited 2 February 2012).

54 *See* id., at 9–10.

55 *See* Asmal, *supra* note 96, at 355.

56 D.W. Nabudere, "Human Rights and Cultural Diversity in Africa" (Paper written for the Association of Law Reform Agencies of Eastern and Southern Africa (ALRAESA), Conference on the Fusion of Legal Systems and Concepts in Africa, 4th-8th September 2005, at the

South Africa recognises the economic and social value of culture. In its policy document the DAC declared:

> Culture is a resource that has the potential to generate significant economic and social benefits for a young developing nation. However, this potential has often gone unnoticed in so far as the contribution to the economy is concerned. It is therefore important to ensure that strategies are developed to ensure this potential is exploited. The industry has potential to be internationally competitive as well as the potential to create employment and offer opportunities for rural and urban development and job creation. To ensure this is achieved government need to craft policies which will support such initiatives.[57]

Although the Convention on the Diversity of Cultural Expressions renewed South Africa's efforts to award much-needed recognition to the value of culture, research done by the Cultural Strategies Group of the former Department of Arts, Culture, Science and Technology (DACST) in the late nineties already documented the advantages of a well-established cultural industry, namely economic significance, creating a South African identity, allowing for distinctiveness in an age of globalization, innovation and creativity, growth in tourism, and social development.[58]

Three months before South Africa ratified the Convention on the Diversity of Cultural Expressions, the DAC, the South African National Commission for UNESCO, and UNISA hosted a national conference at Sun City in South Africa on "Cultural Diversity for Social Cohesion and Sustainable Development.[59] According to the conference announcement, the conference was a "major step forward in adopting an action plan for Africa and the Diaspora on Cultural Diversity for social cohesion and sustainable development."[60] The purpose was to

---

Imperial Resort Beach Hotel, Entebbe), *available at* www.justice.gov.za/alraesa/conferences/2005uganda/ent_s4_nabudere.pdf (last visited 2 February 2012).

57 *See* South Africa, Department of Arts and Culture, "Arts and Culture Policy Review: A Background Document on Arts, Culture and Heritage Policy Review Process in South Africa", 31, *available at* www.dac.gov.za/projects/Policy%20Review/Background%20document.doc (last visited 2 February 2012).

58 *See* Department of Arts, Culture, Science and Technology, "The South African Music Industry: Cultural Industries Growth Strategy", at 12–3 (Report to the Department of Arts, Culture, Science and Technology, November 1998), *available at* www.info.gov.za/view/DownloadFileAction?id=70494 (last visited 2 February 2012).

59 *See* Africa and Diaspora Conference on Cultural Diversity for Social Cohesion and Sustainable Development [Africa and Diaspora], "The Sun City Statement and Plan for Action" (Conference held in Sun City, South Africa, 11–15 September 2006), *available at*. www.dac.gov.za/publications/reports/SunCitySTATEMENT_CultDiv.pdf (last visited 2 February 2012).

60 In this context "Diaspora" refers to the African Diaspora which explains the movement of Africans throughout the world. A definition for the African Diaspora was adopted at the AU's Meeting of Experts on the Definition of the African Diaspora on 11–12 April 2005 at Addis Ababa and reads: "The African Diaspora consists of peoples of African origin living outside the continent, irrespective of their citizenship and nationality and who are willing to

unpack the Convention on the Diversity of Cultural Expressions and its importance for the African continent, and it was finally declared that the Convention on the Diversity of Cultural Expressions must be viewed as a practical guide for:

(a) Making available resources for Cultural Diversity, acknowledging culture as the basis for development, cooperation and self determination;
(b) Capacitating sustainable cultural industries and making them relevant to the needs of Africa and the Diaspora;
(c) Integrating the role of culture in economic and social development through exchange and intraregional, inter-regional and South-South partnerships;
(d) Harmonizing cultural policies for Africa and the Diaspora;
(e) Strengthening knowledge production and sharing by using technology to break down barriers of ignorance and foster dialogue between the Continent and the Diaspora;
(f) Preserving and protecting the development and ownership of Cultural Diversity through education, trade, social development, media and cross-sectoral partnerships;
(g) Creating and implementing policies on Cultural Diversity as a fundamental motivating factor for good governance, peace keeping and security in Africa and the Diaspora;
(h) Strengthening the role of culture and traditional knowledge in social cohesion;
(i) Reversing cultural terrorism, restoring and preserving the cultural properties and legacies belonging to Africa and the Diaspora as a critical factor for sustainable development.[61]

After reaching consensus on the speedy ratification of the Convention on the Diversity of Cultural Expressions by African states, and its subsequent integration into those states' domestic law, the conference adopted a plan of

contribute to the development of the continent and the building of the African Union." African Union, "Report of the Meeting of Experts on the Definition of the African Diaspora" (11–12 April 2005), *available at* www.africa-union.org/organs/ecossoc/Report-Expert-Diaspora%20Defn%2013april2005-Clean%20copy1.doc (last visited 2 February 2012). The concept "Cultural Diversity" is not defined in the 2006 African Union Charter for African Cultural Renaissance, *available at* www.africa-union.org/root/au/Documents/Treaties/treaties.htm (last visited 2 February 2012). Considering the fact that this Charter takes its guidance from other international documents, including the Convention on the Diversity of Cultural Expressions, it is only logic that the concept has a similar meaning, namely the "manifold ways" in which cultural groups find expression, including the "varied ways" in which they express these differences (*see* Article 4(1) Convention on the Diversity of Cultural Expressions).

61 *See* Africa and Diaspora, "Significance of the Conference", *supra* note 59.

action that involved the roles and responsibilities of states,[62] civil societies[63] and cultural practitioners,[64] as well as inter-regional and intra-regional bodies.[65] However, in spite of the overall enthusiasm expressed towards the Convention on the Diversity of Cultural Expressions, 28 African countries have ratified it to date.[66]

It is clear from the outcome of the conference that South Africa believes the Convention on the Diversity of Cultural Expressions to have a social and economic value. On the one hand it should be instrumental in promoting the development of the cultural sector and, on the other, it should bring about

---

62 *See* Africa and Diaspora, "Plan of Action, Roles and Responsibilities of States", *supra* note 59 (indicating that states should "a. Accelerate ratification of the Convention on Cultural Diversity and integrate its content in local laws and regulations; b. Develop post-ratification policies and strategies based on inclusion, sustainability and cross-sectoral partnerships; c. Allocate resources and budgets for activities and programmes that protect and promote Cultural Diversity; d. Establish mechanisms for information, research, data collection, monitoring and evaluation; e. Prioritise accountability and report back to Africa and Diaspora on development; f. Empower creative industries through training on rights, intellectual property, patenting, ownership and management.").

63 *See* id., "Plan of Action, Roles and Responsibilities of Citizens – Civil Society," *supra* note 59 (stipulating that citizens and civil society should "a. Compile cultural statistics on NGOs, structures and practitioners within arts and culture; b. Encourage partnerships with all role players including public and private sector on local, regional and international level; c. Form lobby and pressure groups to monitor and evaluate impact of strategies; d. Embark on fund raising initiatives; e. Examine and revitalise the role of indigenous knowledge and traditional leadership.").

64 *See* id., "Plan of Action, Roles and Responsibilities of Cultural Practitioners", *supra* note 59 (asking that cultural practitioners "a. Set and maintain standards of excellence in production and service delivery pertaining to Cultural Diversity; b. Form structures for monitoring, evaluation and lobbying; c. Develop and maintain skills database of artists and practitioners within creative industries; d. Develop and implement inter- and intra-regional research programs on cultural and artistic expression.").

65 *See* id., "Plan of Action, Roles and Responsibilities of Inter- and Intraregional Bodies", *supra* note 59 (arguing that inter- and intraregional bodies could "a. Develop models of best practices from successful arts and culture programs and projects from the Continent and the Diaspora; b. Foster awareness, recognition and cooperation (sic), through collaboration between governments and communities in Africa and the Diaspora; c. Encourage discussion and exchange around policy-making in countries where there are no existing cultural policies; d. Establish a Working Group on Cultural policies to ensure that policy-making, protection and harmonisation stays on the agenda; e. Create awareness programs about links and synergies between Africa and the African Diaspora; f. Avail and create platforms, programmes and resources for youth to ensure and bridge inter-generational gaps and foster posterity.").

66 *See* UNESCO, "Convention on the Protection and Promotion of the Diversity of Cultural Expressions", *available at* http://portal.unesco.org/la/convention.asp?KO=31038&language=E (last visited 2 February 2012). In chronological order these countries are *Djibouti, Togo, Madagascar, Burkina Faso, Senegal, Mali,* Cameroon, Namibia, South Africa, Tunisia, *Niger,* Gabon, *Mozambique,* Kenya, *Benin,* Nigeria, *Guinea* and Zimbabwe, Chad, Sudan, Seychelles, *Ethiopia, Burundi, Congo, Lesotho, Malawi, Angola* and *Central African Republic* (the countries marked in italics are on the UN's List of Least Developed Countries). A total of 122 countries and one organization have ratified, accepted, acceded or approved the *Convention on the Diversity of Cultural Expressions* as on 22 June 2012.

economic prosperity through promoting cultural industries. Whether this is indeed what the Convention on the Diversity of Cultural Expressions will achieve in practice remains to be seen.

From the outset the DAC was eager to have the Convention on the Diversity of Cultural Expressions ratified, but in spite of its aspiration to be one of the first 30 signatories needed to validate the Convention on the Diversity of Cultural Expressions, the legal technicalities of the ratification of international agreements in South Africa prevented it from doing so.[67] To the DAC the main implications of the ratification of the Convention on the Diversity of Cultural Expressions relate to the measures to be taken to obtain equilibrium in the current imbalances in the global trade of cultural goods and services. In other words, it is expected that its ratification would lead to fair trade relations, where all countries' cultural goods would compete globally on a level playing field. At present, there are two main factors that influence South Africa's capacity to compete internationally in the cultural market, these being a lack of resources and a lack of capacity. It is envisaged that the Convention on the Diversity of Cultural Expressions will unlock the resources for capacity building for cultural industries and other areas of the cultural sector and ensure the maintenance of international quality standards that will assist South Africa in having its cultural products compete globally.[68]

South Africa also anticipates that the implementation of the Convention on the Diversity of Cultural Expressions will address the issues related to the influx of foreign products, especially by minimizing foreign imports and by striking a balance between local and foreign products.[69] One of the challenges facing developing African countries (including South Africa) is mapping the infrastructure of financial support mechanisms for the developing world so that all stakeholders can understand how it works.

Additionally, South Africa recognizes the importance of the Convention on the Diversity of Cultural Expressions in facilitating South-South and regional co-operation, as well as the facilitation of the transfer of technology and

---

67 South Africa was only the 37th country to ratify the Convention on the Diversity of Cultural Expressions whereas Djibouti was the first African country to ratify it. *See* id.

68 Uniform international standards do not exist but the guidelines of the International Organization for Standardization established in Switzerland provide a good indication of what is globally regarded as quality and what not. *See* International Organization for Standardization, *available at* www.iso.org/iso/home.html (last visited 2 February 2012).

69 *See* Parliamentary Monitoring Group, "UNESCO Convention on Protection & Promotion of Diversity of Cultural Expression; Policy & Legislative Review: Briefing" (7 November 2006), *available at* www.pmg.org.za/print/8511 (last visited 2 February 2012) (referring R. Matibe, the Deputy Director of the Department of Arts and Culture, briefing the Arts and Culture Portfolio Committee on the background of the Convention on the Diversity of Cultural Expressions); *See also* Parliamentary Monitoring Group, "Explanatory Memorandum – Ratification of the Convention on Protection & Promotion of Diversity of Cultural Expression", *available at* www.pmg.org.za/docs/2006/061107memo.pdf (last visited 2 February 2012).

knowledge to the developing world.[70] The Convention on the Diversity of Cultural Expressions is seen as a promotional tool to encourage the exchange of cultural goods and services between developed and developing countries, and specifically to better the latter's access to the global cultural market. The Convention on the Diversity of Cultural Expressions could serve as an important tool to mainstream the national and international use of culture to effect development in South Africa and other developing countries.[71]

Although there is a general consensus between members of parliament that the Convention on the Diversity of Cultural Expressions will benefit Member States, especially African developing countries, some members of the South African government are sceptical of certain aspects of the Convention on the Diversity of Cultural Expressions. Firstly, the implications of the USA and Israel's refusal to sign the Convention on the Diversity of Cultural Expressions, especially since the USA has the capacity to bombard developing markets with its film industry products and the flow of electronic information, has raised some concerns regarding the effectiveness of the Convention on the Diversity of Cultural Expressions. Secondly, the voluntariness of the contributions of the member countries to the International Fund, has led to some fears regarding the commitment of the countries not contributing to the Fund. Thirdly, some members of parliament are troubled by the fact that the rate of ratification of the Convention on the Diversity of Cultural Expressions ratification has been rather slow, and lastly, there is a concern that the Convention on the Diversity of Cultural Expressions may not be applicable to the protection of linguistic diversity.[72]

The implementation of the Convention on the Diversity of Cultural Expressions in South Africa could also be hampered by other problems the

70 *See* SOUTH AFRICA, DEPARTMENT OF ARTS AND CULTURE, "Strategic Plan 1 April 2003 – 31 March 2003", (14 February 2003), *available at* www.dac.gov.za/publications/strategic_plan/strategic_plan2003-2006.htm (last visited 2 February 2012) (Recently, South Africa was involved in the SA-Mali Project to conserve the ancient manuscripts of Timbuktu. The project was an initiative of NEPAD and is an illustration of Africa taking charge of the preservation of the African heritage).

71 *See* PARLIAMENTARY MONITORING GROUP, *supra* note 69 (in a global context, the EU-ACP Support Programme to Cultural Industries in ACP countries serves as an example of cooperation between the EU and ACP countries in the framework of the Convention on the Diversity of Cultural Expressions). *See also* ACP CULTURES, "The EU-ACP Support Programme to Cultural Industries", *available at* www.acpcultures.eu/?lang=uk&page=index (last visited 2 February 2012) (the general objective of the Programme is to contribute to poverty reduction and sustainable development through the promotion of an enabling environment for creativity, cooperation and exchanges, independence and viability of the cultural sector in the ACP States, as well as the safeguarding of cultural diversity and fundamental cultural values).

72 *See* id. Whether language issues can be included in the definition of cultural expression or not would in all probability depend on the national policies of a particular state. In view of South Africa's rich diversity in languages, cultural expressions and activities would almost certainly include rather than exclude linguistic diversity.

country is currently experiencing, especially in the area of interaction between the various spheres of government. Cultural matters currently fall within functions concurrently within national and provincial legislative competence, as well as within functions belonging exclusively to provincial legislative competence.[73] The fact that municipal governments[74] (the third level of government) are, in contrast, not competent to legislate on cultural matters might create the impression that local government might not have a role to play in the implementation of the Convention on the Diversity of Cultural Expressions.[75]

Additionally, there seem to be conflicting viewpoints on the identity of the main departments for the implementation of the Convention on the Diversity of Cultural Expressions. The main purpose of the DAC is to develop and preserve South African culture with a view to ensuring social cohesion and nation-building. However, the DAC has also been promoting the development of the economic potential of cultural industries in order to provide for job creation, poverty reduction, skills transfer, the development of small businesses and the implementation of the Broad-Black Economic Empowerment strategy.[76] Through this strategy, the Department adds to the Accelerated and Shared Growth Initiative for South Africa (AsgiSA)[77] as well as the Joint Initiative for Priority Skills Acquisition (JIPSA).[78] In contrast to the main purpose of the DAC, one of the purposes of the Department of Trade and Investment (DTI) is

---

73 *See* Constitution, *supra* note 5, Schedule 4 (Part A). In terms of Schedule 5 (Part A) provincial cultural matters fall within exclusive provincial legislative competence. An overlapping of jurisdiction in the case of cultural matters is thus not excluded. In addition, it is also envisaged that implementation of the Convention on the Diversity of Cultural Expressions would impact on local government (municipal structures) and the civil society level, especially in light of the provisions of the Convention on the Diversity of Cultural Expressions that encourage the active participation of civil society to achieve the objectives of the Convention.

74 Municipal governments are also referred to as "local government" in a South African context.

75 South Africa has a three-tier system of government consisting of the national, provincial and local levels of government, which all have legislative and executive authority in their own spheres, and are defined in Section 40(1) of the Constitution as "distinctive, interdependent and interrelated" spheres of government. *See* Constitution, *supra* note 5, Article 40 (1).

76 *See* South Africa, Department: Trade and Industry, "Broad-Based Black Economic Empowerment Unit", *available at* http://beenow.co.za/2010/08/broad-based-black-economic-empowerment-unit/ (last visited 2 February 2012) (the Broad-Black Economic Empowerment Strategy is a government intervention to address the systematic exclusion of the majority of South Africans from full participation in the economy).

77 *See* South African Government Information, "Accelerated and Shared Growth Initiative for South Africa (AsgiSA)" (18 May 2007), *available at* www.info.gov.za/asgisa/asgisa.htm (last visited 2 February 2012) (explaining that the mandate of the South African government is, among others, to halve poverty and unemployment by 2004).

78 *See* Government Communications, "What is JISPA", 1 Vukuzenzele (2006), *available at* www.info.gov.za/vukuzenzele/Pages/jipsa(1).htm (last visited 2 February 2012) (indicating that JIPSA is made up of government, business and labor organizations. It aims to speed up the development of the skills most needed in South Africa to help the economy to grow.).

to utilize culture's economic potential. While the responsibility of the DAC is to focus on the developmental aspect of culture, the responsibility of the DTI is to focus on the economic aspect of culture. Nevertheless, the strategy of the DAC to contribute to AsgiSA and JIPSA clearly has a wider impact than merely in developing culture. These apparent cross-purposes also feature in the literature dealing with the apparent conflict between the objectives of the Convention on the Diversity of Cultural Expressions and the WTO-agreements.[79] The conflict between these two departments of the South African government might frustrate the effective implementation of the Convention on the Diversity of Cultural Expressions on a national level, especially if it is not efficiently managed by the responsible departments.[80]

In addition, effective communication between the South African government departments and the structures of UNESCO may be hampered by various factors. To begin with, the Cluster Office for Angola, Lesotho, Namibia, South Africa and Swaziland is situated in Windhoek, Namibia.[81] Previously the Cluster Office was situated in South Africa. Not having direct access to the decentralized UNESCO structures might hinder South Africa's effective communications with these structures. This might be the reason why South Africa never communicated its wish list pertaining to the International Fund, whist Namibia delivered its wishes on time.[82] Also, the office of South African National Commission for UNESCO is hosted within the offices of another government department, namely the Department of Education, which contributes to the time-consuming and sometimes overly bureaucratic flows of information and decision-making between the South African government and the UNESCO structures.

---

79 *See, e.g.*, A. Khachaturian, "The New Cultural Diversity Convention and its Implications on the WTO International Trade Regime: A Critical Comparative Analysis", 42 *Tex. Int'l L. J.* 191, 191–206 (2006).

80 For a more detailed discussion of the issues, *see e.g.* C. Rautenbach and A.A. du Plessis, "Fragmentation: Friend or Foe in the Effective Implementation of the Convention on the Diversity of Cultural Expressions in South Africa", 34 *SAYIL* 132, 132–58 (2009).

81 This office is also the focal point for the co-operation with the Secretariat of NEPAD.

82 Namibia wants the International Fund to: "Provide financial assistance for the participation of artists/experts in Intergovernmental Committee meetings and related activities; Training of Human and Institutional capacity in Member States especially in developing countries and other countries in need; Supporting and promoting creative talents of artists, specifically those artists without formal art training; Providing financial support to art centers that offer practical training for young artists; Supporting and promoting the role of women artists in their quest to eradicate poverty; Promoting/supporting art education for the youth/ unemployed youth; Assisting Member States to raise awareness through media on the importance of art and culture and their contribution to the development of the economy". *See* UNESCO, Intergovernmental Committee, "Written contributions of Parties on the use of the International Fund for Cultural Diversity," *CE/08/1.EXT.IGC/INF.6A*, at 11 (17 April 2008), *available at* http://unesdoc.unesco.org/images/0015/001598/159800M.pdf (last visited 2 February 2012).

To add to this, the role and nature of arts and culture in social cohesion and nation building are frequently not clearly defined. In poverty stricken countries the cultural industry is more often than not an area where cost-cutting will be applied in order to provide for poverty alleviation. South Africa would need to address these issues before engaging wholeheartedly in the implementation of the Convention on the Diversity of Cultural Expressions at all levels of government and the civil society.

In spite of the good intentions of the Convention on the Diversity of Cultural Expressions, there remains a certain cynicism about its true effect in developing countries. These concerns are raised mainly in the context of global capitalism, where the primary object is to profit from trade and development, whilst the primary aim of the Convention on the Diversity of Cultural Expressions is to preserve cultural diversity.[83]

Another aspect that warrants mention is the fact that the commitments in terms of the Convention on the Diversity of Cultural Expressions are based on good faith, as there are no enforceable legal penalties for non-compliance of the state parties to the provisions of the Convention on the Diversity of Cultural Expressions. The only recourse for non-compliance would probably be the exertion of political influence by other influential Member States. Positive and optimistic assertions by renowned individuals, such as the late Asmal, show recognition of the value and potential of the Convention on the Diversity of Cultural Expressions and a commitment to make it work. In this regard, Asmal declared:

> By adopting UNESCO's newest standard-setting instrument, we have established the most innovative platform for international cultural co-operation that the world has ever known.[84]

3.3. SOUTH AFRICA AS A DEVELOPING COUNTRY

The Convention on the Diversity of Cultural Expressions has an important role to play for developing countries,[85] supporting them in their efforts to preserve and develop their cultural heritage by placing a general responsibility on all parties to be mindful of the specific needs of developing countries,[86] and places

---

83 *See* M. Van Graan, "The Proposed Convention on Cultural Diversity: a Developing World Perspective", *The Power of Culture* (May 2005) *available at* www.krachtvancultuur.nl/en/current/2005/may/convention.html (last visited 2 February 2012).

84 Asmal, *supra* note 96, at 356.

85 The important role of developing countries is evident from the text of the Convention on the Diversity of Cultural Expressions, which refers to developing countries no less than 15 times. *See* Convention on the Diversity of Cultural Expressions, *supra* note 15, Articles 1, 4, 14, 15, 16 and 17.

86 *See* id., Sections 14 and 15.

a specific responsibility on developed countries to give preferential treatment to developing countries under certain circumstances.[87]

When determining the scope and extent of the Convention on the Diversity of Cultural Expressions, especially regarding the allocation of the funds of the International Fund to developing countries, it is necessary to determine which Member States can be classified as "developed" and which as "developing" countries. There is no universal definition for what constitutes a developing country, but it is generally accepted that a developing country is one which has a relatively low overall standard of living, an underdeveloped industrial base, a medium Human Development Index (HDI)[88] score and a moderate Gross National Income (GNI) per capita.[89] However, in spite of these conditions, a country could be in a phase of economic development, and so be labelled a developing country. The WTO[90] does not define developing countries[91] and members of the WTO themselves announce whether they are "developed" or "developing". The only category recognized by the WTO is that of the "least developed countries", which are defined by the UN as such.[92] In general, all

87 *See* id., Sections 16.

88 *See* UNDP, "Human Development Reports", *available at* http://hdr.undp.org/en/statistics/ (last visited 2 February 2012) (according to the 2011 Human Development Index rankings, South Africa shows medium development and ranks 123rd out of 187 countries). *See also* International Human Development Indicator (2011), *available at* http://hdrstats.undp.org/en/countries/profiles/ZAF.html (last visited 2 February 2012).

89 *See* World Bank, "Gross National Income per Capita, Atlas Method and PPP", *available at* http://siteresources.worldbank.org/DATASTATISTICS/Resources/GNIPC.pdf (last visited 2 February 2012) (South Africa ranks 98th on the Gross National Income scale (Atlas method) with an income per capita of 6,100 US dollars).

90 The approval of the Convention on the Diversity of Cultural Expressions immediately raised concerns of conflict between the general aim of the Convention on the Diversity of Cultural Expressions, namely protection against the commodification of cultural diversity and the generally liberal international trade regime endorsed by the WTO. Most of the concerns came from the USA. *See* E.H. Chiang, "The UNESCO Convention on the Protection and Promotion of the Diversity of Cultural Expressions: A Look at the Convention and its Potential Impact on the American Movie Industry", 6 *W. U. Global Studies L. R.* 379, 398–403 (2007); L.R. Helfer, "Toward a Human Rights Framework for Intellectual Property", 40 *U.C. Davis L. Rev.* 971, 1001–7 (2007); L.R. Helfer, "Toward a Human Rights Framework for Intellectual Property", 40 *U.C. Davis L. Rev.* 971, 1001–7 (2007); J.P. Singh, "Culture or Commerce? A Comparative Assessment of International Interactions and Developing Countries at UNESCO, WTO, and Beyond", 8 *Int'l Studies Perspectives* 36–53 (2007); Khachaturian, *supra* note 79, at 191–209; P. Leuprecht, "The Difficult Acceptance of Diversity," 30 *Vermont L. R.* 551, at 560–3 (2006); C.M. Bruner, "Culture, Sovereignty, and Hollywood: UNESCO and the Future of Trade in Cultural Products", 43–53 (Bepress Legal Series, Working Paper No. 1972, 2007), *available at* http://law.bepress.com/expresso/eps/1972 (last visited 2 February 2012).

91 South Africa has been a WTO member since 1 January 1995.

92 The three criteria used by the UN are low income, weak human assets and economic vulnerability. *See* United Nations Conference on Trade and Development, "UN Recognition of the Least Developing Countries", *available at* www.unctad.org/Templates/Page.asp?intItemID=3618&lang=1 (last visited 2 February 2012). Thirty-two of the countries listed by the UN as least developed countries are members of the WTO. *See* World Trade

countries that are not developed countries are regarded as developing countries, including the least developed countries.

Interestingly, South Africa has characteristics of both "developing" and "developed" countries and has been described by the CIA World Fact Book as:

> ... a middle-income, emerging market with an abundant supply of natural resources; well-developed financial, legal, communications, energy, and transport sectors; a stock exchange that is 17th largest in the world; and modern infrastructure supporting an efficient distribution of goods to major urban centres throughout the region.[93]

In 2010 South Africa was ranked 31st out of a total of 214 World Bank Atlas economies of the World Bank as a result of its GNI of 304,591 million dollars.[94] In 2011 the HDI for South Africa was 0.619, which gives it a ranking of 123 out of 187 countries.[95] Notwithstanding South Africa's economic growth and great potential over the last few years, the country is still characterized by a tremendous disparity in incomes and wealth.[96] A very small percentage of the population lives in conditions typical of a highly industrialized society, while a great proportion of the population lives in conditions typical of a developing country.[97] Though there has been a considerable increase in the use of energy in black African households, only about one half of those households use electricity[98] and running water.[99] Furthermore, the unemployment rates of black people are still considerably higher than those of the white population,[100] and the level of education between the two population groups also varies quite

---

Organization, "Least Developing Countries", *available at* www.wto.org/english/thewto_e/whatis_e/tif_e/org7_e.htm (last visited 2 February 2012).

93 Central Intelligence Agency, "The World Factbook: South Africa - Economy", *available at* https://www.cia.gov/library/publications/the-world-factbook/geos/sf.html#Econ (last visited 2 February 2012).

94 *See* Worldbank, "Gross National Income 2010 – Atlas Method", *available at* http://siteresources.worldbank.org/DATASTATISTICS/Resources/GNI.pdf (last visited 2 February 2012).

95 See United Nations Conference on Trade and Development, "Human Development Report 2011 -Sustainability and Equity: A Better Future for All", *available at* http://hdr.undp.org/en/media/HDR_2011_EN_Complete.pdf (last visited 2 February 2012), Table 1.

96 As pointed out by the South African Public Service Commission, there are various official and unofficial surveys pertaining to the level of poverty in South Africa. Be that as it may, the fact that between 40–50% of the South African population lives in poverty cannot be denied, and the rate of poverty remains one of the greatest concerns of the South African government. *See* Public Service Commission, *Report on the Evaluation of Government's Poverty Reduction Programme* 6 (Pretoria: The Public Service Commission, 2007).

97 *See* Du Plessis, *supra* note 14, at 20–1.

98 *See* Statistics South Africa, *supra* note 4, at 82–6 (the use of electricity is mainly for cooking, heating and lighting).

99 *See* id, at 87–9 (piped water in dwelling).

100 *See* id, at 36–50.

noticeably.[101] Poverty levels have not reduced significantly and the burden of HIV/AIDS remains heavy.[102] Nevertheless, South Africa's sustained economic growth and potential over the years has earned it recognition as one of the "emerging and developing economies" of 2008.[103] South Africa does not fall into the category of a least developed country, but also does not entirely qualify as a developing country. For that reason it is extremely important for South Africa and all other developing countries, no matter in what stage of development, that the guidelines on the use of the resources of the International Fund clearly map out what is meant by the expression "developing countries". At this moment, however, the question of whether South Africa is a developing country or not is of only academic importance. South Africa is indeed recognised as a developing country for the purposes of the International Fund for Cultural Diversity and will thus be eligible to apply for funding in line with the operational guidelines.[104]

The exact scope and meaning of the phrase "preferential treatment for developing countries" as contained in Article 16 of the Convention poses another challenge for South Africa and other developing countries. Within the WTO context, there are two kinds of preferential treatment.[105] The arguments pertaining to these types of preferential treatment may be useful in the context of culture. Firstly, preferential treatment entails more lenient implementation schedules to lower trade barriers for developing countries in the cultural sector and, secondly, it requires non-reciprocal, preferential access for developing countries to developed markets in the cultural sector. Preferential access to developed markets would mean, among other things, that developing countries would be able to receive higher prices for their cultural goods than they would

---

101 *See* id, at 36–86.

102 *See* Du Plessis, *supra* note 14, at 23.

103 *See* International Monetary Fund, "World Economic Outlook Report: Database - WEO Groups and Aggregates Information" (April 2008), *available at* www.imf.org/external/pubs/ft/weo/2008/01/weodata/groups.htm#oem (last visited 2 February 2012). As a result of the global crisis South Africa's output declined by 1¾ percent in 2009 and it is estimated that future growth in South Africa will be tempered by its high unemployment rate and other tight credit conditions. *See* International Monetary Fund, "World Economic Outlook: Rebalancing Growth" 67–8 (April 2010), *available at* www.imf.org/external/pubs/ft/weo/2010/01/pdf/text.pdf (last visited 2 February 2012).

104 See UNESCO, "International Fund for Cultural Diversity: Parties to the UNESCO 2005 Convention on the Protection and the Promotion of the Diversity of Cultural Expressions that are recognized by UNCTAD as developing economies, economies in transition and least developed countries" (March 2011), *available at* www.unesco.org/new/fileadmin/MULTIMEDIA/HQ/CLT/pdf/Conv2005_IFCD_developing_Parties.pdf (last visited 2 February 2012).

105 *See* R. Duncan, "World Trade Organization: Issues for Developing Countries", 4–5 (Asia Pacific School for Economics and Management, Working Paper No. 03-1, 2003), *available at* https://digitalcollections.anu.edu.au/ (last visited 2 February 2012) (note that his viewpoint deals with WTO trade policies within the agricultural sector. Similar arguments may be advanced with regard to the cultural sector).

on the open world market, and this can be seen as a form of international aid. As already explained, however, the objectives of the WTO agreements and those of the Convention on the Diversity of Cultural Expressions seem to be in direct conflict in certain areas, and consequently it will be necessary to reach a consensus on the exact meaning of "preferential treatment of developing countries" in the context of the Convention on the Diversity of Cultural Expressions.

South Africa, represented by its expert, Makhanya, certainly has its own perspectives on what the content of preferential treatment for developing countries should be.[106] Makhanya does not agree that preferential treatment is necessarily anti-WTO but argues that it should play a similar role in the cultural domain as that which it currently plays in the domain of trading.[107] In line with many other postcolonial writers, Makhanya places great emphasis on South Africa's political history in his interpretation of preferential treatment. According to him preferential treatment must be read as "redress" or "restoration" and as "a way of expanding [South Africa's] international relations" on the African continent and elsewhere.[108] In other words, his idea of granting preferential treatment to cultural artists, professionals and practitioners, as well as cultural goods and services, as set out in article 16 of the Convention, is narrowed down to include only those categories which have been marginalized because of colonialism.[109] Considering that the Operational Guidelines obliges developed countries to encourage developing countries to "articulate their own needs and priorities", and then to take these needs and priorities into consideration when they set up preferential treatment frameworks and schemes, one could argue that Makhanya's views are not way out of line.[110] In addition, one could argue that in giving preference to marginalized cultures, one might achieve wider and more balanced cultural exchanges as set out in the Operational Guidelines.[111] However, linking culture only to past injustices could result in the unnecessary politicisation of cultural cooperation and trade agreements between Member States. This could enlarge even further the divide between the cultural groups in a country with a young democracy such as South Africa.

---

106 *See* Makhanya, supra note 31.

107 *See* id, at 6.

108 *See* id, at 3.

109 *See* id, at 7.

110 *See* UNESCO, Conference of the Parties, "Operational Guidelines on Preferential Treatment for Developing Countries (Article 16 of the Convention)", §2.3. (June 2009), *available at* www.unesco.org/new/fileadmin/MULTIMEDIA/HQ/CLT/pdf/Conv2005_DO_Art_16_EN.pdf (last visited 2 February 2012).

111 *See* id., at §1.1.

3.4. MOBILIZATION OF CIVIL SOCIETY IN SOUTH AFRICA

Civil society actors in South Africa have been instrumental in the creation of the Convention on the Diversity of Cultural Expressions, and they are now encouraged by the Convention to actively engage in promoting its ratification and implementation globally.[112] In line with this call to mobilize, civil society actors have taken a number of initiatives to ensure the implementation of the Convention on the Diversity of Cultural Expressions in South Africa. For example, they established the South African Coalition for Cultural Diversity (SACCD) on 7 September 2007 at the Southern African Music Rights Organisation (SAMRO)[113] House in Johannesburg.[114] Some of the main aims of the SACCD were to maximize South Africa's participation in the Convention on the Diversity of Cultural Expressions and to facilitate cooperation and the development of joint positions and action among cultural associations from the publishing, film and television, music, live performance and visual arts and crafts sectors.

Elsewhere in Africa another coalition, called the Arterial Network, was established in March 2007 in Senegal.[115] The Arterial Network started as a "dynamic, continent-wide network of non-government organisations, creative industry companies, festivals and individual artists engaged in the African creative sector"[116] but developed over the last four years in a structured network with Chapters in at least 31 of the 53 African countries. At the recent Fifth Intergovernmental Committee Meeting, Arterial Network was the only civil society organization from Africa representing Africa and it is clear that participation from the African continent should be encouraged and promoted on a more aggressive level.

---

112 Reference to civil society is made in Articles 11 (explicit provision), 6, 7, 12, 15 and 19 of the Convention on the Diversity of Cultural Expressions.

113 SAMRO was established in 1961 with the objective to protect the intellectual property of composers and authors, as well as to ensure that composers' and authors' talents are adequately credited both locally and internationally for music usage. The organisation is currently the primary representative of music performing rights in Southern Africa. *See* SAMRO, *available at* www.samro.org.za/ (last visited 2 February 2012).

114 The SACCD consisted of the major players in the South African creative industries, amongst others, SAMRO, the Publishers Association of South Africa (PASA) and the Visual Arts Network of South Africa (VANSA). *See* the official website of the SACCD, *available at* www.saccd.org.za/ (last visited 2 February 2012). The establishment of the SACCD was followed by a meeting of Coalitions and Cultural Professional Committee of Coalitions for Cultural Diversity in association with SAMRO and SACCD with the financial support of the Commonwealth Foundation on 10 September 2007.

115 *See* Arterial Network, *available at* http://arterialnetwork.org/ (last visited 2 February 2012).

116 *See* Arterial Network, "Vision", *available at* http://arterialnetwork.org/about/vision (last visited 2 February 2012).

At two separate meetings held in Johannesburg, South Africa, on 12 August 2010 and Cape Town on 19 August 2010, the South African Chapter of Arterial Network (SACAN) was established.[117] Very soon it became clear that the objectives of the SACCD (established in 2007) and SACAN overlapped quite considerably. An agreement was reached between the SACCD and SACAN resulting in the termination of the SACCD on 21 October 2011 at the conference on "Activating the UNESCO Convention on Cultural Diversity".[118] A number of other important decisions were also taken during the course of the conference. First of all a Civil Society Working Group on the UNESCO Convention (Working Group) consisting of nine civil society members was established.[119] The Working Group operates as a subcommittee of SACAN with its main focus being the implementation of the Convention. Its mandate is:[120]

(a) To consult with the South African creative sector in order to develop strategic plans, priorities and strategies in pursuing the goals and intentions of the UNESCO Convention on the Protection and Promotion of the Diversity of Cultural Expressions.
(b) To implement strategies to deliver concrete outcomes on an annual basis that are consistent with the UNESCO Convention.
(c) To engage with government (national, provincial and municipal), the private sector, international and continental partners (including other formations in the cultural diversity sector) in the implementation and pursuit of strategies aimed at realizing the goals of the Convention.

The Working Group had its first meeting at the conference followed by a second meeting in November 2011 to map out the way forward. One of the main concerns of the Working Group is the relationship between civil society and the South African government. To date government has been slow in engaging with civil society and modalities for engaging civil society in the preparation of the periodical report required in terms of Article 9(a) of the Convention on the Diversity of Cultural Expressions have not been finalized.

Another important development at the conference was the launching of U40-Africa. This network emanates from the activities of the "U40 World Forum", a brainchild of the German Commission for UNESCO and the International

117 *See* Arterial Network, "South African Chapter", *available at* www.arterialnetwork.org/chapters/view/south-africa (last visited 2 February 2012).

118 The significance of this date lies in the fact that it was decided that the date of the conference will be the determining date for the termination of the SACCD.

119 The members of the Working Group consists of two members of the outgoing leadership of the SACCD, two members appointed by SACAN, one nominee of U40-Africa and three delegates to the conference.

120 Author is a member of the Working Group and has access to the documents relevant to the Working Group.

Federation of Coalitions for Cultural Diversity (FICDC), who collectively organized the "U40 World Forum" (12–14 June 2009) at the Second Conference of Parties Meeting held in Paris (15–18 June 2009). The forum brought together 50 young professionals (under 40 years of age) from all over the world to discuss proposals for the implementation of the Convention. Their collective proposals are recorded under the title "Proposals for a Cultural Diversity 2030".[121] The idea of creating an U40-Africa network was concretized during a round table discussion with the South African DAC. The first meeting of the network was held in Pretoria, South Africa on 22 September 2009 during the Fourth World Summit on Arts and Culture (22–25 September) hosted by the DAC. The meeting focused on the vision, mission and future activities of the network and the drafting of proposed statutes. As already said, the formal hosting of U40-Africa took place at the October conference. Future activities of U-40 Africa include the creation of regional chapters, recognition as a non-governmental organization (NGO) by UNESCO and the creation of a global presence in cultural diversity matters.[122]

New developments in South Africa are, however, a course for concern. The effective participation of civil society in cultural governance matters requires that civil society should have proper access to information, especially with regard to cultural matters. The controversial Protection of State Information Bill[123] is currently being debated in parliament. It provides for the protection of certain state information from unlawful disclosure and regulates the manner in which state information may be protected. If passed as legislation it might also have an impact on civil society's right to access cultural diversity information. One specific thing that comes to mind is the four-yearly reports which must be presented to UNESCO by Member States. If these reports are going to be classified as secret information, civil society will not have access to and be able to provide input before the report is submitted to UNESCO. Although it is unlikely that that would happen, the possibility is always there and civil society should guard against this from happening in future.

3.5. IMPLEMENTATION OF THE CONVENTION ON THE DIVERSITY OF CULTURAL EXPRESSIONS IN SOUTH AFRICA

The implementation of the Convention on the Diversity of Cultural Expressions in South Africa will proceed along three lines, some of which have already

121 *See* German Commission for UNESCO, "U40-World Forum 'Cultural Diversity 2030'", *available at* www.unesco.de/.html?&L=1 (last visited 2 February 2012).

122 *See* The Archival Platform, "Report on U40 Africa Network Meeting, Pretoria 22 Sept", *available at* www.archivalplatform.org/news/entry/u40_africa_network (last visited 2 February 2012).

123 *See* Bill No. B6–2010, *available at* www.parliament.gov.za (last visited 2 February 2012).

occurred. First, as a member of the IGC, South Africa participated in the mapping of the operational guidelines for the Convention on the Diversity of Cultural Expressions, including those relating to the International Fund.

Secondly, as a member of the AU and NEPAD, as well as various other international cultural organizations, South Africa should take a leading role in advocating the advantages and operational effect of the Convention on the Diversity of Cultural Expressions for the African community. In its Foreign Policy Document South Africa clearly states its intention to play a leading international role in "the constructive advancement of the new 'economic' world order towards a more equitable set of practices," as well as the impact of the new world order on the African continent.[124]

Thirdly, as a party to the Convention on the Diversity of Cultural Expressions, South Africa must implement the Convention on the Diversity of Cultural Expressions in its domestic law by identifying new arrangements for international, regional and sub-regional co-operation, and by ensuring the participation of civil society in the process. In order to do so, the DAC has already developed a Post Ratification Strategy for the implementation of the Convention on the Diversity of Cultural Expressions.[125] However, during the recent Mzansi's Golden Economy Consultative Conference (14–15 April 2011) hosted by the DAC, the Convention on the Diversity of Cultural Expressions was not even mentioned in the Conference Declaration, although the declaration reiterates the importance of the arts, cultural and heritage sector of South Africa.[126]

The DAC, which is mainly responsible for arts and culture, is key in ensuring the implementation of the Convention on the Diversity of Cultural Expressions.[127] The legislative mandate of the DAC is quite broad and covers a range of institutions[128] and legislation.[129] The vision of the DAC is "to develop

---

124 *See supra* note 16.

125 *See* Wakashe, *supra* note 34, at 5.

126 *See* South Africa, Department of Arts and Culture "Arts and Culture Summit: Conference Declaration", *available at* www.dac.gov.za/media_releases/2011/15-04-2011_2.html (last visited 2 February 2012). For more information on the conference, see South Africa, Department of Arts and Culture, "Mzansi's Golden Economy Consultative Conference Report", *available at* www.dac.gov.za/reports.htm (last visited 2 February 2012).

127 Other government departments, such as the Department of Trade and Industry (DTI), also deal with cultural issues, for example the protection of Indigenous Knowledge Systems.

128 Declared Cultural Institutions are declared as such according to the Cultural Institutions Act (Act No. 119 of 1998). They are corporate bodies that receive an annual subsidy from the DAC.

129 The following acts have been promulgated in the furtherance of the DAC's legislative mandate to date: National Archives and Record Service of South Africa Act (Act No. 43 of 1996); Cultural Institutions Act (Act No. 119 of 1998); Culture Promotion Act (Act No. 35 of 1983); South African Geographical Names Council Act (Act No. 118 of 1998); Heraldry Act (Act No. 18 of 1962); Legal Deposit Act (Act No. 54 of 1997); National Arts Council Act (Act No. 56 of 1997); National Film and Video Foundation Act (Act No. 73 of 1997); National Heritage Council Act (Act No. 11 of 1999); National Heritage Resources Act (Act No. 25 of 1999); PAN

and preserve South African culture to ensure social cohesion and nation-building"[130] and its mission corresponds broadly with the stated objectives of the Convention on the Diversity of Cultural Expressions.[131] It is obvious that the DAC plays a leading role in the arts and culture sector by developing policy objectives and priorities in all spheres of government dealing with cultural issues. It has to ensure the participation of provincial and municipal government, as well as public entities and civil society, in dealing with cultural issues. The DAC is also responsible for resources allocation and management on a national level, international co-operation, funding, and the contribution of the cultural sector to the economy.

The DAC's Post Ratification Strategy includes a review and update of its national legislative frameworks to ensure its alignment with the Convention on the Diversity of Cultural Expressions. In addition, the DAC plans the hosting of national workshops between all spheres of government, civil society and other cultural institutions in order to promote the Convention on the Diversity of Cultural Expressions and its objectives. The DAC will also see to the implementation of the Convention on the Diversity of Cultural Expressions at the grassroots level by aligning programs and projects with a view to promoting cultural diversity and cultural expressions. In addition, the DAC plans to involve the media, disability agencies dealing with cultural practitioners, and rurally based cultural practitioners to promote cultural diversity. In order to realize the objectives of the Post Ratification Strategy, the DAC is to set up a National Steering Committee that will monitor and implement the Post Ratification Strategy on the Convention on the Diversity of Cultural Expressions. The DAC will also be the actor responsible for preparing four-yearly reports to UNESCO under the terms of Article 9 of the Convention on the Diversity of Cultural

---

South African Language Board Act (Act No. 59 of 1995); National Library of South Africa Act (Act No. 92 of 1998); Library for the Blind Act (Act No. 91 of 1998). However, these acts were promulgated before the Convention on the Diversity of Cultural Expressions came into operation and they do not give effect to the Convention as required by Section 213 of the Constitution.

130 *See supra* note 32. The legislative mandate of the DAC is rather broad and covers a range of institutions and legislation. The primary legislative mandate is Sections 16, 30 and 31, as well as Schedule 4 of the Constitution. For other national acts falling under the DAC's jurisdiction, *see* South Africa, Department of Arts and Culture, "Legislation", *available at* www.dac.gov.za/acts.htm (last visited 2 February 2012).

131 *See* Convention on the Diversity of Cultural Expressions, *supra* note 15, Article 1. The mission of the DAC is to "Develop and promote arts and culture in South Africa and mainstream its role in social development; [d]evelop and promote the official languages of South Africa and enhance the linguistic diversity of the country; [i]mprove economic and other development opportunities for South African arts and culture nationally and globally through mutually beneficial partnerships, thereby ensuring the sustainability of the sector; [d]evelop and monitor the implementation of policy, legislation and strategic direction for the identification, conservation and promotion of cultural heritage; [g]uide, sustain and develop the archival, heraldic and information resources of the nation to empower citizens through full and open access to these resources."

Expressions.[132] The DAC has recognized that the implementation of the Convention on the Diversity of Cultural Expressions requires a collaborative effort from each and every person in South Africa by declaring:

> Support from the people is important for the Convention to work. We need to induce active participation and support from NGO's, civil society and the mass media. These groups in particular should play a major role in disseminating the meaning and principles of the Convention to minority cultures at every level and in every genre.[133]

The practical implementation of the Convention on the Diversity of Cultural Expressions will be achieved through the existing programs of the DAC, which are six in total, namely (1) Administration (Corporate Services); (2) Arts and Culture in Society; (3) National Language Service; (4) Cultural Development and International Co-operation; (5) Heritage Promotion; and (6) National Archives, Records, Libraries and Heraldic Services.[134] The Convention on the Diversity of Cultural Expressions plays a role in almost all of these programs. The DAC's Legal Services falling under program (1) above has to ensure compliance with any legislation dealing with culture and is, therefore, also responsible for the legal intricacies pertaining to the Convention on the Diversity of Cultural Expressions as well.[135] The second program, "Arts and Culture in Society", is intended to develop and promote arts and culture in South Africa and to mainstream its role in social development.[136] The third program, which focuses on linguistic diversity in South Africa, develops, promotes and protects the country's official languages through policy formulation, legislation and the implementation of the language policy in order to allow South Africans to realize their language rights.[137]

The practical implementation of the Convention on the Diversity of Cultural Expressions in South Africa is especially evident in the DAC's fourth program. The purpose of this Cultural Development and International Co-operation program is to "improve economic and other development opportunities for South African arts and culture, nationally and globally, through mutually beneficial partnerships." The program recognizes the importance of international co-operation in promoting the diversity of cultural expressions

---

132 *See* Wakashe, *supra* note 34, at 6–8.

133 Id., at 8.

134 South Africa, Department of Arts and Culture "Annual Report: 2010/2011", 20–70 (2011). The doings of the DAC are duly documented in its annual reports. *See* South Africa, Department of Arts and Culture, "Annual Reports", *available at* www.dac.gov.za/annual_report.htm (last visited 2 February 2012).

135 *See* South Africa, Department of Arts and Culture, "Medium-Term Strategic Framework: April 2010 – March 2014", 27, *available at* www.dac.gov.za/publications/strategic_plan/Strategic_Plan2010_2014.pdf (last visited 2 February 2012).

136 *See* id., at 30–4.

137 *See* id., at 35–7.

that improve sustainable economic and other development opportunities for South African arts and culture on a national and global level.[138] Within this program various key objectives within the framework of "Cultural Development", "International Cooperation" and "Investing in Culture" have been identified in the latest strategy plan of the DAC. The objectives under "Cultural Development" deals with the transformation of the cultural sector, the development of skills, institutions and markets, the promotion and protection of the cultural industries sector, the conducting of research and the establishment of a Cultural Observatory. The main objectives under "International Cooperation" are the consolidation of the African Agenda on culture, the promotion of South African arts, culture and heritage globally, the strengthening of South Africa's bilateral relations and contributing to global discourses pertaining to cultural diversity. The modest objective under "Investing in Culture" is the remodelling of this objective, which will not be easy to do. In a previous report the objective, "Investing in Culture", was described as being aimed at providing access to skills and markets as a tool for urban regeneration; rural development and job creation on a national level;[139] and the developing of international relations.[140] This objective has had considerable success and between 2005 and 2007, 5088 jobs have been created through the funding of projects. The beneficiaries consisted of 62% women, 53% youth and 8.5% disabled persons, and 40% of the allocated funds were invested in nodal municipalities in support of Integrated Sustainable Rural Development and Urban Renewal programs. Through important partnerships established nationally and internationally, products developed from several projects have entered mainstream markets and as a result some of the supported projects have already

138 *See* id., at 38–42.

139 ALthough the criteria for funding projects include the ability to address national priorities, namely poverty alleviation, the involvement of women, youth and disabled people, and job creation, it also has an international dimension. The qualifying projects must have the potential to be marketable, be self sustaining, and be community driven, should directly benefit the community in terms of job creation and skills development, and must have the potential to promote tourism. The program is neither meant to replace or fund the Provincial and Local Arts and Culture Programs, nor the role of funding organizations such as National Arts Council, National Film and Video Foundation, the South African Provincial Arts and Culture Councils and the National Heritage Council. *See* South Africa, Department of Arts and Culture, "Investing in Culture Programme,"*available at* www.dac.gov.za/brochures_booklets.htm (last visited 2 February 2012).

140 *See* South Africa, Department of Arts and Culture, "Annual Report: 2006/2007", 54–56 and 61–62 (2007). The countries with which South Africa has signed cultural agreements include Mali, Mozambique, Gabon, Mauritius, Botswana, France, Belarus, Norway, Sweden, United Kingdom and China. As an example, in terms of the South African/Swedish program, funds were allocated to 31 South African organizations which had joint projects with Swedish organizations and to 15 South African organizations which received planning grants for establishing and strengthening partnership with Swedish organizations. The DAC allocated R12 million and the Swedish International Development Cooperation Agency SEK45 million for the period 2004 to 2008.

produced 10% of their allocated project costs. This development was seen as good progress towards sustainability beyond governmental funding and was encouraged by the DAC.[141]

In 2005, the DAC commenced with the reviewing its policies, including its 1996 *White Paper on Arts, Culture and Heritage*, and all the legislation within its jurisdiction. This process was initiated by the South African Minister and Members of the Executive Council's Forums (MINMEC) who mandated the South African Technical Intergovernmental Committee (TIC) to initiate a review of its policies.[142] The TIC established a Policy Review Committee, which in turn mandated a Policy Review Task Team to develop and facilitate the Policy Review Process. Cheadle Thompson & Haysom Inc was eventually contracted by the DAC to review the legislation with DAC ministers.[143] The specific terms of reference were to "review the heritage laws for divergence, duplication and inconsistency" in relation to the existing national policy documents and Constitution, and other applicable laws.[144] Cheadle Thompson & Haysom Inc submitted a lengthy report to the DAC in 2009.[145] According to the report some of the main challenges are to develop outdated cultural policies and also to address the disjuncture between policy and legislation effectively.[146] They made a number of policy recommendations which have not been instituted yet. Although the Convention on the Diversity of Cultural Expressions formed part of the report, it had not been ratified yet when the report was compiled, and it did not influence the recommendations of the panel. One could thus only speculate on the question of whether or not the Convention would have influenced the outcome of the report had it been ratified by South Africa when the review was done.

So far South Africa has also endeavoured to satisfy its obligation to advocate for the importance of the protection and promotion of the diversity of cultural expression through education and public awareness as required by Article 10 of the Convention on the Diversity of Cultural Expressions. This is done, for

141 *See* id., at 61.

142 MINMECs are informal intergovernmental structures that arose soon after South Africa began its experiment in decentralizing government. Due to the constitutionally dispersed nature of authority, provinces and national government have original as well as exclusive responsibilities to develop policies, legislate, and act within their specified areas of competence. In terms of Section 1 of the Intergovernmental Relations Framework Act (Act No. 13 of 2005), the definition of a MINMEC is "a standing intergovernmental body consisting of at least a Cabinet member and members of the provincial Executive Councils responsible for functional areas similar to those of the Cabinet member." *See* T. Rapoo, "Concealed Contest: MINMECs and the Provincial Debate" (Policy Brief No. 18, 1999), *available at* www.cps.org.za/18.htm (last visited 2 February 2012).

143 *See* South Africa, Department of Arts and Culture, "Review of Heritage Legislation Report", *available at* www.dac.gov.za/reports.htm (last visited 2 February 2012).

144 *See* id., at 5.

145 See id.

146 *See* id., at 23–1.

example, through South Africa's participation in different multilateral fora such as UNESCO, INCP, the Commonwealth Foundation,[147] the South African Development Community (SADC)[148] and the AU. Such participation is significant for the development and shaping of global discussions pertaining to cultural diversity. In addition, South Africa hosted the third All Africa, Diaspora and World Festival of the Arts and Culture (FESTAC) in February 2010. The relationship between government and civil society remains, however, a point of concern for the effective implementation of the Convention domestically.

To date, South Africa has shown an unparalleled commitment to ensuring the implementation of the Convention on the Diversity of Cultural Expressions on a domestic level, and it is hoped that this enthusiasm will not be hampered by needless political agendas and power struggles between individuals and government structures.

4. CONCLUDING REMARKS

South Africa's participation in the birth of the Convention on the Diversity of Cultural Expressions clearly demonstrates the country's political influence in international organizations and of the negotiation and technical skills of the South African representatives in addressing international issues.

The Convention on the Diversity of Cultural Expressions recognizes the dual nature of cultural goods and services, and identifies measures that should be identified by Member States in order to ensure the promotion and protection of cultural diversity.[149] It is evident that there might be overlap or even conflict between the objectives of the Convention on the Diversity of Cultural

147 The Commonwealth Foundation is an intergovernmental organization, resourced by and reporting to Commonwealth governments, and guided by Commonwealth values and priorities. Its mandate is to strengthen civil society in the achievement of Commonwealth priorities, including the promotion of arts and culture. *See* COMMONWEALTH FOUNDATION, "Visions and Values", *available at* www.commonwealthfoundation.com/Aboutus/Visionsandvalues (last visited 2 February 2012).

148 The SADC has been in existence since 1980. It was initially formed as a loose alliance of nine states known as the Southern African Development Coordination Conference (SADCC), with the main aim of coordinating development projects in order to lessen economic dependence on the then apartheid South Africa. After apartheid, South Africa became a member and the current Member States include Angola, Botswana, the Democratic Republic of Congo, Lesotho, Madagascar, Malawi, Mauritius, Mozambique, Namibia, Seychelles, South Africa, Swaziland, United Republic of Tanzania, Zambia and Zimbabwe. The current agenda of the SADC is based on various principles, such as development orientation; subsidiarity; market integration and development; facilitation and promotion of trade and investment and variable geometry. *See* SOUTH AFRICAN DEVELOPMENT COMMUNITY, "SADC Profile", *available at* www.sadc.int (last visited 2 February 2012).

149 *See* KHACHATURIAN, *supra* note 79, at 192.

Expressions and those of the WTO trade regime, which would necessitate the balancing of conflicting values.

Although there might be criticisms raised in regard to the Convention on the Diversity of Cultural Expressions as a legal instrument,[150] its political meaning is clear, namely to counter the effects of globalism, especially in the context of developing countries. Considering South Africa's political standing within the international community of states and the African continent, it must ensure that an adequate environment is created for the Convention on the Diversity of Cultural Expressions to flourish.

South Africa has quite an impressive legislative and policy framework dealing with arts and culture,[151] and although the Convention on the Diversity of Cultural Expressions has not yet been incorporated into domestic law, South Africa is committed to fulfilling its international responsibilities in terms of the Convention. Although one has the impression that government departments are engaging with the Convention on the Diversity of Cultural Expressions behind the scenes, the fact that the Convention on the Diversity of Cultural Expressions has not been incorporated in the domestic law of South Africa remains a problem for the direct application of the Convention in South Africa. In addition, the fragmented approach to the application of the Convention on the Diversity of Cultural Expressions and the lack of cooperation between government departments and between government and civil society might further frustrate the effective application of the Convention on a domestic level.

Although South Africa experiences other difficulties such as poverty and HIV/AIDS, the country has a Cultural Ministry which is dedicated to the implementation of the Convention on the Diversity of Cultural Expressions on all levels. In 2008, the former Minister of Arts and Culture, Z. Pallo Jordan said the following:

---

150 It does not offer definitions for culture and cultural identity, and its relation to other international agreements is murky. *See* Bruner, *supra* note 90, at 8.

151 These frameworks include a legislative framework comprising of the White Paper on Arts, Culture and Heritage of 1996; the Constitution (with its Bill of Rights), Schedules 4 and 5 of the Constitution dealing with the jurisdictions of the national and provincial governments; and various other national legislation. Included in the legal framework is the Commission for the Promotion and Protection of the Rights of Cultural, Religious and Linguistic Communities Act, which was established under Chapter 9 (Sections 181, 185 and 186) of the Constitution as well as the Commission for the Promotion and Protection of the Rights of Cultural, Religious and Linguistic Communities Act (Act No. 19 of 2002). The establishment of various statutory bodies provides for additional frameworks for the protection of the cultural sector, namely the National Arts Council; the National Film and Video Foundation; the National Heritage Council; Business Arts South Africa; the Lottery Fund; the Pan South African Language Board, the Provincial Language Committees; the National Language Service (at the DAC); and the National Cultural Institutes, including the Robben Island Museum, Nelson Mandela Museum and the Albert Luthuli Museum. *See also supra* note 129 (legislation listed).

> Through UNESCO, South Africa is playing a significant role in shaping the international cultural landscape. This vindicates our strategy for international relations which seeks to place South Africa among the key players in global cultural affairs. South Africa has honed her skills on the issues of cultural diversity, intangible heritage and indigenous knowledge.[152]

In contrast to previous international agreements, the Convention on the Diversity of Cultural Expressions has been embraced by political leaders with great enthusiasm and interest. It is probably too early to foretell whether this euphoria will continue but considering the activities of the DAC, other cultural organizations and individuals, it would certainly be safe to say that South Africa is, at least, committed to making the Convention on the Diversity of Cultural Expressions work.

---

152 Z. P. Jordan, Former Minister of Arts and Culture, "Budget Vote Speech at the Parliament" (6 June 2008), *available at* www.dac.gov.za/speeches/minister/Speech06June2008.htm (last visited 2 February 2012).

TABLE OF INTERNATIONAL TREATIES AND CONVENTIONS

Agreement for Facilitating the International Circulation of Visual and Auditory Materials of an Educational, Scientific and Cultural Character, 10 December 1948, 197 *U.N.T.S.* 3

Agreement on the Importation of Educational, Scientific and Cultural Materials, with Annexes and Protocol annexed, 22 November 1950, 131 *U.N.T.S.* 25 (1952)

Agreement on Agriculture, 15 April 1994, *LT/UR/A-1A/2*

Agreement on Safeguards, 15 April 1994, *LT/UR/A-1A/8*

Agreement on Subsidies and Countervailing Measures, 15 April 1994, *LT/UR/A-1A/9*

Agreement on the Application of Sanitary and Phytosanitary Measures, 15 April 1994, LT/UR/A-1A/12

Agreement on the Importation of Educational, Scientific and Cultural Materials, 17 June 1950, *available at* http://portal.unesco.org/en/ev.php-URL_ID=12074&URL_DO=DO_TOPIC&URL_SECTION=201.html (last visited 2 February 2012) and its *Nairobi Protocol* of 26 November 1976

Agreement on Trade-Related Aspects of Intellectual Property Rights, 15 April 1994, *LT/UR/A-1C/IP/1*

American Convention on Human Rights, 22 November 1969, 1144 *U.N.T.S.* 123

Berne Convention for the Protection of Literary and Artistic Works, 9 September 1886, 828 *U.N.T.S.* 211 (last revised at Paris, 24 July 1971)

Consolidated Versions of the Treaty on European Union and of the Treaty establishing the European Community, *C 321 E/2*, *available at* http://eur-lex.europa.eu/LexUriServ/LexUriServ.do?uri=OJ:C:2006:321E:0001:0331:EN:pdf (last visited 2 February 2012)

Consolidated Versions of the Treaty on European Union and the Treaty on the Functioning of the European Union, *OJ 2008/ C 115/1*, *available at* http://eur-lex.europa.eu/LexUriServ/LexUriServ.do?uri=OJ:C:2008:115:0001:0012:EN:PDF (last visited 2 February 2012)

Constitution of the United Nations Educational, Scientific and Cultural Organisation, 16 November 1945, 52 *UNTS* 275

Convention (IX) concerning Bombardment by Naval Forces in Time of War, 18 October 1907, 3 *Martens Nouveau Recueil (ser. 3)* 604, *available at* www.icrc.org/ihl.nsf (last visited on 2 February 2012)

Convention (IV) Respecting the Laws and Customs of War on Land and its Annex: Regulations concerning the Laws and Customs of War on Land, 18 October 1907, 3 *Martens Nouveau Recueil (ser. 3)* 461, *available at* www.icrc.org/ihl.nsf (last visited on 2 February 2012)

Convention for Facilitating the International Circulation of Films of an Educational Character, 11 October 1933, 1 *L.N.T.S.* 333
Convention for the Protection of Cultural Property in the Event of Armed Conflict, 14 May 1954, 249 *UNTS* 240 and its Protocol (1954)
Convention on the Exchange of Official Publications (1958)
Convention on the Means of Prohibiting and Preventing the Illicit Import, Export and Transfer of Cultural Property, 14 November 1970, 823 *UNTS* 231
Convention Concerning the Protection of the World Cultural and Natural Heritage, 16 November 1972, *available at* http://portal.unesco.org/en/ev.php-URL_ID=13055&URL_DO=DO_TOPIC&URL_SECTION=201.html (last visited 2 February 2012)
Convention Against Torture and Other Cruel, Inhuman or Degrading Treatment or Punishment, 10 December 1984, 1465 *UNTS* 85
Convention on the Rights of the Child, 20 November 1989, *UN Doc. A/44/49*
Convention on the Protection of the Underwater Cultural Heritage, 2 November 2001, *UNESCO Doc.MISC/2003/CLT/CH/4*
Convention for the Safeguarding of the Intangible Cultural Heritage, 17 October 2003, *U.N. Doc. MISC/2003/CLT/CH/14*
Convention on the Protection and Promotion of the Diversity of Cultural Expressions, 20 October 2005, *U.N. Doc. CLT-2005/CONVENTION DIVERSITE-CULT REV.*
Covenant on Economic, Social and Cultural Rights, 16 December 1966, 993 U.N.T.S. 3
European Convention for the Protection of Human Rights and Fundamental Freedoms, 4 November 1950, *ETS* No. 5
General Agreement on Tariffs and Trade, 30 October 1947, 55 U.N.T.S. 194 (1947)
General Agreement on Tariffs and Trade 1994, 15 April 1995, *LT/UR/A-1A/1/GATT/1*
General Agreement on Trade in Services, 15 April 1994, LT/UR/A-1B/S/1
ILO Convention (No. 169) concerning Indigenous and Tribal Peoples in Independent Countries, 27 June 1989, 28 *I.L.M.* 1382
International Convention concerning the Use of Broadcasting in the Cause of Peace, 23 September 1936, 186 *L.N.T.S.* 301
International Convention for the Protection of Performers, Producers of Phonograms and Broadcasting Organisations, Article 3, 26 October 1961, 496 *U.N.T.S.* 44 (1961)
International Convention on the Elimination of All Forms of Racial Discrimination, 21 December 1965, 660 *UNTS* 195
International Convention on the Elimination of All Forms of Discrimination Against Women, 18 December 1979, 1249 *UNTS* 13
International Convention on the Harmonized Commodity Description and Coding System, 14 June 1983, 1503 *UNTS* 167, Annex
International Convention on the Protection of the Rights of All Migrant Workers and Members of Their Families, 18 December 1990, GA Res. 45/158, *A/RES/45/158*
International Covenant on Civil and Political Rights, 16 December 1966, 999 *U.N.T.S.* 171
Framework Convention for the Protection of National Minorities, 1 February 1995, *ETS 157* (1995)
Marrakesh Agreement Establishing the World Trade Organization, 15 April 1994, LT/UR/A/2

Protocol to the Agreement on the Importation of Educational, Scientific and Cultural Materials, 26 November 1976, 1259 *U.N.T.S.* 3 (1982)
Treaty of Lisbon amending the Treaty on European Union and the Treaty establishing the European Community, 13 December 2007, *OJ C 306* (17 December 2007)
Understanding on Rules and Procedures Governing the Settlement of Disputes, 15 April 1994, Marrakesh Agreement Establishing the World Trade Organization, Annex 2, Legal Instruments – Results of the Uruguay Round, 33 *I.L.M.* 1125 (1994)
Universal Copyright Convention, 6 September 1952, 216 *UNTS* 133
Vienna Convention on the Law of Treaties, 23 May 1969, 1155 *UNTS* 331

TABLE OF CHARTERS, DECLARATIONS, RECOMMENDATIONS, AND RESOLUTIONS

African Charter on Human and Peoples' Rights, 27 June 1981, 21 *I.L.M.* 58 (1982)

Cultural Charter for Africa, 5 July 1976, *available at* www.africa-union.org/root/au/Documents/Treaties/Text/Cultural_Charter_for_Africa.pdf (last visited 2 February 2012)

Charter of Fundamental Rights of the European Union, 7 December 2000, *OJ 2000/C 364/01*

Charter for African Cultural Renaissance, 24 January 2006, *available at* www.au.int/en/sites/default/files/CHARTER_FOR_AFRICAN_CULTURAL_RENAISSANCE.pdf (last visited 2 February 2012)

Declaration of Principles of International Cultural Co-operation, 4 November 1966, *available at* http://unesdoc.unesco.org/images/0011/001140/114048e.pdf#page=82 (last visited 2 February 2012)

Declaration on Race and Racial Prejudice, 27 November 1978, *available at* http://portal.unesco.org/en/ev.php-URL_ID=13161&URL_DO=DO_TOPIC&URL_SECTION=201.html (last visited 2 February 2012) and www2.ohchr.org/english/law/race.htm (last visited 2 February 2012)

Declaration on the Rights of Persons belonging to National or Ethnic, Religious and Linguistic Minorities, 18 December 1992, *Resolution 47/135*

Declaration concerning the Intentional Destruction of Cultural Heritage, 17 October 2003, *available at* http://portal.unesco.org/en/ev.php-URL_ID=17718&URL_DO=DO_TOPIC&URL_SECTION=201.html (last visited on 2 February 2012)

European Charter for Regional or Minority Languages, 5 November 1992, *ETS 148* (1992)

Mexico City Declaration on Cultural Policies, 26 July – 6 Augustus 1982, *available at* http://portal.unesco.org/culture/en/files/35197/11919410061mexico_en.pdf/mexico_en.pdf (last visited on 2 February 2012)

Recommendation on the Status of Scientific Researchers, 20 November 1974, *available at* http://unesdoc.unesco.org/images/0011/001140/114040e.pdf#page=166 (last visited 2 February 2012)

Recommendation on Participation by the People at Large in Cultural Life and their Contribution to It, 26 November 1976, *available at* http://unesdoc.unesco.org/images/0011/001140/114038e.pdf#page=145 (last visited 2 February 2012)

Recommendation concerning the Status of the Artist, 27 October 1980, *available at* http://portal.unesco.org/en/ev.php-URL_ID=13138&URL_DO=DO_TOPIC&URL_

SECTION=201.html (last visited 2 February 2012) and http://unesdoc.unesco.org/images/0011/001140/114029e.pdf#page=144 (last visited 2 February 2012)

Recommendation 1043 (1986) on Europe's Linguistic and Literary Heritage, 19 September 1986, *available at* http://assembly.coe.int/main.asp?Link=/documents/adoptedtext/ta86/erec1043.htm (last visited 2 February 2012)

Recommendation on the Safeguarding of Traditional Culture and Folklore, 15 November 1989, *available at* http://portal.unesco.org/en/ev.php-URL_ID=13141&URL_DO=DO_TOPIC&URL_SECTION=201.html (last visited 2 February 2012)

Recommendation concerning the Promotion and Use of Multilingualism and Universal Access to Cyberspace, 2003, *available at* http://portal.unesco.org/ci/en/files/13475/10697584791Recommendation-Eng.pdf/Recommendation-Eng.pdf (last visited 2 February 2012)

United Nations Declaration on the Rights of Indigenous Peoples, 13 December 2007, *A/RES/61/295*

Universal Declaration of Human Rights, 10 December 1948, GA Res. 217A (III), *UN Doc. A/810*

Universal Declaration on Cultural Diversity, 2 November 2001, *available at* http://portal.unesco.org/en/ev.php-URL_ID=13179&URL_DO=DO_TOPIC&URL_SECTION=201.html (last visited 2 February 2012)

United Nations Declaration on the Rights of Indigenous Peoples, 13 December 2007, *A/RES/61/295*

TABLE OF OPERATIONAL GUIDELINES

UNESCO, General Assembly, "Operational Directives for the Implementation of the Convention for the Safeguarding of the Intangible Cultural Heritage" (2008, as amended 2010), *available at* www.unesco.org/culture/ich/index.php?lg=en&pg=00026 (last visited 2 February 2012)

UNESCO, Conference of the Parties, "Operational Guidelines" (June 2009), *available at* www.unesco.org/new/en/culture/themes/cultural-diversity/diversity-of-cultural-expressions/the-convention/operational-guidelines/ (last visited 2 February 2012)

——, "Approval of the Operational Guidelines for the Implementation of the Convention and Future Activities of the Committee", *CE/09/2 CP/210/7* (30 March 2009), *available at* http://unesdoc.unesco.org//0018/001826/182661E.pdf (last visited 2 February 2012)

——, "Operational Guidelines on Education and Public Awareness (Article 10 of the Convention)" (June 2009), *available at* www.unesco.org/new/fileadmin/MULTIMEDIA/HQ/CLT/pdf/Conv2005_DO_Art_10_EN.pdf (last visited 2 February 2012)

——, "Operational Guidelines on Cooperation for Development (Article 14 of the Convention)" (June 2009), *available at* www.unesco.org/new/fileadmin/MULTIMEDIA/HQ/CLT/pdf/Conv2005_DO_Art_14_EN.pdf (last visited 2 February 2012)

——, "Operational Guidelines on Preferential Treatment for Developing Countries (Article 16 of the Convention)" (June 2009), *available at* www.unesco.org/new/fileadmin/MULTIMEDIA/HQ/CLT/pdf/Conv2005_DO_Art_16_EN.pdf (last visited 2 February 2012)

——, "Operational Guidelines on the Use of the Resources of the International Fund for Cultural Diversity (Article 18 of the Convention)" (June 2009), *available at* www.unesco.org/new/fileadmin/MULTIMEDIA/HQ/CLT/pdf/Conv2005_DO_Art_18_EN.pdf (last visited 2 February 2012)

UNESCO, Intergovernmental Committee for the Protection of World Cultural and Natural Heritage, *Operational Guidelines for the Implementation of the World Heritage Convention*, (January 2008), *available at* http://whc.unesco.org/archive/opguide08-en.pdf (last visited on 2 February 2012)

TABLE OF FREE TRADE AGREEMENTS

Canada-Israel Free Trade Agreement, 1 January 1997, *available at* www.international.gc.ca/trade-agreements-accords-commerciaux/agr-acc/israel/toc-tdm.aspx?lang=eng&view=d (last visited 2 February 2012)

Canada-United States Free-Trade Agreement, 4 October 1988, 27 *I.L.M.* 281 (1988)

Israel-United States Free Trade Area Agreement, 19 August 1985, *24 I.L.M. 657*

North American Free Trade Agreement between the Government of Canada, the Government of Mexico and the Government of the United States, 17 December 1992, 32 *I.L.M.* 605 (1993)

United States-Korea Free Trade Agreement, 30 June 2007, *available at* www.ustr.gov/agreements/trade-agreements/fta/final-text (last visited 2 February 2012)

TABLE OF EUROPEAN LEGISLATIVE ACTS, CONCLUSIONS, RECOMMENDATIONS AND RESOLUTIONS

Conclusions of the Council and of the Representatives of the Governments of the Member States, meeting within the Council, on the Work Plan for Culture 2008–2010, 10 June 2008, *OJ 2008 C 143/9*

Conclusions of the Council and of the Representatives of the Governments of the Member States, meeting within the Council, on the Work Plan for Culture 2011–2014, 2 December 2010, *OJ 2010 C 325/1*

Council Decision 2008/211/EC on the Principles, Priorities and Conditions contained in the European Partnership with Bosnia and Herzegovina and Repealing Decision 2006/55/EC, 18 February 2008, *OJ 2008 L 80/18*

Council Decision on the Conclusion of the Convention on the Protection and Promotion of the Diversity of Cultural Expressions, 18 May 2006, *OJ 2006 L 201/15*

Council Directive 89/552/EEC on the Coordination of Certain Provisions Laid Down by Law, Regulation or Administrative Action in Member States Concerning the Pursuit of Television Broadcasting Activities, 3 October 1989, *OJ 1989 L 298/23*

Council Directive 89/552/EEC on the Coordination Certain Provisions laid Down by Law, Regulation or Administrative Action in Member States Concerning the Pursuit of Television Broadcasting Activities, 3 October 1989, *OJ L 298* as amended by European Parliament and Council of European Union, "Directive 97/36/EC of the European Parliament and of the Council of 30 June 1997 amending Council Directive 89/552/EEC on the Coordination of Certain Provisions Laid Down by Law, Regulation or Administrative Action in Member States Concerning the Pursuit of Television Broadcasting Activities", 30 July 1997, *OJ L 202*

Council Regulation (EC) No. 40/94 of 20 December 1993 on the Community Trade Mark, Articles 64–72, 14 January 1994, *OJ L 11* as amended

Council Regulation (EC) No. 509/2006 of 20 March 2006 on Agricultural Products and Foodstuffs as Traditional Specialities Guaranteed, 31 March 2006, *OJ L 93* as amended

Decision 508/2000/EC of the European Parliament and of the Council of 14 February 2000 establishing the Culture 2000 Programme, *OJ 2000 L 63/1*

Decision 1855/2006/EC of the European Parliament and of the Council of 12 December 2006 establishing the Culture Programme (2007–2013), 30 July 1997, *OJ L 202*

Directive 2007/65/EC of the European Parliament and of the Council amending Council Directive 89/552/EEC on the Coordination of Certain Provisions Laid Down by

Law, Regulation or Administrative Action in Member States Concerning the Pursuit of Television Broadcasting Activities, 11 December 2007, *OJ 2007 L 332/27*

European Parliament Resolution on Cultural Industries, 4 September 2003, *P5_TA-PROV(2003)0382*

European Parliament Resolution on the Risks of Violation, in the EU and especially in Italy, of Freedom of Expression and Information (Article 11(2) of the Charter of Fundamental Rights), 22 April 2004, *P5_TA(2004)0373*

Protocol on Cultural Cooperation, [2011] *OJ L 127/1418*

Recommendation from the Commission to the Council to Authorise the Commission to Participate, on behalf of the Community, in the Negotiations within UNESCO on the Convention on the Protection of the Diversity of Cultural Contents and Artistic Expressions, 1 September 2004, *SEC (2004) 1062*, *available at* http://ec.europa.eu/avpolicy/docs/ext/mandat_en.pdf (last visited 2 February 2012)

Resolution on Preserving and Promoting Cultural Diversity: The Role of the European Regions and International Organisations such as UNESCO and the Council of Europe, 14 January 2004, *OJ 2005 C 92E/322*

Resolution on Working towards a Convention on the Protection of the Diversity of Cultural Content and Artistic Expression, 14 April 2005, *OJ 2006 C33E/591*

Resolution of the Council on a European Agenda for Culture, 16 November 2007, *OJ 2007 C 287/1*

BIBLIOGRAPHY

1. MONOGRAPHS & EDITED VOLUMES

Adorno, Th. W., *The Culture Industry* (London: Routlegde, 1991)

—— and Horkheimer, M., *Dialectic of Enlightenment* (London: Verso, 1997)

Balasubramanyam, V.N. and Greenaway, D. (ed.), *Trade and Development: Essays in Honour of Jagdish Bhagwati* (New York: St. Martin's Press, 1996)

Benjamin, W., "Das Kunstwerk im Zeitalter seiner technischen Reproduzierbarkeit", in R. Tiedemann and H. Schweppenhäuser (eds.), *Walter Benjamin - Gesammelte Schriften*, Vol. I, 2nd ed. (Frankfurt am Main: Suhrkamp., 1978)

Bently, L. and Sherman, B., *Intellectual Property Law*, 3nd ed. (Oxford: Oxford University Press, 2009)

Blake, J., *Developing a New Standard-setting Instrument for the Safeguarding of Intangible Cultural Heritage: Elements for Consideration* (Paris: UNESCO Printing, 2002)

——, *Commentary on the UNESCO 2003 Convention on the Safeguarding of Intangible Cultural Heritage* (Leicester: Institute of Arts and Law, 2006)

Brems, E. (ed.), *Conflicts Between Fundamental Rights* (Antwerp: Intersentia, 2008)

Breunig, C., *Kommunikationspolitik der UNESCO: Dokumentation und Analyse der Jahre 1946 bis 1987* (Konztanz: Universitätsverlag Konstanz, 1987)

Brown, M.F., *Who Owns Native Culture?* (Cambridge, Mass.: Harvard University Press, 2003)

Croome, J., *Reshaping the World Trading System: A History of the Uruguay Round* (Geneva: World Trade System, 1995)

Cornish, W. and Llewelyn, D., *Intellectual Property: Patents, Copyright, Trade Marks and Allied Rights*, 7th ed. (London: Sweet and Maxwell, 2010)

Cowan, T., *Good and Plenty: The Creative Successes of American Arts Funding* (Princeton: Princeton University Press, 2006)

Dalziel, P. and Saunders, C., with Fyfe, R. and Newton, B., *Sustainable Development and Cultural Capital* (Wellington: Statistics New Zealand, 2009)

Donders, Y.M., *Towards a Right to Cultural Identity?* (Antwerp: Intersentia, 2002)

Drahos, P., *A Philosophy of Intellectual Property* (Aldershot: Dartmouth, 1996)

Dutfield, G., *Intellectual Property, Biogenetic Resources and Traditional Knowledge* (Sterling: Earthscan, 2004)

Echols, M., *Food Safety and the WTO: The Interplay of Culture, Science and Technology* (The Hague: Kluwer Law International, 2001)

Eeckhout, P., *External Relations of the European Union - Legal and Constitutional Foundations* (Oxford: Oxford University Press, 2004)

Fijalkowski, A. and Cameron J. (eds.), *Trade and the Environment: Bridging the Gap* (London: Cameron May, 1998)

Francioni, F., (ed., with F. Lenzerini), *Commentary to the 1972 World Heritage Convention* (Oxford: Oxford University Press, 2008)

Gagne, G. (ed.), *La diversité culturelle: Vers une convention internationale effective?* (Québec: Fides, 2005)

Gibson, J., *Community Resources: Intellectual Property, International Trade and Protection of Traditional Knowledge* (Aldershot: Ashgate, 2005)

Goldstein, P., *International Copyright: Principles, Law, and Practice* (New York, Oxford University Press, 2010)

——, *Copyright's Highway: From Gutenberg to the Celestial Jukebox* (Stanford: Stanford University Press, 2003 (rev. ed.))

Graber, Ch. B., *Handel und Kultur im Audiovisionsrecht der WTO: Völkerrechtliche, ökonomische und kulturpolitische Grundlagen einer globalen Medienordnung* (Bern: Stämpfli, 2003)

Guibault, L.C.R., *Copyright Limitations and Contracts: An Analysis of the Contractual Overridability of Limitations on Copyright* (The Hague: Kluwer Law International, 2002)

Hirao, M., *Shouhyouhou [Trademark Law]*, 1st rev. ed. (Tokyo: Gakuyo Shobo, 2006)

Hoekman, B. and Kostecki, M., *The Political Economy of the World Trading System: The WTO and Beyond*, 2nd ed. (Oxford: Oxford University Press, 2001)

Hoffman, B.T. (ed.), *Art and Cultural Heritage: Law, Policy and Practice* (Cambridge: Cambridge University Press, 2005)

Howkins, J., *The Creative Economy: How People Make Money From Ideas* (London: Penguin, 2002)

Irwin, D.A., Mavroidis, P.C. and Sykes, A.O., *The Genesis of the GATT* (Cambridge: Cambridge University Press, 2008)

Ivey, B., *Arts, Inc.: How Greed and Neglect Have Destroyed Our Cultural Rights* (Berkeley: University Press of California, 2008)

Jackson, J.H., *World Trade and the Law of GATT* (Indianapolis: Bobbs-Merrill, 1969)

——, *The World Trading System: Law and Policy of International Economic Relations*, 2nd ed. (Cambridge, Mass.: The MIT Press, 1997)

Landes, W.M. and Posner, R.A., *The Economic Structure of Intellectual Property Law* (Cambridge: Belknap Press of Harvard University Press, 2003)

Lévy, R.B.F., *Les compétences culturelles de la Communauté Européenne* (Aix-en-Provence: Presses universitaires d'Aix-Marseille, 2004)

Linderfalk, U., *On the Interpretation of Treaties: The Modern International Law as Expressed in the 1969 Vienna Convention on the Law of Treaties* (Dordrecht: Springer, 2007)

Loman, J.M.E., et al., *Culture and Community Law: Before and After Maastricht* (Deventer: Kluwer Law and Taxation, 1992)

Lotman, Y.M., *Universe of the Mind – A Semiotic Theory of Culture* (A. Shukman (trans.)) (Bloomington: Indiana University Press, 1990)

Lotz, A.D., *The Television Will Be Revolutionized* (New York: New York University Press, 2007)

Lucas, A. and Lucas, H.-J., *Traité de la propriété littéraire et artistique*, 3rd ed. (Paris: Litec, 2006)

Kaser, M., *Römisches Privatrecht*, 15th ed. (Munich: Beck, 1989)

Klein, U., *The Business of Art Unveiled: New York Art Dealers Speak Up* (Frankfurt am Main: Peter Lang Publisher, 1994)

Kroeber, A.L. and C. Kluckhohn, C., *Culture – A Critical Review of Concepts and Definitions* (Cambridge, Mass.: Peabody Museum, 1952)

Macaulay, T.B., *The Life and Works of Lord Macaulay: Complete in Ten Volumes*, Edinburgh edition (London: Longmans, Green and Co., 1896)

Malraux, A., *L'esquisse d'une psychologie du cinéma* (Paris: Gallimard, 1946) (1939)

Mavroidis, P., *The General Agreement on Tariffs and Trade: A Commentary* (Oxford: Oxford University Press, 2005)

Merryman, J.H., Elsen, A.E. and Urice, S.K., *Law, Ethics, and the Visual Arts*, 5th ed. (The Hague: Kluwer Law International, 2007)

Neuwirth, R.J., *The Cultural Industries in International Trade Law: Insights from the NAFTA, the WTO, and the EU* (Hamburg: Verlag Dr. Kovač, 2006)

Noam, E., *Television in Europe* (Oxford: Oxford University Press, 1991)

Office of the U.S. Trade Representative (ed.), *U.S. National Study on Trade in Services: A Submission by the United States Government to the General Agreement on Tariffs and Trade – Motion Pictures* (Washington D.C.: Office of the US Trade Representative, 1984)

Olstrom, E., *Governing the Commons: The Evolution of Institutions for Collective Action* (Cambridge: Cambridge University Press, 1990)

Orwell, G., *Nineteen Eighty-Four* (London: Penguin Books, 2000)

Psychogiopoulou, E., *The Integration of Cultural Considerations in EU Law and Policies* (Leiden: Martinus Nijhoff Publishers, 2008)

Palmeter, D.N. and Mavroidis, P.C., *Dispute Settlement in the World Trade Organization: Practice and Procedure* (Cambridge: Cambridge University Press, 2004)

Richieri Hanania, L., *Diversité culturelle et droit international du commerce* (Paris: La Documentation française, 2009)

Rundell, J. and Mennell, St. (eds.), *Classical Readings in Culture and Civilization* (London: Routledge, 1998)

Schechter, R.E. and Thomas, J.R., *Intellectual Property: The Law of Copyrights, Patents and Trademarks* (St. Paul: West Publishing Company, 2003)

Scott, D., *Refashioning Futures: Criticism after Post-Coloniality* (Princeton: Princeton University Press, 1999)

Seitel, P. (ed.), *Safeguarding Traditional Cultures: A Global Assessment* (Washington D.C.: Center for Folklife and Cultural Heritage Smithsonian, 2001)

Sell, S.K., *Private Power, Public Law: The Globalization of Intellectual Property Right* (Cambridge: Cambridge University Press, 2003)

Sekhar, A. and Steinkamp, A. (eds.), *Mapping Cultural Diversity – Good Practices from Around the Globe: A Contribution to the Debate in the Implementation of the UNESCO Convention on the Protection and Promotion of the Diversity of Cultural Expressions*, 2009, *available at* www.unesco.it/_filesDIVERSITAculturale/_DUK.pdf (last visited 2 February 2012)

Sen, A., *Development as Freedom* (Oxford: Oxford University Press, 1999)

Smiers, J., *Arts under pressure – Promoting Cultural Diversity in the Age of Globalization* (The Hague: Hivos, 2003)

Shuibhne, N.N., *EC Law and Minority Language Policy: Culture, Citizenship and Fundamental Rights* (The Hague: Kluwer Law International, 2002)

Stenou, K., *UNESCO and the Issue of Cultural Diversity: Review and strategy, 1946–2004 – A study based on official documents*, 2004, *available at* http://unesdoc.unesco.org////154341mo.pdf (last visited 2 February 2012)

Tamura, Y., *Chosakukenho gaisetsu [Copyright Law]*, 2nd ed. (Tokyo: Yuhikaku, 2001)

Throsby, D., *Economics and Culture* (Cambridge: Cambridge University Press, 2001)

——, *The Economics of Cultural Policy* (Cambridge: Cambridge University Press, 2010)

Towse, R., *Creativity, Incentive and Reward: An Economic Analysis of Copyright and Culture in the Information Age* (Cheltham: Edward Elgar Publishing, 2001)

——, (ed.), *A Handbook of Cultural Economics* (Cheltham: Edward Elgar Publishing, 2003)

UNESCO, UNESCO, *A Guide to the Operation of the Agreement on the Importation of Educational, Scientific and Cultural Material*, 4th ed., (Paris: UNESCO Publishing, 1969)

——, *Guide pratique de la Décennie mondiale du développement Culturel 1988–1997* (Paris: Unesco Printing, 1987)

——, *World Culture Report 1998: Culture, Creativity and Markets* (Paris: UNESCO Publishing, 1998)

——, *World Culture Report 2000: Cultural Diversity, Conflict and Pluralism* (Paris: UNESCO Publishing, 2000)

——, *Culture, Trade and Globalization: Questions and Answers* (Paris: UNESCO Publishing, 2000)

Vaidhyanathan, S., *Copyrights and Copywrongs: The Rise of Intellectual Property and How It Threatens Creativity* (New York: New York University Press, 2003)

Velthuis, O., *Talking Prices: Symbolic Meanings of Prices on the Market for Contemporary Art* (Princeton: Princeton University Press, 2005)

von Lewinski, S. (ed.), *Indigenous Heritage and Intellectual Property: Genetic Resources, Traditional Knowledge and Folklore*, 2nd ed. (Aphen aan de Rijn: Kluwer Law International, 2008)

Voon, T., *Cultural Products and the World Trade Organization* (Cambridge: Cambridge University Press, 2007)

Williams, T.G., *The History of Commerce* (London: L. Pitman, 1926)

World Commission on Culture and Development, *Our Creative Diversity: Report of the World Commission on Culture and Development* (Paris: UNESCO Publishing, 1995)

World Commission on Environment and Development, *Our Common Future* (Oxford: Oxford University Press, 1987)

WTO Secretariat, *A Handbook on the GATS Agreement* (Cambridge: Cambridge University Press, 2005)

2. JOURNAL ARTICLES, BOOK CHAPTERS AND PRESENTATIONS

Acheson, K. and Maule, C., "Canadian Content Rules: A Time for Reconsideration" 16 *Canadian Public Policy* 284 (1990)

——, "International Agreements and the Cultural Industries", 6 *North American Outlook* 1 (1995)

Adorno, Th. W., "Culture and Administration", in Th. W. Adorno (ed.), *The Culture Industry: Selected Essays on Mass Culture*, 1991, 107

Aikawa-Faure, N., "UNESCO Convention for the Safeguarding of Intangible Cultural Heritage - from its Adoption to the First Meeting of the Intergovernmental Committee", in Kokuritsu Binkazai Kikou, Tokyo Bunkazai Kenkyujo and Mukei Bunka Isanbu (eds.), *Safeguarding Intangible Cultural Heritage: International Cooperation and the Role of Japan*, 13 (2008), *available at* www.tobunken.go.jp/~beino/pdf/sympo/07KeynoteSpeech2Aikawa.pdf (last visited 2 February 2012)

Ahn, D., "Linkages between International Financial and Trade Institutions – IMF, World Bank and WTO", 34 *Journal of World Trade* 1 (2000)

——, "Legal and Institutional Issues of Korea-EU FTA: New Model for Post-NAFTA FTAs?" *GEM Policy Brief* (October 2010), *available at* http://gem.sciences-po.fr////_KOREU%20FTA%20201010.pdf (last visited 2 February 2012)

Alben, E., "GATT and the Fair Wage: A Historical Perspective on the Labor-Trade Link", 101 *Columbia Law Review* 1410 (2001)

Alexander, P.J., "Product Variety and Market Structure: A New Measure and a Simple Test", 32 *Journal of Economic Behavior and Organization* 207 (1997)

Altwegg, J., Artenschutz für Schönes: Die Unesco spricht: Kultureller Protektionismus soll erlaubt sein", *Frankfurter Allgemeine Zeitung* 35 (9 June 2005)

Anand, S. and Sen, A., "*Sustainable Human Development: Concepts and Priorities*", *available at* www.undp.org.in/hdrc/APRI/Event/Colombo/resources/ppr/sustainable%20human%20development%20abstract.pdf (last visited 2 February 2012)

Ashworth, G.J., Graham, B., and Tunbridge, J.E., *Pluralising Pasts: Heritage, Identity and Place in Multicultural Societies*, 2007, 8

Baker, E.C., "International Trade in Media Products", in N. Elkin-Koren and N.W. Netanel (eds.), *The Commodification of Information*, 2002, 267

Bal, S., "International Free Trade Agreements and Human Rights: Reinterpreting Article XX of the GATT", 10 *Minnesota Journal of Global Trade* 62 (2001)

Balassa, C., "Trade Issues in the Motion Picture Industry" (unpublished report prepared for the Office of the United States Trade Representative (1981) (one file with C. Balassa)

——, "International Cooperation to Improve Trade Rules", 6(4) *North America Outlook* 25 (1998)

——, "America's Image Abroad: The UNESCO Cultural Diversity Convention and U.S. Motion Picture Exports" (Paper Presented at a conference held in Washington, D.C. by the Curb Center for Art, Enterprise and Public Policy at Vanderbilt, on April 24, 2008)

BENHAMOU, F. and S. PELTIER, S., "How Should Cultural Diversity Be Measured? An Application Using the French Publishing Industry", 31 *Journal of Cultural Economics* 85 (2007)

——, FLÔRES JR., R.G. and PELTIER, S., "The Use of Diversity in Cultural Economics: Theoretical and Applied Considerations" (11–13 Dec. 2008) (paper presented at "Conference on Models of Cultural Dynamics and Diversity", Paris School of Economics, Paris, France), *available at* www.cepr.org/meets/wkcn/2/2393/papers/Benhamou.pdf (last visited 2 February 2012)

BENKLER, Y., "Intellectual Property and the Organization of Information Production", 22 *International Review of Law and Economics* 81 (2002)

——, "Through the Looking Glass: Alice and the Constitutional Foundations of the Public Domain", 66 *Law and Contemporary Problems* 173 (2003)

BEPPU, D., "When Cultural Value Justifies Protectionism: Interpreting the Language of the GATT to Find a Limited Cultural Exception to the National Treatment Principle", 29 *Cardozo Law Review* 1765 (2008)

BERGSTEN, C.F., "Speech before the Trilateral Commission: The Backlash against Globalization" (9 May 2000), *available at* www.petersoninstitute.org/publications/papers/paper.cfm?ResearchID=377 (last visited 2 February 2012)

BERNIER, I., "Cultural Goods and Services in International Trade Law", in D. BROWNE, ed., *The Culture/Trade Quandary – Canada's Policy Options*, 1998, 108

——, "La première réunion d'experts gouvernementaux sur l'avant-projet de convention sur la protection de la diversité des contenus culturels et des expressions artistiques de l'UNESCO: Les implications pour la suite de la négociation" (2004), *available at* www.diversite-culturelle.qc.ca/fileadmin/documents/pdf/chronique04–12.pdf (last visited 2 February 2012)

——, "Trade and Culture," in P.F.J. MACRORY, A.E. APPLETON, and M.G. PLUMMER (eds.), *The World Trade Organization. Legal, Economic and Political Analysis*, 2005, Vol. III, 747

——, "An Important Aspect of the Implementation of the Convention on the Protection and Promotion of the Diversity of Cultural Expressions: the International Fund for Cultural Diversity"" (2007), *available at* www.diversite-culturelle.qc.ca/fileadmin/documents/pdf/fonds-diversite-culturelle-eng.pdf (last visited 2 February 2012)

——, "The Unesco Convention on the Protection and Promotion of the Diversity of Cultural Expressions: A Cultural Instrument at the Junction of Law and Politics" (2008), *available at* www.diversite-culturelle.qc.ca//documents//du-droit_eng.pdf (last visited 2 February 2012)

BETTIG, R.V., "Concentration in the Copyright Industries", in P.K. YU (ed.), *Intellectual Property and Information Wealth: Issues and Practices in the Digital Age*, Vol. I (Copyright and Related Rights), 2007, 361

BHAGWATI, J., "Culture and Trade: America's Blindspot", in J. BHAGWATI (ed.), *The Wind of the Hundred Days: How Washington Mismanaged Globalization*, 2002, 209

BHALA, R., "Clarifying the Trade-Labor Link", 37 *Columbia Journal of Transnational Law* 11 (1998)

BOILEAU, J., "Baroud d'honneur", *Le Devoir* (12 October 2005), *available at* www.ledevoir.com//10//92377.html. (last visited 2 February 2012)

Bonnet, H., "L'œuvre de l'institut international de coopération intellectuelle", 61 *Recueil des Cours* 457 (1937)

Boswell, J., *Boswell's Life of Johnson*, Ch. G. Osgood (ed.), 1917, *available at* www.gutenberg.org/files/1564/1564-h/1564-h.htm (last visited 2 February 2012)

Boyle, A. and Freestone, D., "Introduction", in A. Boyle and D. Freestone (eds.), *International Law and Sustainable Development* 12 (1999)

Brooks, E., Note, "Cultural Imperialism vs. Cultural Protectionism: Hollywood's Response to UNESCO Efforts to Promote Cultural Diversity", 5 *Journal of International Business and Law* 112 (2006)

Broude, T., "Taking 'Trade and Culture' Seriously: Geographical Indications and Cultural Protection in WTO Law", 26 *University of Pennsylvania Journal of International Economic Law* 623 (2005)

——, "Conflict and Complementarity in Trade, Cultural Diversity and Intellectual Property Rights", 2 *Asian Journal of WTO & International Health Law and Policy* 345 (2007)

Bruner, C.M., "Culture, Sovereignty, and Hollywood: UNESCO and the Future of Trade in Cultural Products", 40 *New York Journal of International Law and Policy* 351 (2008)

Buchsbaum, J., "'The *Exception Culturelle* is Dead.' Long Live Cultural Diversity: French Cinema and the New Resistance", 47 *Framework: The Journal of Cinema and Media* 5 (2006)

Burri-Nenova, M., "Trade and Culture: Making the WTO Legal Framework Conducive to Cultural Considerations", 5 *Manchester Journal of International Economic Law* 2 (2008)

Buzzini, G. P., and Condorelli, L., "List of World Heritage in Danger", in Francioni (ed., with Lenzerini), *Commentary to the 1972 World Heritage Convention*, 2008, 175

Carmody, C., "When 'Cultural Identity was not at Issue': Thinking About Canada – Certain Measures Concerning Periodicals", 30 *Law & Policy in International Business* 231 (1999)

Castonguay, A., "151 Countries Support UNESCO's Draft Convention on the Diversity of Cultural Expressions. Only the U.S. and Israel Voted Against It", *Le Devoir* (18 October 2005), *available at* www.ledevoir.com//10/18/92872.html (last visited 2 February 2012)

Chiang, E.H., "The UNESCO Convention on the Protection and Promotion of the Diversity of Cultural Expressions: A Look at the Convention and Its Potential Impact on the American Movie Industry", 6 *Washington University of Global Studies Law Review* 379 (2007)

Choe Sang-Hun, "As Surprised Opponents Protest, South Korea Pushes U.S. Trade Pact Through Parliament", *The New York Times* 10 (23 November 2011)

Choi, W.-M., "Screen Quota and Cultural Diversity: Debates in Korea-US FTA Talks and Convention on Cultural Diversity", 2 *Asian Journal of WTO & International Health Law & Policy Journal* 267 (2007)

Craufurd Smith, R., "Community Intervention in the Cultural Field: Continuity or Change?", in R. Craufurd Smith (ed.), *Culture and European Union Law*, 2004, 19

——, "From Heritage Conservation to European Identity: Article 151 EC and the Multi-faceted Nature of Community Cultural Policy", 32 *European Law Review* 48 (2007)

——, "The UNESCO Convention on the Protection and Promotion of the Diversity of Cultural Expressions: Building a New World Information and Communication Order?", 1 *International Journal of Communication* 24 (2007)

Cremona, M., "Defending the Community Interest: The Duties of Cooperation and Compliance", in M. Cremona and B. de Witte (eds.), *EU Foreign Relations Law – Constitutional Fundamentals*, 2008, 125

Coalition Française pour la Diversité Culturelle, "The French Coalition Hail Successful Conclusion of UNESCO Negotiations for Treaty on Cultural Diversity in spite of the Hostility of the United States, 8 June 2005", 5(19) *The Diversity of Cultural Expressions Newsletter* (Archives) (20 June 2005), *available at* www.diversite-culturelle.qc.ca/index.php?id=110&L=1&tx_bulletinsirre_pi1[year]=2005&tx_bulletinsirre_pi1[idbulletin]=32&cHash=be3338b4f4 (last visited 2 February 2012)

Cocq, E. and Lévy, F., "Les Marchés Audiovisuels Dans les Pays en Développement. Bilan Statistique Centré Sur 11 pays – Chine, Corée du Sud, Inde, Philippines, Thaïlande, Costa Rica, Mexique, Salvador, Burkina Faso, Sénégal, Nigeria", in UNESCO, *Tendances des Marchés Audiovisuels: – Perspectives Régionales – Vues du Sud, CI/COM/2006/PUB/10*, 2006

Coleman, E., "Cultural Property and Collective Identity", in S. Herbrechter and M. Higgins (eds), *Returning (to) Communities: Theory, Culture and Political Practice of the Communal*, 2006, 161

Coombe, R., "Protecting Cultural Industries to Promote Cultural Diversity: Dilemmas for International Policymaking Posed by the Recognition of Traditional Knowledge", in K. Maskus and J. Reichman (eds.), *International Public Goods and Transfer of Technology Under a Globalized Intellectual Property Regime*, 2005, 599

Cooper, W.H. (coordinator), "The U.S.-South Korea Free Trade Agreement (KORUS FTA): Provisions and Implications", *CRS Report for Congress* 41 (30 November 2011), *available at* http://fpc.state.gov///.pdf (last visited 2 February 2012)

Cottier, T., "Die völkerrechtlichen Rahmenbedingungen der Filmförderung in der neuen Welthandelsorganization WTO-GATT", 38 *Zeitschrift für Urheber- und Medienrecht* 749 (1994)

Cowen, T., "French Kiss-Off: How Protectionism Has Hurt French Films", *Reason*, July 1998, *available at* www.reason.com/news/show/30691.html (last visited 2 February 2012)

Cunningham, C.B., "In Defense of Member States Culture: The Unrealised Potential of Article 151(4) of the EC Treaty and the Consequences for EC Cultural Policy", 34 *Cornell International Law Journal* 119 (2001)

Curtis, J.S., "Culture and the Digital Copyright Chimera: Assessing the International Regulatory System of the Music Industry in Relation to Cultural Diversity", 13 *International Journal of Cultural Property* 59 (2006)

Das, D.K., "Debacle at Seattle: The Way the Cookie Crumbled", 34 *Journal of World Trade* 181 (2000)

DATTU, R., Journey from Havana to Paris: The Fifty-Year Quest for the Elusive Multilateral Agreement on Investment", 24 *Fordham International Law Journal* 275 (2000)

DEACON, H., *Legal and Financial Instruments for Safeguarding our Intangible Heritage*, available at www.international.icomos.org/victoriafalls2003/papers/C3–2%20-%20 Deacon.pdf (last visited 2 February 2012)

DEMSETZ, H., "The Private Production of Public Goods", 13 *Journal of Law and Economics* 293 (1970)

DE SCHUTTER, O., and TULKENS, F., "Rights in Conflict: the European Court of Human Rights as a Pragmatic Institution", in E. BREMS (ed.), *Conflicts Between Fundamental Rights*, 2008, 169

DE WITTE, B., "The Cultural Dimension of Community Law", in Academy of European Law (ed.), *Collected Courses of the Academy of European Law*, Vol. IV-1, 1993, 229

——, "Trade in Culture: International Legal Regimes and EU Constitutional Values", in G. DE BÚRCA and J. SCOTT (eds.), *The EU and the WTO: Legal and Constitutional Issues*, 2001, 237

——, "Non-Market Values in Internal Market Legislation", in N.N. SHUIBHNE (ed.), *Regulating the Internal Market*, 2006, 61

DICKSON, D.M., "September Trade Gap Widened 18.2 Percent", *The Washington Times* 1 (14 November 2009)

DIETZ, A., "Cultural Diversity and Copyright", 16 *Les Cahiers de propriété intellectuelle (Hors série)* 109 (2004)

DJIAN, J.-M., "Un laboratoire devitalise", *Le Monde Diplomatique* 26 (October 2005), *available at* www.monde-diplomatique.fr//10/DJIAN/12801 (last visited 2 February 2012)

DONALDSON, J.D., "'Television Without Frontier': The Continuing Tension Between Liberal Free Trade and European Cultural Integrity", 20 *Fordham International Law Journal* 90 (1996)

DONDERS, Y., "The legal framework of the right to take part in cultural life", in Y. DONDERS AND VL. VOLODIN (eds.), *Human Rights in Education, Science and Culture: Legal Developments and Challenges*, 2007, 231

——, "The History of the UNESCO Convention on the Protection and Promotion of the Diversity of Cultural Expressions", in H. SCHNEIDER and P. VAN DEN BOSSCHE (eds.), *Protection of Cultural Diversity from a European and International Perspective*, 2008, 1

DOUGLAS, N., "Political Structures, Social Interaction and Identity Changes in Northern Ireland", in B. GRAHAM (ed.), *In Search of Ireland: A Cultural Geography*, 1997, 151

DOWD, T.J., "Concentration and Diversity Revisited: Production Logics and the U.S. Mainstream Recording Market, 1940–1990", 82 *Social Forces* 1411 (2004)

DU PLESSIS, A. and RAUTENBACH, C., "Legal Perspectives on the Role of Culture in Sustainable Development" 13 *Potchefstroom Electronic Law Journal* 26 (2010)

DUPUY, P.-M., "A Doctrinal Debate in the Globalization Era: On the "Fragmentation" of International Law", 1 *European Journal of Legal Studies* 1 (2007)

EHRING, L., "GATT Article IV", in R. WOLFRUM and P.-T. STOLL (eds.), *Max Planck Commentaries on World Trade Law*, Vol. 5, 2009

Elliott, L. and Luce, E., "US and Europe Clear Obstacles to GATT Deal", *The Guardian (London)* 1 (15 December 1993)

Faini, R., de Melo, J. and Zimmermann, K.F., "Trade and migration: an introduction", in R. Faini and J. de Melo & K.F. Zimmermann (eds.), *Migration – The Controversies and the Evidence*, 1999, 1

Francioni, F., "Thirty Years On: Is the World Heritage Convention Ready for the 21st Century?", XII *Italian Yearbook of International Law* 13 (2002)

Ferri, D., "EU Participation in the UNESCO Convention on the Protection and Promotion of the Diversity of Cultural Expressions: Some Constitutional Remarks", 3 *European Diversity and Autonomy Papers – EDAP* (2005), *available at* www.eurac.edu/documents/edap/2005_edap03.pdf (last visited 2 February 2012)

——, "Preamble", in Francioni (ed., with Lenzerini), *Commentary to the 1972 World Heritage Convention*, 2008, 11

——, and Lenzerini, F., "The Future of the World Heritage Convention: Problems and Prospects", in Francioni (ed., with Lenzerini), *Commentary to the 1972 World Heritage Convention*, 2008, 401

Farnsworth, C.H., "U.S. is Changing Its Tune on Liberalization of Trade", *New York Times* (29 October 1990), *available at* www.nytimes.com/1990/10/29/business/international-report-us-is-changing-itstune- (last visited 2 February 2012)

Filipek, J., ""Culture Quotas": The Trade Controversy over the European Community's Broadcasting Directive", 28 *Stanford Journal of International Law* 323 (1992)

Footer, M.E. and Graber, C.B., "Trade Liberalization and Cultural Policy", 3 *Journal of International Economic Law* 115 (2000)

Formentini, S. and Iapadre, L., "Cultural Diversity and Regional Trade Agreements: The Case of Audiovisual Services" (2006), *available at* www.etsg.org///.pdf (last visited 2 February 2012)

Frankel, S., "Trademarks and Traditional Knowledge and Cultural Intellectual Property", in G.B. Dinwoodie and M.D. Janis (eds.), *Trademark Law and Theory: A Handbook of Contemporary Research*, 2008, 433

Frey, B. and Stutzer, A., "What Can Economists Learn From Happiness Research?", 40 *Journal of Economic Literature* 402 (2002)

Frye, T. and Shleifer, A., "The Invisible Hand and the Grabbing Hand", 87 *American Economics Review* 354 (1997)

Fu, W.W., "Concentration and Homogenization of International Movie Sources: Examining Foreign Film Import Profiles", 56 *Journal of Communication* 813 (2006)

——, and Sim, C., "Examining International Country-to-Country Flow of Theatrical Films", 60 *Journal of Communication* 120 (2010)

Fullman, A.R., "Reconcilable Differences: The United States versus the Canadian Perspective Towards UNESCO's Convention on the Protection of the Diversity of Cultural Contents and Artistic Expressions" (Master's Thesis, George Mason University, December 2005), *available at* www.aimeefullman.com/Reconciliable_Differencespdf.pdf (last visited 2 February 2012)

Galenskaya, L., "International Co-operation in Cultural Affairs", 198 *Recueil des Cours* 265 (1986)

Gao, H., "The Mighty Pen, the Almighty Dollar, and the Holy Hammer and Sickle: An examination of the conflict between trade liberalization and domestic cultural policy with special regard to the recent dispute between the US and China on restrictions on certain cultural products", 2 *Asian Journal of WTO & International Health Law and Policy* 313 (2007)

Garnham, N., "Afterword: The Cultural Commodity and Cultural Policy", in S. Selwood (ed.), *The UK Cultural Sector: Profile and Policy Issues*, 2001, 445

Germann, Ch., "Diversité culturelle à l'OMC et l'UNESCO à l'example du cinéma" (2004) *Revue Internationale de Droit Économique* 325

——, "Towards a *Global Cultural Contract* to Counter Trade Related Cultural Discrimination", in N. Obuljen and J. Smiers (eds.), *The UNESCO Convention on the promotion and protection of the diversity of cultural expressions: Making it work*, 2006, 286

Gervais, D.J., "Collective Management of Copyright and Neighbouring Rights in Canada: An International Perspective", 1(2) *Canadian Journal of Law and Technology* 21 (2002)

Gordon, W.J., "A Property Right in Self Expression: Equality and Individualism in the Natural Law of Intellectual Property", 102 *Yale Law Journal* 1533 (1993)

Gottselig, G.A., "Canada and Culture: Can Current Cultural Policies Be Sustained in the Global Trade Regime?", 5 *International Journal of Commercial Law and Policy* 1 (2000)

Graber, Ch.B., "The New UNESCO Convention on Cultural Diversity: a Counterbalance to the WTO?", 9 *Journal of International Economic Law* 553 (2006)

——, "Substantive Rights and Obligations under the UNESCO Convention on Cultural Diversity", in H. Schneider and P. Van den Bossche (eds.), *Protection of Cultural Diversity from a European and International Perspective*, 2008, 141

Grosheide, F.W., "Cultural Diversity and Copyright Law: Between Good Intentions and Better Functioning", 5 (6–7 October 2008) (paper presented at the "2008 ALAI Conference on Cultural Diversity: Its Effects on Authors and Performers in the Context of Globalisation", Dubrovnik, Croatia), *available at* www2.law.uu.nl/priv/cier/Documenten/Worddoceng/ALAICONFERENCE2008DUBROVNIK CROATIA22%20final.doc (last visited 2 February 2012)

Grossman, G. and Sykes, A., "United States – Definitive Safeguard Measures on Imports of Certain Steel Products", 6 *World Trade Review* 89 (2007)

Guerrier, J., "Négociations commerciales: la position de l'Union Européenne quant aux services audiovisuels", in C. B. Graber, M. Girsberger and M. Nenova (eds.), *Free Trade versus Cultural Diversity*, 2004, 132

Hafner, G., "Pros and Cons Ensuing from Fragmentation of International Law", 25 *Michigan Journal of International Law* 849 (2004)

Hahn, M., "A Clash of Cultures? The UNESCO Diversity Convention and International Trade Law", 9 *Journal of International Economic Law* 515 (2006)

Hall, S., "Whose Heritage? Un-settling 'the Heritage', Re-Imaging the Post-Nation", in J. Littler and R. Naidoo (eds.), *The Politics of Heritage: The Legacies of 'Race'*, 2005, 25

Hanson, G.H. and Xiang, Ch., "International Trade in Motion Picture Services" (January 2008), *available at* http://irpshome.ucsd.edu/faculty/gohanson/TradeinServicesNBER2008.PDF (last visited 2 February 2012)

Handler, R., "Who Owns the Past? History, Cultural Property, and the Logic of Possessive Individualism", in B. Williams (ed.), *The Politics of Culture*, 1991, 63

HARDIN, G., "The Tragedy of the Commons", 162 *Science* 1243 (1968)

HARTLEY, J., "Creative Industries", in J. HARTLEY (ed.), *Creative Industries*, 2005, 1

HAZUCHA, B. and KONO, T., "Conceptualization of Community as a Holder of Intangible Cultural Heritage", in T. KONO (ed.), *Intangible Cultural Heritage and Intellectual Property: Communities, Cultural Diversity and Sustainable Development*, 2009, 145

——, "Community as a Holder of Intangible Cultural Heritage: A Broader Public Policy Perspective", in T. KONO (ed.), *Intangible Cultural Heritage and Intellectual Property: Communities, Cultural Diversity and Sustainable Development*, 2009, 223

——, "Intellectual Property and Cultural Diversity: Two Views on the Relationship between Market and Culture", 26 *Intellectual Property Law and Policy Journal* 39 (2010), *available at*: http://papers.ssrn.com//.cfm?abstract_id=1470103) (last visited 2 February 2012) (English version)

HEYD, D., "Cultural Diversity and Biodiversity: A Tempting Analogy", 13 *Critical Review of International Social and Political Philosophy* 159 (2010)

HILLION, C., "Mixity and Coherence in EU External Relations: The Significance of the 'Duty of Cooperation'" (Centre for the Law of EU External Relations, CLEER Working Papers 2009/2)

——, "Mixity and Coherence in EU External Relations: The Significance of the Duty of Cooperation", in C. HILLION and P. KOUTRAKOS (eds.), *Mixed Agreements Revisited: The EU and its Member States in the World*, 2010, 87

HOLBROOK, M.B. and ADDIS, M., "Art Versus Commerce in the Movie Industry: A Two-Path Model of Motion-Picture Success", 32 *Journal of Cultural Economics* 87 (2008)

HUGHES, J., "The Philosophy of Intellectual Property", 77 *Georgetown Law Journal* 287 (1988)

——, "Copyright and Incomplete Historiographies: Of Piracy, Propertization, and Thomas Jefferson", 79 *Southern California Law Review* 993 (2006)

HUNTINGTON, S.P., "The Clash of Civilizations" 72 *Foreign Affairs* 22 (1993)

HUGENHOLTZ, P.B., GUIBAULT, L. and VAN GEFFEN, S., *The Future of Levies in a Digital Environment*, 2003, *available at* www.ivir.nl/publications/other/DRM&levies-report.pdf (last visited 2 February 2012)

HYUN-KYUNG KIM, C., "Building the Korean Film Industry's Competitiveness: Abolish the Screen Quota and Subsidize the Film Industry", 9 *Pacific Rim Law and Policy Journal* 353 (2000)

KAWASHIMA, N., "The Artist's Resale Right Revisited: A New Perspective", 14 *International Journal of Cultural Policy* (2008)

KISH, K.A., "Protectionism to Promote Culture: South Korea and Japan, a Case Study", 22 *University of. Pennsylvania Journal of International Economic Law* 153 (2001)

KOCKEL, U., "Reflexive Traditions and Heritage Production", in U. KOCKEL and M.N. CRAITH (eds.), *Cultural Heritages as Reflexive Traditions*, 2007, 28

KONO, T., "UNESCO and Intangible Cultural Heritage from the Viewpoint of Sustainable Development", in A. A. YUSUF (ed.), *Standard Setting in UNESCO: Normative Action in Education, Science and Culture*, 2007, 237

——, "The UNESCO Convention for the Protection and the Promotion of the Diversity of Cultural Expressions", in K. ALEXANDER and M. ANDENAS (eds.), *The World Trade Organization and Trade in Services*, 2008, 846

KAUFMAN, A., "Is Foreign Film the New Endangered Species?", *The New York Times* 23 (22 January 2006)

KHACHATURIAN, A., "The New Cultural Diversity Convention and its Implications on the WTO International Trade Regime: A Critical Comparative Analysis", 42 *Texas International Law Journal* 191 (2006)

KIM, J., "The Viability of Screen Quotas in Korea: The Cultural Exception under the International Trade Regime", 26 *Korean Journal of International and Comparative Law* 199 (1998)

KLAMER, A., "Cultural Goods Are Good for More than Their Economic Value", in V. RAO and M. WALTON (eds.), *Culture and Public Action*, 2004, 138

KLEIN, J., "What are Motion Pictures doing for Industry?", 128 *Annals of the American Academy of Political & Social Science* 79 (1926)

KNIGHT, J., "Trade in Higher Education Services: *The Implications of GATS*", *The Observatory on Borderless Education* (March 2002), *available at* http://firgoa.usc.es//files/.pdf (last visited 2 February 2012)

KUR, A. and KNAAK, R., "Protection of Traditional Names and Designations", S. VON LEWINSKI (ed.), *Indigenous Heritage and Intellectual Property: Genetic Resources, Traditional Knowledge and Folklore*, 2nd ed., 2008, 293

LANDLER, M. and WONG, W., "China Says Clinton Harms Relations With Criticism of Internet Censorship", *The New York Times* 4 (23 January 2010)

LEMAISTRE, A. and LENZERINI, F., "Articles 19–26: International Assistance", in F. Francioni (ed., with LENZERINI), *Commentary to the 1972 World Heritage Convention*, 2008, 305

LEE, S.Y., KIM E.-M. and KIM, Y.I., "The Effect of the Korean Screen Quota System on Box Office Performance", 42 *Journal of World Trade* 335 (2008)

——, KIM E-M and JUN, S.H., "On the Exportability of Korean Movies", 13 *Review of Development Economics* 28 (2009)

——, LEE, J. and SOHN, K.H., "The United States – Korea Free Trade Agreement: Path to Common Economic Prosperity or False Promise?", 6 *University of Pennsylvania East Asia Law Review* 112 (2011)

LENZERINI, F., "Lo 'sfruttamento minerario sostenibile' come principio emergente nel diritto internazionale contemporaneo" ['Sustainable Mining' as Emerging Principle of Contemporary International Law], 1 *Rivista Giuridica dell'Ambiente* 165 (2004)

——, "Article 12: Protection of Properties Not Inscribed on the World Heritage List", in F. FRANCIONI (ed., with LENZERINI), *Commentary to the 1972 World Heritage Convention*, 2008, 201

——, "Articles 15–16: World Heritage Fund", in F. Francioni (ed., with LENZERINI), *Commentary to the 1972 World Heritage Convention*, 2008, 269

LEUPRECHT, P., "International Law: The Difficult Acceptance of Diversity", 30 *Vermont Law Review* 551 (2006)

LIEBOWITZ, S.J. and R. WATT, R., "How To Best Ensure Remuneration for Creators in the Market for Music?: Copyright and Its Alternatives", 20 *Journal of Economic Surveys* 513 (2006)

LOCKHART, N. and MITCHELL, A., "Regional Trade Agreements under GATT 1994: An Exception and its Limits", in A. MITCHELL (ed.), *Challenges and Prospects for the WTO*, 2005, 217

LOISEN, J. and DE VILLE, F., "The EU-Korea Protocol on Cultural Cooperation: Toward Cultural Diversity or Cultural Deficit?" 5 *International Journal of Communication* 254 (2011)

LUBINA, K. and SCHNEIDER, H., "The Implementation of Droit de Suite – Inventory and Reflection in the Light of the Community's Cultural Competence", in H. SCHNEIDER and P. VAN DEN BOSSCHE (eds.), *Protection of Cultural Diversity from a European and International Perspective*, 2008, 317

LUCE, E., "The Deal: High Price of Accord in Services Package", *The Guardian (London)* 12 (15 December 1993)

MACEY, J.R., "New Theories of the Regulatory Statecynicism and Trust in Politics and Constitutional Theory", 87 *Cornell Law Review* 280 (2002)

MACMILLAN, F., "The UNESCO Convention as a New Incentive to Protect Cultural Diversity", in H. SCHNEIDER and P. VAN DEN BOSSCHE (eds.), *Protection of Cultural Diversity from a European and International Perspective*, 2008,163

MAGDER, T., "Franchising the Candy Store: Split-Run Magazines and a New International Regime for Trade in Culture", *Canadian-American Public Policy* No. 34 (1998)

MARCEAU, G., "WTO Dispute Settlement and Human Rights", 13(4) *European Journal of International Law* 753 (2002)

MARKS, S., "Defining Cultural Rights", in M. BERGSMO (ed.), *Human Rights and Criminal Justice for the Downtrodden – Essays in Honour of Asbjorn Eide*, 2003, 293

MATSUMOTO, S., "Performers in the Digital Era: Empirical Evidence from Japan", in R. TOWSE (ed.), *Copyright in the Cultural Industries*, 2002, 196

MATTOO, A., "National Treatment in the GATS: Corner-Stone or Pandora's Box?", 31 *Journal of World Trade* 107 (1997)

MATTELART, A., "Cultural Diversity Belongs to Us All", *Le Monde Diplomatique* (15 November 2005), *available at* http://mondediplo.com/2005/11/15/15unesco (last visited 2 February 2012)

MAUERHOFER, V., "3-D Sustainability: An Approach for Priority Setting in Situation of Conflicting Interests Towards Sustainable Development", 64 *Ecological Economics* 496 (2008)

MCCAIN, R., "Defining Cultural and Artistic Goods", in V.A. GINSBURGH and D. THROSBY (eds.), *Handbook of the Economics of Art and Culture*, 2006, 147

MCCLINTOCK, P., "MPAA Specialty Films See Rising Costs", *Variety* (2008), *available at* www.variety.com/article/VR1117981882.html?categoryid=13&cs=1 (last visited 2 February 2012)

MCMILLAN, J., "A Game-Theoretic View of International Trade Negotiations: Implications for the Developing Countries", in K. ANDERSON and B. HOEKMAN, *The Global Trading System*, Vol. 2, 2002, 184

MERRYMAN, J.H., "The Proposed Generalisation of the Droit do Suite in the European Communities", 1 *Intellectual Property Quarterly* 16 (1997)

MITCHELL, A., "A Legal Principle of Special & Differential Treatment for WTO Disputes?" 5 *World Trade Review* 445 (2006)

——, and VOON, T., "Operationalizing Special and Differential Treatment in the WTO: Game Over?" 15 *Global Governance* 343 (2009)

MEYER-BISCH, P., "Les Droits Culturels, Forment-Ils une Catégorie Spécifique de Droits de L'Homme?", in P. MEYER-BISCH (ed.), *Les Droits Culturels, une Catégorie Sous-Développée de Droits de L'Homme, Actes du VIIIe Colloque interdisciplinaire sur les droits de l'homme*, 1993, 17

MOSLER, H., "General Principles of Law", in R. BERNHARDT (ed.), *Encyclopaedia of Public International Law*, 1984, Vol. 7, 89

MURRAY, T.M., "The U.S.-French Dispute over GATT Treatment of Audiovisual Products and the Limits of Public Choice Theory: How an Efficient Market Solution was 'Rent-seeking'", 21 *Maryland Journal of International Law and Trade* 203 (1997)

MUSITELLI, J., "La Convention sur la diversité culturelle: anatomie d'un succès diplomatique" 62 *Revue internationale et stratégique* 10 (2006), *available at* www.diplomatie.gouv.fr//IMG/pdf/0701-MUSITELLI-EN.pdf (last visited 2 February 2012) (English version)

NADEL, M.S., "How Current Copyright Law Discourages Creative Output: The Overlooked Impact of Marketing", 19 *Berkeley Technology Law Journal* 785 (2004)

NETANEL, N.W., "Copyright and a Democratic Civil Society", 106 *Yale Law Journal* 283 (1996)

NETANEL, N.M., "Copyright and 'Market Power' in the Marketplace of Ideas", in F. LÉVÊQUE and H. SHELANSKI (eds.), *Antitrust, Patents and Copyright: EU and US Perspectives*, 2005, 149

NEUWIRTH, R.J., "The Cultural Industries and the Role of Article IV GATT: Reflections on Policy Options for Canada and the EU in the new WTO Round" (2002), *available at* http://papers.ssrn.com//.cfm?abstract_id=1352171 (last visited 2 February 2012)

——, "'United in Divergence': A Commentary on the UNESCO Convention on the Promotion and Protection of the Diversity of Cultural Expressions", 66 *Heidelberg Journal of International Law* 819 (2006)

——, "The European Union and the Culture Industries: From the Common Market to a 'Common Sense'", in D. WARD (ed.), *The European Union & the Culture Industries: Regulation and the Public Interest*, 2008, 241

——, "Der WTO-Bericht zu China – Measures Affecting the Protection and Enforcement on Intellectual Property Rights: ein Kommentar", 58 *Gewerblicher Rechtsschutz und Urheberrecht, Internationaler Teil* 367 (2009)

——, "A Constitutional Tribute to Global Governance: Overcoming the Chimera of the Developing-Developed Country Dichotomy", *European University Institute (EUI) Working Paper LAW* 2010/20 (2010)

——, "The 'Culture and Trade Debate' Continues: The UNESCO Convention in Light of the WTO Reports in China – Publications and Audiovisual Products: Between Amnesia or Déjà Vu?", 44 *Journal of World Trade* 1333 (2010)

——, "(De)Regulating the Creative Economy", 1 *Journal of Creative and Knowledge Society* 44 (2011)

OBULJEN, N., "From Our Creative Diversity to the Convention on Cultural Diversity", in N. OBULJEN AND J. SMIERS (eds.), *UNESCO's Convention on the Protection and Promotion of the Diversity of Cultural Expressions: Making It Work*, 2006, 17

O'Connor, J., "The Definition of the Cultural Industries", 2(3) *European Journal of Arts Education* 15 (2000)
Oppenheimer, A., "Cultural War is Taking Aim at Hollywood", *The Miami Herald* (22 January 2006)
Oppetit, B., "Les tendances régressives dans l'évolution du droit contemporain", in J.-F. Pillebout (ed.), *Mélanges dédiés à Dominique Holleaux*, 1990, 317
Pager, S.A., "Beyond Culture vs. Commerce: Decentralizing Cultural Protection to Promote Diversity Through Trade", 31 *Northwestern Journal of International Law and Business* 63 (2011)
Pagniet, G., "Industries de la culture et développement", 194 *Le Courrier ACP* 42 (2002)
Paterson, R.K. and Karjala, D.S., "Looking Beyond Intellectual Property in Resolving Protection of the Intangible Cultural Heritage of Indigenous Peoples", 11 *Cardozo Journal of International and Comparative Law* 633 (2003)
Peeperkorn, L. and Verouden, V., "The Economics of Competition", in J. Faull and A. Nikpay (eds.), *The EC Law of Competition*, 2007, 3
Perlmutter, S., "Resale Royalties for Artists: An Analysis of the Register of Copyright's Report", 16 *Columbia-VLA Journal of Law and the Arts* 395 (1993)
Pessach, G., "Copyright Law as a Silencing Restriction on Noninfringing Materials: Unveiling the Scope of Copyright's Diversity Externalities", 76 *Southern Caifornia Law Review* 1067 (2003)
Petit, M., "UNESCO Approves the Convention on Cultural Diversity", *Broadcasting Regulation and Cultural Diversity* 1 (4 November 2005)
Phillips, V.J., "Reflections on Intellectual Property, Traditional Knowledge and Cultural Expressions: Indigenous Rights to Traditional Knowledge and Cultural Expressions: Implementing the Millennium Development Goals", 3 *Intercultural Human Rights Law Review* 191 (2008)
Piaskowski, N., "Collective Management in France", *in* D.J. Gervais (ed.), *Collective Management of Copyright and Related Rights*, 2006, 153
Pratt, A.C., "Cultural Industries and Public Policy: An Oxymoron", 11 *International Journal of Cultural Policy* 31 (2005)
Pretty, J., et al., "The Intersections of Biological Diversity and Cultural Diversity: Towards Integration", 7 *Conservation and Society* 100 (2009)
Price, M.E., "Government Policy and Economic Security for Artists: The Case for the Droit de Suite", 77 *Yale Law Journal* 1333 (1968)
Prott, L., "Cultural Rights as Peoples' Rights in International Law", in J. Crawford (ed.), *The Rights of Peoples*, 1998, 93
Psychogiopoulou, E., "The Cultural Mainstreaming Clause of Article 151(4) EC: Protection and Promotion of Cultural Diversity or Hidden Cultural Agenda?", 12 *European Law Journal* 575 (2006)
——, "The 'Cultural' Criterion in the European Commission's Assessment of State Aids to the Audio-Visual Sector" 37 *Legal Issues of Economic Integration* 273 (2010)
Ranaivoson, H., "Measuring Cultural Diversity: A Review of Existing Definitions" (2007), *available at* www.uis.unesco.org/culture/Documents/Ranaivoson.pdf (last visited 2 February 2012)
Reddy, M.B., "The Droit de Suite: Why American Fine Artists Should Have the Right to a Resale Royalty", 15 *Loyola of Los Angelas Entertainment Law Review* 59 (1995)

Redgwell, C., "Article 2: Definition of Natural Heritage", in Francioni (ed., with Lenzerini), *Commentary to the 1972 World Heritage Convention*, 2008, 63

Régibeau, P. and Rockett, K., "The Relationship Between Intellectual Property Law and Competition Law: An Economic Approach", in S.D. Andermann (ed.), *The Interface Between Intellectual Property Rights and Competition Policy*, 2007, 505

Regourd, S., "Le Projet de Convention sur la Diversité Culturelle: Vers une Victoire à la Pyrrhus…", 226 *Légipresse* 115 (2005)

Rey, G., "Les Tendances et Perspectives du Marché Audiovisuel en Colombie, au Pérou et au Venezuela", *in* UNESCO, *Tendances des Marchés Audiovisuels: - Perspectives Régionales - Vues du Sud, CI/COM/2006/PUB/10*, 2006

Richieri Hanania, L. and Ruiz Fabri, H., "Comment on Article 8 and Comment on Article 17", in S. Von Shorlemer (ed.), *Commentary on the 2005 UNESCO Convention on the Protection and Promotion of the Diversity of Cultural Expressions*, 2012

Riding, A., "Next lone U.S. dissent: Cultural diversity pact", *The New York Times* (12 October 2005)

——, "U.S. all but alone in opposing Unesco cultural pact", *The New York Times* (20 October 2005), *available at* www.nytimes.com//10/20/world/americas/20iht-unesco.html (last visited 2 February 2012)

Ruiz Fabri, H., "Analyse et Commentaire Critique de l'Avant-Projet de Convention sur la Protection de la Diversité des Contenus Culturels et des Expressions Artistiques dans la Version Soumise pour Commentaires et Observations aux Gouvernements des Etats Membres de l'UNESCO" (2004), *available at* www.francophonie.org/IMG/pdf/Analyse_et_commentaire_av-projet_convention_protection_div_contenus_cult_et_expr_artistiques.pdf (last visited 2 February 2012)

——, "Reflections on Possible Future Legal Implications of the Convention", in N. Obuljen and J. Smiers (eds.), *The UNESCO Convention on the promotion and protection of the diversity of cultural expressions: Making it work*, 2006, 71

——, "Culture seized by globalization: can international law be of any help? Reflections on possible future legal implications of the UNESCO Convention on the protection and promotion of the diversity of cultural expressions", in A. Reinish and U. Kriebaum (eds.), *The Law of International Relations: Liber Amicorum Neuhold*, 2007, 299

——, "Jeux dans la Fragmentation: la Convention sur la promotion et la protection de la diversité des expressions culturelles" 111 *Revue Générale de Droit International Public* 43 (2007)

Roche, F., "Que reste-t-il de l'exception culturelle après Seattle?", 258 *Regards sur l'actualité* 13 (2000)

Rosenau, J.N., "Governance in the 21st Century", 1 *Global Governance* 13 (1995)

Rowlands, M., "Cultural Rights and Wrongs: Uses of the Concept of Property", in K. Verdery and C. Humphrey (eds.), *Property in Question: Value Transformation in the Global Economy*, 2004, 207

Roy, M., "Beyond the Main Screen: Audiovisual Services in PTAs", in J. A. Marchetti and M. Roy (eds.), *Opening Markets for Trade in Services: Countries and Sectors in Bilateral and WTO Negotiations*, 2009, 340

SALAMBÉRÉ, A., "Attentes des Pays du Sud à l'Égard d'une Convention sur la Diversité des Expressions Culturelles" (speech held at 'Le Dix-Huitièmes Entretiens' du Centre Jacques Cartier – Rhône-Alpes: Le Combat pour la Diversité Culturelle) (5 December 2005), *available at* www.diversite-culturelle.qc.ca/fileadmin/documents/pdf/salambere.pdf (last visited 2 February 2012)

SAUVÉ, P. and STEINFATT, K., "Towards Multilateral Rules on Trade and Commerce: Protective Regulation or Efficient Protection", in PRODUCTIVITY COMMISSION (ed.), *Achieving Better Regulation of Services*, 2001, 323, *available at* www.cid.harvard.edu/cidtrade/Papers/Sauve/sauveculture.pdf (last visited 2 February 2012)

SCAFIDI, S., "Intellectual Property and Fashion Design", in P.K. YU (ed.), *Intellectual Property and Information Wealth: Issues and Practices in the Digital Age*, Vol. I (Copyright and Related Rights), 2007, 115

SCHEPERS, St., "The Legal Force of the Preamble to the EEC Treaty", 6 *European Law Review* 356 (1981)

SCHLOEMANN, H.L. and OHLHOFF, St., "'Constitutionalization'and Dispute Settlement in the WTO: National Security as an Issue of Competence", 93 *American Journal of International Law* 424 (1999)

SCHOTT, J.J., BRADFORD, S.C. and MOLL, T., "Negotiating the Korea–United States Free Trade Agreement" 4 *Policy Briefs in International Economics* 1 (2006), available at www.iie.com/publications/pb/pb06-4.pdf (last visited 2 February 2012)

SCOVAZZI, T., "Articles 8–11: World Heritage Committee and World Heritage List", in FRANCIONI (ed., with LENZERINI), *Commentary to the 1972 World Heritage Convention*, 2008, 148

SCULLY, K., "The Most Dangerous Game: U.S. Opposition to the Cultural Exception", 36 *Brooklyn Journal of International Law* 1183 (2011)

SEARS, L.J., "Comment", 43 *Current Anthropology* 147 (2002)

SEVILLE, C., "Copyright in Perfumes: Smelling a Rat", 66 *Cambridge Law Journal* 49 (2007)

SINCLAIR, J., "Culture and Trade: Some Theoretical and Practical Considerations", in E.J. MCANANY and K. T. WILKINSON (eds.), *Mass Media and Free Trade: NAFTA and the Cultural Industries*, 1997, 38

SIWEK, S.E., *Engines of Growth: Economic Contributions of U.S. Intellectual Property Industries*, 2005, *available at* www.nbcuni.com/About_NBC_Universal/Intellectual_Property/pdf/Engines_of_Growth.pdf (last visited 2 February 2012)

SHAFFER, G.C. and POLLACK, M.A., "Hard vs. Soft Law: Alternatives, Complements, and Antagonists in International Governance", 94 *Minnesota Law Review* 706 (2010)

SLATTERY, E.K., "Preserving the United States' Intangible Cultural Heritage: An Evaluation of the 2003 UNESCO Convention for the Safeguarding of the Intangible Cultural Heritage as a Means to Overcome the Problems Posed by Intellectual Property Law", 16 *DePaul-LCA Journal of Art and Entertainment Law* 201 (2006)

SMIERS, J., "A Convention on Cultural Diversity: From WTO to UNESCO", *Media International Australia* 81 (2004), *available at* www.uq.edu.au/emsah/mia/issues/miacp111.html#smiers (last visited 2 February 2012)

SMITH, E., "'Avatar' Opens Strongly, in Test for Industry – James Cameron's 3-D Sci-Fi Movie, a Costly Bet on New Film-Making Technology, Takes in $232.2 Million Globally", *Wall Street Journal (Eastern edition)* B.6 (21 December 2009)

SMITH, J. A. and DALE, H., "Cultural Diversity and Freedom at Risk at UNESCO", *The Heritage Foundation Web Memo No. 885* (17 October 2005), *available at* www.heritage.org/Research/InternationalOrganizations/wm885.cfm. (last visited 2 February 2012)

SNEDDON, C., HOWARTH, R.B. and NORGAARD, R.B., "Sustainable Development in a Post-Brundtland World, 57 *Ecological Economics* 253 (2006)

SOHN, Y. and KOO, M.G., "Securitizing trade: the case of the Korea-US Free Trade Agreement", 11 *International Relations of the Asia-Pacific* 433 (2011)

STEIN, K.C.C., "The Management and Resolution of Cross Border Disputes as Canada/U.S. Enter the 21st Century: Telecommunications and Culture: Transborder Freedom of Information or Cultural Identity?", 26 *Canadian – US Law Journal* 313 (2000)

STÉNOU, K., *UNESCO and the Issue of Cultural Diversity: Review and Strategy, 1946–2004* (2004), revised version, *available at* www.unesco.org/culture/culturaldiversity/docs_pre_2007/unesco_diversity_review_strategy_1946_2004_en.pdf (last visited 2 February 2012)

STOKES, B., "Tinseltown Trade War", 1991 *National Journal* 434

STOLL, P.-T. and VON HAHN, A., "Indigenous Peoples, Indigenous Knowledge and Indigenous Resources in International Law", in S. VON LEWINSKI (ed.), *Indigenous Heritage and Intellectual Property: Genetic Resources, Traditional Knowledge and Folklore*, 2nd ed., 2008, 7

SUNSTEIN, C.R., "Television and the Public Interest", 88 *California Law Review* 499 (2000)

SUTHERLAND, P. *et al.*, "The Future of WTO: Addressing Institutional Challenges in the New Millennium", (2004), *available at* www.wto.org/english/thewto_e/10anniv_e/future_wto_e.pdf (last visited 2 February 2012)

SYMONIDES, J., "Cultural Rights", in J. SYMONIDES (ed.), *Human Rights – Concepts and Standards*, 2000, 175

TAUBMAN, A., "Genetic Resources", in S. VON LEWINSKI (ed.), *Indigenous Heritage and Intellectual Property: Genetic Resources, Traditional Knowledge and Folklore*, 2nd ed., 2008, 181

TAYLOR, K., "Our Sad Little Stand to Protect Canadian Culture", *Globe and Mail* (4 June 2005), *available at* www.friends.ca/news-item/3254 (last visited 2 February 2012)

TAYLOR, M. and TOWSE, R., "The Value of Performers' rights: An Economic Approach", 20 *Media, Culture & Society* 631 (1998)

THOMAS, J., "US Deeply Disappointed by Vote on UNESCO Diversity Convention", *News Blaze*, 21 October 2005, *available at* http://newsblaze.com/story/20051021224840nnnn.nb/topstory.html (last visited 2 February 2012)

THROSBY, D., "Linking Culture and Development Models: Towards a Workable Concept of Culturally Sustainable Development", in World Commission on Culture and Development, Commissioned Paper (1994)

——, "Culture, Economics and Sustainability", 19 *Journal of Cultural Economics* 199 (1995)

——, "Linking Cultural and Ecological Sustainability", 8 *International Journal of Diversity in Organisations, Communities and Nations* 15 (2008)

——, "Culture in Sustainable Development: Insights for the Future Implementation of Art. 13", CE/08/Throsby/Art.13 (14 January 2008), *available at* http://unesdoc.unesco.org/images/0015/001572/157287e.pdf (last visited 2 February 2012)

——, "Modelling the Cultural Industries", 14 *International Journal of Cultural Policy* 217 (2008)

Tichenor, F.A., "Motion Pictures as Trade Getters", 128 *Annals of the American Academy of Political & Social Science* 84 (1926)

Towse, R., "Copyright and Economic Incentives: An Application to Performers' Rights in the Music Industry", 54 *KYKLOS* 369 (2001)

——, "Partly for the Money: Rewards and Incentive to Artists", 54 *KYKLOS* 473 (2001)

——, "Copyright and Cultural Policy for the Creative Industries", in O. Granstand (ed.), *Economic, Law and Intellectual Property: Seeking Strategies for Research and Teaching in a Developing Field*, 2003, 419

——, "Copyright and Artists: A View from Cultural Economics", 20 *Journal of Economic Surveys* 567 (2006)

——, "Copyright and Creativity: An Application of Cultural Economics", 3 *Review of Economic Research on Copyright Issues* 83 (2006)

——, "Human Capital and Artists' Labour Markets", in V. Ginsburgh and D. Throsby (eds.), *Handbook of the Economics of the Arts and Culture*, 2006, 865

——, "Why Has Cultural Economics Ignored Copyright?" 32 *Journal of Cultural Economics* 243 (2008)

Tsai Yu Lin, "Exploring the Link Between Trade and Cultural Protection in the Context of Anti-Dumping", 42 *Journal of World Trade* 563 (2008)

Trachtman, J.P., "Trade and… Problems, Cost-Benefit Analysis and Subsidiarity", 9 *European Journal of International Law* 32 (1998)

Udo, V.E. and Jansson, P.M., "Bridging the Gaps for Global Sustainable Development: A Quantitative Analysis", 90 *Journal of Environmental Management* 3700 (2009)

Vadi, V.S., "When Cultures Collide: Foreign Direct Investment, Natural Resources, and Indigenous Heritage in International Investment Law", 42 *Columbia Human Rights Law Review* 797 (2011)

van Beek, W.E.A. and Jara, F., "'Granular Knowledge'" Cultural Problems with Intellectual Property and Protection", in F.W. Grosheide and J.J. Brinkhof (eds.), *Intellectual Property Law 2002: Articles on Cultural Expressions and Indigenous Knowledge*, 2002, 35

Van Grasstek, C., "Le Traitement des Biens et des Services Culturels dans les Accords Commerciaux Internationaux", in UNESCO, *Tendances des Marchés Audiovisuels: – Perspectives Régionales – Vues du Sud, CI/COM/2006/PUB/10*, 2006

Vanhees, H., "Directive 2001/84/EC – Directive on the Resale Right for the Benefit of the Author of an Original Work of Art", in T. Dreier and B. Hugenholtz (eds.), *Concise European Copyright Law*, 2006, 405

Van Uytsel, S., "Inventory Making and Fairy Tales: Safeguarding of Intangible Cultural Heritage in Historical Perspective", in T. Kono (ed.), *Intangible Cultural Heritage and Intellectual Property: Communities, Cultural Diversity and Sustainable Development*, 2009, 113

——, and Kono, T., "Intangible Cultural Heritage Identified: Inventories as an Essential Part of the Safeguarding Process", in T. Kono (ed.), *Intangible Cultural Heritage and Intellectual Property: Communities, Cultural Diversity and Sustainable Development*, 2009, 43

——, "Philosophies Behind the Intangible Cultural Heritage Convention: Equality in Heritage Protection, Community Recognition and Cultural Diversity" (2012), *available at* http://papers.ssrn.com/sol3/papers.cfm?abstract_id=2001835 (last visited 2 February 2012)

Varona, A.E., "Changing Channels and Bridging Divides: The Failure and Redemption of American Broadcast Television Regulation" 6 *Minnesota Journal Journal of Law, Science and Technology* 1 (2004)

Veron, L., "Hollywood and Europe: A Case of Trade in Cultural Industries, the 1993 GATT Dispute" (Columbia International Affairs Online, Working Papers CIAO Date 4/99), *available at* www.ciaonet.org/wps/ue/vel (last visited 2 February 2012)

——, "La mise en œuvre de la Convention sur la diversité des expressions culturelles Portée et enjeux de l'interface entre le commerce et la culture", 42 *Revue Études internationales* 493 (2011)

Von Shorlemer, S., "Promoting International North-South Cooperation in the Framework of the UNESCO Convention on the Protection and Promotion of the Diversity of Cultural Expressions: First Steps 2007–2010" (document prepared for the conference on Cultural Diversity - Europe's Wealth. Bringing the UNESCO Convention to Life, 26–28 April 2007, Essen), *available at* www.unesco.org/culture/culturaldiversity/Schorlemer_essen_20070427_en.pdf (last visited 2 February 2012)

Voon, T., "UNESCO and the WTO: A Clash of Cultures?" 55 *International and Comparative Law Quarterly* 635 (2006)

Voon, T., "China - Measures Affecting Trading Rights and Distribution Services for Certain Publications and Audiovisual Entertainment Products", 103 *American Journal of International Law* 710 (2009)

——, "China and Cultural Products at the WTO", 37(3) *Legal Issues of Economic Integration* 253 (2010)

Wager, H., "Copyright and the Promotion of Cultural Diversity", in H. Schneider and P. Van den Bossche (eds.), *Protection of Cultural Diversity from a European and International Perspective*, 2008, 193

Wang, H., "What do Trading Rights and General Exceptions Mean for China? Some Observations of China-Audiovisual Services", 12 *Gonzaga Journal of International Law* 3 (2009)

Weinstock, N., "Asserting Copyright's Democratic Principles in the Global Arena", 51 *Vanderbilt Law Review* 217 (1998)

Wines, M., "China Issues Sharp Rebuke to U.S. Calls for an Investigation on Google Attacks", *The New York Times* 6 (26 January 2010)

Wouters, J. and De Meester, B., "UNESCO's Convention on Cultural Diversity WTO Law: Complementary or Contradictory?" (Institute for International Law, Working Paper No. 73, 2005)

——, "Cultural Diversity and the WTO: David Versus Goliath", in H. Schneider and P. Van den Bossche (eds.), *Protection of Cultural Diversity from a European and International Perspective*, 2008, 85

——, "The UNESCO Convention on Cultural Diversity and WTO Law: A Case Study in Fragmentation of International Law", 42 *Journal of World Trade* 205 (2008)

Wright, C., "Reconciling Cultural Diversity and Free Trade in the Digital Age: A Cultural Analysis of the International Trade in Content Items", 41 *Akron Law Review* 399 (2008)

X, "UNESCO Overwhelmingly Approves Cultural Diversity Treaty", 9(36) *BRIDGES Weekly Trade News Digest* (2005), *available at* http://ictsd.net/i/news/bridgesweekly/6211/ (last visited 2 February 2012)

X., "Google, don't be evil?", *Xinhuanet* (29 January 2010), *available at* http://news.xinhuanet.com///2010–01/29/c_13155970.htm (last visited 2 February 2012)

Yecies, B.M., "Parleying Culture Against Trade: Holywood's Affairs with Korea's Screen Quotas", 38 *Korea Observer* 1 (2007), *available at* http://ro.uow.edu.au/cgi/viewcontent.cgi?article=1119&context=artspapers (last visited 2 February 2012)

Yusuf, A.A., "Article 1: Definition of Cultural Heritage", in Francioni (ed., with Lenzerini), *Commentary to the 1972 World Heritage Convention*, 2008, 23

Yu, P.K., "Traditional Knowledge, Intellectual Property, and Indigenous Culture: An Introduction", 11 *Cardozo Journal of International & Comparative Law* 239 (2003)

——, "Cultural Relics, Intellectual Property, and Intangible Heritage", 81 *Temple Law Review* 433 (2008)

——, "Sinic Trade Agreements", 44 *University of California at Davis Law Review* 953 (2011)

Yupsanis, A., "The Concept and Categories of Cultural Rights in International Law – Their Broad Sense and the Relevant Clauses of the International Human Rights Treaties", 37 *Syracuse Journal of International & Commercial Law* 207 (2010)

3. DOCUMENTS AND REPORTS PREPARED BY GOVERNMENTAL ORGANIZATIONS, INTERNATIONAL ORGANIZATIONS AND NON-PROFIT ORGANIZATIONS

Agency for Cultural Affairs, "Administration of Cultural Affairs in Japan – Fiscal 2009", *available at* www.bunka.go.jp/english/index.html (last visited 2 February 2012)

Committee on Economic, Social and Cultural Rights, "General Comment No. 4, The Right to Adequate Housing", *E/1992/23* (1991)

——, "General Comment No. 12, The Right to Adequate Food", *E/C.12/1999/5* (1999)

——, "General Comment 13: The Right to Education", *E/C.12/1999/10* (1999)

——, "General Comment No. 14, The Right to the Highest Attainable Standard of Health", *E/C.12/2000/4* (2000)

——, "General Comment 15: The Right to Water", *UN Doc. E/C.12/2002/11* (2002)

——, "General Comment 17: The Right of Everyone to Benefit from the Protection of the Moral and Material Interests Resulting from any Scientific, Literary or Artistic Production of Which He or She is the Author", *UN Doc. E/C.12/GC/17* (2005)

——, "General Comment 18: The Right to Work", *UN Doc. E/C.12/GC/18* (2006)

Commission of the European Communities, "Proposal for a Council Decision on the Conclusion of the UNESCO Convention on the Protection and Promotion of the Diversity of Cultural Expressions", *COM (2005)* 678 (7 December 2005)

Communication by France, "For a new European Union external cultural strategy", December 2009, *available at* www.diplomatie.gouv.fr/fr/IMG/pdf/2009-12-21_Communication_France_Strategie_culturelle_exterieure_ENG.pdf (last visited 2 February 2012)

Communication from the Commission to the Council and the European Parliament, "Towards an International Instrument on Cultural Diversity", *COM (2003) 520* (27 August 2003)

Communication from the Commission to the European Parliament, the Council, the European Economic and Social Committee and the Committee of the Regions, "On a European Agenda for Culture in a Globalising World", *COM (2007) 242* (10 May 2007)

Communication of the European Community and its Member States to UNESCO, "On the Preliminary Draft UNESCO Convention on the Protection of the Diversity of Cultural Contents and Artistic Expressions" (15 November 2004), *available at* http://trade.ec.europa.eu/doclib/docs/2004/december/tradoc_120449.pdf (last visited 2 February 2012)

Communication to the Council and to the European Parliament, "On the General Approach to Enable ENP Partner Countries to Participate in Community Agencies and Community Programmes", *COM (2006) 724* (4 December 2006)

Council of Europe, "Explanatory Report to the Framework Convention for the Protection of National Minorities, Explanatory Report", *available at* http://conventions.coe.int/Treaty/EN/Reports/Html/157.htm (last visited 2 February 2012)

Council of the European Union, "Draft Council Decision Authorising the Commission to Participate, on behalf of the Community, in the Negotiations within UNESCO on the Convention on the Protection of the Diversity of Cultural Contents and Artistic Expressions", *13840/04 CULT 103* (29 October 2004), *available at* http://register.consilium.eu.int/pdf/en/04/st13/st13840.en04.pdf (last visited 2 February 2012)

——, Press Release: 2616th Council Meeting, Education, Youth and Culture, *14380/04 (Presse 310)* (15–16 November 2004), *available at* www.consilium.europa.eu/ueDocs/cms_Data/docs/pressData/en/educ/82679.pdf (last visited 2 February 2012)

——, "Code of Conduct between the Council, the Member States and the Commission on the UNESCO Negotiations on the Draft Convention on the Protection of the Diversity of Cultural Contents and Artistic Expressions", *5768/05 CULT 4* (31 January 2005), *available at* http://register.consilium.europa.eu/pdf/en/05/st05/st05768.en05.pdf (last visited 2 February 2012)

——, "Code of Conduct between the Council, the Member States and the Commission for the participation of the Community and its Member States in meetings regarding the implementation of the Convention on the Protection and Promotion of the Diversity of Cultural Expressions", *5914/07* (1 February 2007), *available at* http://ec.europa.eu/culture/documents/pdf/code_conduct_council_en.pdf (last visited 2 February 2012)

Department for Culture, Media and Sport, *Department for Culture, Media and Sport*, *available at* www.culture.gov.uk/ (last visited 2 February 2012)

EC, Audiovisual and Media Policies, "The General Agreement on Trade in Services (GATS) and the Doha Development Agenda", *available at* http://ec.europa.eu/avpolicy/ext/multilateral/gats/index_en.htm (last visited 2 February 2012)

European Commission, "Fair Compensation for Acts of Private Copying" (14 February 2008), *available at* http://ec.europa.eu/internal_market/copyright/docs/levy_reform/background_en.pdf (last visited 2 February 2012)

——, "Staff Working Paper on the External Dimension of Audiovisual Policy", *SEC (2009) 1033* (14 July 2009)

——, "Green Paper on the online distribution of audiovisual works", *COM (2011) 427* (13 July 2011)

——, "Communication to the Council, the European Parliament, the Economic and Social Committee and the Committee of Regions on Certain Legal Aspects relating to Cinematographic and Other Audiovisual Works", *COM (2001) 534* (26 September 2011)

European Audiovisual Observatory, *Focus 2010: World Film Market Trends*, www.obs.coe.int/online_publication/reports/focus2010.pdf (last visited 2 February 2012)

GATT, "Application of GATT to International Trade in Television Programmes", *L/1615* (16 November 1961)

——, "Application of GATT to International Trade in Television Programmes", *L/1646* (21 November 1961)

——, "Application of GATT to International Trade in Television Programmes", *L/1686* (18 December 1961)

——, "Application of GATT to International Trade in Television Programmes: Report of the Working Party", *L/1741* (13 March 1962)

——, "Application of GATT to International Trade in Television Programmes – Revised United States Draft Recommendation", *L/1908* (10 November 1962)

——, "Application of GATT to International Trade in Television Programmes – Proposal by the Government of the United States", *L/2120* (18 March 1964)

GATT, Group of Negotiations on Services, Working Group on Audiovisual Services, "Matters Relating to Trade in Audiovisual Services: Note by the Secretariat", *MTN.GNS/AUD/W/1* (4 October 1990)

GATT, Uruguay Round Group of Negotiations on Services, "Scheduling of Initial Commitments in Trade in Services: Explanatory Note", *MTN.GNS/W/164* (3 September 1993)

GATT Decision of 25 June 1971, "Generalized System of Preferences", *BISD18S/24* (28 June 1971)

GATT Decision of 28 November 1979, "Differential and More Favourable Treatment Reciprocity and Fuller Participation of Developing Countries", *L/4903* (3 December 1979)

German Commission for UNESCO, "U40-World Forum 'Cultural Diversity 2030'", *available at* www.unesco.de/.html?&L=1 (last visited 2 February 2012)

Human Rights Committee, "General Comment 23, Article 27 (Fiftieth Session, 1994)", *Compilation of General Comments and General Recommendations Adopted by Human Rights Treaty Bodies, U.N. Doc. HRI/GEN/1/Rev.1* (1994)

International Network for Cultural Diversity, "Proposed Convention on Cultural Diversity" (2003), *available at* www.indc.net (last visited 2 February 2012)

——, "Draft Convention on Cultural Diversity", *available at* www.incd.net/.html (last visited 2 February 2012)

——, "Statement on the Position of the European Union in the negotiations on the Convention on the Protection of the Diversity of Cultural Contents and Artistic Expressions", *available at* www.incd.net/docs/Europeanposition.htm (last visited 2 February 2012)

International Network of Cultural Policies, "Draft International Convention on Cultural Diversity by the Working Group on Cultural Diversity" (2003), *available at* www.incp-ripc.org (last visited 2 February 2012)

Intellectual Property Office, "Our Mission", *available at* www.ipo.gov.uk/about/whatwedo.htm (last visited 2 February 2012)

Office of the United Nations High Commissioner for Human Rights, "Declaration on the Rights of Indigenous Peoples", *available at* www.ohchr.org/english/issues/indigenous/declaration.htm (last visited 2 February 2012)

Organization for Security and Co-operation in Europe, "Document of the Copenhagen Meeting of the Conference on the Human Dimension of the CSCE", 29 June 1990, *available at* www.osce.org/documents/odihr/2006/06/19392_en.pdf (last visited 2 February 2012)

Organisation International de la Francophonie, "Centre de lecture et d'animation culturelle: 20 ans d'expérience dans le pays francophone", *available at* www.francophonie.org/IMG/pdf/CLAC_Francais-2.pdf (last visited 2 February 2012)

——, "Oslo Recommendation Regarding the Linguistic Rights of National Minorities", 1 February 1998, *available at* www.osce.org/documents/hcnm/1998/02/2699_en.pdf (last visited 2 February 2012)

Parliamentary Questions, "Written Question by Ruth Hieronymi (PPE-DE) to the Commission, "UNESCO Convention on the Protection and Promotion of the Diversity of Cultural Expressions" (8 November 2007), *available at* www.europarl.europa.eu/sides/getDoc.do?pubRef=-//EP//TEXT+WQ+P-2007–5554+0+DOC+XML+V0//EN (last visited on 25 November 2011)

Permanent Delegation of the Russian Federation with UNESCO, "Address by H.E. Ms Eleonora Valentinovna Mitrofanova, Chairperson of the Executive Board of UNESCO, Permanent Delegate of the Russian Federation to UNESCO" (2 November 2011), *available at* www.unesco.mid.ru/pr_e_73.html (last visited 2 February 2012)

The Cultural Industries Sectoral Advisory Group on International Trade (SAGIT), "An International Agreement on Cultural Diversity – A Model for Discussion" (September 2002), *available at* www.international.gc.ca/trade-agreements-accords-commerciaux/assets/pdfs/sagit_eg.pdf (last visited 2 February 2012)

UN Conference on Trade and Employment, "Havana Charter for an International Trade Organization and Final Act and Related Documents", *UN Doc ICITO/1/4/1948* (Havana November 21, 1947 to March 24, 1948)

UNCTAD, "Report of the Expert Meeting on Audiovisual Services: Improving Participation of Developing Countries", *TD/B/COM.1/56* (4 December 2002)

——, "World Creative Economy Report 2008: The challenge of assessing the creative economy towards informed policy-making", *available at* www.unctad.org//docs/cer_en.pdf (last visited 2 February 2012)

——, "World Creative Economy Report 2010: Creative Economy: A Feasible Development Option", *available at* www.unctad.org//docs/_en.pdf (last visited 2 February 2012)

UNESCO, "Working Paper of the Meeting of Government Representatives to Prepare a Draft Declaration on Race and Racial Prejudice", *Doc. SS-77/CONF.201/1* (18 August 1977)

——, "Intergovernmental Conference on Cultural Policies for Development" (Stockholm, 30 March – 2 April, 1998), *available at* http://portal.unesco.org/culture/en/ev.php-URL_ID=18717&URL_DO=DO_TOPIC&URL_SECTION=201.html (last visited 2 February 2012)

——, "The Final Report on the Intergovernmental Conference on Cultural Policies" CLT-98/Conf.210/5 (31 August 1998), *available at* unesdoc.unesco.org/images/0011/001139/113935eo.pdf (last visited 2 February 2012)

——, "Main Lines of an Action Plan for the Implementation of the UNESCO Declaration on Cultural Diversity" (2001), *available at* http://unesdoc.unesco.org/images/0012/001271/127160m.pdf (last visited 2 February 2012)

——, "Draft Resolution submitted by the United States of America on the Desirability of drawing up an international standard-setting instrument on cultural diversity", *Doc. 32 C/COM.iv/DR.5 Paris* (2003)

——, "Preliminary Study on the Technical and Legal Aspects Relating to the Desirability of a Standard-Setting Instrument on Cultural Diversity," *32 C/52 No. 34* (18 July 2003)

——, "Preliminary Draft of a Convention on the Protection of the Diversity of Cultural Contents and Artistic Expressions", *CPL/CPD/2004/CONF-201/2* (July 2004)

——, "Oral Report of the Rapporteur, Mr. Artur Wilczynski" (Closing Session of the First Intergovernmental Meeting of Experts on the Preliminary Draft Convention on the Protection of the Diversity of Cultural Contents and Artistic Expressions, 20–25 September 2004), *available at* www.unesco.org/culture/culturaldiversity/docs_pre_2007/oral_report_wilczynski_en_25092004.pdf (last visited 2 February 2012)

——, "Preliminary Draft Convention on the Protection of the Diversity of Cultural Contents and Artistic Expressions", *CLT/CPD/2004/CONF.607/6* (23 December 2004)

——, "Preliminary Report of the Director-General Containing Two Preliminary Drafts of a Convention on the Protection of the Diversity of Cultural Contents and Artistic Expressions", *CLT/CPD/2005/CONF.203/6* (3 March 2005)

——, "Preliminary Draft of a Convention on the Protection of the Diversity of Cultural Contents and Artistic Expressions", *171 EX/INF.18* (April 2005)

——, "Preliminary Report By the Director-General Setting Out the Situation to be Regulated and the Possible Scope of the Regulating Action Proposed, Accompanied by the Preliminary Draft of a Convention on the Protection of the Diversity of Cultural Contents and Artistic Expressions", *Doc. 33 C/23* (4 August 2005), *available at* http://portal.unesco.org/culture/en/files/28182/1124818579333C23_Eng.pdf/33C23 _Eng.pdf (last visited 2 February 2012)

——, "Diversity of Cultural Expressions", *available at* www.unesco.org/new/en/culture/themes/cultural-diversity/2005-convention (last visited 2 February 2012)

——, "30 Frequently Asked Questions Concerning the Convention on the Protection and Promotion of the Diversity of Cultural Expressions", *CLT/CEI/DCE/2007/PI/32, available at* http://unesdoc.unesco.org/images/0014/001495/149502E.pdf (last visited 2 February 2012)

——, "Ten Keys to the Convention on the Protection and Promotion of the Diversity of Cultural Expressions", *CLT/CEI/DCE/2007/PI/32* (2005)

——, "Tendances des Marchés Audiovisuels: – Perspectives Régionales – Vues du Sud", *CI/COM/2006/PUB/10* (2006)

——, "17 New Projects Get Funding From the IFCD", *available at* www.unesco.org//en///diversity/expressions/international-fund/ (last visited 2 February 2012)

——, "Convention on the Protection and Promotion of the Diversity of Cultural Expressions", *available at* http://portal.unesco.org//.asp?=31038&=E (last visited 2 February 2012)

——, "Conference of Parties", *available at* www.unesco.org//en/culture//cultural-diversity/cultural-expressions/meetings/conference-of-parties/ (last visited 2 February 2012)

——, "Contributions to the IFCD", *available at* www.unesco.org/new//culture/themes/diversity/expressions// (last visited 2 February 2012)

——, "Intergovernmental Committee", *available at* www.unesco.org//en/culture//cultural-diversity/expressions//rgovernmental-/ (last visited 2 February 2012)

——, "Reflections on Cultural Diversity – Conferences and Round Tables", *available at* http://portal.unesco.org/culture/en/ev.php-URL_ID=35258&URL_DO=DO_TOPIC&URL_SECTION=201.html (last visited 2 February 2012)

——, "The Global Alliance on Cultural Diversity", *available at* http://portal.unesco.org/culture/en/ev.php-URL_ID=24468&URL_DO=DO_TOPIC&URL_SECTION=201.html (last visited 2 February 2012)

——, "The Stockholm Conference", *available at* http://portal.unesco.org/culture/en/ev.php-URL_ID=18717&URL_DO=DO_TOPIC&URL_SECTION=201.html (last visited 2 February 2012)

——, "The World Heritage List", *available at* http://whc.unesco.org/en/list (last visited on 2 February 2012)

UNESCO, Executive Board, "Preliminary Study on the Technical and Legal Aspects relating to the Desirability of a Standard-setting Instrument on Cultural Diversity", *166 EX/28* (12 March 2003)

—— "Participation of the European Commission in the Intergovernmental Meeting of Experts (Category II) on the Preliminary Draft Convention on the Protection of the Diversity of Cultural Contents and Artistic Expressions", *170 EX/37* (12 September 2004)

—— Executive Board, "Participation of the European Community in the Intergovernmental Meeting of Experts (Category II) on the Preliminary Draft Convention on the Protection of the Diversity of Cultural Contents and Artistic Expressions", *171 EX/47* (17 March 2005)

UNESCO, General Assembly, "Desirability of Drawing Up an International Standard-Setting Instrument on Cultural Diversity", *Resolution 32 C/34* (13 October 2003), *available at* http://unesdoc.unesco.org/images/0013/001331/133171e.pdf (last visited 2 February 2012)

UNESCO, General Conference (20th session), "Draft Declaration on Race and Judicial Prejudice", *Doc. 20 C/18*, Annex, Explanatory Report (25 September 1978)

——, "Opportunité de l'elaboration d'un instrument normatif international concernant la diversité culturelle", *32 C/52* (18 July 2003)

UNESCO, Institute for Statistics, "Measuring the Diversity of Cultural Expressions: Applying the Stirling Model of Diversity in Culture" (2011), *available at* www.uis.unesco.org/Library/Documents/tp6-11.pdf (last visited 2 February 2012)

UNESCO, Intergovernmental Committee for the Promotion and Protection of the Diversity of Cultural Expressions, "Preparation of Guidelines on the Use of the Resources of the International Fund for Cultural Diversity", *CE/07/1.IGC/6* (25 October 2007), *available at* www.unesco.org/culture/culturaldiversity/december07/igc1_6_en.pdf (last visited 2 February 2012)

——, "Role and participation of civil society in the implementation of the provisions of the Convention (Decision 1 IGC 5C)", *CE/07/1.IGC/Dec. Rev* (13 December 2007), *available at* http://unesdoc.unesco.org/images/0015/001584/158430e.pdf (last visited 2 February 2012)

——, "Secretariat's Report of Activities 2011", *CE/11/5.IGC/213/INF.3* (27 November 2011)

——, "Fifth Ordinary Session – Decisions", *CE/11/5.IGC/213/Dec.* (7 December 2011)

UNESCO, Intergovernmental Meeting of Experts, "Resolution 34: Desirability of Drawing Up an International Standard-Setting Instrument on Cultural Diversity", *CLT/CPD/2004/CONF.201/5* (17 October 2003), *available at* http://portal.unesco.org/culture/en/files/21974/10902326553Eng-Resolution32C34-conf.201-5.pdf/Eng-Resolution32C34-conf.201-5.pdf (last visited 2 February 2012)

UNESCO, First Meeting of Experts (category VI) on the First Draft of an International Convention on the Protection of the Diversity of Cultural Contents and Artistic Expressions, "Report", *CLT/CPD/2003-608/01*, (20 February 2004)

——, Third Meeting of Experts (category VI) on the First Draft of an International Convention on the Protection of the Diversity of Cultural Contents and Artistic Expressions, "Report", *CLT/CPD/2004/603/5* (23 June 2004)

——, "Issues Arising in Connection with the Implementation of the World Heritage Convention", *Doc. CC-77/CONF.001/4* (9 June 1977), *available at* http://unesdoc.unesco.org/images/0003/000309/030934EB.pdf (last visited on 2 February 2012)

UNESCO, World Heritage Committee, *Decision 31 COM 7B.11*, WHC-07/31.COM/24 (31 July 2007)

——, "Historic Centre of Cordoba", *available at* http://whc.unesco.org/en/list/313 (last visited on 2 February 2012)

United Nations, "Central Product Classification Version 1.1", *Statistical Papers, Series M, No. 77* (2004)

United Nations, Commission on Human Rights, "Globalization and Its Impact on the Full Enjoyment of Human Rights: Report of the High Commissioner for Human Rights Submitted in Accordance with Commission on Human Rights Resolution 2001/32", *E/CN.4/2002/54* (15 January 2002)

United Nations, International Law Commission, "Fragmentation of International Law: Difficulties Arising from the Diversification and Expansion of International Law – Report of the Study Group – Finalized by Martti Koskenniemi", *A/CN.4/L.682* (13 April 2006)

United States Mission to UNESCO, "UNESCO Convention Could Limit Freedom of Cultural Expressions and Trade" (20 October 2005), *available at* http://geneva.usmission.gov/Press2005/2010Oliver.htm (last visited 2 February 2012)

US Department of State, "The Convention on the Protection and Promotion of the Diversity of Cultural Expressions", *Fact Sheet* (11 October 2005), *available at* www.state.gov/r/pa/prs/ps/2005/54690.htm (last visited 2 February 2012)

US Department of State, Bureau of International Information Programs, "U.S. Opposed 'Deeply Flawed' U.N. Cultural Diversity Convention" (21 October 2005), *available at* www.america.gov/st/washfile-english/2005/October/20051020170821GLnesnoM3.670901e-02.html (last visited 2 February 2012)

US Department of State, Foreign Press Center Roundtable, "UNESCO Cultural Diversity Convention: The US View", 27 September 2005, *available at* www.fpc.state.gov/fpc/54039.htm (last visited 2 February 2012)

US Department of State, Office of the Spokesman, "The Convention on the Protection and Promotion of the Diversity of Cultural Expressions", 11 October 2005, *available at* www.state.gov/r/pa/prs/ps/2005/54690.htm (last visited 2 February 2012)

US, Office of the United States Trade Representative, "Foreign Trade Barriers Report: Europe" (1998), *available at* www.ustr.gov/assets/Document_Library/Reports_Publications/1998/1998_National_Trade_Estimate/asset_upload_file841_2758.pdf (last visited 2 February 2012)

WIPO, Intergovernmental Committee on Intellectual Property and Genetic Resources, Traditional Knowledge and Folklore, "The Protection of Traditional Knowledge: Draft Objectives and Principles" *WIPO/GRTKF/IC/10/5* (2 October 2006), *available at* www.wipo.int/edocs/mdocs/tk/en/wipo_grtkf_ic_10/wipo_grtkf_ic_10_5.pdf (last visited 2 February 2012)

——, "The Protection of Traditional Cultural Expressions/Expressions of Folklore: Draft Objectives and Principles" *WIPO/GRTKF/IC/10/4* (2 October 2006), *available at* www.wipo.int/edocs/mdocs/tk/en/wipo_grtkf_ic_10/wipo_grtkf_ic_10_4.pdf (last visited 2 February 2012)

World Bank, "Culture Counts: Financing, Resources, and the Economics of Culture in Sustainable Development – Conference Proceedings" (2000), *available at* www-wds.worldbank.org/external/default/WDSContentServer/WDSP/IB/2000/11/17/000094946_00110405591265/Rendered/PDF/multi_page.pdf (last visited 2 February 2012)

WTO, "Decision on Differential and More Favourable Treatment, Reciprocity, and Fuller Participation of Developing Countries", *L/4903, BISD 26S/203* (28 November 1979)

——, "Canada – Final List of Article II (MFN) Exemptions", *GATS/EL/16* (15 April 1994)

——, "India – Final List of Article II (MFN) Exemptions", *GATS/EL/42* (15 April 1994)

——, "Turkey – Taxation of Foreign Film Revenues: Notification of Mutually Agreed Solution", *WT/DS43/3-G/L/177* (24 July 1997)

——, "Japan – Measures Concerning Sound Recordings: Notification of a Mutually-Agreed Solution", *WT/DS28/4 – IP/D/1/Add.1* (5 February 1997) and *WT/DS42/4-IP/D/4/Add.1* (17 November 1997)

——, "Request for Consultations by the United States: China – Measures Affecting Trading Rights and Distribution Services for Certain Publications and Audiovisual Entertainment Products", *WT/DS363/1, G/L/820, S/L/287* (16 April 2007)

——, "Request for the Establishment of a Panel by the United States", *Doc. WT/DS363/5* (11 October 2007)

——, "China – Measures Affecting Trading Rights and Distribution Services for Certain Publications and Audiovisual Entertainment Products: Request for Consultations by the United States", *WT/DS363/1, G/L/820, S/L/287* (16 April 2007) and Add. 1 (16 July 2007)

——, "Understanding the WTO: The Organization, Members and Observers" (23 July 2008), *available at* www.wto.org/english/theWTO_e/whatis_e/tif_e/org6_e.htm (last visited 2 February 2012)

WTO, "China – Measures Affecting Trading Rights and Distribution Services for Certain Publications and Audiovisual Entertainment Products: Notification of an Appeal by China under Article 16.4 and Article 17 of the Understanding on Rules and Procedures Governing the Settlement of Disputes (DSU), and under Rule 20(1) of the Working Procedures for Appellate Review", *WT/DS363/10* (23 September 2009)

WTO, "China – Measures Affecting Trading Rights and Distribution Services for Certain Publications and Audiovisual Entertainment Products: Notification of an Other Appeal by the United States under Article 16.4 and Article 17 of the Understanding on Rules and Procedures Governing the Settlement of Disputes (DSU), and under Rule 23(1) of the Working Procedures for Appellate Review", *WT/DS363/11* (6 October 2009)

——, "Understanding between China and the United States Regarding Procedures under Articles 21 and 22 of the DSU", *WT/DS362/15* (13 April 2010)

——, "Doha Development Agenda: Negotiations, Implementation and Development", *available at www.wto.org/english/tratop_e/dda_e/dda_e.htm* (last visited 2 February 2012)

——, "List of All Early Announcements Made to WTO", *available at* http://rtais.wto.org/UI/PublicEARTAList.aspx (last visited 2 February 2012)

——, "List of all RTAs", *available at* http://rtais.wto.org//.aspx (last visited 2 February 2012)

——, "Member Sector/Matrix Report: Communications Services", *available at* http://tsdb.wto.org/matrixlist.aspx (last visited 2 February 2012)

——, "Regional Trade Agreements", *available at* www.wto.org//_e/region_e/region_e.htm (last visited 2 February 2012)

——, "Regional Trade Agreements Notified to the GATT/WTO and in Force: By Date of Entry into Force", *available at* http://rtais.wto.org/UI/PublicPreDefRepByEIF.aspx (last visited 2 February 2012)

WTO, Committee on Trade and Development, "Implementation of Special and Differential Treatment Provisions in WTO Agreements and Decisions", *WT/COMTD/W/77* (25 October 2000)

——, "Reclaiming Development in the WTO Doha Development Round", *WT/COMTD/W/145* (1 December 2005)

WTO, Consultative Board, "The Future of the WTO: Addressing Institutional Challenges in the New Millennium" 2004, *available at* www.wto.org/english/thewto_e/10anniv_e/future_wto_e.pdf (last visited 2 February 2012)

WTO, Council for Trade in Services, "Audiovisual Services: Background Note by the Secretariat", *S/C/W/40* (15 June 1998)

——, "Communications from the United States: Audiovisual Services", *S/C/W/78* (8 December 1998)

——, "Communication from Israel: Review of Article II Exemptions / Replies to Questions Posed on Israel's MFN Exemptions in the Area of Audiovisual Services in the Course of the Review of MFN Exemptions", *S/C/W/158* (10 July 2000)

——, "Communication from the United States: Audiovisual and Related Services", *S/CSS/W/21* (18 December 2000)

——, "Communication from Japan: The Negotiations on Trade in Services", *S/CSS/W/42* (22 December 2000)

——, "Communication from Canada: Canadian Initial GATS Sectoral/Modal/Horizontal Negotiating Proposals", *S/CSS/W/46* (14 March 2001)

——, "Guidelines for the Scheduling of Specific Commitments under the General Agreement on Trade in Services (GATS): Adopted by the Council for Trade in Services on 23 March 2001", *S/L/92* (28 March 2001)

——, "Communication from Switzerland: GATS 2000, Audio-visual Services", *S/CSS/W/74* (4 May 2001)

——, "Communication from Brazil: Audiovisual Services", *S/CSS/W/99* (9 July 2001)

——, "Communication from Hong Kong China, Japan, Mexico, the Separate Customs Territory of Taiwan, Penghu, Kinmen and Matsu, and United States: Joint Statement on the Negotiations on Audiovisual Services", *TN/S/W/49* (30 June 2005)

——, "Audiovisual Services: Information Note by the Secretariat", *JOB(05)/192* (19 September 2005)

WTO, Council for Trade-Related Aspects of Intellectual Property Rights, "The Protection of Traditional Knowledge and Folklore: Summary of Issues Raised and Points Made – Note by the Secretariat (Revision)", *P/C/W/370/Rev.1* (9 March 2006)

WTO, Dispute Settlement Body, "Minutes of Meeting Held in the Centre William Rappard on 10 December 2003", *WT/DSB/M/160* (27 January 2004)

WTO, General Council, "Agreement between the WTO and the IMF and the World Bank", *WTO Doc. WT/L/194* (18 November1996) and its Addendum, *WT/L/194/Add.1* (18 November 1996)

——, "Decision Adopted by the General Council on 1 August 2004", *WT/L/579* (2 August 2004)

——, "Doha Work Programme", *WT/L/579* (2 August 2004)

WTO, Ministerial Conference, "Ministerial Declaration adopted on 14 November 2001", *WT/MIN(01)/DEC/1* (20 November 2001)

——, "Implementation-Related Issues and Concerns – Decision of 14 November 2001", *WT/MIN (01) 17* (20 November 2001)

WTO, Ministerial Conference, "Doha Work Programme: Ministerial Declaration Adopted on 18 December 2005", *WT/MIN(05)/DEC* (22 December 2005)

WTO, Secretariat, "Services Sectoral Classification List – Note by the Secretariat", *MTN.GNS/W/120* (10 July 1991)

——, "Summary of the Provisions contained in the Uruguay Round Agreements for the Differential and More Favourable Treatment of Developing and Least Developed Countries", *available at* www.wto.org/english/tratop_e/devel_e/anexii_e.doc. (last visited 2 February 2012)

WTO, Committee on Trade and Development, "Implementation of Special and Differential Treatment Provisions in WTO Agreements and Decisions", *WT/COMTD/W/77* (25 October 2000)

——, "Special and Differential Treatment for Least-Developed Countries", *WT/COMTD/W/135* (5 October 2004)

WTO Press Release, "Ministerial Conference approves Russia's WTO membership" (16 December 2011), *available at* www.wto.org//_e/_e/_rus_16dec11_e.htm (last visited 2 February 2012)

WTO Press Release, "WTO membership of Montenegro and Samoa approved" (17 December 2011), *available at* www.wto.org//_e/_e/_wsm_17dec11_e.htm (last visited 2 February 2012)

WTO, Working Party on GATS Rules, "Report of the Meeting of 17 September 2007: Note by the Secretariat", *S/WPGR/M/59* (2 October 2007)

——, "Report of the Meeting of 10 November 2009: Note by the Secretariat", *S/WPGR/M/66* (25 January 2010)

——, "Report of the Meeting of 22 June 2011: Note by the Secretariat", *S/WPGR/M/74* (19 July 2011)

4. WTO DECISIONS

4.1. *Appellate Body Reports*

Appellate Body Report, "Japan – Taxes on Alcoholic Beverages", *WT/DS10/AB/R, WT/DS11/AB/R, WT/DS8/AB/R* (4 October 1996)

Appellate Body Report, "Canada – Certain Measures Concerning Periodicals", *WT/DS31/AB/R* (30 June 1997), *available at* www.wto.org/english/tratop_e/dispu_e/cases_e/ds31_e.htm (last visited 2 February 2012)

Appellate Body Report, "European Communities – Measures Concerning Meat and Meat Products (Hormones)", *WT/DS48/AB/R* (16 January 1998)

Appellate Body Report, "United States – Import Prohibition of Certain Shrimp and Shrimp Products", *WT/DS58/AB/R* (12 October 1998)

Appellate Body Report, "Argentina – Safeguard Measures on Imports of Footwear (EC)", *WT/DS121/AB/R* (14 December 1999)

Appellate Body Report, "Turkey – Restrictions on Imports of Textiles and other Clothing Products", *WT/DS34/AB/R* (22 October 1999)

Appellate Body Report, "Canada – Certain Measures Affecting the Automotive Industry", *WT/DS139/AB/R, WT/DS142/AB/R* (19 June 2000)

Appellate Body Report, "United States – Safeguard Measures on Imports of Fresh, Chilled or Frozen Lamb Meat from New Zealand and Australia", *WT/DS177/AB/R, WT/DS178/AB/R* (1 May 2001)

Appellate Body Report, "United States – Definitive Safeguard Measures on Imports of Certain Steel Products", *WT/DS248/AB/R, WT/DS249/AB/R, WT/DS251/AB/R, WT/DS252/AB/R, WT/DS253/AB/R, WT/DS254/AB/R, WT/DS258/AB/R, WT/DS259/AB/R*, (10 November 2003)

Appellate Body Report, "European Commission – Conditions for Granting Tariff Preferences to Developing Countries", *WT/DS246/AB/R* (7 April 2004)

Appellate Body Report, "United States – Measures Affecting the Cross-Border Supply of Gambling and Betting Services", *WT/DS267/AB/R* (3 March 2005)

Appellate Body Report, "Brazil – Measures Affecting Imports of Retreaded Tyres", *WT/DS332/AB/R* (3 December 2007)

Appellate Body Report, "China – Measures Affecting Trading Rights and Distribution Services for Certain Publications and Audiovisual Entertainment Products", *WT/DS363/AB/R* (21 December 2009)

4.2. *Panel Reports*

Panel Report, "Japan – Taxes on Alcoholic Beverages", *WT/DS10/R, WT/DS11/R, WT/DS8/R* (11 July 1996)

Panel Report, "Canada – Certain Measures Concerning Periodicals", *WT/DS31/R* (14 March 1997)

Panel Report, "Argentina – Definitive Safeguard Measure on Imports of Preserved Peaches", *WT/DS238/R* (14 February 2003)

Panel Report, "European Communities – Measures Affecting the Approval and Marketing of Biotech Products", *WT/DS291/R* (29 September 2006)

Panel Report, "Brazil – Measures affecting Imports of Retreaded Tyres", *WT/DS332/R* (12 June 2007)

Panel Report, "China – Measures Affecting Trading Rights and Distribution Services for Certain Publications and Audiovisual Entertainment Products", *WT/DS363/R* (12 August 2009)

5. EUROPEAN JUDICIAL DECISIONS

5.1. *European Court of Justice*

Case C-181/73, *R.&V. Haegeman v the Belgian State*, [1974] E.C.R.-449

Case 170/78, *Commission of the European Communities v United Kingdom of Great Britain and Northern Ireland*, [1983] E.C.R. 2265

Case 407/85, *3 Glocken GmbH and Gertraud Kritzinger v USL Centro-Sud and Provincia autonoma di Bolzano*, [1988] E.C.R. 4233
Case 286/86, *Ministère public v Gérard Deserbais*, [1988] E.C.R. 4907
Case 178/84, *Commission v. Germany*, [1987] E.C.R. 1227
Case C-379/87, *Groener*, [1989] E.C.R. 3967
Case C-459/03, *Commission v Ireland (MOX Plant)*, [2006] E.C.R. I-4635
Case C-250/06, *United Pan-Europe Communications Belgium and Others*, [2007] E.C.R. I-11135
Case C-222/07, *Unión de Televisiones Comerciales Asociadas (UTECA) v Administración General del Estado*, [2009] E.C.R. I-01407
Opinion 2/91, Convention N° 170 of the International Labour Organisation concerning Safety in the Use of Chemicals at Work, [1993] E.C.R. I-1061
Opinion 1/94, Competence of the Community to Conclude International Agreements concerning Services and the Protection of Intellectual Property, [1994] E.C.R. I-5267

5.2. *Opinion of the Advocate General*

Opinion of Advocate General Kokott delivered on 4 September 2008, Case C-222/07, Unión de Televisiones Comerciales Asociadas (UTECA), *available at* www.curia.eu.int (last visited 2 February 2012)

5.3. *European Commission*

European Commission, Decision of 24 August 2010 on State Aid N 164/2010, Germany, Leipziger Reit- und Rennverein Scheibenholz
European Commission, Decision of 13 December 2010 on State Aid N 122/2010, Hungary, Danube Cultural Palace
European Commission, Decision of 23 February 2011 on State Aid N 446/2010, France, Aide aux projects pour les nouveaux medias
European Commission, Decision of 11 May 2011 on State Aid 32643 (2011/N), Spain, State aid to Basque museums
European Commission, Decision of 11 May 2011 on State Aid 30649 (N 2011), Denmark, State aid to the Danish Shellfish Centre
European Commission, Decision of 4 April 2011 on State aid 32144 (N 2011), Spain, State aid to dance, theatre and poetry
European Commission, Decision of 4 April 2011 on State Aid SA.32119 (2011/N), Spain, State aid to activities in the theatre and circus sectors
European Commission, Decision of 19 April 2011 on State Aid 32549 (N 2011), Espagne, Subventions pour le développement de l'usage de la langue basque dans la vie sociale
European Commission, Decision of 19 April 2011 on State aid 32266 (N 2011), Spain, Aid for the promotion of the Basque language at the workplace
European Commission, Decision of 11 December 2007 on State Aid C 47/06 (ex N 648/05), Tax credit introduced by France for the creation of video games (2008/354/EC), *OJ 2007 L 118/16*
European Commission, Decision of 31 August 2010 on State Aid N 96/2010, Austria, Austrian film support scheme

6. HUMAN RIGHTS COURT DECISIONS

6.1. *European Court of Human rights*

EUROPEAN COURT OF HUMAN RIGHTS, *Chapman v. the United Kingdom*, 18 January 2001, no. 27238/95

6.2. *Inter-American Court on Human Rights*

INTER-AMERICAN COURT ON HUMAN RIGHTS, *Yanomami Indians in OAS*, Inter-Am C.H. Res. No. 12/85, Case No. 7615

INTER-AMERICAN COURT ON HUMAN RIGHTS, *The Mayagna (Sumo) Indigenous Community of Awas Tingi v. the Republic of Nicaragua*, 31 August 2001, Inter-Am. C.H.R, Series C, No. 79

INTER-AMERICAN COMMISSION ON HUMAN RIGHTS, *Maya Indigenous Communities and their Members v. Belize*, 5 October 2000, IACHR Report No. 78/00, case No. 12.053

INTER-AMERICAN COMMISSION ON HUMAN RIGHTS, *Maya Indigenous Communities of the Toledo District Belize*, 12 October 2004, IACHR Report No. 40–04, case No. 12.053